ROUTLEDGE HANDBOOK OF SUSTAINABLE AND REGENERATIVE FOOD SYSTEMS

T0320240

This handbook includes contributions from established and emerging scholars from around the world and draws on multiple approaches and subjects to explore the socio-economic, cultural, ecological, institutional, legal, and policy aspects of regenerative food practices.

The future of food is uncertain. We are facing an overwhelming number of interconnected and complex challenges related to the ways we grow, distribute, access, eat, and dispose of food. Yet, there are stories of hope and opportunities for radical change towards food systems that enhance the ability of living things to co-evolve. Given this, activities and imaginaries looking to improve, rather than just sustain, communities and ecosystems are needed, as are fresh perspectives and new terminology. The *Routledge Handbook of Sustainable and Regenerative Food Systems* addresses this need. The chapters cover diverse practices, geographies, scales, and entry-points. They focus not only on the core requirements to deliver sustainable agriculture and food supply, but go beyond this to think about how these can also actively participate with social-ecological systems. The book is presented in an accessible way, with reflection questions meant to spark discussion and debate on how to transition to safe, just, and healthy food systems. Taken together, the chapters in this handbook highlight the consequences of current food practices and showcase the multiple ways that people are doing food differently.

The *Routledge Handbook of Sustainable and Regenerative Food Systems* is essential reading for students and scholars interested in food systems, governance and practices, agroecology, rural sociology, and socio-environmental studies.

Jessica Duncan is Associate Professor in the Rural Sociology Group, Wageningen University, the Netherlands.

Michael Carolan is a Professor in the Department of Sociology, Colorado State University, USA.

Johannes S.C. Wiskerke is Professor and Chair of the Rural Sociology Group, Wageningen University, the Netherlands.

ROUTLEDGE HANDBOOK OF SUSTAINABLE AND REGENERATIVE FOOD SYSTEMS

Edited by Jessica Duncan, Michael Carolan, and Johannes S.C. Wiskerke

LONDON AND NEW YORK

First published 2021
by Routledge
4 Park Square, Milton Park, Abingdon, Oxon OX14 4RN
605 Third Avenue, New York, NY 10017

First issued in paperback 2023

Routledge is an imprint of the Taylor & Francis Group, an informa business

British Library Cataloguing-in-Publication Data
A catalogue record for this book is available from the British Library

Library of Congress Cataloging-in-Publication Data
Names: Duncan, Jessica, editor. | Wiskirke, Johannes SC, editor. | Carolan, Michael S., editor.
Title: Routledge handbook of sustainable and regenerative food systems / edited by Jessica Duncan, Michael Carolan, and Johannes SC Wiskirke.
Identifiers: LCCN 2019058532 (print) | LCCN 2019058533 (ebook) | ISBN 9781138608047 (hardback) | ISBN 9780429466823 (ebook)
Subjects: LCSH: Food security. | Food supply. | Sustainable agriculture.
Classification: LCC HD9000.5 .R6796 2020 (print) | LCC HD9000.5 (ebook) | DDC 338.1/9–dc23
LC record available at https://lccn.loc.gov/2019058532
LC ebook record available at https://lccn.loc.gov/2019058533

ISBN: 978-1-03-257039-6 (pbk)
ISBN: 978-1-138-60804-7 (hbk)
ISBN: 978-0-429-46682-3 (ebk)

DOI: 10.4324/9780429466823

Typeset in Bembo
by Swales & Willis, Exeter, Devon, UK

Publisher's Note
The publisher has gone to great lengths to ensure the quality of this reprint but points out that some imperfections in the original copies may be apparent.

CONTENTS

Contents

FIGURES

TABLES

CONTRIBUTORS

Editors

Jessica Duncan is Associate Professor in Rural Sociology at Wageningen University (the Netherlands). She researches relationships between governance mechanisms, food provisioning, the environment, and the actors that interact across these spaces. She sits on the editorial board for the journal *Sociologia Ruralis* and acts as an advisor and researcher with Traditional Cultures Project (USA).

Michael Carolan is a Professor of Sociology and Associate Dean of Research and Graduate Affairs. Other appointments include: Distinguished Fulbright Research Chair, University of Ottawa, Canada; Professor of Political Science (Status-Only), University of Toronto, Canada; and Research Affiliate, Centre for Sustainability, University of Otago, Dunedin, New Zealand.

Johannes S.C. Wiskerke is Professor and Chair of Rural Sociology at Wageningen University. His research activities focus on a) the dynamics and socio-economic impacts of multifunctional agriculture, b) alternative food networks and their impact on rural and regional development, and c) urban food provisioning and city region food policies. Currently he is involved in two research projects: a Horizon 2020 project exploring urban–rural relations and synergies (ROBUST) and a project titled Urbanizing in Place.

Contributors

Patricia Natividad Álvarez is a research scientist (PhD candidate) and an international development worker. She has worked for 12 years in international development programs and projects in Africa and Latin America, especially in local capacity building, gender, human mobility, rural development and monitoring & evaluation.

Holly Amos is a dietitian and candidate in the Dalhousie University Master of Marine Management. With a passion for local, sustainable food systems and aligning human and environmental health, she views the food system as an avenue to support mutually beneficial relationships between individual, community, and environmental wellbeing.

Megan Bailey is Assistant Professor and SSHRC Canada Research Chair with the Marine Affairs Program at Dalhousie University. Megan's research is motivated by notions of equity and fairness, and a belief that the way humans use the ocean, and the resources within, should be governed in ways that ensure ecological resilience and social wellbeing.

André Eduardo Biscaia de Lacerda is a research scientist and Research Station Manager in Embrapa Forestry. He has worked for 15 years in ecology and forestry research, conducting multidisciplinary projects on biodiversity, sustainable forest management, genetics, and community-based agroforestry in Southern Brazil.

Alison Blay-Palmer is the Director of the Laurier Centre for Sustainable Food Systems at Wilfrid Laurier University in Waterloo, Canada. She is the lead investigator for Food: Locally Embedded Globally Engaged (FLEdGE) a Canadian-based international partnership engaged in research and knowledge sharing to enhance food system sustainability. The partnership includes more than 130 individuals and 89 organizations. She is also co-lead for Urbal with co-applicant Dr. E. Valette (CIRAD, Montpellier, France), a research project developing a methodology to map innovation pathways for sustainable urban food being tested in 12 urban food innovation labs in eight cities. She also works with the RUAF Global Partnership on the City Region Food System with the UN Food and Agriculture Organization.

Kelly Bronson is a Canada Research Chair in Science and Society at University of Ottawa. She is a social scientist studying science-society tensions that erupt around controversial technologies (GMOs, fracking, big data) and their governance. Her research aims to bring community values into conversation with technical knowledge in the production of evidence-informed decision-making. She has published her work in regional (Journal of New Brunswick Studies), national (Canadian Journal of Communication) and international journals (Journal of Responsible Innovation, Big Data and Society). She has just finished writing a book on big data and artificial intelligence in agriculture.

Abel Cassol is a Professor of Rural Sociology and Development at the Federal University of Pelotas (UFPel), Pelotas, Rio Grande do Sul, Brazil. He works as a researcher in the Group on Agriculture, Food and Development Studies (GEPAD/CNPq).

Aude Chesnais is a Senior Researcher for non-profit organization Village Earth. She has worked for over ten years on issues of engagement in sustainability with Lakota communities in South Dakota, US. She uses participatory and decolonial methods to design locally useful research that brings visibility to Indigenous sustainable innovation. She is now working on a research project aiming at determining a national food sovereignty index on tribal land.

Jennifer Clapp is a Canada Research Chair and Professor in the School of Environment, Resources and Sustainability at the University of Waterloo. Her most recent books include Food, 3rd edition (2020), *Speculative Harvests: Financialization, Food, and Agriculture* (with S. Ryan Isakson, 2018), and *Hunger in the Balance: The New Politics of International Food Aid* (2012).

Anna Davies (FTCD, MRIA) is Chair of Geography, Environment and Society at Trinity College Dublin, Ireland. Widely published in the fields of environmental governance and sustainable development, she has advised national governments, international organizations, and grassroots sustainability organizations.

Lisa Deijl was trained as an anthropologist. She became fascinated with regenerative food systems as the solution to a lot of the world's problems and obtained an MSc in Organic Agriculture from Wageningen University. She now works for a Dutch NGO that, through EU subsidies, pays farmers for biodiversity protection.

Maria del Milagro Nuñez-Solis was a New Zealand Development Scholarship student and earned a Master in Applied Science – International Rural Development at Lincoln University. Originally from Costa Rica, she researches different coffee communities' realities, with interests in alternative and diverse economies, food studies, and gender in transformative approaches to agriculture.

Dries de Moor is lecturer in social work and researcher on conceptions of quality of life at care farms at the Research Centre for Social Support and Community Care at the Faculty of Health and Social Studies, HAN University of Applied Sciences, Nijmegen, the Netherlands.

Angga Dwiartama is Assistant Professor at the School of Life Sciences and Technology, Institut Teknologi Bandung, Indonesia. His research focuses on understanding the sustainability and resilience of agriculture and food systems, as also the growth of alternative food movements in Indonesia.

Rebecca A. Ellis is a PhD candidate in Geography at Western University and a member of the Rotman Institute of Philosophy. Her current research examines human/bee relationships using a political ecology approach. She is a permaculture practitioner, community organizer, and lover of bees of all kinds.

Tomaso Ferrando is Research Professor at the University of Antwerp (Law and Research Group and Institute of Development Policy). Previously, he lectured in law at the University of Bristol Law School and at the University of Warwick School of Law. Before obtaining his PhD in law at the University of Sciences Po Paris, he was research fellow at the Institute for Global Law and Policy at Harvard Law School and visiting researcher at the University of Cape Town and at the Universidade of São Paulo. Tomaso researches and works on the legal construction of a global food system that starves, overfeeds, and depletes the planet, and engages with the right to food and food systems as a commons as legal and political alternatives to the dominant food paradigm.

María Cristina Omonte Ferrufino, has led multidisciplinary action research projects in rural areas of Bolivia, on topics related to sustainable family farming, family and child nutrition, participatory methodologies and strengthening of local capacities, with a focus on revaluation of local resources and local knowledge for the last decade.

Mikelis Grivins, dr.soc., is a researcher at Baltic Studies Centre in Latvia. Grivins has been involved in studying foraging, agri-food systems, and sustainability transition in Central and Eastern Europe. His current research addresses the role of wild product gathering and untapped potential of non-timber forest products in the European countryside. Grivins is the chair of Latvian Sociological Association and the convenor of pan-European research study group 'Alternative food supply networks in Central and Eastern Europe'.

Jan Hassink is senior researcher at Wageningen Plant Research. His research deals with the social aspects of agriculture and food practices, nature and health, and citizen initiatives. He has a specific interest in the transition perspective, social change, and social entrepreneurship.

Elisabeth Hense is Associate Professor for Spirituality Studies at Radboud University. From a humanities perspective her research focuses on societal renewal in the Netherlands, especially renewal in the fields of agriculture and gardening. She is a fellow of the European SPES Institute and substitute chair of the Research Institute of the German Carmelites.

Mariaelena Huambachano is an Assistant Professor, Civil Society and Community Studies, at the University of Wisconsin, Madison. Mariaelena is an Indigenous scholar, food sovereignty and environmental justice advocate. She is also an active member of the United Nations Permanent Forum on Indigenous Issues. Her research focuses on Indigenous transnational comparative studies at the interface between cultural and agrobiodiversity, proving a new approach to understand traditional knowledge, biocultural heritage, and public policies. She is currently working on a book project titled 'Indigenous Food Sovereignty, Sustainability, and Justice' and in an international community-based project, 'Our Right to Food Sovereignty', with community partners in Aotearoa New Zealand, Peru, USA and Ecuador.

Rositsa T. Ilieva is the Director of Food Policy Monitor at the CUNY Urban Food Policy Institute in New York and author of *Urban Food Planning* (Routledge, 2016). For nearly a decade, her research has focused on the integration of just and sustainable food systems goals in the domains of urban policy, design, and planning in the US, Europe, and elsewhere.

Antonio A.R. Ioris is a reader and director of the MSc in Environment and Development at the School of Geography and Planning, Cardiff University. Recent research projects have focused on agribusiness expansion and 'agrocultural' frontiers in the Amazon, land-based tensions between Indigenous peoples and agribusiness farmers, and the resistance to mainstream development.

Joost Jongerden is an Associate Professor at Rural Sociology, Wageningen University, the Netherlands and project professor at the Asian Platform for Global Sustainability and Transcultural Studies at Kyoto University, Japan. He studies the ways in which people develop alternatives to market- and state-induced insecurities. This he refers to as 'Do-It-Yourself-Development'. A list of his publications is available at https://joostjongerden.academia.edu/.

Charles Z. Levkoe is the Canada Research Chair in Sustainable Food Systems and Associate Professor in the Department of Health Sciences at Lakehead University. His community-engaged research uses a food systems lens to better understand the importance of, and connections between, social justice, ecological regeneration, regional economies, and active democratic engagement.

Joseph Macharia is a PhD candidate at Queensland University and Technology, Business School, Australia. His research interest relates to digital technologies, particularly the intersection between entrepreneurship and agriculture for development. He is the founder of Mkulima Young, an online platform that connects farmers to markets across Africa.

Ana Moragues-Faus is a Senior Research Fellow at University of Barcelona and a visiting fellow at the Sustainable Places Institute, in Cardiff University. She engages in action-research processes and combines a set of critical theories such as political ecology and participative justice to support the development of more just and sustainable food systems.

Caitlin Morgan is a PhD candidate in Food Systems at the University of Vermont. She has an MS in Food Systems, also from UVM, and a BS in Conservation and Resource Studies from the University of California at Berkeley.

Angela Moriggi is a social scientist working for transdiciplinary research projects on rural and urban sustainability. She is external PhD candidate at Wageningen University and Marie Curie Fellow of the project SUSPLACE (Sustainable Place Shaping). Her research focuses on various dimensions of social change, employing participatory and action-oriented research approaches.

Cheryl Morse is Associate Professor of Geography and a member of the Environmental Program and the Food Systems Graduate Faculty at the University of Vermont. She is a rural geographer who researches human–environment interactions. Specifically, her work is concerned with how people perceive, co-produce, and experience rural places. She has published in the fields of rural studies, migration, health geographies, and youth geographies.

Evelyn R. Nimmo is a multi-disciplinary researcher, currently working as a post-doctoral Fellow in the Department of History at the State University of Ponta Grossa (UEPG), Brazil. Dr. Nimmo's research experience and interests include community-based approaches to environmental history and exploring gender in relation to traditional ecological knowledge.

Stefano Pascucci is Professor in Sustainability and Circular Economy at the University of Exeter Business School, UK. He is research fellow at the Environment and Sustainability Institute (ESI), and research affiliate at Exeter Centre for the Circular Economy (ECCE), University of Exeter. He is also Visiting Researcher at the Department of Business Management and Organization (BMO) at Wageningen University (the Netherlands). He holds a PhD in agricultural economics, and then specialized in topics related to institutional analysis and sustainability connected to entrepreneurship, organization studies, innovation, and value chain management. His research focuses particularly on food and agribusiness, sustainability, and circular economy. He is particularly concerned about the analysis of the interplay between sustainability, (community-based) entrepreneurship, innovation, and value chain configurations. He has published, among others, in the *Journal of Business Venturing, Journal of Business Ethics, Journal of Cleaner Production, Agriculture and Human Values, Food Policy,* and *Agricultural Systems.*

Archana Patnaik is an Assistant Professor at Department of Humanities and Social Sciences, Indian Institute of Technology, Kharagpur. She is interested in research with an interdisciplinary perspective in areas of community-based natural resource management and common studies, law and society, sociology of science and technology, gender and technology.

Nazmun Ratna is a senior lecturer at Lincoln University. She is a development economist and is currently working as a food security and gender expert for a project on improving the availability of fresh vegetables in local markets serving nutritionally vulnerable consumers in Bangladesh, India, and Tanzania.

Christopher Rosin is a senior lecturer in political ecology at Lincoln University (New Zealand). He has published research on yerba mate in South America and the pastoral and horticulture sectors in New Zealand. He is currently involved in an interdisciplinary project to design future productive landscapes in New Zealand.

Joshua Sbicca is Assistant Professor of Sociology at Colorado State University. His research and teaching focus on food politics, food justice, social movements, and inequalities. He is the author of *Food Justice Now! Deepening the Roots of Social Struggle*. He is also a co-editor of *A Recipe for Gentrification: Food, Power, and Resistance in the City*.

Sergio Schneider is a Full Professor of Sociology of Rural Development and Food Studies and work at the Federal University of Rio Grande do Sul (UFRGS), Porto Alegre, Rio Grande do Sul, Brazil. He holds a CNPq research scholarship for high scientific productivity in Brazil, PQ1D.

María Mayer de Scurrah is the Director of the YANAPAI group, a Peruvian NGO that researches agriculture and nutrition in Peru's Central Highlands. She holds a PhD in plant breeding with 20 years of work at the International Potato Center (CIP) and 9 years at the "South Australian Research and Development Institute". She aims to achieve a better integration between agriculture and nutrition of the high Andean population, as well as to enhance the adaptation of the high Andean population to climate change, both by strengthening the management and use of agrobiodiversity.

Saverio Senni is associate professor at the Tuscia University (Italy) teaching Rural Development Policy. His research deals with multifunctional agriculture and rural development processes, focusing from a socio-economic perspective on the social and inclusive role of agricultural practices. He was member of the Management Committee of COST Action 'Green Care in Agriculture'.

Stephen Sherwood is lecturer/researcher in Knowledge, Technology, and Innovation at Wageningen University (the Netherlands) and EkoRural (Ecuador). Steve studies self-organized, self-harmful organization associated with agriculture and food, in particular that associated with mass pesticide poisoning, degradation of soils, and agrobiodiversity, and the proliferation of chronic disease.

Tammara Soma is an Assistant Professor (Planning) at the School of Resource and Environmental Management at Simon Fraser University. She is the co-founder and Research Director of the Food Systems Lab (foodsystemslab.ca), the first social innovation lab to tackle food waste in Canada. Her current project focuses on addressing farm culls and surplus in Southern BC, an interactive community food asset mapping project, the social as well as human dimensions of digital agriculture. She is co-editor of the *Routledge Handbook on Food Waste*.

Andrew Spring is a Research Associate in Northern Knowledge Networks, Associate Director of the Laurier Centre for Sustainable Food Systems, and an Adjunct Professor in Geography and Environmental Studies at Wilfrid Laurier University, Waterloo, ON. His research explores climate change adaptation and sustainable food systems with communities in Canada's North.

Phoebe Stephens is a PhD candidate at the University of Waterloo. With the support of the Pierre Elliott Trudeau Foundation and the Social Sciences and Humanities Research Council of Canada, Phoebe investigates the potential of social financing mechanisms for sustainable food systems. Phoebe's work has been published in several interdisciplinary peer-reviewed journals.

Paul V. Stock's research emphasizes care by farmers through agriculture. His most recent book (with D. Bryon Darby and Tim Hossler) *New Farmers 2014/2018* (2019) documents diverse farm practices through a combination of photography, design, and sociology. He is Associate Professor of Sociology and the Environmental Studies Program at the University of Kansas.

Lukas Szrot's current book-length work in progress focuses on how culture, religion, and values shape views of environmental change in the US. He has also written on theoretical and methodological issues in sociology and the social psychology of belief. Dr. Szrot is an Assistant Professor of Sociology at Bemidji State University.

Amy Trubek is Professor in the Nutrition and Food Sciences department at the University of Vermont and Faculty Director for University of Vermont's graduate program in Food Systems. Trained as a cultural anthropologist and chef, her research interests include the history of the culinary profession, globalization of the food supply, the relationship between taste and place, and cooking as a cultural practice. She is the author of three books: *Haute Cuisine: How the French Invented the Culinary Profession* (2000), *The Taste of Place: A Cultural Journey into Terroir* (2008), and *Making Modern Meals: How Americans Cook Today* (2017).

Marc Wegerif is Lecturer in Development Studies in the Department of Anthropology and Archaeology, University of Pretoria, focusing on agrarian transformation and food systems. He has over 30 years of development sector work experience from project level to national and international policy and advocacy. His doctorate was obtained with the Rural Sociology Group at Wageningen University.

Tony Weis is an Associate Professor of Geography at Western University whose research is broadly located in the field of political ecology. He is the author of *The Ecological Hoofprint: The Global Burden of Industrial Livestock* (2013) and *The Global Food Economy: The Battle for the Future of Farming* (2007).

Michael Woods is Professor of Human Geography at Aberystwyth University, Wales, UK. His research focuses on the global countryside, rural policy and politics, and rural–urban relations, including through the ERC GLOBAL-RURAL and Horizon 2020 ROBUST projects. He is a former editor of the *Journal of Rural Studies*.

1

REGENERATING FOOD SYSTEMS

A social-ecological approach

Jessica Duncan, Michael Carolan, and Johannes S.C. Wiskerke

Introduction

The future of food is uncertain. Rising levels of malnutrition, inequality, and environmental degradation point to the failure of food systems to deliver safe and healthy food for all. As this book goes to press, roughly one in five people around the world are under lock-down we collectively face down the Covid 19 pandemic. Yet people still need to eat. This has proven hard for some as supply chains buckle under the weight of households hording foodstuffs. Meanwhile, meat processing plants are closing, as workers, without health care, fall ill and die. To say nothing of the waste, like the US dairy farmers who had to dump millions of gallons of milk once under contract to any of the thousands of schools shut for the remainder of the academic year. Crises always highlight the core flaws of any system. As Covid-19 remains fresh in our minds, we hope these limits turn into opportunities as we realize the need for new way of thinking about we organize food systems.

As a concept, sustainability has evolved a great deal since the late 20th century, expanding beyond academia to become 'an orthodoxy for discourses' across the public and private sectors (Axinte et al. 2019, 120). There is quite broad agreement about the multi-dimensional nature of sustainability as a concept in so far as it includes the pursuit of social equity, the creation of human welfare (often through economic means), and the maintenance of a natural resource base (Béné et al. 2019, 123). The so-called Brundtland Report (1987, para. 23) added a time dimension: that we must ensure sustainable development 'meets the needs of the present without compromising the ability of future generations to meet their own needs'.

The 2030 Agenda for Sustainable Development, launched in 2016, builds on these developments and puts forwards a global plan of action. With the formal adoption of the 17 interconnected Sustainable Development Goals (SDGs), governments are tasked with developing pathways towards social, economic, and environmental dimensions of sustainability. The ambition of a regenerative food system is in line with the SDGs and reflects the realization that radical, systemic changes are needed if we are ever meet those ambitious but existentially necessary goals. To be *regenerative* implies a degree of cumulative emergence – a more-than-the-sum-of-the-parts type of outlook that is interested in more than maintenance.

The SDGs have set the international agenda for addressing sustainable development and they reflect a complex and broad view of sustainability, albeit with limitations. Practical strategies for achieving these aims remain unspecified and discussions around sustainability are frequently

1

Table 1.1 Relations between regenerative food systems and the SDGs

Goal	Relation to regenerative food systems
Goal 1: No Poverty	A core value of regeneration must be to regenerate fair, equitable systems, where food producers receive a fair price for their products and where consumers have access to healthy foods at an affordable price. This will require a redistribution of financial flows in the food system and a radical change away from (who) profits in the food value chain.
Goal 2: Zero Hunger	Achieving food security – ensuring stable access to healthy and culturally appropriate foods at all times, for all people – through sustainable practices must be a top priority for decision makers around the world. Working towards regenerative food systems allows for an opening up of possible pathways to meet this goal while ensuring that solutions are grounded in local contexts and are working with the entire food system to regenerate soils, seeds, health and sustainable diets, and vibrant communities.
Goal 3: Good Health and Wellbeing	Regeneration of healthy foods and healthy systems is at the core of regenerative food systems. Key to regenerative food systems is recognizing the importance of wellbeing for regenerative systems and how to regenerate practices and relations that promote wellbeing.
Goal 4: Quality Education	Holistic education includes food literacy but also literacy in how to navigate the food landscape. Regenerative food systems require educational pathways that iteratively link back into the livelihoods, capabilities, and desires of communities and cannot be imposed from outside.
Goal 5: Gender Equality	The majority of food producers around the world are women yet they maintain unequal access to land, financing, education, and other resources. Equality, regardless of gender, is fundamental for maintaining food systems that regenerate values of fairness and equity. This principle must also extend across races, religions, abilities, and sexualities.
Goal 6: Clean Water and Sanitation	Regenerative food systems do not contribute to the pollution of water further, they are attuned to the responsible use of water.
Goal 7: Affordable and Clean Energy	Clean energy that is accessible to all will be needed to support regenerative food systems from farm to fork. A transition to clean energy will involve trade-offs and may lead to negative societal impacts in the short term, particularly for more vulnerable segments of society. However, acting now is likely to lead to less negative impacts than acting later, when it will arguably be too late. Ensuring that support systems are in place to limit the impacts on people will also be fundamental in the short to medium time. Funding this will be a challenge but feasible, for example through new approaches to taxation.
Goal 8: Decent Work and Economic Growth	Regenerative food systems are designed to give more meaning to existing food systems jobs. This entails a shift wherein there is broad societal recognition and appreciation of work across the food system and changes in payment and profit structures.
Goal 9: Industry, Innovation, and Infrastructure	Industry can play a key role in expanding or scaling up regenerative food system practices and principles but it is important that the concept of regeneration in relation to food systems not become co-opted by industry. This is fundamentally about practices. Similarly, investment in infrastructure can facilitate the uptake and integration of regenerative food practices.
Goal 10: Reduced Inequality	A regenerative food system has values of fairness and equity at its core. Reduced inequality relates to other goals such as access to food, gender equality, access to education and quality work with fair wages.

(Continued)

Table 1.1 (Cont.)

Goal	Relation to regenerative food systems
Goal 11: Sustainable Cities and Communities	Regenerative food systems are key to sustainable cities and communities and are useful for advancing the three pillars of sustainability: ecological, social, economic. Cities are key leaders in food system transition and need to be actively developing integrated policies that move beyond sustainability towards regeneration.
Goal 12: Responsible Consumption and Production	The link between responsible consumption and production is key within regenerative food systems. For food production to be viable, there is a need for appropriate markets.
Goal 13: Climate Action	We are facing a climate emergency. Concrete and rapid change is needed from governments, the private sector, and broader society. Conventional agriculture is a major contributor to climate change. Regenerative food systems need to ensure that greenhouse gas emissions are limited. These will be different depending on eco-region. There is no single best solution. We also recognize that there may be contradictions when it comes to what is best for the climate and best for biodiversity. These contradictions need to be made explicit and democratic processes are needed to make difficult decisions.
Goal 14: Life Below Water	The sea provides a range of food products that are fished and harvested. Doing this in a sustainable manner, with a view to regeneration, is fundamental for not only maintaining but regenerating fish stocks and marine environments.
Goal 15: Life on Land	The goal of protecting, restoring, and promoting sustainable use of terrestrial ecosystems is fundamentally aligned with the objectives of regenerative food systems.
Goal 16: Peace and Justice, Strong Institutions	The promotion of peaceful and inclusive societies is a core value of regenerative systems. Food insecurity and hunger are on the rise and conflict contributes to this. We can expect greater conflicts as the impacts of climate changes increase and there is more migration. Regenerative food systems that are adaptable to climatic changes and climatic variability are fundamental to limiting conflict, particularly in areas of protracted crisis.
Goal 17: Partnerships for the Goals	There is a clear need to strengthen means of implementing systemic change towards sustainable and regenerative systems through global partnerships. Indeed, an integrated approach that sees cities, nations, regions, and international actors working together in a comprehensive and coherent way is needed to pave pathways to regeneration. At the same time, it is fundamental that local contexts are respected and one-size-fits-all solutions are avoided.

reduced to the environmental dimension (Béné et al. 2019, 123). Further, progress towards achieving SDG 2 – to end hunger, achieve food security and improved nutrition, and promote sustainable agriculture – is far from positive. Data from 2016 suggest that the number of chronically undernourished people in the world increased to 815 million, up from 777 million in 2015 (FAO et al. 2017). That same year, 21 countries experienced high or moderately high domestic prices for one or more staple cereal food commodities (UN 2017, 4). Aid allocated to agriculture from member countries of the Development Assistance Committee of the Organization for Economic Cooperation and Development (OECD) remains where it was in the late 1990s, at 7 per cent. The prospects of achieving a sustainable future are looking bleak.

One challenge is that, despite international agreement around 17 goals and 169 targets, sustainability remains a contested and political concept and process (Béné et al. 2019, 124; Eakin et al. 2017, 3). While most agree that our food system is failing, what the failure is about is less clear (for a summary see Béné et al. 2019) due to competing interpretations of key problems, solutions, and competing interests (Béné et al. 2019; Moragues-Faus, Sonnino, and Marsden 2017). Further, understandings of sustainability and food systems are informed by the underlying values that shape how experts view and interpret the world (Béné et al. 2019, 117; Eakin et al. 2017; Foran et al. 2014). Some experts point to the inability of the system to feed future populations, calling for a closing of the yield gap and investments in existing supply chains. Others are concerned about the inability of the system to deliver a healthy diet and call for a closing of the nutrient gap. There are those who are concerned about the inability of the system to produce equal and equitable benefits and call for enhanced grassroots autonomy. And there are those who think that the greatest failure is about impacts on the environment and push for a reduction of the 'food-print'. Others see the failure as a mix of some or all these perspectives.

We acknowledge that the root of the problem is not narrative or conceptual, but we also know that how we talk about these challenges matters. From where we stand, it is clear that we need better concepts and new stories that position us as part of nature; not as sustainers of nature, but as active participants in an integrated cycle of regeneration. We need examples that refer to processes of enhancing the ability of living beings to co-evolve in ways that allow for diversity, complexity, and creativity (Mang and Haggard 2016, xiv); that invoke images of participating with the environment in harmony with ecological systems, instead of images of doing less damage (Reed 2007).

Sustainability, in its dominant form, is primarily an exercise in efficiency. With regeneration, we push for a shift in focus: to fundamentally rethink and redesign our food and related practices so that they (re)build and contribute to (i.e. regenerate) soil fertility, community cohesion, integrated policies, or sustainable diets, to name but a few. We accept that this concept will certainly be subject to many of the same tensions, challenges, and limitations as the concept of sustainability. However, unlike the verb sustain – to support or to cause something to continue – the verb regenerate means to produce or create. We argue for moving beyond 'supporting' and 'maintaining' towards 'creating' is what is needed – to engage in a politics and to afford practices that *add* to the world (Carolan 2013). While we need to move beyond business as usual, we also need to regenerate the systems that have been adversely impacted. This more adequately reflects the values and principles that are needed to move towards safe, just, healthy, and diverse food systems. Towards this end, we conceptualize regeneration as a holistic approach that moves past neutral environmental impact towards the creation of effects for a mutually supportive symbiosis across the food system (Axinte et al. 2019). From this approach, the human–nature dualism dissolves, making analytic and practical space for co-creating and co-evolving. It forces an engagement with the production of life, and on the ways this is cultivated.

Six principles for regenerative food systems

While many of the chapters in this handbook address practices which may be considered niche, it is important to note that these are not merely 'alternative' food systems: these are systems which foster agro-bio-socio-economic diversity. In turn, these chapters address many of the key challenges facing food systems (e.g. climate change, changing demographics, labour, access to land; soil fertility, displacement, animal welfare, food waste, health, and justice).

Taken as a whole, these chapters point to a number of key practices and ideas that would appear central to advancing regenerative food systems. We present them here as principles for regenerative food systems, noting that these are not exclusive or clear-cut principles, but rather dynamic and cross-cutting.

The six principles are:

1) Acknowledging and including diverse forms of knowing and being
2) Taking care of people, animals, and the planet
3) Moving beyond capitalist approaches
4) Commoning the food system
5) Promoting accountable innovations
6) Long-term planning and rural–urban relations

Principle 1: to acknowledge and include diverse forms of knowing and being in the world

Many chapters in this handbook speak to the need to embrace diverse approaches to research, including Indigenous and traditional ecological knowledges. Towards this end, Levkoe et al. (Chapter 2) bring in an explicitly normative agenda for regenerative food system research that builds on theories and practices of decolonization, feminism, post-capitalism, co-production of nature and knowledge, and engaged scholarship to enhance a more traditional political economy approach. This aligns well with the arguments put forward by Chesnais (Chapter 5) on the need for cultural appropriateness in the development of regenerative practices. Going more specific, Dwiartma (Chapter 3) and Huambachano (Chapter 4) present traditional and Indigenous practices to illustrate the ways these can move us towards more sustainable and regenerative food systems. Blay-Palmer et al. (Chapter 6) show how existing frameworks including the Right to Adequate Food, the UN Declaration on the Rights of Indigenous People, and the Convention for the Safeguarding of Intangible Cultural Heritage can function to support Indigenous and traditional food systems. They argue that protecting cultural heritage is key to advancing regenerative food systems. In terms of including diverse forms of knowing in policy making and governance processes, Deijl and Duncan (Chapter 7) call for critical reflection and action when it comes to the design and roll-out of participatory food policy processes. They argue that policies for regenerative food systems need to be participatory and co-produced by a diversity of stakeholders and that meaningful and that representative co-production is needed.

Principle 2: taking care of people, animals, and the environment

A regenerative food future must have justice at its core. Towards this end, Stock and Szrot (Chapter 8) present a reflection on justice in relation to regenerative food systems, arguing that justice is a struggle to reshape reality in ways which allow for people to flourish. Looking specifically at labor, Sbicca (Chapter 9) explores tensions between food labor and technology by positioning these in class struggle. Engaging with class is key to position visions of regenerative labor alongside actually existing economic conditions, both historically and contemporarily. Hassink and colleagues (Chapter 10) focus on caring in agriculture. Using care ethics as a tool to analyse agricultural and food practices that aim to reconnect with society and nature, they argue that caring agriculture can transition approaches of control towards ones of partnership and respect, values which must be at the core of any regenerative food system. Weis and Ellis (Chapter 11) turn to current debates on the role of animals in regenerative food systems and map out arguments for different forms of farming that take care of animals. Taking a different position in relation to animals, Amos and Bailey (Chapter 12) look at the management of fisheries, highlighting how our food systems are embedded within socio-cultural, economic, and ecological contexts. Focusing on examples from Canada they make a case for considering food systems as a part of complex environmental and human systems (sometimes referred to as social-ecological systems). In so doing, opportunities open up to align human health and wellbeing with environmental health.

Principle 3: to overcome capitolocentrism when it comes to understanding how people access food

As Levkoe et al. explain (Chapter 2), capitalocentrism refers here to the positioning of all market processes with reference to capitalism. With this principle we dare people to think and look beyond the constraints of capitalism to uncover myriad practices (existing and potential) that contribute to regenerative food systems. Schneider and Cassol (Chapter 13) place the discussion on agri-food markets within the broader scope of economic sociology, highlighting the analytical approaches to markets that have been mobilized by leading schools of contemporary sociological thinking. In so doing they uncover possibilities for dialogue and expand the explanatory potential of markets. Wegerif's (Chapter 14) contribution offers a more concrete entry point into thinking about how markets function in a non-capitolocentric way, through the concept of a symbiotic food system. Symbiotic food systems are organized around how people arrange their economic activities to meet their daily needs. Importantly, the concept includes reflections on the management of the tension between the individual striving to look after themselves and working in solidarity for the mutual benefit of the others involved.

Davies (Chapter 15) also highlights the importance of looking at what people do and how they organize to access food in her chapter on sharing. By mapping the digital traces of contemporary food sharing initiatives, she highlights a diversity of practices that exist, but are often overlooked, and which advance key tenets of a more sustainable and regenerative food system. Taking a broader view, Stephens and Clapp (Chapter 16) consider the impact of financial systems on food systems, and examine how social finance could potentially support more regenerative food systems in the context of financialization in the agri-food sector. Social finance refers to investment for social and environmental return, rather than purely for financial gain. This relates to questions raised by Carolan (Chapter 17) who, looking at smaller-scale entrepreneurs, calls for more discussion around businesses whose owners seek to maximize profit, particularly in light of the pro social trade-offs. Carolan also highlights the numerous ways that small-scale food entrepreneurs can become trapped in cycles of debt, while reminding us that gender dynamics need to be explicitly addressed in efforts to build regenerative food systems. While many innovations and practices exist outside of and or in opposition to capitalist approaches, we are also reminded that many people are working to make ends meet and to build businesses within a capitalist framework. For example, Nuñez-Solis et al. (Chapter 18) provide a case for individualised market strategies to support regenerative food systems based on their research into coffee production in Costa Rica. They show how some small-scale producers are moving away from international cooperative marketing structures (i.e. Fair Trade), opting instead for individualized, market-based strategies.

Principle 4: a commoning of the food system

As Ferrando (Chapter 19) explains, commoning the food system calls for qualifying food as a non-commodity, and as part of a commons. In this vision, food is a non-commodity at the center of an ecological organization structured around the principles of anti-colonialism, anti-patriarchy, equality, social justice, and on the recognition of the inherent co-construction of nature and society as intrinsically connected. This approach provides a conceptual entry point to engage not only with the status quo but also with the idea of multiple food systems that are both common and communing. The latter is argued to be a central process of interacting that is key as we move towards regenerative food systems.

Grivins (Chapter 20) builds on the idea of commoning food by considering foraging practices in relation to regenerative food systems. He argues that foraging also usefully creates new linkages between categories that are often perceived as contradictory – environment and person, the local and the global, the past and the present, and the traditional and the modern. Patnaik and Jongerden (Chapter 21) also challenge the view of food as a commodity by showing how conservation and sharing of landrace varieties and use of sustainable farming methods helped communities to interact and rebuild their farms. Their case study shows how seed sharing and collection through the space of commons can lead to the restoration, rebuilding, and regeneration of agricultural practices informed by traditional, Indigenous knowledge in ways that are beneficial for small-scale farmers and key to promoting regenerative food systems. Natividad and colleagues (Chapter 22) provide insights into different modes of management of life in agriculture and food by examining agrobiodiversity as the product of an aesthetic order. In so doing, they show how a situated reordering of food systems can contributes to the possibility of more regenerative agriculture, food, and nutrition.

Principle 5: accountable innovations that advance regenerative and just food systems

When thinking about regenerative food systems, it is clear that innovations are needed: business as usual is not an option (IAASTD 2009). In this context, we understand innovations as new forms of social practice and organization, as well as new or improved technological products and processes. Accountability is linked to what is seen as legitimate in a political culture; to what citizens in a specific setting and time period deem acceptable. This can be complicated when we consider that so many of the problems we face when it comes to food systems can be classified as 'wicked problems': problems of extreme consequence to humanity (and the earth) that are difficult or impossible to solve (Conklin 2006; Duncan 2015; Rittel and Webber 1974). This in turn links to the first principle, acknowledge and include diverse forms of knowing and being in the world. We recognize this only complexifies an already complicated matter, but as Einstein reminds us, 'We can't solve problems by using the same kind of thinking we used when we created them'.

Harnessing the positive potential for innovation to advance regenerative food systems means also recognizing that some innovations may contribute to environmental degradation, disrupt livelihoods, and exacerbate inequalities (UNCTAD 2017). As such, the innovations which are supported (with time, labor, financing, and policy support) need to account for social, ecological, economic impacts. Accountable innovation demands we ask key questions, such as what kinds of innovation are both needed and capable of being regenerative; queries that ultimately hinge on processes and principles of social inclusivity and political transparency (Bronson 2019; Eastwood et al. 2017; van der Burg, Bogaardt, and Wolfert 2019). Processes that rely on co-production or citizen science could provide useful guidance here.

While it is clear that more thinking is needed as to how to hold private actors accountable to the wider society, it is also clear that we need to ensure that innovations (be they technical or social) are acceptable to the communities where they are being implemented, that they address root problems (not just symptoms), and that they are transparent in terms of who gets what, why, and how.

One key development within food systems innovations that aims to tackle root problems builds on the circular economy. Pascucci (Chapter 23) explains that circular economy is based on a number of key principles: resources need to circulate in closed loops; renewable energy should be used where possible; and diversity should be celebrated. He also highlights, importantly, that in discussions around food and circular economy, there is a polarization around two narratives, each of which leads to the identification of very different food futures. Using a food systems design approach he suggests two possible pathways for transitions: globalized industrial ecology and networked agro-ecology.

Bronson (Chapter 24) takes a closer look at the tools and technologies emerging in the field of digital agriculture. The research shows that, in the current economic and legal order, these innovations do not yet support regenerative purposes but are rather reproducing a number of social and cultural food system challenges. Yet it is also clear that there is an opportunity to shape digital innovations and their infrastructures for a diversity of food system actors. We reiterate here the importance of accountable innovation.

Macharia (Chapter 25) presents possibilities for new pathways for innovation at the farm level. Exploring relationships between digital technologies, medium-scale farmers, and the phenomenon of telephone farming he shows how digitalization can change business processes. These digital technologies engender specific effects which in turn reshape the debate on how we think and talk about agri-food-based technologies.

Principle 6: the importance of planning for the advancement of regenerative food systems

Regenerative food systems require thoughtful, deliberate, and long-term planning. Central to planning for regenerative food systems is rethinking the rural/urban divide. Woods (Chapter 26) usefully considers the significance of rural–urban linkages in current and future food systems. This is fundamental as food is at the core of the rural–urban relation. Contemporary food systems involve rural–urban interactions that stretch over longer distances, and in turn create dependencies between non-adjacent localities. While urban agriculture is gaining much needed attention, it is clear that the global countryside feeds an increasingly urbanized global population. In turn, Woods notes that a transition to more sustainable forms of farming is likely to involve the relocation of food production back closer to urban markets, including the reinvigoration of urban and peri-urban agriculture.

Morse et al. (Chapter 27) address some of these concerns by taking a landscape perspective on planning. In their chapter they highlight the promise of working landscape policy approaches for engaging public support for progressive food production policies. Their reflections illustrate the importance of funding, culture, place, and human–environmental interactions in developing appropriate policies. Further, taking a landscape view to planning pushes people out of silos and allows for improved dialogue around the possibilities and potential of landscapes for regenerative ends. Ilieva (Chapter 28) expands on this idea: by taking a foodshed approach to food-city co-evolution she presents clear reasons why planning for regenerative food systems is a vital new frontier in city planning and agri-food planning more broadly.

Soma (Chapter 29) brings us back to a circular economy approach and challenges us to reflect on the categorization of food and waste. In so doing, she aims to provide alternative ways to view and value food. From the perspective that food waste is a resource, Soma outlines how waste can be managed better in a regenerative food system, without losing sight of unequal and uneven waste collection. In explaining how food waste can become a resource within a circular food system, she also draws attention to the urgent need to revitalize biodegradable food packaging.

Finally, Ionis (Chapter 30) presents a broader reflection on the relations between food insecurity and the market-based globalized world. He reminds us that in our current state of climate and food crises, efforts are underway to present these as non-political crises that can be overcome through the incorporation of more production areas and more input-intense technologies. He usefully reminds us that crises are moments where we need to react.

While developing this book we repeatedly asked ourselves: do we need a new label? With agroecology, permaculture, climate smart agriculture, ecological intensification, sustainable intensification, do we really want to engage with yet another concept. Since you are reading this, you have already figured out that the answer is yes. There are two main reasons we came to this decision.

First, we note that regenerative is emerging as a new buzz word in the agri-food domain and it is important for us to get a handle on what it means and how it can be usefully applied. The term regenerative is one that is emerging in some scientific disciplines – spatial design for example (Cole 2012a, 2012b; Mang and Haggard 2016), but also in the sociology of food and agriculture – and we look at it as a step beyond sustainability. This leads us to the second reason. We identified an opportunity to participate in the shaping of this concept, from a socio-ecological perspective, to help move us beyond some of the limits of sustainability. As explained above, we need a concept that can better reconcile relations between the social and environmental; one that actively locates society and community in its models. We can see value in the concept insofar as it can challenge the dominant scientific mindset that is busy with input/output level analysis and de-political constructions of sustainability (Duncan 2015, 2016). This handbook thus moves us beyond the boundaries of sustainability, to focus less on maintaining systems, towards practices that build and regenerate ecosystems, communities, and cultures. Regenerative approaches to food systems seek to understand and implement practices that reinstate and regenerate over time. These approaches take into account not only farming systems, but also farm families, fishers, pastoralists, workers, migrants, rural communities, landscapes, and regions and ecosystems. They are key to our collective food futures.

Discussion questions

1. We have proposed six principles to inform a transition towards regenerative food systems. Can you think of other principles and reflect on what they would add?
2. We argued that thinking about regeneration moved us beyond the nature–culture binary and allows for thinking around co-creation. Can you think of examples of what this kind of thinking looks like in practice?
3. How does a 'regenerative' lens complicate recent investments by industry to promote sustainability along the supply chain?

Recommended reading

Carolan, M. 2016. (2012) *The Sociology of Food and Agriculture*, 2nd edition. Oxon: Routledge.

Cole, Raymond J. 2012a. "Regenerative Design and Development: Current Theory and Practice." *Building Research and Information* 40 (1): 1–6. doi:10.1080/09613218.2012.617516.

Eakin, Hallie, John Patrick Connors, Christopher Wharton, Farryl Bertmann, Angela Xiong, and Jared Stoltzfus. 2017. "Identifying Attributes of Food System Sustainability: Emerging Themes and Consensus." *Agriculture and Human Values* 34 (3): 757–73. doi:10.1007/s10460-016-9754-8.

IPES Food. 2015. *The New Science of Sustainable Food Systems: Overcoming Barriers to Food Systems Reform.* Leuven: International Panel of Experts on Sustainable Food Systems. www.ipes-food.org/_img/upload/files/NewScienceofSusFood.pdf.

Maye, D. and J. Duncan. 2017. "Sustainable Food System Transitions: European Perspectives and Research Agenda." *Sociologia Ruralis* 57 (3): 267–73. doi:10.1111/soru.12177.

Wiskerke, J.S.C. and S. Verhoeven. 2018. *Flourishing Foodscapes: Designing City-Region Food Systems.* Amsterdam: Valiz Publishers.

References

Axinte, Lorena F., Abid Mehmood, Terry Marsden, and Dirk Roep. 2019. "Regenerative City-Regions: A New Conceptual Framework." *Regional Studies, Regional Science* 6 (1): 117–29. doi:10.1080/21681376.2019.1584542.

Béné, Christophe, Peter Oosterveer, Lea Lamotte, Inge D. Brouwer, Stef de Haan, Steve D. Prager, Elise F. Talsma, and Colin K. Khoury. 2019. "When Food Systems Meet Sustainability – Current Narratives and Implications for Actions." *World Development* 113 (January): 116–30. doi:10.1016/j.worlddev.2018.08.011.

Bronson, Kelly. 2019. "Looking through a Responsible Innovation Lens at Uneven Engagements with Digital Farming." *NJAS – Wageningen Journal of Life Sciences*, April: 100294. doi:10.1016/j.njas.2019.03.001.

Brundtland, G. 1987. *Report of the World Commission on Environment and Development: Our Common Future.* New York: United Nations. https://sustainabledevelopment.un.org/content/documents/5987our-common-future.pdf.

Carolan, Michael S. 2013. "The Wild Side of Agro-Food Studies: On Co-Experimentation, Politics, Change, and Hope." *Sociologia Ruralis* 53 (4): 413–31.

Cole, Raymond J. 2012a. "Regenerative Design and Development: Current Theory and Practice." *Building Research and Information* 40 (1): 1–6. doi:10.1080/09613218.2012.617516.

Cole, Raymond J.. 2012b. "Transitioning from Green to Regenerative Design." *Building Research and Information* 40 (1): 39–53. doi:10.1080/09613218.2011.610608.

Conklin, Jeffrey. 2006. *Dialogue Mapping: Building Shared Understanding of Wicked Problems.* Chichester: Wiley Publishing.

Duncan, Jessica. 2015. "'Greening' Global Food Governance." *Canadian Food Studies* 2 (2): 335–44. doi:10.15353/cfs-rcea.v2i2.104.

Duncan, Jessica. 2016. "Governing in a Post-Political Era: Civil Society Participation for Improved Food Security Governance." In *Advances in Food Security and Sustainability*, volume 1, edited by David Barling, 137–61. Burlington, VT: Academic Press.

Eakin, Hallie, John Patrick Connors, Christopher Wharton, Farryl Bertmann, Angela Xiong, and Jared Stoltzfus. 2017. "Identifying Attributes of Food System Sustainability: Emerging Themes and Consensus." *Agriculture and Human Values* 34 (3): 757–73. doi:10.1007/s10460-016-9754-8.

Eastwood, C., L. Klerkx, M. Ayre, and B. Dela Rue. 2017. "Managing Socio-Ethical Challenges in the Development of Smart Farming: From a Fragmented to a Comprehensive Approach for Responsible Research and Innovation." *Journal of Agricultural and Environmental Ethics*, December. doi:10.1007/s10806-017-9704-5.

FAO, IFAD, UNICEF, WFP, and WHO. 2017. *The State of Food Security and Nutrition in the World 2017. Building Resilience for Peace and Food Security.* Rome. www.fao.org/3/a-I7695e.pdf.

Foran, Tira, James R.A. Butler, Liana J. Williams, Wolf J. Wanjura, Andy Hall, Lucy Carter, and Peter S. Carberry. 2014. "Taking Complexity in Food Systems Seriously: An Interdisciplinary Analysis." *World Development* 61 (September): 85–101. doi:10.1016/j.worlddev.2014.03.023.

IAASTD. 2009. *Synthesis Report of the International Assessment of Agricultural Knowledge, Science and Technology for Development.* Washington, DC. https://wedocs.unep.org/handle/20.500.11822/7862 (accessed Mar. 2020).

Mang, Pamela, and Ben Haggard. 2016. *Regenerative Development and Design: A Framework for Evolving Sustainability.* Hoboken, NJ: Wiley.

Moragues-Faus, Ana, Roberta Sonnino, and Terry Marsden. 2017. "Exploring European Food System Vulnerabilities: Towards Integrated Food Security Governance." *Environmental Science and Policy* 75 (September): 184–215. doi:10.1016/j.envsci.2017.05.015.

Reed, Bill. 2007. "Shifting from 'Sustainability' to Regeneration." *Building Research and Information* 35 (6): 674–80. doi:10.1080/09613210701475753.

Rittel, Horst W.J. and Melvin M. Webber. 1974. "Dilemas in a General Theory of Planning." *Policy Sciences* 4: 155–69.

UN. 2017. *Progress towards the Sustainable Development Goals: Report of the Secretary-General (E/2017/66).* New York: United Nations.

UNCTAD. 2017. *New Innovation Approaches to Support the Implementation of the Sustainable Development Goals.* Geneva. https://unctad.org/en/pages/PublicationWebflyer.aspx?publicationid=1775.

van der Burg, Simone, Marc-Jeroen Bogaardt, and Sjaak Wolfert. 2019. "Ethics of Smart Farming: Current Questions and Directions for Responsible Innovation towards the Future." *NJAS – Wageningen Journal of Life Sciences*, March: 100289. doi:10.1016/j.njas.2019.01.001.

2

A POLITICAL ECONOMY FOR REGENERATIVE FOOD SYSTEMS

Towards an integrated research agenda

Charles Z. Levkoe, Ana Moragues-Faus, and Jessica Duncan

Introduction

The political economy of food has catalysed a critical analysis within food studies.[1] Scholars have used political economy to analyse food systems dynamics, and to argue that food, and food systems, cannot be understood as abstract concepts outside of social relationships (see for example Bernstein 2010, 2017; Buttel 2001; Fine 1994; Friedmann 1993). In turn, political economy has been fundamental to understanding the power dynamics inherent within the development of the global food systems that have replaced subsistence agriculture and regional markets over the past centuries. Constantly evolving, political economy helps to uncover power relations across all aspects of food systems along with related social and ecological influences and impacts. While the political economy of food is multifaceted, analysis tends to focus on the role that capital and the state have played in restructuring agriculture and fisheries along with grassroots efforts to develop more sustainable food systems within the context of (late) capitalism. As the challenges facing food systems continue to evolve, it is important to reflect on the value of political economy as a research tool for advancing regenerative food systems, as these are desperately needed.

Climate change has increased rates of species extinction, loss of biodiversity, and increased inequality threatening food systems and the social and ecological health of all life on earth. In 2019, the world's leading climate scientists published a report through the United Nations' Intergovernmental Panel on Climate Change (IPCC) warning that, in just over a decade, global warming will increase risks of drought, floods, extreme heat and poverty, with devastating impacts on hundreds of millions around the globe (IPCC 2019). Food systems researchers are increasingly recognizing the links between food, well-being, and the planet's health. Recently, reports from the International Panel of Experts on Sustainable Food Systems (IPES-Food 2015, 2016, 2017) and the EAT-Lancet Commission (Willett et al. 2019) warned of the dangers of current food systems trends that put profits over social and ecological health. Recognizing these new realities, we suggest that scholars must seriously consider the possibilities for a political economy of regenerative food systems – that is, food systems that feed people, work with nature, and are controlled by those that grow, harvest, and forage for food. Our understanding of regenerative food systems is based in systems thinking and rooted in ideals of food sovereignty and agroecology (Rosset and Altieri 2017; Wittman et al. 2010). It is above all fundamentally concerned with building healthy people, healthy communities, and a healthy planet.

In this chapter, we present a brief review of the evolution of the political economy of food systems research. We argue that while there are significant gaps in the ways that this existing framework has addressed sustainable food systems, scholars should continue to engage with political economy in order to critically address the flows of power. Building on a critical review of the literature and reflecting on our own scholarship, and recognizing that justice must remain at the foundation of any analytical framework, we propose potential hybridizations of the political economy approach to food systems with other conceptual developments. These include decolonizing approaches, feminist groundings, post-capitalist approaches, co-production of knowledge and nature, and engaged scholarship. We argue that, when combined with a more traditional political economy framework, these approaches expand the potential for research to advance regenerative food systems. As such, integrating innovative theoretical and practical perspectives along with related methodological tools offers new and exciting horizons.

Evolution of a political economy of food systems

Political economy to food systems was adopted in the 1980s as an approach to identify the multiple relations between people, capital, and space that contributed to ill health, inequity, and ecological degradation (Buttel 2001; Friedmann 1982; Marsden et al. 1996). Political economy approaches have since gained popularity in the study of food systems in part due to the focus on power relations and the resulting socio-material inequalities. According to Collinson (2003, 10), political economy analyses concentrate on "the interaction of political and economic processes in a society: the distribution of power and wealth between different groups and individuals, and the processes that create, sustain and transform these relationships over time." Bernstein (2017, 8) has put forward questions to uncover the key relations of power with respect to social interactions and the ways they impact and influence decision-making across food systems. He asks: Who owns what? Who does what? Who gets what? What do they do with it? Usefully, these can be applied "across different sites and scales, from individual farming households through village, local and national socioeconomic units of investigation to the world economy" (Bernstein 2017, 8). These simple questions align with a political economy approach insofar as they help up uncover relations of power and the various ways social relations impact and influence decision-making across food systems.

A political economy approach to food systems is further distinguished by its analysis of food as part of both political and economic processes. Moreover, the dynamics of food systems are understood in terms of relations of power and not simply material goods and outcomes. Political economy approaches have incorporated wide historical and geographical perspectives, helping to explain why and how power changes over time, and how the activities of one group affect others (Collinson 2003:10). As such, political economy approaches are used to understand the economic and political dynamics that affect issues such as access, availability, production, harvesting, and consumption.

A political economy approach has also been used to analyse food systems processes at different scales, with a particular focus on agriculture. An example of this is the study of farmers' strategies through a range of structuralist approaches which include exploring the *agrarian question* and the class position of food producers (Goodman and Watts 1997). Over time food systems scholars have adapted political economy approaches to address gaps and emerging issues. The so-called consumption turn in food systems research (part of the broader cultural turn in geography and other disciplines) offered new approaches and tools for analysing power relations and addressed questions of value and quality across the food chain. This focus on consumption served to highlight gaps in the political economy scholarship that had been focused primarily on a structural analysis of agricultural production (Buttel 2001). Adapting to these new perspectives, political economy scholars started to address the agency of food producers, retailers and consumers along with the role of culture and identity within food politics (Goodman and DuPuis 2002; Lockie and Kitto 2000). These approaches expanded the scope of political economy by stressing the need to address issues of identity and incorporate behavioral perspectives. In so doing they provided new ways of accounting for agency in theorizing change.

Despite this, many critics warned of insufficient engagement with feminist theory, postcolonial theory, critical race studies, and social constructivism (Galt 2013). Scholars have also argued that political economy approaches have failed to appreciate new ecological conditions within food systems and been insufficient in their recognition and, in turn, conceptualizations of the role of nature (Boyd et al. 2001; Galt 2013). For example, the focus on human agency brought about by the consumption turn ignored the role of non-human actors in food systems and lamented an omission of nature in explaining prospects for societal change. Many of these critical elements are addressed by the increasingly influential field of political ecology (Perreault et al. 2015), which more fully integrates ideas of nature into its analysis and is expanding in many directions including urban political ecology, feminist political ecology, and the political ecology of food (see below). A recognition of co-production of knowledge and nature has been championed by diverse theoretical perspectives, from political ecology to social innovation. Food systems researchers are increasingly aware of the need to mobilize this concept as a means to incorporate nature more fully in political economy debates. For that purpose, political ecology perspectives are considered particularly useful, along with other concepts such as socio-natures, insofar as they examine the historically situated process through which nature and society are materially and discursively co-productive of one another (Aeberhard and Rist 2009; Alkon 2013).

Despite these limits, we maintain a commitment to political economy insofar as it is useful for continuing to identify and critique socio-economic and political dynamics of food systems by exposing how power operates across multiple scales. Furthermore, we recognize that by-passing socio-economic and political relations can contribute to actively reproducing social inequalities (Gibson-Graham 2006; Gregson 1995; Winter 2003). However, we contend that an explicitly political and normative agenda is required to advance a research agenda that can move us towards regenerative and equitable food systems. In what follows we put forward a proposal for a hybrid approach for understanding food system dynamics that builds on the strengths of political economy. Such hybrid approaches have been championed notably within cultural geography and post-structural sociology and include the theories that supersede structure/agency dichotomies (Busch and Juska 1997; Lockie 2002; Wilkinson 2006) and embrace socio-ecological perspectives to bridge society and nature (Moragues-Faus and Marsden 2017).

Expanding the political economy of sustainable food systems

From this brief review, it is clear that the lines of political economy are increasingly blurring its contours. We note the continued value and use of established political economy approaches but also recognize a need to continue to expand and evolve in order to address the changing social and ecological context. Expanding political economy for regenerative food systems requires an integrated approach to research and action. We here argue that it calls for an explicit and critical normative positioning that is grounded in a justice perspective. Further, it must not only recognize the value of different perspectives, but also acknowledge and account for different ways of knowing alongside traditional forms of academic knowledge that has dominated political economy to date. There is also the need to value historical approaches that map cultural flows and help to elucidate how narratives and socio-ecological conditions are created (and to be prepared to discard those that do not serve normative objectives). In the following subsections, we present a sample of approaches and methods we deem fundamental to a regenerative food systems research agenda that can contribute to a political economy approach (and vice versa). For each, we also provide examples from our own research experiences to reflect on how these theoretical tools add valuable insights to conceptualize and enact sustainable food system practices while highlighting the challenges arising in an application of these frameworks.

Decolonizing approaches

Broadly speaking decolonization is a deeply political process that refers to the theoretical and practical contestation and (re)imagining of western and colonial narratives and social relations. Decolonizing approaches refer to disconnecting from systems that have contributed to the violence (and in many cases genocide) against Indigenous people (Smith 2013). Applied to research, decolonization is a recognition that academic ways of knowing are implicated in the colonial and imperial project and have furthered the marginalization and oppression of Indigenous people around the globe. Furthermore, it is a recognition that research can be a process of healing and revitalization for communities and Indigenous–settler relationships (Kovach 2015; Wilson 2009).

Decolonizing approaches recognize the impacts of the dominant food system on Indigenous peoples and their traditional territories (Grey and Patel 2015; Kepkiewicz and Dale 2019). When discussing food systems, it is essential that researchers acknowledge that political economy approaches are rooted in colonial knowledge and an uncritical use can risk further epistemic violence (Teo 2010). This means addressing the power relations inherent in the control and ownership of land, water, and seeds that have been appropriated from Indigenous peoples through violence, disposition, and displacement. The history of the dominant food system is synonymous with the history of colonialism and consolidation of power (Mintz 1986). Furthermore, colonial structures (i.e. settler-colonialism) and exploitative relationships are reproduced in everyday practices – including through research. Decolonization must involve a process of supporting Indigenous resurgence, self-determination, sovereignty, and nationhood, the repatriation of Indigenous land, and the reimagining of all our relationships to land and water (Corntassel 2012; Tuck and Yang 2012). Decolonization can contribute to political economy's commitment to identifying and challenging the dominant capitalist, industrial food system through acknowledging and addressing the impact on Indigenous communities and traditional territories (Grey and Patel 2015; Kepkiewicz and Dale 2019; Morrison 2011).

The project "Understanding our Food Systems: Building Food Sovereignty in Northwestern Ontario[2]" is an example of a decolonizing approach. The project was led by the Indigenous Food Circle, a network of Indigenous-led and Indigenous-serving organizations in the Thunder Bay region, Canada (Levkoe et al. 2019d). Beginning in 2017, a coordinating team of scholar-activists and community-based practitioners worked with fourteen First Nations with the goal to rebuild Indigenous food systems and work towards food sovereignty. The project and the coordinating team facilitated the development of relationships through continuous communication and networking, while providing support for action projects established by each First Nation (see Levkoe et al., 2019c). This project stands against research that has been conducted by academics or consultants that furthers the settler-colonial project. Projects like Understanding our Food Systems that are led by First Nations and rooted in food sovereignty and action-based outcomes demonstrate opportunities to decolonize research.

Feminist groundings

Feminist research has contributed novel methodological approaches that work to challenge and unravel dominant notions of research, allowing for more expansive sources and forms of knowledge to emerge. These perspectives have enriched food systems research and political economy perspectives for decades. This is not least because in nearly all societies gender has, and continues to, play a central role in defining roles and responsibilities related to the production, manufacturing, provisioning, eating, and disposal of food (Bock and Duncan 2017). Feminist researchers focus on ways that everyday practices, affective/emotional relationships, and the micro-politics of control can help elucidate the multiscale co-constitution of inequalities, from the body to the community to the global level. This approach has had a major impact on understanding how power contributes to the reproduction of the neoliberal globalized food system (Elmhirst 2011; Hayes-Conroy and Hayes-Conroy 2013; Truelove 2011). Feminist approaches are particularly useful in exploring embodied ways of knowing (and eating) (see for example Bryant and Jaworski 2011; Epstein 1996). Recent debates situate the focus on the intersectionality of gender, class, race, and other subjectivities as lenses to understand the historical constitution and current reproduction of foodscapes (Moragues-Faus and Marsden 2017). Lewis (2015, 423) writes, "taking intersectionality into account also means fully embracing interdisciplinarity." Such approaches to the study of food serve to elucidate understandings of power as well as resistance. Cunniff Gilson's (2015) work has shown how the application of feminist theory through core concepts such as vulnerability, relationality, and dependency are key to not only understanding injustices in contemporary food systems but also pursuing food justice. For her, a feminist approach helps resolve the tension between critiques of the industrial food system and critiques of the sociocultural politics of food and health. Given that food practices are gendered and that women commonly face higher risks and greater burdens from the impacts of climate change in situations of poverty, and the majority of the world's poor are women, a political economy of regenerative food systems has much to gain from integrating feminist groundings.

Taking a feminist approach to understanding changing access to land for pastoralists in Gujarat India, the research of Duncan and Agarwal (2017) focused on women in order to better understand challenges they face in exercising or maintaining their rights. Using ethnographic data and an analytic framework building on sociological theories of practices they analyse a typical day in the lives of the women in areas impacted by land grabbing. In so doing they identified specific ways in which the loss of access to land, and corresponding loss of livestock, impacted the lives of pastoralist women, particularly related to work and to domestic practices that a more traditional household perspective would perhaps not have captured. The research found that the knowledge and skills making up the traditional social practices of pastoralists were being rapidly replaced and it was unclear whether they could be re-routinized. For many of the women this loss of lifestyle, culture, and heritage, but also their identity, was a tragedy. However, the research also found that many women struggled with the trade-offs of losing traditional practices but perceived gains, for example, around improved access to formal education for children, including girls.

Post-capitalist approaches

Food production has been increasingly capitalized and industrialized, resulting in the alienation of people from the food system. This separation has been identified as a fundamental concern of unsustainability in the modern food system (Trauger and Passidomo 2012). Yet at the same time much of the food systems scholarship, including political economy research, has been accused of falling into a "capitalocentric trap." Capitalocentrism refers here to the positioning of all market processes with reference to capitalism as "fundamentally the same as (or modelled upon) capitalism, or as being deficient or substandard imitations; as being opposite to capitalism; as being the complement of capitalism; as existing in capitalism's space or orbit" (Gibson-Graham 1996, 6). As a result, this approach tends to ignore or hide the diversity of ways people actually get, distribute, and access food.

In response, post-capitalist approaches draw on a range of interdisciplinary fields (e.g. poststructuralism, postcolonialism, decolonization, and feminism) to provide a critique of capitalist development and produce alternative narratives and action rooted in equity and justice. Gibson-Graham's (1996, 2006) work on post-capitalist politics has bloomed into a diverse and community economies approach that proposes an evolving set of theory and actions to understand and assess innovations outside capitalist parameters (Community Economies Collective 2001; Gibson-Graham et al. 2018). Increasingly, the diverse economies framework has been utilized in food systems research to avoid totalizing approaches and reproducing top-down, capitalist-centric narratives (Davies et al. 2017; Larner 2003), and to inspire new political opportunities (Cameron and Wright 2014; Crossan et al. 2016; Harris 2009; Sarmiento 2017). A post-capitalist politics supports the "(re)negotiation of the economic basis of agriculture and generates new subjectivities directed toward a more integrated, interdependent and cooperative economy of agriculture" (Trauger and Passidomo 2012, 282). Post-capitalist projects need to be locally specific but tend to share three core elements: a politics of language which calls for developing new, richer local languages of economy and of economic possibility; a politics of the subject, which includes cultivating ourselves and others as subjects of non-capitalist development; and a politics of collective action, that entails working collaboratively to produce alternative economic organizations and spaces in place (Gibson-Graham 2006, x).

The post-capitalist lens has been used to empower alternative food networks, but also to criticize the dominant food system. Its core premise is that identifying and supporting a more diverse and potentially transformative array of initiatives can produce a more sensitive approach to understanding food practices in terms of labor arrangements, property structures, types of transactions, and enterprise models. The diverse economies framework makes visible everyday practices and in turn empowers their capacity to enact change.

Research on the informal and social economy of food in Northwestern Ontario, Canada, reveals a series of initiatives that focus on sharing and exchanging food as far more than simply economics (Nelson et al. 2019). For example, the Aroland Youth Blueberry Initiative located in Aroeland First Nations engages youth in the community to work with adults and elders to pick wild blueberries. Beyond selling the berries at a major regional farmer's market, the youth learn environmental stewardship, practice traditional harvesting techniques, engage in intergenerational knowledge exchange, support local programs with the profits, and enhance the communities' wellbeing and self-determination. In another case study, the work of Cloverbelt Local Food Coop, a regional online food coop, goes well beyond retail sales. The initiative supports a healthy local food system in rural communities, provides education opportunities, provides livelihood for residents, and strengthens social ties within and between communities. Nelson et al. (2019) argue that these case studies simultaneously work within and outside of the neoliberal economy and demonstrate "their influence on re-spatializing and re-socializing conventional food system approaches as they provide social, economic and environmental benefits to their local and regional communities" (Nelson et al. 2019, 55). In turn, these initiatives demonstrate alternatives that work within and alongside dominant market structures and challenge the dominant capitalist narrative.

Co-production of knowledge and nature

Co-production is championed by diverse theoretical perspectives, from political ecology to social innovation. Food studies are increasingly aware of the need to mobilize this concept as a means to incorporate nature more fully in political economy debates. For that purpose, political ecology perspectives are considered particularly useful, along with other concepts such as socio-natures, insofar as they examine the historically situated process through which nature and society are materially and discursively co-productive of one another (Aeberhard and Rist 2009; Alkon 2013). Using historically and geographically contextual approaches, political ecology adds to a political economy approach by "guiding researchers to pay attention not only to the 'ecology' or science of the topic at hand, but also to the agency of ideas and the actions of social, economic, and discursive power across scales" (Kull et al. 2015, 123). Importantly, it is an explicitly political approach that acknowledges wider political controversies about the nature of ecological risk and the influence of political actors upon knowledge production (Forsyth 2005, 165).

Recently Moragues-Faus and Marsden (2017) identified ways that political ecology perspectives can underpin a revised critical food scholarship based on understanding place-based socio-natures, addressing the politics of scale and inequality and co-producing knowledge and change. For example, an action-research process with emerging sustainable food cities has contributed to unpack how nature and society are co-productive of each other, as well as the role that knowledge and framing play in fostering change. Specifically, working with a network of 60 plus UK cities has contributed to celebrate the diversity of socio-ecological flows that make up British urban foodscapes, and therefore contest pre-imposed imaginaries of what a sustainable food city should look like (Moragues-Faus 2019; Moragues-Faus and Carroll 2018). Instead, this collaborative work has focused on empowering place-based and participatory definitions of sustainability for example by co-producing a non-prescriptive indicators toolbox to measure progress in sustainable food cities (Moragues-Faus and Marceau 2018). Among others, research with the UK Sustainable Food Cities Network has also contributed to understand how different communication, organization and knowledge co-production tools contribute to create cross-scalar, collective, and distributive agencies (Moragues-Faus and Sonnino 2019). This work has also sparked critical reflection on the need to develop better mechanisms to put at the centre of reframing and transforming food systems those currently with "no-voice," such as groups experiencing food poverty, or different ethnicities, which generally continue to be excluded from these processes (Moragues-Faus 2019).

Engaged scholarship

Engaged scholarship aims to bridge the gaps between academic research and teaching and civil society and social movement efforts. Broadly, it refers to a range of approaches to studying complex social problems that are relevant and can be applied to experiences of people, communities, organizations, and policy makers (Peterson 2009). Building on the previous four subsections that discuss decolonization, feminism, post-capitalist approaches, and the co-production of knowledge and nature, an engaged approach to research, teaching, and action demands accountability from the people under study. According to a scoping literature review conducted by Beaulieu et al. (2018), engaged scholarship is characterized by core values of social justice and civic engagement along with principles that include high-quality scholarship, reciprocity, identified community needs, boundary-crossing, and democratization of knowledge. While not all engaged scholarship is the same, transformative approaches within regenerative food systems work can act as a democratizing countermovement to mobilize diverse ideas, resources, and experiences that leads to progressive social change (Goemans et al. 2018; Levkoe et al. 2016; Swords et al. 2010). This is categorically different than approaches that assume academics play an objective or neutral role by conducting research as experts. At one level, it demands academics abandon preconceived ideas along with beliefs about how outcomes will benefit what they already believe to be true. While political economy can inform engaged scholarship, the specific ways it might be used should be determined by the research process itself along with those involved.

This is particularly important in the field of sustainable food systems, as many scholars have been active in engaged research, teaching and action (see for example Andrée et al. 2016; Levkoe et al. 2019b). For example, Levkoe et al. (2019a) propose three core principles for engaged researchers studying food sovereignty: people (humanizing research relationships), power (equalizing power relations), and change (pursuing transformative orientations). While these principles may fit very closely with a political economy framework, they also build on feminist, post-capitalist, and co-production of knowledge and nature perspectives. Integrating engaged scholarship and political economy means getting out of the classroom or institution and engaging with people and processes on a personal level. Teaching can also adopt engaged scholarship through embedding students in local communities through action-research projects (Levkoe et al. 2019b; Moragues-Faus et al. 2015). These examples challenge the long-standing academic culture and power dynamics of the "ivory tower" that separate scholarship from social change work. This also demands that institutions take responsibility for their local foodscapes and that academics become scholar-activists and take a position on their work that goes beyond objectivity.

Discussion and conclusion: political economy as a tool for food system change

Political economy has played a key role in the evolution of food systems research. While it has continued to evolve, as an approach, it is not without critique (Duncan et al. 2019). We note that while there are gaps in the ways that political economy has addressed sustainable and regenerative food systems, food systems scholars should continue to engage with political economy in order to critically address key relations of power. However, to remain attentive to changing contexts, we have introduced other approaches which we have found useful for addressing noted shortcomings. Further, we see the explicit introduction of decolonizing, feminist, post-capitalist, co-produced, and engaged research as fundamental to a research agenda that expands the scope of political economy of regenerative food systems. We note that these are not the only approaches that can, or should be, pursued for a comprehensive research agenda for a renewed political economy of regenerative food systems. We propose these because they have proven useful in our own work to expand our inquiries and deepen our analysis and impact. We also recognize that their application is not unproblematic and that each approach brings a new set of questions and concerns. Precisely, we advocate for a sensitive regenerative food systems scholarship that is in constant flux, critique, and (re)evolution.

First, when it comes to decolonization, we recognize that the use of the term can be seen as problematic. As Tuck and Yang (2012, 3) note, decolonization is not a metaphor for how to improve research but rather it is about the repatriation of Indigenous land and life. In this vein, we must consistently question the role of settlers conducting research in an Indigenous context. While there may be good intentions, Indigenous research led by settlers and/or academics can easily reproduce settler-colonial dominance (especially when using research towards career advancement). Further, while we have noted that research can be a process of healing and revitalization, it can also erode such processes. Building knowledge, skills, and trust to do this kind of research takes time, patience, and a great deal of listening. It may also entail sharing outcomes through non-academic channels or not at all. This can create tensions for researchers, particularly early-stage researchers, who need to meet specific institutional outputs.

Second, recognizing that food systems impact men and women differently, and in turn, understanding the impact of changing food systems on women, is fundamental to advancing sustainable food systems. However, as critical scholarship works to move beyond binary constructions of gender, more thinking needs to take place about what a critical and contemporary feminist research agenda will entail. Certainly openness, listening, and flexibility will be core principles. Moving forward however, research needs to remain conscious about the history of white, western feminism dominating other feminisms, and continue to address concerns around cultural relativism.

We find it important also to state that, from our own experiences, conducting research as women comes with its own risks. Both female authors have experienced forms of sexual harassment while conducting fieldwork. We recognize that these experiences are likely to be heightened when issues of race, class, sexuality, and (dis)ability are taken into account (especially for junior or pre-tenure scholars). In our own research these experiences have gone undocumented and unreported; inscribed in our minds but absent from analysis and discussion. A feminist research agenda opens up space for addressing these experiences and developing actions to end them.

Third, in applying a political economy perspective we need to acknowledge the broad range of alternative food initiatives as well as everyday forms of resistance seeking to transform current unjust and unsustainable foodscapes, as highlighted by feminist and post-capitalist scholars (Gibson-Graham 2006; Truelove 2011). Further, key questions emerge around how to reconcile the transformational power of these micro-practices with the cross-scalar power dynamics that reproduce an unjust food system. The diverse economy framework highlights how the interactions of buying groups with supermarkets do not necessarily rely on capitalist relations, rather they can rely on unpaid labour and accessible food in order to deliver healthy foodstuffs to vulnerable communities. At the same time, across geographies and scales, retailers play a key role in sustaining unjust and unsustainable food practices. It remains to be addressed how to reconcile reading and empowering diversity at cross-scalar geometries of power that actively shape wide-reaching food system transformation. Further, we must ensure that political economy research does not feed the capitalocentric narratives that capitalism is everywhere and therefore impossible to escape (Cameron and Wright 2014).

Fourth, while a political ecology pushes forward traditional political economy questions around how and what knowledge is produced as well as contestation around the processes through which knowledge is legitimated and appropriated, when it comes to food systems research, questions related to co-production remain. We need to address for example how we conduct research with/on the powerful. Are co-productive processes the best way to research in every circumstance? With whom are we co-producing and are we creating new elites and continuing to reproduce exclusion dynamics? A sensitive regenerative food scholarship requires engagement with these questions and developing a caring culture within academia that supports and champions vulnerable groups also within the academic community. This includes expanding the types and geographies of the concepts we cite (e.g., publicly value) to rightfully acknowledge local knowledges and research communities (Leff 2015).

Finally, engaged scholarship calls for explicit recognition of positionality, with researchers being reflexive in terms of where, how, and when they fit into the research. This means not only explicitly recognizing bias and connections to the research, but also the potential power dynamics at play and their implications. While the examples we provide highlight the value of engaged scholarship, we recognize that this is not always the most appropriate or feasible approach. We recognize that not all scholars are willing or able to adopt the position of scholar-activist. Echoing concerns raised in our discussion around decolonization, we note that efforts of scholars to engage in engaged research do not always end well. Often researchers and communities face different timelines, objectives, processes, and pathways that cannot always be reconciled and which can sometimes be revealed too late in the process. We also warn that reflexivity is useful to a point, and that we should avoid an inward turn leaving us too focused on our individual positionality and identity (Routledge and Driscoll Derickson 2015).

Building on a critical review of the literature and a reflection of our own scholarship, we have proposed potential hybridizations of the political economy of food with other conceptual developments in food systems research, including decolonizing approaches, feminist groundings, post-capitalist approaches, place-based co-production of knowledge and nature, and engaged scholarship. We have argued that, when combined with a more traditional political economy framework, these approaches expand the potential for research to advance sustainable food systems. In turn, integrating innovative theoretical and practical perspectives along with related methodological tools offers new and exciting horizons for the political economy of regenerative food systems.

Discussion questions

1. We have proposed a series of approaches to expand the political economy based on our own work. Are there additional approaches that might advance a research agenda for regenerative food systems?

2. Are there specific elements of food systems that this approach is better suited towards? Why?
3. How might our proposed agenda for regenerative food systems contribute to research you are involved with?

Notes

1 This chapter was adapted from Duncan et al. (2019).
2 For more information on the Understanding Our Food Systems project see www.understandingour foodsystems.com.

Further readings

Bernstein, H. 2017. Political economy of agrarian change: Some key concepts and questions. *RUDN Journal of Sociology, 17*(1), 7–8.

Community Economies Collective. 2001. Imagining and enacting non- capitalist futures. *Social Review, 28*, 93–135.

Smith, L. T. 2013. *Decolonizing methodologies: Research and indigenous peoples.* London: Zed Books Ltd.

Trauger, A. and Passidomo, C. 2012. Towards a post-capitalist-politics of food: Cultivating subjects of community economies. *ACME: An International E-Journal for Critical Geographies, 11*(2), 282–303.

Tuck, E. and Yang, K. W. 2012. Decolonization is not a metaphor. *Decolonization: Indigeneity, Education and Society, 1*(1), 1–40.

References

Aeberhard, A. and Rist, S. 2009. Transdisciplinary co-production of knowledge in the development of organic agriculture in Switzerland. *Ecological Economics, 68*(4), 1171–1181.

Alkon, A. H. 2013. The socio-nature of local organic food. *Antipode, 45*, 663–680.

Andrée, P., Kepkiewicz, L., Levkoe, C. Z., Brynne, A., and Kneen, C. 2016. Learning, food, and sustainability in community-campus engagement: Teaching and research partnerships that strengthen the food sovereignty movement. In J. Sumner (Ed.), *Learning, food, and sustainability* (pp. 133–153). New York: Palgrave Macmillan.

Beaulieu, M., Breton, M., and Brousselle, A. 2018. Conceptualizing 20 years of engaged scholarship: A scoping review. *PLoS One, 13*(2), e0193201.

Bernstein, H. 2010. *Class dynamics of agrarian change.* Halifax: Fernwood Publishing.

Bernstein, H. 2017. Political economy of agrarian change: Some key concepts and questions. *RUDN Journal of Sociology, 17*(1), 7–8.

Bock, B. B. and Duncan, J. 2017. Gender and food practices – From seed to waste, an introduction. In B. Bock and J. Duncan (Eds.), *2016 yearbook of women's history* (vol. 36, pp. 1–14). Hilversum: Uitgeverij Verloren.

Boyd, W., Prudham, W. S., and Schurman, R. A. 2001. Industrial dynamics and the problem of nature. *Society and Natural Resources, 14*(7), 555–570.

Bryant, L. and Jaworski, K. 2011. Gender, embodiment and place: The gendering of skills shortages in the Australian mining and food and beverage processing industries. *Human Relations, 64*(10), 1345–1367.

Busch, L. and Juska, A. 1997. Beyond political economy: Actor networks and the globalization of agriculture. *Review of International Political Economy, 4*(4), 688–708.

Buttel, F. H. 2001. Some reflections on late twentieth century agrarian political economy. *Sociologia Ruralis, 41*(2), 165–181.

Cameron, J. and Wright, S. 2014. Researching diverse food initiatives: From backyard and community gardens to international markets. *Local Environment, 19*(1), 1–9.

Collinson, S. 2003. *Power, livelihoods and conflict: Case studies in political economy analysis for humanitarian action.* London: Overseas Development Institute. Available at: www.odi.org.uk/resources/download/241.pdf

Community Economies Collective. 2001. Imagining and enacting non-capitalist futures. *Social Review, 28*, 93–135.

Corntassel, J. 2012. Re-envisioning resurgence: Indigenous pathways to decolonization and sustainable self-determination. *Decolonization: Indigeneity, Education and Society, 1*(1), 86–101.

Crossan, J., Cumbers, A., McMaster, R., and Shaw, D. 2016. Contesting neoliberal urbanism in Glasgow's community gardens: The practice of DIY citizenship. *Antipode, 48*(4), 937–955.

Cunniff Gilson, E. 2015. Vulnerability, relationality, and dependency: Feminist conceptual resources for food justice. *IJFAB: International Journal of Feminist Approaches to Bioethics, 8*(2), 10–46.

Davies, A. R., Edwards, F., Marovelli, B., Morrow, O., Rut, M., and Weymes, M. 2017. Making visible: Interrogating the performance of food sharing across 100 urban areas. *Geoforum, 86,* 136–149.

Duncan, J. and Agarwal, M. 2017. 'There is dignity only with livestock': Land grabbing and the changing social practices of pastoralist women in Gujarat, India. In S. Shortall and B. Bock (Eds.), *Cosmopolitan rural gender relations; international perspectives on gender and rural development* (pp. 52–75). Boston, MA: CABI.

Duncan, J., Levkoe, C. Z., and Moragues-Faus, A. 2019. Envisioning new horizons for the political economy of sustainable food systems. *IDS Bulletin, 50*(2), 37–56.

Elmhirst, R. 2011. Introducing new feminist political ecologies. *Geoforum, 42,* 129–132.

Epstein, M. J. 1996. Consuming performances: Eating acts and feminist embodiment. *TDR, 40*(4), 20–36.

Fine, B. 1994. Towards a political economy of food. *Review of International Political Economy, 1*(3), 519–545.

Forsyth, T. 2005. The political ecology of the ecosystem approach for forests. In J. Sayer and S. Maginnis (Eds.), *Forests in landscapes: Ecosystem approaches for sustainability* (pp. 165–176). London: Earthscan.

Friedmann, H. 1982. The political economy of food: The rise and fall of the postwar international food order. *American Journal of Sociology, 88,* S248–S286.

Friedmann, H. 1993. The political economy of food: A global crisis. *New Left Review, 197,* 29–57.

Galt, R. E. 2013. Placing food systems in first world political ecology: A review and research agenda. *Geography Compass, 7*(9), 637–658.

George, S. 2017. *Shadow sovereigns: How global corporations are seizing power.* Cambridge: John Wiley & Sons.

Gibson-Graham, J. K. 1996. *The end of capitalism (as we knew it).* Minneapolis, MN: University of Minnesota Press.

Gibson-Graham, J. K. 2006. *A postcapitalist politics.* Minneapolis, MN: University of Minnesota Press.

Gibson-Graham, J. K., Cameron, J., Dombroski, K., Healy, S., Miller, E., and the Community Economies Collective. 2018. Cultivating community economies: An essay for the next system project. Available at: https://thenextsystem.org/cultivating-community-economies.

Goemans, M., Levkoe, C. Z., Andrée, P., Changfoot, N., and Christopherson-Cote, C. 2018. Learning to 'walk the talk': Reflexive evaluation in community-first engaged research. *Engaged Scholar Journal: Community-Engaged Research, Teaching, and Learning, 4*(2), 61–84.

Goodman, D. and DuPuis, E. M. 2002. Knowing food and growing food: Beyond the production–consumption debate in the sociology of agriculture. *Sociologia Ruralis, 42*(1), 5–22.

Goodman, D. and Watts, M. 1997. Agrarian questions: Global appetite, local metabolism: Nature, culture, and industry in Fin-de-Siecle Agro-Food Systems. In D. Goodman and M. Watts (Eds.), *Globalising food: Agrarian questions and global restructuring* (pp. 1–24). London: Routledge.

Gregson, N. 1995. And now it's all consumption? *Progress in Human Geography, 19*(1), 135–141.

Grey, S. and Patel, R. 2015. Food sovereignty as decolonization: Some contributions from Indigenous movements to food system and development politics. *Agriculture and Human Values, 32*(3), 431–444.

Guthman, J. 2008. Neoliberalism and the making of food politics in California. *Geoforum, 39*(3), 1171–1183.

Harris, E. 2009. Neoliberal subjectivities or a politics of the possible? Reading for difference in alternative food networks. *Area, 41,* 55–63.

Hayes-Conroy, J. and Hayes-Conroy, A. 2013. Veggies and visceralities: A political ecology of food and feeling. *Emotion, Space and Society, 6,* 81–90.

IPCC [Intergovernmental Panel on climate Change]. 2019. *Climate change and land.* United Nations. Available at www.ipcc.ch/report/srccl/

IPES-Food [International Panel of Experts on Sustainable Food Systems]. 2015. *The new science of sustainable food systems: Overcoming barriers to food system reform.* International Panel of Experts on Sustainable Food Systems. Available at www.ipes-food.org/images/Reports/IPES_report01_1505_web_br_pages.pdf

IPES-Food [International Panel of Experts on Sustainable Food Systems]. 2016. *From uniformity to diversity: A paradigm shift from industrial agriculture to diversified agroecological systems*. International Panel of Experts on Sustainable Food systems. Available at www.ipes-food.org/images/Reports/Uniformity ToDiversity_FullReport.pdf

IPES-Food [International Panel of Experts on Sustainable Food Systems]. 2017. *Unravelling the food–health nexus: Addressing practices, political economy, and power*. International Panel of Experts on Sustainable Food Systems. Available at www.ipes-food.org/images/Reports/Health_FullReport.pdf

Kepkiewicz, L. and Dale, B. 2019. Keeping 'our' land: Property, agriculture and tensions between Indigenous and settler visions of food sovereignty in Canada. *Journal of Peasant Studies*, 46(5), 983–1002.

Kovach, M. 2015. Emerging from the margins: Indigenous methodologies. In L. Brown and S. Strega (Eds.), *Research as resistance: Critical, indigenous and anti-oppressive approaches* (pp. 43–64). Toronto: Canadian Scholars' Press.

Kull, C., Arnauld de Sartre, X., and Castro-Larrañaga, C. 2015. The political ecology of ecosystem services. *Geoforum*, 61, 122–134.

Larner, W. 2003. Neoliberalism? *Environment and Planning D: Society and Space*, 21, 509–512.

Leff, E. 2015. The power-full distribution of knowledge in political ecology. In G. B. Tom Perreault and J. McCarthy (Eds.), *The Routledge handbook of political ecology* (pp. 64–75). London and New York: Routledge.

Levkoe, C. Z., Andrée, P., Bhatt, V., Brynne, A., Davison, K., Kneen, C., and Nelson, E. 2016. Collaboration for transformation: Community–campus engagement for just and sustainable food systems. *Journal of Higher Education, Outreach and Engagement*, 20(3), 23–61.

Levkoe, C. Z., Brem-Wilson, J., and Anderson, C. R. 2019a. People, power, change: Three pillars of a food sovereignty research praxis. *Journal of Peasant Studies*, 46(7), 1389–1412.

Levkoe, C. Z., Erlich, S., and Archibald, S. 2019b. Campus food movements and food system transformation: Mobilizing community-campus partnerships for the real food challenge in Canada. *Engaged Scholar Journal: Community-Engaged Research, Teaching, and Learning*, 5(1), 57–76.

Levkoe, C. Z,, McLaughlin, J., Strutt, C., and Ng, V. 2019c. Understanding our food systems: Food sovereignty in Northwestern Ontario. Phase II final report. A report for the Thunder Bay District Health Unit and the Ontario Ministry of Health and Long-Term Care. Thunder Bay, ON.

Levkoe, C. Z., Ray, L., and McLaughlin, J. 2019d. The indigenous food circle: Reconciliation and revitalization through food in Northwestern Ontario. *Journal of Agriculture, Food Systems and Community Development*, 9(B), 101–114.

Lewis, D. 2015. Gender, feminism and food studies. *African Security Review*, 24(4), 414–429.

Lockie, S. 2002. 'The invisible mouth': Mobilizing 'the consumer' in food production-consumption networks. *Sociologia Ruralis*, 42(4), 278–294.

Lockie, S. and Kitto, S. 2000. Beyond the farm gate: Production-consumption networks and agri-food research. *Sociologia Ruralis*, 40(1), 3–19.

Marsden, T., Munton, R., Ward, N., and Whatmore, S. 1996. Agricultural Geography and the political economy approach: A review. *Economic Geography*, 72(4), 361–375.

Mintz, S. W. 1986. *Sweetness and power: The place of sugar in modern history*. London: Penguin.

Moragues-Faus, A. 2019. Towards a critical governance framework: Unveiling the political and justice dimensions of urban food partnerships. *Geographical Journal*, 186(1), 73–86.

Moragues-Faus, A. and Carroll, B. 2018. Reshaping urban political ecologies: An analysis of policy trajectories to deliver food security. *Food Security*, 10(6), 1337–1351.

Moragues-Faus, A. and Marceau, A. 2018. Measuring progress in sustainable food cities: An indicators toolbox for action. *Sustainability*, 11(1), 1–17.

Moragues-Faus, A. and Marsden, T. 2017. The political ecology of food: Carving 'spaces of possibility' in a new research agenda. *Journal of Rural Studies*, 55, 275–288.

Moragues-Faus, A., Omar, A., and Wang, J. 2015. Participatory action research with local communities: Transforming our food system. 18 November 2015. Food Research Collaboration Policy Brief.

Moragues-Faus, A. and Sonnino, R. 2019. Re-assembling sustainable food cities: An exploration of translocal governance and its multiple agencies. *Urban Studies*, 56, 778–794.

Morrison, D. 2011. Indigenous food sovereignty: A model for social learning. In H. Witman, A. A. Desmarais, and N. Wiebe, (Eds.) *Food sovereignty in Canada: Creating just and sustainable food systems* (pp. 97–113). Halifax: Fernwood.

Nelson, C., Stroink, M., Levkoe, C. Z., Kakagemic, R., McKay, E., Streutker, A., and Stolz, W. 2019. Understanding social economy through a complexity lens in Northwestern Ontario: Four case studies. *Canadian Food Studies/La Revue Canadienne Des Études Sur L'alimentation, 6*(3), 33–59.

Perreault, T., Bridge, G., and McCarthy, J. 2015. *The Routledge handbook of political ecology*. Oxford: Routledge.

Peterson, T. H. 2009. Engaged scholarship: Reflections and research on the pedagogy of social change. *Teaching in Higher Education, 14*(5), 541–552.

Rosset, P. M. and Altieri, M. A. 2017. *Agroecology: Science and politics*. Black Point: Fernwood.

Routledge, P. and Driscoll Derickson, K. 2015. Situated solidarities and the practice of scholar-activism. *Environment and Planning D: Society and Space, 33*(3), 391–407.

Sarmiento, E. R. 2017. Synergies in alternative food network research: Embodiment, diverse economies, and more-than-human food geographies. *Agriculture and Human Values, 34*(2), 485–497.

Smith, L. T. 2013. *Decolonizing methodologies: Research and indigenous peoples*. London: Zed Books Ltd.

Swords, A. C. S. and Kiely, R. 2010. Beyond pedagogy: Service learning as movement building in higher education. *Journal of Community Practice, 18*(2–3), 148–170.

Teo, T. 2010. What is epistemological violence in the empirical social sciences? *Social and Personality Psychology Compass, 4*(5), 295–303.

Trauger, A. and Passidomo, C. 2012. Towards a post-capitalist-politics of food: Cultivating subjects of community economies. *ACME: An International E-Journal for Critical Geographies, 11*(2), 282–303.

Truelove, Y. 2011. (Re-)conceptualizing water inequality in Delhi, India through a feminist political ecology framework. *Geoforum, 42*(2), 143–152.

Tuck, E. and Yang, K. W. 2012. Decolonization is not a metaphor. *Decolonization: Indigeneity, Education and Society, 1*(1), 1–40.

Wilkinson, J. 2006. Network theories and political economy: From attrition to convergence? In T. Marsden and J. Murdoch (Eds.), *Between the local and the global: Confronting complexity in the contemporary agri-food sector* (pp. 11–38). Oxford: Emerald Group Pub Ltd.

Willett, W., Rockström, J., Loken, B., Springmann, M., Lang, T., Vermeulen, S., et al. 2019. Food in the anthropocene: The EAT–Lancet Commission on healthy diets from sustainable food systems. *The Lancet, 393*(10170), 447–492.

Wilson, S. 2009. *Research as ceremony*. Halifax: Fernwood Publishing.

Winter, M. 2003. Geographies of food: Agro-food geographies–making reconnections. *Progress in Human Geography, 27*(4), 505–513.

Wittman, H., Desmarais, A., and Wiebe, N. 2010. *Food sovereignty: Reconnecting food, nature and community*. Halifax: Fernwood Publishing.

3

INDIGENOUS LIVELIHOOD

Angga Dwiartama[1]

Introduction

It is commonly understood that food has its story. Food as appears on our plate today is constructed through a long and complex network of production, packaging, processing, and distribution, in which different agricultural commodities, foodstuffs, and ingredients combine seamlessly together. Take a bag of branded potato chips, for example, and see how the hidden network behind this product links potatoes in the Netherlands, industrial salt in Australia, and palm oil in Indonesia. Behind the scenes, various actors – farmers, traders, food industries, nutritionists, governments – play their role in the process (Carolan 2017).

What is also apparent, although less often discussed, is that food has its *history*. What, and how, we eat has a long story behind it. Food, in its material and symbolic senses, is formed out of a mixture of various cultural roots. Notice restaurants and food stalls across most cities in the world, and you will find a range of geographically embedded food products, from Italian espresso to Chinese noodles. So-called modern food was once traditional, indigenous food that has become assimilated to modern lifestyles, popularized, and commodified into its current state. Lind and Barham (2004) give the example of tortilla, which started out as a traditional cuisine in Mexico but is now a feature of our fast food industry.

It is therefore clear that food has both spatial and temporal dimensions. The rise (and demise) of our modern food system is the result of a wide range of economic activities built upon a long historical process that involves narratives of dominance and exploitation, migration (Mintz 1986), assimilations, and religious encounters (Aregay 1988). One of the most renowned literatures on this subject is Sidney Mintz's *Sweetness and Power* (1986): sugar has historically been linked with the slave trade in Africa, colonial plantation in the Caribbean, and industrial revolution in London.

If learn something from the past, it is that we need to scrutinize the future and sustainability that this modern food system leads us to. Many studies have shown that the global food system is displacing local food cultures in many places, against the advice of indigenous community groups and local food movements. Western diets diminish the importance of local cuisine and have a deteriorating effect on our health through obesity, diabetes, and other non-communicable diseases (Kuhnlein and Receveur 1996). At the other end of the spectrum, globalization of food has also taken a toll on ecosystems in many regions in the world through unsustainable practices of industrial agriculture (Altieri 2002; Norgaard 1984). Communities are detached from their local ecologies, native plants are disappearing and replaced by invasive exotic species, and deforestation in the tropics makes way for new plantations and large-scale agricultural lands.

The degenerative effects of our globalized, modern food system on both society and environment require a regenerative remedy. As this book argues, this goes beyond sustainability narratives. Critics of sustainability posit that the concept (=to sustain) necessitates that a system should be predictable and relatively stable over a course of time (Folke et al. 2002). Research on agricultural sustainability therefore focuses on the ability either to predict and model the future through various scenarios or to develop proxies that may indicate the potential impacts of a particular action in the long run (Bell and Morse 2012). However, in an already compromised and ever-complex world where disturbances occur capriciously, sustainability becomes obsolete, and thus concepts like resilience (Folke et al. 2002) and regeneration (Dahlberg 1993) come into play.

When sustainability is about maintaining a particular practice whilst allowing the system to function well in the future, then I argue that the best proven examples of sustainability are those which have been practiced consistently for generations and stood the test of time. This is exemplified by traditional food systems of many indigenous peoples. Ellis and Wang (1997) illustrate this neatly as they document a traditional rice production system in Tai Lake district in China that has been producing rice for millennia with an increasing trend of productivity. However, the article also comes with a warning – in the 1960s, while production rose rapidly due to an introduction of chemical fertilizer, the ecology began to crumble as the river became polluted. This shows that whilst indigenous agri-food systems have proven to be sustainable, it is not easy to be resilient and regenerative in the face of modern challenges. Berkes et al. (2000) demonstrate the way indigenous peoples' traditional knowledge is able to help them anticipate the changing environment through what they term 'adaptive knowledge'.

This chapter aims to explore traditional/indigenous practices in the agri-food systems and illustrate the way in which traditional/indigenous livelihoods can help us learn to move towards more sustainable and regenerative food systems. This chapter is structured as follows. The second part talks about the definition and scope of indigenous food systems, through two bodies of literature that extensively discuss this topic. In the third part, I will use an empirical case study of an indigenous community group in Indonesia to show how their sustainable and regenerative practices offer a solution for many of the problems we are facing. The last part of this chapter will conclude with a reflection on ways to create compatibility between traditional practices and modern values, with a few questions to move forward.

Indigeneity and sustainability

Traditional, indigenous, native, and local food systems are often used interchangeably to address systems of food provisioning that have its roots in the local or native people. The International Labor Organization (ILO) is best known to be an international organization that has particular concern for the rights of indigenous peoples in terms of labor conditions specifically and broader issues of identity, customs, and land in general. The ILO Convention No. 169/1989 provides subjective and objective criteria that define indigenous people. Subjectively, indigenous people are people who identify as belonging to the group. Objectively, indigenous people:

descend from populations, who inhabited the country or geographical region at the time of conquest, colonisation or establishment of present state boundaries. They retain some or all of their own social, economic, cultural and political institutions, irrespective of their legal status.

(ILO 1989, Article 2)

Traditional or indigenous food systems, consequently, endeavor 'to identify all food within a particular culture available from local natural resources and culturally accepted' (Kuhnlein and Receveur 1996: 418). An indigenous food system is a cultural product of indigenous people through their interaction with their local ecology.

Viergever (1999) distinguishes between indigenous and local in the way in which the former seem to be able to maintain their own distinct cultures despite a strong pressure to integrate with the larger society. In contrast, local communities may not have a cultural identity that sets them apart from the larger society. To illustrate, a local food system may resist globalization of food through its own production, distribution, and marketing system, but the type of food produced, the method of production, and the market mechanism may not be substantially different from the modern food system elsewhere. An indigenous food system, on the other hand, has distinct practices (e.g. hunting and gathering, swidden cultivation or traditional pasture) as well as products (titi bird in New Zealand; Moller et al. 2004). Traditional and indigenous, on the other hand, are more often closely related,[2] with traditional implying a temporal dimension, i.e. demonstrating practices that are constructed and perpetuated over generations, whereas indigenous implies a spatial one.[3]

In the literature, there are at least two schools of thought that extensively discuss indigenous agri-food systems. One substantial body of literatures on indigenous/ traditional food systems is that of Harriet Kuhnlein and her colleagues in the Centre for Indigenous Peoples' Nutrition and Environment (CINE) (Kuhnlein 2003; Kuhnlein et al. 2009; Turner and Turner 2007), which focuses on the consumption and nutrition side of indigenous peoples' food systems. Another body of literatures on traditional agricultural knowledge focuses on the production side of the food system (Altieri 2002; Norgaard 1984), advocating sustainable practices that promote conservation, restore ecological balance, and build up soil quality in the long run. Although these two bodies of literatures intersect in many aspects, the emphases and challenges are put differently. This chapter will discuss each in more detail and follow with an empirical case study that combines both frameworks.

On the nutrition side of the systems, Kuhnlein and her network document the way in which many indigenous groups across the developing world have in fact provided alternatives to the unhealthy foods we eat in our modern setting. This starts from utilizing what is available at the indigenous peoples' local ecologies through their traditional food system. For many, this can range from 35 species/varieties of plants and animals in Maasai, Kenya to 387 species/varieties in Karen, Thailand (Kuhnlein et al. 2009). These species provide rich nutritional values, even to the level of micronutrients (Kuhnlein 2003). Compare this with our daily modern diet that uses fewer than 20 species of animals/plants as food. In addition, this food diversity also reduces the community's dependency on a particular food product, and so increases their resilience towards hazards that may inhibit their access to that particular food (Kuhnlein and Receveur 1996).

Traditional food system knowledge and practice not only delves into the type of food the indigenous peoples eat, but also the way they acquire, process, and consume them. In a case of the Desana indigenous group in the Amazon, foods are acquired seasonally from nature, and so the diet of Desana varies from month to month (Cotton and Wilkie 1996). The extraction of forest resources relies on cues provided by local indicators. So, for instance, after seasonal heavy rains and the peach palm blooms, Desana people begin to collect certain fruits, collect mushrooms, and set fish traps. Food preparation also becomes an important aspect of traditional food systems. In Hopi indigenous people in North America (Kuhnlein and Receveur 1996), households combine various foods through more than 70 ways of preparations. This is meant not only for the palate, but also because some forms of food source need to be processed in a particular manner to retain nutrients or remove toxins from the food.

The other body of literature deals with traditional agricultural knowledge, which attempts to maintain balance between crop production and local ecological functions while also eliminating dependency on mechanization and external inputs typical of modern agriculture. Traditional agriculture is practiced in about one quarter of the world's population, largely in resource-poor areas such as in the tropical regions (Cotton and Wilkie 1996). In many indigenous communities, methods like terraces, polycultures, and agroforests have contributed to a rich repository of multifunctional agricultural practices that not only produce sufficient food for the community, but also conserve soil, biodiversity, and ecosystem integrity (Altieri 2002; Gliessman 2006). These practices are what Stephen Gliessman (2006) and Miguel Altieri (2002) termed agroecology; a concept that has begun to have pertinence in alternative farming systems all around the world. In his book, Gliessman (2006) notes how traditional agriculture shares a lot of similarities with its local natural ecosystem, as he said:

> The greater the structural and functional similarity of an agroecosystem to the natural ecosystems in its biogeographic region, the greater the likelihood that the agroecosystem will be sustainable
>
> *(Gliessman 2006, 288)*

Agronomists and ecologists take a particular interest in traditional agriculture systems (as compared to other traditional means of acquiring food), because of their compatibility and contribution to providing an alternative means of producing food. Consequently, new forms of agriculture such as organic, permaculture, System of Rice Intensification (SRI), agroforest, and natural farming are likely inspired by traditional agriculture practices.

As well as the discussions of traditional agri-food systems in the two bodies of literature factors are identified that contribute to the degradation of traditional knowledge and indigenous people. Turner and Turner (2007) identifies two major factors that play a part in this demise, one on the production side and the other on the consumption side. The first relates to the peoples' loss and limitation of access to land and natural resources. While access may not necessarily be lost, traditional management practices may be disappearing due to their incompatibility with the modern value system. For instance, slash-and-burn and swidden cultivation are prohibited in some forest areas because it is seen as a threat to conservation, despite the fact that these practices are not the main reason behind land degradation and transformation (Sunderlin and Resosudarmo 1996).

At the consumption end, introduction of new foods as well as globalization and domination of mainstream food systems contribute to the dietary change of indigenous people. Kuhnlein and Receveur (1996) document this change in diets among indigenous people across the world and identifies some of the non-communicable diseases that follow, such as obesity, anemia, cancer, alcoholism, and cases of malnourishment. In one case in

Papua New Guinea, diets consisting of various staple roots and fish were replaced with imported rice and tinned meat. Not only did this affect the community's lifestyle and health, but also increased their dependence on external source of diets that are subject to uncontrollable price fluctuations. In another case in Botswana, the community's nomadic life that could provide hundreds of dietary variations was replaced with a sedentary life in settlements and diets consisting mainly of maize. Ironically, many of these changes were also pushed by government programs aiming to achieve national food security by promoting a single national staple food and one way of producing it, as exemplified in the case of Indonesia (see also Dwiartama et al. 2016). This is how the story goes.

Empirical case study: rice-based indigenous community in West Java, Indonesia

With a population of about 261 million people, Indonesia positions itself as the fourth largest country in the world, owing to its economic growth and agricultural intensification in the 1970s that resulted in a rapid increase of its population in the past half century. From this total population, 54 percent inhabits the island of Java, an area of only 6 percent of the total landmass of the country. Indonesia's agricultural sector contributes to around 13 percent of the GDP and 34.3 percent of the total labor force, with a total of 24 million households working in mostly small-scale agriculture, based on the 2013 country's agriculture census. There are over 300 distinct native ethnic groups, but the two major groups by far are Javanese (those originating from the central and eastern part of Java, but currently inhabiting almost all part of Indonesia due to transmigration program) and Sundanese (a group mainly inhabiting the western part of Java), differentiated mainly on the basis of their dialects. In terms of cultural practices, however, the major ethnic groups have become modernized in such a way that they no longer possess any distinct traits that would identify them as indigenous people.

In various laws and regulations, the Indonesian government has made a clear definition of who indigenous people are. In the Law No. 32/2009 on the protection and management of natural environments, an indigenous group is defined as a group of people that inhabits a particular geographical region for generations, are bound to their place, exhibit a strong tie with their ecology, and possess a value system that regulates the economic, political, and social aspects of their internal life. In theory, the government has indeed attempted to protect the existence of indigenous people through instruments such as the Agrarian Law (No. 5/1960) and Forestry Law (No. 41/1999), particularly creating a clear delimitation of indigenous lands and establishing indigenous formal institutions.

This notwithstanding, the rights of many small indigenous community groups across the vast archipelago are still left unprotected. This leads to the establishment of Aliansi Masyarakat Adat Nusantara (AMAN), a national alliance of indigenous people, which claims to represent more than 2,000 indigenous community groups that cover around 12 million people in Indonesia. Some, for instance in the depth of Papua and Borneo, are almost untouched by economic development and live in a very traditional manner. Others, on the other hand, such those living in the island of Java, interact closely with modern life to the extent that the latter provides strong pressures on the very existence of these community groups. This chapter seeks to show how these indigenous people are able to adapt and be resilient to those pressures while still thriving so as to offer regenerative agriculture and food practices as an example for the surrounding modern communities.

The case of Kasepuhan Ciptagelar

I use a case study of Kasepuhan Ciptagelar (*kasepuhan* is a Sundanese term that literally means 'place of the elders'), a Sundanese cultural enclave located remotely inside a nature reserve area, the Halimun-Salak National Park (Dwiartama 2014; Dwiartama et al. 2016). The area is 180 km south of Jakarta, Indonesia's capital city. The community group consists of around 30,000 individuals living in 568 scattered villages around Mount Halimun, at elevations between 700 and 1,200 meters above sea level (Soemarwoto 2007). They are mainly farmers, practicing rice agriculture for subsistence, although they do not label themselves as such because, in their perspective, rice growing is an obligation of all members of the society regardless of their main professions. Indeed, in addition to rice farming that is the backbone of the community's social life, many work in a range of employment sectors, from school teachers, government officials, traders, to commercial farmers (the main commodities of this region are palm sugar, cardamom, and cloves).

It is difficult to estimate the total area of Kasepuhan, as the practices of swidden agriculture provide the community with a flexible land base through opening of new forest areas, although documents show that the area that this indigenous group lives in covers around 5,000 hectares of land. The community faces challenges as their cultural space is located within a national park that has strict rules of forest access. Due to this, their practice of swidden agriculture (*huma*, or dryland rice farming) has been reduced significantly and replaced by *sawah* (wetland rice agriculture). Thus, to this point, we can still witness two types of rice farming system in Kasepuhan, with *sawah* dominating paddy fields at the lower altitude and *huma* dominating fields in the highlands. The area is practically inaccessible by normal means of transport due to the tropical montane forest surrounding the area. This inaccessibility is perhaps one of the reasons why they can still maintain their culture undisturbed.

Rice is undoubtedly central to the lives of the Kasepuhan people. Kasepuhan's traditional agri-food system centered on rice production and consumption has contributed to the community resilience and food security for generations (Dwiartama 2014). For them rice is irreplaceable, saying that 'without rice, we could not live'. Within their cosmology, life is seen as a cycle – a metaphor that is also represented in their rice agricultural activities, from preparation to planting, harvesting, consuming, and preparing for the next year in an annual cycle. At the final stage of the rituals, they have what is called *seren taun*, a ceremony open to all members of the community (and even to outsiders as a tourism event) to celebrate the achievement of their harvests and to plan for the coming year. Rice is personified by Nyai Pohaci Sanghyang Asri, the goddess of rice and fertility, somewhat similar to the depiction of Ceres in the Roman mythology.

The agriculture side of the system

The regenerative character of Kasepuhan's agri-food system comes from both sides of the chain. Kasepuhan's agricultural system that utilizes hundreds of local *javanica* rice varieties[4] has been around the community for centuries and is able to fulfil the staple need of its people. Rice production is treated in reverential manner to the extent that it should be kept traditional (and organic), with prohibitions on the use modern technology such as tractors, chemical fertilizers, pesticides, and high-yielding rice varieties. There are three factors at the production end that keep this regenerative system effective: land use system, synchronous planting, and rice landrace diversity.

The first factor is the community's conception of land ownership and landscape management. Agricultural land in Kasepuhan is not privately owned (in fact, a proportion of their land belongs to the state in the form of a national park). Farmland can be exchanged between community members, but not bought and sold. This communal ownership enables a more flexible way of managing their landscape. In their traditional value, Kasepuhan assigns half of the 5,000 hectares of land as a bequest forest (*hutan titipan*) that cannot be touched whatsoever. This is similar to the state's designation of conservation forest. Another large proportion of the area (30 percent) is dedicated as cover forest (*hutan tutupan*), an area that must be kept forested, and can only be utilized in a limited manner, such as with the non-timber forest products. Lastly, the open landscape (*hutan bukaan*) covers 20 percent of the total area, which functions as gardens, settlements, and importantly rice terraces (both dry and wetland) that account for half of the total open landscape. This shows the importance of rice agriculture in the community life.

Rice agriculture in Kasepuhan is practiced over a strict protocol. Each year, Abah (literally means father), the community leader, along with his counsellors, decides for the whole community when the beginning of the planting season is, particularly through their reading of astronomic signs.

> We see stars, there are two: *kidang* and *kerti*. They become our reference point. When the two lines up with our position, we can start the planting period. The stars, in one year, only pass us three to four times.
>
> *(Abah, community leader, from an interview in a short*
> *documentary about Kasepuhan; Laksono 2015)*

Synchronous planting does not necessarily mean planting at the same time. In fact, with a wide region varying in altitude and ecological characteristics, planting is not simultaneous. During every harvest festival (*seren taun*), Abah and his counsellors make recommendations about which varieties of rice should be planted in which locations in the next season, taking into considerations the varieties' traits, climate, and the ecology. This is done in such a way that, although planting period differs from place to place within the region, harvest will still be simultaneous. This is critical because pest outbreaks will then be prevented.

> What makes [our paddy fields] safe from pests is that we harvest rice simultaneously. ... Here, when we grow rice, of course there are pests, but there won't be any outbreak, because after our harvest, there will be no more resources to eat and automatically the number will lower again.
>
> *(Abah, ibid.)*

Rice diversity is the third of the key factors. The rice production protocol in Kasepuhan is made so that genetic diversity can still be maintained in the region through an in-situ conservation process (Soemarwoto 2007). This study has recorded that, by 2014, the community had around 500 landraces (or varieties) of rice, classified on the basis of their relative sacredness and characteristics of the grain (*buhun*, ancient; *biasa*, regular; or *ketan*, glutinous), their affinity with a water-soil regime (in *sawah* or *huma*), and the elevation at which they are planted. On each patch of land, every individual is obliged to plant more than one rice variety in combination, one of which should be an ancient type. They believe that this acknowledges their ancestors and cultural identity. As it turns out, keeping this genetic diversity enables the community to produce new landraces from cross-pollination.

People identify these new landraces from the people's use of a finger-knife (*etem*) to cut off the rice stalk during harvest. As opposed to a sickle (or combine harvesting machine) that can cut stalks efficiently, a finger-knife requires the farmer to cut each stalk individually – a painstaking effort but it comes with a benefit of 'feeling' each stalk and noticing new traits that emerge (e.g. thicker hairs, harder stalk, taller stature). A new rice landrace is usually identified in the field and brought and announced during the harvest festival under a new landrace name, if the elders agree.

The food side of the system

At the consumption end, three more factors are influential in shaping a more sustainable food system in Kasepuhan: an effective barn, a traditional milling apparatus, and a strict prohibition on selling rice. In order to maintain (rice) food security, Kasepuhan possesses 8,000 rice barns (or *leuit*) that guarantee the availability of rice for at least three years. There are two types of barns. In every household, a family is obliged to own an individual rice barn roughly the size of a small room. It is normally placed adjacent to the family's house, although there are also groups of rice barns located in a separate place from the houses. The structure of each rice barn looks like a small house with high stilts. The barn is designed and maintained in a particular humidity so as to keep the stored rice grains dry. Rice is stored in tied bundles and attached to the stalks. This prevents the grains from deteriorating. The second barn is the communal one, a large house-like barn located at the center of the main village, close to *Abah*'s house (*imah gede*, literally, the large house). This communal barn is named *leuit si jimat*, or the sacred barn. During every harvest period, each household must give a small part of their harvest yields to the communal barn. If later anyone experiences a harvest failure, he/she could borrow rice bundles from the communal barn and pay for the same number of bundles they borrowed after the next harvest period. This helps to strengthen the social capital and to some extent achieve community food security.

The second factor is the way the indigenous people still use traditional rice milling techniques in a form of long mortar and pestle made from a certain type of timber, called *lisung* and *halu*. Using both apparatuses, women usually pound the rice bundles to detach rice grains from the stalks and remove the chaffs (outer husks) of the grains. In many modern rice agricultural areas, this practice has long been replaced by rice hullers and polishers, which can de-husk rice more efficiently and create a better taste and appearance of white rice. In Kasepuhan, machinery is not allowed, so the old practice remains. What results from this is that the indigenous people in fact consume a healthier form of rice that is richer in vitamin B, bran, and fiber due to the incomplete process of de-husking. Because this brown rice is higher in fiber and proteins, the people are more easily satiated, eat less rice, and consequently have a lower risk of diabetes and other non-communicable diseases. Not only that, their eating less rice also helps maintain their rice stocks in their barns.

Lastly, their resilient food system is also the result of their viewpoint about rice, which for them is as sacred as life itself. Their reverential relations with rice (and consequently other food as well) forbids them from throwing away left-over rice or even selling rice (in any form). Each has its own implication. First, not throwing away rice means that there is no concept of waste in Kasepuhan. People usually process left-over rice as rice crackers or mix it with other ingredients to be used as feeds for fish and poultry. Secondly, not selling rice means that they are less inclined to cash, or at least keep rice from being a market commodity. This is in stark contrast from my findings in a more modernized rice agricultural society in Java, in which farmers sell premium rice for a much higher price to the external market so that they can purchase lower quality rice for themselves (Dwiartama 2014). One of the community elders explains:

> Rice is life itself. So, when someone sells rice, it is as if he/she sells their life, and when his/her life has been sold – when we talk about life, we talk about the spirit, here, we consider this as a great sin. Someone selling rice, in any form, is as if this someone has taken away a life. Or, we can also say that it is equal to killing another being.
>
> *(Yoyo, community elder, from an interview in a short documentary*
> *about Kasepuhan; Laksono 2015)*

The six factors in the whole chain of *Kasepuhan*'s traditional agri-food system (keeping a communal land ownership, planting and harvesting synchronously, maintaining genetic diversity, keeping a communal rice barn, retaining rice qualities through traditional processing techniques, and a respectful attitude towards rice) help the indigenous people to regenerate and sustain their social-ecological system whilst achieving a community food and nutritional security. It is, however, not to say that they are free from threats and troubles. Some of these threats come as external factors, in the form of regulatory pressures from the state, cultural commodification through tourism activities, and the introduction of modern values and practices (including a stronger inclination towards cash). This creates an internal fracture within the indigenous community, partly as more and more young people leave their traditional values in search of a better life in the cities, or more and more processed food products appearing in the villages may replace the traditional diets. This is not peculiar to Kasepuhan, as I will discuss in the last section of this chapter.

Reflections: towards regenerative food systems through indigenous practices

One of the key issues in the increasing threat to indigenous livelihood is the incompatibility between traditional values of indigenous peoples and the modern value system. Land ownership is among the recurring problems (see e.g. Chamberlin 2010 as he puts in his book title: *if this is your land, where are your stories?*). The case study provided has shown that collective land ownership is required not only to guarantee a sustainable and manageable rice production in the region, but also to build a sense of collective belonging within the indigenous community. Conflicts between indigenous people and the state or the private sector often take place around the issue of land tenure and boundaries of indigenous land (Li 2007). Along with the development of new frontiers for housing, plantations and industrial complexes, indigenous lands are decreasing and marginalized, which ends up being a threat against the integrity of the indigenous peoples.

Another form of incompatibility is demonstrated through what Stroma Cole (2007) discusses as cultural commodification. In her study of cultural tourism in eastern parts of Indonesia, Cole identifies that cultural commodification and loss of authenticity become an issue experienced by indigenous people aiming to improve their livelihood through economic development. What transpires from tourism is a situation whereby indigenous people, in order to maintain their attraction, begin to perceive themselves as a representative of an ethnic way of life that freezes them from any socio-economic changes and a better livelihood (although Cole also argues that cultural commodification also creates an identity that enables indigenous people to utilize their political resources for the better).

Kasepuhan Ciptagelar provides a good example of how indigenous people can build a good relationship with urban community groups without being scared of losing their traditional values or their existence. *Abah*, who is now 35 years old and has become the community leader since he was 21 years old, does not shrink from technological advancement. In fact, with the help of urban artists and activists, the community is able to adopt new digital technologies through the establishment of community radio stations, opening access to internet (now the central hall in the village has full broadband internet access) and even run their own television channels. They also produce their own electricity through micro-hydro-electrical machinery spread in streams around the villages. This is all done to create a balance between their traditional and modern values. School children learn about their own culture through the internet, television, and radio station. On the other hand, they are also aware of the threats that modern values pose to their culture, so they make efforts to conserve their culture in many ways. Among the most recent traditional-modern engagements in Kasepuhan is an attempt of a group of university scholars, with the permission of *Abah*, to decode the traditional knowledge system through an interdisciplinary approach that includes astronomy, geography, ecology, anthropology, linguistics, and art (similar to what e.g. Moller et al. 2004 worked on in the Maori in New Zealand).

This chapter agrees that indigenous people, and consequently indigenous food systems, are facing real threats to their existence. However, the solution is not to isolate them in their pockets of communities away from modern values. It is by realising what is compatible or not between the two value systems that we can then build a platform for a rural-urban linkage towards a more regenerative food system. Through this platform, we can learn to be more open to traditional practices at both ends of the agri-food system while at the same time helping indigenous people to attain their rights and safeguard them from the threats posed by the modern value system.

Discussion questions

1. Can you trace the historical origin behind your favorite dishes? How much do they link with traditional knowledge and practices?
2. How has our modern value system impacted the health and wellbeing of different, often marginalized, community groups all over the world?
3. Can you think of incompatibilities and compatibilities between traditional and modern value systems?
4. Do you think our society has been romanticizing indigenous communities and livelihoods too much?
5. What do you think about situating indigenous people and traditional practices as a tourist attraction?

Notes

1 Angga Dwiartama is Assistant Professor at the School of Life Sciences and Technology, Institut Teknologi Bandung (ITB), Indonesia; dwiartama@sith.itb.ac.id.
2 With this regard, Berkes et al. (2000) see indigenous knowledge as being adaptive, rather than traditional in a static/belong-to-the-past sense. For the sake of the discussion, I will use traditional and indigenous to refer to the same idea without providing any nuance to either concept.
3 From the Latin word *indigena* which bears the meaning 'originating from a particular place' (Merriam-Webster dictionary).

4 *Javanica* rice varieties differ from the modern high-yielding varieties in that they have tall plant stature, hard stalks, and low shattering of their grains from the inflorescence. This characteristic is central to the way traditional rice farming is practiced in *Kasepuhan*. For instance, the low shattering trait enables the community to store rice stalks in bundles within their rice barns, which are important so that rice can be stored for years without any significant deterioration in quality (see Dwiartama 2014).

Further reading

Altieri, M. A. (2002). Agroecology: the science of natural resource management for poor farmers in marginal environments. *Agriculture, Ecosystems and Environment, 93*, 1–24.

Berkes, F., Colding, J., and Folke, C. (2000). Rediscovery of traditional ecological knowledge as adaptive management. *Ecological Applications, 10*(5), 1251–1262.

Cotton, C. M., and Wilkie, P. (1996). *Ethnobotany: principles and applications* (No. Sirsi) i9780471955375. Chichester: John Wiley & Sons.

Kuhnlein, H. V., Erasmus, B., and Spigelski, D. (2009). *Indigenous peoples' food systems: the many dimensions of culture, diversity and environment for nutrition and health*. Rome: Food and Agriculture Organization of the United Nations.

Semali, L. M., and Kincheloe, J. L. (Eds.). (1999). *What is indigenous knowledge? Voices from the Academy*. New York: Garland Pub.

References

Altieri, M. A. (2002). Agroecology: the science of natural resource management for poor farmers in marginal environments. *Agriculture, Ecosystems and Environment, 93*, 1–24.

Aregay, M. W. (1988). The early history of Ethiopia's coffee trade and the rise of Shawa. *Journal of African History, 29*(1), 19–25.

Bell, S., and Morse, S. (2012). *Sustainability indicators: measuring the immeasurable?* Abingdon, Oxon: Routledge.

Berkes, F., Colding, J., and Folke, C. (2000). Rediscovery of traditional ecological knowledge as adaptive management. *Ecological Applications, 10*(5), 1251–1262.

Carolan, M. S. (2017). *No one eats alone: food as a social enterprise*. Washington, DC: Island Press.

Chamberlin, J. E. (2010). *If this is your land, where are your stories? Finding common ground*. Toronto: Vintage Canada.

Cole, S. (2007). Beyond authenticity and commodification. *Annals of Tourism Research, 34*(4), 943–960.

Cotton, C. M., and Wilkie, P. (1996). *Ethnobotany: principles and applications* (No. Sirsi) i9780471955375. Chichester: John Wiley & Sons.

Dahlberg, K. A. (1993). Regenerative food systems: broadening the scope and agenda of sustainability. In P. Allen (Ed.), *Food for the future* (pp. 75–102). New York: John Wiley & Sons.

Dwiartama, A. (2014). *Investigating resilience of agriculture and food systems: insights from two theories and two case studies* (Doctoral dissertation, University of Otago).

Dwiartama, A., Rosin, C., and Campbell, H. (2016). Understanding agri-food systems as assemblages: worlds of rice in Indonesia. *Biological Economies: Experimentation and the Politics of Agri-Food Frontiers.* 10.4324/9781315731124

Ellis, E. C., and Wang, S. M. (1997). Sustainable traditional agriculture in the Tai Lake Region of China. *Agriculture, Ecosystems and Environment, 61*(2–3), 177–193.

Folke, C., Carpenter, S., Elmqvist, T., Gunderson, L., Holling, C. S., and Walker, B. (2002). Resilience and sustainable development: building adaptive capacity in a world of transformations. *Ambio, 31*(5), 437–440. https://doi.org/citeulike-article-id:1524120

Gliessman, S. R. (2006). *Agroecology: the ecology of sustainable food systems*. London: CRC press.

International Labor Organization (ILO). (1989). *Indigenous and tribal peoples convention No. 169*. Opened for signature 27 June 1989, entered into force 5 September 1991.

Kuhnlein, H. V. (2003). Micronutrient nutrition and traditional food systems of indigenous peoples. *Food, Nutrition and Agriculture, 33*, 33–37.

Kuhnlein, H. V., and Receveur, O. (1996). Dietary change and traditional food systems of indigenous peoples. *Annual Review of Nutritions, 16*, 417–442.

Kuhnlein, H. V., Erasmus, B., and Spigelski, D. (2009). *Indigenous peoples' food systems: the many dimensions of culture, diversity and environment for nutrition and health*. Rome: Food and Agriculture Organization of the United Nations.

Laksono, D. D. (2015). *Kasepuhan Ciptagelar* [documentary]. Produced by Watchdoc Documentary. Accessed at www.youtube.com/watch?v=ZV0NkADi2dc.

Li, T. M. (2007). Practices of assemblage and community forest management. *Economy and Society, 36*(2), 263–293. 10.1080/03085140701254308

Lind, D., and Barham, E. (2004). The social life of the tortilla: food, cultural politics, and contested commodification. *Agriculture and Human Values, 21*(1), 47–60.

Mintz, S. W. (1986). *Sweetness and power: the place of sugar in modern history*. London: Penguin.

Moller, H., Berkes, F., Lyver, P. O. B., and Kislalioglu, M. (2004). Combining science and traditional ecological knowledge: monitoring populations for co-management. *Ecology and Society, 9*(3), 1–15.

Norgaard, R. B. (1984). Traditional agricultural knowledge: past performance, future prospects, and institutional implications. *American Journal of Agricultural Economics, 66*(5), 874–878.

Soemarwoto, R. (2007). Kasepuhan rice landrace diversity, risk management, and agricultural modernization. In R. Ellen (Ed.), *Modern crises and traditional strategies: local ecological knowledge in Island Southeast Asia* (vol. 6, pp. 84–111). New York: Berghahn Books.

Sunderlin, W. D., and Resosudarmo, I. A. P. (1996). *Rates and causes of deforestation in Indonesia: towards a resolution of the ambiguities*. Bogor: CIFOR.

Turner, N. J., and Turner, K. L. (2007). Traditional food systems, erosion and renewal in Northwestern North America. *Indian Journal of Traditional Knowledge, 6*(January), 57–68.

Viergever, M. (1999). Indigenous knowledge: an interpretation of views from indigenous peoples. In L. M. Semali and J. L. Kincheloe (Eds.), What is indigenous knowledge?: voices from the Academy (pp. 333–359). New York: Garland Pub.

4

INDIGENOUS GOOD LIVING PHILOSOPHIES AND REGENERATIVE FOOD SYSTEMS IN AOTEAROA NEW ZEALAND AND PERU

Mariaelena Huambachano

Introduction

Recognition of Indigenous good living philosophies is on the rise. Global development agendas, such as the United Nations Sustainable Development Goal (SDGs), highlight the significance of local solutions – not least, those embedded in traditional ecological knowledge (TEK) – for global sustainable development (United Nations Department of Economic and Social Affairs, UNDESA 2015). TEK refers to the enduring body of knowledge and practices of Indigenous peoples related to the natural environment of a specific geographic area, acquired mostly through oral history and experiential learning from one generation to the next over thousands of years (Cajete 2000; Durie 2003; LaDuke 1994). These sets of understandings, interpretations, and meanings of the environment manifest a unique 'Indigenous good living philosophy,' which contains insights about biodiversity conservation, environmental governance strategies, and political traditions that arise from hundreds of years of collective memories, and trial and error experiences (Gudynas 2011; LaDuke 1994; Lajo 2011).

Indigenous good living philosophies are rooted in cosmovision: a collectivistic, holistic, and spiritual approach to all beings, humans and non-humans (sea, mountains, rivers, etc.), interconnected to the natural world (Durie 2003; LaDuke 1994). Two of the most important yet under-recognized Indigenous good living philosophies are found in Oceania among the Māori people of Aotearoa with the concept of Mauri Ora that translates to 'Good Life' in English (Marsden 2003; Morgan 2006), and similarly, in Latin America among the Quechua people of Peru in the notion of Allin Kawsay, which translates to 'Living Well' in English and 'Buen Vivir' in Spanish (Lajo. 2012, Quijano 2011, Huambachano 2015). However, existing research on food policy has paid little attention to the lived experiences and responses to traditional food systems of Indigenous peoples, and their pivotal role in the framing of a more sustainable and equitable food system model (La Vía Campesina 2015; McMichael 2009).

In this context, the aim of this chapter is to understand how Quechua and Māori communities are continuing to pursue and realize sustainable food systems grounded on Indigenous good living philosophies. And what challenges continue to exist for Indigenous peoples? According to a definition provided by the Food and Agriculture Organization of the United Nations (FAO 2016),

> a sustainable food system (SFS) is a food system that delivers food security and nutrition for all in such a way that the economic, social and environmental bases to generate food security and nutrition for future generations are not compromised.
>
> *(FAO 2016, 1)*

The definition postulates the aim of a food system that is economically viable (economic sustainability); it provides broad-based benefits for all members of society (social sustainability); and it does not deplete the natural environment (environmental sustainability). While the SFS concept is a modern term to address unsustainable agriculture, this is not an unfamiliar notion for Indigenous peoples, but rather an enduring good living philosophy that requires ongoing attention to maintaining a balance between ecological, economic, and social systems.

To address the research questions of this study, I developed the Khipu Model (KM) described in Huambachano (2017). Briefly, the KM is based on an Andean knowledge-keeping system, which is an intricate and colourful knotted-string device mainly used by the Inca to record both statistical and narrative information (Urton 2003). I adapted the configuration of the Andean khipu to use it as a source of knowledge production that privileges Indigenous ways of knowing and being. The model draws on participatory action research methodology, TEK, values, and principles of kaupapa Māori, which is a Māori research framework (Smith 1999), and the body of scholarship addressing Indigenous research methods (Kovach 2009; Pihama et al. 2002; Wilson 2008).

Data collection tools that emerged from the KM included three Indigenous gatherings, and two talking circles with elders, Indigenous community leaders, and people engaged in traditional food systems in both countries. The study was conducted in Peru and New Zealand between March 2014 and July 2018. In Peru, the Quechua communities that took part of our research were Choquecancha and Rosaspata. Similarly, the Māori iwi (tribes) of Ngāti Hine and Ngāti Porou in the North Island of the country took part of this investigation. Preliminary gatherings with research partners took place in both countries to inform the formulation of questions, research topics, and to identify key research partners for data collection purposes.

Interview protocols, location for gatherings, taking circles, and availability of research partners were discussed at the beginning of Indigenous gatherings and talking circles. The study partners cited throughout this chapter are Quechua and Māori knowledge holders[1] of traditional foods, knowledge, and practices of cultural traditions associated with sustainable food systems. The analysis of the empirical evidence is through the lens of the TEK theory, which studies Indigenous peoples' knowledge systems embedded in their cosmovisions (Battiste 2002; Berkes and Folke 2002; Cajete 2000; Deloria 2005; LaDuke 1994; McGregor 2009).

Indigenous peoples, specifically Quechua and Māori, have long been concerned that colonial approaches to food systems, for example, industrial agriculture[2] that treats food as a commodity disregards their rights to self-determination because we have an obligation to enhance the natural world just as the natural world (as our kin) has an obligation to enhance our lives. But also, industrial agriculture disrupts Indigenous peoples' spiritual, cultural, and physical relationships to ancestral lands that are fundamental for our wellbeing (Coté 2016; Huambachano 2018; Hutchings 2015; Whyte 2016b). For Indigenous peoples, the land is the foundation of their social, political, legal, and economic systems and cultural identification manifested in their good living philosophies (Huambachano 2018). However, power and control of assets specifically of land use for agricultural purposes around the world have shifted massively from governments to the private sector (Borras et al. Kay 2008).

I have argued (see Huambachano 2015, 2017, 2018) that good living philosophies of Indigenous peoples of Peru (Allin Kawsay) and Aotearoa (Mauri Ora) contain valuable teachings about resilient food systems, biodiversity preservation, and agroecological practices. Pieced together, Indigenous good living principles encapsulate principles of food sovereignty to maintain the integrity of not only Indigenous food systems but also of humanity overall (Huambachano 2018). Consequently, a food sovereignty framework directs me to analyse the emergence of Quechua and Māori peoples' good living philosophies and their vital role in framing a more sustainable and regenerative food system. La Via Campesina frames 'the right to food sovereignty' as a collective human right encompassing 'the right to self-determination, the right to permanent sovereignty over natural resources and the right to development' (Claeys 2012, 849). In this study, I do not claim to speak for the Quechua or Māori people, but instead I draw on their teachings and wisdom generously shared by each of them, and from the knowledge I have attained from my kinship relations and lived cultural experiences as an Indigenous woman of Peru and who has lived in Aotearoa too.

This chapter begins with a description of Indigenous good living philosophies followed by the analysis of the philosophical foundations of Allin Kawsay and Mauri Ora. Subsequently, I discuss the role of Indigenous good living philosophies and Indigenous food sovereignty in relation to regenerative food systems. The conclusion draws together the threads of the argument that Indigenous peoples' good living philosophies herald an Indigenous food sovereignty model to preserve the health of the natural world, food systems, and overall human wellbeing.

Indigenous good living philosophies: Allin Kawsay and Mauri Ora

From all geographic regions of the world such as the African, Oceanian, North American, and South American regions, Indigenous peoples are the holders of TEK and practices for sustainable development, especially agrobiodiversity preservation for sustainable food systems imbued in Indigenous good living philosophies (LaDuke 1994; Lajo 2012). Examples of good living principles are found, for example, in Aotearoa New Zealand (Mauri Ora), in the highlands of Peru (Allin Kawsay), in Central America in Costa Rica, (Laman Laka), and in North America, (Minobimaatisiiwin) the the good life approach of the Anishinabeg and Cree people. (Jaramillo 2010; LaDuke 1994; Lajo 2012). All these Indigenous terms, sometimes translated as Indigenous notions of 'Living well', more broadly refer to a concept that summarizes Indigenous worldviews or cosmovisions, and how we ought to live well.

An Indigenous worldview or cosmovision denotes a holistic view of nature encompassing know-how systems for resource management and biodiversity preservation (Dávalos 2008; LaDuke 1994; Lajo 2011). The good living philosophies of some Latin American countries such as Peru known as Allin Kawsay and in Ecuador and Bolivia referred to Sumaq Kawsay or Buen Vivir in Spanish have begun to gain notoriety within the discourse of Indigenous models of sustainable living and economic development. Particularly, the President of Bolivia Evo Morales questions whether the Sumaq Kawsay provides the basis for an alternative 'good living' approach. It is an approach that does not solely focus on economic growth but rather places an emphasis on holistic wellbeing (Dávalos 2008; Huambachano 2015; Lajo 2012; Walsh 2010). Therefore, it is prudent to understand the theoretical foundations of Allin Kawsay and Mauri Ora and their contribution in the discourse of regenerative food systems.

Quechua people and Allin Kawsay/Buen Vivir/Good living

In the Andean world, Allin Kawsay has been passed on from generation to generation through oral history (Lajo, 2012). The Sumaq or Allin Kawsay (in the Quechua language) or Suma Qamaña (in the Aymara language) expresses *the good-living philosophies of practice* of the Indigenous peoples of Peru, Ecuador, and Bolivia (Dávalos 2008; Lajo 2012; Quijano 2011). Allin Kawsay is the Quechua phrase widely recognized in the highlands of Peru, which is where this research took place and therefore Allin Kawsay is the phrase used to refer to the good-living philosophy of the Quechua people of Peru. Allin Kawsay reflects the core conceptions of Andean cosmovision, such as the concept of interconnectedness with the cosmos, human and non-human world leading to a stage of equilibrium with nature.

Javier Lajo is one of the very few Indigenous Peruvian scholars who has written extensively about Allin Kawsay, and he defines it as:

A philosophy for the sustainable use of the natural resources available on Pacha-mama, and managed accordingly to sustainability principles of reciprocity, duality and the application and transmission of a state of equilibrium with Pachamama, human and all living things.

(Lajo 2011, 5)

This study on Quechua people and traditional agricultural system shows that Quechua farmers still harvest the many varieties of Andean crops such as potatoes, corn, quinua, and other staples such as oca and qañiwa,[3] adopting traditional practices entrenched in the Allin Kawsay philosophy. As Sonia Tito from Choquecancha stated:

Allin Kawsay is our philosophy of living well with Pachamama and with all our relations, human and non-human (rivers, mountains), and spiritual beings too. We have learnt from our parents and grandparents' key principles such as ayni (reci-procity) and yananti (solidarity). Also, we manage our land according to ayllu system (governance).

All these principles and values have been passed on from one generation to the other. Allin Kawsay is our ideology of sustainable living because if it were not for Allin Kawsay, we would not know about resource management and ecosystem pro-tection. No systems of natural law and order in our community.

This narrative expresses teachings about sustainable use of the natural resources available on Pachamama, and managed according to sustainability principles; principles of reciprocity, community and family solidarity; and the application and transmission of ancestral knowledge.

Māori people and Māuri Ora

Mauri according to (Morgan 2006, 3) refers to the 'binding force between the physical and spiritual'. Mauri is not a stand-alone concept; rather is inextricably linked to other energies that derive from the spiritual realm therefore its complementation with 'Ora', which means energy in Māori and pieced together form the Māori philosophical system of Mauri Ora (Durie 2003; Pohatu 2010; Morgan 2016). Percy Tipene of Ngāti Hine explained to me that:

> Mauri ora is about holistic well-being and it is important to protect the Mauri; and thus the health of the various elements of your 'mahinga kai' to ensure the quality and integrity of the food it produces is high and that the people who consume it are healthy.[4]

This narrative makes references to the concept of Mauri Ora in the realm of sustainable food systems, in which elder Percy Tipene explains that shifts in mauri (life-force, life spirit) of any part of the environment, for example through human use, would cause changes in the mauri of immediately related components, and as a result, the whole system is eventually affected. Since time immemorial, Indigenous peoples have honoured this intimate understanding of the relationship between humans and the ecosystem, and the need to maintain a harmonious equilibrium within this connection. Additionally, social/political and cultural orders and ethical principles such as reciprocity (you take only what you need, and you leave the rest) are instances of Indigenous peoples' responsible interactions with the ecosystems to preserve the integrity of Mother Earth's ecosystems (Battiste 2002, Berkes 2012 Kimmerer 2013; Pierotti and Wildcat 2000).

This study argues that for Indigenous good living philosophies to be recognized at international domains as an Indigenous sustainable development approach, it is necessary for the interwoven human–nature and spiritual relationships, natural laws, and cultural principles imbued in such good-living philosophies to be understood within the legal framework of the UN Declaration on the Rights of Indigenous Peoples (2011). Specifically, in Article 3: Indigenous peoples' right to self-determination, in Article 11: Indigenous peoples have the right to practice and revitalize their cultural traditions and customs, and Article 32, Indigenous peoples have the right to regulate and establish priorities for the use of their territories for development. The governments of Ecuador and Bolivia have taken the lead in advocating the philosophy of sumaq kawsay as an alternative economic development to the current neoliberal economic model (Huanacuni 2010).

Also, empirical studies on the role of Indigenous good living philosophies in safeguarding food systems have been carried out by Indigenous scholars. For example, in Huambachano's (2018) study of Quechua and Māori peoples' well-being ideologies and food security, she argues that the food security framework of Quechua and Māori resonates with conceptions of food sovereignty. She furthers outlines a set of cultural and ecological values of Quechua and Māori that ensures that both the rights of individuals and the human rights to food and Indigenous collective food relations are achieved without compromising the sustainability of the ecosystems. For the Quechua people: *Ayni* (reciprocity), *ayllu*: (collectiveness), *yanantin*: (equilibrium), and *chaninchay* (solidarity). For Māori people: *Kaitakitanga* (guardianship), *koha* (reciprocity), *tikanga* (ethics), and *wairuatanga* (spirituality). These fundamental cultural values work seamlessly together, infusing and revitalizing Quechua and Māori traditional food systems.

Also, Native American scholar Charlotte Coté (Nuu-Chah-nulth) describes how through the Indigenous philosophy of hishuk'ish tsawalk (everything is one), uu-a-thluk (taking care of), and iisaak (respect) her nation is regenerating community wellbeing by mending the broken spiritual and cultural relationship to food systems that they have been subjected to through settler colonialism (Coté 2016). Building up on these empirical studies, I argue that Indigenous philosophies of wellbeing enact practices of food sovereignty that articulate an alternative regenerative food system model.

Indigenous food sovereignty revival: Māori and Quechua

To counteract the oppressive industrial global food security model there has been a food sovereignty movement sweeping across the Indigenous world from North America and from Oceania to Latin America (Coté 2016; LaDuke 1999; Huambachano 2018; Morrison 2011; Whyte 2016a). But before I discuss Indigenous food sovereignty, it is important here to make a distinction between the concept of food sovereignty coined by La Via Campesina in 1996 and later refined at the 2007 Forum for Food Sovereignty in Selingue, Mali, during which 500 delegates from over 80 countries adopted the Declaration of Nyeleni. According to the 2007 Declaration of Nyéléni (2007, 1), food sovereignty encompasses:

> The right of peoples, communities, and countries to define their own agricultural, labour, fishing, food and land policies which are ecologically, socially, economically and culturally appropriate to their unique circumstances. It includes the true right to food and to produce food, which means that all people have the right to safe, nutritious and culturally appropriate food and to food-producing resources and the ability to sustain themselves and their societies.

This definition asserts the 'right' of nations and peoples to control their food systems, food cultures, and environment. The 'rights'-based discourse embedded in La Via Campesina calls for a fundamental shift towards the right of all peoples to healthy and culturally appropriate food and the right to define their own food and agricultural systems (Coté 2016; Hoover 2017; Huambachano 2018). While the conception of food sovereignty resonates with the aspirations of Indigenous peoples the collective rights and cultural responsibilities that Indigenous people have with their kinship system human and non-human relatives are not emphasised within the framing of rights as legal entitlements (Coté 2016; Huambachano 2018; Morrison 2011).

First Nations scholar Dawn Morrison (Secwempec) explains Indigenous food sovereignty as:

> Food is a gift from the Creator. In this respect, the right to food is sacred and cannot be constrained or recalled by colonial laws, policies or institutions. Indigenous food sovereignty is ultimately achieved by upholding our long-standing sacred responsibilities to nurture healthy, interdependent relationships with the land, plants and animals that provide us with our food.
>
> *(Morrison 2011, 100)*

Building up from Morrison's Indigenous food sovereignty definition, Indigenous scholars (see Coté 2016; Hoover 2017; Huambachano 2018; Whyte 2016) argue that Indigenous food sovereignty efforts are not only forms of resistance against colonial-capitalist legacies.

They also represent a resurgence of Indigenous epistemologies and ontologies encompassing Indigenous cultural (e.g. kinship relations), political (e.g. governance structures), legal (e.g. authority status of non-human kin), and economic (e.g. locally based economies) institutions as part of the larger process of decolonization and self-determination. Corntassel and Bryce (2011) argue that Indigenous food sovereignty is the result of Indigenous resurgence in foregrounding customary laws and practices informing Indigenous ways of life and food systems. The set of Indigenous customary laws, ethical principles, and kinship governing structures is what Daigle (2019) describes as Indigenous political and legal orders that frame Indigenous form of authority and governance.

I argue, it is Quechua and Māori peoples' cosmovisions and TEKs embedded in their good living philosophies that provide them with the basis to claim not only their rights to land, and resources contained therein, but to honour the responsibilities and obligations with their extended kinship system that are physical and spiritual health and wellbeing. In the case of Quechua peoples, since pre-colonial times they have exercised their right to self-govern their ancestral terrains and decide collectively what they want to produce and consume through a collective ownership system referred to as *ayllu* (community in English and *comunidad de los Andes* in Spanish) (Lajo 2011).

I observed during fieldwork for this study that all Quechua communities still administer their territories in a collectivistic way alongside chacras (farms) or small plots allotted to individual families. In doing so they do not own the land but have collective property rights to it.

In the ayllu system apus (sacred mountains), mayu (rivers), and qochas (lakes), as well as the history, stories, and spirit of a place have roles to play in maintaining the sacred balance of the ayllu to ensure that all members of the ayllu have access to sufficient and nutritious food. Thus, through the ayllu system, the Quechua people of Peru exercise their rights to self-determination to govern their territories according to their cultural, political, and legal traditions – life in the Andes cannot be otherwise. Peru is signatory to a series of international law instruments such as the International Labour Organization or ILO 169, and the United Nations Declaration on the Rights of Indigenous Peoples (UNDESA 2015).

However, currently Indigenous peoples of Peru have limited state legal recognition, with the exception of native communities being legally recognized in the Peruvian Constitution under the law decree 89 (Huambachano 2017). This limited land rights landscape poses challenges for Quechua people's self-determination to continue having access to land for food production. As Eusebio[5] stated:

> I am afraid that the government would come here one day and change our ances-
> tral land system and so my land will be given to big food corporations. These com-
> panies will exploit Pachamama all year round without having any kind of
> consideration for her well-being.

Thus, it can be argued that for Quechua people food sovereignty means having control over land, resources, and cultural knowledge. If they lose their land that means they lose agency over their food systems and cultural identity. In Aotearoa, Māori Indigenous autonomy and sovereignty over their ancestral territories is acknowledged in the Te Tiriti o Waitangi (Treaty of Waitangi in English). On 6 February 1840 the Treaty of Waitangi was signed between Māori leaders, known as rangatira, and the British Crown (Mutu 2018). Self-determination, in Durie's (1995, 45) terms, 'captures a sense of Māori ownership and active control over the future'.

Durie (1995) argues that the Treaty of Waitangi supports Māori rights to self-determination in order to conceptualize their governing policies and to engage in policy implementation oriented to wellbeing in their own affairs. However, discrepancies in the English and Māori versions over the notion of sovereignty have long been the subject of debate, and as soon as the Treaty of Waitangi was signed Māori had to endure dispossessions of their land. As Lionel from the Papatūānuku marae (tribe) explains:

> The loss of tribal land in the 19th century due to land being taken against our will and the involvement of our Māori soldiers in the Second World War was further exacerbated by land confiscations that resulted in the loss of many Māori's tūranga-waewae (a place to stand). It was our land! The government confiscated Māori land from our soldiers that went to war.[6]

In the 1940s, the European intervention produced two principal effects: Māori had lost most of their land, and what was left was no longer under the control of powerful political groups such as iwi or hapu. By 1950s, New Zealand witnessed a Māori exodus from rural to urban areas heralded by the dispossession of Māori land (Jackson 2000; Mutu 2018). All of the Māori research participants indicated that they are reluctant to sell their land, as eloquently described by one of the research participants: 'I am tangata whenua – the people of the land and without land I don't have any sense of belonging. So we fought and are fighting the Crown tirelessly to preserve our land.'

It was Māori peoples' strong bond with whenua that motivated Māori peoples' activism specifically in the 1960s and 1970s to stop the sale of Māori land, and key examples are the Land March in 1975 and Bastion Point in 1977 (Jackson 2000; Mutu 2018). Bastion Point is a coastal area of land in Auckland city in the Northern part of Aotearoa, and holds cultural and historical significance for Māori people because it highlighted the resilient attitude of Māori against forced land alienation by pākehā (European descendants) in the late 1970s. The protests started on 5 January 1977 and ended on 25 May 1978 (507th day) when 222 protesters were evicted and arrested by police, but this did not end there and these land protests bolstered Māori peoples' aspirations to enact their land sovereignty rights (Jackson 2000; Walker 1991). The examples above give evidence of Quechua and Māori peoples' struggles post-colonization to enact collective-self-determination over their food landscapes and cultural knowledge, which ultimately threaten food sovereignty.

Conclusion

This study provides evidence of the vital role that Indigenous good living philosophies play in the revitalization of Indigenous food sovereignty of Quechua and Māori people. Allin Kawsay and Mauri Ora construct a theoretically informed approach to living well guiding Quechua and Māori traditional food systems. It is Quechua and Māori collectivistic capabilities and knowledge embedded in their good-living philosophies that provide them with the basis to claim their rights to land and resources contained therein, and these rights are held by the community's customary law, values, and customs.

The value of food for these two Indigenous groups is at the core of their cultural identity, knowledge and social-political structures because for us food has culture, history, stories, it has relationships, that tie us to our food. In this sense, food is more than a commodity: it is sacred; food is sacred because it originates from all our relatives (human and non-human), holding cultural meaning inherently linked to rights to preserve a connection with all our kinship system. For example, each year the activities associated with foods such as harvesting ceremonies, dances like pow wows and communal food festivals, renew the family, community, cultural, political, and social relationships that connect Indigenous peoples, with all community members (plants, rivers, and spiritual beings). Thus, collective food relations represent, besides the obtaining of food for purposes of livelihood, an essential aspect of cultural identity.

It is fundamental to take into account that many Indigenous peoples view the right to food as a collective one and they are demanding not just food with a calorie count purpose, but their rights to sufficient, healthy, and culturally appropriate food. These two Indigenous groups continue to fight to have autonomy to grow their foods according to their cultural knowledge systems. Therefore, the revitalization of Indigenous food systems is a critical tool in preserving Indigenous culture, wellbeing, and thereby their rights to healthy food systems. More broadly, Allin Kawsay and Māuri Ora hold social, political, economic and cultural frameworks guiding their ways of life. These Indigenous good living philosophies contain teachings on food sovereignty, and how to live in harmonious and reciprocal relationships with Mother Earth, and with each other to ensure the reproduction of the cycles of life in its full vitality and diversity.

Discussion questions

1. What is the relationship between Indigenous knowledge and food production?
2. How Quechua and Māori communities are continuing to pursue and realise regenerative food systems grounded in Indigenous good living philosophies?
3. Is Indigenous knowledge a key for improving food security? What challenges continue to exist for Indigenous peoples.
4. What is the contribution of Indigenous peoples' knowledge to the challenges of international food security?

Notes

1 In this chapter, I use the term 'knowledge holders' to denote Quechua and Māori people who have extensive knowledge on the study topics and who are authorities in their community. This term does not exclude people who may not be of the age of an elder but who are important thinkers and leaders within the Māori and Andean world.
2 Industrial agriculture is characterized by large-scale farming and the adoption of scientific-technological systems such as the use of Genetically Modified Organisms (GMOs) (McMichael 2009).
3 Leonel Hotene, personal interview December 2016.
4 Percy Tipene, personal interview July 2015.
5 Petronila Quispe, personal interview March 2015.
6 Eusebio Tito, personal interview December 2017.

Further readings

Altieri, M.A. (2016). Agroecological principles for sustainable agriculture. In N. Uphoff (Ed.), *Agroecological Innovations: Increasing Food Production with Participatory Development* (pp. 40–46). Sterling, VA: Earthscan Publications.

Huambachano, M. (2019). Indigenous food sovereignty: Reclaiming food as sacred medicine in Aotearoa New Zealand and Peru. *New Zealand Journal of Ecology*, 43(3), 1–17 https://newzealandecol ogy.org/nzje/3384.pdf

Kawharu, M. (2010). Environment as marae. In R. Selby, P. Moore, and M. Mulholland, (Eds.), *Kaitiaki: Māori and the Environment* (pp. 221–239). Wellington: Huia.

McGregor, D. (2004a). Coming full circle: Indigenous knowledge, environment and our future. *American Indian Quarterly*, 28(3–4), 385–410.

Whyte, K.P. (2016). Indigenous food sovereignty, renewal and settler colonialism. In M. Rawlinson and C. Ward, Routledge (Eds.), *The Routledge Handbook of Food Ethics* (pp. 1–31). Abingdon, Oxon: Routledge Taylor & Francis Group.

References

Altieri, M.A. and Toledo, V.M. (2011). The agroecological revolution in Latin America: Rescuing nature, ensuring food sovereignty and empowering peasants. *Journal of Peasant Studies*, 38(3), 587–612.

Battiste, M. (2002). *Indigenous Knowledge and Pedagogy in First Nations Education: A Literature Review with Recommendations*. Ottawa: Apamuwek Institute.

Berkes, F. (2012). *Sacred Ecology*. New York: Routledge.

Berkes, F. and Folke, C. (2002). Back to the future: Ecosystem dynamics and local knowledge. In L. H. Gunderson and S. Holling (Eds.), *Panarchy: Understanding Transformations in Human and Natural Systems* (pp. 121–146). Washington, DC: Island Press.

Borras, S.M., Jr., Edelman., M., and Kay, C. (2008). Transnational agrarian movements confronting globalization. *Special Issue of Journal of Agrarian Change*, 8, 1–2.

Claeys, P. (2012). The creation of new rights by the food sovereignty movement: The challenge of institutionalizing subversion. *Sociology*, 4(5), 844–860.

Cajete, G. (2000). *Native Science: Nature Laws of Interdependence*. Santa, FE: Clear Light Publishers.

Battiste, M. (2011). *Reclaiming Indigenous Voice and Vision*. Vancouver: UBC Press.

Battiste, M., and Henderson, J. (2000). *Protecting Indigenous Knowledge and Heritage: A Global Challenge*. Saskatoon: Purich.

Corntassel, J. and Bryce, C. (2011). Practicing sustainable self-determination: Indigenous approaches to cultural restoration and revitalization. *Brown Journal of World Affairs*, 18, 151.

Coté, C. (2016). 'Indigenizing' food sovereignty: Revitalizing indigenous food practices and ecological knowledges in Canada and the United States. *Humanities*, 5(3), 57.

Dávalos, P. (2008). El Sumak Kawsay (Buen Vivir) y las censuras del desarrollo. Retrieved from http:// alainet.org/active/23920.

Daigle, M. (2019). Tracing the terrain of Indigenous food sovereignties. *Journal of Peasant Studies*, 46(2), 297–315.

Deloria, V. (2005). Indigenous peoples. In W. Schweiker (Ed.), *The Blackwell Companion to Religious Ethics* (pp. 552–559). Oxford: Blackwell Publishing.

Declaration of Nyéléni (2007). La Via Campesina and Declaration of Nyéléni. Retrieved https://viacam pesina.org/en/declaration-of-nyi/

Durie, M. (2003). *Nga Kahui Pou Launching Māori Futures*. Wellington: Huia Press.

Durie, M.H. (1995). Beyond 1852: Maori, the state, and a New Zealand constitution. *Sites*, 30, 31–47.

Gudynas, E. (2011). Buen Vivir: Today's tomorrow. *Development*, 54(4), 441–447.

Hoover, E. (2017). 'You can't say you're sovereign if you can't feed yourself': Defining and enacting food sovereignty in American Indian community gardening. *American Indian Culture and Research Journal*, 41(3), 31–70.

Huambachano, M. (2015). Indigenous knowledge and food security. *International Journal of Food Studies: An Interdisciplinary Journal*, 5(3), 33–47.

Huambachano, M. (2017). Through an indigenous lens food security is food sovereignty: Case studies of Maori people of Aotearoa and Andean people of Peru. Unpublished PhD thesis, University of Auckland, New Zealand.

Huambachano, M. (2018). Enacting food sovereignty in Aotearoa New Zealand and Peru: Revitalizing indigenous knowledge, food practices and ecological philosophies. *Journal of Agroecology and Sustainable Food Systems*, 42(9), 1003–1028.

Huanacuni, F. (2010). *Good Living/Living Good: Andean Philosophy, Politics, Strategies and Regional Experiences*. Lima, Peru: Andean Coordinating committee of Indigenous Organizations.

Hutchings, J. (2015). *Te Mahi Mā Ra Hua Parakore: A Mā Ori Food Sovereignty Handbook*. Ō taki, Aotearoa/New Zealand: Te Tā kupu, Te Wā nanga o Raukwa.

Jackson, M. (2000). Where does sovereignty lie? In C. James (Ed.), *Building the Constitution* (pp. 21–38). Wellington: Institute of Policy Studies, Victoria University of Wellington.

Jaramillo, E. (2010). Mother Earth and 'Living Well' – New analytical and strategic paradigms for Indigenous struggles. Retrieved from www.iwgia.org/publications/search-pubs?publication_id=470

Kimmerer, R. (2013). *Braiding Sweetgrass: Indigenous Wisdom, Scientific Knowledge and the Teachings of Plants*. Minneapolis, MN: Milkweed Editions.

Kovach, M. (2009). *Indigenous Methodologies: Characteristics, Conversations, and Contexts*. Toronto: University of Toronto Press.

LaDuke, W. (1994). Traditional ecological knowledge and environmental futures. *Journal of International Environment and Policy*, 5, 127–135.

LaDuke, W. (1999). *All our Relations: Native Struggles for Land and Life*. Minneapolis, MN: South End Press.

Lajo, J. (2011). Un model Sumaq Kawsay de gobierno. Retrieved from http://alainet.org/active/49164&lang=es.

Lajo, J. (2012). Cosmovision Andina: Sumaq Kawsay-ninchik o Nuestro Vivir Bien. Retrieved from http://alainet.org/active/59345&lang=es

La Vía Campesina. (2015). *Annual Report 2015*. Harare: Author.

Marsden, M. (2003). *The Woven Universe: Selected Readings of Rev. Māori Marsden*. Ōtaki: The Estate of Rev. Māori Marsden.

McGregor, D. (2004b). Coming full circle: Indigenous knowledge, environment and our future. *American Indian Quarterly*, 28(3–4), 385–410.

McGregor, D. (2009). Linking traditional knowledge and environmental practice in Ontario. *Journal of Canadian Studies/Revue D'études Canadiennes*, 43(3), 69–100.

McMichael, P. (2009). A food regime analysis of the 'world food crisis'. *Agriculture and Human Values*, 26 (4), 281–295.

Morgan, T.K. (2006). Decision-support tools and the indigenous paradigm. *Engineering Sustainability*, 159 (ES4), 169–177.

Morrison, D. (2011). Indigenous food sovereignty: A model for social learning. In A.A. Desmarais, N. Wieber, and H. Wittman (Eds.), *Food Sovereignty in Canada: Creating Just and Sustainable Food Systems* (pp. 97–113). Vancouver: Fernwood Publishing.

Mutu, M. (2018). Behind the smoke and mirrors of the Treaty of Waitangi claims settlement process in New Zealand: No prospect for justice and reconciliation for Māori without constitutional transformation. *Journal of Global Ethics*, 14(2), 208–221.

Orange, C. (1987). *The Treaty of Waitangi*. Wellington: Bridget Williams Books.

Pierotti, R. and Wildcat, D. (2000). Traditional ecological knowledge: The third alternative (commentary). *Ecological Applications*, 10(5), 1333–1340.

Pohatu, Y.W. (2010). Mauri: Rethinking human wellbeing. *MAI Review*, 3, 1–12.

Quijano, A. (2011). ¿Sistemas alternativos de producción? *Producir Para Vivir: Los Caminos de la Producción No Capitalista*, 8, 369–399.

Smith, G.H. (1997). The development of Kaupapa Maori: Theory and Praxix. Unpublished doctoral thesis, University of Auckland, New Zealand.

UNDESA. (2015). Investing in development: A practical plan to achieve the Millennium development goals report. Retrieved from http://unmillenniumproject.org/documents/MainReportComplete-lowres.pdf

United Nations Permanent Forum for Indigenous Issues (UNPFII). (2011). *Permanent Forum on Indigenous Issues: Report on the Tenth Session of the Economic and Social Council*. Retrieved from http://un.org/esa/socdev/unpfii/documents/session_10_report_EN.pdf

United Nations Food and Agriculture Organization (UN FAO). (2016). Sustainable Food Systems Report. Retrieved from http://fao.org/3/ca2079en/CA2079EN.pdf

Urton, G. (2003). *Signs of the Inka Khipu: Binary Coding in the Andean Knotted-string Records*. Austin, TX: University of Texas Press.

Walker, R. (1991). The genesis and transformation of the Waitangi tribunal. In A. Pawley (Ed.), *A Man and a Half: Essays in Pacific Anthropology and Ethnobiology in Honour of Ralph Bulmer*, Memoir No. 48. (pp. 615–624). Auckland: The Polynesian Society.

Walsh, C. (2010). Development as Buen Vivir: Institutional arrangements and (de)colonial entanglements. *Development*, 53(1), 15–21.

Whyte, K.P. (2016a). Our ancestor's dystopia now. Indigenous conservation and the anthropocene. In U. Heise, J. Christensen, and M. Niemann (Eds.), *Routledge Companion to the Environmental Humanities* (pp. 1–9). Abingdon, Oxon: Routledge Taylor & Francis Group.

Whyte, K.P. (2016b). Indigenous food sovereignty, renewal and settler colonialism. In M. Rawlinson and C. Ward, Routledge (Eds.), *The Routledge Handbook of Food Ethics* (pp. 1–31). Abingdon, Oxon: Routledge Taylor & Francis Group.

Wilson, S. (2008). *Research is Ceremony: Indigenous Research Methods*. Winnipeg: Fernwood Publishing.

5

BEYOND CULTURALLY-SIGNIFICANT PRACTICES

Decolonizing ontologies for regenerative food-systems

Aude Chesnais

Introduction

Food is about people and ways of living; in essence, food is cultural. Our contemporary global food system is threatened by hegemonic practices that promote industrial monopolies, dependency on global food markets, and monocropping which destroys food diversity and threatens health through heavy chemical use. We are also losing the cultural and thus the social meaning of food, leading to systemic aberrations that now endanger our food future and ultimately our planet's survival. Such irrationality is constructed historically and culturally engrained. The path cannot be set for a global sustainable food system without understanding the political economy of its cultural norms.

Regenerative practices are emerging as part of a deeply reflexive effort to bring about a truly sustainable future. Instead of maintaining existing systemic configurations, regenerative development aspires to create resilient and adaptive structures for communities to thrive now and in the future (Plaut et al. 2016). This comprehensive approach is a call for inclusivity, holistic thinking, and systemic change. It builds upon and incorporates ethical principles from a diversity of sources and bears many similarities to existing concepts such as traditional ecological knowledge (TEK) (Pickering Sherman et al. 2010; Ross et al. 2011). As a blooming movement worldwide, it is increasingly gaining credit and legitimacy, one successful project at a time. However, in practice, the ecological transition is lived in struggle and often falls back to monopolistic practices and western-centric economic principles, failing to emerge as a legitimate alternative to a destructive global mode of food production.

What would it take for a global shift to occur? What is the role of culture? Can we envision a global culture of sustainability? In this chapter, I discuss the role of cultural significance in the development and expansion of regenerative practices. From 10 years of research with grassroots food-systems practitioners in the Lakota reservations of Pine Ridge and Cheyenne River in South Dakota, I use two case studies looking at water and buffalo restoration projects to exemplify how the stakes behind regenerative practices might well extend beyond a simple need for cultural diversity. To that end, I tie the question of culture to the political economy of the commodified world-system. Cultural significance might carry the seeds of a true systemic shift, if it enables a profound deconstruction of the colonial global food system. The discussion evolves into the possibilities for a global decolonial project to shape a culturally-significant regenerative food system that goes beyond a utilitarian organization of natural resources and consumption. I conclude using my experience as a researcher and community-based development facilitator to offer practical solutions at the local and global scale.

Lakota culture and land use history

Whether destructive or regenerative, food practices are anchored in the conception of land as a means of production and subsequently as a cultural norm. Such conceptions are intertwined with policy-making, which is shaped by and shapes new food practices. A particular sense of place and connection to the land can be created, induced, or impaired. A look at historical patterns in the land of the Lakota nations in South Dakota sheds light on how these changes operate. In what locals call "Indian country" or the "Rez",[1] a historical shift took place through the methodical destruction of the practical relevance of one mode of production and the imposition of another.

Indeed, many locals argue that the Lakota way of life and more generally the cultural practices of the Great Plains tribes were mostly achieved through "ethnocide",[2] i.e. the cultural demise that followed the legally orchestrated destruction of their livelihood. As in many indigenous contexts around the world, that shift occurred through the coercive move from a nomadic and collective use of land to a commodified one. Preceding the surrender of the last free Lakota bands, a federal campaign encouraged soldiers, settlers, and anyone with a rifle to kill wild bison (Lueck 2002) whether for hide or sport. The purpose was publicly known, shown through the words of this army officer: "every buffalo dead is an Indian gone". Shortly after the mid-nineteenth century, most buffalos had disappeared from the Great Plains, leaving remaining bands of free Native[3] tribes starving, and thereby providing a strong leverage to push them into accepting meager pieces of land that they could call theirs. The reservation system started to take shape.

We can clearly identify how those events and the practice of treaty signing occurred as a by-product of cultural domination (Price 1994). Even if decision-making had occurred fairly – which it rarely did – a nomadic mode of production disappears at the very moment where it agrees to split and occupy specific pieces of land. In 1887, the Allotment Act forcibly parceled collective territories allocated to the Great Sioux reservation into individual lots. This promoted the colonial process by further commodifying land, disabling the nomadic lifestyle, and imposing the shift to an agrarian utilitarian model; thus deeply harming the cultural relevance of the Lakota economic and social model (Biolsi 1995; Brewer and Dennis 2018).

The commodification of land in Indian country precipitated the destruction of a way of life, the relevance of its cultural markers, and imposed a western model that sees natural resources and people as instrumental to economic gain. Over the past 150 years, that shift has profoundly transformed the Lakota food system (Jewell 2008). From a heavily active lifestyle and diet that was gathered and hunted from local surroundings, Lakotas were forced to become reliant on the basic commodities and funds distributed by the federal government as a cynical "compensation" for the theft of their land, lives, and culture.

Cultural resistance to land commodification: challenging colonial epistemologies

Colonial power is most appropriately defined as a material capacity to destroy ways of life and subsequently the relevance of social-cultural norms. It starts as a material feature anchored in practical livelihood pillars such as land. Modifying relations to land creates new divisions of labor and means of exchange. Borrowing from Polanyian concepts (Polanyi 2001), the imposition of a capitalist relation to the means of production involves imposing conceptions such as money and, in the case of Indian country, diverging conceptions of time, creating cultural dissonance with profound socio-economic repercussions. For instance, the concept of "Indian time" refers to a slow-paced practice involving social relations, widely incompatible with the utilitarian notion of a capitalist "work day" (Pickering 2004).

The colonial cultural shift takes root once the material conditions imposed by colonial forces provide enough leverage to completely alter ways of life and thus the relevance of accompanying cultural practices. In the case of the Great Plains, such a shift occurred through the relocation to reservations, itself a by-product of combined efforts to exterminate buffalos by army and settlers. However, that profound change did not occur without resistance, and changes in cultural norms do not imply their complete annihilation but rather foster transformations that can powerfully equip modern initiatives of social change.

First, although the forced commodification and privatization of land accompanied coercive policies implementing capitalist agricultural practices, it was met with silenced community opposition in the form of collectivist cultural norms incompatible with capitalist accumulation. As the then colonial administration comments:

> A serious drawback in the work of civilizing these or any Indians … is found in the universal custom of relatives and connections by marriage considering that what one has belongs to all. As such relations are usually very numerous and for the most part idle and improvident, no one family can accumulate anything. Let a man be in receipt of a salary, no matter how large, or let him by industry raise a crop, and he gets no real benefit from it. His own relations and those of his wife swarm down upon him and consume everything, so that he has nothing for his industry. This is not only discourages any attempt to be industrious and to accumulate property, especially things that can be used for food, but it puts a premium on idleness and unthrift, for he who idles not only saves his muscle, but fares as well as does he who works.
>
> *(Commissioner of Indian Affairs 1896, 291)*

Lakotas had been coerced onto "the path of civilization" which, from the colonizer's perspective, represented the only framework in which they could have any existence at all. Rejoicing at the civilizing effects of the Allotment Act on the Lakota, Commissioner Collier also proclaimed: "any laws must protect these individual property rights in living allottees and their heirs". The Lakotas' "guardian" had spoken, and because his voice was the only one through which Lakotas could exist in the eyes of the western capitalist knowledge system, the discourse was quietly framed as: how Lakotas should, but cannot, assimilate into a capitalist mode of production. The focus is on a supposed lack of skills rather than the coercion of different cultural models into one hegemonic lifestyle and worldview.

This extends beyond the destruction of a culture, livelihood, and replacement of a mode of production into how the capitalist narrative infiltrated indigenous relations of production (Schulz 2017). Since this process was generalized worldwide through colonialism, our current world-system can be perceived as a cultural hegemon that installed developmentalism as the most salient global cultural project, imposed through ethnocide and epistemicide (Escobar 2016; Grosfoguel 2011; Mignolo 2007). It defines one culture, one way to see the world, one way to consider social relations and the economy. Some scholars deny the existence of western monoculturalism (Law 2015). I do not dismiss the existence of western cultural pluralism, but rather consider the cultural practices that accompanied developmentalism through colonialism and formed a hegemonic ontology that characterized natural resources as means of production.

The globalization of western culture still impacts how we define development projects, management, and entrepreneurship, subsequently affecting how we evaluate local projects' success and resilience. The marginalization of indigenous projects' worldwide provides proof of this pattern (Chesnais 2017). Solutions to global livelihood issues such as climate change and destructive mass agriculture remain currently heard and validated within that one model, at best considering alternative worldviews as nice supplements to mainstream sustainable initiatives. This is even highlighted through the need to address culturally-significant practices in sustainability. Indeed, when do we feel the need to debate cultural appropriateness? When other cultural frameworks are visibly undermined. This only occurs if one cultural framework takes too much space and dominates the narrative. Any discussion about cultural significance is a question of cultural dominion and thus a matter of coloniality.

Yet, peripheral colonial spaces might hold significant keys to deeply transform utilitarian relations towards a regenerative model. In silence or through politicized social movements, cultural resistance has survived in indigenous contexts (Corntassel 2012; Fenelon 1998; Fenelon and Hall 2008; Taiaiake and Corntassel 2005), and manifests today at the heart of local grassroots development. The first part of this resistance is ontological; it can be seen in the surprising endurance of specific cultural worldviews towards the land (Pickering and Jewell 2008). Despite land privatization, it is still referred to as a collective notion. An interesting observation is related by Cook-Lynn (1993):

> The Sioux or Lakota ... often spoke of the disappearance of their people. When I answered that census figures showed their population increasing, they countered that parts of their reservations were continually being lost. They concluded there could be no more Indians when there was no more Indian land. Several older men told me that the original Sacred Pipe given the Lakota in the Beginning was getting smaller. The Pipe shrank with the loss of land. When the land and Pipe disappeared, the Lakota would be gone.
>
> *(Schusky 1981)*

This demonstrates how Lakota traditional cultural norms perceive culture as embedded in the natural environment and see the colonization and loss of land as a loss of culture, which endangers not only the material but the survival of the people as a whole. It highlights the symbolic dimension of land from a Lakota standpoint, which does not distinguish between the spiritual and physical properties of land.

From a culturally appropriate standpoint, the commodification of land is accompanied by a desacralization of land, which participates in cultural loss from colonial trauma. The modern existence and endurance of Lakota culture and the emergence of new cultural norms is heavily impacted by power dynamics. Modern utilitarian developmentalism is locally lived and perceived as a colonial continuum.

By contrast, Lakotas' struggles and projects establish different ways of relating to the world, exemplified in our case study below. These ways not only serve practical livelihoods but are also markers of cultural alternatives to utilitarian developmentalism, translating into different ways of being. For De Sousa Santos (2014) and others (Blaser 2014; Escobar 2016; Grosfoguel 2007; Maldonado-Torres 2011; Mignolo 2012; Schulz 2017), these "epistemologies of the South" are arising worldwide as ontological struggles; claiming a right to exist despite the hegemonic economic cultural model. For instance, in Lakota country, local conceptions of land, labor, and time are less representative of a culturally inherent inability to transition to a utilitarian use of natural resources than an enduring expression of cultural difference and its right to exist (see Pickering 2004). Cultural specificities stand as barriers in reaction to cultural hegemonization, and point to alternative models of being in and relating to the natural world, from which our global model in peril could greatly benefit.

Regenerating land through culturally-significant grassroots revolutions

Lakota tribal members are increasingly taking part in local land-based projects aimed at sustainability and self-sufficiency, which entail unique features not found in western sustainability initiatives. Such features affect projects' shape, funding, deadlines, outcomes, and the way they are conducted and managed (Chesnais 2017). After navigating and overcoming the tricky tribal land-tenure system, a growing number of local individuals have claimed their historical piece of land or obtained land use permissions to engage in grassroots initiatives. This pattern indicates that local people see in those forms of development something far more appealing than other forms of business.

Food security always plays a fundamental part in these initiatives, and is usually present along with housing, energy, and educational projects. Examples of sustainable food projects involve any combination of the following: 1) returning the buffalo, 2) restoring local water cycles, 3) growing food using permaculture principles, 4) sharing knowledge through sustainable food-system events, 5) involving youth in local projects, 6) reviving traditional food gathering practices, 6) reviving traditional cooking, and 7) reviving or recreating ceremonies surrounding food. Here, I particularly address the growing practices of 1) restoring water cycles and 2) returning the buffalo.

An enduring interest in water and water access in "Indian country" has engaged many tribal members in water protection movements. The recent anti-pipeline movements such as the Lakota reservation of Standing Rock gave visibility to long underground battles for Indigenous Nations. The extensive history of environmental hazards polluting Native aquifers and streams creates a documented case of environmental injustice undermining food systems (Barker 2015; Fenelon 1997; Simpson 2003). Major challenges throughout different Indian reservations include uranium, oil, and pesticide contamination in tribal water systems and/or local in-site sources and desertification from settlers' artificial dams.

These issues affect water access and quality and birth a myriad of issues affecting personal health and the capacity to landscape private land into self-sufficient havens. Growing responses have been 1) political protesting and general disapproval, 2) the search for alternative sources of clean water on family land, and 3) engaging in holistic projects to recover land moisture and impact local water cycles. The latter is particularly interesting as it yields totally innovative projects in shape and vision.

Indeed, non-acquainted outsiders would be surprised to hear grassroots projects' managers talk about "restoring water cycles". What can it possibly mean practically? What is the scope of such projects? In practice, local grassroots practitioners seek to implement short-term landscaping tools to alter and restore soil moisture and thus positively impact the retention of water to deter floods and improve local plant diversity and yield. In the sites I witnessed, waterscaping occurs in two steps. Step 1 observes terrain typology and identifies techniques needed to optimize soil water retention. Step 2 implements these tools. Techniques include the construction of small successive wooden dams on steep pieces of land. After several years, transformations are clearly visible; native plants return to desolate lands, soil quality and moisture is visibly improved, life returns. Water restoration landscaping is a growing practice present throughout Indian country and beyond.[4]

The second type of project I discuss is about bringing back the buffalo. Reservations in the Great Plains increasingly raise tribal herds (Mcdonald 2001). Pine Ridge counts approximately 300 heads. Organizations such as the Inter-Tribal Buffalo Council help tribes recover buffalo herds on tribal land, most of it for conservation and not livestock purposes. Tribes raise buffalo for other meanings than immediate profit gain, in this case, for culture and soil. Agricultural studies link buffalo grazing with increased land restoration, while cows have a documented record of damaging the fragile upper layer of Great Plains soil (Chesnais 2010).

According to local project managers, buffalo also participate in soil conservation. While they graze freely, they increase soil malleability and increase rainwater retention. Thus, raising buffalo is not simply a question of wildlife conservation but also soil conservation, making it a multifaceted part of ecosystem preservation. Other groups on the reservation raise buffalo, such as the Knife Chief Buffalo Nation, a branch of a late buffalo cooperative that brought together several families around ethical and culturally appropriate buffalo raising. Buffalo are raised exclusively on pasture and grass, without hormones. The few killed for meat follow cultural and spiritual ceremonies using all parts of the animal.

Cultural specificities in sustainable practices as alternative worldviews

What is unique about these water and buffalo projects? Could not the above descriptions fit many sustainable land restoration and food projects? First, by traditional Lakota standards, what I presented could be seen as the "wasicu" (wa-shee-tshoo) or white/western way of knowing. I gave a linear descriptive and task-based presentation of projects and their function. It is difficult to fit Lakota projects in western boxes. They simply do not fit. Crucial elements such as relational and spiritual aspects have a predominant place that barely exist as peripheral coating in mainstream development proposals. A truly traditional Lakota description would take its time and follow a storytelling format, including moral cues and relational interactions between natural elements and people. Complex field operations are debated during the implementation stage, but not as part of the overall vision.

Since this chapter's format requires some description for knowledge exchange, the best culturally-appropriate alternative might look like this. In the Lakota language, water can be translated as "Mní" (maneeh) and buffalo translates as "Tatanka" or "Pte". Language matters because it contains cultural cues that do not translate literally. This is not a shift to different words, but to a different cultural understanding of being in the world; an ontological shift. "Mní" and "Tatanka" are not cultural substitutions for "business as usual". They define distinct worldviews and profoundly affect cultural, social and economic structures, from which we could benefit (see Yates et al. 2017).

Most local grassroots initiatives present a variation of what one project manager defined as the "seven tenets". The vision, or agenda, of a project states:

> Our guidance comes from the Lakota medicine wheel, which is our traditional symbol of the interconnectedness of our world. The medicine wheel represents not only the seven physical directions of north, east, south, west, sky, earth and inner self, but also the unity of the different races among humans with the spiritual and physical realms, Earth's basic elements, as well as the basic human needs … which are Food, fire, water, shelter, people, spirit, self.
>
> *(Bryan Deans, in Chesnais 2017)*

These tenets aim towards "a good quality life", reflecting culturally-relevant aspects of the Lakota ethos. Interpreting them from a western framework is misleading and simplifies processes that entail more nuances when described by Lakotas. When describing water, a water advocate on the Cheyenne River reservation states:

> So, I'm here to speak for Mní (water) as I know it. And Mní is water … Mní is Lakota word for water. And what it means is mní: "I live" or "we live" … Mní … is our first home. When we're in our Ina, our mother's stomach, we live in water. Mní is our first medicine. We're told when we're born … our mother puts the mní to our lips. It's our first medicine … So, this is something as Lakota, we're born with that knowledge. We all are, whether we're Lakota or what race, or nationality we are (whether consciously or not).
>
> *(Candace Ducheneaux, in Chesnais 2017)*

Mní is perceived as a relative, in the physiological and spiritual sense. Projects pertaining to the Mní/Water tenet aim at protecting or restoring the relation with water. Their features demonstrate a holistic understanding of water, from the straightforward goal of facilitating local access to clean water to more macro goals such as restoring water cycles and protecting water for the next seven generations.

Similarly, Lakotas traditionally relate to "Pte" or the buffalo nation as a relative, another living species with whom to maintain peaceful relations in sharing land and livelihood; a worldview that endures today. In one study, most Lakota respondents expressed a desire for living on the land, restoring wildlife, and a connectivity between humans and animals who are equally valued in their right to exist (Pickering Sherman et al. 2010, 512). In the aftermath of the cultural loss of physically losing a lifestyle connected to bison after their extermination, Lakotas see the return of the buffalo as bringing back the spirit of their people. Raising buffalo is thus not simply another business activity but a modern practice for cultural survival, building a solid and somewhat familiar cultural base to reinvent new ways of being Lakota in the twenty-first century. The nomadic way of life completely dependent on "Pte" for subsistence might be over, but people define new practices regenerating parts of that relationship to culturally exist.

For example, the killing process of "Pte" involves ceremonies that revitalize cultural traditions, such as youth rites of passage, where young boys get to perform a "first kill" after three days of ritual praying in sweat lodges for purification and guidance. The teen arrives on the pasture armed with a rifle, wearing an eagle feather, focused and invested with an important task. He patiently waits for the arrival of the animal. The young bull presents itself. He shoots and kills him. This is not an act of greed for economic gain but an act of conscience. The animal is cut and bled on the pasture, his body transported for processing, and every part put to use.

These practices are also about learning from nature to improve human lives. Lakotas historically depended on observing wildlife behavior for survival. These observations help create that sense of relationship and respect to other species, thus thought of as "animal nations". It endures as knowledge production and exchange creating innovative contemporary projects. A traditional example of biomimicry, for instance, Lakotas often say that the buffalo who is meant to die will present itself and face the hunter; a claim based on knowledge of typical herd behavior. Bison herds adopt protective practices when confronted with danger. The elderly and young stay in central positions surrounded by healthy adults, while young bulls occupy the dangerous periphery.

This knowledge is present throughout Lakota culture and emerges when they articulate grassroots projects for contemporary survival. Outsiders can witness it in casual conversation with project managers. Valuable traditional environmental knowledge permeates their projects' vision and shape if we only listen. The relation to "Pte" also extends to its connection to "Mní" as buffalos impact the water retention of the soil. In my research, small dams used in water restoration projects are referred to as inspired from the beaver nation. That knowledge is complex and includes layers of kinship between various animal and plant nations, relations considered less tangible from a western cultural framework.

This knowledge attained cultural relevance through immediate application to Lakota hunts, lifestyles, and survival. It emerges today as a cultural revival tool informing highly innovative self-sufficient practices that take the form of regenerative food projects that are cultural in essence. For Lakota grassroots practitioners, working with water and buffalo is ultimately about repairing and strengthening relationships, improving kinship with living beings and revitalizing cultural identity. It is a culturally-specific project with economic, environmental, and social goals. This relational-based model affects perceptions of time, whereby projects are usually conceived on a 300 year or seven generations model, which links back to knowledge and cultural transmission.

The weight of cultural diversity in defining systemic alternatives

To analyze and define regenerative practices and systemic alternatives, it is crucial to consider food-systems projects as complex cultural and ontological struggles. In post-colonial communities, it translates as the right to exist and operate from a different worldview with other relations to nature. In Lakota country, that struggle takes shape as the decommodification of land and of the various relationships with other living nations. It draws from a kinship model of understanding the natural world to define alternatives to an economic mode of production perceived as invasive, misfit, and an enduring marker of colonial oppression. The decommodification of people's relation to nature and cultural innovative practices together form an alternative economic model that is a decolonial process.

Acknowledging culturally-significant practices within the matrix that bore them is necessary for a comprehensive understanding of grassroots regenerative projects. But that is only the first step. It requires opening up to different ways of thinking and being. In conservation practices, progress has been made towards reviving traditional indigenous knowledge or TEK and indigenous views on stewardship of nature to inform mainstream development practices (see Pickering Sherman et al. 2010; Ross et al. 2011).

However, such progress remains peripheral in regards to the history of suppressing or silencing indigenous conservation practices and knowledge through western hegemonic cultural domination (Bassi et al. 2008; Turner et al. 2000). The mainstream utilitarian economic culture continues to damage global ecosystems and to dismiss the people who manage them differently. Such a disproportionate cultural hegemon not only increases inter-cultural clash, division, and misunderstanding, but also prevents the emergence of true viable systemic alternatives to our unsustainable mode of production. Yet, a paradigmatic shift in western knowledge production is needed, confirmed by the recent UN report giving a twelve-year deadline to alter the course of our mode of production or face unprecedented ecosystem crash (Masson-Delmotte et al. 2019).

Western epistemologies widely theorize the best processes for systemic change. For instance, Plaut et al. (2016) state a necessity to shift from a mechanistic to an ecological worldview. However, much local development still compartmentalizes complex systems into parts. The Brundtland report (United Nations Brundtland Commission 1987) divided sustainability into three distinct pillars, when in practice they inform and overlap with each other. This leads to partial thinking and fosters the division between organizations targeting the environment, the economy, or the social, thus still conceived as competing elements (Schulz 2017).

Such division could benefit from considering indigenous frameworks and their relational understanding of ecology, people, and economy to generate efficiency in creating change. This knowledge has developed more holistic projects due to cultural understanding of kinship relations to nature. They also create less dependence on the economic pillar and demonstrate frugal innovation due to other factors such as the pressure induced by economic strain in post-colonial environments. Consequently, they must rely on other skills beyond financial pressure to lead projects to completion. The barriers to project completion that western developmentalist culture asserts are lifted through culturally appropriate, or decolonial, technology.

As in our case study, relational-based models often lengthen projects' duration, but fit into sustainable design for land regeneration that truly includes future generations. In such a frame, there is no room for half measures and progressive environmental degradation mitigation. It causes a complete shift of the economic model and its culture. In this context, cultural specificities are revealed as being more than superficial add-ons to sustainability to ensure fair cultural diversity; instead, transforming the global cultural narrative carries seeds of sustainable transition.

From decolonial identity struggles towards a global culture of sustainability

Throughout this chapter, we have seen how the relevance of socio-economic norms is maintained and altered through culture and cultural identity. The same process of identity production can point towards a global culture of sustainability. Lakota identity has been affected by the colonial process and has defined itself both separately and in reaction to colonial trauma and ethnocide. The history of Native identity in the US evolved back and forth from assimilation to cultural resistance (Fenelon 1997; Fenelon and Hall 2008). Identity is not linear, but multiple and fluid. Maalouf defines identity as sets of allegiances that overlap and are highly dependent within and between groups' perspectives (Maalouf 2001).

Project managers often see themselves as both culturally traditional and innovative, Lakotas and citizens of the world. Such combinations occur endogenously and differ from outsiders' perspectives. Through defining their own sets of allegiances in spite of western perceptions, contemporary Lakota grassroots practitioners exercise the power to "rename" in colonial contexts (Duarte and Belarde-Lewis 2015); it challenges historical power dynamics, hegemonic economic culture and allows alternative ontologies to emerge with specific associated identities that unite in wider social movements.

Such phenomena can be observed in various colonial contexts worldwide: hundreds of Native nations from North and South America joined forces in a historical collaboration to protect water from pipelines in the Standing Rock reservation, North Dakota. That unified protest resonates with similar struggles against environmental injustice and social inequalities. In India, thousands of "quiet revolutions" occur in rural areas to regenerate local land and decommodify resources (Manier 2015).

A new environmentally aware and active indigenous identity is rising (Adelson 2001; Bauer 2016; Corntassel 2012; Escobar 2016; Fenelon and Hall 2008; Huambachano 2018; Martiniello 2015; Taiaiake and Corntassel 2005; Waziyatawin 2012). Moreover, Indigenous peoples throughout the world identify and network with various groups that belong to drastically different cultural frameworks. Recently, Hopi "Raincatchers" travelled to indigenous/Amazigh communities in Morocco where they trained local youth in water restoration practices. That interconnection extends beyond ecological agendas. It translates into a new culture of global sustainability bringing together indigenous groups through a global indigenous identity.

Social media have greatly improved indigenous activists' capacity to network and demonstrate support to particular causes. On these platforms, Lakota project managers express commonalities and support struggles such as the Irish resistance against British hegemony or Palestinian struggles against Israeli settler colonialism. Indigenous activists relate to anti-imperialist stakes throughout the world, revealing their projects' vision and shape. Research shows that local native projects demonstrate a detachment from the capitalist mode of production which expresses a form of identity allegiance (Chesnais 2017; Fenelon and Hall 2008). In other words, they are committed to finding alternatives to a capitalist mode of production, collectively identified as colonial oppression, and support similar claims globally.

Although these projects in the so-called developing world originate from critical living conditions, they often start through an identity process: the need for cultural singularity from practices attributed to the western development model, a decolonial endeavor. Consequently, real systemic alternatives are not likely to emerge through material struggle but rather as a countercultural decolonial project. But how can such a project foster a global sustainable culture?

Postcolonial theory has often expressed the relationship between colonialism and the installation of hegemonic capitalism but often fails to consider relationality in terms of its capacity to create and maintain viable cultural alternatives to global capitalism. By contrast, concepts such as "epistemologies of the South" (De Sousa Santos 2014) start from the relation between colonialism and the utilitarian perception of nature induced by global capitalism to open the door to theorize decolonial systemic change. Similarly, Escobar (2018) and others (Querejazu 2016; Schulz 2017) describe the coming of a "pluriverse", a theoretical projection into a world-system where emerging alternative projects are seen as alternatives to relate to natural resources and take their rightful place in global decision-making (Escobar 2018).

In conclusion, indigenous struggles produce sustainable systems out of the very decolonial process they have undertaken against hegemonic thought and culture. Systemic transformation originates in identity struggles and cultural stakes that subsequently change the production model. It is because they are formed in cultural opposition of a model that is truly unsustainable that they now rise as the most relevant sustainable movement for our global future. Practically, it invites us to involve and give legitimacy to indigenous alternatives (Querejazu 2016). As development practitioners and academics, it requires us to welcome different worldviews, especially if they question our western-centric conceptions of land, labor, money, and time, and allow them to alter the knowledge production that currently supports the global mode of production.

What can we learn? Culturally-significant/decolonial ideas for a regenerative future

Designing regenerative practices means reflecting more deeply upon the mechanisms of our global food system, not simply as a provider of food and food values, but as a shaper of entire worldviews. I have conceptualized cultural appropriateness as a decolonial political project aimed at providing space for alternatives to the dominant economic culture. As seen in this chapter, indigenous practices and cultural norms can become an essential source of inspiration because 1) they are born from the decolonial struggle against destructive capitalism and 2) they provide viable and low-cost alternatives for self-sufficient holistic living. We can learn from these efforts, but questions remain. How can we construct a unified vision for a sustainable future while acknowledging cultural specificities worldwide? What does it mean for establishing working collaborations? Based on our discussion, a truly sustainable global food system needs *both* of the following dimensions:

1) A localized interpretation of cultural relevance (i.e. no single "recipe" for local development)
2) A global unifying goal

Our capacity to define a culturally appropriate local vision and a unifying global vision lies the potential success of a global regenerative system. These two dimensions can create the roadmap.

The first dimension should challenge the hegemonic worldview and adopt a decolonial approach to local development. In practice, calls for projects and development initiatives should refrain from assumptions and/or impositions of what projects should look like but instead follow a principle-based approach (Bopp and Bopp 2006). Local projects can be defined by local communities to follow local deadlines, conceptions of work and time, etc. From experience, taking the time and space to define vision with key actors is essential, although challenging.

Cultural norms play a major role in identifying the correct process to follow. For instance in "Indian country", two factors impact what appropriate local decision-making looks like: 1) the concept of "Indian time" that refers to a slow pace of life where social relations take time to build and where meetings cannot start by "going straight to the point" and 2) the local concept of decision-making, where dissent is most strongly expressed by "not showing up" (Price 1994). This precludes the common local development practice to invite people for consultation or debate.

Once key actors are gathered, techniques can be put in place to define local vision, through participatory methods such as those taught by NGO Village Earth, which implies a lengthy set of roundtables where individual visions are efficiently translated into long-term, mid-term, and short-term goals.[5] Participatory practices already exist among development practitioners (Pimbert 2006; Salvador et al. 2005; Stanton 2014; Tobias et al. 2013) and we only need to select methods that follow our general decolonial guideline.

The second aspect consists in building a unifying global vision, which is far more challenging. Part of addressing that challenge requires networking and building alliances. This work has long begun and is creating momentum around grassroots events. For example, the recent third permaculture summit organized by the Oglala Lakota Cultural and Economic Revitalization Initiative[6] successfully took place in summer 2019. It connects knowledges and knowhows between people from the reservation, other tribes and outsiders while working on constructing a self-sufficient site. The summit took place within relation building and extensive social time such as meal-sharing and storytelling.

Such collaborations reflect the collaborative sense of unity that indigenous people are building throughout the world. They rally around a common goal, which can be seen as a set of identity allegiances; to a non-fossil fuel future, to locally grown food, to anti-imperialist wars, to the cry of climate refugees. This global consciousness is growing stronger with the sense of urgency given by climate change. It seems to have developed not in spite, but in response to corporate monopolies, imperialist thinking, and conspicuous consumption. It is building on non-utilitarian views of natural resources and a desire to halt damaging growth and "return to the roots". In essence, such a project is about fighting cultural hegemony and revitalizing various indigenous cultural frameworks.

It is also being met with a conservative backlash, seen through the rising criminalization of environmental protests (De Sousa Santos 2014). This leaves us with a challenging question. Indeed, if this unifying project is to deconstruct hegemonic thought, it must be inclusive. Yet, what happens if one cultural framework promotes the denial of others? Must such dissent be allowed a voice and partake in the process, to the risk of monopolizing the discourse? It seems that in our vision, there is no place for monopolies and ontological violence. The idea of a cultural pluriverse described by authors such as Escobar (2018) takes inspiration from contemporary Latin American Native designs and describes the path away from a capitalist relation to the world towards a more relational ontology as a construction of collective autonomy in networks of interdependent communities. Freedom is enjoyed individually but respects the freedom of others, not through good will but through a strong social contract enforced by kinship and solidarity-based policy-making.

Being able to deconstruct hegemonies and define a global culture of sustainability will define whether we succeed or fail in altering our future. These philosophical questions need to be answered practically. Far from utopian, contemporary scholarly and practitioners' work (Bopp and Bopp 2006; Duarte and Belarde-Lewis 2015; Escobar 2018; Mignolo 2012; Schulz 2017; Wright 2010; Yates et al. 2017) already contain the answers that we need in order to rally the world around a regenerative culture for all.

Discussion questions

1. How do we deconstruct cultural hegemony?
2. How can we foster a global culture of regeneration?
3. How can we create real spaces for indigenous voices?

Notes

1 The "Rez" is a widely accepted nickname to refer to the inherently colonial word "reservations". Similarly, although the term "Indian" is considered as deeply offensive, it is often used by native

peoples when referring to their territories in the term "Indian country". See (Yellow Bird, 1999) for a discussion on appropriate terminology.

2 See (Jaulin, 1970) for a discussion of "ethnocide".

3 Although individuals have different opinions on appropriate terminology, the terms "native" and "indigenous" are widely acknowledged as being appropriate when referring to all First Nations (see Yellow Bird, 1999).

4 See the Hopi Raincatchers group in Hopi land.

5 See www.villageearth.org.

6 See www.OLCERI.org.

Further reading

Escobar, A. (2016). Thinking-feeling with the earth: Territorial struggles and the ontological dimension of the epistemologies of the south. *AIBR Revista de Antropologia Iberoamericana*, 11(1), 11–32.

Grey, S. and Patel, R. (2015). Food sovereignty as decolonization: Some contributions from Indigenous movements to food system and development politics. *Agriculture and Human Values*, 32(3), 431–444.

Querejazu, A. (2016). Encountering the pluriverse: Looking for alternatives in other worlds. *Revista Brasileira de Política Internacional*, 59(2), 16.

References

Adelson, N. (2001). Re-imagining aboriginality: An indigenous people's response to social suffering. *Transcultural Psychiatry*, 37(March), 11–34.

Barker, A.J. (2015). 'A direct act of resurgence, a direct act of sovereignty': Reflections on idle no more, indigenous activism, and Canadian settler colonialism. *Globalizations*, 12(1), 43–65.

Bassi, M., Bhatt, S., Bedrani, S., Bo, L., Bumacas, D., Budhatoki, P. and Stevens, S. (2008). Recognising and supporting indigenous and community conservation: Ideas and experiences from the grassroots. CEESP Briefing note.

Bauer, K. (2016). Land versus territory: Evaluating indigenous land policy for the Mapuche in Chile. *Journal of Agrarian Change*, 16(4), 627–645.

Biolsi, T. (1995). The birth of the reservation: Making the modern Indian among the Lakota. *American Ethnologist*, 22(1), 28–53.

Blaser, M. (2014). Ontology and indigeneity: On the political ontology of heterogeneous assemblages. *Cultural Geographies*, 21(1), 49–58.

Bopp, M. and Bopp, J. (2006). *Recreating the world: A practical guide to building sustainable communities*. Calgary: Four Worlds Press.

Brewer, J.P. and Dennis, M.K. (2018). A land neither here nor there: Voices from the margins and the untenuring of Lakota lands. *GeoJournal*, 84, 571–591.

Chesnais, A. (2010). A feasibility study for the establishment of a bison meat processing facility on the Pine Ridge Reservation, SD. Report, Village Earth, May.

Chesnais, A. (2017). *Wolakota: The face of ReZilience in "post"-colonial America*. Colorado State University, doctoral dissertation.

Cook-Lynn, E. (1993). Who Gets to Tell the Stories? *Wicazo Sa Review*, 9(1), 60–64.

Corntassel, J. (2012). Re-envisioning resurgence: Indigenous pathways to decolonization and sustainable self-determination. *Decolonization: Indigeneity, Education, and Society*, 1(1), 86–101.

De Sousa Santos, B. (2014). *Epistemologies of the South: Justice against epistemicide*. New York: Routledge.

Duarte, M.E. and Belarde-Lewis, M. (2015). Imagining: Creating spaces for indigenous ontologies. *Cataloging and Classification Quarterly*, 53(5–6), 677–702.

Escobar, A. (2016). Thinking-feeling with the earth: Territorial struggles and the ontological dimension of the epistemologies of the south. *AIBR Revista de Antropologia Iberoamericana*, 11(1), 11–32.

Escobar, A. (2018). *Designs for the pluriverse: Radical interdependence, autonomy, and the making of worlds*. Durham, NC: Duke University Press.

Fenelon, J.V. (1997). From peripheral domination to internal colonialism: Socio-political change of the Lakota on standing rock. *Journal of World-Systems Research*, 3, 259–320.

Fenelon, J.V. (1998). *Culturicide, resistance and survival of the Lakota*. New York: Routledge.

Fenelon, J.V. and Hall, T.D. (2008). Revitalization and indigenous resistance to globalization and neoliberalism. *American Behavioral Scientist*, 51(12), 1867–1901.

Grosfoguel, R. (2007). The epistemic decolonial turn: Beyond political-economy paradigms. *Cultural Studies*, 21(2–3), 212–223.

Grosfoguel, R. (2011). Decolonizing post-colonial studies and paradigms of political economy: Transmodernity, decolonial thinking, and global coloniality. *Transmodernity*, 1(1), 214.

Huambachano, M. (2018). Enacting food sovereignty in Aotearoa New Zealand and Peru: Revitalizing indigenous knowledge, food practices and ecological philosophies. *Agroecology and Sustainable Food Systems*, 42(9), 1003–1028.

Jaulin, R. (1970). *La paix blanche*. Paris: Seuil.

Jewell, B. (2008). The food that senators don't eat: Politics and power in the Pine Ridge food economy. Unpublished thesis, Colorado State University.

Law, J. (2015). What's wrong with a one-world world? *Distinktion: Scandinavian Journal of Social Theory*, 16(1), 126–139.

Lueck, D. (2002). The extermination and conservation of the American bison. *Journal of Legal Studies*, 31 (S2), S609–S652.

Maalouf, A. (2001). *In the name of identity: Violence and the need to belong*. New York: Arcade.

Maldonado-Torres, N. (2011). Thinking through the decolonial turn: Post-continental interventions. *Transmodernity: Journal of Peripheral Cultural Preservation in the Luso-Hispanic World*, 1(2), 1–18.

Manier, B. (2015). *Made in India: Le laboratoire ecologique de la planete*. Paris: Premier parallele.

Martiniello, G. (2015). Food sovereignty as praxis: Rethinking the food question in Uganda. *Third World Quarterly*, 36(3), 508–525.

Masson-Delmotte, V., Zhai, P., Pörtner, H.-O., Roberts, D., Skea, J., Shukla, P.R. and Waterfield, T. (2019). *Global warming of 1.5°C: An IPCC special report on the impacts of global warming*. Paris: Technical Support Unit.

Mcdonald, J.L. (2001). Bison restoration in the Great Plains and the challenge of their management. *Great Plains Research*, 11(1), 103–121.

Mignolo, W.D. (2007). Delinking: The rhetoric of modernity, the logic of coloniality and the grammar of de-coloniality. *Cultural Studies*, 21(2–3), 449–514.

Mignolo, W.D. (2012). *Local histories/global designs: Coloniality, subaltern knowledges, and border thinking* (vol. 9). Princeton, NJ: Princeton University Press.

Pickering, K. (2004). Decolonizing time regimes: Lakota conceptions of work, economy, and society. *American Anthropologist*, 106(1), 85–97.

Pickering, K. and Jewell, B. (2008). Nature is relative: Religious affiliation, environmental attitudes, and political constraints on the Pine Ridge Indian Reservation. *Journal for the Study of Religion, Nature and Culture*, 2(1), 135–158.

Pickering Sherman, K., Lanen, J. and Sherman, R.T. (2010). Practical environmentalism on the Pine Ridge Reservation: Confronting structural constraints to indigenous stewardship. *Human Ecology*, 38 (4), 507–520.

Pimbert, M. (2006). Transforming knowledge and ways of knowing for food sovereignty and bio-cultural diversity. Conference on Endogenous Development and Bio-Cultural Diversity Lied.

Plaut, J., Dunbar, B., Gotthelf, H. and Hes, D. (2016). Regenerative development through LENSES with a case study of Seacombe West. *Environment Design Guide*, 88, 1–19.

Polanyi, K. (2001). *The great transformation: The political and economic origins of our time*. Boston, MA: Beacon Press.

Price, C. (1994). Lakotas and Euroamericans contrasted concepts of chieftainship and decision-making authority. *Ethnohistory*, 41(3), 447–463.

Querejazu, A. (2016). Encountering the pluriverse: Looking for alternatives in other worlds. *Revista Brasileira de Política Internacional*, 59(2), 16.

Ross, A., Pickering, K., Snodgrass, J.G., Delcore, H.D. and Sherman, R. (2011). *Indigenous peoples and the collaborative stewardship of nature*. Walnut Creek, CA: Left Coast Press.

Salvador, E., Bacon, C., Mendez, E., Brown, M., Salvador, E., Bacon, C. and Brown, M. (2005). *Participatory action research and support for community development and conservation: Examples from shade coffee landscapes in Nicaragua and El Salvador*. Research Center Brief #6. Berkeley, CA: Center for Agroecology and Sustainable Food Systems.

Schulz, K.A. (2017). Decolonizing political ecology: Ontology, technology and "critical" enchantment. *Journal of Political Ecology*, 24(1), 127–143.

Simpson, L. (2003). Toxic contamination undermining indigenous food-systems and indigenous sovereignty. *Pimatiziwin: A Journal of Aboriginal and Indigenous Community Health*, 1(2), 130–134.

Stanton, C.R. (2014). Crossing methodological borders: Decolonizing Community-Based Participatory Research. *Qualitative Inquiry*, 20(5), 573–583.

Taiaiake, A. and Corntassel, J. (2005). Being indigenous: Resurgences against contemporary colonialism. *Government and Opposition*, 597–614. Oxford: Blackwell Publishing.

Tobias, J.K., Richmond, C.A.M. and Luginaah, I. (2013). Community-based participatory research (Cbpr) with indigenous communities: Producing respectful and reciprocal research. *Journal of Empirical Research on Human Research Ethics*, 8(2), 129–140.

Turner, N.J., Ignace, M.B. and Ignace, R. (2000). Traditional ecological knowledge and wisdom of aboriginal peoples in British Columbia. *Ecological Society of America*, 10(5), 1275–1287.

United Nations Brundtland Commission (1987). *Report of the world commission on environment and development: Our common future*. New York: United Nations.

Waziyatawin, A.W. (2012). The paradox of Indigenous resurgence at the end of empire. *Decolonization: Indigeneity, Education and Society*, 1(1), 68–85.

Wright, E.E.O. (2010). *Envisioning real utopias*. London: Verso.

Yates, J.S., Harris, L.M. and Wilson, N.J. (2017). Multiple ontologies of water: Politics, conflict and implications for governance. *Environment and Planning D: Society and Space*, 35(5), 797–815.

Yellow Bird, M. (1999). What we want to be called: Indigenous peoples' perspectives on racial and ethnic identity labels. *American Indian Quarterly*, 23(2), 1.

6

TRADITIONAL FOOD, THE RIGHT TO FOOD, AND SUSTAINABLE FOOD SYSTEMS

Alison Blay-Palmer, Andrew Spring, Evelyn R. Nimmo, and André Eduardo Biscaia de Lacerda

Introduction

Locally, rights-based approaches have contributed to reducing the marginalization of vulnerable populations such as small-scale farmers, pastoralists and fisherfolk. The increased confidence in collectively demanding our rights without fear of violence has resulted in mobilization and organization for a stronger voice. The greater visibility of our struggles has resulted in reducing further injustice.

(Mohammad Ali Shah, Pakistan Fisherfolk Forum – PFF)

The RtAF [Right to Adequate Food] has served to connect seemingly disparate struggles and peoples in different parts of the world, turning what might otherwise be local issues with little international appeal, into an interconnected global fight for human rights. By uniting fisherfolk in Uganda with pastoralists in India and "raising our voices for one another, we can put pressure on governments not to act against any human rights activist. If you act against one, you act against us all."

(Lalji Desai, World Alliance of Mobile and Indigenous Peoples – WAMIP; in Carrigan 2014, 15–16)

As Mohammad Ali Shah and Lalji Desai make clear in the above quotations, rights-based approaches can help weave communities together into global networks for resistance and change (Carrigan 2014). Existing frameworks including the Right to Adequate Food (RtAF), the UN Declaration on the Rights of Indigenous People, and the Convention for the Safeguarding of Intangible Cultural Heritage support Indigenous and traditional food systems. Protecting cultural heritage can also support transformation towards increasingly sustainable food systems (SFS) and provide pathways to share good practices, lessons learned, and empower individuals and communities. Identifying common purpose across communities within regional food systems can amplify the voice of these networks (Carrigan 2014; also Blay-Palmer et al. 2015; Holt Giménez and Shattuck 2011; Levkoe 2011).

Why sustainable food systems?

A sustainable food systems (SFS) framing provides a coherent entry point for considering how the Right to Adequate Food and Nutrition can be met through traditional food systems. SFS are just and equitable, safeguard cultural heritage through access to healthy, nutritious, culturally appropriate food produced and procured from local food sources that keep material resources circulating in local communities and regenerate ecosystems including soil, water quality, and biodiversity. SFS enable people to participate in democratic processes that are accountable, transparent, and participative (Blay-Palmer and Koc 2010; Pirog et al. 2014). SFS offer pathways to transformation in the face of the industrial food system that are resulting in sky-rocketing levels of diet-related disease, climate change, increasing income divides, and biodiversity loss (Heynen et al. 2012; Ilbery and Maye 2005; Shukla et al. 2019; Knezevic et al. 2017; Renting et al. 2003). These impacts are amplified in many Indigenous communities. For example, limited access to traditional food can lead to the increased prevalence of chronic and acute disease and other diet-related health conditions (Council of Canadian Academies 2014; Damman et al. 2008). While acknowledging the risks of setting up false binaries by juxtaposing one food system against another (e.g., industrial/conventional vs. traditional: e.g. Goodman 2004; Ilbery and Maye 2005) and the need for hybrid food system approaches as intermediary spaces between the conventional and alternative food systems and that work progressively towards sustainability goals (Ilbery and Maye 2005), it is increasingly recognized in the face of shared global challenges that structural reform is needed to move away from destructive industrial food supply chains (Carolan 2018).

It is also increasingly recognized that we have much of the conceptual knowledge and practical tools that could be combined to realize multiple benefits simultaneously and move towards system transformation (Blay-Palmer et al. 2018; Gottlieb and Joshi 2010). For example, sustainable diets connect nutrition with ecologies while also respecting cultural heritage (Lang and Rayner 2012; Mason and Lang 2017). They can also improve ecosystem wellbeing and deal with the "double nutrition burden" that includes a lack of nutrients through access to quality food. Public procurement can help can help provide healthy food to marginalized consumers and stabilize demand for producers (Agyeman and Alkon 2011; Sonnino 2009).

More specifically, access to indigenous traditional diets, harvesting, gathering, and food growing can protect personal and community wellbeing. As well, traditional knowledge founded on relationships to the land and food harvesting point to ways to both mitigate and adapt to climate change (O'Dea 1992; Uaay et al. 2001 in Damman et al. 2008, 136; Right to Food and Nutrition Watch 2014, 11). Traditional diets can provide: enhanced individual and community health and wellbeing especially for children and youth mitigating the double burden of disease; community cohesion through, for example, traditional sharing of food and knowledge transfer from elders to youth; and enhanced ecosystem wellbeing through improved land stewardship including natural resource management (Damman et al. 2008; Spring et al. 2018). As Damman et al. (2008) explain, "respect for indigenous peoples' right to adequate food, within the context of their general human rights and their indigenous specific rights, may curb the development of chronic disease in their communities". Respecting and protecting the Right to Food and Indigenous Rights opens spaces to hear these important lessons. It also raises questions about the complementarity and/or tensions between individual rights and collective approaches foundational to many indigenous belief systems.

Rights, international conventions, and indigenous food systems

The Right to Adequate Food and Nutrition (RtAFN), a foundational dimension to the realization of SFS, is recognized in several international declarations and conventions (Riol 2016). As a foundational staring point, the Right to Food as a basic human right is stated in Article 25 of the 1948 Universal Declaration of Human Rights as "everyone has the right to a standard of living adequate for the health and well-being of himself and of his family, including food." Nearly 60 years later, the UN Declaration on the Rights of Indigenous Peoples (UNDRIP) adopted in 2007 "establishes a universal framework of minimum standards for the survival, dignity and well-being of the indigenous peoples of the world" (United Nations 2007). The declaration includes two particularly relevant paragraphs to consider:

> Recognizing that respect for indigenous knowledge, cultures and traditional practices contributes to sustainable and equitable development and proper management of the environment, [and] …
>
> Indigenous peoples have the right to maintain, control, protect and develop their cultural heritage, traditional knowledge and traditional cultural expressions, as well as the manifestations of their sciences, technologies and cultures, including human and genetic resources, seeds, medicines, knowledge of the properties of fauna and flora, oral traditions … They also have the right to maintain, control, protect and develop their intellectual property over such cultural heritage, traditional knowledge, and traditional cultural expressions.

Control and maintenance by indigenous communities of cultural heritage is one dimension of determining food security that is especially pertinent for this discussion. The Convention for the Safeguarding of the Intangible Cultural Heritage adopted by the UN in 2003 recognizes the pressures, intolerance, and threats faced, the importance of dialogue, and the role of inter-generational knowledge exchange to the safeguarding of intangible cultural heritage in the context of globalization pressures:

> *Recognizing* that communities, in particular indigenous communities, groups and, in some cases, individuals, play an important role in the production, safeguarding, maintenance and re-creation of the intangible cultural heritage, thus helping to enrich cultural diversity and human creativity,
>
> *Considering* the need to build greater awareness, especially among the younger generations, of the importance of the intangible cultural heritage and of its safeguarding …[1]

Knowledge about food harvesting, growing, preparation, preservation, sharing, and celebration are all practices associated with cultural heritage. Realizing these rights means respecting and protecting indigenous and traditional food systems as part of cultural heritage and traditional knowledge and practices including the importance of sharing this knowledge between elders and youth. Realizing and protecting these rights will happen in different ways in different places. For example, in northern Manitoba, Canada, to realize food security and sovereignty there is the need

> to ensure that Indigenous peoples have unimpeded access to their traditional geographical hunting, trapping, fishing, and harvesting areas, and that these areas be protected from development projects that lead to contamination of water, flora,

and fauna is essential. Furthermore, it is also crucial to facilitate opportunities for inter-generational knowledge transfer in traditional hunting, harvesting, and cooking techniques within fields such as health and education to improve access to, and utilization, of traditional foods.

(Wendimu et al. 2018, 68)

To enable this access, indigenous peoples need to, "self-determine their own food and surrounding political and economic systems" (Wendimu et al. 2018, 67). Given this complexity, a holistic, food systems approach would help to connect the key considerations into a more coherent approach consistent with many indigenous worldviews (Geniusz 2009). To accomplish this so that changes are community defined and guided, the approach needs to be people-focused and reach across the food system, including and building from individual knowledge about food production, processing, and distribution for change,

> Special efforts must be made to ensure the genuine participation of all people, particularly the poor and the marginalized, in the decisions and actions that are of concern to them in order to improve self-reliance and assure positive results. All relevant sectors of government should act in concert with communities and, as appropriate, with NGOs. Community involvement should lie not only in their indicating their perceived priorities but also in planning, managing and evaluating community based interventions.
>
> *(Wendimu et al. 2018, 68)*

This requires knowledge about what is needed on the ground and to provide policy consistency across scales so that those systems can move towards sustainable transformation. This is an imperative in the context of Truth and Reconciliation in Canada so that colonial power systems that articulate across scales are continuously identified, called out, and deconstructed (Desmarais and Wittman 2014; Morrison 2011). As Bragdon explains,

> At present there does not appear to be a coherent understanding of the international architecture for food security, of what needs to be done by governments collectively, and the freedom governments need domestically to ensure the food security of their own populations without harming the needs of others. Given the current state of global food security, it is incumbent upon governments to provide more than just an enabling environment for markets and the private sector.
>
> *(Bragdon 2015, 1)*

This enabling environment demands a move from industry-centric linear, input–output approaches to circular, integrated relationships (Bragdon 2015, 6).

> A transformation of the energy matrix and the food system is required, contributing to food sovereignty, as called for by La Via Campesina and built upon during the Forum for Food Sovereignty, in Nyéléni in 2007. This called for food systems to be in the hands of the people and at the service of humanity, where small-scale producers (who produce 70–80% of the world's food) play a crucial role.
>
> *(Right to Food and Nutrition Watch 2017, 67–68)*

Food sovereignty is founded on respecting the right to food self-determination for smallholders, peasants (*campesina*), and more recently marginalized consumers. If we look to the food sovereignty movement, La Via Campesina, we see the assertion of peasant rights to land and self-determination for self-sustaining agriculture and food systems (Nyéléni 2007; Patel 2009). Agroecology is one well-recognized way forward to the achievement of food sovereignty. The circular processes in agroecology that recycle nutrients and biomass require farmers to have control over the land, water, seeds, and related biodiversity (Cedeño 2014, 48; HLPE 2019). The community and social dimensions of agroecology also need to be supported through the realization of human rights as well as related policies and programs (Leyva and Lores 2018).

While rights are being extended to some peasant landowners, we do not see the same rights being recognized for hunter-gatherer food communities. Hunter-gatherer food systems rely on ecosystem health on a large scale. And complexities arise when the ecosystems, as well as migratory routes for food sources, cross geopolitical and jurisdictional boundaries and where the obligation of the state to protect wildlife conflicts at times with the livelihoods of communities. If the food system is ultimately determined by the health of the ecosystem, managing that ecosystem becomes instrumental in the sustainability and long-term viability of the communities that the system supports. Therefore, the ultimate success of conservation of natural capital, such as the long-term health of the animals communities depend on, may lie in a regional approach, with other jurisdictions supporting similar initiatives, as well as studies to help understand ecosystem impacts under a changing climate regime. It again appears that the community level is insufficient when dealing with certain parts of the community's food system. The complex mix of scale, livelihoods, and natural capital play a key role in the food system (Dahlberg 1993).

An example of reforms from Argentina provides some guidance about moving forward. As part of their 1994 constitutional reform, Argentina granted constitutional standing to previously ratified treaties that provide a framing in support of the right to food.[2] Collectively, these treaties provide reference points to enable the RtAF. A missing dimension is regional supportive policy and programs, as well as federal commitment to making this happen in the face of political and economic elites (Damman et al. 2008). The Argentinian example underscores that multi-scale policy coherence founded on the Right to Food is foundational for food sovereignty to have a chance at being realized (Patel 2011). Networks of communities are needed so that voices are amplified in the move to build more SFS. Food sovereignty, multi-scale governance mechanisms, and related programs that embed and respect the Right to Food help protect traditional food and cultural heritage for both food harvesters and farmers. Indigenous peoples and cultural heritage can be central to food security solutions, protect biodiversity, and help regenerate ecosystems. A rights-based approach to respect and protect traditional food growing and harvesting provides a way forward for food and nutrition security as well as for cooling the planet. "Future policy decisions to cope effectively with the causes of global warming must put forward human rights before any technical measures. Global warming is after all, a problem of climate justice" (Cedeño 2014, 49). Using small-scale farmers (SSF) as an example of how to secure rural livelihoods, it is important to ensure "informed, continued and effective participation in decision-making processes. SSF need to be involved in the developing the policies that support them" (Bragdon 2015, 16). This applies equally to indigenous food harvesters and offers the basis for comparison developed in the balance of this chapter. In the Canadian context,

In addition to the idea that Food is sacred, these discussions have emphasized the importance of Participation at individual, family, community, and regional levels. Self-determination refers to the "freedom and ability to respond to our own needs for healthy, culturally-adapted indigenous foods. It represents the freedom and ability to make decisions over the amount and quality of food we hunt, fish, gather, grow and eat" (Morrison 2011: 100). Finally, Legislation and policy reform attempts to "reconcile Indigenous food and cultural values with colonial laws, policies and mainstream economic activities" (101).

(Desmarais and Wittman 2014)

While there has been some success in getting policy-alignment in more southern communities in Canada, northern communities have not received the same attention.

In the following sections, case studies provide two examples of community-based research as the basis for solidarity using a rights-based approach. The first is a small First Nation community in the Northwest Territories of Canada and responds to a call from Desmarais and Wittman (2014) in the context of food sovereignty in Canada that "requires a critical engagement with a new politics of possibility. This involves reconsidering and reframing concepts of collective political will, appropriate authority, governance, self-determination, solidarity, and individual and collective rights" (2014, 1154). The second example describes traditional agroforestry approaches in Brazil, adding to existing work including research by Schneider and Niederle (2010). These localized cases help us to understand more about the basis for global networks that could foster the realization of the Right to Food, safeguard intangible cultural heritage, and foster more ecologically sound food systems. The cases offer insights into parallel challenges faced by both communities. For example, both case studies demonstrate the lack of community capacity and the need for more coherent locally relevant food sensitive policies, for example, protected land status and economic supports founded on community engagement by policy-makers. Together, this adds to what we understand about the basis for solidarity through the Right to Food for locally appropriate traditional food systems.

Case studies

This section reports ongoing research projects in southern Brazil and the Northwest Territories in Canada. Both projects are part of a Canadian partnership, FLEdGE (Food: Locally Embedded, Globally Engaged) funded through the Social Sciences and Humanities Research Council of Canada. The partnership includes 89 organizations and 132 individuals and enables knowledge sharing opportunities between partners.

In both Brazil and the NWT, research was initiated at the invitation of the communities. In the NWT participants included active land users and harvesters, community Band Council members and elders. In Brazil, community participants included: small-scale erva-mate farmers, local representatives of family farmers' unions, researchers from national and regional agricultural research/outreach agencies and universities, and non-governmental organizations. Information was gathered using participatory action research approaches so that research responds to the needs and visions of communities and adds to local capacity based on community defined goals. As appropriate, the research projects used on-the-land camps, oral history interviews and farm visits, focus groups, community meetings, and/or interviews to gather information. In both projects, the work builds on long-standing embedded relationships between the researchers and communities.

Traditional food systems: Canada's Northwest Territories

Kakisa, located in the Canada's Northwest Territories (NWT), is home to the Ka'a'gee Tu First Nation (KTFN). This small Dene community has a strong link to the surrounding land, lakes, and water that make up their traditional territory. The land is a source of cultural and spiritual wellbeing, and is the basis of the community's food system, which continues to be based on subsistence harvesting – hunting, fishing, and gathering. Like many communities across the northern regions of Canada, there are concerns regarding the impacts of climate change and development pressures on the health of the land, waters, and animals. With communities across Canada's north experiencing alarmingly high rates of food insecurity, climate change is another stressor on an already compromised system (Council of Canadian Academies 2014). A research partnership between the KTFN and researchers from Wilfrid Laurier University started in 2014 with a project to examine the impact of climate change on the community's food system, the access and availability of traditional foods, and explore opportunities to build a better food system. Community members described changes in weather, water, and animal distributions, but also more uncertainty and risk associated with being on the land and harvesting traditional foods. As part of a participatory action research approach, the community was able to identify several key projects and initiatives to increase access to and availability of affordable and healthy foods for everyone. This community vision of a more sustainable food system includes: fostering stronger relationship between youth and elders; increased access to healthy foods, and increased stewardship of the environment. Overall, community members in Kakisa, identified reestablishing connections to the land and each other, but with the addition of modern tools and infrastructure as the basis of health and sustainable food system moving forward (Spring et al. 2018).

However, identifying what needs to be done and building the community's vision for their food system are two different things. Community members face many challenges, and many of these were captured as part of ongoing collaboration with the community focusing on identifying what barriers are limiting the ability to achieve their desired food system. Research in Kakisa uses a modified Community Capital Framework (CCF) to describe community food systems in terms of available or depleting capitals (Spring et al. 2018). The CCF is based on seven dimensions of capital contained within a community: natural, social, cultural, political, built, financial, and human. In the CCF, as interpreted here, the capitals are viewed as overlapping systems that interact with one another and can be used to create capitals or resources that contribute to healthy, vibrant communities, economies, and ecosystems (Emery and Flora 2006; Flora et al. 2004). This approach is compatible with other emerging definitions of food systems, including complex adaptive systems (Stroink and Nelson 2013), the sustainable rural livelihoods framework (Scoones 2009) and systems of systems (Blay-Palmer et al. 2016; Hipel et al. 2010) and are defined by place and local circumstances (Marsden 2012).

Many projects that have been implemented in Kakisa over the past few years have built on the community's social capital and experience working with a variety of organizations. For example, the community expressed a great deal of interest in growing food. Using connections in the region, the Northern Farm Training Institute, a local organization that demonstrates the feasibility of farming in the NWT, has helped to facilitate food growing workshops and planting gardens with the local school for the past few years. Although there are some issues with community participation, lack of knowledge of food growing and history of both good and bad experiences in growing food, the community is committed to having food growing as part of their food system and as a way to rely less on food imported from the south that is expensive and tends to be highly processed so unhealthy (Simba and Spring 2017). But with gardens and other initiatives, this small community of approximately 50 people lacks capacity to carry out much of their vision for their food system. Graduate students and researchers have been able to fill some of this capacity by contributing to grant writing, facilitating on-the-land camps that connect youth and elders, and mapping and recording traditional knowledge and stories from elders as per the community's vision (Kok 2020). These projects have built social, cultural, and human capitals, which are important parts of the food system, but do not tackle some of the more important issues facing the community.

Kakisa lacks political capital in terms of local decision-making over resources, which is a key capital of the food system. Located in the Dehcho region of the NWT, there is currently no comprehensive land claim agreement in place in the region, the community has limited ways it can have a say in, and protect, their land. The KTFN Band Council is responsible for advocating on behalf of the community but is limited due to the size of the community, with few community members able to attend the numerous meetings in the region. The community works closely with organizations, communities, and government in the region but often lacks the regional organization mandated as part of land claim agreements to act on behalf of their community. One option that the KTFN has been pursuing for years is obtaining protected areas status for their traditional lands, a designation that would ensure the land is locally-managed to conserve biodiversity and ecosystem health, establish a land management authority, and protect traditional land uses (NWT Protected Area Strategy Advisory Committee 1999). The KTFN allocates available capitals, including their time (human), social capital, and financial resources, to establish their rights to oversee the management of their traditional territory in the hopes of protecting their lands for future generations (Spring 2018).

In Kakisa, often conversations about food systems focus on what can be done with the capitals that exist in the community, and what can be achieved through partnerships with other institutions and organizations. The community is happy to see some of the successes and programs scaled out to regional levels to see other communities become engaged in similar food systems initiatives. This is a bottom-up approach that involves working together and sharing knowledge with others as part of the next steps of many of the projects being implemented. But that approach is dependent on the availability of capitals required, not to mention interest and relationships with partners. Having policies in place to support the community's vision would greatly impact the current food system. The community is allocating so much of its available resources to creating the frameworks for protection and stewardship of their lands, supporting on-the-land learning and sharing of traditional knowledge to support the next generation of harvester. Stewardship could see harvesters and land uses supported as guardians, or environmental monitors of their traditional territories, protecting the land while bringing food home to be shared with the community. What has been done through this innovative partnership between the community and academic partners has created the capacity to slowly build these resources, often through competitive funding opportunities. But imagining what could be accomplished for community food systems in the NWT through national adoption of rights-based conventions could provide transformational reference points.

Traditional food systems: erva-mate in Brazil

In Southern Brazil, traditional agroforestry systems have continued for generations on small-scale family farms that are made up of diverse mosaics of food crops, vegetable gardens, and managed and natural forests. Despite their small size (less than 50 ha), family farms supply a significant share of food production to the domestic market, including 87% of manioc, 70% of beans, 46% of corn, 58% of milk, 50% of poultry, 59% of pork, and 30% of cattle (Rocha et al. 2012). Non-wood forest products produced through traditional agroforestry systems, which include erva-mate (yerba mate; *Ilex paraguariensis*) extraction, native fruits, and often livestock grazing (Hanisch 2019), are critical to the farm's income and security, as they provide a relatively secure return with minimal input. These traditional systems have also been pivotal to the conservation of about 20–25% of secondary forests in a region that has approximately 1% of the original forest cover (Castella and Britez 2004; Vibrans et al. 2012). Maintaining the forest cover is essential not only to the farms, as it protects local biodiversity (natural pest control) and water availability, but also for the regions in which these systems exist, providing the ecosystem services necessary for urban and peri-urban areas. Through oral history interviews and farm visits to document traditional knowledge with small-scale erva-mate producers, along with community workshops including producers, local and national agricultural research and outreach agencies, universities, and NGOs, this case study examines the tensions between small-scale farmers in Southern Brazil, the implementation of policies at the local and regional level, and the application of legal restrictions related to forests and forest products, and how these play out in terms of producers' right to define their own food and agricultural systems.

Traditional erva-mate production has its roots in Guaraní indigenous cultural food practices but has undergone significant transformation since first contact with the Spanish in the sixteenth century (Nimmo and Nogueira 2019). In the last 30 years, increases in consumption of erva-mate have led to pressures to modernize production through the use of monoculture stands, chemical fertilizers, and pesticides. Despite this growing pressure, traditional erva-mate producers in Southern Paraná State and Northern Santa Catarina State have maintained the agroforestry systems in which erva-mate thrives. As a shade-tolerant species, erva-mate produces well in the understory environment of the iconic Araucaria Forest of the region, with little need for fertilizers or pesticides because of the natural interactions in the forest environment (Chaimsohn and Souza 2013). For many of the interviewed participants, the agroecological practices that inform erva-mate agroforestry production spill over into all areas of the farm, including limited use of pesticides and synthetic fertilizers, as well as cultivation of heirloom seeds and rotational grazing, among others. However, small-scale farmers face challenges related to the lack of value given to their products and continued pressure to move toward conventional agriculture to increase yields, despite the problems inherent in monocrop systems (i.e., debt, mechanization, market fluctuation, food insecurity). Over the last 15 years, several innovative policy initiatives have been developed in Brazil to improve income and food security on small-scale farms, while the Right to Food was added to the country's constitution in 2010 (Rocha et al. 2012). Yet how these policies play out at the local level, and the challenges faced in terms of producers' autonomy in decision-making, remain hidden from wider narratives about the success of Brazil's right to food initiatives.

Two programs in particular have had a significant economic impact on small-scale producers in our study region. One program is the National Food in Schools Program (Programa Nacional de Alimentação Escolar, PNAE) which began in the 1950s to provide food to children in public schools and modified in 2003 with the requirement that 30% of the food included in the program come from local and organic producers (Ferreira de Moura 2017). This program serves over 40 million children per day and every municipality throughout Brazil participates (Rocha et al. 2012). Another program, the National Food

Acquisition Program (Programa de Aquisição de Alimentos, PAA), implemented in 2003, sources 100% of the food from local family farms to be distributed in government-run institutions including daycares, hospitals, food banks, among others. These programs, along with National Program for Strengthening Family Agriculture (Programa Nacional de Fortalecimento da Agricultura Familiar, PRONAF) are pillars of the government's Fome Zero strategy to combat hunger and food insecurity (Rocha et al. 2012). The traditional systems that producers have maintained on family farms, including agroforestry systems, diverse crops, and organic vegetable gardens, have been essential in not only meeting this demand, but also ensuring that these farming families remain food secure. However, the majority of small-scale farms are unable to consistently produce a sufficient amount on their individual farms to meet the requirements of the government programs. Local Family Farmers Unions (FETRAF) have stepped in, working with SSFs to develop and organize cooperatives to meet the program's needs locally. The development of these co-ops and production networks has strengthened community ties and offered new economic opportunities, for example through organic fairs, while also supporting their continuation.

The effects of these policies on small-scale farms and their local communities can be seen through the maintenance of traditional knowledge systems, the inclusion of younger generations in family farming practices, support for the local economy, and access to healthy fresh produce and food for lower-income families. However, these policies have created a reliance on government to fund local, small-scale production, without a consideration of scaling-out these systems and enabling farmers to become independent of government funds. The precarity of these programs is clearly shown through the different ways in which policies are envisioned at the government level and how they are implemented on the ground. For example, the wide-reaching graft scandal that engulfed the government led the Federal Public Prosecutor to run a fine-tooth comb over all government contracts, including those with local co-ops developed to fulfill the PNAE and PAA programs. Irregularities in the contracts, for example the substitution of one product for another due to fluctuations in crops and harvests, were interpreted as criminal offences and 11 leaders of co-ops were imprisoned for several months (https://noticias.uol.com.br/cotidiano/ultimas-noticias/2013/09/24/pf-cumpre-11-mandados-de-prisao-em-operacao-contra-desvio-do-fome-zero-no-pr.htm). Although all of those imprisoned from Paraná State have been exonerated, the disruption of the leadership and the cutting off of public funds due to the investigation, along with recent budget cuts, left hundreds of small-scale farmers (SSFs) who relied on the program without an income, while also affecting access to local produce and food security for the families that received produce. As noted above, these programs are a significant part of Brazil's Fome Zero strategy to address the Zero Hunger Sustainable Development Goal outlined by the UN, and their disruption puts the country's ability to meet these goals in jeopardy. Many of the SSFs in these municipalities have reverted to tobacco or other fertilizer and pesticide reliant monoculture crops, while others managed to continue with erva-mate or other products, selling in local fairs. Clearly, the creation of legal and policy mechanisms and their application do not consider the realities of agricultural production, particularly for small-scale farms.

Tensions between the law and SSFs in the region are also evident considering the Forest Code[3] and the severe restrictions placed on the use of forests. Restrictive laws put in place since the 1960s (Brazil 1965, 2006) have been essential in the fight against deforestation; however, these laws do not consider the realities of traditional agroforestry practices that have been in place for over 100 years, nor were they developed in consultation with those farmers that have conserved forests on their properties. As noted above, the few remnants of

Araucaria Forest are concentrated in Southern Paraná and Northern Santa Catarina States partly because of the continuation of erva-mate production in agroforestry systems. Yet, the law restricts any type of forest management within these ecosystems, i.e., removal of trees, and limited ability to harvest fire-wood or other non-wood forest products. Rather than working with communities to support stewardship and sustainable management of the forests, which is already part of erva-mate producers' traditional practice, farmers feel that the environmental agency disproportionately police their activities and refuse their requests to manage the forest. This situation has created antagonism not only between small-scale farmers and the agency but also with the forest. Erva-mate producers who use the forest biome are caught in a difficult position between the law and practice. In order to avoid problems in the future, for example the inability to remove spontaneous tree regeneration, farmers actively remove seedlings, thus impoverishing the forest composition and threatening the continuation of the biome.

Despite the tensions between policy and practice, grassroots initiatives that support SSFs' agricultural autonomy, cultural heritage, and continuation of traditional systems are flourishing in the region. For example, the region is home to a thriving network of heirloom (*crioulo*) seed collection and exchange which is essential for community building, knowledge sharing, and sustaining local food biodiversity. Many of the SSFs are actively involved in planting local varieties of corn, popcorn, beans, pumpkin and squash, rice, among others. These seed fairs were born out of a collective consciousness of the need to preserve local food biodiversity and traditional practices in the region and have grown significantly over the years. Meanwhile, local chapters of FETRAF have partnered with EMATER (Paraná State's agricultural outreach agency) to develop a program to transition farmers away from tobacco and into other agroecological crops and the Public Prosecutor of Labour (Ministério Público do Trabalho) is beginning to support such practices. Many of those hired to do this outreach are young women, providing not only important employment opportunities, but also enabling young women to play an active role in the transition toward more sustainable practices in the region. In Brazil, although women play a crucial, yet often hidden, role in family agriculture (UN Women 2019), women are proportionately more likely to leave family farms and migrate to the cities, leaving some rural areas with a gender difference of up to 10% (Oxfam Brasil 2016). Programs that hire women to get involved in activities surrounding SSF are important, as they begin to combat the pervasive stereotypes that women are not farmers and that small-scale farming isn't a valuable or viable career choice. Our ongoing engagement with these communities is beginning to see greater participation of young women, yet more need to get involved in local farmers unions and their voices need to be included in decision-making, while also providing mentoring opportunities for other young women.

Despite the successes of and international attention given to Brazil's Fome Zero programs, there is a real need to invert the top-down approaches of agricultural research/ outreach and policies must consider the realities of small-scale farms and their families, building policies and practices in collaboration. For example, through our ongoing partnership project, researchers from Embrapa Forestry (Brazil's national forest research company) are developing and testing models of forest restoration that are economically viable and enable farmers to move away from conventional agricultural practices, such as monocultures and pesticides. These models are being developed in collaboration with small-scale erva-mate producers and based on traditional knowledge of the forest that we are documenting through oral history interviews. Forest products are important aspect of these models, along with trees for wood production: *Mimosa scabrella*, bracatinga, and other native fruit tree species that adhere to the restrictive Forest Code while also offering avenues of agricultural innovation. Projects like ours that focus on valuing and documenting the voices and knowledge of farmers using traditional agroforestry systems are urgently required, not only so that their products and culture can be valued by society, but their important role in rural and urban ecological wellbeing is recognized and appreciated. Our continued engagement with farmers, family farmers unions, NGOs, and regional and national government agencies is beginning to bear fruit, with the Public Prosecutor of Labour of Paraná supporting the creation of a strategic council (*Observatório*) made up of civil society, government, and research agencies to inform policies and support the development and expansion of traditional erva-mate production.

Clearly, SSFs face many challenges in relation to their right to define their own food and agricultural systems. This is compounded by pressure to move to monoculture crops, including transgenic soy, corn, and tobacco, some of which comes from government agricultural and outreach agencies. With the inauguration of a far-right government in 2019, this pressure is only likely to grow as representatives of the agribusiness and forestry sectors have been given prominent positions in government, most of whom have little appreciation for the previous government's policies in relation to SSFs. The future of programs supporting SSFs, for example through access to credit (PRONAF), and policies such as PNAE and PAA is unclear, which will have a direct impact on food security and the right to adequate food for both farmers and the communities in which they live. The grassroots and community initiatives already in place, the local chapters of Family Farmers Unions, and partnerships across communities, unions, and research institutions, such as the partnership we have fostered, will be essential to confront the challenges SSFs are likely to face in the coming years.

Common threads: discussion and conclusion

The examples from northern Canada and southern Brazil point to commonalities that could provide the basis for community engaged and connected action founded on human rights through the protection and support of networks of sustainable food systems as opportunities for regeneration. Rights focused networks can create new, or add to existing, networks. Examples of how to enact change in this way come from many sources. New paths forward are emerging through global-local articulations including the Occupy Movement and the 2019 Climate Action Strikes. La Via Campesina as a global movement is an exemplar for enacting political and food systems change (Desmarais 2012). Agroecology education programs in Nicaragua that build on the Brazilian MST (Landless Workers Movement) and the Cuban ANAP (Asociación Nacional de Agricultores Pequeños), identify educational approaches that move the focus from the individual to the territory. In these cases, agroecological education becomes a way to bring about change as farmers educate farmers about technical farming practices as well as the participation and interrogation of social processes. Scaling this up is supported by territorial mediators including the presence of the social movement itself, schools, facilitators, methods for social activation, and organizational structures, as well as access to land, positive experiences with agroecology, and direct access to consumers (McCune et al. 2017). In our case studies, there are parallels with Guardian Programs in the NWT and the regional networks of farmers in Brazil. In reflecting on the two case studies, points of commonality become apparent:

1. That there are shared challenges and opportunities for these communities and their food systems;
2. That there are multiple dividends from these traditional food systems;
3. That there is the basis for building rights-based networks of common practice to enable transformative SFS.

First, both communities have strong cultural links to the land through their food systems. And, while these food systems foster water, soil, and biodiversity relying on cultural diversity, they are adversely impacted by the economic and environmental effects of globalization including development pressures and climate change. These global scale pressures and food system industrialization also negatively impact food security and health. Shared responses to the challenges are the inner-community building of youth and elder connections through the valuing and sharing of traditional knowledge and the valorization of cultural and biocultural diversity (Pimbert 2017). The case from Brazil lays out the local support for diverse seeds, growing systems, and cultural systems through direct-sell fairs and markets and regional extension services as well as support to transition to agroecological practices from tobacco farming. Pluriactivity economically also provides more robust formal and informal economic supports making the communities better able to self-determine their food systems in keeping with food sovereignty approaches. This pluriactivity is consistent with research by Schneider and Niederle (2010) where Brazilian dairy farmers develop autonomy and minimize risk by: using their own crops to feed their animals; consume, trade, or direct sell the food they produce and process through value-added food products (e.g. cheese) and kitchen gardens; diversify crops and value streams; and, as a result, experience increased valorization and improved opportunities for women and youth. Taken together there is refocusing from export to self-provisioning.

Framing food as systems that include ecological, cultural, and economic dimensions helps to support cooperatives and regional networks as important tools for raising community impact and viability. These food networks address other dimensions of sustainable food systems in particular cultural and economic considerations that have positive ecological implications. For example, traditional food systems provide solutions to pressing issues including climate change, un(der)employment of youth and women, social inclusion, and ecological regeneration and can offer ways to engage with other types of food systems. However, it is up to national governments to assume their duty of care and provide a rights-based enabling environment. As Bragdon says,

> Putting SSF [small scale farmers, but for this chapter also traditional farmers and traditional harvesters] innovation at the center in considering policy options does not exclude collaborative research efforts. Indeed, synergies between "formal" sector actors, particularly public research institutions, and small-scale innovation systems are likely to be important to the health and resilience of food systems. The point is to ensure the synergies empower SSF and represent collaboration and part-nership and do not cause the displacement of SSF. Ensuring relationships are equit-able and do not displace SSF – a group serving not only private but public interests – is the role of the public sector and public policy.
>
> *(2015, 9)*

There is very specific overwhelming support for traditional food and cultural heritage in existing declarations and conventions – what is lacking is the political will to enact, respect, and protect at all or consistently nationally and through international regulations. For example, in the wake of the Truth and Reconciliation Call for Action in Canada released in 2015, there is clear call for compliance with international agreements. This could include the adoption and ratification of, for example, the UN Convention for the Safeguarding of the Intangible Cultural Heritage. Unfortunately, while there is interest in supporting the harmonization of Canadian law with the UN Declaration on Rights of Indigenous Peoples, currently there is not enough support to make this a reality. The law that would have made this a reality (Bill C-262) was not passed in June 2019 and so would need to be revived following the national election in the fall of 2019 (Rogers 2019). As well, the only example of Indigenous self-governed community in the Northwest Territories was launched in 2016 in Deline on Great Bear Lake. While this process took decades to be realized and the self-government process still under development the implications for sustainable food systems point to self-determination of resource management, land stewardship, and revitalization of language and culture (Spring 2018). In Brazil, where traditional food production systems face pressures to industrialize production especially in context of the 2019 far-right government and the future of existing national programs including PRONAF and PAA are uncertain, existing links to local groups (FETRAF and EMATER) could help to continue the tangible, grassroots enactment of the Right to Food. Regional initiatives supportive of traditional food systems also provide ongoing space for these programs to persist. Additionally, the tensions between small-scale farmers in Southern Brazil, the implementation of policies supportive of traditional food systems at the local and regional level, and the application of legal restrictions related to forests and forest products create contested spaces for producers and how they are able to realize the right to define their own food and agricultural systems.

There is a corresponding need for accountability,

> human rights treaties must be at the core of mandatory regulation at the international level. Looking ahead, our major challenge is thus the important task of making them truly enforceable at all levels. Locally, it is crucial to continue increasing human rights accountability through mechanisms such as social auditing and people's tribunals. So far, people's mobilization remains the paramount form of human rights accountability. At the national level, the right to food is not fully justiciable everywhere yet and mandatory regulation on all relevant policy fields – as those included in the Guidelines – is still lacking. Finally, at the international level, it is necessary to complete the architecture of the international human rights system with a world court for human rights ... the Guidelines can be effectively hardened when social movements claim, monitor and implement them themselves.
>
> *(Suárez and Aubry 2014, 25)*

Possible ways to move forward include action plans with specific timelines, indicators of progress, and allocation of responsibilities. Implementation is key. The former UN Rapporteur on the Right to Food, de Schutter, explains the need for clarity and accountability:

> What must be done is to adopt an action plan with clear timelines for the implementation of each action to be taken, clear indicators to measure progress, and a clear allocation of responsibilities. In this way, no single part of government can avoid having to account for failing to take the measures it is expected to take. That

idea is a very powerful one. And in countries that have adopted such national strategies, it has acquired some degree of impact. Again however, the implementation of this idea is very uneven from region to region. Even in Latin America, where many countries have adopted a framework law on the RtAF, and have for the most part adopted national strategies, it is not clear whether there is always independent monitoring of the implementation of these strategies. It is also unclear whether there are any sanctions associated with non-compliance for the timelines that are set. So there is certainly still work to be done.

(De Schutter 2012, 18–19)

In commenting on agricultural investment as a tool for food sovereignty, McKeon explains the need for iteration between top-down and bottom-up approaches is key so that the

two must be mutually reinforcing, with local and national mobilization providing the popular energy for global policy work that otherwise would be reduced in its legitimacy and its urgency and, in return, accessing outside support for local struggles. National accountability backed by political mobilization is the indispensable complement for globally negotiated guidance …

(McKeon 2014, 31)

It is also critical for

a participatory human rights-based approach that transforms "victims" into "actors," resulting in the promotion of self-determination instead of dependency … In short, community engagements that protect local knowledge in relation to sustainable food systems must be protected; these activities can and do trigger a multitude of activities that have mobilized women, men and children to solve common post-crisis challenges, thus further contributing to the restoration of communities' self-reliance.

(Cedeño 2014, 39)

Respecting and protecting the Right to Food and the Rights of Indigenous Peoples opens spaces to hear these important lessons. It also raises questions about the complementarity and/or tensions between individual rights and collective approaches foundational to many indigenous worldviews that requires more attention with cultural heritage as one dimension of determining food security that is especially pertinent in the face of globalization (United Nations Declaration on the Rights of Indigenous Peoples in 2003). This chapter points to the need the Right to Food and the Rights of Indigenous Peoples as requiring support at all policy scales with appropriate policies and programs to embed and protect these rights in the context of ever-shifting government priorities. Global knowledge sharing and support networks, including La Via Campesina, offer platforms for realizing these rights across scales.

Discussion questions

- How can networks be created to enable knowledge sharing that could support more recognition of the Right to Food?
- (How) do indigenous worldviews align with more individual human rights?

- How can gender and youth be brought more centrally into consideration in research linked to the Right to Food and traditional food systems?

Notes

1 The "intangible cultural heritage" means the practices, representations, expressions, knowledge, skills – as well as the instruments, objects, artifacts, and cultural spaces associated therewith – that communities, groups, and, in some cases, individuals recognize as part of their cultural heritage. This intangible cultural heritage, transmitted from generation to generation, is constantly recreated by communities and groups in response to their environment, their interaction with nature and their history, and provides them with a sense of identity and continuity, thus promoting respect for cultural diversity and human creativity. (UNESCO 2003).

2 Including International Covenants of 1966 on Economic on Social and Cultural Rights (ICESCR) and on Civil and Political Rights (ICCPR), the Convention on the Elimination of all Forms of Racial Discrimination (CERD), the CRC, the American Declaration of the Rights and Duties of Man, the American Convention on Human Rights, and the ILO 169.

3 Updated and improved in 2012, the Forest Code is the main legal instrument for regulating land use on private rural lands in Brazil. "The Forest Code establishes two main types of land under environmental protection: Permanent Protection Areas (PPA) and Legal Reserves (LR). PPAs provide absolute protection of environmentally significant areas, such as riparian zones of rivers and hilltops. Legal Reserves are the areas in which rural landowners are required to set aside a proportion of their land that must maintain native vegetation. The proportion that must be set aside varies according to property size and location. Within the Amazon as much as 80% of a property must be set aside, whereas it is 35% in the parts of the Cerrado which fall within the legal definition of Amazonia, and 20% in the rest of rural Brazil" (https://www.globalcanopy.org/sites/default/files/docu ments/resources/Brazil's%20Forest%20Code%20briefing.pdf).

Further reading

Gaarde, I. 2017. *Peasants Negotiating a Global Policy Space: La Vía Campesina in the Committee on World Food Security.* New York: Routledge.

Riol, K.S.C. 2016. *The Right to Food Guidelines, Democracy and Citizen Participation: Country Case Studies.* New York: Routledge.

Sebastia, B. 2016. Eating traditional food: politics, identity and practices. In *Eating Traditional Food.* New York: Routledge, pp. 15–33.

References

Agyeman, J. and Alkon, A.H. eds. 2011. *Cultivating Food Justice: Race, Class, and Sustainability.* Cambridge, MA: MIT Press.

Blay-Palmer, A. and Koc, M. 2010. Imagining sustainable food systems: the path to regenerative food systems. In A. Blay-Palmer (ed.), *Imagining Sustainable Food Systems.* Abingdon, Oxon: Routledge.

Blay-Palmer, A., Santini, G., Dubbeling, M., Renting, H., Taguchi, M. and Giordano, T. 2018. Validating the city region food system approach: enacting inclusive, transformational city region food systems. *Sustainability, 10*(5), 1680.

Blay-Palmer, A., Sonnino, R. and Custot, J. 2016. A food politics of the possible? Growing sustainable food systems through networks of knowledge. *Agriculture and Human Values, 33*(1), 27–43.

Bragdon, S. 2015. Reinvigorating the public sector: the case of food security, small-scale farmers, trade, and intellectual property rules. Colloquium Paper 64. *Policy.*

Brazil. 1965. Law n° 4,771, 15 September. Institui o novo Código Florestal. Diário Oficial da União, Brasília, DF, 16 set 1965. Seção 1, p. 9529.

Brazil. 2006. Law n° 11,428, 22 December. Dispõe sobre a utilização e proteção da vegetação nativa do Bioma Mata Atlântica, e dá outras providências. Diário Oficial da União, Brasília, DF, 26 December 2006.

Carolan, M. 2018. *The Real Cost of Cheap Food.* Abingdon, Oxon: Routledge.

Carrigan, A. 2014. The "rights" time: Civil society reflections on the right to Adequate Food. In Right to Food and Nutrition Watch, *Ten Years of the Right to Food Guidelines: Gains. Concerns and Struggles*. Washington, DC: Bread for the World, FIAN International, and Interchurch Organisation for Development Cooperation, p. 13. Available at: www.righttofoodandnutrition.org/ten-years-right-food-guidelines-gains-concerns-and-struggles

Castella, P.R. and Britez, R.M. eds. 2004. *A floresta com araucaria no Paraná: Conservacão e diagnóstico dos remanescentes florestais*. Brasília, DF: Ministério do Meio Ambiente.

Cedeño, A.M. 2014. Responses to climate change challenges on food production: strengthening resilience or increasing dependence. In Right to Food and Nutrition Watch, *Ten Years of the Right to Food Guidelines: gains. Concerns and Struggles*. Washington, DC: Bread for the World et al., p. 46. Available at: www.righttofoodandnutrition.org/ten-years-right-food-guidelines-gains-concerns-and-struggles

Chaimsohn, F.P. and Souza, A.M. 2013. *Sistemas de Produção Tradicionais e Agroflorestais de Erva-Mate No Centro-Sul Do Paraná e Norte Catarinense*. Ponta Grossa, Brazil: IAPAR.

Council of Canadian Academies. 2014. *Aboriginal Food Security in Northern Canada: An Assessment of the State of Knowledge*. Ottawa: The Expert Panel on the State of Knowledge of Food Security in Northern Canada, Council of Canadian Academies.

Dahlberg, K.A. 1993. Regenerative food systems: Broadening the scope and agenda of sustainability. In Patricia Allen (ed.), *Food for the Future: Conditions and Contradictions of Sustainability*. New York: John Wiley & Sons, pp. 75–102.

Damman, S., Eide, W.B. and Kuhnlein, H.V. 2008. Indigenous peoples' nutrition transition in a right to food perspective. *Food Policy, 33*(2), 135–155.

De Schutter, O. 2012. *World Trade Organization and the Post-Global Food Crisis Agenda: Putting Food Security First in the International Trade System*. New York: United Nations Publications.

Desmarais, A.A. 2012. Building food sovereignty: A radical framework for alternative food systems. *Critical Perspectives in Food Studies*, 359–377.

Desmarais, A.A. and Wittman, H. 2014. Farmers, foodies and first nations: getting to food sovereignty in Canada. *Journal of Peasant Studies, 41*(6). 1153–1173.

Emery, M. and Flora, C. 2006. Spiraling-up: Mapping community transformation with community capitals framework. *Community Development, 37*(1), 19–35.

Ferreira de Moura, I. 2017. Antecedentes e Aspectos Fundantes da Agroecologia e da Produção Orgânica Na Agenda das Políticas Públicas no Brasil. In R.H.R. Sambuichi, I.F. de Moura, L.M. de Mattos, M.L. de Ávila, P.A.C. Spínola and A.P. Moreira da Silva (eds.), *A Política Nacional de Agroecologia e Produção Orgânica no Brasil: Uma trajetória de luta pelo desenvolvimento rural sustentável*. Brasilia: Ipea, pp. 25–52.

Flora, C., Flora, J. and Fey, S. 2004. *Rural Communities: Legacy and Change*. 2nd ed. Boulder, CO: Westview Press.

Food and Agriculture Organization. 1996. *Rome Declaration on World Food Security and World Food Summit Plan of Action: World Food Summit 13–17 November 1996*. Rome: FAO.

Geniusz, W.M. 2009. *Our Knowledge is Not Primitive: Decolonizing Botanical Anishinaabe Teachings*. Syracuse, NY: Syracuse University Press.

Goodman, D. 2004. Rural Europe redux? Reflections on alternative agro-food networks and paradigm change. *Sociologia ruralis, 44*(1), 3–16.

Gottlieb, R. and Joshi, A. 2010. *Food Justice*. Cambridge, MA: MIT Press.

Hanisch, A.L., Negrelle, R.R.B., Bonatto, R.A., Nimmo, E.R. and Lacerda, A.E.B. 2019. Evaluating sustainability in traditional silvopastoral systems (Caívas): looking beyond the impact of animals on biodiversity. *Sustainability, 11*(11). 3098. doi:10.3390/su11113098.

Heynen, N., Kurtz, H.E. and Trauger, A. 2012. Food justice, hunger and the city. *Geography Compass, 6* (5), 304–311.

Hipel, K.W., Fang, L. and Heng, M. 2010. System of systems approach to policy development for global food security. *Journal of Systems Science and Systems Engineering, 19*(1), 1–21.

HLPE = High Level Panel of Experts on Food Security and Nutrition. 2019. *Other Innovative Approaches for Sustainable Agriculture and Food Systems that Enhance Food Security and Nutrition*. Rome: Committee on World Food Security.

Holt Giménez, E. and Shattuck, A. 2011. Food crises, food regimes and food movements: rumblings of reform or tides of transformation? *Journal of Peasant Studies, 38*(1), 109–144.

Ilbery, B. and Maye, D. 2005. Food supply chains and sustainability: evidence from specialist food producers in the Scottish/English borders. *Land Use Policy*, 22(4), 331–344.

Knezevic, I., Blay-Palmer, A., Levkoe, C.Z., Mount, P. and Nelson, E. eds. 2017. *Nourishing communities: From fractured food systems to transformative pathways.* Cham: Springer.

Kok, K. 2020. Monitoring environmental change using a participatory modified photovoice approach with Indigenous knowledge holders in Kakisa, Northwest Territories. *Theses and Dissertations* (Comprehensive). 2233. https://scholars.wlu.ca/etd/2233

Lang, T. and Rayner, G. 2012. Ecological public health: the 21st century's big idea? An essay by Tim Lang and Geof Rayner. *Bmj*, 345, e5466.

La Via Campesina: International Peasant's Movement. Organisation. 2011. https://viacampesina.org/en/watch-and-screen-our-new-video/

Levkoe, C.Z. 2011. Towards a transformative food politics. *Local Environment*, 16(7), 687–705.

Leyva, Á. and Lores, A. 2018. Assessing agroecosystem sustainability in Cuba: a new agrobiodiversity index. *Elementa: Science of the Anthropocene*, 6, 80. doi:10.1525/elementa.336.

Marsden, T. 2012. Food systems under pressure: regulatory instabilities and the challenge of sustainable development. In G. Spaargaren, P. Oosterveer and A. Loeber (eds.), *Food Practices in Transition: Changing Food Consumption, Retail and Production in the Age of Reflexive Modernity.* New York: Routledge.

Mason, P. and Lang, T. 2017. *How Ecological Nutrition Can Transform Consumption and The Food System.* Abingdon, Oxon: Routledge.

Maye, D., Holloway, L. and Kneafsey, M. 2007. *Alternative Food Geographies.* New York: Elsevier.

McCune, N., Rosset, P.M., Salazar, T.C., Saldívar Moreno, A. and Morales, H. 2017. Mediated territoriality: Rural workers and the efforts to scale out agroecology in Nicaragua. *Journal of Peasant Studies*, 44(2), 354–376.

McKeon, N. 2014. *Food Security Governance: Empowering Communities, Regulating Corporations.* Abingdon, Oxon: Routledge.

Morrison, D. 2011. Indigenous food sovereignty – a model for social learning. In H. Wittman, A. A. Desmarais and N. Wiebe (eds.), *Food Sovereignty in Canada: Creating Just and Sustainable Food Systems.* Halifax: Fernwood Publishing, pp. 97–113.

Nelson, E. and Tovar, L.G. 2017. Navigating spaces for political action: victories and compromises for Mexico's local organic movement. In I. Knezevic et al. (eds.), *Nourishing Communities.* Cham: Springer, pp. 165–181.

Nimmo, E.R. and Nogueira, J.F.M.M. 2019. Creating hybrid scientific knowledge and practice: the Jesuit and Guaraní cultivation of Yerba Mate. *Canadian Journal of Latin American and Caribbean Studies.* doi:10.1080/08263663.2019.1652018.

NWT Protected Area Strategy Advisory Committee. 1999. *The Northwest Territories Protected Areas Strategy: A Balanced Approach to Establishing Protected Areas in the Northwest Territories.* Kakisa: KTFN.

Nyéléni. 2007. Forum for Food Sovereignty.

O'Dea, K. 1992. Obesity and diabetes in "the land of milk and honey". *Diabetes/Metabolism Reviews*, 8 (4), 373–388.

Oxfam Brasil. 2016. *Terrenos da Desigualdade: Terra, agricultura e desigualdades no Brasil rural.* https://oxfam.org.br/publicacao/terrenos-da-desigualdade-terra-agricultura-e-desigualdade-no-brasil-rural/ (Accessed March 25, 2020).

Patel, R. 2009. Food sovereignty. *Journal of Peasant Studies*, 36(3), 663–706.

Patel, R. 2011. *The Value of Nothing: How to Reshape Market Society and Redefine Democracy.* London: Granta.

Pimbert, M.P. ed. 2017. *Food Sovereignty, Agroecology and Biocultural Diversity: Constructing and Contesting Knowledge.* Abingdon, Oxon: Routledge.

Pirog, R., Miller, C., Way, L., Hazekamp, C. and Kim, E. 2014. The local food movement: setting the stage for good food. MSU Center for Regional Food Systems (for more information contact: Rich Pirog, MSU Center for Regional Food Systems (rspirog@ msu. edu), p. 3.

Renting, H., Marsden, T.K. and Banks, J. 2003. Understanding alternative food networks: exploring the role of short food supply chains in rural development. *Environment and Planning A*, 35(3), 393–411.

Right to Food and Nutrition Watch. 2014. *Ten Years of the Right to Food Guidelines: Gains. Concerns and Struggles.* Washington, DC: Bread for the World, FIAN International, and urch Organisation for Development Cooperation. www.righttofoodandnutrition.org/ten-years-right-food-guidelines-gains-concerns-and-struggles

Right to Food and Nutrition Watch. 2017. The way forward 2017. www.righttofoodandnutrition.org/files/R_t_F_a_N_W_2017_ENG_10.pdf

Riol, K.S.C. 2016. *The Right to Food Guidelines, Democracy and Citizen Participation: Country Case Studies.* Abingdon, Oxon: Routledge.

Rocha, C., Burlandy, L. and Maluf, R. 2012. Small farms and sustainable rural development for food security: the Brazilian experience. *Development Southern Africa, 29*(4), 519–529. doi:10.1080/0376835X.2012.715438.

Rogers, S. 2019. https://nunatsiaq.com/stories/article/canadas-undrip-legislation-headed-for-defeat/

Schneider, S. and Niederle, P.A. 2010. Resistance strategies and diversification of rural livelihoods: The construction of autonomy among Brazilian family farmers. *Journal of Peasant Studies, 37*(2), 379–405.

Scoones, I. 2009. Livelihoods perspectives and rural development. *Journal of Peasant Studies, 36*(1), 171–196.

Shukla, P.R. et al. 2019. *Climate Change and Land: An IPCC Special Report on Climate Change, Desertification, Land Degradation, Sustainable Land Management, Food Security, and Greenhouse Gas Fluxes in Terrestrial Ecosystems.* Paris: IPCC.

Simba, M. and Spring, A. 2017. Growing a garden in Kakisa. *Northern Public Affairs, 5*(1), 24–26.

Sonnino, R. 2009. Quality food, public procurement, and sustainable development: the school meal revolution in Rome. *Environment and Planning A, 41*(2), 425–440.

Spring, A. 2018. Capitals, climate change and food security: Building sustainable food systems in northern Canadian Indigenous communities. PhD thesis. Wilfrid Laurier University, Waterloo, Canada.

Spring, A., Carter, B. and Blay-Palmer, A. 2018. Climate change, community capitals, and food security: building a more sustainable food system in a northern Canadian boreal community. *Canadian Food Studies/La Revue canadienne des études sur l'alimentation, 5*(2), 111–141.

Stroink, M.L. and Nelson, C.H. 2013. Complexity and food hubs: Five case studies from Northern Ontario. *Local Environment,* 18(5), 620–635.

Suárez, S. and Aubry, F. 2014. Rethinking the voluntary vs. binding divide:A reflection after 10 years of the voluntary guidelines on the right to Food. In Right to Food and Nutrition Watch, *Ten Years of the Right to Food Guidelines: Gains. Concerns and Struggles.* Washington, DC: Bread for the World et al. www.righttofoodandnutrition.org/ten-years-right-food-guidelines-gains-concerns-and-struggles

UNESCO. 2003. https://ich.unesco.org/en/convention

United Nations. 2007. *UN Declaration on the Rights of Indigenous Peoples.* www.un.org/development/desa/indigenouspeoples/declaration-on-the-rights-of-indigenous-peoples.html

UN Women. 2019. *Progress of the World's Women 2019–2020: Families in a Changing World.* www.onumulheres.org.br/wp-content/uploads/2019/06/Progress-of-the-worlds-women-2019-2020-en.pdf

Vibrans, A.C., McRoberts, R.E., Lingner, D.V., Nicoletti, A.L. and Moser, P. 2012. Extensão original e atual da cobertura florestal de Santa Catarina. In A.C. Vibrans, L. Sevegnani, A.L.D. Gasper, and D. V. Lingner (eds.), *Diversidade e conservacão dos remanescentes florestais.* Blumenau, Brazil: Edifurb, pp. 65–78.

Wendimu, M.A., Desmarais, A.A. and Martens, T.R. 2018. Access and affordability of "healthy" foods in northern Manitoba? The need for Indigenous food sovereignty. *Canadian Food Studies/La Revue canadienne des études sur l'alimentation, 5*(2), 44–72.

7

CO-CREATIVE GOVERNANCE OF AGROECOLOGY

Lisa Deijl and Jessica Duncan

Introduction

One pathway we can take to create regenerative food systems is agroecology. Agroecology is receiving increased recognition and attention from governance institutions as a possible solution to the multiple crises that exist in food policy today (Parmentier 2014). However, agroecology as practice, movement, and science, is interpreted in different ways by different groups (Pimbert 2015). This chapter maps current discourses around agroecology and considers how key groups behind these discourses are more or less able to influence related policy processes. This is relevant because those who can influence the policy-making process affect the outcomes of said process (Swyngedouw 2005). As this chapter will show, transdisciplinary co-creation of knowledge is a core principle of agroecology. We in turn argue that in order to reflect this and other tenants of agroecology, the governance of agroecology should be inclusive of all knowledge producers.

To explore a governance process wherein these issues play out, this chapter presents the results of a discourse analysis applied to the FAO Regional Symposium on Agroecology for Sustainable Agriculture and Food Systems for Europe and Central Asia which took place in Budapest, Hungary from 23 to 25 November 2016. All of the formal interventions at the symposium were recorded and made available online. One of the authors attended the symposium as an invited speaker. The analysis considers the discourses of scientists, farmers, policy-makers, and civil society organizations (CSOs), and how they were able or unable to participate in the process, and what effect this had on the outcome of the symposium. As such, the aim of this chapter is to signal potential threats to agroecological principles when they are translated into policy-making processes and to give recommendations as to what a co-created governance process could look like.

Agroecology as a pathway to regenerative food systems

The central idea of agroecology is to view an agricultural production system as a modified ecosystem: an agroecosystem. The concept of the agroecosystem highlights that like any other ecosystem, agricultural production systems are shaped by dynamic processes that strive towards an equilibrium of energy and nutrients (Gliessman 2015).

What agroecology aims to do is '[apply] ecological concepts and principles to the design and management of sustainable agro-ecosystems' (Altieri 2014, 2). Key to an agroecological production system is that it fits the local environment by its very design, in contrast to models which propose a one-size-fits-all solution. Further, these systems regenerate themselves, rather than being dependent on external inputs (Rosset and Altieri 1997).

Scientists have used the term agroecology to refer to the application of ecological principles to agriculture since the 1920s (FAO 2018, 6). Often a distinction is made between agroecology as a science, practice, and social movement (Silici 2014). The first use of the term agroecology is attributed to work that the Russian agronomist Bensin published in 1928, demarcating the start of agroecology as a science. Wezel et al. (2009) place the consolidation of the scientific discipline in the 1970s, when the concept of the agroecosystem was introduced. Wezel et al. (2009, 506) also propose that it was at this time that agroecology emerged as a practice, explaining that

> one of the origins of agroecology as a practice was laid during the 1980s in Latin America. … Agroecology helped local farmers to improve their Indigenous farming practices as an alternative to a high input, chemical-intensive agriculture promoted by international corporations.

Lastly, the origin of agroecology as a social movement is placed in the 1990s (Silici 2014). It was also around this time that the peasants' movement La Vía Campesina was founded, and coined the term 'food sovereignty', which they defined as 'the right of each nation to maintain and develop its own capacity to produce its basic foods respecting cultural and productive diversity' (La Vía Campesina 1996, as cited in Patel 2009, 665).

While this three-part division is widely acknowledged, there are also theorists that do not agree with it, nor with the linear timeline as outlined here. These scholars argue that the three facets cannot be separated, especially not the movement from the science. They argue that those who see agroecology solely as a science present agroecology falsely as a technological fix for the problems of the mainstream agri-food system, whereas a holistic fix should include tackling the social and institutional frameworks that uphold that system (Gonzalez De Molina 2013). For example, Gliessman (2015, xii), writes:

> It became obvious to me as an agroecologist that we needed to expand the scope of the field beyond the growing and eating of food. We needed to find a political voice, align closely with social movements, and focus on developing a grassroots and community-based alternative food system that could grow outward and eventually make the industrial food system obsolete.

Thus, there is contention in the academic literature on the issue of whether or not agroecology as a science should have a political aim. At a time when policy-makers are willing to promote agroecology, it is important to reflect on which version of this story is put forward by scientists of agroecology. As Weingart (1999) notes, scientists have long had a powerful position in policy-making processes.

Another point of contention is the question of how researchers and policy-makers should relate to the actual practitioners of agroecology in the process of knowledge production. As agroecological production methods are so attuned to their local environment, the creativity, knowledge, and skills of farmers are of vital importance to agroecological production systems

(Coolsaet 2016). This is a point often raised by non-European scholars, who critique the attribution of agroecology to European science. Altieri and Holt-Giménez (2016, 2) note:

> Although many northern academics claim that the term Agroecology was first coined by European scientists … at the beginning of the 20th century, the roots of agroecology lie in the ecological rationale of indigenous and peasant agriculture still prevalent in many parts of the developing world. Thirty years ago, Latin American agroecologists argued that a starting point for new, pro-poor agricultural development strategies were the very systems that traditional farmers had developed over centuries.

It is clear that farmers have contributed massively to the body of knowledge on agroecological production methods, and continue to do so. As noted by Milgroom et al. (2016,7): 'while scientific knowledge aims to be largely explicit, a lot of relevant knowledge and skill in agriculture is tacit, implicit or hidden in (women) farmers' practices and in their heads'. This insight remains poorly addressed in the institutional discourse on agriculture in general. On this topic Wakeford et al. (2016) write: 'mainstream agricultural development has been largely based on scientism [which] ignores or displaces local and indigenous knowledge systems'. This means that if agroecology aims to fundamentally change the food system towards regenerative processes, it should be cautious not to repeat this logic. Instead, to fulfill the transformative potential of agroecology towards regenerative food systems, it is important that people working with agroecology in and across practice, science, and movement come together to jointly co-create knowledge on agroecology and to translate this into food systems policy.

This concept of co-creation has been put forward by a number of academics as a way to understand social innovation processes (Schneider et al. 2012). Social innovation is here defined as: 'the creation of long-lasting outcomes that aim to address societal needs by fundamentally changing the relationships, positions and rules between the involved stakeholders, through an open process of participation, exchange and collaboration with relevant stakeholders, including end-users, thereby crossing organizational boundaries and jurisdictions' (Voorberg et al. 2015, 1334). According to Voorberg et al. (2015) the concepts of co-creation, co-production, and participation overlap in the academic literature, as they refer to the involvement of citizens in social innovation. In their systematic review of the literature on co-creation/co-production, they distinguish three different levels of involvement: the citizen as co-implementer, co-designer, and initiator. The last two more active levels of involvement are more often associated with co-creation than with co-production. We speak of co-creation of knowledge in governance processes of agroecology as we envision high levels of involvement from various, notably affected, stakeholders. In the next section, we present the results of our case study of a policy process related to agroecology. After that, we discuss the degree to which co-creation did or did not take place.

Case study: FAO regional symposium on agroecology

The UN's Food and Agriculture Organization Regional Symposium on Agroecology for Sustainable Agriculture and Food Systems for Europe and Central Asia took place in Budapest, Hungary, in November 2016. The objectives of the symposium, as written in the Participant Handbook (FAO 2016), were:

- To facilitate the exchange of knowledge and experiences among different stakeholders (food producer organizations, academics, private sector, European Union (EU) institutions and representatives from all European and Central Asian countries) on the potential contribution of agroecology to sustainable agriculture and food systems;
- To showcase existing practices and models of agroecology and provide a synthesis of the key elements related to agroecology;
- To identify and define potential entry points and areas of contribution of agroecology in public policies;
- To catalyze international collaboration to develop ways forward for strengthening agroecological practices and programs in the region.

One of the primary expected outcomes of the symposium was for the participants to contribute to recommendations for public policies. A video recording of the whole conference is made publicly accessible by FAO on YouTube. At the start of the symposium there was a 'high-level panel session', with four speeches from representatives of the FAO and the European Commission. The rest of the symposium was made up of six modules with distinct themes, each with their own panels. At the end of each module there was some room for discussion and questions to the panel members from the audience. All those who spoke, in speeches or in the discussion, became part of the discourse analysis. Amongst the speakers we distinguished the following groups:

Scientists: People possessing an academic title or profile and producing scientific work. Their research subjects cover the natural science and social science dimensions of agroecology. They speak on their own behalf as experts and gain legitimacy due to their scientific output and organizational affiliation.

Government officials: The individuals in this group represent national governments, governmental committees, or supra-national government bodies such as the European Commission or FAO.

Farmers: Virtually all individuals in this category are self-employed small producers of agricultural products. Some of them also represent farmer's movements, such as La Vía Campesina.

CSO-representatives: These people represent civil society organizations (CSOs). The term 'civil society organization' is used as an umbrella term to refer to both social movements and NGOs. NGOs are understood to be organizations that represent a specific issue or theme or the interests of certain social groups. In contrast, social movements are recognized as self-organized social actors with a shared identity that have come together to represent their own interests (Duncan 2015, 101–2).

In what follows, we present a discourse analysis based on the interventions of each group described above. By group, the discourse analysis was undertaken on the basis of two sets of codes: how does a group 'characterize agroecology' and what 'recommendations' do they make. The goal was to first discern the different discourses that were represented, and secondly to see which of those had the most influence on the final recommendations. This was followed by the discourse analysis for the official recommendations of the symposium.

Scientists

In this group we observed a division between scientists that characterized agroecology as something technical and those that characterized it as something socio-cultural. In terms of the technical discourse, agroecology is presented as a series of techniques and practices. The focus is on how to make individual production systems more sustainable. The technical discourse considers the farm plot-level and promotes incremental change of food production systems. This discourse is exemplified in this excerpt from the presentation of a French scientist:

> We think about how to use different breeds and different cultivars. At the top right [pointing to a PowerPoint slide] you see that if you have contrasted arrangements of wheat cultivars or if you have mixtures of cultivars, you can change the risks from rust strains. Wheat rust is obviously a risk and you can limit the disease spread by mixing the cultivar or by assembling the cultivar to landscape scale. Another strategy is to use the grasslands and arable crops which provide a sustained resource for the pollinators and that is on the bottom left where you see how the pollinators can actually use a grassland at times where you have no flowers with the crops.

This excerpt is illustrative of many scientific presentations at the symposium which focused on the enumeration of specific agricultural techniques. Our analysis found that this technical style received slightly more emphasis during the symposium than other approaches.

The socio-cultural discourse focuses on the wider political, social, and cultural dynamics influencing how farmers choose to practice their craft. Advocates of this discourse seek to transform, rather than conform to, the dominant agri-food system. Exemplary are these words from a UK scholar:

> Agroecology moved from the field to encompass the whole food system. And one other definition is that agroecology is the ecology of food systems. The different bits that connect seeds to plate, but also the policy and institutional framework that determine the pathways of food systems. Now that formulation actually brought about a change in agroecological practice because it opened up a broader perspective that facilitated the links with farmer organizations, consumers citizen groups and social movements supporting alternative to industrial food and farming. ... There are a lot of normative issues in the choices ahead of us.

In this excerpt, the scientist clearly states how he considers factors beyond the farm level to be of key interest to agroecology. He also explicitly mentions the normativity inherent in making policy choices for agriculture. By contrast, the technical discourse does not address this. In fact, it makes this normativity invisible, as it casts the answer to each question as technological.

Although they are divided as a group, recommendations of this group are overwhelmingly directed at 'research and education'. First, regardless of which discourse they advance, scientists place great importance on the need for more data on the benefits of agroecology. Secondly, they emphasize that science could be a mediator between different kinds of knowledges. Actors that are not identified as scientists are at times seen as an untapped resource. Examples of such an outlook can be found in the words of this researcher:

> Farmers can be considered as researchers. They are knowledge producers and this knowledge can be combined with the knowledge of scientists and other knowledge from other actors.

This quote is illustrative of a vision of science combining 'non-scientific' knowledges to gain new understandings. This approach appears to advocate more co-creative knowledge development.

Government representatives

When compared to researchers, government officials are more univocal in their characterization of agroecology. In the way they speak about agroecology, policy-makers echo the technical scientific discourse discussed above. They speak generally about agroecology as a series of management techniques, for example positioning agroecology as a tool for climate change adaptation and mitigation. Another example of such can be seen in a quote from an Austrian government representative:

> We promote the creation of biodiversity strips, or flowering strips on arable land or grassland. We have now an amount of 70,000 hectares of flowering strips. We also promote the greening of arable land, the direct seeding, the maintenance of rare livestock breeds, rare plants. We also promote the management of species rich meadows and pastures.

In their recommendations, government officials strongly push for 'research and education' and 'government regulated market' solutions. Related to the former, government officials emphasize the need for more education at all levels, but also call for more scientific data and evidence. 'Government regulated market solutions', in turn, favor agroecological production methods over conventional production methods. Possible regulation changes range from changing subsidy structures to changing food sanitation laws which would encourage local processing. Both kinds of recommendations are reflected in the following excerpt from a French government representative:

> There were two observations this afternoon which were very important. First, the agroecological approaches that can respond to this climatic challenge in terms of adaptation for example. In relation to this climatic agenda we would like to trans-form the actual economical model for it to become more favorable to human cap-ital. And another intervention, regarding our evaluation on agricultural system performance. The reason why some people hesitate is economic performance. It's important to prove that an agricultural exploitation can be profitable, but also going beyond the short-term financial benefits.

This representative calls for economic regulations that are more favorable to agroecology, for the main reason that agroecology as a management tool can prepare production systems better for climate change. He also calls for more thinking on how to assess agroecological systems differently, for which scientific work is needed.

Farmers

Contrary to the previously discussed groups, particularly the technical scientists and government representatives, the farmers overwhelmingly emphasize the socio-cultural dimensions and the potential of agroecology to transform the entire food system. The technical perspective is notably absent in their rhetoric. Instead, they speak of agroecology in terms of more 'soft' concepts, such as personal connection to the location of production. For example, one farmer and member of La Vía Campesina, states:

> Every day, our daily work embeds us in these very complex ecosystems and our definition of agroecology includes much more than the scientific practices that may avoid the use of fertilizers or pesticides or these terrible practices put forward by industrialized agriculture. It's much more than that. Because our work is about working really deeply in our landscapes and within the cultural identity of our rural communities and our urban areas to make sure that food is really working with a very holistic system.

Farmers also underscore that they want to be seen as holders and creators of knowledge, and not just as receivers of scientific advice. This focus on the knowledge that exists outside of academia comes back in their recommendations. Like the scientists and government representatives, the most popular recommendation from farmers relate to 'research and education'. However, rather than asking for more scientific data, they proposed that more horizontal ways of knowledge production should be fostered. They emphasized the importance of learning about agroecology. This means not only formal education, but also farmer-to-farmer learning networks, which they maintain should be the main channel through which agroecology is promoted. A farmer from Greece explains:

> Case studies and programs are very important to be emphasized, but we have to keep in mind that they are usually local small-scale prototypes. It's important not only to identify them but also to connect them, scale them, communicate them. To every village, every island, every mountain, the most marginalized places.

Furthermore, six out of nine farmers that sat on the panels recommended more market regulation. They proposed that the state should shape market dynamics in a way that protects small agroecological farming projects. They also stressed the need for regulation that safeguards the accessibility of genetic and land resources for small farmers. As a French farmer notes:

> Farmers have to have the right to be able to select their own seeds every year. And they must be secured another right, they need to be able to exchange seeds so that they can renew this diversity amongst themselves.

CSO-representatives

Our analysis of the interventions made by CSO representatives shows that they focus on the socio-cultural rather than the technical side of agroecology. In the way that they characterize agroecology, they emphasize the need for changing the way the whole food system is organized. An example of this can be seen in the following quote:

> We should talk about the need of making direct sales to the consumer to avoid that the benefits are taken by third parties. The food logically should be agroecological or organic but they are obviously more expensive. But they should have better prices. It's a change of mentality, I've heard it many times this morning.

To achieve such system reorganization, the CSO-representatives made recommendations that can be categorized as 'government regulated market' and 'research and education'. As an example of the first, the following excerpt highlights how a CSO-representative called for changes in the subsidy structure of the Common Agricultural Policy (CAP) of the European Union:

> The answer to the question of CAP and agroecology, at least from a government perspective is: 'Yes we can, but we don't dare.' Why? Because, in Europe, CAP is the key legislative framework that influences the production, sales and processing of agricultural products. It has made major decisions on the direction of agriculture in Europe. It has encouraged intensification and specialization of production. It has not gone far enough to stimulate agroecological production methods. Agroecological practices and approaches should be recognized and embedded into the CAP framework. We need to provide enough financial provisions to fund the agroecological transitions.

Not unlike the farmers and the scientists, the CSO-representatives' 'research and education' recommendations mostly refer to the activities of CSOs themselves. They emphasize the importance of their educational work. For example, a representative from an Armenian CSO said:

> We have been organizing farmer field schools and also production and usage of compost in small scale farms and I have to say that after the collapse of Soviet Union after 1991, all lands were privatized in Armenia and each person living in a village got a small plot of land without exact knowledge and exact plan how to deal with this land. And here agroecology is very important and an advisory system is also kind of lacking for them how to do ... maybe this seems very small input but still it's very important to help them to carry out all these issues.

Through this statement and others, the importance of on-the-ground learning opportunities for food-producers is stressed. Thus, this is another example of how not only formal education, but also farmer-to-farmer networks were stressed at the symposium.

Table 7.1 presents an overview of the number of people per actor category that put forward one or both characterizations of agroecology, either in panel presentations or as audience members through spontaneous interventions. From this we can see the imbalance in time spent talking about one discourse versus the other by different groups.

In terms of quantifying the recommendations, Table 7.2 outlines proposed recommendations by actor category, focusing broadly on recommendations for research and education and

Table 7.1 Characterization of agroecology by actor category

	Technical		Socio-cultural		Both		Total
	Panel	*Audience*	*Panel*	*Audience*	*Panel*	*Audience*	
Researchers	9	1	6	4	4	0	24
Government officials	3	4	2	3	3	0	15
Farmers	0	0	7	0	1	0	8
CSO-representatives	0	1	5	3	0	2	11

Table 7.2 Quantifying broad recommendations

	Research and education	*Changing public discourse*
Researchers	22 (/26*100% = 85%)	9 (34%)
Government officials	9 (/15*100%=60%)	3 (20%)
Farmers	7 (/8*100%=88%)	4 (50%)
CSO-representatives	8 (/11*100% = 73%)	4 (37%)

Table 7.3 Quantifying market-based interventions

	Regulated market	*Free market*
Researcher	17 (65%)	1 (4%)
Government officials	9 (60%)	3 (33%)
Farmers	7 (88%)	2 (25%)
CSO-representatives	5 (45%)	1 (9%)

for changing public discourse. The category 'research and education' included anything linked to asking for more research funds on agroecology or teaching agroecology methods. Under 'changing public discourse' we included calls for making the public understand the value of agroecologically produced food.

Table 7.3 captures the interventions that focused specifically on markets. Under 'regulated market' we included recommendations to do with taking away economic obstacles for agroecological producers, while under 'free market' recommendations we included recommendations that agroecological production should market itself.

Discourse analysis of the final recommendations

One of the key objectives of the symposium was to reach consensus around a final document of policy recommendations. An analysis of the outcome document in relation to the analysis of the panel presentations serves to identify which of the key discourses most likely to be translated into policy recommendations.

The committee that drafted the recommendations of the symposium was made up of Caterina Batello (FAO), Eva Torremocha (IFOAM), Lusine Nalbandyan (Armenian Women for Health and Healthy Environment), Alexander Wezel (ISARA), Jyoti Fernandes (La Vía Campesina EU), and Michel Pimbert (Coventry University). The draft recommendations were shared with the participants at a session in which amendments could be proposed. After some debate, a final list of 37 recommendations was approved. In what follows, we present and discuss the results of the discourse analysis of this document.

As for the characterization of agroecology, the technical and socio-cultural styles were represented equally. The document focuses equally on the technical basis on the one hand, and the wider food system context on the other. For example:

Technical:

28. Promote and support agroecological practices that reduce external inputs – specifically seeds, fertilizers, pesticides, animal feed and, fossil fuels enhancing the capacity of soil and agroecosystem health to close cycles and maintain productivity, stability and resilience.

Socio-cultural:

3. Promote the establishment of Food Policy Councils at local, regional and national level to foster and allow consumers and food producers participation in decision making processes around the food system, markets and trade.

The majority of the final recommendations fall under 'research and education' which is representative of the interventions given that almost all groups suggested these. However, these types of recommendations focus not only on traditional research, but also on more 'on-the-ground' learning experiences and bridging the two. Consider, for example:

31. Strengthen public research: allocate more funds for public research in this field, favour interdisciplinary research better connecting agricultural, ecological and social sciences. Facilitate changes in research organisations (incentives and rewards, ways of working and the training of scientists and professionals) and enable farmers and citizens' participation in research including in their community and in governance of research: setting upstream research priorities, the allocation of funds, and participation in production of knowledge and in risk assessments.

Furthermore, an important role is taken up by recommendations coded under 'change public discourse'. These types of recommendations urge policy-makers to raise awareness about agroecology amongst the general public. They also aim at giving recognition to non-dominant forms of knowledge, such as traditional knowledge and cultural practices. The prominence of this type of recommendation is interesting, since it was not the most important intervention for any of the groups. An example of this type of recommendation is:

26. Recognise, value, support and document ancestral knowledge and modern innovations, traditions, pastoralists and peasants' local wisdom. Include participatory action research, the co-production of oral and written knowledge and cultural practices that addresses the true needs of communities, and particularly considers the needs of women, indigenous peoples, vulnerable groups, and youth. Ensure that innovations and the products of research remain in the public and collective domains according to Article 9 in the International Treaty on Plant Genetic Resources for Food and Agriculture (ITPGRFA).

Lastly, there are the 'regulated market' recommendations. In comparison to the amount of emphasis these received from different groups, market issues received relatively little attention in the final recommendations. An example of a formulation of a 'regulated market' recommendation is:

2. Improve and develop a policy and economic framework within agricultural policies that supports and allows farmers to implement agroecological practices and make the transition to agroecological farming systems in the Common Agricultural

Policy (CAP) and in other food and agricultural related policies and programs throughout the Region. Direct payments should be made depending upon protecting and enhancing biodiversity.

Discussion

By analyzing the interventions of panelists and participants and the final recommendations, a conflict clearly emerges between technical and socio-cultural characterizations of agroecology. The group that was most divided by this conflict was the group of scientists. This directly reflects the conflict amongst scholars of agroecology that was identified in the literature. Furthermore, we saw a sharp difference in the way the scientists and government representatives spoke about agroecology versus the way farmers and CSO-representatives did. The majority of the first two groups employed a technical discourse, while the latter unanimously spoke of agroecology as a transformative socio-cultural force.

It is noteworthy that the discourses of scientists and government representatives align so closely, as it seems to demonstrate the powerful position that scientists hold in informing policy-making. This position has been described by different authors with different names (for example: linear model of expertise (Beck 2010), knowledge transfer paradigm (Anderson and McLachlan 2015)). Inviting farmers and CSO-representatives to give their input to the policy-making process seems to challenge this traditional structure, and suggests a step towards co-creative governance. However, just being invited to speak does not immediately make an impact if one is not being heard. It could even damage future co-creation if people feel that it is not worth their time to participate.

The technical discourse advocates incremental change, usually focused on changing the methods of production on the field and farm level. Absent in this narrative are any of the challenges that producers face before and after production in the field, such as access to seeds and markets. This is problematic because by focusing solely on the farm itself, farming businesses are treated in isolation from the food system as a whole. This ignores the reality that outside forces like subsidies and market dynamics determine farmers' production choices to a great extent. If this is not recognized, and only technical solutions are pursued, scaling agroecology up and out will be difficult. Moreover, the effectiveness of such solutions will be minimal if they are not integrated into the reality of the food system (Gonzalez De Molina 2013). Leaving the relations between the stakeholders in the food system as they are and only changing the techniques of individual farmers cannot be called social innovation, in the way that it was defined by (Voorberg et al. 2015). On the other hand, accepting agroecology as transformational – as was recommended by civil society groups – indeed implies a shift in power relations between stakeholders. In order to make this happen, agroecology needs firm political commitment.

The place to demonstrate such commitment would have been in the final recommendations document of the symposium. However, the final recommendations were reasoned from a place that uneasily tries to reconcile the two perspectives on agroecology. Both the technical ('technological solutions are enough') and socio-cultural ('we must change the whole food system') discourses are used as points of departure. This is problematic because, as has been shown, these are not compatible positions. The former refuses to recognize normativity in food systems structures, while the latter expresses a very clear call for the acknowledgment of norms and values about distribution of power and resources. Presenting these opposing discourses as compatible within the recommendations creates a false sense of consensus, or: a 'consensus frame'. Mooney and Hunt (2009, 470) write about consensus frames and note that because 'meaning is nuanced by the discursive context in which it is situated, the same phrase can be used quite differently by various claims-makers'. Exactly this happened to the term 'agroecology' at the symposium. Agroecology became a word that means different things to different people, while the fundamental difference was not addressed. As a result, the final recommendations do not accurately reflect that the majority of the assembly was backing the socio-cultural discourse and that the technical discourse is overrepresented.

The final recommendations document does recognize that there is knowledge creation outside of science. Greatest emphasis is placed on 'research and education'-related recommendations which also cover including and using the knowledge of farmers and indigenous communities. After that, the most emphasized recommendations fall under the theme of 'changing public discourse', which aim at recognizing the knowledge of non-scientists.

So, is this co-creative governance? It is definitely important that these kinds of recommendations are taken up in an official FAO policy document. It might be the key step to a form of governance that includes the producers of food in the process. However, we would argue that the final product of this symposium does not go much further than paying lip service to the practitioners of agroecology. After all, the document gives least attention to those recommendations that would have the most impact: those that urge governments to regulate the market in favor of regenerative food systems.

Given that all groups recommended governments intervene in markets to make them more accessible for agroecological producers, one might have expected a firm stance in the recommendations calling for exactly this. Instead, such recommendations remain poorly defined. Thereby, the document contains verbal commitment to the idea of agroecology as a transdisciplinary and transformative field of action and research, but the structural changes that are needed to make this idea a reality are not adequately addressed.

Conclusion

At the UNFAO Regional Symposium on Agroecology for Sustainable Agriculture and Food Systems for Europe and Central Asia, co-creative governance was not completely achieved, despite having a range of stakeholder groups contributing to the process, with the explicit objective for policy-makers to learn from their knowledge and experiences. We conclude that the characterization of, and the recommendations for, agroecology that were presented by impacted stakeholders were not successful at effecting robust policy recommendations. The discourse of a group of scientists and government representatives ended up drowning out the voices of those who were invited to share their lived experiences.

In this chapter, we have presented agroecology as a key component of a regenerative food system that has been shaped by generations of practice by farmers and by the research of scientists. The case study demonstrates that in this policy processes the insights of farmers and other practitioners can have less weight than those of scientists. This is an obstacle to the translation of agroecological principles into policy. What we are less clear on is whether this is because the interventions of scientists are seen as more legitimate, or whether they are less 'radical' in that they conform more easily to the status quo and thus more easily translated into policy recommendations. We can however surmise that, in calling for more research and education, scientists reinforce not only the consensus frame, but provide policy-makers with the rationale for delaying more difficult policy decisions, for example related to regulating markets, in the name of needing more research. Further, we can conclude that when scientists present agroecology to policy-makers as a series of management techniques, it undermines the political struggle that needs to happen for social innovation of the food system to take place. It shifts focus away from the perspectives and knowledge of those actors who have played an integral role in shaping it, and makes it into something that conforms to rather than transforms the food system.

In the case study we saw that two opposing discourses emerged during the symposium and that there was no time or space to explore or expand on the conflicts, contradictions, and tensions between them. This in turn limited fruitful interaction and precluded a truly political discussion. Based on this, we conclude that conflicts that arise between competing discourses for sustainable food systems should not be avoided, but be given a central place in the policy process. As such, a regenerative food future requires policy processes that are not only capable of co-creating knowledge but also include mechanisms for critical reflection on whose voices are heard and translated into policy. Further, processes are needed to identify and facilitate the conflicts that emerge from competing visions of the pathways that exist to move towards this future.

Discussion questions

1. In this chapter we focused on regional-level and global-level policy processes. How might the conclusions differ if we had focused on a local or national level policy process?
2. We have argued that co-creation as part of a participatory policy process is fundamental for regenerative agriculture. What else needs to be considered in the organization of policy processes for regenerative agriculture?
3. Should participatory policy processes for regenerative agriculture ensure that everyone has a seat at the table? Should everyone have an equal voice at the table or should some people have more influence than others?
4. How should co-creation in policy-making be organized practically? Who should decide which stakeholders to invite and who should safeguard the co-creation process?
5. How can the exchange of knowledge of different stakeholder groups be facilitated better in policy processes?

Further reading

Altieri, M. A. (2014b) 'Agroecology: Principles and Strategies for Designing Sustainable Farming Systems', available at: www.agroeco.org/doc/new_docs/Agroeco_principles.pdf
Gliessman, S. (2015b) *Agroecology: The Ecology of Sustainable Food Systems*. Boca Raton, FL: CRC Press.
Patel, R. (2009b) 'Grassroots Voices: What Does Food Sovereignty Look Like?', *Journal of Peasant Studies*, 36(3): 663–706.

Works cited

Altieri, M. A. (2014a) *Agroecology: Principles and Strategies for Designing Sustainable Farming Systems*. www.agroeco.org/doc/new_docs/Agroeco_principles.pdf

Altieri, M. A. and Holt-Giménez, E. (2016) *Agroecology 'Lite:' Cooptation and Resistance in the Global North.* https://foodfirst.org/agroecology-lite-cooptation-and-resistance-in-the-global-north/ (Accessed: 23 October 2018).

Anderson, C. R. and McLachlan, S. M. (2015) 'Transformative Research as Knowledge Mobilization: Transmedia, Bridges, and Layers', *Action Research*, 14(3): 295–317. doi: 10.1177/1476750315616684.

Beck, S. (2010) 'Moving beyond the Linear Model of Expertise? IPCC and the Test of Adaptation', *Regional Environmental Change*, 11(2): 297–306. doi: 10.1007/s10113-010-0136-2.

Coolsaet, B. (2016) 'Towards an Agroecology of Knowledges: Recognition, Cognitive Justice and Farmers' Autonomy in France', *Journal of Rural Studies*, 47(A): 165–171. doi: 10.1016/j.jrurstud.2016.07.012.

Duncan, J. (2015) *Global Food Security Governance: Civil Society Engagement in the Reformed Committee on World Food Security.* London: Routledge.

FAO (2016) *Participant Handbook: Regional Symposium on Agroecology for SustainableAgriculture and Food Systems for Europe and Central Asia.* Budapest: FAO. www.fao.org/fileadmin/user_upload/reu/europe/documents/Events2016/ageco/BOOKLET.pdf

FAO (2018) *Catalysing Dialogue and Cooperation to Scale up Agroecology: Outcomes of the FAO Regional Seminars on Agroecology.* Rome: FAO. www.fao.org/3/i8992en/I8992EN.pdf

Gliessman, S. (2015a) *Agroecology: The Ecology of Sustainable Food Systems.* Boca Raton, FL: CRC Press.

Gonzalez De Molina, M. (2013) 'Agroecology and Politics. *How to Get Sustainability? About the Necessity for a Political Agroecology*', 37(1): 45–59 doi: 10.1080/10440046.2012.705810.

Jasanoff, S. and Wynne, B. (1998) 'Science and Decisionmaking', pp. 1–87, in Rayner, S. and Malone, E. L. (eds), *Human Choice and Climate Change.* Columbus, OH: Battelle Press.

Milgrom, J., Bruil, J. and Leeuwis, C. (2016) 'Co-creation in the Practice, Science and Movement of Agroecology', *Farming Matters*, 31(1): 6–8.

Mooney, P. H. and Hunt, S. A. (2009) 'Food Security: The Elaboration of Contested Claims to a Consensus Frame', *Rural Sociology*, 74(4):469–497. doi: 10.1526/003601109789864053.

Parmentier, S. (2014) *Scaling-up Agroecological Approaches: What, Why and How?* Brussels: Oxfam-Solidarite. www.oxfamsol.be/fr/scaling-agroecological-approaches-what-why-and-how

Patel, R. (2009a) 'Grassroots Voices: What does Food Sovereignty Look Like?', *Journal of Peasant Studies*, 36(3): 663–706.

Pimbert, M. (2015) 'Agroecology as an Alternative Vision to Conventional Development and Climate-Smart Agriculture', *Development*, 58(2–3): 286–298. doi: 10.1057/s41301-016-0013-5.

Rosset, P. M. and Altieri, M. A. (1997) 'Agroecology versus Input Substitution: A Fundamental Contradiction of Sustainable Agriculture', *Society and Natural Resources*, 10(3): 283–295. doi: 10.1080/08941929709381027.

Silici, L. (2014) *Agroecology, What it is and What it has to Offer.* London: IIED.

Schneider, F., Steiger, D., Ledermann, T., Fry, P. and Rist, S. (2012). 'No-Tillage Farming: Co-creation of Innovation through Network Building', *Land Degradation and Development*, 23(3): 242–255. doi: 10.1002/ldr.1073.

Swyngedouw, E. (2005) 'Governance Innovation and the Citizen : The Janus Face of Governance-beyond-the-State', *Urban Studies*, 42(11): 1991–2006.

Voorberg, W. H., Bekkers, V. J. J. M. and Tummers, L. G. (2015) 'A Systematic Review of Co-Creation and Co-Production: Embarking on the Social Innovation Journey', *Public Management Review.* 17(9): 1333–1357. doi: 10.1080/14719037.2014.930505.

Wakeford, T. et al. (2016) 'Strengthening People's Knowledge', *Farming Matters*, 32(1): 40–43.

Weingart, P. (1999) 'Scientific Expertise and Political Accountability: Paradoxes of Science in Politics', *Science and Public Policy*, 26(3): 151–161.

Wezel, A. et al. (2009) 'Agroecology as a Science, a Movement and a Practice. A Review', *Agronomy for Sustainable Development*, 29(4): 503–515. doi: 10.1051/agro/2009004.

8

JUSTICE

Paul V. Stock and Lukas Szrot

Introduction

In writing about "Justice" in the context of regenerative food systems, we begin with Goodman et al. (2012, 24): "The alternative food movement would be more effective ... if it worked with a more reflexive notion of justice, one based on a clearer understanding of the complexities of justice in its various and contradictory meanings." In essence, the food justice movement goes forward with various and diverse meanings of justice without critically interrogating what *justice* is. Food justice mimics the same tactics and aspirations as environmental justice, which cribbed them from the civil rights movement without visiting the ontological assumptions or the teleological goals. As Goodman et al. argue, the food justice movement offers a "pervasive but unexamined conception of justice" (2012, 24). To address this, we explore what justice might mean before offering some reflections on justice for regenerative agriculture.

Toward a thicker description of justice

Perhaps asking *what justice is* evokes a half-forgotten undergraduate philosophy course or raises the likelihood of being passed over in relative silence by *practical* readers. However, a concept of justice left unexamined risks unintended and unforeseen consequences. Though none of the ideas presented in this section are particularly novel, together they elicit a *thicker description* of justice by contextualizing environmental and food justice in an account of *the good* rooted in the human person.[1]

Typical accounts of justice begin with the egalitarian account delineated in Rawls' (Rawls 1971) *A Theory of Justice*. Put pithily, if self-interested individuals were to bake a new society from scratch, and each of them knew nothing about the capacities they would possess in said society, their recipe would include an account of justice that was actively and consistently focused on improving the lot of the least advantaged through strong social welfare and redistribution efforts.[2] Such a definition is helpful, if *thin*. A thicker description of justice requires, among other things, a more coherent account of human persons embedded in a complex social fabric.

Rawls' description can be thickened by drawing upon the pragmatist tradition that places that individual within a complex of socio-economic relations (see Dewey 1999). This move "anchors" liberal individualism in the possibility of political, economic, and cultural relations for the *common good* (pp. 36, 52, 60–78). Dewey's (1999) vision offers a glimpse of a human who is more than a self-interested rational actor,[3] but ultimately he hangs his hopes for justice on "enlightened" political-economic restructuring. Fraser (2003) corrects for this apparent *economism* by addressing the politics of recognition. In defining justice in terms of one's ability to fully participate in society, Fraser's vision of justice is flexible enough to be applied to matters of practical scope, and open-ended enough to address the *capacities* of human beings as stakeholders who can and should participate on parity with one another in its realization. However, Fraser's work remains thin in two important regards. The first source of this thinness relates to the horizons of human agency in a *broken* world (Smith 2011, 75–8). Specifically, tragedy inheres in the world, including *but not limited to* tragic trade-offs involved in moral and political decisions (Hook 1974); there is a *pinch* between the real and ideal which cannot be firmly and finally resolved, and humans must make choices based on incomplete information and ever-changing circumstances.[4]

It is not enough to note that even the most democratic efforts to make the most humane decisions toward furthering *justice* involve difficult and painful trade-offs. An account of justice which more fully takes *tragedy* into account requires a re-examination of how (social) reality is construed. We may not share definitions of a social problem, but a shared idea of the reality which undergirds efforts to seek justice must exist in the first place, and as such, must arise out of a deeper sense of the tragic. Drawing upon Smith:

> If we want to understand human persons and social life adequately, we will have to account not only for powerful capacities and conditions of personal thriving but also what, for lack of a better word, we might call brokenness … we humans characteristically suffer some kind of brokenness or disorder or alienation that prevents the realization of our completeness, perfection, integration, and wholeness. Every culture, philosophy, and religion has developed some account or another of what I am calling *brokenness* … Not to do so, I suggest, would be, literally, out of touch with reality – because something like brokenness is part of our reality.
>
> *(Smith 2011, 76–7)*

Bringing together both *weak* social constructivism[5] and this realist account of *brokenness*: tragedy, brokenness, the pinch are not mere consequences of human decision-making. Instead, brokenness is better understood as a *property* of a *real world* that exists *prior to* human beings' respective experiences of it. This raises the harrowing possibility that, "Moral and political 'problems' are intractable; they cannot be solved …. History is not encouraging about solutions to moral and political problems; yet it offers examples of a temporary and partial resolution" (Stivers 2008, 100). Secondly, Fraser (2003, 29–32), in her effort to "sociologize" justice, is keen to move away from conceptions of "the good" as too psychologically rooted. This move leaves the promise of group-level outcomes as a means of framing justice *sans* a fuller accounting of the personal agents responsible for, and beholden to, these outcomes.

A thicker account of justice, then, would begin with "the good," rooted in a detailed account of human capacities and purposiveness (see, for example, Bell 2018). While we, with the pragmatists, take for granted that more democracy is preferable to less, we seek to describe what kinds of humans would be more, or less, able to live in and contribute to a realization of justice. Surely human beings are, and ought to be, democratic stakeholders and rational actors, but we are more. It is here that accounts of justice enter real-life human bodies, minds, and efforts.

The blandest of insights is that the decision-making capacities of deliberative bodies run up against the physical limitations of their constituents. Such limitations are evident in real-life experiments in democratic deliberation, in which

> my biggest meeting … my longest meeting … I don't even remember what it was about at this point. I realized later that in some ways it was not democracy because it was the people who could stay awake the longest who became the winners.
>
> *(Agger 2009, 207)*

Persons eat, sleep, care for children, and work (to name just a few limits); real and inescapable physical strain is thereby placed on political commitments. This is especially true when those political commitments involve maintaining, cultivating, and rearing living and breathing animals, plants, and ecosystems. How then is justice conceived related to the environment and food?

Environmental justice

Environmental justice refers to the pursuit of just access and enjoyment of the biological necessities for living a life towards flourishing. As persons, people in any kind of community should be assured the ability to breathe clean air, drink clean water, grow food within soil that is unpolluted or harm-filled, and eat fish, plants, and animals without fear of poisoning.

Typical US narratives of the environmental justice movement/study of environmental injustice/environmental racism revolve around the emergent movements that helped catalyze the civil rights movement and the extremely white and bourgeois environmental movements (Taylor 1992). The majority of those narratives trace the emergence of the environmental justice movement to the Love Canal crisis (toxic-waste-dumps-turned-into-suburbia tactic) and the proposed toxic waste incinerator in Warren County, NC (let's-put-the-toxic-stuff-in-the-poorest-blackest-county-in-the-state tactic).[6] In both instances, citizens organized to protest the conditions imposed upon them to seek redress and justice – moving away from the toxic dump covered up with houses or the prevention of the siting of a toxic waste dump.

At the same time, national and international non-governmental organizations developed – like Greenpeace – to tackle ecosystem and global level conservation issues. Taylor (1992, 39) describes the irony of the "big" environmental groups bending over backwards to save whales and owls and significant landscapes and ecosystems:

> but we have yet to see an environmental group champion the cause of homeless-ness in humans or joblessness as issues on which it will spend vast resources. It is a strange paradox that a movement which exhorts the harmonious coexistence of people and nature, and worries about the continued survival of nature (particularly loss of habitat problems), somehow forgets about the survival of humans (especially those who have lost their "habitats" and "food sources").

What Taylor offers here is the paradox of environmental justice movements seeking justice for animals and ecosystems while at the same time ignoring some persons. While we know that no movement is really all-encompassing, it is an important lacuna to examine. We have multiple examples to challenge at least the chronological narrative of emergent environmentalism in line with concerns over inequity along race, ethnicity, class, and gender and sexuality. And in many ways, these challenges precede what we often term the environmental movement, much less the environmental justice movement. For example, the movement against the consistent dumping of mercury into the sea that caused numerous illnesses among the population in and around Minamata on the island of Kyushu, Japan began in the 1950s (Mishima 1992). Guha (2000) gives voice to the idea of the environmentalism of the poor that most clearly illustrates the interactions of race, class, and gender, that attend to the victims of environmental injustice.

Rob Nixon (2011) picked up this idea of the environmentalism of the poor, and clarified that often these injustices evolve over long periods of time, rendering the effects invisible in many ways rendering blame difficult or impossible to assign. The environmentalism of the poor, with a much greater emphasis on women's roles and lives, places people's livelihoods within a stronger interaction between the social and environmental dimensions. Nixon interrogates, as literature, the work of activist-writers in the testimonial tradition. These books offer testimonials or a witness (like in court proceedings to a crime). For example, Ken Saro-Wiwa's diverse writing on the damage of Shell and the Nigerian government, laying waste to people and places in the Niger Delta over decades offers a witness account to the slow violence of petro-governance. Slow violence describes "violence that occurs gradually and out of sight ... that is dispersed across time and space" (p. 2). Because slow violence is "spectacle deficient" (p. 47) witnesses, like Saro-Wiwa, are often the only way for others elsewhere to "see" and comprehend the damage that has been done.

We would like to flip the idea of witness for this idea of thinking about justice in relationship to regenerative agriculture. While the testimonial tradition does important work of documenting what is wrong, to think of witness as not the one who does the seeing of the unjust, but the one who is seen doing justice offers us pathways forward: in the case of this handbook, then who are the ones who are *doing* justice? Who offers *real* examples of regenerative agriculture? In regard to climate change, Kevin O'Brien (2017) documents examples of nonviolent activists or witnesses we can learn from. As O'Brien declares,

> The value of these witnesses is not that they offer answers to the present challenge but instead that they model a thoughtful moral response to other cases of structural violence. They offer guides – but not a plan – for a twenty-first century movement seeking climate justice.
>
> *(11)*

Kathleen Dean Moore (2016) offers that we need to "distinguish between morality of prohibition [you can't, don't] and a morality of affirmation [what you do to save, protect, grow something you value]" (p. 18). In this mode, witnesses of environmental justice, food justice, and regenerative agriculture become important models that we can learn from. This also helps pivot our research agendas (not completely) away from merely critiquing what is bad or negative related to the environment, food, and regenerative agriculture: "The morality of affirmation is a soaring invitation to affirm what you believe is good and just and beautiful and right, and to align your life to those values" (Moore 2016, 18). And we would add to the end the phrase, "for others to see." In this light, the recent emphases (recent, that is, in mainstream conversations) for diversity, equity, and inclusion become important places to identify witnesses – for too long ignored – for justice in environmental, food, and regenerative agriculture circles.

Food justice

As a starting point, Gottlieb and Joshi (writing in 2010) defined food justice as the achievement of "ensuring that the benefits and risks of where, what, and how food is grown and produced, transported and distributed, and accessed and eaten are shared fairly" (6). Another makes the stakes clearer by describing food justice as "the struggle against racism, exploitation, and oppression taking place with the food system that addresses inequality's root causes both within and beyond the food chain" (Hislop 2014, 9). Alkon and Guthman (2017) help trace food justice's similarities to the environmental justice movement, where it's both a movement and a burgeoning area of inter- and transdisciplinary scholarship.

In issues of food systems, justice retains a central place, often described of in terms of rights or security. Typical descriptions refer to food security as an overarching goal to secure access to the right number of calories for everyone (Carolan 2011). Much of the work on food justice focuses on the producers and workers of the food systems that includes both the push for increased wages for fast food workers, but most notably (and historically) a push to secure wage and safety protections for agricultural workers. The discrepancy of agricultural and food laborers being paid less, and remaining exempt from minimum wage laws, comes from the historical reality that farmworkers and food servers were jobs historically dominated by people of color.

Gottlieb and Joshi (2010, 223) describe that food justice works at "multiple layers" simultaneously. We see this in the emergent (but also absented, as Santos (2007) would argue) voices involved in food systems work around the world. On one hand, Slow Food emerged as a cultural preservationist movement from Italy that resonates with many as elitist and racist (Piatti 2015). On the other, Slow Food's goals mimic those of the food sovereignty movement of protecting local culture, markets, recipes, and communities (La Via Campesina 2005). The Landless Peasants of Brazil (MST) and the wider networks of food sovereignty activism around the world (Wald 2015) work under the premise that local agitation connected globally can challenge the international food systems connected to Western and global marketplaces sold under the banner of Free Trade. Many of these groups try to live out the worlds and systems they would like to see in place, something others have called a prefigurative politics of food or food utopias (Stock 2015). Internationally, the shift is toward either sovereignty or re-peasantization. Both push for a radical departure from top-down development programs for international food growing and distribution (Nelson and Stock 2018).

In many ways, food justice and the related movements aim to address the slow violence inherent in the food system (Cock 2013; McConnell 2015). Cock (2013, 10) argues, "Food insecurity involves a form of 'slow violence' because its damaging effects on the human body are not only relatively invisible, but it means an erosion of human capacities and potentials that occurs gradually over time." Both food sovereignty and groups explicitly agitating for food justice aim to counter the extreme concentration in the global food and agricultural system (Howard 2016). In an interesting take on food justice, Kerssen and Brent (2017, 308) articulate the importance of land when they write, "It is difficult to imagine transformative change in the food system without government support … for redistributive and restorative land reform". While an oft-discussed topic in the rest of the world, land reform is not often at the top of the United States' agenda, nor that of many other accelerated economies of the world.[7] But just as food sovereignty draws from the experiences and injustices in the Global South so too does the experience and injustice of land reform stem from the Global South again like the Landless Peasant Movement (MST) in Brazil (for example, see *Soil, Struggle and Justice* (2014): www.youtube.com/watch?v=eq3KJMLH3Bk).

Ivan Illich (1973, 99ff.) argues in *Tools for Conviviality* that one tool to establish a more just (i.e. convivial) society will be the recovery of legal procedures. As Wiebe and Wipf (2011, 5) point out, "sustainable food production and genuine food security are a function of community-based control over the food system". In the realm of food production we have examples of local cities changing policy to support pollinators and household food production, as well as lawyers tackling the complex web of policies involved in supporting regenerative agriculture (Head 2017). Above all, though, solutions and the hope of solutions will be rooted not in an abstract hope that humanity survives, but in specific concern for actual persons in actual places.

Personalism

As a philosophical theory, personalism takes as the starting point persons, not individuals, as actors with a telos, a goal or purpose to flourish. For Christian Smith (2010),

> Personalism thus rejects the human image constructed and promoted by individualistic liberalism, libertarianism, social contractarianism, rational choice theory, and exchange theory. Persons do not exist first as self-contained selves who subsequently engage and exchange with other selves in order to secure some outcome or consume some benefit. Persons, instead, are originally, constitutively, and inescapably social, interactive, and communicative in origin and being. Sociality helps constitute the essential character of personhood. For starters, the human bodies from which personhood emergently arises into ontological being are not only produced by but essentially are the commingling of two preexistent human bodies through the intimate meeting of personal relation.
>
> *(Smith 2010, 67–8)*

Personalism relies on presuming that all persons have dignity. Any violence that undermines that dignity, whether interpersonal or governmental, thus violates that dignity.

> Dignity recognizes and describes persons as innately precious and inviolable. Because of this dignity, human persons are naturally worthy of certain kinds of moral treatment by themselves and in their mutual relations – in particular, of respect, justice, and love. The ontology of personhood makes it morally true that persons are creatures that are worthy of being treated with respect, justice, and love. In the nature of things, persons should give other persons the recognition and honor of respect. Persons ought to provide other persons what they rightly deserve in justice. And persons should care for the genuine well-being of other persons in love.
>
> *(Smith 2015, 55)*

As Levinas (1985, 90) cautions then, "Justice, exercised through institutions, which are inevitable, must always be held in check by the initial interpersonal relationship." For our purposes here, personalism helps us recognize regenerative agriculture as a way for persons to coordinate and create systems of agriculture and food production with an aim towards human flourishing.

Personalism for regenerative agriculture: introducing Bernard Charbonneau's political ecology

Bernard Charbonneau's unique contribution via personalism and an emphasis on freedom helps us rethink justice especially in the context of food production with an emphasis on radically local (up to regional) solutions. As a founding political ecologist and just recently translated into English from French, Charbonneau, first published in 1980, pre-dates Klein's call that climate change changes everything by "identifying the global character of the threats to nature and human freedom, and in insisting on radical bottom-up alternatives" (Stephens 2018, xv, on Charbonneau). Charbonneau (2018) outlines a dialogical relationship when he argues,

> To recognize nature is to accept the whole of it, warts and all ... that is given over to absurdity, necessity and death: practicing an *amor fati* that is the opposite of resignation to fate; whereas fleeing it by embellishing it amounts to a denial of it. The love of Nature with a capital N, identified with perfect Totality, is not love.
>
> *(58)*

Just as we often see a "love" of nature turned into protection and tourism (pp. 59–60), do those forces also become destructive, thus undermining the relationship between nature and freedom. It is only in recognizing the power of nature as the real, actual, physical home and life-giving place of being human can we pursue actual freedom from our knowledge of nature, from the state, and from institutions that seek to undermine that freedom. "Freedom is but a sham if it fails to take into account the necessities [clean air, clean water, access to land for food] ruling any reality" (Charbonneau 2018, 80). This absolute recognition of the reality that political lives are premised on reinforces the value of thinking about persons living on a planet. Charbonneau's great intellectual friend Jacques Ellul (1964) would characterize those forces seeking to undermine freedom (and by extension the health of the planet) as *technique*. Not just capitalism, but the emergence in the twentieth century of all sorts of physical and psychological systems in search of control that Ellul describes as *technique* undermine human freedom and contribute to the destruction of the planet. In agriculture, both the scale and intensification of fossil fuel-based methods of production demonstrate technique (for example see Scott 1998, especially chapter 8). Both Ellul and Charbonneau conclude that an emphasis on specific relationships with specific persons and specific places (for example, both demonstrated and organized against a waterfront development near their home) as the antidote to the totalitarian (from both Left and Right, Charbonneau 2018, 92) impulse of modernity. The ecological personalism that animates most of their work has little expression in English environmental and agricultural thought. Truly regenerative agricultural solutions in the future will require social and cultural transformations that put care of others and the planet radically at the center of concern and action. We offer the Catholic Worker movement's farms as a witness to the kinds of work necessary to enjoy a truly regenerative food production systems that privileges justice.

The Catholic Worker movement's farms as examples of personalist justice in agriculture

The Catholic Worker movement originated during the Great Depression in New York City as a newspaper dedicated to social justice issues inflected with Catholic doctrine. Dorothy Day had been a socialist-leaning journalist prior to the founding of *The Catholic Worker* in 1933. While oriented toward issues of homelessness, unions, and other important issues, Dorothy was a late-comer to Catholicism, converting in the wake of the birth of her daughter in the late 1920s. A meeting with Peter Maurin, an unconventional and itinerant theologian, shaped not only the Catholic Left, but social movements of all kinds since their meeting in the early 1930s. Peter, born a peasant, spent time in Paris involved in vibrant discussions of Catholic social justice and personalism. Peter brought with him a very French and European interpretation of social justice teaching that did not resonate as much within US Catholics or politics. The combination of Peter's French personalism and Dorothy's pragmatism created a theory and model of social change that defies typical categorization for social movement theorists and activists alike.

After the initial publication of the newspaper documenting recent strikes and crises, the newspaper offices soon became a place to offer cups of coffee, space to relax, clothing, and room on the floor for sleeping. Soon other places were rented, eventually becoming the basis for the hospitality house model of the Catholic Worker movement (Murray 1990). There's never been a constitution or a board of directors, and the movement has tried to retain a horizontal and decentralized organizational structure.

From the beginning, Dorothy Day and Peter Maurin outlined a three-point plan with the houses of hospitality as a central feature. Second was the publication of *The Catholic Worker*. It has been in continuous circulation since May 1, 1933. In addition to the newspaper from the New York City houses – where Dorothy Day made her home (with voluminous travel as both speaker and tourist and activist) – Day, Maurin, and subsequent editors encouraged each and every house to publish their own. This has included newspapers, newsletters, email newsletters, memoirs, letters between houses (often published in the publications themselves) all in pursuit of an open dialogue in pursuit of social justice, but has also subsequently formed much of the backbone of a theory in action of the Catholic Worker. The third point of the Peter's vision for society was the pursuit of what we would now call self-sufficiency with the establishment of communal farms.

The Catholic Worker farms

The Catholic Worker movement established their first farm in 1936 in Easton, Pennsylvania.[8] While the venture ended around 1945, the hallmarks of many later Catholic Worker farms were established at this first Catholic Worker farm. These included support for those physically and mentally challenged, a retreat for those from the city, crafts and skill-based workshops, some growing of food, and a place for activism. While the farm never got close to the Rule that dictated Benedictine monks' lives in terms of the balance of prayer, work, and sleep that Peter Maurin pushed for, the farm became a place to learn how to grow and preserve food, provide respite for those in need of rest, opportunity for intergenerational sharing of stories, home bases for other kinds of activism and resistance, and a general meeting place in the community (Stock 2014). Many of those ideas have played out at the roving farm affiliated with the Catholic Worker houses in New York City. Peter Maurin Farm, 22-acres on Staten Island, quickly became one of the most successful farm ventures following its establishment in 1950. As Father Duffy, a Catholic Worker-aligned priest, wrote ("Food, Farming, and Freedom", *CW*, Oct. 1952, 3):

> The object of the project is to build up healthy human beings on healthy soil and with healthy food and to make as many of them as possible, free men and free women who can live as God intended them, and as they desire to live in a world of peace and reasonable abundance on their way to eternity.

There, in plain language, is the Catholic Worker's personalist stance that connects the real gifts of the planet with the pursuit of human freedom and thus a regenerative agriculture for both the soil and the soul. Even the *Catholic Worker*'s review of the USDA's annual yearbook focused on soil made sure to point out that the care of the soil was a "moral issue." ("Book Reviews", *CW* 1958: January). The closure of Peter Maurin Farm in 1964 scattered the Catholic Worker's farm project further up the Hudson to a derelict mansion in need of significant repair. That, combined with the late 1960s social upheaval, meant that not much farming happened between leaving Staten Island and the establishment of a second Peter Maurin Farm in Marlboro, NY, in 1979. That farm still operates today and serves as both a rural hospice retreat as well as a garden producing vegetables for the New York City area houses' soup kitchens and other hospitality outlets.

Dorothy Day, in a witnessing of personalism (often referred to as nonviolent anarchism in the newspaper and by its adherents), made environmental issues paramount to her pacifism and activism even if she did not write about them as such. Two visits help illustrate this. First, Dorothy visited Koinonia farm in Georgia, where the founders emphasized an interracial agricultural commune in 1957 and wrote about her near death by gunshot and the developing relationship between Koinonia and the Catholic Worker in the late 1950s (featured in the *Catholic Worker* newspaper between September 1956 through May 1957). The second instance comes a few years later, during a strike in 1973, when Dorothy Day visited California in solidarity with the American Farmworkers Union. In the iconic photograph, Day is framed by two sheriff's deputies (https://exhibits.stanford.edu/fitch/catalog/gp115vj7135). Around 75 years old at the time, Day was doing one of her last bits of travel, something that she was known for, and she spent it on a picket line supporting union workers in their pursuit of justice. While not having the academic language of food justice at the time, clearly the American Farmworkers, in solidarity with allies, were working for safe food and safe working conditions while also agitating for a place at the wider table of justice. The Catholic Worker movement and their farms, since the 1930s, have advocated for similar things that continue to this day.

One final example is the congregation of Catholic Worker farms in the bioregion called the Driftless region of the central United States (the region that comprises SE Minnesota, SW Wisconsin, and NE Iowa). These four farms – New Hope (outside Dubuque), IA, Lake City (MN), Ananthoth Community Farm (Luck, WI), and St. Isidore (Cuba City, WI) – share interests in growing food, volunteerism, voluntary poverty, race-related activism, justice, and sustainability in its largest sense. Specifically, Catholic Workers affiliated with these farms have protested against frack sand mining along the Mississippi River,[9] committed civil disobedience against pipelines,[10] hosted conferences on working towards justice with Indigenous groups and other minority groups, volunteered in local communities, and hosted retreats. All of these activists demonstrate a witness and willingness to work towards justice often centered around food and land issues. As The Greenhorns video (https://vimeo.com/204248108) illustrates, there is also an intergenerational component at the St. Isidore Farm. These contemporary examples of personalist regenerative agriculture offer witness to what is possible by living in and within community.

Conclusions

The CW embody both the testimonial witnessing that Nixon and others document as important, but also the physical and embodied witness of life lived in pursuit of justice to be seen by others. To live in a morally affirmative way, Kathleen Dean Moore (2016) asserts, is to live a life able to be seen by others that demonstrates what is right specifically in regards to our planet. To be morally affirmative means to live out what one cares about; it does not mean pointing fingers (this is moralizing) or saying the world is doomed (this is cynicism). The Catholic Worker farms act as witnesses of justice in relationship to a regenerative food systems through their actions of growing food, confronting racial inequity, and power imbalances in their local communities, as well as by offering hospitality to everyone. In many ways, the CW illustrate Goodman et al.'s (2012) call for reflexive justice.

> Reflexive justice brings activism back to the imperfect politics of process and away from the perfect and privileged politics of standard setting. Rather than creating an alternative economy for the homogenous few, reflexive localism could work across difference, and thereby make a difference, for everyone.
>
> *(Goodman et al. 2012, 32)*

Thus, it is *persons* – not stakeholders, rational actors, deliberative bodies, demographic categories, or identity groups – who directly bear the brunt of injustices, or share in the fruits of a more just and sustainable food system. Persons share numerous *capacities* in which justice can be rooted – Smith (2011, 42–55) lists 30 such capacities while also noting that "there are no doubt others that matter" (p. 43). Two specific *normative principles* are highly relevant here – *gregariousness* and *human dignity*.

Regarding the first, the primary distinction between the "individual" and the "person" lies in the conception of human beings as *relational* parts of an *emergent* social whole (Smith 2011, 30–1). The social cosmos arises out of the collective relationships of the persons within it, taking on new properties. As societies emerge out of relationships between persons, persons emerge out of biological processes, which emerge out of chemical processes, which emerge out of physical processes. The end result of this chain of processes and emergent properties is that *gregariousness* – human sociality – inheres in human personhood.[11] Persons are not infinitely malleable blobs of clay molded by faceless "structural" forces. We are "centers with purpose" in Smith's terms (2011, 78–81). The social world in which persons interact is formed by the relationships between these centers with purpose, even as it comes to take on new properties.

An account of human dignity follows from this conception: as centers with purpose, persons ought not be treated as things; persons ought not be treated as means, but only as ends unto themselves. Following from this conception of persons: persons have natural rights which must be respected; persons have the right to be free to develop their talents, to flourish, and to be able to help others to do the same; and perhaps most importantly, the social world exists to develop the personhood of all its members (Smith 2011, 436–7).

Thus, an ethic rooted in duty and dignity of persons, and contextualized in a real and "broken" world, offers a *thicker* account of personhood, connecting the person to the social, and the capacities of the former to the possibilities that inhere in the latter. The alternative – justice formulated at the level of group claims, stakes, and outcomes *sans* an account of persons – risks shipwreck on the tumultuous seas of a broken world. Justice framed in implicitly consequentialist terms risks turning a quest for egalitarian social relations into an insoluble in-group/out-group power struggle (Stivers 2008, 78–85). Justice, though an ongoing struggle, is not merely a struggle against unjust structures or policies or social relations. Justice is a struggle to reshape – with the agency and limitations of human persons, however fallibly and temporarily – reality itself, along lines more conducive to the flourishing of human persons.

And in this sense, a personalist-based regenerative agriculture belies categorization of Right and Left. As Charbonneau (2018) argues,

> While it recruits its militants in a leftist milieu that dreams of a perfect society, on the ground the ecological movement defends what is: those trees, those villages, this culture. It is at once revolutionary, because it demands of society a radical change of direction, and conservative: at every moment, we find it in the paradox.
>
> *(149)*

In this sense the Catholic Worker movement's farms offer a witness uncharacterizable in today's politics and is potentially best seen in the light of what is not-yet-become or as a prefigurative politics. As Michael Harrington argued in the *Catholic Worker* newspaper in 1951 (July-August, 3), "[a] green revolution, of a non-violent movement toward a humanitarian society based on production for human dignity" was necessary. As a living witness of how we can live in community and caring for one another, particularly those most damaged or broken by this broken world, working to dismantle patriarchy and racism through the land and community, the Catholic Workers and their allies on farms and in communities across the United States and the world offer living, breathing, real lives in pursuit of justice most often through people's stomachs whether with shared cups of coffee, warm, nutritious soup, meals conjured from the backyard garden, the Catholic Worker farm, or recovered from the grocery store dumpster.

O'Brien, reflecting mainly on climate change, but relevant here, asks: "So what can we do? We can work against the violence of climate change. We can work to become witnesses, leaving a legacy of resistance from which future generations can learn" (2011, 204–5). This is the emergent and prefigurative hope of regenerative agriculture. Catholic Workers on farms offer one form of witness. Those doing regenerative agriculture, especially those surrounded by those NOT doing regenerative agriculture, serve as witnesses of justice as well that we are all looking to learn from.

Discussion questions

1. What other stories of regenerative agriculture witnesses should we be sharing with one another?
2. How do urban and rural divisions act as barriers to discussing regenerative agriculture in urban-based settings?
3. How might assumptions about what human beings "really are" animate, and limit, discussions of food justice?
4. What can the kinds of "real-world" exemplars of justice, these witnesses, presented in this chapter offer in terms of how we understand, and behave toward, both the earth, and one another?
5. Defining justice can seem paradoxical. How can one work toward justice without first having a clear idea of what justice is? On the other hand, without having concrete examples of what justice looks like, how can one define, theorize, and/or write about justice?

Notes

1 Geertz 2001. See also Ryle. 1949. Since we use the terms *thick* and *thin* in a specific manner which is attributable to the work of the anthropologist Clifford Geertz or the philosopher Gilbert Ryle:, *thick description* is an attempt to systematically contextualize *behavior*. Justice, then, is an effort toward changing human behaviors at the social level. As such, we attempt to contextualize justice in currents of pragmatism, critical realism, and personalism.

2 Rawls 1971. Rawls' work is more complex and nuanced than the description above allows for. A helpful contemporary summary (and critique) of Rawls can be found in Rodgers 2011, 182–5.

3 Rawls' theory of justice assumes a conception of the human as "liberal individual" (Rodgers 2011, 183–4). A "thicker" conception of the human person *than that provided by liberal individualism* as related a "thicker" social world *than that delimited by the nature of economic relations* underpins the vision of food justice laid out in this chapter.

4 Glaude 2007, 20–30; Hook 1974, 5–13; this view is ostensibly more compatible with the pragmatism of William James than that of John Dewey, as pointed out by Hilary Putnam (1992). The term *pinch* comes from James' formulations of pragmatist ethics, and will be used further in this section. Glaude disputes this distinction between James and Dewey, as well as Putnam's framing of the issue – I set aside these complexities because Putnam points to a central tension between the "good" and the "right" which sets the stage for the remainder of the argument.

5 For a critical realist account of social constructivism, see Smith 2011, 122. For a pragmatist effort to harmonize *ontological* realism and *conceptual relativism*, see Putnam. 1987.

6 In an unexplored potential irony, Warren County was also home to an institutional attempt at creating a racially integrated community from the ground up: Soul City, North Carolina (Strain 2004). The attempts at building Soul City (mostly from the 1970s through the 1990s) bridge the smoldering Civil Rights movement in the wake of the assassinations of King, Malcolm X, and Bobby Kennedy and the emergent environmental justice movement. In many ways, strains of the Civil Rights movement were privileging environmental justice issues all along, particularly in the work of the American Farmworkers Union tackling workplace and food safety issues, in which Dolores Huerta also forged important relationships with the women's movement and the Black Panther Party, whose school lunch program continues to be run by the USDA (Minkoff-Zern 2017). Such environmental issues such as safety from toxic chemicals and the right to healthy food, while central to the movements at the time, tend to get overshadowed in the mythologization of movement founders and celebrities.

7 Joe Brewer's work on Native American *re*possession is an important argument in this respect (see for example Brewer and Dennis 2019).

8 This section relies heavily on Stock's work on the Catholic Worker movement with special attention on the Catholic Worker farms (Stock 2009, 2010, 2012, 2014, 2016).

9 Hydraulic fracturing of oil or gas utilizes a process whereby chemicals, water, and fine grain sand are pumped under high pressure into the rock formations containing the oil or gas to fracture that same rock and thus release the fossil fuels. The kind of sand used in the process more often than not comes from quarries dug nearby rivers.

10 https://www.uscatholic.org/articles/201909/catholic-worker-devotes-her-energy-environmental-activism-31817

11 Kathleen Dean Moore (2016, 35) puts it this way: "If there is a fact true of human beings – today, as always – I would suggest it is this: that we want to love and be loved, delight and be delighted, give and be given, in the back-and-forth relatedness that earns us a meaningful place in the pantheon of all being."

Further reading

Alkon, Alison Hope, and Julie Guthman, eds. 2017. *The New Food Activism: Opposition, Cooperation, and Collective Action*. Oakland, CA: University of California Press.

Anderson, Molly. "Charting Growth to Good Food." www.researchgate.net/publication/264719667_CHARTING_GROWTH_TO_GOOD_FOOD_DEVELOPING_INDICATORS_AND_MEASURES_OF_GOOD_FOOD_-_FINAL_PROJECT_REPORT.

Charbonneau, Bernard. 2018. *The Green Light: A Self-Criticism of the Ecological Movement*. Translated by Christian Roy. London: Bloomsbury.

Gottlieb, Robert, and Anupama Joshi. 2010. *Food Justice*. Cambridge, MA: MIT Press.

Smith, Christian. 2011. *What is a Person?* Chicago, IL: University of Chicago Press.

References

Agger, Ben. 2009. *The Sixties at 40: Leaders and Activists Remember and Look Forward*. Boulder, CO: Paradigm Publishers.

Alkon, Alison Hope, and Julie Guthman, eds. 2017. *The New Food Activism: Opposition, Cooperation, and Collective Action*. Oakland, CA: University of California Press.

Bell, Michael Mayerfeld. 2018. *City of the Good: Nature, Religion, and the Ancient Search for What is Right*. Princeton, NJ: Princeton University Press.

Brewer, Joseph P., and Mary Kate Dennis. 2019. "A Land Neither Here Nor There: Voices from the Margins and the Untenuring of Lakota Lands." *GeoJournal*, 84: 571–591.

Carolan, Michael. 2011. *The Real Cost of Cheap Food*. London: Routledge.

Charbonneau, Bernard. 2018. *The Green Light: A Self-Criticism of the Ecological Movement*. Translated by Christian Roy. London: Bloomsbury.

Cock, Jacklyn. 2013. "Addressing the 'Slow Violence' of Food Insecurity: The Case of Gauteng, South Africa." In *The Food Crisis: Implications for Labor*, edited by Christoph Scherrer and Debdulal Saha, 2: 9–28. Labor and Globalization. München: Rainer Hampp Verlag.

Dewey, John. 1999. *Individualism, Old and New*. Amherst, MA: Prometheus Books.

Ellul, Jacques. 1964. *The Technological Society*. New York: Vintage.

Fraser, Nancy. 2003. "Social Justice in the Age of Identity Politics: Redistribution, Recognition, and Participation." In *Redistribution or Recognition? A Political-Philosophical Exchange*, edited by Nancy Fraser and Axel Honneth, 7–109. New York: Verso.

Geertz, Richard. 2001. "Thick Description: Toward an Interpretive Theory of Culture." In *Contemporary Field Research: Perspectives and Formulations*, edited by Robert Emerson, 2nd ed., 55–75. Long Grove, IL: Waveland Press.

Glaude, Eddie S. 2007. *In a Shade of Blue: Pragmatism and the Politics of Black America*. Chicago, IL: Chicago University Press.

Goodman, David, E. Melanie DuPuis, and Michael K. Goodman. 2012. "Coming Home to Eat? Reflexive Localism and Just Food." In *Alternative Food Networks: Knowledge, Practice, and Politics*, 11–32. Abingdon, Oxon: Routledge.

Gottlieb, Robert, and Anupama Joshi. 2010. *Food Justice*. Cambridge, MA: MIT Press.

Guha, Ramachandra. 2000. *Environmentalism: A Global History*. New York: Longman.

Head, John W. 2017. *International Law and Agroecological Husbandry: Building Legal Foundations for a New Agriculture*. Earthscan Food and Agriculture Series. Abingdon, Oxon; New York: Routledge.

Hislop, Rasheed Salaam. 2014. *Reaping Equity: A Survey of Food Justice Organizations in the USA*. Davis, CA: University of California.

Hook, Sidney. 1974. *Pragmatism and the Tragic Sense of Life*. New York: Basic Books.

Howard, Philip H. 2016. *Concentration and Power in the Food System: Who Controls What we Eat?* 3. London: Bloomsbury Publishing.

Illich, Ivan. 1973. *Tools for Conviviality*. New York: Perennial.

James, William. 1891. "The Moral Philosopher and the Moral Life." *International Journal of Ethics*, 1(3): 330–354.

Kerssen, Tanya M., and Zoe W. Brent. 2017. "Grounding the U.S. Food Movement." In *The New Food Activism: Opposition, Cooperation, and Collective Action*, edited by Alison Hope Alkon and Julie Guthman, 284–315. Oakland, CA: University of California Press.

La Via Campesina. 2005. "Seven Principles to Achieve Food Sovereignty." www.nfu.ca/sites/www.nfu. ca/files/Principles%20of%20Food%20Sovereignty.pdf.

Levinas, Emmanuel. 1985. *Ethics and Infinity: Conversations with Philippe Nemo, Trans*. Pittsbugh, PA: Duquesne University Press.

McConnell, Jonathan. 2015. "Slow Violence and the Eschatological Crisis of Agriculture". In *The Peace of Nature and the Nature of Peace: Essays on Ecology, Nature, Nonviolence, and Peace*, edited by Andrew Fiala, 101–8. Leiden: Brill.

Minkoff-Zern, Laura-Anne. 2017. "Farmworker-Led Food Movements Then and Now." In *The New Food Activism: Opposition, Cooperation, and Collective Action*, edited by Alison Alkon and Julie Guthman, 157–78. Oakland, CA: University of California Press.

Mishima, Akio. 1992. *Bitter Sea: The Human Cost of Minamata Disease*. Tokyo: Kosei Publishing Co.

Moore, Kathleen Dean. 2016. *Great Tide Rising: Towards Clarity and Moral Courage in a Time of Planetary Change*. Berkeley, CA: Counterpoint.

Murray, Harry. 1990. *Do Not Neglect Hospitality: The Catholic Worker and the Homeless*. Philadelphia, PA: Temple University Press.

Nelson, Jon, and Paul Stock. 2018. "Repeasantisation in the United States." *Sociologia Ruralis*, 58 (1): 83–103. https://doi.org/10.1111/soru.12132.

Nixon, Rob. 2011. *Slow Violence and the Environmentalism of the Poor*. Cambridge, MA: Harvard University Press.

O'Brien, Kevin J. 2017. *The Violence of Climate Change: Lessons of Resistance from Nonviolent Activists*. Washington, DC: Georgetown University Press.

Piatti, Cinzia. 2015. "Slow Food Presidia: The Nostalgic and the Utopian." In *Food Utopias*, edited by Paul Stock, Michael Carolan, and Christopher Rosin, 88–106. London: Routledge.

Putnam, Hilary. 1987. *The Many Faces of Realism*. Chicago, IL: Open Court.

Putnam, Hilary. 1992. *Renewing Philosophy*. Cambridge, MA: Harvard University Press.

Rawls, John. 1971. *A Theory of Justice*. Cambridge, MA: Harvard University Press.

Rodgers, Daniel T. 2011. *Age of Fracture*. Cambridge, MA: Belknap University Press of Harvard University Press.

Ryle, Gilbert. 1949. *The Concept of Mind*. Chicago, IL: University of Chicago Press.

Santos, Boaventura de Sousa. 2007. "The World Social Forum: Toward a Counter-Hegemonic Globalisation." In *The World Social Forum: Challenging Empires*, edited by Peter Wateman and Jen Sai, 235–245. Montreal, Canada: Black Rose. Editors Peter Waterman and Jai Sen.

Scott, James C. 1998. *Seeing Like a State: How Certain Schemes to Improve the Human Condition Have Failed*. New Haven, CT: Yale University Press.

Smith, Christian. 2010. *What Is a Person?: Rethinking Humanity, Social Life, and the Moral Good from the Person Up*. University of Chicago Press.

Smith, Christian. 2011. *What Is a Person?* Chicago, IL: University of Chicago Press.

Smith, Christian. 2015. *To Flourish or Destruct: A Personalist Theory of Human Goods, Motivations, Failure, and Evil*. University of Chicago Press.

Stephens, Piers H.G. 2018. "Forward" to Bernard Charbonneau, *The Green Light: A Self-Criticism of the Ecological Movement*. Translated by Christian Roy. London: Bloomsbury.

Stivers, Richard. 2008. *The Illusion of Freedom and Equality*. Albany, NY: State University of New York Press.

Stock, Paul V. 2009. *The Original Green Revolution: The Catholic Worker Farms and Environmental Morality*. Fort Collins, CO: Colorado State University.

Stock, Paul V. 2010. "Catholic Worker Economics: Subsistence and Resistance Strategies of Householding." *Bulletin for the Study of Religion* 40 (1): 16–25.

Stock, Paul V. 2012. "Consensus Social Movements and the Catholic Worker." *Politics and Religion* 5 (1): 83–102.

Stock, Paul V. 2014. "The Perennial Nature of the Catholic Worker Farms: A Reconsideration of Failure." *Rural Sociology* 79 (2): 143–73. https://doi.org/10.1111/ruso.12029.

Stock, Paul V. 2015. "Contradictions in Hope and Care." In *Food Utopias: Reimagining Citizenship, Ethics and Community*, edited by Paul Stock, Michael Carolan, and Christopher Rosin, 171–94. Abingsdon, Oxon: Routledge/Earthscan.

Strain, Christopher. 2004. "Soul City, North Carolina: Black Power, Utopia, and the African American Dream." *Journal of African American History* 89 (1): 57–74.

Taylor, Dorceta. 1992. "Can the Environmental Movement Attract and Maintain the Support of Minorities." In *Race and the Incidence of Environmental Hazards: A Time for Discourse*, edited by Paul Mohai and Bunyan Bryant, 38: 28–54. Boulder, CO: Westview Press.

Wald, Nave. 2015. "Towards Utopias of Prefigurative Politics and Food Sovereignty: Experiences of Politicised Peasant Food Production." In *Food Utopias: Reconsidering Citizenship, Ethics and Community*, edited by Paul Stock, Michael Carolan, and Christopher Rosin, 107–25. Abingdon, Oxon: Routledge/Earthscan.

Wiebe, Nettie, and Kevin Wipf. 2011. "Nurturing Food Sovereignty in Canada." In *Food Sovereignty in Canada: Creating Just and Sustainable Food Systems*, edited by Hannah Wittman, Annette Aurelie Desmarais, and Nettie Wiebe, 1–12. Winnipeg: Fernwood Pub.

9

LABOR REGENERATION

Work, technology, and resistance

Joshua Sbicca

Introduction

In the techno-utopian future of artificial intelligence, robots will be flipping burgers. Goodbye low-wage greasy jobs. Hello sparkling sanitized pushbutton work. Popular culture has long had a conflicted fascination with fast-food. On one hand, fast-food encapsulates the height of industrial rationality. Uniform ingredients and recipes replicated across space. Chain X in location one offers the same options in location two, ad infinitum. On the other hand, fast-food represents the mundanity of labor stripped of creativity. Workers perform rote tasks to provide a predictable product with little remuneration. Indeed, these jobs were long imagined as part-time work carried out by high schoolers, jobs better left to people climbing their way up the occupational ladder. Or better yet, jobs that could be eliminated by machines.

An era-defining representation of these issues plays out in *Back to the Future* and *Back to the Future 2*. Marty McFly's brother, Dave, works at Burger King, a symbol for the popularity of fast-food and the demise of independent diners like Lou's Café. Lou's Café had formerly been a hangout spot for teenagers back in 1955, but by 1985 it was Lou's Aerobic Fitness Center. Corporate power colonizes retail landscapes. However, predicting the hipster revival of previous eras of cool, when Marty McFly travels to the future in 2015, this building is nostalgically reanimated as the Café 80's. There are no workers, only hanging television screens, floating electronic celebrity heads, ready to take your order. Modeled on Max Headroom, a fictional artificial intelligence character from the 1980s, Michael Jackson, Ronald Reagan, and Ayatollah Khomeini jostle with each other to sell customers food. Ronald Reagan quickly engages Marty McFly as he looks around, saying, "Welcome to the Café 80's where it's always morning in America even in the afternoon. Our special today is mesquite grilled sushi," as Ayatollah Khomeini, with flames burning in the background commands repeatedly, "You must have the special!" Interestingly, industrial food remains, in the simulacra of Pepsi product placement; Marty McFly interrupts, "Stop! All I want is a Pepsi." An automatic pop-up machine then immediately serves up that sugary fizzy cola.

The vision of this film is striking. Many fast-food chains, malls, and airports now have electronic kiosks with screens where customers can place their orders. The ennui of isolated interaction with digital representations of food without the need to talk to a human before steaming dumplings arrive on your table separates the eater from work. Companies are adopting such labor-saving technology to reduce labor costs and maximize profits. But what if we were to think about saving-labor technology? The first definition of *technology* in the Merriam-Webster Dictionary simply states, "the practical application of knowledge especially in a particular area." What if we applied knowledge to the practical support of workers themselves?

As a sociologist, I am drawn to the work of Herbert Marcuse (1998), who wrote extensively on technology as a social process that is open to change. He defines technology "as a mode of production, as the totality of instruments, devices and contrivances which characterize the machine age" (41). While technology as a whole can lead to domination and control, especially in the context of industrial capitalism, where its primary purpose is to help produce profit, specific technologies can also be involved in the quest for human liberation. As Marcuse (1969) wrote in reference to the student revolt of 1968,

> They have again raised a specter … of a revolution which subordinates the development of productive forces and higher standards of living [e.g. through technology] to the requirements of creating solidarity for the human species, for abolishing poverty and misery beyond all national frontiers and spheres of interest.
>
> *(ix–x)*

No revolution has managed to achieve this vision, but many struggles abound.

In the world of *Back to the Future*, the revolution is a coup of machines over workers, ostensibly freeing up leisure time to bask in the glow of neon screens and consume without social interaction. The Hayekian vision of freedom to consume as the penultimate expression of liberty, instead of freedom from labor exploitation, reverberates in contemporary debates over the role of technology in the food system. Proponents of technological modernization often claim that automating food labor processes is about saving money, eliminating monotonous tasks, creating new jobs in manufacturing, service, and management, and increasing the planning and rationalization of labor (Rifkin 1995; Segal 2005). But this does not shake the fundamental dilemma that Marcuse identifies, namely that technology in the service of productive forces is primarily to generate profit under capitalism. This abuts social and ecological needs (Schnaiberg 1980). The problem is not about technology per se. Without re-embedding the economy (and its associated technologies) in socioecological systems, labor will remain in the service of capitalism, either in the guise of facilitating the consumption of industrial food through corporate fast-food chains or as the overseers of machines put to work for the same ends (cf. Polanyi 1957).

This chapter takes on some of the tensions between food labor and technology by placing them squarely within the realities of class struggle. Doing so positions visions of regenerative labor alongside actually existing economic conditions, both historically and contemporarily. The notion of regeneration moves beyond the need for social reproduction under capitalism, which centers earning wages to pay for goods to care for oneself to keep working. A focus on regenerative labor asks what kind of economy can set in motion labor relations that improve *and* sustain society's workforce. This shift in focus offers a means to think through the gains and aspirations of labor movements. Workers have fought to advance their interests since the rise of industrial capitalism. This includes issues pertaining to safety, gender equity, and fair wages, as well as workplace democracy and sharing diverse work tasks. Instead of merely working as wage slaves where labor is commodified when sold for a wage, many workers have designed cooperative modes of labor that embed exchange in social relations. This alternative view of labor extends well beyond physical tasks and elevates creativity, freedom, and social and ecological ethics. In their most utopian moments, workers have sought for nothing less than a regenerative labor process that restores workers' source of energy without the exploitation of capitalism that extracts more value than it returns. Indeed, the famous socialist slogan, "From each according to their ability, to each according to their needs," suggests a desirable regenerative goal to strive for: worker's basic needs are met so that work is pleasurable and inventive instead of compelled.

The scholarship on labor in the food system offers many insights into the problems workers face, but fewer attempts to reflect on what leads to successful advances for workers and to imagine future economic alternatives. This is understandable. *The Communist Manifesto* (Marx and Engels 1998) is a cautionary tale in predicting the future for workers. That said, it also provides a template for theorizing and visioning what will improve labor for all people. Might engaging with the idea of regenerative labor produce some insights? Only if it remains grounded in the historical and sociological conditions food chain workers experience and fight to overcome. This creates a check on armchair philosophizing. Indeed, much of the research on food chain workers focuses on their material realities, hopes, and struggles. Before proceeding into an extended discussion of some of the tensions between food workers and machines (and their owners), and what this offers in terms of visioning and implementing regenerative labor practices, it is important to first acknowledge previous scholarly insights.

How do we move forward with what we know about food labor?

With the advent of agriculture, farmers' labor is one of the bases for social reproduction. Historically, scholars in the United States have focused on the effect of the industrialization of agriculture on farmers and farming communities, which suggests largely detrimental outcomes to socioeconomic and environmental conditions and community social fabric (Lobao and Stofferahn 2008). Going a step further, commodity systems analysts work to identify how the labor process in commodity systems is fundamental to shaping farming communities (Friedland et al. 1981). Globally, development studies have focused on the effects of globalization on peasant farmers, especially the neoliberal restructuring of agriculture and the undermining of livelihoods as well as the labor of smallholder families (Sen 1966; Ellis 1988; Netting 1993; McMichael 2008). Relatedly in anthropology, there are many eye-opening accounts of plantation agriculture systems (Mintz 1960; Bourgois 1989; Ortiz 1999). Where there have been studies on food chain workers, namely those that sell their labor for a wage, they tend to be labor histories (Daniel 1982; Ruíz 1987; Wells 1996; Fink 1998; McWilliams 1999). These often focus on specific experiences and struggles of farmworkers and meatpacking and food processing workers, with lesser focus on food retail workers in grocery stores, markets, and restaurants (cf. Walker 2004 and Jayaraman 2013 for an exceptions).

Theoretically, there has been an increasingly critical orientation to the study of labor in food systems over the past three decades as neoliberal economic restructuring alongside technological intensification has fundamentally altered food chain work (Besky and Brown 2015). For anthropologists, geographers, and sociologists, this has meant paying greater attention to the intersections between how capital structures labor within the food system and its gendered and racialized patterns (Mitchell 1996; Sachs 1996; Walker 2004; Harrison 2011; Holmes 2013; Ribas 2015). This includes topics such as the ethnic succession of farmworkers in the context of the push-pull forces of immigration, state-sanctioned racist discrimination and violence against food chain workers, sexual harassment faced by women in the workplace, threats to reproductive health due to pesticide exposure, ethnoracial inequities in changing food occupations, and more. This body of work centers the need to account for how the marginality of workers is not universal. For example, the deportability of undocumented Latinx farmworkers threatens the stability of employment in a way that is different than the pressures women farmers face navigating male-dominated agriculture.

While the lesson of much of the critical literature on food labor is that capitalism undervalues workers and that colonial, racist, and patriarchal institutions further marginalize the hands that feed people, workers also fight back. In California, despite the power of capitalist industrial agriculture to reshape ecological and social systems over the last 100 years, food chain workers across sectors have agitated for better remuneration, safe working conditions, and workplace respect (Walker 2004). For example, farmers organized into cooperatives to ensure fair prices, cannery workers fought to collectively bargain, and butchers unionized for better pay and benefits. California has been, and continues to be, a site for contentious food labor struggles whose lessons are instructive elsewhere (Guthman 2004, 2008). In addition to some of these place-based historical accounts are studies of specific movements, campaigns, and strategies. Farmworker struggles, especially those of the United Farm Workers and the Coalition of Immokalee Workers, are well known (Ganz 2009; Marquis 2017). Lesser known are the stories of meatpacking and food processing workers, as well as grocery retail and restaurant workers (Ruíz 1987; Sbicca 2018; Chatelain 2020).

Germane to this chapter is the fact that beyond looking at whether labor in conventional food systems is just is the question of whether sustainable and alternative food systems model labor justice. One noteworthy set of studies has asked tough questions about labor relations in contexts such as food movement non-profits, sustainable farming internships and businesses, domestic fair-trade initiatives, and local food organizations and businesses (Brown and Getz 2008; Sbicca 2015a; Biewener 2016; Ekers et al. 2016). In brief, there is no guarantee that just because there are strong ecological values or commitments to food system change underpinning these efforts that this translates to fair labor practices (Sbicca 2015b). It might actually be harder to implement labor justice given the economic precariousness of initiatives vis-à-vis conventional food competitors and ideological preferences for volunteer association even when that reproduces class differences. Additionally, the food justice literature has been particularly focused on labor questions, although there has been a decline in these studies in recent years (Glennie and Alkon 2018). This is more reason to recommit investigating those approaches to, and visions of, food labor that approximate or activate regeneration.

Marx informs, in one way or another, most studies of food chain workers. That is, these studies usually begin with a political economy analysis that centers power relations between bosses and workers. This is understandable in the context of the historical precarity of food labor under capitalism (Holt-Giménez 2017). While a strict Marxist view might call for the workers of the world to unite to overthrow capitalism and level the class playing field, this oversimplifies the diversity of workers in the food system and obstructs the need to tie universal demands to particular conditions and social experiences of groups of food chain workers (cf. chapters on labor and workers in Alkon and Guthman 2017). The language of regeneration opens the space for greater nuance and aligns with some of Marcuse's (1969) insights on the need to move beyond the hunt for some specific historical agent of revolution. Instead, he contends, "Revolutionary forces emerge in the process of change itself; the translation of the potential into the actual is the work of political practice." As I discuss more below, one way that we can begin to imagine more regenerative, perhaps even revolutionary labor is by accounting for the diversity of food chain worker struggles within the realities of common challenges. The experience of food chain workers as surplus labor helps set up why the question of technology advances such a discussion.

The precarity of food system labor

No regenerative food labor is possible without considering that food chain workers are at the bottom of the occupational hierarchy. There are 21.5 million workers in the food system in the United States. This is the largest employment sector. One out of every seven workers is a food chain worker. Looking at their occupational position in the larger economy contextualizes the current scale and need for these workers, the barriers they face, and therefore the basis for any regenerative labor vision.

Despite the centrality of food labor to the overall economy and sustenance of society, food chain workers are often disposable and replaceable. As a reserve army of labor, namely a class of usually women and people of color workers that enter and leave jobs according to businesses' drive for profit maximization under capitalism, they experience greater exploitation than many other workers. Indeed, in the restaurant industry, annual employee turnover varied between 56 percent to 80 percent over the ten years to 2016 compared to 40 percent to 49 percent in the overall private sector (Steinman 2018). Not only do restaurants rely on a flexible workforce that can continually fill these positions, but they also benefit from a vast part-time workforce vulnerable to economic recessions that faces mechanization pressures to eliminate certain kinds of tasks altogether (Jayaraman 2013). In this respect, the restaurant industry relies on a reserve pool of workers that it simultaneously helps to create. Similar pressures face other food chain workers as well.

As Americans continue to spend more money eating out than at home and as the share of disposable income spent on food remains historically low, the percent of people working in the food system is increasing (Food Chain Workers Alliance and Solidarity Research Cooperative 2016; Okrent et al. 2018). And yet, food chain workers' median annual wage, $16,000, is far below the median across all other industries at $36,468. Because of this, food chain workers rely more on public assistance than the average worker. For instance, they incongruously use the Supplemental Nutrition Assistance Program more than the average worker, and require greater public health insurance, energy and rent subsidy, and welfare support (Food Chain Workers Alliance and Solidarity Research Cooperative 2016). There are also racial, class, and gender inequalities: most food chain workers are not in management positions, which is reinforced by the gatekeeping role of those at the top of companies. Seventy-two percent of CEOs are white males, 14 percent are white women, and the rest are people of color (Food Chain Workers Alliance and Solidarity Research Cooperative 2016). Coupled with major gender and racial wage gaps and working in some of the most dangerous occupations in the United States, these disparities reveal how far the food system is from fully caring for workers.

But there is nothing inevitable about this state of affairs. Large surplus pools of workers are the byproduct of how capitalism organizes labor relations. As Fred Magdoff and Harry Magdoff (2004) note, "there would be no surplus of labor if everyone had enough to eat, a decent place to live, health care, and education, and workers had shorter work hours and longer vacations so they could have more leisure and creative time." While mechanization of rote tasks and technological innovation that reduces human toil may create more opportunities to achieve some of these goals, the way these currently operate in food service suggests some underlying contradictions. In response, many food chain workers have pushed for initiatives to expand our collective social responsibility to ensure we all have access to the resources needed for a dignified human existence.

Fast-food workers, machines, and the fight for dignity and respect

In the service-based economy of countries like the United States, where millions of people work in precarious low-wage jobs with few benefits or the opportunity for promotion, the tension between machines and workers continues to play out. It is unclear whether machines are truly the savior proponents often portray them as: technologies that will increase leisure time and free workers from drudgery. In many respects, our technological overdevelopment has come at the cost of social and political underdevelopment (Boggs and Boggs 2008). For example, "just-in-time" scheduling not only compels a more flexible workforce with little employment stability, it requires a cyborg-like attachment to portable devices that notify workers at a second's notice, like restaurant servers, that there is an available shift. If anything, this techno-management strategy has the consequence of compelling people into second jobs, instilling insecurity in daily scheduling of family responsibilities and leisure opportunities, shortening shifts, and pushing people to always be on call for only part-time work (Schwartz et al. 2015). In brief, technology may be framed to support workers, but its consequences may in fact oppose workers.

On the frontlines of food labor struggles in the United States is the largely women and people of color led Fight for $15 movement. Started by fast-food workers, this movement sparked a nationwide demand for at least a fifteen-dollar minimum wage and the right to form a union. As Terrence Wise, a Black fast-food worker, explained during a conference call with other movement participants about the economic stress of his job:

> My kids are living in poverty. It's hard getting just the basic necessities, and they truly are the reason I fight … It makes me angry, and you should be angry, that these billion-dollar corporations are robbing from my kids and your kids. So we're going to have to stand up and fight back.
>
> *(Greenhouse 2014)*

From the perspective of workers, it seems obvious that their work is treated as disposable despite its role in feeding people and that it should be paid more. The average CEO of a fast-food company earned $23.8 million in 2013, while the average fast-food worker earned less than $19,000 (Ruetschlin 2014). Moreover, with 52 percent of all fast-food workers dependent on public assistance of some kind, taxpayers are subsidizing CEO salaries and shareholder profits to the tune of $153 billion a year (Shah 2015). This raises the question of whether or how workers capture more of the value of their work. Taking his inspiration from the civil rights and women's suffrage movements, Mr. Wise said:

> Those things weren't given to us. People faced hoses and beatings. Some people even died. We have to bring the same pressure for today's times and make the companies listen to us. We have to do whatever it takes to win.
>
> *(Greenhouse 2014)*

And wins have piled up for the Fight for $15 movement. First, the movement has transformed the conversation about minimum wage in the United States. Instead of waiting on the benevolence of companies and politicians to raise the minimum wage, workers have organized around a discrete demand that is well above the federal minimum wage (although still not enough to live on in many states and cities). Second, workers won raises for nearly 12 million workers in 2016 (Fight for 15 n.d.). This has legitimized the movement's demands to the point where it was discussed and debated in the 2016 race for president. Bernie Sanders, for example, adopted the call for a $15 federal minimum wage. Over a four-year period since the start of the Fight for $15 movement, at least 21 states passed minimum wage laws above the federal level, which is $7.25 an hour, and 41 localities have passed minimum wage laws above their state's level (Blake 2018). All of this in the face of at least 24 states that have passed "pre-emption bills" to prevent these increases from taking place, which in some cases appears as white revanchism against low-income communities of color (Blake 2018). Third, major companies have begun to voluntarily increase their base pay in response to the shifts in the economy instigated by workers. Last, and perhaps most important the Fight for $15 movement has shown the power of a multi-ethnoracial working-class movement. In the vein of the late civil rights Poor People's Campaign and more recently its revival under Reverend William Barber II, movements for racial and economic justice are joining to build power at scales necessary to advance labor justice.

The response to some of the most marginalized workers in the United States by fast-food CEOs is telling. In brief, CEOs are little concerned with the social consequences of deepening the industrialization of food production; displacing workers without adequate investment in just transitions; and atomizing people into hyper-consumers with no solidarity with workers. In early 2018, Jack in the Box CEO Leonard Comma announced that, because of minimum wage gains made by workers, the company believed it was now affordable to cut workers and replace them with kiosks. Red Robin also said it will "save" $8 million by substituting machines for workers, "Probably the most challenging thing we're facing in the industry right now is labor costs," said Red Robin CFO Guy Constant (Taylor 2018). He made over $1.7 million in total compensation in 2017. As for Andy Puzder, the former CEO of Carl's Jr. and Hardee's and first pick to be Secretary of Labor under Donald Trump who withdrew after widespread opposition by labor groups and women's groups concerned with domestic abuse allegations, he is overtly hostile to workers. Referring to the benefit of machines over people, "'They're always polite, they always upsell, they never take a vacation, they never show up late, there's never a slip-and-fall, or an age, sex, or race discrimination case'" (Taylor 2016). The cold cash calculation places dollars above workers, a zero-sum approach that cares more for pleasing shareholders than some of the worst paid employees in the United States. Expressing his opposition to increasing the minimum wage, "Does it really help if Sally makes $3 more an hour if Suzie has no job?" (Taylor 2016).

This tension between technology and labor dovetails with some of the challenges of moving from sustainable food systems to regenerative food systems. Sustainability is often understood as a tripartite system composed of environmental, economic, and social practices. It is also a buzzword that is easily coopted (Goldman 2005). Fast-food companies can claim, and often do, that they are using more "sustainable" ingredients, by which they mean ingredients that are less ecologically harmful or healthier. Consider the shift in the past decade by Wendy's to "Certified Sustainable Palm Oil," "Reduce Antibiotics," "Sustainable Beef Production," "Source Only Cage-Free eggs," "Eliminate Gestation Stalls," and "Reduce Energy Consumption" (Wendy's n.d. a). This corporate branding has the effect of selling the consumer on a product that is ostensibly better for the environment and our bodies. Left out of the frame are workers, especially those actually selling that "sustainable" product. But in a neoliberal context where consumers are socialized into the belief that their influence rests in buying power, labor is but an afterthought. This is a false dichotomy between the hands that feed us and our health. We may be eating better environmentally but tasting the economic and labor inequities of how that food arrived on our table. For example, Wendy's public statements suggest that the role of their workers is to serve customers. Under the jobs section of their website, "Why should you work at Wendy's" they state simply that workers will learn, "The keys to making food that's Deliciously Different™; How to put a smile on everyone's face, even your own; That sometimes all you need is a high five and a hamburger" (Wendy's n.d. b). How about a raise and a union? Or at least some cooperative control over the machines?

Designing for regenerative food labor

Perhaps in some foreseeable future when artificial intelligence rules the world, there really will be no need for people to physically sweat to produce, prepare, and serve food. In the meantime, back to the present if you will, we might begin to imagine the first steps toward regenerative food labor. Marcuse recognized nearly 50 years ago that we have reached the technical capacity to fully support workers beyond just the need to earn a living. However, there is still the question of what this means in practice. Marcuse (1969, 91) offers a possible answer:

> The social expression of the liberated work instinct is *cooperation*, which, grounded in solidarity, directs the organization of the realm of necessity [e.g. food] and the development of the realm of freedom [e.g. being free to think about what to do with food].

The lessons of fast-food workers versus machines and their corporate owners suggests that there are both actually existing institutional steps to restructure labor relations and conceptual leaps we can make to begin prefiguring something new entirely.

Regenerative labor entails the need for a holistic praxis that integrates health, the environment, and labor (cf. White 2018). Working with food and plants directly links the cultivation of ecosystems with sustenance. In the middle of these mutually reinforcing or damaging relationships are people, both workers and eaters. Regeneration would require that workers are not only capable of creative labor with enough free time to enjoy the food, animals, and plants under their care, but that the environment is nourished and generating healthy food. At the point of production, it is important to center the labor experience, but this will also entail support from consumers (Goodman and DuPuis 2002; Alkon and Guthman 2017). For counterexample, the application of certain classes of pesticides or herbicides creates a host of problems for ecosystems, workers, and public health. While these agricultural practices manipulate nature to provide jobs and food, they also undermine the conditions for regenerating these same systems. In brief, regenerative labor requires conviviality with food, animals, plants, and the health of the environment and eaters, not alienation. How might we make strides in this direction?

At a minimum, in the here and now, we cannot forget to establish the conditions for regenerative food labor with tools we know work (Aronowitz 2014). While to go back to the peak of the labor movement and its power in the mid-1950s currently seems inconceivable, there are clear benefits to expanding unionization. Unionization not only increases pay and benefits and greater accountability of companies to workers, it improves pay for workers in highly unionized places and industries. And specifically, for women, immigrants, and people of color, unions have been critical to upward class mobility (Rosenfeld 2015). They also create a space for solidarity that bridges social boundaries. At their best, as democratic and deliberative spaces, they empower members to view their work as a collective endeavor that fosters political skills and opportunities for civic engagement beyond the market.

Even if unionization were not to increase, but workers began to cooperatively and collectively restructure their jobs and industries, this could produce similar outcomes and would push back against a division of labor that unfairly distributes rote and creative jobs (cf. the case of Mondragon Cooperative Corporation: Bamburg 2017). There are many prefigurative examples of this in the food system. Cooperative farms, greenhouses and producer groups, food hubs, food distributors, and food retailers, and in some cases open source food-tech startups can help foster more solidarity economies that revalue labor (Anderson et al. 2014; Loh and Agyeman 2019). As this pertains to technology, it could open space for workers most impacted by technological shifts to have a say in the design and use of technology. As it currently stands, for example with companies like Grubhub and subsidiaries like Uber Eats, these technologies rely on a flexible and precarious labor force, in this case to deliver food from many restaurants that exploit their workers. What if the food businesses were cooperatively owned and operated cooperatively controlled apps?

Labor power that comes from unionization or cooperation can translate to new policy. The eight-hour work day, overtime protections, child labor laws, collective bargaining, and solidarity with gender and racial justice movements, are some of the positive legacies of the labor movement. While still within the framework of capitalism that compels the selling of labor for a wage, there have been and continue to be opportunities to carve out space for more regenerative labor relations. One promising idea is to reduce work hours without reducing pay. There is over 50 years of wage stagnation in the United States despite an increase in worker productivity, which means workers are giving more than they are receiving. Working less would allow for more creative aspirations and reduce the stress associated with having to work extra to keep up with declining purchasing power. A related idea is the universal basic income. There are examples at national, regional, and local levels to provide a rights-based regular cash payment to individuals that is unconditional and nonwithdrawable. Although based on distributing oil and gas revenues, The Alaska Permanent Fund is an example of a direct cash payment to nearly all Alaskan residents. This idea could be extended more broadly to all residents of a country with the goal of reducing economic inequality by taxing large companies and the rich. Food chain workers would especially benefit from these changes as more good jobs would become available, which would help reduce the pool of surplus labor.

Conceptually, these examples suggest the need to rethink our categories and the realm of the possible in relation to regeneration. Marxist notions of surplus value, for example, can move beyond the idea that value produced by workers gets accumulated by owners to reinvest in capital circulation. Instead, we might think about surplus in the diverse economy sense (Gibson-Graham 2006). Taking cooperatives as an example, the reinvestment of surplus, economic or otherwise, back into a cooperatively owned and run structure means that the social value of distributing the products of labor equitably comes before exploitation. In essence, we cannot think about regenerative food labor without also considering regenerative modes of exchange.

Centering regenerative labor offers a chance to more squarely discuss democratic socialism and horizontalism. While both focus on the importance of sharing power and involving people in the decision-making processes that most affect their lives, the former sees a strong role for the state while the latter focuses on direct political participation and is skeptical of representative forms of democracy. I see room for both in moving our conversation from a sustainable food system to a regenerative food system. As Erik Olin-Wright (2010) argues, capitalism will not disappear overnight. We cannot smash our way out of it. Instead, there is a critical need for taming capitalism's excesses and eroding its foundations. This requires taking seriously critiques of neoliberalism that argue for reaffirming the importance of using government to its fullest to ensure universal *and* equitable access to all the basic human needs that society produces (Alkon and Guthman 2017). At the same time, movements like Occupy Wall Street show why we cannot wait for government either (Gitlin 2012). People have the power to self-organize in ways that are more economically just and provide goods and services without institutional mediators.

Translated to the case at hand, food chain workers need to be prefiguring the transition to a postcapitalist future, but in the meantime also have labor protections and labor rights enforcement. Organizations like the HEAL (Health, Environment, Agriculture, Labor) Food Alliance builds coalitions and organizes campaigns that advance food justice. The first stop on their ten-point platform (shout out to the Black Panther Party), is "Ensure Dignity for Food Workers and their Families" (HEAL Food Alliance n.d.) For example, HEAL Food Alliance works as a national Good Food Purchasing Policy (GFPP) partner, an initiative that can help reduce the prevalence of poverty wages in local food systems. The GFPP requires public institutions and local government to adopt procurement policies that comply with maintaining a valued workforce (in addition to support for local economies, nutritional health, environmental sustainability, and animal welfare). This holistic praxis is the essence of regenerative labor. The work of organizing for a better food system goes together with working to provide food for human sustenance and culture.

Maybe instead of turnkey industrial food chains with floating celebrity-head-screens that sell people monotonous and interchangeable food-like substances, cooperative neighborhood enterprises can exchange a cornucopia of certifiably fair food with local individuals and institutions. Giving ourselves the freedom to imagine alternatives is a necessary first step. Regeneration is not so much about achieving freedom *from* the grind of work, but rather is about freedom *to* work in ways that allow for creativity, connection, and cooperation.

Discussion questions

1. Can we create the conditions for regenerative food labor without transitioning out of capitalism? If so, how? If not, why?
2. What can the fights of food chain workers for economic justice teach us about the advantages of a regenerative framework over a sustainability framework?
3. How does interrogating food labor in relationship to technology help to point out socioeconomic and political contradictions that need resolution on the path to regeneration?
4. How might a food system reliant on regenerative labor increase leisure time to engage in other pursuits? Relatedly, might forms of food-based care work (e.g. breastfeeding, shopping, cooking) be better supported if the products of food chain workers' labor were regenerative of health and wealth?

Further reading

Alkon, Alison Hope, and Julie Guthman. (eds). 2017. *The New Food Activism: Opposition, Cooperation, and Collective Action*. Berkeley, CA: University of California Press.

Ekers, Michael, Charles Z. Levkoe, Samuel Walker, and Bryan Dale. 2016. "Will work for food: Agricultural interns, apprentices, volunteers, and the agrarian question." *Agriculture and Human Values*. 33(3): 705–720.

White, Monica M. 2018. *Freedom Farmers: Agricultural Resistance and the Black Freedom Movement*. Chapel Hill, NC: University of North Carolina Press.

References

Alkon, Alison Hope, and Julie Guthman. (eds). 2017. *The New Food Activism: Opposition, Cooperation, and Collective Action*. Berkeley, CA: University of California Press.

Anderson, C. R., L. Brushett, T. W. Gray, and H. Renting. 2014. "Working together to build cooperative food systems." *Journal of Agriculture, Food Systems, and Community Development*. 4(3): 3–9.

Aronowitz, Stanley. 2014. *The Death and Life of American Labor: Toward a New Worker's Movement*. New York: Verso.

Bamburg, Jill. 2017. "Mondragon through a critical lens." *Medium*. https://medium.com/fifty-by-fifty/mondragon-through-a-critical-lens-b29de8c6049. Accessed 5/9/2019.

Besky, Sarah, and Sandy Brown. 2015. "Looking for work: Placing labor in food studies." *Labor: Studies in Working-Class History of the Americas*. 12(1–2): 19–43.

Biewener, Carole. 2016. "Paid work, unpaid work, and economic viability in alternative food initiatives: Reflections from three Boston urban agriculture endeavors." *Journal of Agriculture, Food Systems, and Community Development*. 6(2): 35–53.

Blake, John. 2018. "The fight for $15 takes on the 'Jim Crow economy'." www.cnn.com/2018/04/13/us/fight-for-15-birmingham/index.html. Accessed 10/11/2018.

Boggs, James and Grace Lee Boggs. 2008. *Revolution and Evolution in the Twentieth Century*. New York: Monthly Review Press.

Bourgois, Phillipe. 1989. *Ethnicity at Work: Divided Labor on a Central American Banana Plantation*. Baltimore, MD: Johns Hopkins University Press.

Brown, Sandy, and Christy Getz. 2008. "Towards domestic fair trade? Farm labor, food localism, and the 'family scale' farm." *GeoJournal*. 73(1): 11–22.

Chatelain, Marcia. 2020. *Franchise: The Golden Arches in Black America*. New York: Liveright Publishing.

Daniel, Cletus E. 1982. *Bitter Harvest, a History of California Farmworkers, 1870–1941*. Berkeley, CA: University of California Press.

Ekers, Michael, Charles Z. Levkoe, Samuel Walker, and Bryan Dale. 2016. "Will work for food: Agricultural interns, apprentices, volunteers, and the agrarian question." *Agriculture and Human Values*. 33(3): 705–720.

Ellis, Frank. 1988. *Peasant Economics: Farm Households in Agrarian Development*. Cambridge: Cambridge University Press.

Fight for 15. n.d. "The fight for $15: We made history in 2016." https://fightfor15.org/fight-15-made-history-2016/. Accessed 10/11/2018.

Fink, Deborah. 1998. *Cutting into the Meatpacking Line: Workers and Change in the Rural Midwest*. Chapel Hill, NC: University of North Carolina Press.

Food Chain Workers Alliance and Solidarity Research Cooperative. 2016. *No Piece of the Pie: U.S. Food Workers in 2016*. Los Angeles, CA: Food Chain Workers Alliance.

Friedland, William, Ann Barton, and Robert Thomas. 1981. *Manufacturing Green Gold: Capital, Labor, and Technology in the Lettuce Industry*. Cambridge: Cambridge University Press.

Ganz, Marshall. 2009. *Why David Sometimes Wins: Leadership, Organization, and Strategy in the California Farm Worker Movement*. Oxford: Oxford University Press.

Gibson-Graham, J.K.. 2006. *A Postcapitalist Politics*. Minneapolis, MN: University of Minnesota Press.

Gitlin, Todd. 2012. *Occupy Nation: The Roots, the Spirit, and the Promise of Occupy Wall Street*. New York: It Books.

Glennie, Charlotte, and Alison Hope Alkon. 2018. "Food justice: Cultivating the field." *Environmental Research Letters*. 13(7): 073003.

Goldman, Michael. 2005. *Imperial Nature: The World Bank and Struggles for Social Justice in the Age of Globalization*. New Haven, CT: Yale University Press.

Goodman, David, and E. Melanie DuPuis. 2002. "Knowing food and growing food: Beyond the production–consumption debate in the sociology of agriculture." *Sociologia Ruralis*. 42(1): 5–22.

Greenhouse, Steven. 2014. "Strong voice in 'Fight for 15' fast-food wage campaign." *New York Times*. www.nytimes.com/2014/12/05/business/in-fast-food-workers-fight-for-15-an-hour-a-strong-voice-in-terrance-wise.html. Accessed 9/19/2018.

Guthman, Julie. 2004. *Agrarian Dreams? The Paradox of Organic Farming in California*. Berkeley, CA: University of California Press.

Guthman, Julie. 2008. "Neoliberalism and the making of food politics in California." *Geoforum*. 39: 1171–1183.

Harrison, Jill Lindsey. 2011. *Pesticide Drift and the Pursuit of Environmental Justice*. Cambridge, MA: MIT Press.

HEAL Food Alliance. n.d. "Our platform for real food." https://healfoodalliance.org/strategy/the-real-food-platform/. Accessed 2/25/2019.

Holmes, Seth. 2013. *Fresh Fruit, Broken Bodies: Migrant Farmworkers in the United States*. Berkeley, CA: University of California Press.

Holt-Giménez, Eric. 2017. *A Foodie's Guide to Capitalism: Understanding the Political Economy of What we Eat*. New York: Monthly Review Press.

Jayaraman, Saru. 2013. *Behind the Kitchen Door*. Ithaca, NY: Cornell University Press.

Lobao, Linda, and Curtis W. Stofferahn. 2008. "The community effects of industrialized farming: Social science research and challenges to corporate farming laws." *Agriculture and Human Values*. 25(2): 219–240.

Loh, Penn, and Julian Agyeman. 2019. "Urban food sharing and the emerging Boston food solidarity economy." *Geoforum*. 99: 213–222.

Magdoff, Fred, and Harry Magdoff. 2004. "Disposable workers: Today's reserve army of labor." *Monthly Review Press*. https://monthlyreview.org/2004/04/01/disposable-workers-todays-reserve-army-of-labor/. Accessed 2/25/19.

Marcuse, Herbert. 1969. *An Essay on Liberation*. Boston, MA: Beacon Press.

Marcuse, Herbert. 1998. *Technology, War and Fascism*, ed. Douglas Kellner. New York: Routledge.

Marquis, Susan L. 2017. *I am Not a Tractor! How Florida Farmworkers Took on the Fast Food Giants and Won*. Ithaca, NY: Cornell University Press.

Marx, Karl, and Friedrich Engels. 1998. *The Communist Manifesto*. New York: Signet Classic.

McMichael, Philip. 2008. "Peasants make their own history, but not just as they please …" *Journal of Agrarian Change*. 8(2–3): 205–228.

McWilliams, Carey. 1999. *Factories in the Field: The Story of Migratory Farm Labor in California*. Berkeley, CA: University of California Press.

Mintz, Sidney Wilfred. 1960. *Worker in the Cane: A Puerto Rican Life History*. New Haven, CT: Yale University Press.

Mitchell, Don. 1996. *The Lie of the Land: Migrant Workers and the California Landscape*. Minneapolis, MN: University of Minnesota Press.

Netting, Robert McC. 1993. *Smallholders, Householders: Farm Families and the Ecology of Intensive, Sustainable Agriculture*. Stanford, CA: Stanford University Press.

Okrent, Abigail M., Howard Elitzak, Timothy Park, and Sarah Rehkamp. 2018. *Measuring the Value of the U.S. Food System: Revisions to the Food Expenditure Series*. Technical Bulletin No. 1948. Washington, DC: United States Department of Agriculture.

Ortiz, Sutti. 1999. *Harvesting Coffee, Bargaining Wages: Rural Labor Markets in Columbia*. Ann Arbor, MI: University of Michigan Press.

Polanyi, Karl. 1957. *The Great Transformation*. Boston, MA: Beacon Press.

Ribas, Vanesa. 2015. *On the Line: Slaughterhouse Lives and the Making of the New South*. Berkeley, CA: University of California Press.

Rifkin, Jeremy. 1995. *The End of Work: The Decline of the Global Labor Force and the Dawn of the Post-Market Era*. New York: G.P. Putnam Sons.

Rosenfeld, Jake. 2015. "The rise and fall of US labor unions, and why they still matter." *The Conversation*. https://theconversation.com/the-rise-and-fall-of-us-labor-unions-and-why-they-still-matter-38263. Accessed 2/25/19.

Ruetschlin, Catherine. 2014. *Fast Food Failure: How CEO-to-Worker Pay Disparity Undermines the Industry and the Overall Economy*. New York: Dēmos.

Ruíz, Vicki L. 1987. *Cannery Women, Cannery Lives: Mexican Women, Unionization, and the California Food Processing Industry, 1930–1950*. Albuquerque, NM: University of New Mexico Press.

Sachs, Carolyn. 1996. *Gendered Fields: Rural Women, Agriculture, and Environment*. Boulder, CO: Westview Press.

Sbicca, Joshua. 2015a. "Food labor, economic inequality, and the imperfect politics of process in the alternative food movement." *Agriculture and Human Values*. 32(4): 675–687.

Sbicca, Joshua. 2015b. "Farming while confronting the other: The production and maintenance of boundaries in the borderlands." *Journal of Rural Studies*. 39: 1–10.

Sbicca, Joshua. 2018. *Food Justice Now! Deepening the Roots of Social Struggle*. Minneapolis, MN: University of Minnesota Press.

Schnaiberg, Allan. 1980. *The Environment: From Surplus to Scarcity*. New York: Oxford University Press.

Schwartz, Ari, Michael Wasser, Merrit Gillard, and Michael Paarlberg. 2015. *Unpredictable, Unsustainable: The Impact of Employers' Scheduling Practices in D.C.* Washington, DC: D.C. Jobs With Justice.

Segal, Howard P. 2005. *Technological Utopianism in American Culture*. Syracuse, NY: Syracuse University Press.

Sen, Amartya K. 1966. "Peasants and dualism with or without surplus labor." *Journal of Political Economy*. 74(5): 425–450.

Shah, Khushbu. 2015. "52 percent of fast food workers need government assistance to make ends meet." *Eater*. www.eater.com/2015/4/13/8403905/52-percent-fast-food-workers-public-assistance-food-stamps-study. Accessed 10/9/2018.

Steinman, Seth. 2018. "The reasons restaurant employees leave, and how to manage turnover." *Upserve: Restaurant Insider*. https://upserve.com/restaurant-insider/3-common-reasons-restaurant-employee-turnover/. Accessed 2/25/2019.

Taylor, Kate. 2016. "Fast-food CEO says he's investing in machines because the government is making it difficult to afford employees." *Business Insider*. www.businessinsider.com/carls-jr-wants-open-auto mated-location-2016-3. Accessed 10/22/2018.

Taylor, Kate. 2018. "America's fast-food chains are contemplating replacing minimum wage workers with robots: And it could lead to a crisis." *Business Insider*. www.businessinsider.com/minimum-wage-increases-spur-fast-food-chains-to-consider-automation-2018-1. Accessed 10/11/2018.

Walker, Richard. 2004. *The Conquest of Bread: One Hundred Fifty Years of Agribusiness in California*. New York: New Press.

Wells, Miriam. 1996. *Strawberry Fields: Politics, Class, and Work in California Agriculture*. Ithaca, NY: Cornell University Press.

Wendy's. n.d. a. "What we value." www.wendys.com/what-we-value. Accessed 10/12/2018.

Wendy's. n.d. b. "Find jobs." https://careers.wendys.com/. Accessed 10/12/2018.

White, Monica M. 2018. *Freedom Farmers: Agricultural Resistance and the Black Freedom Movement*. Chapel Hill, NC: University of North Carolina Press.

Wright, Erik Olin. 2010. *Envisioning Real Utopias*. New York: Verso.

10

CARING AGRICULTURAL AND FOOD PRACTICES

Jan Hassink, Angela Moriggi, Saverio Senni, Elisabeth Hense, and Dries de Moor

Introduction

European agriculture has undergone significant changes over the past century, especially since WWII. To accommodate the economies of scale of the food industry and to remain economically profitable, farmers had to increase farm size, efficiency, and external inputs, while minimizing labor use per hectare. As a result, environmental problems, homogenization of the landscape, outbreaks of animal diseases, and poor animal welfare gave the agricultural sector a negative reputation (Meerburg et al. 2009). Growing concerns regarding nature conservation and the environment, and increasing demands from new social functions, such as housing and recreation, have put pressure on the sector (Hermans et al. 2010). Moreover, since 1990, an expanding EU has resulted in increased competition. Following the 1992 MacSharry reforms – which led to budgetary pressures, liberalization of the global food trade, and a call for sustainable development (Grin and Marijnen 2011) – farmers have become increasingly aware that real change is needed if they are to survive. Such change would ideally also address growing societal concerns about food safety, animal welfare, biodiversity, and landscape and environmental quality (Meerburg et al. 2009).

In response to such growing concerns, many European rural areas started experimenting with different forms of multifunctional agriculture (Wilson 2008). This meant complementing food production functions with other activities that could meet societal demands, such as therapeutic and social inclusion practices, recreation and landscape services (Durand and van Huylenbroeck 2003; Hassink and Van Dijk 2006). Since then, the number of farms providing high-quality healthcare services has grown exponentially (Hassink 2017).

These forms of multifunctional agriculture have paved the way to alternative farming models to the dominant agricultural paradigm, combining agroecology principles with a more ethical approach that re-connects humans among themselves and with the ecosystem (Shiva 2016). Their context-dependent nature, tied to place-based values and conditions, constitutes a double-edged sword for care and social farms. Because of their place embeddedness, such practices are hard to generalize, and thus their viability remains contested (van der Ploeg 2008). On the other hand, as they respond to the needs and assets of the localities where they develop, care and social farms may offer virtuous examples of regenerative agriculture, where both humans and the ecosystem can thrive (Moriggi, et al. 2020).

Meanwhile, in response to the overwhelming specialization and mechanization of agriculture and food production, "alternative" food networks and practices have also emerged. Their representatives draw attention to the possibility to "resocialize" and "respatialize" food, through supposedly "closer" and more "authentic" relationships between producers, consumers, and their food (Marsden et al. 2000; Renting et al. 2003). Examples of such networks are (combinations of) community supported agriculture (CSA), biodynamic and permaculture farming, and urban farming initiatives.

Against a background of marginalization and vulnerability for small-scale agricultural sector and rural areas, these practices represent a shift towards a caring regenerative agriculture, one that sees plants and animals as community members, rather than commodities, and that wishes to move from an attitude of control towards one of partnership and respect (Wells and Gradwell 2001; Leck et al. 2014). Such experiments show the potential for people to live in resonance with nature, following its rhythms, challenges, changes, and local particularities (Rosa 2016, 453–472). In this view, human beings are "response-able" for nature and have the capacity to live interconnectedly with animals, plants, and nature in its entirety, and care for it thoughtfully (Nussbaum 1998, 201)

To deepen the knowledge for current stakeholders and future entrepreneurs and to address agricultural and rural development policies in a better way, we believe that the practices outlined above are worth investigating further, with special attention to the underlying principles of regeneration and caring. Regenerative forms of agriculture focus generally on the conservation of the natural resource base and the use of technical and ecological measures like abandoning tillage and fostering biodiversity (Rhodes 2017; La Canne and Lundgren 2018). The possible social and caring implications of regenerative forms of agriculture have not received much attention, which makes our exploration of caring aspects of regenerative forms of agriculture even more valuable.

We use care ethics as a tool to explore and analyse agricultural and food practices aiming to reconnect with society and nature.

We start by exploring ideas about and conceptualizations of care from a theoretical perspective, and we focus on the conceptualization offered by Tronto, which we believe to be particularly useful in understanding the regenerative potential of caring forms of agricultural and food practices. The empirical section focuses on different cases of caring forms of agriculture and food production. We describe the aspects and relationships of caring involved, and we examine the challenges that emerge when fully striving to put the principles of caring into practice. By doing so, we hope to expand the current knowledge of regenerative forms of agriculture, and contribute to the debate on its potentials and limits.

Exploring changing ideas about care

Until recently, care was considered mainly to belong to the private and feminine sphere. Feminist literature has brought care work under scrutiny, showing its relevance to the public sphere (Tronto 1993). Feminist environmental care ethics are currently being picked up eagerly in various scholarly debates, especially given their emphasis on empowering communities in terms of resilience and resourcefulness, with an eye on future generations (Whyte and Cuomo 2017). In recent philosophical, economic, and sociological approaches, care has been described as a fundamental human capacity that transcends the private sphere and reaches out to other human beings, as well as non-humans.

The notion that people can engage in non-instrumental and non-manipulative relationships with nature is by no means new. Indigenous cultures have long claimed the interdependence of all forms of life. Symbiotic relationships with places have been sources of identity, community, and spirituality, through which people have experienced resilience, reciprocity, harmony, solidarity, and collectivity (Whyte and Cuomo 2017; Franklin 2018).

Several spiritual traditions have long called for a harmonious relationship with nature, and their teachings are now being revived all over the world. Recent (feminist) theology has also developed an eco-spiritual approach, emphasizing the concepts of stewardship for creation (Edwards 2011) and kinship with creation (Johnson 2014). The aim of living in harmony with nature is also expressed in renewed attention in eco-spiritual reflections on Hinduism (Dwivedi 2006), and the idea that all life is one is used to promote Hindu-oriented eco-spirituality (Singh 2013). In addition, one of the most basic teachings of Buddhism involves the interdependence of all beings (Gross 1997), and Islam is also engaged in the debate on ecology (Foltz 2009), with Muslims being told to respect for nature and not waste natural sources (Duh 2010). As such, all major religions encourage people to have a caring relationship with nature, although they are far from being a revolutionary engine for the desired changes.

Following our literature review, we define "care" as the ability to being responsible for, attending to, being concerned for or about, and paying watchful attention to the object of care (Wells and Gradwell 2001). This is not merely relevant for the health and social sector. For Tronto, caring includes "everything that we do to maintain, continue and repair 'our world' so that we can live in it, looking for the needs of ourselves as well as for those of our environment" (Tronto 1993, 103). Tronto also indicates that care is a set of values as well as concrete practices. In her understanding, a caring process is composed of five stages and connected values. The first stage of the caring process is **caring about**. It starts with *attentiveness*, the ability of someone or some group to notice caring needs that were previously unsatisfied. Suspending self-interest and adopting the perspective of others allows us to care about something or somebody. The recognition of unmet needs may lead to the second phase of **caring for**, when a feeling of *responsibility* is triggered that leads to concrete caring activities. Within the ethics of care, responsibility is not seen as a burden or obligation, but rather as a recognition of the relational nature of human life. Indeed, the feeling of responsibility is the result of a practice of relationality: by interacting with other people, we feel increasingly responsible *for* them. The third phase involves the actual work of care, **care giving**. Care work is not just a technical exercise, but rather a moral practice requiring *competence*. The fourth phase is **care receiving**, where, ideally, there is an open dialogue between care givers and care receivers that is characterized by *responsiveness* and leads to a good quality of the care being provided. Through this process, new needs may be acknowledged, after which the care process continues and a new care cycle begins. Not all care receivers may be able to respond, and the care process may be asymmetrical in nature, which is why Tronto includes a fifth phase, one should encompass the entire care process: **caring with**, which aligns with the moral value of *solidarity* and means that care practices should be designed and implemented in such a way as to recognize the care receivers' dignity and knowledge, to create the necessary conditions for empowerment (Tronto 1993; Faden et al. 2013).

In her study focused on Green Care practices in Finland, (Moriggi et al. 2020) widens Tronto's conceptualization to include care *for* and *with* the environment, in particular the capacity of Green Care practices to shape places in regenerative ways, as a result of two main dynamics: (1) **caring for places**: when green care activities are initiated for place-based reasons – to sustain and (re)generate places via a specific kind of socio-spatial practices; (2) **caring with people (in places):** when the people involved, through empowering caring practices, become partners of a new social model and shape places in new ways, ideally contributing to social justice and inclusion. Both processes of "caring for" and "caring with" are not limited either to people or to the environment, which is particularly interesting when we see the relationship with a place as one of "caring with," and the *responsiveness* of the place also plays a role.

The concept of caring *with* people highlights the regenerative potential of the caring process, namely the possibility to empower care receivers and care givers alike, based on the principles of solidarity, which involve self-determination, choice, and deliberation on the part of those who receive care, respecting their knowledge and dignity. On the other hand, it requires an attitude of experimentation and constant adaptation to the needs and capacities of the people involved (Moriggi et al. 2020). In the long run, empowerment can contribute to social justice, breaking down barriers against physical, emotional, and societal inclusion, and promoting independence and citizenship (Barnes 2008; Keyes et al. 2015). Research shows that care givers involved in Green Care practice also feel empowered by the caring relationship, when such principles are implemented (Hassink et al. 2010), benefitting in particular from the process of learning constantly at an everyday level, as well as the feeling of self-worth, joy, and reward that the practice of relationality with both humans and more-than-humans gives them (Moriggi et al. 2020).

At the same time, this continuous learning process can be challenging (Faden et al. 2013). In practice, care and empowerment do not always match. Indeed, there are many examples where disempowerment is experienced by care receivers, not only because they have no leverage in the relationships with care professionals, but also in the discrimination and stigmatization they experience in everyday life (Barnes 2008), while care givers can feel disempowered by inadequate structural conditions, and by institutionalized standards and habits that place the entire burden of care on just a few individuals (Mol et al. 2010).

Last, but not least, caring, as any other activity, should be also analysed from an economic perspective, considered in its true etymological meaning, the ancient Greek word *oikonomia* (Leshem, 2016) that could be translated as "taking care of the house." But for such a task neoclassical economic theory offers little help with a marginal role given to interpersonal relations, reciprocity, and gratuity among human beings. Therefore a different theoretical framework is requested, such as the civil economy concept (Zamagni 2008). The central idea of civil economy is to look at the experience of human sociality, with everything that such experience implies, within the economic life (Bruni and Zamagni 2007). Civil economy hence looks at economic and social relationships from a perspective in which cooperation, reciprocity, gratuity, gifts, and intrinsic motivations are fundamental, and it tells us that principles "other" than profit and instrumental exchange can – if you want – find a place inside the economic activity (Nelson 2011). A relevant point of the civil economy paradigm that appears interesting in a contest of activities related with care is the attention given to the relational goods (Gui and Sugden 2005) which are fundamental in care-based human relations. According to such perspectives markets must also take into account the relational goods being generated or destroyed by economic activities (Gui and Sugden 2005). The cases studies presented below, focusing also on social and human relationships, represent valuable examples of civil economy in practice.

Caring agricultural and food practices

In this section, we use the conceptualization of care to explore and analyse sustainable agricultural and food practices aimed at reconnecting agriculture with society and moving from an attitude of control towards building a partnership with the natural and social environment. We first describe the main characteristics and principles of some of the major practices that are rooted in the agricultural and food domain and that have the potential to incorporate caring practices in their everyday operations. The practices involved have the potential to incorporate caring practices as they focus on strengthening relationships, harmony among citizens, community health and vitality, and social and ecological embeddedness, to connect to the local environment and local economy and enhance people's attentiveness to others (Curry 2002). As such caring agricultural and food practices incorporate not only individual people but also communities, other living beings, like farm animals, crops, and their natural environments in the widest sense, including soils and landscapes.

Potentially promising connective practices wanting to incorporate caring practices are Community Supported Agriculture (CSA), urban agriculture, permaculture, care and social farming, and organic and biological-dynamic (biodynamic) farming.

Community Supported Agriculture (CSA) is a partnership between farmers and community members working together to create a local food system (Wells and Gradwell 2001). Members typically pay a seasonal fee to the farmer in advance of the growing season in return for a weekly share of the produce. The aim is to share the risks and rewards of farming more equitably, by building on reciprocity, trust, and collective benefits (van Oers et al. 2018). CSA shareholders have the opportunity to become more involved through farm visits, work parties, etc. (Fieldhouse 1995).

Urban agriculture: Urban agriculture has been defined as the growing, processing, and distribution of food and other products through intensive plant cultivation and animal husbandry in and around cities (Kaufman and Bailkey 2000). Urban farms can serve multiple functions that extend beyond food production (Poulsen et al. 2017).

Permaculture is defined as an integrated and evolving design system of plants and animal species that involves a conscious design and maintenance of agriculturally productive ecosystems with the diversity, stability, and resilience of natural ecosystems. It is the harmonious integration of landscape and people, providing food, energy, shelter, and other material and non-material requirements, in a sustainable way (Mollisson 1988), based on the ethical principles of caring for the earth, caring for people, setting limits on population and consumption, and redistributing surplus (Suh 2014).

Care farming and social farming involves a combination of agricultural production and care and social services. Care farms and social farms use agricultural resources to provide care and health services to people with various needs, to promote social inclusion, rehabilitation, employment, education etc. In some countries, like the Netherlands, care services are a paid service (Hassink and Van Dijk 2006).

Organic farming and biological dynamic farming. Organic farming emphasizes the naturalness and sustainability of farming by abstaining from the use of fertilizers and pesticides. Biological dynamic farming is a form of agriculture that focuses not only on healthy foods, but also on realizing harmonious interactions in agriculture and promoting a spiritual development of mankind through cosmic forces. It involves a connection between plants and the environment in its broadest sense, by creating awareness of all life on earth and the spiritual individuality that exists in all of us (Kirchman 1994; Koepf 2007).

These practices vary in focus, from connecting people to the culture of food, bringing farmers and consumers together, connecting food production to the urban population, connecting agriculture to people with special needs, and focusing on a cosmic awareness. Some of these practices (CSA, urban farming, and care/social farming) have already been associated with an ethical approach to care (Wells and Gradwell 2001; Kneafsly et al. 2008; Leck et al. 2014) as the motivations of producers and consumers include caring about aspects of food production that affect the natural environment, people, and animal welfare. That does not mean, however, that all initiatives incorporate a broad caring approach.

Inspiring cases in the Netherlands and Italy

In this section, we now describe several cases in rural and urban settings in the Netherlands and Italy, which are inspiring in the way they incorporate a wide range of care aspects in their practice, based on interviews with the initiators of the cases.

In our discussion of the empirical cases involving care practices, we look at how the different cases incorporate different care elements in their everyday operations, and at the initiators' vision, their challenges, and their contribution to more caring agricultural practices and a more caring society. We examine how these practices relate to the care ideas and identify points of contention. Furthermore, we look at the extent to which the various cases *are attentive to* and *connect with* the community, the environment, farm animals, and vulnerable people, and we examine to what extent caring practices are responsive and empowering. Finally, we discuss what has to be done (and how) to move from sustainable towards regenerative practices.

Care farm "het Liessenhuus": care for vulnerable people in a rural setting in the Netherlands

Care farm "het Liessenhuus" is a small-scale provider of day services for children, young adults, and adults, located in the rural eastern part of the Netherlands. The farmer's aim is to provide customized support to participants who can't participate in regular education or labour, due to learning disabilities, psychiatric, and/or social problems. To empower them, the farmer and his colleagues, try to figure out what interests each participant at the farm (e.g. plants, animals, engineering, farm shop, etc) in order to give them responsibility and a learning process based on inner motivation. As a community "het Liessenhuus" aims for social justice in a broader sense. Together with a number of other care farms in the region, the farm donates some of its crops to the foodbank, as part of the mission to provide healthy fresh food to people who normally cannot afford it, as well as empowering the participants by showing them they contribute to society and to the greater good. The farm sells fresh eggs and vegetable boxes, which customers can sign up for. Although the production of food is limited, it is viewed as an important source of empowerment as the participants develop skills and self-esteem through their part in the process, and as a source of social justice. Indeed, through the foodbank, people with a low income get access to fair and healthy food (biological food is expensive in the Netherlands). For "het Liessenhuus" the entire sale of agricultural products contributes less than 2% to the total income, whereas the rest is payment for the care services based on a contract with the municipality. Equality and reciprocity are important values at het Liessenhuus. The care farmer expects himself and his colleagues to set a good example for the participants: "If the participant has the competence to teach you, as a new farmer, how to feed the animals, you'll experience a reversed relationship when it comes to self-assurance." Giving feedback and showing the bigger picture of food production are designed to stimulate the participants' competences, according to the farmer: "Addressing the value of work is important: you have to tell the boy cleaning the stables that, thanks to him, there is manure for the crops, which means he is making an important contribution to the vegetable boxes." In their experience, care farmers need to have a creative, flexible, and neutral state of mind in order to align their activities to the range of attention spans amongst the participants, and to adapt to the calls of nature. They have to be willing to learn, in part due to the hybrid nature of care farms, where the focus is both on the clients and on the wellbeing of the plants and animals.

Care and biodynamic farm "Ruimzicht": care for people and the planet in a rural setting in the Netherlands

This biological dynamic dairy farm and garden, located in the eastern part of the Netherlands, provides educational and care services. Its mission is to provide care for the earth, the soil, plant life, animals, and people, in a biological and evolutionary sense. The farmers want to care for and support people who are searching for themselves and what they want to be. A strong belief in the deep connection between all life, the earth, and the cosmos gives them an intrinsic motivation to do what must be done. The farmers and gardener aim for balance, and a healthy and vital planet, and such principles guide them and their practices. This implies a minimum use of mechanical methods that require fossil fuel, believing that their approach is better for the soil, plants, and animals, and also for the food they produce. Methods like mulching and reduced tillage are designed to generate a moist and fertile soil, to preserve a healthy soil life, with no chemicals being used, only that which nature provides. In this way, a circular and local chain of production is generated, with the garden yielding around 110 vegetable boxes every week. For the gardener, the boxes are a way to share the story that involves the subscribers and their experiences. The boxes are accompanied by a newsletter, with recipes, personal experiences from the people working at the farm, and tips on how to care for our planet. Animal and plant care is reflected in decisions like respecting the family relations within the herd of cows, and letting plants and seeds complete their circle of life. This opposes conventional efficiency-based methods, such as separating calves in an early stage from their mothers to raise milk production, or faster growth of crops, in order to maximize profits for humans solely. According to the farmer, "We don't have to artificially orchestrate. It has all been figured out already. A herd of cows functions best and provides the best milk if it really is a herd: a family." Biodiversity and following nature's principles are the guiding principles, which also create challenges, like a lack of manpower and a struggle against the capitalist system: "As long as supermarket chains push farmers to produce near, or even under, cost prices, we are a long way from realizing a critical mass in true biological production." According to the gardener, consumers have been indoctrinated: "They are misled by the 'lowest price guarantees' of the supermarkets." Although the farmers put their heart and soul into it, and work very hard for very little, it is rewarding. Ruimzicht provides educational activities and care to anyone sympathizing with their vision. For educational purposes a five-day farmschool program can be attended by groups from primary schools, so the children will learn their food can be produced in an environment-friendly way. Also, single-parent families can subscribe for a holiday program to learn at the farm and enjoy and connect with their children. Besides these regular activities, "Ruimzicht" intends to provide care for anyone who feels the farm is a place to learn or recover, in spite of any diagnoses, target groups, and the regular care-system. Openness and a willingness to learn, for farmers and participants alike, are necessary to establish co-workership and personal development. As the gardener explains: "I believe everyone tries to tell us something. Everyone is like a mirror. And it's my own task to figure out what I can learn from other people. ... And then talk about it, that's the challenge." Anyone who feels attracted to the principles of the farm is welcome to participate, regardless of their capacities.

The seeds of life: solidarity for people in an urban setting in Italy

The social cooperative *Seeds of Life* ("Semi di Vita") started in 2011 in Casamassima, a neighbourhood of the Metropolitan City of Bari, in the south-eastern region of Italy. The initiator, Angelo Santoro, decided to change his life during the economic crisis and started a care-oriented farming project. At that time, care farming, or social agriculture, as it is called in Italy, was growing rapidly. Farming first began on 2,000 square meters owned by the Casamassima Municipality, and involved a family association of marginalized disabled youths. A vegetable garden was considered the best way to integrate the youngsters in the local community. At first, mentally disabled youths worked at the care farm; later also convicted teenagers started working on the farm. Neither Angelo nor his partners had an agricultural background, but they were all deeply inspired by solidarity and altruistic motivations. Local civic groups, families, and individuals informally supported the initiative's first steps. One of the first challenges was to protect the land and crops from the pesticides being used by the conventional farmers around them. In 2014, the care farming project moved to a run-down part of the city that had been built in the 1950s and that had a number of social problems, including the presence of crime.

It was in that neighbourhood that Angelo and his partners were given a 2 hectare piece of land owned by a religious institution that has been abandoned for years, and it is there that the Seeds of Life social cooperative was formed. Within a short time-frame they managed to make the cooperative a place where people in a fragile social condition could feel at home. An important decision was to allow local residents to use part of the land that had been made available to the cooperative, with the remaining part being used to grow figs, prickly pears (or Indian figs), and vegetables, including different kinds of local varieties of peppers (sweet and hot), and some olive trees.

One problem they encountered early on was people's habit of picking what they needed from an area that for years had been a "no man's land." It was only after the local parishes were involved that people started to respect the boundaries of the new cooperative. The parcels on which locals were allowed to grow produce helped secure that respect, as someone was always present on the land. Although overall turnover continues to be modest (€60,000 in 2018), revenues are growing, to a large extent thanks to processed products that have a greater added value and that are sold under the trademark "Bontà Comune" (Common Goodness),[1] with 20% of sales coming from fresh vegetables, 50% from processed produce, and the remaining 30% from social projects. Thanks to these percentages the cooperative is classed as a "social agriculture operator" according to Italian legislation involving social agriculture (no. 141/2015).

Seeds of Life has recently expanded the farming activity on 26 hectares in the nearby Valenzano municipality, an area confiscated from organized crime. Here a fig cultivation project is planned, for the positive market value that that fruit guarantees. The aim is to strengthen the cooperative's economic sustainability, usually a weak point when initiatives depend on volunteers who tend to have personal and altruistic motivations and to actively participate in actions to support legality in the area.

Food garden Rotterdam: caring for people and nature in an urban setting in the Netherlands

The Food Garden is an initiative that was started in 2010 in the Delfshaven neighbourhood on a 0.7 hectare abandoned area in Rotterdam in the Netherlands. After a major building project was cancelled as a result of the economic crisis, the urban farm project was able to put the unused land to good use for the next five years. The Food Garden is located next to the office of the Food Bank Rotterdam, an organization providing free food packages to low-income households. At the start, the main aim was to supply the Food Bank Rotterdam with fresh and healthy fruit and vegetables, which the Food Garden was able to realize for several years in a row, to which new objectives were added over time: i) reintegration of people with difficulties entering the labor market by letting them produce food, ii) mobilizing people and encouraging them to take part, and iii) developing the area into an urban platform where urban development issues and social issues are connected. The Food Garden has adopted permaculture principles, with the interaction between people and nature as a central objective, stimulating local biodiversity and a maximum yield for the people involved.

The Food Garden is a foundation that is financially dependent on fundraising, municipal subsidies, and sponsors. The work in the garden is carried out by three employees working on a freelance basis, and about 45 volunteers. All in all, the people involved are a very diverse group. The Food Garden provides them with structure and meaningful work. In particular, for people who are dependent on support, it is an important experience to be able to contribute to the production of healthy food for people who may need the help even more than they do. The social element appears to be very important to the participants: the respect of the community, the social interactions, and social support. According to the initiator, a key factor in the farm's success is the heterogeneity of the group and the informal approach, giving people trust and confidence. The project leader also emphasizes that the core of the project is growing healthy food, not providing care. According to him, people are not included because they deserve to be pitied, but because they can make a real contribution to the project, which makes for a more equal relationship, which is different compared to conventional care. In his view, relations in conventional care are defined in a contract between a care giver and a care receiver, which is not the kind of relationship he prefers. The Food Garden is also keen to safeguard its small-scale, informal identity.

One of the challenges, next to having continuous access to land, was to acquire funds from the city of Rotterdam. It was impossible to secure a contract with the city to provide social and healthcare services, because they were unable to meet all the formal requirements. To gain access to care funds from the city of Rotterdam for daycare activities, a collaboration was formed with Pluspunt, an established social care organization.

Findings: underlying principles of the different practices and the case studies

We have selected cases from different practices that have adopted a wide range of approaches to providing care (see Table 10.1). The case studies involve different types of

Table 10.1 Provides an overview of the underlying principles of the cases and their care activities

Case	Liessenhuus	Ruimzicht	Seeds of Life	Food Garden
Type of farm	Care farm based on organic principles	Care farm based on biodynamic and CSA principles	Care farm in a urban context	Urban farm based on permaculture principles
Principles guiding the farmer's practices	Social justice, mutual learning, individuality of each participant	Healthy vital planet. Holistic learning, reflection, personal development	Solidarity, respectful relationships, legality	Cooperation, nature, and people
Care for community: underpinning principles and practices	Safety and social inclusion	Involvement and education of the community	Support from community	Food for food bank; encouraging people to participate; urban platform for social and developmental issues
Care for environment	Biological, seasonal	Care for the earth, soil, plant life: mulching	Organic farming and biodiversity	Permaculture; creating a food forest; healthy soil
Care for farm animals	Respect for natural needs	Respect for natural needs	Animals not present	Animals not present
Care for vulnerable citizens	Discover what interests them, equal relationship	Support in what they want to be; personal development	Educate and integrate in community	Re-integration equal relationship; contribution to useful work; creating a community
Care for food	Fresh food for people via foodbank	Food experience, education	Community growing vegetables	Fresh vegetables
Challenges	Little production	Lack of workforce; deal with capitalist system	Creating a safe place; influence conventional agriculture	Access to land; budget for social services

agriculture and food production, where people care about the needs of other people, the community and the wider environment. The farms provide a rich context where, through meaningful tasks that connect to people's personal interests, and through the natural processes of life and death, growth and change, people learn to care and (inter)act with nature.

The cases discussed above share some underlying principles: participation, reintegration, and education of vulnerable citizens (care receivers), while developing an equal relationship with them. Care receivers are not seen as clients (or even patients), but as co-producers, and their requirements, knowledge, interests, and visions serve as starting points. The farmers told us how they learn from their interaction with care receivers, describing caring for vulnerable people as an open interaction between partners. This allows for a socio-economic model in which everyone contributes and is valued for their useful work, based on mutual dependency rather than power dynamics, creating the necessary conditions to establish caring relations that empower care receivers. As such, the cases clearly illustrate how care can be organized through practices that are constituted and shaped by their participants (Conradi 2015), rather than through the delivery of services and goods to passive recipients. The targets of the interventions, now commonly referred to as "client groups" or "consumers," can become active participants whose agency and role are worth highlighting (Barnes 2008).

The selected cases also exemplify care for the community and the environment. They vary in how that is done. Care for the community involves: donating fresh vegetables to the food bank, encouraging people to participate, giving them the opportunity to grow vegetables themselves, educating them about healthy food, and creating a platform for social innovation. In the case of "het Liessenhuus," a safe haven is also offered for young adults to work and learn, stimulating their personal reintegration as part of the surrounding community. "Seeds of Life" and the "Food Garden" regenerate abandoned urban areas into community places where people meet and grow fresh vegetables. "Ruimzicht" tries to create awareness of how all living beings, plants, the earth, and the cosmos are connected, leading by example in all they do, by telling the story and by inviting everyone to come on board.

Two of the cases focus mainly on the interaction between nature and people, with caring for the environment being an explicit objective, illustrated by care for soil organisms, reduced use of fossil fuel, biodiversity, and the creation of a food forest. "Seeds of Life" has in fact adopted organic farming and is keen to stimulate biodiversity.

All initiatives provide access to healthy and fresh food, especially for vulnerable people, and involve and educate people on this topic. Only at "Liessenhuus" and "Ruimzicht" are farm animals part of the farm.

The main challenges for the initiatives are a lack of funds, a lack of manpower, the challenges involved in creating a safe place, and gaining access to land.

The various case studies show that altruism, reciprocity, selflessness, and responsibility are important motivations for farmers and other initiators of "care-oriented" agricultural or food practices. In the cases discussed above, care for people with special needs, for the community, and for the wider ecosystem are all integrated. This fits the concept of the civil economy where social relationships and cooperation are considered important aspects of economic activities (Gui and Sugden 2005). The cases illustrate how their economic activities are based on caring relationships with participants, communities, and the environment.

The practices and cases discussed above are also examples of location-based practices reflecting a discourse of reconnection and re-territorialization, providing an alternative to the dominant discourse of competitive thinking in the agricultural and food sector (Horlings and Marsden 2014). We should keep in mind that not all location-based practices include a similar wide range of caring behaviors.

The cases illustrate different ways to finance activities. The Dutch care farms are contracted by municipalities to provide useful activities to people needing support. The "Food Garden" established a collaboration with a care organization to gain access to funding. "Seeds of Life" also combines income from the sales of agricultural products with social services, while generating additional financial value by introducing an ethical trade mark.

Discussion and conclusion

The motivations of farmers and the market play a crucial role in fostering regenerative approaches to food production, creating market arenas where consumers and clients become "partners" in a new social model (Carbone and Senni 2010). The farmers in our cases have deeply rooted altruistic motivations, based on feelings of solidarity. The farmers are attentive to people's individual needs and always willing to learn. Research often focuses on the farmers' financial motivations to such an extent that we risk ignoring or neglecting other objectives that drive their actions (Gasson 1973; Carbone and Senni 2010). In particular when it comes to diversification in agriculture, non-pecuniary objectives often play a role in addressing farm decisions, in particular involving family farms or small cooperative farms, where the "caring activities" are part of the social business model. Meanwhile, citizens are supposed not to be passive clients and consumers, but members who are actively involved. Farmers and other participants learn from each other in relationships characterized by reciprocity, trust, and cooperation (van Oers et al. 2018). In this respect, it can be questioned whether donating fresh vegetables to the food bank is an act of stimulating participation, empowerment, and co-production of the beneficiaries or whether it keeps them in a dependent position.

An important question is to what extent these kinds of care initiatives can influence the dominant agricultural and food systems, and help bring about a transition from sustainable towards regenerative agricultural and food practices that create healthy environments, communities, and people, as well as improve the resources being used, and that encourage continual on-farm innovation designed to generate environmental, social, economic, and spiritual wellbeing (Mendez et al. 2013). Practices like CSA, urban agriculture, permaculture, care farming, and organic and biodynamic farming are well suited to be part of this transition, in particular when based on holistic principles. The cases discussed in this chapter are illustrations of the regenerative practices in question, which can empower care receivers, care givers, and communities alike, regenerate abandoned land and improve environmental quality.

It remains to be seen to what extent new practices can actually challenge the dominant agricultural and food systems (Jones et al. 2003; Alkon and Norgaard 2009), one of the main challenges being how to sustain and scale up in an increasingly corporate-dominated industry. Indeed, initiatives may struggle to attract resources (money, land, manpower) and new participants, to secure the approval and support from parties and municipalities, and to incorporate wider interests and commitments in their negotiations (van Oers et al. 2018). To influence the dominant agricultural and food systems, innovations should emphasize and monitor their contribution to solving wicked problems in our societies and redefining how we eat and grow food, build communities, improve public health, and reduce social and economic inequality (Cox et al. 2008). Working together and coming up with a joint strategy for gaining support and changing dominant systems would make sense, since the different regenerative initiatives and practices share many underlying caring values and can inspire stakeholders in the agricultural and food domain.

Discussion questions

1. Should connective practices like community supported agriculture, permaculture, social farming, urban farming, and biological dynamic farming join forces to challenge dominant agricultural and food systems?
2. Should policy makers support caring agricultural and food practices financially for their contribution to more inclusive, social, and healthy societies?

3. Should social, spiritual, and caring values become important elements in the curriculum for future farmers in order to foster regenerative approaches and new social models in agriculture and food production?

Note

1 www.madeinmasseria.it/bonta-comune.

Further reading

Curry, J.M. (2002). Care theory and "caring" systems of agriculture. *Agriculture and Human Values* 19, 119–131.

de Moor, D. and Hermsen, M. (2018). Achieving happiness at care farms in the Netherlands. *Journal of Social Intervention: Theory and Practice* 27, 4–23. doi:10.18354/jsi.545.

Hassink, J., Elings, M., Zweekhorst, M., Nieuwenhuizen, N.v.D. and Smit., A. (2010). Care farms: attractive empowerment-oriented and strengths-based practices in the community. *Health and Place* 24, 423–430.

Moriggi, A. (2019). Exploring enabling resources for place-based social entrepreneurship: a participatory study of Green Care practices in Finland. *Sustainability Science*. doi:10.1007/s11625-019-00738-0.

van Oers, L., Boon, W.P.C. and Moors, E.H.M. (2018). The creation of legitimacy in grassroots organisations. A study of Dutch community supported agriculture. *Environmental Innovation and Societal Transitions*. doi:10.1016/j.est.2018.04.002.

References

Alkon, A.H. and Norgaard, K.M. (2009). Breaking the food chains: an investigation of food justice activism. *Sociological Inquiry* 79 (3), 289–305.

Barnes, M. (2008). Care, deliberation and social justice. In: Dessein, J. (ed.), *Farming for health. Proceedings of the Community of Practice Farming for Health, 6–9 November 2007, Ghent, Belgium*, pp. 27–37. Merelbeke, Belgium: ILVO.

Bruni, L. and Zamagni, S. (2007). *Civil economy: efficiency, equity, public happiness*, vol. 2. Oxford: Peter Lang.

Carbone, A. and Senni, S. (2010). Consumers attitude toward ethical food: evidence from social farming in Italy. In: Dessein, J. and Bock, B. (eds.), *The economics of green care in agriculture*, pp. 76–84. Loughborough: Loughborough University.

Conradi, E. (2015). Redoing care: societal transformation through critical practice. *Ethics and Social Welfare* 9 (2), 113–129. doi:10.1080/17496535.2015.1005553.

Cox, R., Holloway, L., Venn, L., Dowler, L., et al. (2008). Common ground? Motivations for participation in a community-supported agricultural scheme. *Local Environment* 13 (3), 203–218.

Curry, J.M. (2002). Care theory and "caring" systems of agriculture. *Agriculture and Human Values* 19, 119–131.

Duh, A.A. (2010). Religion's role in the development, ecology and climate change: an Islamic perspective, Presentation at the Conference on the role of Religion in Development – Focus on Ecology and Climate Change, Finnish Evangelical Lutheran Mission. 22 April, Helsinki.

Dwivedi, O.P. (2006). Hindu religion and environmental well-being. In: *The Oxford handbook of religion and ecology*, pp. 160–184. Oxford: Oxford University Press.

Durand, G. and van Huylenbroeck, G. (2003). Multi-functionality and rural development: a general framework. In: van Huylenbroeck, G. and Durand, G. (eds.), *Multifunctional agriculture. A new paradigm for European agriculture and rural development*, pp. 1–16. Burlington: Ashgate.

Edwards, D. (2011). *Ecology at the heart of faith: the change of heart that leads to a new way of living on earth.* New York: Orbis Books.

Faden, R.R., Kass, N.E., Goodman, S.N., Pronovost, P., Tunis, S., and Beauchamp, T.L. (2013). An ethics framework for a learning health care system: a departure from traditional research ethics and clinical ethics. *Ethical Oversight of Learning Health Care Systems, Hastings Center Report Special Report* 43 (1), S16–S27. doi:10.1002/hast.134.

Fieldhouse, P. (1995). Community shared agriculture. *Agriculture and Human Values* 13 (3), 43–47.

Foltz, C.R. (2006) Islam. In: Gottlieb, R.S. (ed.), *The Oxford handbook of religion and ecology.* Oxford: Oxford University Press 2006.

Franklin, A. (2018). Spacing natures: resourceful and resilient community environmental practice. In: Marsden, T. (ed.), *The SAGE handbook of nature*, pp. 267–285. London: SAGE Publications.

Gasson, R. (1973). Goals and values of farmers. *Journal of Agricultural Economics* 24 (3), 521–542.

Grin, J. and Marijnen, E. (2011). Global threats, global changes and connected communities in the global agrofood system. In: Brauch, H. et al. (eds.), *Coping with global environmental change, disasters and security. Hexagon series on human and environmental security and peace*, vol. 5, pp. 1005–1018. Berlin, Heidelberg: Springer.

Gross, R.M. (1997) Buddhist resources for issues of population, consumption, and the environment. In: Tucker, M.E. and Williams, D.R. (eds.), *Buddhism and ecology: the interconnection of dharma and deeds*, pp. 155–172. Cambridge, MA: Harvard University Press.

Gui, B. and Sugden, R. (eds.). (2005). *Economics and social interaction: accounting for interpersonal relations.* Cambridge: Cambridge University Press.

Hassink, J. (2017). Understanding care farming as a swiftly developing sector in the Netherlands. PhD thesis, University of Amsterdam.

Hassink, J., Elings, M., Zweekhorst, M., Nieuwenhuizen, N.V.D., and Smit, A. (2010). Care farms: attractive empowerment-oriented and strengths-based practices in the community. *Health and Place* 24, 423–430.

Hassink, J. and Van Dijk, M. (2006). *Farming for health: green-care farming across Europe and the United States of America.* Wageningen, the Netherlands: Springer.

Hermans, F., Horlings, I., Beers, P.J., et al. (2010). The contested redefinition of a sustainable countryside: revisiting Frouws' rurality discourses. *Sociologia Ruralis* 50 (1), 46–63.

Horlings, L.G., and Marsden, T.K. (2014). Exploring the "new rural paradigm" in Europe: eco-economic strategies as a counterforce to the global competitiveness agenda. *European Urban and Regional Studies* 21 (1), 4–20.

Johnson, Elizabeth A. (2014). *Ask the Beasts: Darwin and the God of Love.* London: Bloomsbury.

Jones, P., Shears, P., Hillier, D., Comfort, D., and Lowell, J. (2003). Return to traditional values? A case study of slow food. *British Food Journal* 105 (4/5), 297–304.

Kaufman, J.L., and Bailkey, M. (2000). *Farming inside cities: entrepreneurial urban agriculture in the United States.* Cambridge, MA: Lincoln Institute of Land Policy.

Keyes, S.E., Webber, S.H., and Beveridge, K. (2015). Empowerment through car: using dialogue between the social model of disability and an ethic of care to redraw boundaries of independence and partnership between disabled people and services. *ALTER, European Journal of Disability Research* 9, 236–248.

Kirchman, H. (1994). Biological dynamic farming – an occult form of alternative agriculture? *Journal of Agricultural and Environmental Ethics* 7 (2), 173–187.

Kneafsly, M., Cox, R., Holloway, L., Dowler, E., Venn, L., and Tuomainen, H. (2008). *Reconnecting consumers, producers and food. Exploring alternatives.* Oxford and New York: Berg.

Koepf, H. (2007). What is bio-dynamic agriculture? *Biodynamics* 261, 27–29.

La Canne, C.E., and Lundgren, J.G. (2018). Regenerative agriculture: merging farming and natural resource conservation profitably. *PeerJ* 6, e4428. doi:10.7717/peerj.4428.

Leck, C., Evans, N., and Upton, D. (2014). Agriculture who cares? An investigation of "care farming" in the UK. *Journal of Rural Studies* 34, 313–325.

Leshem, D. (2016). Retrospectives: what did the ancient Greeks mean by oikonomia? *Journal of Economic Perspectives* 30 (1), 225–238.

Marsden, T., Banks, J., and Bristow, G. (2000). Food supply chain approaches: exploring their role in rural development. *Sociologia Ruralis* 40, 424–438.

Meerburg, B.G., Korevaar, H., Haubenhofer, D.K., Blom-Zandstra, M., and van Keulen, H. (2009). The changing role of agriculture in Dutch society. *Journal of Agricultural Science* 147, 511–521.

Mendez, V.E., Bacon, C.M., and Cohen, R. (2013). Agroecology as a transdisciplinary, participatory and action-oriented approach. *Agroecology and Sustainable Production Systems* 37, 3–18.

Mol, A., Moser, I., and Pols, J. (2010). Care: Putting practice into theory. In: Mol, A., Moser, I., and Pols, J. (Eds.), *Care in practice: On tinkering in clinics, homes and farms*, pp. 7–27. Bielefeld: Transcript-Verlag.

Mollisson, B. (1988). *Permaculture: a designer's manual.* Sisters Creek, Tasmania: Tagari.

Moriggi, A., Soini, K., Bock, B., and Roep., D. 2020. Caring *in, for,* and *with* nature: an integrative framework to understand Green Care practices. Submitted to a Special Issue of *Sustainability*.

Nelson J.A. 2011. The relational economy: A Buddhist and feminist analysis. In: Laszlo Zsolnai (Ed.), *Ethical principles and economic transformation: a Buddhist approach*, pp. 21–33, Dordrecht: Springer.

Nussbaum, M. (1998). *Gerechtigkeit oder Das gute Leben*. Frankfurt: Suhrkamp.

Poulsen, M.N., Neff, R.A. and Winch, P.J. (2017). The multifunctionality of urban farming: perceived benefits for neighbourhood improvement. *Local Environment* 22 (11), 1411–1427.

Puig de la Bellacasa, M. (2010). Ethical doings in naturecultures. *Ethics, Place and Environment: A Journal of Philosophy and Geography* 13 (2), 151–169. doi:10.1080/13668791003778834.

Renting, H., Marsden, T., and Banks, G. (2003). Understanding alternative food networks: exploring the role of short food supply chains in rural development. *Environment and Planning A* 35, 393–411.

Rhodes, C.J. (2017) The imperative for regenerative agriculture. *Science Progress* 100 (1), 80–129.

Rosa, H. (2016). *Resonanz: eine Soziologie der Weltbeziehung*. Berlin: Suhrkamp.

Shiva, V. (2016). *Earth democracy: justice, sustainability and peace*. London: Zed Books.

Singh, R.P.B. (2013). Ecological cosmology in Hindu tradition for the 21st century. In: Sharma, A. and Khanna, M. (eds.), *Asian perspectives on the world's religions after September 11*, pp. 245–259. Santa Barbara CA: ABC-CLIO, Inc..

Suh, J. (2014). Towards sustainable agricultural stewardship: evolution and future directions of the permaculture concept. *Environmental Values* 23, 75–98.

Tronto, J. (1993). *Moral boundaries: a political argument for an ethic of care*. New York and London: Routledge.

Tronto, J.C. (2013). *Caring democracy: markets, equality, and justice*. New York and London: New York University Press.

van der Ploeg, J.D. (2008). *The new peasantries: struggles for autonomy and sustainability in an era of empire and globalization*. London: Earthscan.

van Oers, L.M., Boon, W.P.C., and Moors, E.H.M. (2018). The creation of legitimacy in grassroots organisations. A study of Dutch community supported agriculture. *Environmental Innovation and Societal Transitions*. doi:10.1016/j.est.2018.04.002.

Wells, B.L., and Gradwell, S. (2001). Gender and resource management: community supported agriculture as caring-practice. *Agriculture and Human Values* 18 (1), 107–119. doi:10.1023/A.

Whyte, K.P. and Cuomo, C. (2017). Ethics of caring in environmental ethics: indigenous and feminist philosophies. In: Gardiner, S.M. and Thompson, A. (eds.), *The Oxford handbook of environmental ethics*, pp. 234–247. Oxford: Oxford University Press.

Wilson, G.A. (2008). From "weak" to "strong" multi-functionality: conceptualising farm-level multifunctional transitional pathways, *Journal of Rural Studies* 24, 367–383.

Zamagni, S. (2008). Reciprocity, civil economy, common good. In: *Pursuing the common good: how solidarity and subsidiarity can work together*, pp. 467–502. Vatican. City: Pontifical Academy of Social Sciences.

11

ANIMAL FUNCTIONALITY AND INTERSPECIES RELATIONS IN REGENERATIVE AGRICULTURE

Considering necessity and the possibilities of non-violence

Tony Weis and Rebecca A. Ellis

Introduction: from multifunctionality to meatification and back – or somewhere else?

The domestication of livestock was an important part of the development of agriculture in many parts of the world, as well as being fundamental to the rise of herding cultures (Altieri et al. 2015; Fagan 2017; Fairlee 2010; Mazoyer and Roudart 2006). This historical significance is reflected in the diverse venerations of livestock animals and consumption in different cultures (Harris 1978). The interspecies relation between humans and animals used and consumed in agriculture and herding was distinctive from much the earlier domestication of dogs or the semi-domestication of cats.[1] These changing interspecies relations were also bound up in momentous social transformations, in particular formative class and gendered power imbalances and divisions of labour (Fagan 2017).

In farming and herding, animals were no longer simply prey, but rather were made to serve multifunctional roles and afforded heightened protection from predators and enhanced food supplies, including through fallowed land, crop stubble, managed pasture, the supply of household food wastes, and (to limited extents) primary products of cultivated land. In other words, they were mostly fed through from complementary land uses rather than harvested crops. The multifunctionality of domesticated animals can also be understood as a range of use values obtained by farming and herding societies. While the nature of multifunctionality varied across bioregions and cultures, in general use values involved combinations of: coerced labour on- and off-farms (e.g. tillage, haulage); condensed nutrients for fertilization and fuel; and bodily products for clothing (wool, down, skins) and nutrition (milk, eggs, flesh). Agricultural societies also came to rely upon the roles that both semi-domesticated and wild species play in pollination, most notably bees, who create a range of valuable products in addition to their invaluable effort transferring pollen grains.

Although animals had some and often considerable degrees of autonomy, the interspecies relation in farming and herding was always one of dominance (Nibert 2013). In addition to coercing labour, taking bodily products, and killing short of full lifespans, this dominance also involved some restriction of movement and manipulation of breeding. In considering the changes to agriculture wrought by industrialization, it is also important to stress that whatever the precise nature of the multifunctionality there was always a strong degree of spatial, cognitive, and emotional proximity between use values and individual animals. Proximity was such that people either knew the animals whose work they relied on and whose flesh and reproductive outputs they consumed or at least had a strong sense of the conditions under which they lived (Weis 2013).

Across much of the world, the interspecies relations in agriculture today are radically different than those that prevailed over the 10,000 history of farming and herding. The industrialization of livestock production has disarticulated soaring populations of animals from landscapes, led by chickens and pigs, and confined them to enclosures that few people ever see inside of. In industrial systems, the historic multifunctionality of animals has been replaced by the sole imperative of accelerating bodily growth and reproductive outputs. The acceleration of weight gain, laying, and lactation has been accomplished through a range of changes including great increases in density, restrictions in mobility, genetic enhancement, artificial insemination techniques, and vast flows of feed crops, pharmaceuticals, and other inputs. The ensuing surge in productivity has underpinned the meatification of diets, which describes the momentous rise in the per capita consumption of animal flesh and products, encapsulated in the fact that the average person on a world scale (with large global disparities between high- and low-income countries) now eats nearly twice as much animal flesh than roughly two generations ago.[2] The dramatic expansion in the size of livestock operations and acceleration of animal lives has also transformed the nature of human labour within spaces of breeding (which include artificial insemination[3] and physical mutilations like de-beaking), growing (though these are extensively automated), and slaughter and packing (which face greater barriers to automation, at least for now, and involve high risks of sudden and chronic stress injuries along with the psychosocial strain of immersion in spaces filled with misery, pain, and killing). Taken together, the changes in the scale and nature of industrial production along with the changes in the spatial, cognitive, and emotional distance from animals in consumption can be seen to constitute a revolution in interspecies relations (Weis 2013).

There is overwhelming evidence that the revolution in livestock production and consumption bears heavily on a range of problems including climate change, biodiversity loss, and animal suffering (Crist et al. 2017; D'Silva and McKenna 2018; Imhoff 2011; Lymberry 2014; Machovina et al. 2015; Nibert 2013; Springmann et al. 2018, 2016). This is made worse by the consensus that this trajectory is also leading to worsened health outcomes, as a major factor in increasing rates of non-communicable diseases (NCDs), gross disparities in access to food, and mounting risks of antibiotic resistance (Dinu et al. 2016; Lim et al. 2012; Popkin 2009; Springmann et al. 2016; Wallace 2016).

In short, there is no doubt that confronting industrial livestock production and de-meatification are pivotal to any hope of building regenerative agro-food systems. There is, however, heated debate about where this should lead, with two alternative routes commonly posed. The first route entails some degree of animal multifunctionality and therefore some but less consumption of animal-based foods, sometimes framed as ethical omnivory or ethical vegetarianism. The second route is towards the complete abolition of all animal coercion and consumption, or veganism. This chapter examines the core logic of both cases, giving attention to the ethical implications of domestication and the interspecies relations of animals in mixed farming and pastoralism and the possibilities of non-violence, which are a crucial aspect of competing visions. In giving attention to the possibilities of non-violent interspecies relations, we also consider whether there might be space for a third possibility in which some animals can play functional roles within regenerative agricultural cycles without being exploited or killed.

Less but some: the case for the enduring multifunctionality of animals

For many and probably most advocates of regenerative agriculture and related fields of agroecology and permaculture,[4] the multifunctionality of livestock animals in mixed farming is not simply a relic of the pre-modern world. On the contrary, it is seen to involve biological and physical efficiencies that can and should be enhanced through conscious design. At the heart of this case is the ability of animals to turn organic wastes from crop production and households, and unusable biomass from fallowed fields and uncultivated areas into combinations of labour power, fertilizer, fuel, fiber, skins, and useable nutrition, which has the potential to reduce or eliminate external sources of locomotion and fertilization, along with the associated fossil fuel budgets and greenhouse gas emissions (Altieri et al. 2015; Fairlee 2010; Webster 2018).

From this perspective, the course of de-industrializing livestock production should aim to either maintain the multifunctional roles of animals where they still exist or restore them where they have been lost, though clearly at much lower population densities and with much less consumption than in industrial systems. Some argue that holistic or managed grazing by cows, sheep, and goats can help to restore soils and certain degraded ecosystems, particularly in arid and semi-arid grasslands and mountain ranges that cannot be easily cultivated, and where ruminants can mimic the function of large, non-domesticated herbivores that have been extirpated or declined in population (Holmgren 2002; Starhawk 2004; Toensmeier 2016). Toensmeier (2016) makes a case for silvopastoral systems that integrate grazing livestock with food-bearing and other valuable tree species, arguing that this can have an important role in carbon sequestration and hence climate change mitigation.

For those who insist upon the multifunctionality of animals in agriculture, there remains a divide between those who see the consumption of animal flesh as necessary and those who claim it can be avoided. The former group argues that the biophysical efficiency of integrating livestock in mixed farms depends upon killing and consuming bodies for food, which is why Fairlee (2010) (a permaculture practitioner and advocate) refers to meat as a 'benign indulgence' and why Pollan (2008) contends that, while people should eat *mostly* plants, this also entails eating *less but some* animal flesh, milk, eggs, and honey. The ethical vegetarian case accepts that some animals are needed in regenerative agricultural systems but hopes that it can occur without violence, which could conceivably involve allowing animals to peaceably 'retire' and live into old age after their labour power, laying, or lactation has waned.[5] Many meat-eaters in turn refute this appeal to non-violence, insisting that consuming the flesh of dead animals is part of what it means to be human. For instance, in a well-known critique of vegetarianism, Plumwood (2000) insists that refusing meat falsely 'demonizes' the nature of predation by humans and other animals.[6]

While human necessity is always at the forefront of how the use of livestock is justified, at any scale, this case is often paired with an argument that some advantages are conferred to animals (food supplies, safety, and in some cases shelter), as well as a promise that caring stewardship is at the very least possible. The population growth of livestock species is sometimes touted as an indication of what they have 'won' from their dependence upon humans over millennia, which also implies that they have no plausible exit from it. Starhawk (2004, 116), a well-known permaculture advocate, clearly encapsulates this sense of irreversibility:

> sheep, cows, chickens, and our other domesticated animals have now coevolved with us for thousands of years. Were we to stop eating them, they would not live happy, productive, fulfilled animal lives; they would cease to exist as species and become extinct.

Furthermore, because humans have increased the genetic diversity of domesticated animals through the long history of selective breeding, some also point to the fact that so-called heritage breeds can only be sustained with continuing human management and use (with the importance of doing so posed against the radical genetic narrowing associated with industrial livestock production) (FAO 2007; Hoffmann 2011).

The claim that benign stewardship is possible relates to the nature of multifunctionality and the intimacy that comes with relatively low populations, where farmers and herders know their animals as individual beings and have an interest in their longevity. At a basic level, it assumes that livestock animals can have a reasonably good life before the 'one bad day' where it ends. Although it will always be impossible to define precisely what a 'good' life would be for farmed animals, in its fullest expression this might entail allowing animals to live with considerable agency and autonomy in their daily lives, affording sufficient rest where labour is forced, and having other use values for farming (e.g. fertilizer, pollination), nutrition (e.g. eggs, milk, honey), and fiber (e.g. wool) accrue through partly managed but reasonably normal – or 'biologically appropriate' – species behaviours. A basic guideline for this general goal is encapsulated by the influential farmer-activist Joel Salatin (2017), who describes his farming as seeking to respect the '"pigness" of the pig.' For Salatin, this means allowing his pigs to scavenge for part of their diet, select reproductive partners, live in social groups of their own choosing, and wander around relatively freely, rooting, digging, sun-bathing, dirt-bathing, and wallowing in mud (see also Salatin 2011; Webster 2018).

Some go further still and argue that the stewardship of livestock can not only respect the 'animalness of the animal' but can approach a similar sort of companionship and mutual affection as exists between humans and animals like dogs and cats in many cultures. Despite the obvious barriers to analyzing and proving this, there is growing empirical evidence to suggest that certain domesticated animals (and not only dogs and cats) can develop emotional bonds to humans, including the ability to understand and respond to human displays of emotions (Nawroth et al. 2019; Proops et al. 2018). It is most plausible for humans to express affection for labouring animals such as horses, donkeys, and oxen, but it is also conceivable for animals that cannot be known as individuals such as honeybees.[7] To the degree that affective relationships between small farmers and their livestock can exist it can constitute another objection to industrialization.

Transcending the use of animals: the case for abolition

For people who seek to abolish all use of animals, domestication is not an immutable interspecies relation. Rather, it is seen to mark something of an 'original sin' from more egalitarian and less ecologically destructive gatherer–hunter cultures (Mason 1993; Nibert 2013). While technologically-limited hunters drove the extinction of many large animal species prior to the rise of agriculture, and wrought considerable ecological change through fire, the rise of agriculture and herding unleashed more systematic and much larger scale conversions of forests and grasslands. This not only reduced habitat for other species but involved a continued assault on predators, which now threatened not only humans but livestock too.

Abolitionists reject the idea that enhanced protection from predators and augmented feeding environments were advantageous for livestock, and that long-term population growth and geographic dispersion reflects a species-level advantage bestowed by domestication, as some evolutionary biologists have argued (Thomas 2017). Rather, they insist, these ostensible gains need to be understood in relation to the diminished status of animals as 'living stock', one of the first forms of property. This entailed coercive violence from the start, as a degree of physical mutilation goes back to the early stages of domestication, such as the branding of skin to mark individual beings as property. These relations entailed death short of a full lifespan, restricted autonomy, and arduous labour. The longstanding phrase 'beasts of burden' underscores the difficulty of work and accompanying condescension, and for many animals the main respite from hard labour has been immobility, tied to posts or the inside of sheds. In this light, population growth and dispersion were not advantageous to these species, much as one could hardly defend the institution of slavery by pointing to a rising population of slaves (Spiegel 1996). Rather, they indicate a highly detrimental trajectory: a narrowing and descending path that became harder to escape over time, as long-term artificial selection for docility and human use values exacerbated dependence upon human-managed environments. Abolitionists also regularly stress the role these interspecies relations of dominance had in the rise of class and gender inequalities (Adams 2010; Francione 2008; Mason 1993; Nibert 2013), with Nibert's (2013) evocative term 'domesecration' meant to convey a sense of multifaceted descent.

In short, whether considering past or present contexts, abolitionists argue that any imagery of benign stewardship in farming and herding cannot stand up to the primacy of use values and the property status of livestock. On top of disputing whether farm animals can be granted reasonably good lives, they also insist that the 'one bad day' cannot be reduced to a caveat. For animals, this not only obviously terminates the possibility of any further enjoyment of life but is bound to affect the social lives of small groups. For humans, there is no way to reconcile affection for an animal with the knowledge that one will eventually kill and consume its flesh; there is only cognitive dissonance. This cognitive dissonance is seen to extend to the vegetarian hope of non-violence, which fails on two primary grounds. First, there are bound to be 'excess' males (e.g. cattle, water buffalo, goats, and chickens) where they do not have the same nutritional functionality as their female counterparts and cannot be justified solely for composting wastes into fertilizer, though some male cattle and water buffalo can be made to work. Second, female cows, buffalo, and goats get exploited through accelerated and sometimes forcible impregnation, as their value generating milk increases when they are kept in continual cycles of pregnancy or lactation, which can also involve the removal of young and the breaking of motherly bonds.

Beyond the moral philosophical case, abolitionists also stress the need to challenge the matter of necessity. The nutritional defense for consumption of meat, eggs, and dairy has never been shakier, as there is abundant evidence from research on nutrition and epidemiological patterns that plant-based diets can bring wide-ranging health benefits (Dinu et al. 2016; Lim et al. 2012; Popkin 2009; Springmann et al. 2016). The stronger defense for consuming animal products lies on the side of production and the fact that, as indicated earlier, most advocates of regenerative agriculture and allied fields see the need to integrate small populations of livestock for their role cycling organic wastes, grasses, and other matter into valuable fertilizer.

However, for abolitionists, the historic multifunctionality of animals in agriculture and pastoralism was often far from sustainable over the long term, as is powerfully evidenced in the many once fertile lands that are now deserts, like the so-called 'Cradle of Civilization' (Montgomery 2007). Furthermore, there are new, urgent imperatives as the earth enters the epoch of the Anthropocene (or Capitalocene) in which biophysical conditions are moving far beyond the parameters that have prevailed over the past 10,000 years. A central, inescapable goal is to strive for large reductions in GHG emissions and large increases CO_2 sequestration capacity through aggressive re-naturalization efforts, which are also crucial to ebb the loss of biodiversity. These point very clearly at the need to source nutrition as efficiently as possible, and there is an extensive literature demonstrating that plant-based diets tend to generate far less GHG emissions and command far less land and resources than meat-centered diets (Crist et al. 2017; Poore and Nemeck 2018; Springmann et al. 2018, 2016).

For abolitionists, any animal activity in agriculture would have to be undirected with any use values deriving from the autonomous activity of animals, such as through their role in pollination or rescued farm animals generating manure, with farm sanctuaries also having a critical educational role in relation to industrial livestock production (Gillespie 2019). Although the use of insect-killing chemicals would seem to be incompatible with the ethical aspiration to avoid intentional harm, many vegans are focused primarily on mammals and birds and are willing to abide pesticide and inorganic fertilizer use in industrial agriculture – a clear reflection of which is the fast-expanding scope of non-organic vegan products. Some vegans are also vesting great hopes in high-technology meat-substitutes that rely on genetic modification and gene editing, including both plant-based 'meats' and cloning or 'test-tube' meat.[8] Yet while substitutes based on industrial monocultures might be at the forefront of growing vegan demand, and this might have some considerable benefits in relation to cycling the products of monocultures through industrial livestock, further discussion of these implications lies beyond the scope of this chapter as this is not compatible with any conception of regenerative agriculture.

There is, however, a marginal but growing movement of vegan organic (or 'veganic') farming and vegan permaculture that seeks to align the broad aspirations of regenerative agriculture with the desire to avoid all harm and killing in food production. Although there is a degree of fuzziness about the definition, the basic premise of veganic agriculture is that it cannot involve any exploitation, conception of animals as property, or reliance in any directed way, and must also avoid the use of GMO seeds, pesticides, and fossil fuel-derived inputs which reverberate on animals in unintended ways (Seymour; forthcoming). Although difficult to track, around 50 farms in the United States self-identify as veganic (out of almost 13,000 certified organic farms).[9] Veganic agriculture practitioners avoid the use of all by-products from livestock production including manure, bloodmeal, bone meal, and fish emulsions. Instead, they premise their regenerative production on methods such as the use of plant-based green manures and composting and nutrient and mineral inputs from non-animal sources such as kelp, lime, gypsum, and the meal of nitrogen-rich seed plants.

The aim of avoiding all harm and killing presents a number of difficult practical challenges, most of all how to control undesirable or 'pest' species and how to return sufficient nutrients to soils, which reverberate in difficult ethical questions, such as whether it is ethical to encourage pest predators or take any bee products if it can be done without harm to the bees (Seymour forthcoming). These dilemmas grow with scale. For instance, veganic farmers try to control non-human animals from consuming crops with a combination of physical barriers (such as the use of floating row covers and fruit socks) and by indirectly encouraging the presence of wild predator species, approaches that are generally practiced in contexts of relative isolation. If veganic farms were to become more prevalent across landscapes it is possible that some of these approaches could be less viable or it could magnify demand for damaging synthetic materials, such the use of plastics in row covers, which is a growing concern with large-scale organic production. The greater relative labour intensity on veganic farms poses another set of questions for the prospects of scaling up, especially in light of how poorly paid waged labour in agriculture in general tends to be (though the challenge of fairly remunerating farmers and workers lies far beyond the terrain of veganic agriculture alone).

In sum, there are no definitive blueprints that might guide the development of a cruelty-free, plant-based food system, and its growth will depend upon the flourishing of practical experiments and the sharing of knowledge. Two indications of the fledgling nature of this movement can be seen in the growth of vegan permaculture design courses[10] and in efforts to establish basic standards and a Stockfree certification (that includes seventeen categories) for veganic farmers, which is now available in both the US and UK. There may be more hope in this movement scaling out rather than scaling up, especially if it is based on an integration of animal rights, environmentalism, and workers' rights within agriculture.

Integrating without exploiting animals

There is compelling evidence that moving towards plant-based diets and away from the heavy consumption of flesh, milk, and eggs will be highly beneficial to the environment, human health, and other animals (Crist et al. 2017; Dinu et al. 2016; Lim et al. 2012; Poore and Nemeck 2018; Popkin 2009; Springmann et al. 2018, 2016). But it is not yet clear whether regenerative agro-food systems can function on any significant scale without some animal functionality. Regardless of how compelling the ethical case for veganic agriculture may be, it is possible that some integration of domesticated and semi-domesticated animals may be necessary, either in present transitions towards regenerative agricultural systems or in a radical future where they have moved from the margins to the center.

The case of bees is a good example of both transitional and long-term dilemmas if reducing or eliminating animal exploitation is prioritized in regenerative agriculture. As noted, some conceptions of veganic agriculture exclude the keeping of honeybees, and all exclude the consumption of honey or human use of beeswax (Seymour forthcoming). However, the combination of industrialized agriculture, habitat loss, and climate change are driving the steady decline of wild bees to a point where some wild species of bees and other insects are bound for extinction (Lister and Garcia 2018). This decline means that semi-domesticated honeybees are increasingly essential to the pollination of a range of annual and tree crops, and this dependence seems bound to increase, not only for agriculture but also within relatively self-organizing ecosystems. While the management of honeybees for pollination does not have to entail the use of their honey or beeswax, the necessity of one function does impel conversations about whether gathering these products for human use could be benign or if it is inherently exploitative.

Attempts to reduce or eliminate the exploitation of animals in regenerative agricultural systems also present difficult challenges for fertilization, as animal manure has been a primary mechanism for sustaining soil fertility through millennia and could help to rehabilitate land degraded by excessive tillage, erosion, and chemical inputs. Although there are a range of other effective practices for maintaining or improving soil health that do not rely on animals, including composting systems based on the decay of plants, treated humanure, and green manures (plants that add nutrients to the soil while growing as well as when decaying), in practice these are often coupled with the use of some animal manure. In the absence of animal manure, it is unclear whether these practices could suffice on a large scale and within all climates. The challenge of fertilization without animals is further complicated by the fact that nutrient cycles within trophic webs have been widely disrupted by environmental change, including the massive declines of wild animal populations known as de-faunation (Dirzo et al. 2014). Domesticated animals now comprise the large majority of all mammalian and bird biomass on earth (Bar-On et al. 2018) and, as with honeybees and pollination, it is possible that the ecological functions (e.g. cycling nutrients, dispersing seeds) of some extinct or declining species could be substituted by similar more abundant species, including domesticated animals – which would also raise prospects of animals becoming feral and evolving in new directions (Thomas 2017). Re-substituting the labour of animals such as oxen, horses, and donkey for some of the locomotion of tractors and other large vehicles could also conceivably have a role in reducing dependence on fossil fuels and ensuing GHG emissions.

The practical and moral questions surrounding animal functionality in regenerative agriculture are problematized still further by the fact that domestication has, for better or worse, made many animals dependent on humans for food, protection from predators, and shelter during certain seasons (indeed, as noted, domesticated animals comprise a large and growing share of all animal life). While the breeding of animals for characteristics that benefit industrialized livestock agriculture certainly increases the misery of the individual animal and is not in the interest of the species as a whole, so-called heritage breeds of domesticated farm animals tend to be more resilient animals with some, such as sheep, goats, and honeybees, better able to live in relative (though not complete) autonomy from humans. Striving to end all management of animal populations in farming landscapes would imply that heritage breeds of domesticated animals, which have been affected by millennia of human intervention, will eventually die out. In the contexts of the extinction spasm and defaunation, in which many wild animals are struggling within habitat patches that are too small, fragmented, and altered by climate change, it may be that heritage breeds of domesticated animals are best equipped to survive in highly altered and fragmented landscapes, in turn helping maintain a degree of large animal diversity in the short term – and perhaps expand it in the longer term as some become feral, thereby helping to re-diversify an ecologically impoverished world.

The recognition that some animal functions in agriculture might be necessary, or that heritage breeds have a right to existence after long histories of domestication, does not mean that the goal of enhancing animal autonomy and reducing exploitation as far as possible need be abandoned. On the contrary, Donaldson and Kymlicka (2010) argue that, while the course of domestication has been driven by human priorities at the expense of the interests of those animals being changed, drawing them into exploitative and violent interspecies relations, justice now requires repositioning domesticated animals as full members – indeed co-citizens – within the interspecies societies humans have created. This entails conferring the rights of residency, inclusion in consideration of the public good (as far as possible, given that they can obviously not articulate it for themselves), and the right to exercise agency over as much of their lives as possible.[11] Contrary to many animal abolitionists, Donaldson and Kymlicka (2010, 63) argue that it would be 'premature to claim that the best or only way to redress the injustices suffered by domesticated animals is to seek their extinction.'[12]

Donaldson and Kymlicka's (2010) moral philosophical case for granting co-citizenship to domesticated animals draws heavily on the premise that people who need assistance and external advocates in order to live and participate in society, such as young children and intellectually disabled individuals, should still maintain irrevocable citizenship rights. Further, they insist that interdependencies between species need not be inherently undignified or unnatural for other animals, which resonates with longstanding feminist critiques of masculinist theories that reify independence and individualism. One indication that some interspecies dependence is inevitable can be seen in the fact that some wild and liminal animals flourish in human-created spaces, and it is likely that even if humans had never proceeded with selective breeding some animals would have chosen to live in community with humans, a case strengthened by recent debates about the agency of dogs in forging relationships with humans (Hare and Woods 2013).

Donaldson and Kymlicka (2010) acknowledge that conferring citizenship rights on domesticated animals does not necessarily exclude all functionality with respect to humans, stressing that just and equitable participation in societies entails performing beneficial roles for others beyond solely one's self-interest. Some basic considerations for assessing what animal functions could be compatible with their model of co-citizenship include those that involve free choice and agency, cause no harm, and do not relegate animals to a position of structural inferiority (i.e. akin to second class citizenship). From this, they insist that companionship, grazing 'services' (e.g. manure), honey, and guardian roles could be obtained by humans without exploitation or harm to their co-citizens, who in turn receive some discernible benefits. They also suggest that in limited cases eggs, wool, and beeswax might be used,[13] but in no cases could this model justify the use of domesticated animals for meat, dairy, or hard labour.

Conclusions

This chapter started from a premise that there is overwhelming evidence that trajectory of livestock production and consumption on a world scale is highly destructive, inequitable, and inhumane. In light of the urgency of climate change, biodiversity loss, and soil degradation, the magnitude of non-communicable disease, and the immense scale of animal suffering, the need to reduce livestock production and move towards plant-based diets is undeniable. From this premise, we have considered debates about where this should lead in terms of the functionality of animals in regenerative agriculture systems, including both practical and moral dimensions.

The fact that most visions of regenerative agriculture accept the necessary functionality of domesticated animals is not surprising in light of the 10,000-year history of agriculture. Yet however entangled interspecies relations are between humans and domesticated animals, the history of domestication does not in itself represent a defense, whether we view it in light of past injustices, present uncertainties (such as the precariousness of agriculture in a rapidly warming world), or the hope of transcending all exploitation and intentional violence in a way that runs beyond the ostensible 'one bad day'. Reflecting these concerns, a small group of veganic farmers and vegan permaculturists are striving to fashion regenerative practices that do not exploit animals, though this movement is still in its infancy and small in scale, and in general there has been insufficient imagination and applied ecological research in relation to the importance of the subject (Seymour forthcoming).

In facing up to the daunting challenge of transforming agro-food systems, we can draw inspiration from the fact that they have never been static but rather always bound up with changes in social and interspecies relations, environmental conditions, and technological development. Domesticated animals have been an important part of agrarian change from the progress of civilizations to the past and present deterioration of environmental conditions, and to contest the nature of prevailing interspecies relations – and commit to an ethic of care and multispecies flourishing – could help to inspire radical social change based on a fundamentally different conception of abundance than that of growth, profits, and accumulation (Collard et al. 2015). So while the extent to which animal functions will remain necessary or can be transcended in regenerative agricultural systems is unsettled, the goal of eliminating all animal exploitation and intentional violence should still guide innovation.

Discussion questions

1. What does the multifunctional role of animals in mixed farming systems entail?
2. How has the domestication of livestock animals been justified in philosophical terms?
3. Why do those seeking to end animal use in agriculture argue that the long history of domestication should not make it unassailable?
4. Given that the biophysical conditions of the planet are moving beyond anything experienced in the 10,000 history of agriculture, how much should the historic multifunctionality of animals inform future-oriented practices?
5. Is the elimination of all harming and killing in agriculture a desirable goal in or philosophical terms? Is it plausible in practical terms? What are the central challenges?

Notes

1 The semi-domestication of cats was also important to the early origins of agriculture, in helping guard grains surpluses from rodents.
2 There are large global disparities in meatification between high- and low-income countries, with much of the anticipated growth in meat consumption in the coming decades expected to unfold in the middle, in fast-industrializing countries (Nibert 2013).
3 Davis (2017) insists this is better understood as interspecies sexual assault.
4 Agroecology draws together traditional farming knowledge, modern ecological science, and pro-peasant politics (Altieri et al. 2015). Permaculture has been described as 'an international grassroots movement characterized by its focus on holistic regenerative design and practice for sustainable human settlements' (Ferguson and Lovell 2017). We do not intend to diminish the distinctions between these visions and associated advocacy, but we believe it is safe to assume they share enough commonality in the conception of livestock multifunctionality to be considered together for the purposes of this chapter.
5 There are undoubtedly some vegetarians who feel more aligned with vegans in principle but remain vegetarian more for practical rather than moral reasons. The point here is that the ontological basis of vegetarianism necessarily accedes to some use of animals in agriculture.
6 Eaton (2002) provides a counter-critique of Plumwood's argumentation, insisting that she misinterprets some of the radical permutations and implications of ethical vegetarianism in western thought and advocacy.
7 There are several cultural practices about honeybees, particularly in cultures where beekeeping has been an important, longstanding practice. For example, there was a tradition of 'talking to the

bees' in parts of Europe and northeastern parts of the United States, telling individual colonies about family deaths and other significant life events (English 2018).

8 The 'Impossible Burger' is the most celebrated example of this, with market valuation surging on its crossover into mainstream markets such as fast-food giant Burger King.

9 Mona Seymour's project to map veganic farms in the US can be found at https://veganic.world/farm-map/. Further information on the movement can be found at the Veganic Agriculture Network www.goveganic.net/.

10 More detail on what this certification entails can be found at https://stockfreeorganic.net/. Examples of vegan permaculture design courses can be found at https://spiralseed.co.uk/vegan-permaculture/.

11 In this framework, they suggest that wild animals which avoid humans should be treated as sovereign nations and liminal animals highly autonomous within human landscapes (e.g. racoons, squirrels, and rats) should be treated as denizens. In all cases, animals must be understood to possess basic, universal rights to be free from intentional harm, exploitation, and (as far as possible) habitat destruction.

12 There is less moral justification to sustain industrial breeds because they have been bred for such rapid growth that they are often left disabled or in pain on rare occasions when they are removed from industrial settings and allowed to age.

13 When it comes to bodily products such as eggs, wool, honey, and beeswax, the deciding factor in terms of use versus exploitation may be the commoditization of the product. A similar ethical line is crossed when human bodily products are commoditized such as blood donation, human ova, sperm, and hair.

Further reading

A wide-ranging collection on many closely-related subjects:
- D'Silva, J., and C. McKenna (eds.) (2018): *Farming, Food and Nature: Respecting Animals, People and the Environment*. London: Routledge.

On the long history of domestication:
- Fagan, B. (2017): *The Intimate Bond: How Animals Shaped Human History*. London: Bloomsbury.
- Nibert, D.A. (2013): *Animal Oppression and Human Violence: Domesecration, Capitalism and Global Conflict*. New York: Columbia University Press.

On the permaculture case for animals:
- Fairlee, S. (2010): *Meat: A Benign Extravagance*. White River Junction, VT: Chelsea Green.

On the destructive trajectory of meatification and industrial livestock production:
- Wallace, R. (2016): *Big Farms Make Big Flu: Dispatches on Infectious Disease, Agribusiness, and the Nature of Science*. New York: Monthly Review Press.
- Weis, T. (2013): *The Ecological Hoofprint: The Global Burden of Industrial Livestock*. London: Zed.

On the connection between human oppression and the exploitation of animals:
- Adams, C. (2010[1990]): *The Sexual Politics of Meat: A Feminist-Vegetarian Critical Theory*. New York and London: Bloomsbury.

On a co-citizenship model of interspecies relations and animal entitlements.
- Donaldson, S., and W. Kymlicka (2010): *Zoopolis: A Political Theory of Animal Rights*. Oxford: Oxford University Press.

Works cited

Adams, C. (2010 [1990]): *The Sexual Politics of Meat: A Feminist-Vegetarian Critical Theory*. New York and London: Bloomsbury.

Altieri, M., C.I. Nicholls, A. Henao, and M.A. Lana (2015): 'Agroecology and the design of climate farming system.' *Agronomy for Sustainable Development*, 35(3), 869–890.

Bar-On, Y.M., R. Phillips, and R. Milo (2018): 'The biomass distribution on Earth.' *PNAS*, 115(25), 6506–6511.

Collard, R., J. Dempsey, and J. Sundberg (2015): 'A manifesto for abundant futures.' *Annals of the Association of American Geographers*, 105(2), 322–330.

Crist, E., C. Mora, and R. Engelman (2017): 'The interaction of human population, food production, and biodiversity protection.' *Science*, 356(6335), 260–264.

D'Silva, J., and C. McKenna (eds.) (2018): *Farming, Food and Nature: Respecting Animals, People and the Environment*. London: Routledge.

Davis, K. (2017): 'Interspecies sexual assault: A moral perspective.' *Animal Liberation Currents*. July 12. Available at: www.animalliberationcurrents.com/interspecies-sexual-assault/

Dinu, M., R. Abbate, G.F. Gensini, A. Casini, and F. Sofi (2016): 'Vegetarian, vegan diets with multiple health outcomes: A systematic review with meta-analysis of observational studies.' *Critical Reviews in Food Science and Nutrition*, 57(17), 3640–3649.

Dirzo, R., H.S. Young, M. Galetti, G. Ceballos, N.J. Isaac, and B. Collen (2014): 'Defaunation in the Anthropocene.' *Science*, 345(6195), 401–406.

Donaldson, S., and W. Kymlicka (2010): *Zoopolis: A Political Theory of Animal Rights*. Oxford: Oxford University Press.

Eaton, D. (2002): 'Incorporating the other: Val Plumwood's integration of ethical frameworks.' *Ethics and the Environment*, 7(2), 153–180.

English, C. (2018): 'Telling the bees.' *JStor Daily*, September 5, Available at: https://daily.jstor.org/telling-the-bees/

Fagan, B. (2017): *The Intimate Bond: How Animals Shaped Human History*. New York: Bloomsbury.

Fairlie, S. (2010): *Meat: A Benign Extravagance*. White River Junction, VT: Chelsea Green.

FAO (2007): *The State of the World's Animal Genetic Resources for Food and Agriculture*. Rome: FAO Commission on Genetic Resources for Food and Agriculture.

Ferguson, R.S., and S.T. Lovell (2017): 'Livelihoods and production diversity on US permaculture farms.' *Agroecology and Sustainable Food Systems*, 41(6), 588–613.

Francione, G.L. (2008): *Animals as Persons: Essays on the Abolition of Animal Exploitation*. New York: Columbia University Press.

Gillespie, K. (2018): *The Cow with Ear Tag #1389*. Chicago, IL: University of Chicago Press.

Hare, B. and V. Woods (2013): *The Genius of Dogs: How Dogs are Smarter than you Think*. New York: Plume.

Harris, M. (1978): *Cows, Pigs, Wars and Witches: The Riddles of Culture*. New York: Vintage.

Hoffmann, I. (2011): 'Livestock biodiversity and sustainability.' *Livestock Science*, 139(1–2), 69–79.

Holmgren, D. (2002): *Permaculture: Principles and Pathways Beyond Sustainability*. Hepburn: Holmgren Design Services.

Imhoff, D. (ed.) (2011): *The CAFO Reader: The Tragedy of Industrial Animal Factories*. Berkeley, CA: University of California Press.

Lim, S.S., et al. (2012): 'A comparative risk assessment of burden of disease and injury attributable to 67 risk factors and risk factor clusters in 21 regions, 1990–2010: A systematic analysis for the *Global Burden of Disease* Study 2010.' *The Lancet*, 380(9859), 2224–2260.

Lister, B.C., and A. Garcia (2018): 'Climate-driven declines in arthropod abundance restructure a rainforest food web.' *PNAS*, 115, 44.

Lymberry, P. (2014): *Farmageddon: The True Cost of Cheap Meat*. New York: Bloomsbury.

Machovina, B., K.J. Feeley, and W.J. Ripple (2015): 'Biodiversity conservation: The key is reducing meat consumption.' *Science of the Total Environment*, 536, 419–431.

Mason, J. (1993): *An Unnatural Order: The Roots of Our Destruction of Nature*. New York: Simon & Schuster.

Mazoyer, M., and L. Roudart (2006): *A History of World Agriculture: From the Neolithic Age to the Current Crisis*. New York: Monthly Review Press.

Montgomery, D. (2007): *Dirt: The Erosion of Civilizations*. Berkeley, CA: University of California Press.

Nawroth, C., J. Langbein, M. Coulon, V. Gabor, S. Oesterwind, J. Benz-Schwarzburg, and E. von Borell (2019): 'Farm animal cognition – linking behavior, welfare and ethics.' *Frontiers of Veterinary Science*, 12, 2.

Nibert, D.A. (2013): *Animal Oppression and Human Violence: Domesecration, Capitalism and Global Conflict*. New York: Columbia University Press.

Plumwood, V. (2000): 'Integrating ethical frameworks for animals, humans, and nature: A critical feminist eco-socialist analysis.' *Ethics and the Environment*, 5(2), 285–322.

Pollan, M. (2006): *The Omnivore's Dilemma: A Natural History of Four Meals*. New York: Penguin.

Pollan, M. (2008): *In Defence of Food: An Eater's Manifesto*. New York: Penguin.

Poore, J., and T. Nemeck (2018): 'Reducing food's environmental impacts through producers and consumers.' *Science*, 360(6392), 987–992.

Popkin, B. (2009): 'Reducing meat consumption has multiple benefits for the world's health.' *Archives of Internal Medicine*, 169(6), 543–545.

Proops, L., K. Grounds, A.V. Smith, and K. McComb (2018): 'Animals remember previous facial expressions that specific humans have exhibited.' *Current Biology*, 28(9), 1428–1432.

Sage, C. (2012): *Environment and Food*. New York: Routledge.

Salatin, J. (2011): *Folks, This Ain't Normal: A Farmer's Advice for Happier Hens, Healthier People, and A Better World*. New York: Center Street.

Salatin, J. (2017): *The Marvelous Pigness of Pigs: Respecting and Caring for All God's Creation*. New York: FaithWords.

Seymour, M. (forthcoming). 'Envisioning a vegan agriculture.' In: P. Hodge, A. McGregor, Y. Narayanan, S. Springer, O. Veron, and R.J. White (eds.), *Vegan Geographies: Ethics beyond Violence*.

Spiegel, M. (1996 [1988]): *The Dreaded Comparison: Human and Animal Slavery*, 2nd ed. New York: Mirror Books.

Springmann, M., et al. (2018): 'Options for keeping the food system within environmental limits.' *Nature*, 562, 519–525.

Springmann, M., H.C.J. Godfray, M. Rayner, and P. Scarborough (2016): 'Analysis and valuation of the health and climate cobenefits of dietary change.' *PNAS*, 113(15), 4146–4151.

Starhawk (2004): *The Earth Path: Grounding Your Spirit in the Rhythms of Nature*. New York: HarperCollins.

Steinfeld, H., P. Gerber, T. Wassenaar, V. Castel, M. Rosales, and C. de Haan (2006): *Livestock's Long Shadow: Environmental Issues and Options*. Rome: FAO.

Thomas, C. (2017): *Inheritors of the Earth: How Nature is Thriving in an Age of Extinction*. New York: PublicAffairs.

Toensmeier, E. (2016): *The Carbon Farming Solution: A Global Toolkit of Perennial Crops and Regenerative Agriculture Practices for Climate Change Mitigation and Food Security*. White River Junction, VT: Chelsea Green.

Wallace, R. (2016): *Big Farms Make Big Flu: Dispatches on Infectious Disease, Agribusiness, and the Nature of Science*. New York: Monthly Review Press.

Webster, J. (2018): 'Green and pleasant farming: Cattle, sheep and habitat.' In: J. D'Silva and C. McKenna (eds.), *Farming, Food and Nature: Respecting Animals, People and the Environment*. London: Routledge, pp. 101–106.

Weis, T. (2013): *The Ecological Hoofprint: The Global Burden of Industrial Livestock*. London: Zed.

12

LINKING SMALL-SCALE FISHING AND COMMUNITY CAPITALS

The case of Atlantic cod

Holly Amos and Megan Bailey

Introduction

Marine and freshwater ecosystems offer a multitude of opportunities for food production, from seaweed mariculture, to fish farming, to wild capture fisheries. Indeed, as the global population approaches the projected 9.7 billion by 2050 (United Nations Department of Economic and Social Affairs 2019), and as the differential impacts of land versus aquatic animal food production are uncovered (Hilborn et al. 2018), the role of fish and seafood in meeting global food and nutritional security is expected to increase (Duarte et al. 2009). Additional "solutions" to feeding 9 billion by 2050 include adopting a systems approach to food. Sustainable food systems have been suggested as a way to produce an adequate quantity and quality of food to feed the world. Framed as a tool for building food security and ensuring that sustainable production continues, they are seen as an improvement upon conventional food production practices that cause environmental degradation through poor water and soil management practices, intensive production, monoculture, and reduced biodiversity (Godfray and Garnett 2014).

However, our food systems are embedded within socio-cultural, economic and ecological contexts. Therefore, they should be considered as a part of the complex environmental and human systems (sometimes referred to as social-ecological systems). By considering food systems as a part of broader environmental and human systems we can begin to see that aligning human health and wellbeing with environmental health is necessary to support sustainable food production for years to come. There has been international recognition of the need to consider the interconnectedness of human health and wellbeing and environmental health (Environment and Climate Change Canada, 2016; UNDP, 2016a, 2016b), however, this has yet to be seen in policy in Canada for food production generally, and for marine food production specifically.

Marine food production is not just about contributing to a food supply, but the very practice of fishing has deep cultural roots in coastal Canada, contributing to both individual as well as community wellbeing (Newell and Ommer 1999). Thinking then about how marine food production is part of the larger social-ecological system that recognizes both ecosystem and human dimensions becomes an imperative for developing fisheries policies to reinforce those benefits. It is this type of food system, one that simultaneously contributes to ecosystem and human health that we consider to be a regenerative food system as it links with notions originally put forward by Dahlberg three decades ago (1993). Dahlberg espoused we develop or return to a decolonized approach to industrial agriculture, Indigenous food systems, and a health-based instead of productivity-based model to food production in order to move toward regenerative food systems. This third model, one with a health focus, lends itself well to an exploration of the connectivity between human and ecological systems within the context of fisheries production.

When a food system meets a community's needs, be they health, social, cultural, natural, political, and/or economic needs, community wellbeing is supported. But at the same time, when the needs of the community are not met and community wellbeing suffers, so too does the food system. This connectivity between wellbeing and food systems reinforces that a food system reform that presupposed a linear relationship between these two things will not go far enough. Rather, regenerative food systems, which recognize circularity, have the potential to support community wellbeing through providing various ecosystem services and meeting community needs in a way that goes beyond sustainability to actively support improved health in the connected systems. We suggest that this creates a sort of positive feedback loop where community wellbeing supports regenerative food systems, and vice versa.

Unfortunately, much of Canada's fisheries policies do not appear to have been developed with human health and wellbeing in mind, but rather have supported neoliberal reforms including privatization and fleet rationalization. These reforms have disproportionately favoured the large-scale fishing sector, to the detriment of social health (Bennett et al. 2018; Pinkerton and Davis 2015), thereby not supporting regenerative marine food systems. In this chapter, we argue that the small-scale fishing sector is worthy of policy prioritization as it is well-positioned to contribute to regenerative food systems. We explore how small-scale fisheries contributed to community wellbeing, through a case study of the Newfoundland northern cod fishery collapse in the 1990s and the changes to community wellbeing, measured though community capitals, following the collapse. We argue that, should the recovery of the collapsed cod stocks be realized, fisheries should not be managed so as to be merely sustainable, but to be regenerative. We chose this example as it clearly demonstrates the community wellbeing consequences of a crisis in the food system, and the need for an approach that goes beyond sustainable food systems in the event of opening up a fishery, to one that supports the improved health and regeneration of the fishery and of the community.

We first provide a background on small-scale fisheries in Canada, and a small narrative on Canada's iconic cod collapse. We then discuss the community capitals models, and its potential in helping us to understand how, if managed appropriately, Canadian small-scale fisheries can contribute to regenerative food systems in Canada. Our focus in this chapter is specifically on community wellbeing, and while we recognize that wellbeing is not the only component of a regenerative food system, we think it is a vital component that has so far been ignored in many fisheries policies, and food policies more broadly. Fisheries management has long kept its feet grounded in concepts and approaches to ecological sustainability, but it's clear that this alone does not allow fish as food and fish harvesters as food producers to receive the policy attention they deserve.

Small-scale fisheries and Newfoundland

There is no universally accepted definition of small-scale fisheries (Soltanpour et al. 2017). Perhaps given that any given fishery anywhere in the world is unique in its catch, methods, resources, and the surrounding socioeconomic and political conditions, it is impractical to try to encompass all of these factors in one definition. Nevertheless, researchers and policymakers alike have attempted to do so. The Food and Agriculture Organization of the United Nations (FAO) defines small-scale fisheries as "traditional fisheries using relatively small amount of capital and energy, relatively small fishing vessels, but varying from gleaning or a one-man canoe in poor developing countries, to more than 20 meters trawlers, seiners, or long-liners in developed ones" (FAO in Soltanpour et al. 2017). This definition leaves plenty of room for the inclusion or exclusion of a wide range of fishing methods and fishing communities.

While Canada as a whole has favoured corporatization and privatization of its fisheries, Atlantic Canada's fishing sector still retains a strong small-scale contingent. This is largely due to three Fisheries and Oceans licensing policies for Atlantic Canada that act as controls to prevent monopolies in the fishery. It should be noted that Canada's Arctic and Pacific fisheries have separate policies to regulate license holders and their activities.

- The *Fleet Separation Policy*, established 1979, dictates that companies may not hold licenses for fishing boats less than 19.8m length overall (LOA) in the Atlantic fisheries (Fisheries and Oceans Canada 1996). This policy prevents processors, distributors, and others from outside of the fishery from monopolizing the fishery by owning all of the fishing operations.
- The *Owner-Operator Policy*, established 1989, supports Atlantic Canada's small-scale fisheries by requiring that license owners must also be the operator of their fishing vessel (Fisheries and Oceans Canada 2010). This prevents the buying-up of licenses and quota by organizations or individuals hoping to make a profit off of someone else's work.
- The *Policy for Preserving the Independence of the Inshore Fleet in Canada's Atlantic Fisheries (PIIFCAF)* seeks to strengthen the Fleet Separation and Owner Operator Policies through "promot[ing] a commercial fishery in Atlantic Canada with a strong independent inshore sector" (Fisheries and Oceans Canada 2010).

These policies support a fishery sector that prioritizes the inshore sector and small-scale production, promoting the small-scale model of a fisher getting a license and fishing on his/her own boat for his/her own profit. This is a stark contrast to Canada's Pacific fisheries where corporations can buy up vast quantities of quota and essentially own a large proportion of a fishery. These provisions for Atlantic fisheries were recently codified in law and protected under Fisheries Act reform, which passed on June 21, 2019. The Newfoundland cod fishery, discussed below provides a case study of one of these uniquely small-scale Atlantic fisheries.

For the purposes of the case study below, the community referred to includes all of those who have a connection, whether economic, social, cultural, or otherwise, to the cod fishery. This would include fish harvesters, processors, retailers, families, and others living in the community. Given that in small fishing villages the fishery may have been the industry that prompted settling the community and continues to sustain the community, nearly every individual would have some level of connection to the fishery.

Case study: Newfoundland's northern cod fishery

Figure 12.1 The fishery has been an important part of the establishment and history of many towns along the coast of Newfoundland, including in the capital city of St. John's.

Photo credit: Cod fish curing in Southside, St. John's, Newfoundland. *NL Collection, Provincial Resource Library, St. John's.*

Newfoundland's Atlantic cod (*Gadus morhua*) fishery went from famous to infamous. Those travelling through the Grand Banks in the 1400s recalled tales of cod stocks so abundant that they slowed ships. These stocks were fished by domestic Canadian and foreign fleets for hundreds of years with long lines and boxed nets (Figure 12.1). By the 1960s the cod abundance started to fall. Advancements like freezer vessels and trawling took their toll on the northern cod stocks and by 1992 the spawning stock had dropped to 7% of the historical abundance (Higgins 2009).

The decline in cod stocks raised concern for government, scientists, and fishers. Governments responded to these concerns by cooperating in the North Atlantic Fisheries Organization (NAFO) to set harvest limits (total allowable catches, TACs), which nations continued to exceed (Higgins 2009). With the extension of Canada's exclusive economic zone (EEZ) to 200nm under the 1982 United Nations Convention on the Law of the Sea (UN 1982), Canada gained more control of the cod stocks within their waters but continued to overfish, and foreign nations continued to overexploit the stocks just outside of Canada's EEZ. Additionally, scientific advice was largely ignored, and in some cases greatly overestimated the abundance of cod due to scientific error (Higgins 2009; May n.d.). Fishers voiced concern to government officials, arguing that they had noticed their catch declining, even for the same amount of effort (or more) (Higgins 2009). Despite the voiced concerns and apparent attempts at management, there was insufficient action to prevent the collapse of Atlantic cod stocks throughout Atlantic Canada, known as the northern cod stocks, off the coast of Newfoundland and Labrador.

On July 2, 1992 the Department of Fisheries and Oceans announced a moratorium on the northern cod fishery. Citing ecological causes for the decline in cod stocks, the Minister of Fisheries announced a two-year moratorium to allow the stocks to recover. After the moratorium the fishery was expected to return to its former glory with renewed fish stocks to exploit. Unfortunately, the moratorium more or less remains in place 26 years later, and its impact is still felt in the province (Bavington 2010). While it is unclear if the fishery will ever recover to its former productive potential, there were recently signs that things were looking up (Rose et al. 2015). In 2015, increases in the cod population and sizes of individual fish seemed promising (Rose et al. 2015), leading to a favourable assessment of one part of the fishery operating in a region off Newfoundland (in management terms known as the 3Ps region) to be certified as "sustainable" against the fisheries standard of the Marine Stewardship Council (MSC) (Blythe-Skyrme, Nichols, and Angel, 2016). MSC is largely viewed as the gold standard in eco-certifications, and currently almost 15% of total fisheries production carries the MSC logo. The MSC model works by certifying what are called "units of assessment", and in the case of northern cod this unit is made up of Icewater Seafood Inc. and Ocean Choice International. However, in 2017 certification was voluntarily suspended because of ongoing concerns with stock decline.

Assessing community wellbeing through the community capitals framework

Here, we explore the connection between the Newfoundland northern cod fishery and regenerative food systems by invoking the community capitals framework. Community wellbeing is a multifaceted concept with complex interactions between a multitude of factors that contribute to each domain (social, economic, environmental, human, cultural, and political). Wellbeing is often discussed as a continuum from individual to global wellbeing, with community wellbeing falling somewhere in between (Mccrea et al. 2014). Each level of wellbeing has aspects that may be exclusive to that level or may be relevant along the continuum. We consider community wellbeing in the context of small fishing communities, including the geographic and social connections that link directly to that community through the Community Capitals Framework (CCF, Figure 12.2). In this way, we are assuming that i) a regenerative food system is one that contributes to community capitals (and vice versa); and that ii) community capitals are necessary but not sufficient contributors to community wellbeing. The CCF was selected for its use in considering community assets (usually to assess community development) (Mattos 2015), as well as previous applications in assessing community wellbeing (Mccrea et al. 2014). In this way we seek to answer how the fishery contributed to wellbeing by assessing how community capitals changed when the fishery was gone, and we go on to discuss how we can think about regenerative food systems as those that contribute to community capitals, thus supporting community wellbeing.

The CCF usually focuses on the strengths, or assets, in a community. To assess the contribution of the cod fishery to community wellbeing we have considered assets that the fishery contributed by exploring the deficits that were left with the moratorium. Within each domain of the framework a set of dimensions are defined, which were derived from dimensions used in similar studies of community wellbeing. Additional dimensions have been added to capture factors unique to the Newfoundland cod fishery (Table 12.1).

Table 12.1 The domains and dimensions of the community capitals framework as applied in analyzing the contribution of the Newfoundland northern cod fishery to community wellbeing

Domain	Dimension
Natural Capital	• Sustainable Resource Use*
	• Environmental Stewardship
Economic Capital	• Employment*
	• Income*
	• Business Opportunities*
Social Capital	• Social Connectedness*
	• Social Participation*
Human Capital	• Individual Health Status
	• Health Services*
	• Education*
Cultural Capital	• Arts and Culture
	• Patterns of Daily Life
	• "Kiss the cod"
Political/Governance Capital	• Trust
	• Agency*

*- Dimensions identified by an asterisk have been adopted or adapted from McCrea et al. 2014; Fey et al. 2006.

Figure 12.2 Community capitals associated with Newfoundland's cod fishery.

The following sections will explore the contributions of each domain of the adapted Community Capitals Framework to community wellbeing in the small-scale northern cod fishery of Newfoundland. We start with natural capital and how a reduction in this asset has had knock-on effects for decades.

Natural capital

Natural capital refers to the environmental resources within or used by a community. Natural capital includes dimensions such as healthy ecosystems, sustainable natural resource exploitation, and a connection to the environment. Each of these dimensions contributes to community wellbeing, often indirectly through supporting other forms of capital, such as economic and social capital, for example jobs in natural resource extraction. Historically, the northern cod fishery is an example of the unsustainable use of natural capital, with direct links to a loss of community wellbeing. The overfishing that occurred resulted in a moratorium on the fishery, with many negative impacts for all other domains of community capitals. The cod stocks off Newfoundland were fished hard for centuries using both small- and large-scale gear. While often touted as more sustainable due to the prevalence of multispecies fisheries, less resource-intensive equipment, and a lower catch capacity, there is no guarantee that a small-scale fishery supports natural capital more than a large-scale fishery (Kolding et al. 2014; Soltanpour et al. 2017). To maintain natural capital, any fishery, small- or large-scale, must operate sustainably. Unsustainable fishing depletes stocks, threatens the ecosystem balance, and degrades natural capital. If a small-scale fishery is managed sustainably, and if attention is paid to potentially regenerative aspects of the fishery, then this dimension of natural capital can contribute to other domains of the framework.

Given the reliance of communities on the cod fishery, environmental stewardship could be considered a dimension of natural capital. Fostering environmental stewardship could be protective of community wellbeing moving forward, as it may be more likely to lead to a preservation of natural capital. The scientific community is still unable to agree on whether or not the cod fishery will ever recover (Sguotti et al. 2019). Concerns about the management of snow crab and shrimp stocks have also recently arisen, with a fear that they may face the same fate (Murphy 2017).

It is worth noting that the loss of natural capital in Newfoundland's cod fishery had a domino effect. In studies of natural resource dependent communities, it has been found that the community's natural capital contributes to social and economic capital, as the social network and economic status of the community are closely tied to the resource (Fey et al. 2006). Additionally, natural capital alone does not provide community wellbeing, and actually this is true of all assets. Assets need to be present, but so too do the capabilities to access and benefit from those assets (see the work of Sen 2000). This leads to the conclusion that cod in the water is not enough to contribute to the wellbeing of fishing communities.

Economic capital

Economic capital includes the economic assets that a community has that support the community to flourish and fulfill their full potential (Wiseman and Brasher 2008). Dimensions of economic capital include stable employment, income, and opportunities for economic development. Small-scale fisheries can contribute to economic capital through providing employment in the fishery and in related sectors (i.e. fish processing, dock work), through providing income opportunities, and through providing opportunities for economic growth in the fishery and in related sectors.

The Newfoundland northern cod fishery collapse caused significant economic hardship in the province. The hardships that followed made apparent the contribution of the fishery to the economic capital, and thereby the wellbeing of fishing communities. Newfoundland's cod fishery provided employment for an estimated 12% of the province's labour force with approximately 30,000 jobs directly and indirectly involved in the fishery, jobs which were lost due to the moratorium (Higgins 2008). When the moratorium was announced not only were fish harvesters out of work, but fish processing plants and docks were forced to lay off employees too. While snow crab and other shellfish fisheries expanded after the moratorium, the unemployment rate remains high throughout Newfoundland and Labrador, estimated at 14.2%, or twice the national average, in 2018 (Statistics Canada 2018).

It's important to note that fisheries tend to be seasonal, making the contribution of fisheries to economic assets difficult to assess. In Newfoundland, fishers were familiar with the seasonal nature of the work. In fact, the reference to "fishing for stamps" began emerging in the 1950s and refers to the familiar pattern of fishing during the on-season in order to qualify for employment insurance payments in the off-season (Canada National Archives in Lund 1995). Prior to the cod fishery moratorium, in Newfoundland, 44% of fishers' income was from employment insurance (Department of Fisheries and Oceans in Lund, 1995). Thus, the fishery provided income during the fishing season and access to employment insurance in the off-season. Managing a fishery with attention to the extent to which it supports *improved* employment opportunities from the status quo may be an important principle in thinking of fisheries as part of regenerative food systems.

Support programs such as the Northern Cod Adjustment and Rehabilitation Program (NCARP) and later The Atlantic Groundfish Strategy (TAGS) were established to support those who lost work due to the moratorium. The NCARP ended in 1994 and was replaced with TAGS. TAGS funds dried up in 1998, earlier than anticipated due to high residual unemployment. The financial support for NCARP was "based on [fishers'] average unemployment insurance earnings from 1989–1991" (Higgins 2009) with the prerequisite that recipients had to enroll in retraining programs to assist them in gaining employment outside of the fishery (Higgins 2008). However, there has been widespread criticism that the retraining programs were poorly suited to meet the needs of the target groups and were ineffectual in equipping participants for entry into another market area (Globe and Mail 1998; Higgins 2008).

The story of Newfoundland's cod fishery provides a tale of a precarious cycle of *fishing for stamps*, to year-round support payments from government, to government funds drying up. Thus, while the cod fishery provided a source of (questionably) stable income, the moratorium left many without adequate income or opportunities to gain it. Overcapitalization (too much investment in capital) in a fishery is a danger to the stability of economic, social, and ecological assets in a community. Two weeks before the moratorium, Glenn Winslowe, a cod fisherman, invested $1,000,000 CAD in a larger boat and equipment to expand his operation (CBC News The National 2017). With the cod fishery suddenly closed, those who invested in gear such as large trawlers that were ideal for the cod fishery were left with the remaining debt. While the government attempted to provide financial support for those forced out of the fishery, these previously incurred costs remained (Higgins 2008). Yet overcapitalization remains on the east coast, with the lobster fishery being a prime example, where economically attractive activities lead to more investment at the expense of social and ecological risks (Steneck et al. 2011).

Social capital

Social assets include connections, a sense of community, and involvement within that community. Social capital contributes to community wellbeing through providing the social networks, support, and resilience to survive shocks to other types of capital, and providing a sense of identity within the community. The cod fishery in Newfoundland contributed greatly to the social capital of small fishing communities, specifically by providing opportunities for community involvement and a reason to remain in the community (Figure 12.3). Social connectedness is an important aspect of community wellbeing as it allows individuals to feel a part of the community, to receive and to contribute to the support and networks within the community. Small-scale fisheries can contribute to social connectedness through providing direct connections, such as a working relationship, or indirect connections, such as supporting family and friends to remain in a community. As we discuss below, many of the social implications of the cod fishery moratorium are interconnected with other domains of community capital.

In the 15 years following the cod moratorium there was an 11% drop in Newfoundland's population (Government of Newfoundland and Labrador in Schrank and Roy 2013). Some smaller fishing communities saw as much as a 30% drop in population (Murray et al. 2005), with this outmigration being mostly young people leaving in search of better opportunities (Canadian Policy Research Network in Power et al. 2014). A recent study on young people's perceptions of the fishery closure in Newfoundland found that they perceive little opportunity for them to stay in their communities and make a living without the fishery (Power et al. 2014). In a cod moratorium report that aired on the

Figure 12.3 The cod fishery provided employment in fishing, fish processing (pictured here) and in other roles to support the fishery as well as a sense of social identity associated with fishing towns.

Photo credit: Men processing cod fish. *NL Collection, Provincial Resource Library, St. John's.*

Canadian Broadcasting Corporation (CBC), a resident of a Newfoundland fishing community stated that "it's like someone died in the family" (Anon. in CBC News The National 2017) in reference to the outmigration of community members. This results in a sense of missing community connections and a town that lacks the social capital that once was there.

Here we consider community participation to include engagement in the community that is inclusive of employment, social participation, interactions with other community members, and contributing to the local economy through spending in the community: essentially, participation in the daily activities of life within the community. Small-scale fisheries support this through providing various types of capital, including the economic capital for employment and spending and the social capital to retain enough people for a community to be sustained. The Newfoundland cod fishery provides an example of an interesting form of community participation. Schrank (2005) suggests that "work sharing" is possibly still occurring. This refers to the practice of fish harvesters working only until they are eligible for employment insurance and then resigning in order to allow family or friends to take their "turn" working until they qualify for employment insurance too. This cycle allows more community members to qualify for support payments by sharing a job between multiple people. Unfortunately, this means that there is a perpetual reliance on government support and a loss of economic capital to grow businesses and opportunities in the area. However, perhaps this sharing of employment has permitted some social capital to be retained in communities that were hit hard by the cod moratorium. Perhaps the ability to share employment and then to access employment insurance has allowed more people to remain in the communities, participating socially and economically. While there are arguments to be made for the infeasibility of this system, we would be remiss to ignore that this may be a strategy to retain social capital.

Human capital

In discussing human capital in this chapter we will focus on human health and education. Communities with a healthy population are more able to "flourish and fulfill their full potential." It should be acknowledged that there are other forms of human capital, however we focus on human health due to its direct relevance to community wellbeing, and in line with Dahlberg's (1993) third tenant of regenerative food systems.

There are several ways that small-scale fisheries can contribute to health, and thereby community wellbeing, that are quite intuitive (i.e. providing food, providing financial resources to access health services). However, there are few data around the contributions of the cod fishery to this dimension of the community capital domain. Some of the difficulty in assessing the impact of the cod fishery (and subsequent moratorium) on individual and community health is the lack of data to compare pre- and post-moratorium conditions. While changes in health with the closure of the fishery are discussed below, it should be noted that the causes and interactions of these changes require further exploration.

Small-scale fisheries can have mixed implications for individual's health. As we discussed earlier, a common characteristic of the small-scale fisheries in Atlantic Canada is the cycle of working, receiving employment insurance, and working again. Research elsewhere has shown that the uncertainty of this type of work could negatively impact the mental health of individuals and thereby impact their contributions to community wellbeing (Moscone et al. 2016). In the period following the moratorium (1995–2001) self-reported health and emotional wellbeing in Newfoundland's small fishing communities improved (Murray et al.

2005). While there are many other factors that may have contributed to these improvements, it is an interesting correlation. Interviews with those impacted by the collapse may provide insight into the emotional health shift. In an interview with The National (2017), Glenn Winslowe, the cod fisherman mentioned above, talks about the fury and upset felt by him and his crew when the moratorium was announced. However, he continues to explain that with time the emotions have settled, and many have accepted that the moratorium was necessary and likely should have come earlier.

As is often seen when populations shift geographically (in the case of Newfoundland from fishing communities to other opportunities around the nation and abroad), there has been a shift in the government services in the area. Due to outmigration, Newfoundlanders have to travel greater distances to access health services (Murray et al. 2005). This is concerning given the concurrent trend of an aging demographic (Power et al. 2014). As people age, they tend to require more health services and often more urgent care. With farther to travel in order to receive care there may be negative consequences for individuals' health, and perhaps more incentive to abandon small fishing towns for more populated centres. Thus, the loss of social and economic capital has contributed to a loss of human (health) capital in small fishing communities, thereby compromising community wellbeing.

Education, whether formal or informal, contributes to human capital through providing knowledge and skills that may be useful in a community. Additionally, education in areas such as finance and resource management could support other forms of capital in small fishing communities, such as educating fishers on financial options available to them or the complexity of ecosystem interactions. This is not to imply that fishers currently lack this knowledge, but rather that the availability of education around these topics may, in some cases, be of benefit. The Newfoundland cod fishery itself did provide human capital through hands-on, skills-based education opportunities, such as learning fishing techniques or the seasonal movements of the fish. With the collapse of the fishery it was necessary to turn to other education opportunities. The NCARP and TAGS both required that recipients participate in retraining programs to be eligible for financial support. As previously mentioned there have been criticisms of these programs for being ill-suited to the intended audience and not providing useful skills (Higgins 2008), however for some they offered the opportunity to gain a formal education that was not previously accessible (Murray et al. 2005).

Cultural capital

Cultural capital is understood here to include assets that preserve heritage, arts, culture, and the history of a community. Small-scale fisheries are often touted as important for preserving the cultural heritage of fishing communities (Soltanpour et al. 2017). With numerous small fishing villages throughout Atlantic Canada the fishing culture is prevalent around the coasts, including in Newfoundland (Figure 12.4). Insights from Newfoundlanders suggest that cod played an important role in the daily life in their communities and that cod fishery collapse was the end of a way of life (CBC The National 2017; Murphy 2017).

The arts can play an important role in preserving cultural heritage and promoting cultural connection. The incorporation of fishing culture into arts is prevalent throughout the history of Atlantic Canada. From music to textiles to literature, the fishing life is well represented. In Newfoundland, the cod fishery has featured prominently in art for centuries. Newfoundland's folk music has always celebrated fishing. But since the moratorium a darker tone has been noted, with dozens of songs mentioning the post-moratorium struggles

Figure 12.4 The cod fishery was an important part of daily life in Newfoundland's fishing villages, including Quidi Vidi, for several centuries prior to the collapse of the fishery. The importance of the fishery became ingrained in the culture and history of these communities.

Photo credit: Fish drying in Quidi Vidi, Newfoundland. *NL Collection, Provincial Resource Library, St. John's.*

(Navaro in Gzowski 1995). The usual hard-knock-life themes of Newfoundland folk music had in some cases adopted a "protesting" feel, as discussed by Anita Best and Peter Narvaez in a Canadian Broadcasting Corporation radio segment with Peter Gzowski about the impact of the cod ban on Newfoundland's music culture (1995). In addition to the musical history of Newfoundland, the cod fishery has been featured in literature for many years, from the journals of early explorers to authors who write about Newfoundland today (Dundas 2014). The cod fishery continues to contribute to the cultural capital of communities through the arts.

Much of the culture of fishing communities comes from the patterns of life that the fishery demands. From fishing in the on-season, drying fish on clothes lines, to repairing nets and boats in the off-season, the life of small fishing communities revolves around the fishery. The cod fishery of Newfoundland was so ingrained in culture that it has become a symbol for the Newfoundland culture and life through "Kiss the cod" practices. For nearly five decades the traditional ceremony of "screeching in" visitors to the island has been practiced across Newfoundland. The ceremony involves a shot of Newfoundland Screech Rum followed by the kissing of a cod fish, allowing visitors to become honorary Newfies (Ferreira 2015; International Traveller n.d.). While there is some disagreement about whether the tradition is a fun ritual or a mockery of Newfoundland culture, it has become nonetheless a recognized and often celebrated tourist activity (Ploughman 2018) that speaks to the close connection between the cod fishery and Newfoundland culture. This example also shows the strong link between capitals: By commodifying the cultural capital of the cod fishery, economic capital is reinforced.

Political/governance capital

Political capital considers the agency, or decision-making power, that the community has as well as the ability of the community to express views and have those views heard. Political capital contributes to community wellbeing through providing a sense of control and self-determination, rather than a feeling that the community is subject to the conditions around it.

The Newfoundland northern cod fishery moratorium provides an example of the negative implications of a top-down fishery management system that did not support community political capital. This has led us to include the dimension of (dis)trust to political capital as it is prevalent in the literature on the cod fishery. Especially in a sector which relies on government stock assessments, fisheries management plans, government licensing, and government regulations for fishing within the EEZ, trust in political and governance processes is vital.

In a famous quote from the day prior to the moratorium announcement, John Crosbie, the Federal Fisheries Minister, told a crowd of angry fish harvesters "I didn't take the fish from the God damn water," essentially suggesting that the fishers were to blame. The moratorium that followed the next day greatly undermined trust between fishing communities and the government. In retrospect, the announcement of the moratorium was to be expected. Fishers had been warning for years that the stocks were not doing well, but their complaints went unacknowledged (Higgins 2009). It's important to note here that the small-scale sector was blaming the large-scale and largely offshore sector for population declines, and hence, what they had wanted were regulations that would curb the offshore fleet. However, on July 2, 1992, it was a shock to fishing communities that even the small-scale sector would be shut down. An article from the Globe and Mail (1998) demonstrates the feelings of unjust governance in the fishery as the Newfoundland Minister of Rural Revitalization is quoted asking the federal government "What price do you expect us to pay for your mismanagement?".

Agency is an important concept in considering how political capital contributes to community wellbeing. Without any decision-making power a community is subject to whatever decisions are imposed on them. In the context of small-scale fisheries, agency can come in the form of fisher participation on management groups or community-based fisheries management. The Newfoundland cod fishery is an example of a fishery where fishers lacked agency, were unable to influence decisions even though they had raised concerns, and were ultimately negatively impacted. The cod collapse is thus an example of the top-down management of a small-scale fishery in which the communities lacked political capital. Had political capital been nurtured through a fisheries management approach that supported community co-management, decisions to reduce the burden of the collapse could have been made in a more transitional way.

Conclusion

The Newfoundland cod fishery is a unique case study to explore how small-scale fisheries can contribute to community wellbeing. It is often difficult to tease out the contribution of a food production system on wellbeing outcomes, however the collapse of the fishery allowed for observing, measuring, and assessing the wellbeing consequences of *not* having the food production system in the community. The community capitals framework has allowed us to explore how the fishery contributed (or not) to community assets, including physical, social, economic, human, cultural, and political capital. The point is that the assumption that fisheries management is about managing fish is simplistic and dangerous. Having enough fish in the water to sustain a fishery is not supportive of a regenerative food system. Rather a food system that links health and wellbeing outcomes to management of the system is necessary. In this way, managing a fishery so that it not only sustains a fish population but contributes positively to community capitals will require a new paradigm of fisheries management in Canada. Should cod stocks recover, and should a substantial commercial fishery open, paying attention to these dynamics will be essential.

Discussion questions

1. As in land-based food production, arguments abound about whether the small-scale fish harvester can really produce enough fish to feed the world. What kind of balance, if any, is needed between large and small scale fisheries activities to balance regenerative food systems and ones that produce on industrial scales?
2. Do one or two community capitals stand out as more important than the others when thinking about fisheries and regenerative food systems?
3. The contribution of fish to food security is often framed as one of fish quantity. But if we think about the practices of fishing and fish production, in addition to the fish itself, how can we think about the contribution of fisheries to food security?
4. Capture fisheries production differs from most land-based food production in that the activities exploit and impact a shared resource, the ocean, rather than privately owned resources, such as land and crops. What potential challenges and opportunities exist for fisheries in regenerative food systems, given that the resource being exploited is not exclusively owned by those profiting from it?

Further reading

Bavington, D. (2010). *Managed annihilation: An unnatural history of the Newfoundland cod collapse.* Vancouver: UBC Press.

Bennett, N., Kaplan-Hallam, M., Augustine, G., Ban, N., Belhabib, D., Brueckner-Irwin, I., … Bailey, M. (2018). Coastal and Indigenous community access to marine resources and the ocean: A policy imperative for Canada. *Marine Policy*, *87*, 186–193.

Kolding, J., Béné, C., and Bavinck, M. (2014). Small-scale fisheries: Importance, vulnerability and deficient knowledge. In S. Garcia, J. Rice and A. Charles (Eds.) *Governance of marine fisheries and biodiversity conservation: Interaction and coevolution*, pp. 317–331. Wiley Blackwell: Hoboken, NJ.

Mccrea, R., Walton, A., and Leonard, R. (2014). A conceptual framework for investigating community wellbeing and resilience. *Rural Society*, *23*(3), 270–282.

Pinkerton, E., and Davis, R. (2015). Neoliberalism and the politics of enclosure in North American small-scale fisheries. *Marine Policy*, *61*, 303–312.

References

Bailey, M. (2018). Coastal and Indigenous community access to marine resources and the ocean: A policy imperative for Canada. *Marine Policy*, *87*, 186–193.

Bavington, D. (2010). *Managed annihilation: An unnatural history of the Newfoundland cod collapse.* Vancouver: UBC Press.

Bennett, N., Kaplan-Hallam, M., Augustine, G., Ban, N., Belhabib, D., Brueckner-Irwin, I., … Bailey, M. (2018). Coastal and Indigenous community access to marine resources and the ocean: A policy imperative for Canada. *Marine Policy*, *87*, 186–193.

Blythe-Skyrme, R., Nichols, J., and Angel, J. (2016). *MSC sustainable fisheries certification Canada / Newfoundland 3Ps Atlantic Cod Fishery-Public Certification Report*. Retrieved from https://fisheries.msc. org/en/fisheries/canada-newfoundland-3ps-cod/@@assessment-documentsets?documentset_name= Public+certification+report&assessment_id=FA-00957&phase_name=Public+certification+report +and+certificate+issue&start_date=2014-05-20&title=Initial+Assessment

CBC News The National. (2017). Newfoundland cod fishery: Lessons not learned? [Video]. Retrieved from www.youtube.com/watch?v=0sFmT8IXGhw

Dahlberg, K. (1993). A transition from agriculture to regenerative food systems. *Futures*, *26*(2), 170–179. doi:10.1016/0016-3287(94)90106-6

Duarte, C., Holmer, M., Olsen, Y., Soto, D., Marbà, N., Guiu, J., … Karakassis, I. (2009). Will the oceans help feed humanity? *BioScience*, *59*(11), 967–976. doi: 10.1525/bio.2009.59.11.8

Dundas, D. (2014). Michael Crummey says Sweetland is about mortality. *The Star Halifax*, August 19. Retrieved from www.thestar.com/entertainment/books/2014/08/19/michael_crummey_says_swee tland_is_about_mortality.html

Environment and Climate Change Canada. (2016). *Achieving a sustainable future: A federal sustainable development strategy for Canada 2016–2019* (Cat.: En4-136/2016E-PDF). Gatineau, QC: Canada. Environment and Climate Change Canada.

Ferreira, V. (2015). Tis the rum, me son: Screech-in ceremonies bring waves of tourists, celebrities to St. John's pub. *The National Post*, May 15. Retrieved from https://nationalpost.com/life/food/tis-the-rum-me-son-screech-in-ceremonies-bring-waves-of-tourists-celebrities-to-st-johns-pub

Fey, S., Bregendahl, C., and Flora, C. (2006). The measurement of community capitals through research. *Online Journal of Rural Research and Policy*, *1*(1), 1.

Fisheries Act. (1985). R.S.C. F-14. Retrieved from Justice Laws Website: https://laws-lois.justice.gc.ca/ eng/acts/f-14/

Fisheries and Oceans Canada. (1996). *Commercial fisheries licensing policy for eastern Canada- 1996*. Retrieved from www.dfo-mpo.gc.ca/fm-gp/policies-politiques/licences-permis/index-eng.htm

Fisheries and Oceans Canada. (2010). *Preserving the independence of the inshore fleet in Canada's Atlantic fisheries*. Retrieved from http://dfo-mpo.gc.ca/fm-gp/initiatives/piifcaf-pifpcca/piifcafqa-pifpccaqr-eng.htm

Globe and Mail. (1998). Newfoundlanders seek help over cod fishery collapse. April 23. *The Globe and Mail (1936–Current)*. Retrieved from http://ezproxy.library.dal.ca/login?url=https://search-pro quest-com.ezproxy.library.dal.ca/docview/1146788409?accountid=10406

Godfray, H. C. J., and Garnett, T. (2014). Food security and sustainable intensification. *Philosophical Transactions of the Royal Society B: Biological Sciences*, *369*(1639), 20120273. doi:10.1098/ rstb.2012.0273

Government of Canada. (1992, July 2). Crosbie announces first steps in northern cod recovery plan [media release]. Retrieved from www.cdli.ca/cod/announce.htm

Gzowski, P. (1995). Newfoundland artists respond to cod ban [Radio]. CBC Radio (Producer), *Morningside*. CBC Radio.

Higgins, J. (2008). *Economic impacts of the cod moratorium*. Heritage Newfoundland and Labrador. Retrieved from www.heritage.nf.ca/articles/economy/moratorium-impacts.php

Higgins, J. (2009). *Cod moratorium*. Heritage Newfoundland and Labrador. Retrieved from www.heri tage.nf.ca/articles/economy/moratorium.php

Hilborn, R., Banobi, J., Hall, S. J., Pucylowski, T., and Walsworth, T. E. (2018). The environmental cost of animal source foods. *Frontiers in Ecology and the Environment*, *16*(6), 329–335. doi: 10.1002/ fee.1822

International Traveller. (n.d.). *Kiss the cod and become an honourary Canadian in Newfoundland*. Retrieved from www.internationaltraveller.com/100-kiss-the-cod-in-newfoundland/

Kolding, J., Béné, C., and Bavinck, M. (2014). Small-scale fisheries: Importance, vulnerability and deficient knowledge. In S. Garcia, J. Rice and A. Charles (Eds.) *Governance of marine fisheries and biodiversity conservation: Interaction and coevolution*, pp. 317–331. Wiley Blackwell: Hoboken, NJ.

Leeder, J. (2018). Newfoundland cod stocks suffer serious and surprising decline. *The Globe and Mail*, March 23. Retrieved from www.theglobeandmail.com/canada/article-newfoundland-cod-stocks-suffer-serious-decline-report/

Long, R. D., Charles, A., and Stephenson, R. L. (2015). Key principles of marine ecosystem-based management. *Marine Policy*, *57*, 53–60.

Lund, L. (1995). "Fishing for stamps": The origins and development of unemployment insurance for Canada's commercial fisheries, 1941–71. *Journal of the Canadian Historical Association, 6*(1), 179–208. doi:10.7202/031093ar

MacPherson, I. (2013). The Antigonish movement. *The Canadian Encyclopedia*. Retrieved from www.the canadianencyclopedia.ca/en/article/antigonish-movement

Mahoney, S. (1995). Inquiries for a sustainable future: A decision-making approach to the study of selected Canadian issues – the disappearance of the northern cod. Learning for a Sustainable Future. Retrieved from www.lsf-lst.ca/media/cod.en.pdf?phpMyAdmin=27c4ca48e56t67ceba5e

Mattos, D. (2015). Community capitals framework as a measure of community development. University of Nebraska-Lincoln, September 2. Retrieved from https://agecon.unl.edu/cornhusker-economics/2015/community-capitals-framework

May, A. (n.d.) The collapse of the northern cod. *Newfoundland Quarterly, 102*(2), 41–44.

Mccrea, R., Walton, A., and Leonard, R. (2014). A conceptual framework for investigating community wellbeing and resilience. *Rural Society, 23*(3), 270–282.

Moscone, F., Tosetti, E., and Vittadini, G. (2016). The impact of precarious employment on mental health: The case of Italy. *Social Science and Medicine, 158*(C), 86–95.

Murray, M., MacDonald, D., Simms, A., Fowler, K., Felt, L., Edwards, A., ... (2005). *Community resilience in Newfoundland: The impact of the cod moratorium on health and social well-being* (Revised ed., DesLibris. Documents collection). St. John's, Newfoundland: Newfoundland and Labrador Centre for Health Information (Canadian Electronic Library, distributor).

Murphy, R. (2017). Point of view: How the fishery moratorium savaged Newfoundland [The National]. CBC News The National. Retrieved from www.youtube.com/watch?v=QTF68MAujaw

Newell, D., and Ommer, R. (1999). *Fishing places, fishing people traditions and issues in Canadian small-scale fisheries* (DesLibris. Books collection). Toronto, ON: University of Toronto Press.

OECD. (2001). *Total allowable catch (TAC)*. Retrieved from https://stats.oecd.org/glossary/detail.asp?ID=2713

Pinkerton, E., and Davis, R. (2015). Neoliberalism and the politics of enclosure in North American small-scale fisheries. *Marine Policy, 61*, 303–312.

Ploughman, K. (2018). Out with the screech-in. *Downhome Life*, January 16. Retrieved from www.down homelife.com/article.php?id=1905

Power, N., Norman, M., & Dupré, K. (2014). "The fishery went away": The impacts of long-term fishery closures on young people's experience and perception of fisheries employment in Newfoundland coastal communities. *Ecology and Society, 19*(3), 1.

Rose, G., and Rowe, S. (2015). Northern cod comeback. *Canadian Journal of Fisheries and Aquatic Sciences, 72*(12), 1789–1798. doi:10.1139/cjfas-2015-0346

Schrank, W. (2005). The Newfoundland fishery: Ten years after the moratorium. *Marine Policy, 29*(5), 407–420.

Schrank, W., and Roy, N. (2013). The newfoundland fishery and economy twenty years after the Northern Cod Moratorium. *Marine Resource Economics, 28*(4), 397–413.

Sen, A. (2000). *Development as freedom*. London: Anchor.

Sguotti, C., Otto, S. A., Frelat, R., Langbehn, T. J., Ryberg, M. R., Lindegren, M., ... Möllmann, C. (2019). Catastrophic dynamics limit Atlantic cod recovery. *Proceedings of the Royal Society B*. doi:10.1098/rspb.2018.2877

Soltanpour, Y., Monaco, C., and Peri, I. (2017). Defining small-scale fisheries from a social perspective. *Calitatea, 18*, 425–430. Retrieved from http://ezproxy.library.dal.ca/login?url=https://search-pro quest-com.ezproxy.library.dal.ca/docview/2095681189?accountid=10406

Statistics Canada. (2018). Chart 3 unemployment by province, March 2018. Retrieved from https://www150.statcan.gc.ca/n1/daily-quotidien/180406/cg-a003-eng.htm. Accessed March 20, 2020.

Steneck, R. S., Hughes, T. P., Cinner, J. E., Adger, W. N., Arnold, S. N., Berkes, F., ... Worm, B. (2011). Creation of a gilded trap by the high economic value of the Maine lobster fishery. *Conservation Biology, 25*(5), 904–912.

United Nations, Department of Economic and Social Affairs, Population Division (2019). *World population prospects 2019: Highlights* (ST/ESA/SER.A/423).

United Nations Development Program. (2016a). *UNDP support to the implementation of sustainable development goal 14 ocean governance*. Retrieved from https://www.undp.org/content/dam/undp/library/Sustainable%20Development/14_Oceans_Jan15_digital.pdf

United Nations Development Program. (2016b). *UNDP support to the implementation of sustainable development goal 15 protect, restore and promote sustainable use of terrestrial ecosystems.* Retrieved from https://www.undp.org/content/dam/undp/library/Sustainable%20Development/15_Terrestrial%20_Jan15_digital.pdf

United Nations General Assembly. (1982). *United Nations convention on the law of the sea,* December 10. New York: United Nations.

Wiseman, J., and Brasher, K. (2008). Community wellbeing in an unwell world: Trends, challenges, and possibilities. *Journal of Public Health Policy, 29*(3), 353–366.

13

FOOD AND MARKETS

The contribution of economic sociology

Sergio Schneider and Abel Cassol

Introduction

The commoditization of social and economic life is advancing at a rapid pace. Most farmers and families living in rural areas today, whether producers or just residents, are in some way incorporated into goods, services, or information markets. The ways farmers are integrated into markets and the way exchanges take place are very diverse. There is no standard or model, no single path or determined linear direction. Hence it is important to understand how commoditization affects the rural environment and agri-food production and, especially, how farmers and rural dwellers are incorporated into markets.

Nevertheless, several gaps persist in the studies on the commoditization of farmers' lives or, more precisely, on the social processes that lead to their incorporation into markets. Most of the research conducted on this issue focuses on the analysis of the markets proper, such as supply strategies, consumer preferences, price formation, competitiveness, among others. In brief, studies have prioritized the analysis of economic exchanges, mediated by relative prices, between production and consumption agents, to the detriment of a deeper understanding of the peculiar organization of these markets, largely based on reciprocity and/or inter-knowledge, and of the power relations and domination mechanisms present in such spaces. A sociological question remains, particularly regarding markets in rural areas and food and agriculture, that shall be further explored.

The characteristics and mode of operation of agri-food markets raise particularly troubling questions when so-called alternative markets are at stake, especially the niche and proximity markets created by new products that seek greater added value. The same is true for *traditional products*, which gain ground with increasing consumer demand for traditional, typical, regional, or "origin labelled" products characterized by their artisanal or ethical or even sustainability-related (organic, agroecological, etc.) aspects.

A look at the sociological and economic literature shows that the incorporation of individuals into markets was almost always interpreted by scholars as part of the expansion of the social division of labor, which would produce more and more complex social relations. Marxist political economy, for example, attributes to this process the transition from societies and modes of production based on use value to those based on exchange values, in which markets are understood as an essential space for circulation of goods and formation of a society of classes. The functionalist sociology of Durkheim, in turn, realized that the expansion of the markets entailed the formation of a new sociability characterized, according to him, by the organic solidarity. Comprehensive sociology, represented by Weber and Simmel, has perhaps given more weight to the effects of markets, since the authors assert that the market was the vector of implantation of a new rationality that commended the use of money as a mechanism of social interaction (Raud 2005).

In the context of rural sociology, the analysis of farmers' incorporation into markets has also been the subject of several studies. Lenin's pioneering works highlighted the erosive character of commoditization, which would lead peasants to a process of disaggregation and social differentiation. Chayanov, in turn, showed that peasants established relations with the markets to sell their surplus, which allowed them to ensure somewhat autonomously their economic reproduction. Later, in the second half of the twentieth century, Henry Mendras (1978) and Theodor Shanin (1973) noted that peasants' relations with markets comprised an important factor in changing their social status. For Mendras, commoditization is part of the "end of the peasantry" as local communities, while for Shanin the markets promoted the subordination of peasants, claiming their "oppression by external forces" (Shanin 1990).

More recently, Ploeg (1992) has claimed that the commoditization of agriculture does not necessarily have a negative and excluding character. On the contrary, the author shows that, in some cases, commoditization can be beneficial to social reproduction of small-scale farmers, especially insofar as, by entering markets in which they have more control over information, prices, and the supply mechanism, they can improve their autonomy and gain more room for manoeuvre in negotiations (Ploeg 2008).

Given the importance of markets for farmers' social reproduction strategies, studies on agriculture commoditization have shown that public policies can help develop and strengthen markets. Thus, not only can markets be socially constructed, but public policies can play an important role in this process. This leads to the argument that having more and better markets can be critical for rural development generally (Hebink et al. 2015). In addition, especially in North American and European literature on food and sustainability, a discussion has emerged on "new" agri-food markets based on short supply chains between producers and consumers or on alternative food networks (Brunori 2007; Goodman 2009; Goodman et al. 2012; Marsden et al. 2003).

In this context, some issues arise concerning the scope and role of these markets in the development of food systems. Questions are raised as to the scale and the limits and possibilities of local food production for meeting the growing demand for affordable quality products. Similarly, the local and moral character of these sustainable production and consumption practices is questioned (Born and Purcell 2006; Pratt 2007).

However, despite growing concern with investigating the ways and mechanisms through which farmers access and sell their food – which became a latent social and sociological issue – studies have made little progress in analysing the markets proper. Issues surrounding social relations of exchange, stability of transactions, and the problem of the order of such markets have been little theorized in the contemporary context, particularly in agri-food studies (Beckert 2010).

Although the theoretical and analytical framework of the new economic sociology has been applied by studies on sustainable food systems to show the embeddedness of economic relations within the new markets (Fligstein 2001; Krippner 2001; Wilkinson 2019), the role played by local, social, and cultural values in building quality attributions, and the development of more sustainable food production and consumption practices and processes, such studies have theorized little about the nature and functioning of markets. This makes it difficult to produce a cohesive and integrated approach to improve understanding, replicate the diverse researched experiences, and create a set of indicators and variables for public policies to enable sustainable food systems (Sonnino and Marsden 2017).

The present contribution aims to place the discussion on agri-food markets within the broader scope of economic sociology, especially highlighting the analytical approaches to markets that have been mobilized by leading schools of contemporary sociological thinking. We intend to show the possibilities for dialogue as well as the explanatory potential offered by different economic sociology approaches to markets. Thus, we intend to contribute to fill the gap between studies on agri-food markets and the analysis of markets *tout court*.

Locating the studies on agri-food markets

Although not explicitly, studies on contemporary agri-food markets have adopted some approaches from new economic sociology to analyse, interpret, and understand how these supply spheres are constructed and reproduced, what cultural values they mobilize, and what (sustainable) practices they generate. References to the field of economic sociology and its approaches can be found in the studies on sustainable agri-food (Brunori 2007; Goodman et al. 2012; Murdoch et al. 2000).

According to Blay-Palmer and colleagues (2018), there are at least seven dominant conceptual (and empirical) approaches to developing and analysing sustainable agri-food markets and systems: bio-region and foodsheds (Getz 1991; Kremer and Schreuder 2012), alternative agri-food networks (Goodman et al. 2012), short food supply chains (Marsden et al. 2003), rural–urban connections (Guthman 2014), sustainable food systems (Feenestra 1997), territorial development (Caron et al. 2018; Lamine et al. 2012), and city–region agri-food systems (Jennings et al. 2015). We add to these the *nested markets* approach as another example of contemporary analysis of food markets, which we will further discuss in the third section.

Although much of this research comes from the global North, these studies are also gaining room and relevance in the South. In the Brazilian case, works by Marques et al. (2016) and Gazzola and Schneider (2017) are good examples of these different approaches.

While all such studies involve food supply and food markets issues, some of them focus on ecological dimensions of food (bio-region and foodsheds), others on multiple resources (water quality, soil, waste, etc.) related to the development of food systems (urban–rural connections), or highlight their spatial (territorial development) and sustainable dimensions (sustainable food systems). Very few propose to theorize about and/or specifically analyse agri-food markets (Maye and Kirwan 2010). The two approaches that are most likely to theorize about markets and the ways in which food chain actors trade and interact economically are alternative agri-food networks and short supply chains.

The alternative agri-food networks, although being diversely defined, can be understood as sets of relations established between social actors and organizations directly involved in the processes of production, transformation, commercialization, and consumption of foods and that interact while building new spaces for exchange and transaction (Blay-Palmer et al. 2018). Or rather as organized flows of foodstuffs that in some way connect people concerned about their consumption practices with those who want a better price for their food, or who want to produce their food in an unconventional way (Whatmore and Clark 2006).

These networks are central to the main strategies for sustainable regional development (Marsden and Renting 2017). Because they rely on local definitions of quality and interpersonal relationships, they are able to (re)connect food to traditional practices and to local farming, nature, and landscapes, establishing economic processes of production and consumption that value environmental, nutritional, and health characteristics, generating more sustainable and resilient practices (Horlings and Marsden 2014).

Many studies on agri-food networks seek essentially to problematize and demonstrate the social and material construction of "food quality". To that end, three concepts/approaches are mobilized: short food supply chains,[1] convention theory, and the notion of social embeddedness of the economy (Maye and Kirwan 2010).

It is also worth noting that, despite such studies on agri-food networks being strongly influenced by actor-network theories, cultural approaches to economics, and convention theory, few have clearly and deeply theorized around these approaches (Goodman 2002). These studies seek to provide descriptions and detailed analyses of new approaches to food that offer paths to rural development, without caring about theorizing or analysing the markets per se (Maye and Kirwan 2010).

However, some studies on agri-food networks clearly mobilize elements of sociological approaches to economics. In general, processes that build alternatives to the conventional food system claim the need to (re)localize the food production, supply, and consumption dimensions (Goodman et al. 2012). Under this premise, many researchers assert the importance of recovering the cultural aspects and meanings related to these processes – and attributed to food – the role of social networks in strengthening and reconnecting producers and consumers, and the role of social norms and rules in mechanisms of governance and operation of these markets.

As we will see below, these three dimensions – cultural aspects, governance rules and norms, and social networks – are central to discussions on the sociological aspects of the economy and markets. Many studies and researches on agri-food markets highlight that these new spaces have emerged and reproduced in an alternative way, precisely for facilitating a better integration of the actors and the social and cultural recognition of their production and consumption practices.

Thus, the analyses stemming from the new economic sociology (and its various approaches) and from sustainable food systems framework (and its various approaches) are convergent, especially concerning the reading and interpretation of markets. These spaces are no longer seen as mere places for meeting of supply and demand, being now recognized as spaces where the ways of transacting are linked to culture, values, interactions, and social norms, generating (sustainable) characteristic practices and behaviors. Such contextual features, in turn, are what define the quality and distinction of foods commercialized through these markets (Sonnino and Marsden 2006).

An example of this convergence can be seen in studies by Fonte (2008, 2010), who uses a cultural notion of economy to explain the differences in the emergence and in operating characteristics of various agri-food networks in countries of the global North. She shows how culture and traditional and historical knowledge associated to local production have played a key role in revaluing traditional practices of food production and consumption in countries where the process of food industrialization has not been so significant (France, Italy, Greece). In these countries, culture and the web of meanings attributed to food are at the heart of strategies for building sustainable and localized supply networks and systems (Fonte 2008).

Other studies applying a cultural analysis to the economy examine traditional ways of food production and consumption in certain regions, contrasting them with the safety and hygiene requirements imposed on these practices. These studies discuss how the process for establishing food quality often opposes quality to identity (culture), and explore the strategies adopted by small-scale farmers to manage their traditional practices (Allaire 2012; Cruz and Menasche 2013; Muchnik et al. 2005; Pratt 2007).

Differently, Marsden et al. (2000, 2003) analyse the emergence of short food supply chains from the perspective of social networks and the concept of social embeddedness. In brief, these authors claim that the main contribution of these chains lies in the fact that the foods they commercialize reach consumers "embedded with information". Such embeddedness is associated to definitions of food quality, valuing of traditional and/or sustainable modes of production, or willingness to pay better prices for products commercialized through these markets (Goodman et al. 2012). In other words, embeddedness entails the ability to link food to its production sites/regions by means of references to environmental, social, cultural, and health aspects – something that the long/conventional chains do not allow (Lang and Heasman 2009).

This embeddedness, therefore, entails consumers more cognizant of the characteristics of production and able to make reliable associations between food origin and territory, and to identify with the social values of the people who produce the food. Although this embeddedness is certainly also linked to cultural aspects of the food, the short food supply chains approach focuses on the construction of (alternative) networks between actors aimed at the reproduction of sustainable practices associated to agriculture and food.

The economic social networks approach is also applied by studies focused on consumer organizations that buy their food directly from family farmers (via baskets, messaging applications, social media, etc.), the so-called Solidarity Purchasing Groups (GAS – Gruppi di Acquisto Solidale). These researches generally demonstrate how alternative consumer networks, involving interaction and exchanges, are built upon the sharing of values and worldviews around sustainable consumption practices (Beletti and Mancini 2015; Brunori et al. 2012)

Finally, there is a set of researches on agri-food markets that mobilize the institutional approaches of the convention and organizational theories to explain the emergence and governance mechanisms of these networks, showing that the maintenance of such markets is directly linked to a set of social norms that distinguish their products, build their prices, and socially legitimize them (Niederle and Junior 2018). The convention theory is generally used to analyse how food quality is defined, highlighting quality as a construction that stems from a system of negotiations between different "qualities" (Murdoch et al. 2000; Wilkinson 1997). In other words, the modern economy is a space for constant negotiation of rules, norms, and conventions that compete to set the quality of the exchanged goods and products (Callon 1998).

Also adopting an institutionalist approach there are studies that see markets as an aggregate of rules and social norms that are locally appropriated and shared. Such rules drive the construction of collective mechanisms of governance that ascribe stability, distinction, and quality to food (Hebink et al. 2014; Ploeg 2014). These approaches, which have Oström's (1999, 2010) studies as reference, are based on the idea that local markets and their sustainable practices are common pool resources collectively appropriated by the various actors who construct them. These common pool resources, in turn, are responsible for creating competitive conditions for small farm products, insofar as the rules and norms on which they are based lead to new governance patterns that legitimize and distinguish such products (Ploeg 2014). We will look more closely into this approach in the fourth section.

Thus, it seems clear that the various studies on sustainable food systems make use of different approaches to economic sociology to interpret and understand how these spaces are created, what practices they generate, and how they are reproduced. In particular, discussions about markets have gained relevance in the field of agri-food studies. However, this observed convergence requires further analysis of the main sociological approaches to economics. This is what is done in the following.

Economic sociology and markets: networks, institutions, and culture

Sociological approaches to economics generally aim to explain and demonstrate economic actions and their outcomes, by means of the influence of social structures on individual economic behavior. The political, social, and historical dimensions of the economy (neglected by economists) are analysed for understanding different issues as the stability of transactions, formation and functioning of markets, characteristics of economic interactions and exchanges, relations between the State and economic activity, and formation of interests by the actors (Bourdieu 2005).

In general terms, economic sociology can be defined as the sociological perspective applied to economic phenomena, aiming at: understanding the social, political, and cultural relations that comprise economic processes; analysing interactions and connections between the economy and society at large; and studying the institutional and cultural transformations that constitute the social context of the economy (Smelser and Swedberg 2005). Outstanding works with this perspective include White (1981), Granovetter (1973, 1985), Smelser and Swedberg (2005) and Zelizer (2009), in the United States, and Beckert (2009, 2013), Fligstein (2001), Callon (1998) and Steiner (2006), in its European strand.

Economic sociology has asserted the existence of three main social forces – or three social structures – that can be identified and claimed as the most relevant to the sociological explanation of the economy and the understanding of markets: social networks, institutions, and culture (cognitive frames) (Beckert 2010; Dobbin 2004; Fourcade 2007). Thus, each of these approaches has been mobilized to analyse and explain the emergence and operation of markets, formation of prices, values attributed to certain objects, and the role played by actors and organizations in the construction of new spaces of production, marketing, and consumption of foods (Goodman 2002; Marsden et al. 2003; Zelizer 1979).

According to Wilkinson (2019), these structures were differently appropriated and discussed by the American and the European (German) strands of the new economic sociology (NES). While the American strand emerges and consolidates through the critique of neoclassical economics and its abstract definition of the market, claiming the need to understand mercantile dynamics as embedded in social structures (networks and culture), the European strand, especially in Germany, seeks to understand the dynamics of capitalism through an attempt to synthesize those three structures. In other words, while the main emphasis of American economic sociology was on analysing market dynamics (notably through the notions of networks and culture), German economic sociology focused on the idea that markets are central institutions for understanding capitalist dynamics (thus adopting a heterodox and institutionalist perspective). These studies have shown how each of these structures influence economic behavior and actions, and how social networks, institutions, and culture are reproduced and transformed, entailing implications and changes also in the markets and the ways actors transact. Although these social forces are constantly interacting and act together in the emergence, reproduction, and transformation of the markets and the economy, they have been studied and analysed independently by economic sociology –

authors often focus the analysis on one structure ignoring the others or, more commonly, subsume one under another (Beckert 2010).

Our objective here is to analyse each of these social structures separately. Our goal is to analyze each of these social structures separately. Although none can be subsumed by another, because we recognize that economic dynamics are built and operate concomitantly across the three dimensions (social networks, culture, and institutions), we will discuss the contribution of each of these approaches to the study of markets. Then, we present the attempt of synthesis and integration proposed by Beckert (2010), for whom a fourth definition of the market as a field can offer a relational and integrated analysis of these social forces for understanding the dynamics of the economic order. Subsequently, we will present the contemporary and prominent approach of *nested markets* to demonstrate how social networks, culture, and institutions can be integrated to analyse the current food production and consumption processes.

Markets as social networks

The studies of markets as social networks are possibly most used by sociology to interpret the economy. This approach is based on the premise that the positioning of actors (or firms) in relation to others has fundamental influence on economic actions and transactions. In this regard, social relations structure is seen as the main mechanism for guiding economic actions and behavior (Beckert 2010; Granovetter 1985).

To that extent, markets are defined as social structures and sets of actions, embedded in actual networks of social and interpersonal relations. Therefore, networks are examined as an explanatory category to understand economic action, markets, and economic outcomes (Granovetter 2005).

In this perspective, for some authors, social networks are responsible for the construction and emergence of markets (White 1981), while for others, complementarily, they comprise the interactive mechanism that stabilizes the markets. The networks help information circulate, stabilize incentives, and build trust or a "generalized morality" without which markets could not exist (Fourcade 2007; Granovetter 1985). Also, for others like Burt (1992), social networks help explain how the patterns of social relations structure not only markets, but also dependence relationships between actors (and firms).

As we may see, there is a significant variety of interpretations and uses of social networks to analyse the economy and markets. However, despite such theoretical differences, most authors of economic sociology have made just instrumental use of networks to analyse specific and empirical issues involving markets and organizations (Fourcade 2007). Furthermore, methodologies for network analysis have been developed and applied to understand society, in which networks themselves comprise a social structure (Scott and Carrington 2011).

Therefore, network structures are supposed to have clear economic implications, affecting, for example, the economic outcomes, price volatility, and/or performances of organizations and firms (Uzzi 1997). In other words, social structures – by means of interaction networks – affect the economy, especially for three main reasons. First, social networks influence the flow and quality of information. As information is often subtle and difficult to verify, actors tend to choose transacting and interacting with known agents to have more reliable access to information. Secondly, networks are important mechanisms of reward and/or punishment, since these relationships have their impacts amplified when established between agents known to each other. Finally, social networks are important sources of trust, insofar as the sureness that the other will do what is "right" can be reinforced in a context of interpersonal relationships (Granovetter 1985, 2005).

Therefore, the interpretation of markets as networks originates from the capacity of actors to build strategies for commercialization and transaction by establishing interpersonal networks and creating social bonds, on the basis of which economic exchanges are conducted (Nee 2005). This approach is commonly applied in the studies on agri-food markets, especially in the analysis of Alternative Agri-Food Networks and Short Food Supply Chains, as highlighted above.

Markets as institutions

Institutional approaches to markets and the economy also involve "social forces" to understand and explain economic actions and behavior of agents and organizations. Such approaches emphasize the role played by rules, norms (formal and informal), and by social and cultural values in the institutionalization of certain behaviors, standards, and transaction modes used by actors. These studies aim essentially to question how a particular set of social processes is established and reproduced; or how and why certain social arenas (behavior, actions, values) become socially recognized and legitimized (Fourcade, 2007).

As with networks, the definition of institutions is not consensual within institutionalist studies. Some authors define them as concrete structures that involve actual interests of different actors (individual or collective) for the establishment of specific economic transactions. An institution, in this perspective, is defined as "a system of interrelated informal and formal elements – custom, shared beliefs, conventions, norms, and rules – governing social relationships within which actors pursue and fix the limits of legitimate interests" (Nee 2005, 55; Oström 1999).

Other authors, in turn, define institutions in terms of social and cultural values. An institution is not only a legitimized and shared social rule or norm, but also a set of values that *institutionalize*, i.e., ratify and guide certain social and cultural standards of action and transaction (Boltanski and Thevenot 1991; Polanyi 1980). Thus, institutions are a set of values used to assign meaning to actions – they allow the (economic) actors to interpret their actions.

Furthermore, some authors define institutions as practices: patterns of economic behavior (habits) deriving from "systems of established and prevalent social rules that structure social interactions" (Hodgson 2006, 2). In this sense, institutions comprise patterns of social interaction that structure human life, and that materialize through language, laws, and organizations, for example (Hodgson 2006).

Despite these differences, all authors in this approach agree that markets are institutions: spaces that combine social and cultural values or rules, norms, and beliefs, which guide and standardize the way in which economic actors interact and transact and the governance mechanisms that regulate exchanges.

Thus, institutional approaches have been used to interpret and demonstrate the construction of new agri-food markets in terms of social rules and norms that are contested, negotiated, and established among actors. In addition, several analyses have shown how agri-food markets are built on certain local social and cultural values that are conveyed to food, generating distinction and particular qualities for farmers and the products they market (Sonnino 2007).

This is the case with the *nested markets* approach, which is gaining ground in agri-food studies (Milone and Ventura 2015). For this approach, agri-food markets are spaces in which a set of common pool resources influences the definition of governance mechanisms (rules and social norms) that guide and generate new practices and processes of sustainable rural development.

Markets as culture

The perspective that defines markets as culture focuses on enquiring about the cognitive frameworks that allow agents to interpret their economic behavior. In this way, actors interpret and give meaning to social institutions and norms in terms of the implications of their behaviors, making it necessary to examine the structures of meaning in which these actions are embedded and how they contribute to decision making and evaluation by agents and firms in the markets (Beckert 2010). More than this, the cultural and cognitive dimension assumes that, to some extent, actions reflect routine behaviors, and that such behaviors contribute to the social order of markets.

This approach has been used by authors to analyse how culture affects the economy, or vice versa. Works as those of Zelizer, for example, demonstrate how the (moral) value attributed to certain social objects have been modified throughout history, thereby changing their economic use (Zelizer 1979), or how the use of money follows certain social meanings that are culturally established (Zelizer 1989). Other authors apply the cultural approach to economics to identify the mechanisms of stable reproduction of economic institutions (DiMaggio and Powell, 1983), or to analyse the economic performativity, i.e., how the knowledge of the economy is itself a central element for the functioning of markets (Callon 1998).

Although this approach does not establish a common definition of markets, with its authors defining them in various ways, it is possible to assert that the cultural perspective considers markets as spaces in which a set of cultural beliefs, meanings, and norms act guiding the ways actors interact and attribute value and meaning to objects and to their own interactions (Zelizer 2009).

A common point of the cultural approaches is that they analyse the economy (and markets) relationally. The economy and the markets are assumed to be social structures that, therefore, should not be analysed independently from culture or from interpersonal relationships. Thus, the central point of the relational analyses lies in the correspondence between meanings (culture) and the transactions and media of exchange appropriated by the agents (Block 2012). Thus, studies that focus on the processes of interpretation and attribution of meaning to interactions and transacted goods within markets usually include in their analyses the distribution and consumption dimensions, hardly present in other approaches.

In the case of agri-food studies, these approaches have been used, for example, in appreciation of the singularities of certain products (Karpik 2007), as well as in analyses of processes attributing quality to certain foods, especially regarding Geographical Indications and/or Protected Designation of Origin (Allaire 2012; Bérard and Marchenay 2008; Zaneti and Schneider 2016).

Markets as a field (Beckert's attempt to synthesize)

There is still a fourth approach mobilized to explain the social emergence and functioning of markets. This approach defines and analyses markets as a field (Bourdieu 2005; Fligstein 2001).

By considering markets as social arenas for interaction and exchange of goods and services, the definition of economy as a field allows for shifting the emphasis, in the analysis of markets, from the exchange processes and practices to the "social forces" that structure them (Beckert 2010, 609). The notion of field refers to a group of actors (producers, consumers, firms, organizations) that interact in a social arena directing their actions at each other (Fligstein 2001). Agency in the field results from the influence exerted by social forces on actors that are part of it. These forces consist of relationship networks, norms, and rules existing within the field and of the ways to interpret these rules.

Therefore, despite differences in definitions of *field* within the social sciences, scholars agree that markets, when considered as fields, are structured by social forces that increase the stability of interactions and economic transactions (Bourdieu 2005; DiMaggio and Powell 1983; Fligstein 2001). In this sense, this "understanding of markets as fields encompasses conceptualizations that view markets as realms of interaction structured by institutions or by networks or by local cultures" (Beckert 2010, 609).

According to Beckert (2010) this approach enables a synthesis of the three social structures previously analysed by sociological studies of the markets. For this author, defining markets as fields enables analysis of the reciprocal influence that these social forces exert on each other, allowing a better understanding of the dynamics of operation and transformation of markets and the economy. For example, the analysis of institutions can explain how certain values become socially relevant and how this process concomitantly influences the structuring of social networks; or how social networks create and disseminate culture, and establish collective forces for changing institutions; or, finally, how the culture legitimizes and produces the perception of institutions and, at the same time, modifies the perception of the structures and networks of social relations.

Consequently, the definition of markets as fields serves as a theoretical umbrella under which agents are seen as entangled in a set of distinct social forces that locate them in space and in relation to others, provide for the achievement of their goals, as well as limit these opportunities. Thus, the simultaneous analysis of the three social forces (networks, institutions, and culture) enables better understanding of the emergence, stability, and transformation processes of markets and the economy in general (Beckert 2010).

Nested markets – a proposal for analysis of agri-food markets

Among recent contributions to the analysis of contemporary agri-food markets the *nested markets* approach stands out. According to a group of authors, the construction of markets and marketing mechanisms comprises one of the most relevant characteristics of sustainable rural development processes (Hebink et al. 2014; Oostindie et al. 2010; Ploeg 2014; Schneider et al. 2016).

Nested markets are generally seen as mechanisms for food commercialization built on shared social norms and standards collectively appropriated by local actors. Following the perspective adopted by Ostrom (1999, 2010), the analysis of nested markets focuses on the different patterns of governance built and reproduced by farmers and consumers, when developing sustainable food production, marketing, and consumption practices and processes (Hebink et al. 2014; Oostindie et al. 2010; Ploeg 2016; Polman et al. 2010).

In this sense, from the perspective of the nested markets, it is important to investigate how "alternative" rules, norms, and social conventions are constructed, negotiated, reproduced, and legitimized, so as to structure spaces for food commercialization that distinguish their practices and their food from those found in conventional/industrial markets of production and consumption.

In spite of its theoretical origin being related to the economic institutionalist perspective of K. Polanyi – which privileges the analysis of the emergence of social rules and norms that build markets – the nested markets approach calls for a heterodox reading of sustainable food systems and their markets, making use of networks and culture precisely to explain the emergence of such rules.

This approach considers local markets (nested markets) to be embedded in a broader and relational context which also includes the global/conventional markets. What distinguishes the nested markets approach is that it relates the flows of commodities, information, and values that build sustainable local markets to the standards, norms, and rules that reproduce the conventional markets. There would be a multiple and diverse interaction process, a field of contention and power relations where production and consumption alternative practices and processes compete with conventional ones for the acceptance and legitimation of their agri-food products.

According to Ploeg (2016, 23), a nested market

> is a segment of a wider market. It is a specific segment that typically displays different price levels, distributional patterns of the total Value Added and relations between producers, distributors and consumers than those seen in the wider market. This segment is nested in a wider market. It is part of, but at the same time it differs from it.

Nested markets, thus, comprise exchange practices and mechanisms of social interaction between economic agents, which fit inside broader contexts, generally called conventional ones, though differing significantly from these. Such differentiation is attributed to their capacity to build three main elements/characteristics: distinctiveness, socio-material infrastructures, and common pool resources.

The distinctiveness of nested markets lies in two main dimensions: price and quality. Foods commercialized through these markets usually have lower prices when sold directly to consumers. On the other hand, they can also be much more expensive, when commercialized via specialized markets (like local and organic stores) and/or when they are specific to certain regions (PGI, PDO). As to their quality, it is built on factors such as the mode of production (family, traditional, ecological, etc.), the social organization of time and space allowing consumers access to fresh food, or the availability of the product – the more scarce/singular it is, the greater its quality (Ploeg 2016).

The socio-material infrastructures refer to the set of social norms and standards that are created and agreed between actors to make their products available via nested markets. Such infrastructures are essentially responsible for socially legitimizing the traditional knowledge applied to producing local foods and, more than that, for placing them in markets distinguished from the mainstream (Ploeg 2016). That is to say, differentiated products stemming from small-scale farming need distinct markets, so as to attain fairer prices, bring consumers and producers closer, and reduce the transaction costs involved. This process is carried out by mobilizing social norms and standards for action and management, establishing collective agreements and sharing practices and processes among local actors, so as to socially reinforce and legitimize these practices – and markets.

Finally, nested markets are characterized by the share of common pool resources. In these markets, both the distinctiveness and the socio-material infrastructures are collectively appropriated and managed, thus connecting different actors and collective actions that allow the development of mutual benefits.

Objectively, these common pool resources are realized in the possibility for producers to obtain additional benefits, such as better prices, access to specific groups of consumers, access to markets for unique products, and use of local productive resources (Ploeg 2014). In other words, governance and the benefits generated by these food markets are collectively appropriated by local and regional communities, furthering their economies and enhancing the livelihood and reproduction of farmer families (as well as allowing consumers to access healthy and fresh foods). Thus, the nested markets perspective adopts a heterodox approach to markets and the economy, through the lens of three "social structures" that guide economic practices, as discussed above.

Clearly, the element of distinctiveness and its dimensions of price and quality comprise cultural expressions of valorization and attribution of meaning to foods commercialized via nested markets. Empirically, these cultural expressions can be observed through the legitimacy and positive value attributed by consumers to traditional and artisanal modes of production and to ecological and sustainable practices carried out by small-scale farmers. This legitimacy is usually connected to shared political worldviews and cultural values that become materialized in the foods offered by these markets.

In a recent study, we observed that the perceived quality of food products originating from a small-scale agriculture market was built on a shared cultural representation that arose from a positive view on the rural and the family production mode (Cassol 2018). As producers and consumers shared common social origins linked to the rural (since many consumers were born in rural areas or had family members or acquaintances who were farmers) a positive view of the products offered by this market was built, legitimizing traditional modes of production and its foods (Cassol 2018).

As to the dimension of socio-material infrastructure, it is mobilized through the inherent institutional component of food markets creation. By asserting that such markets are based on patterns of governance and on the definition of social norms and standards for their management and economic reproduction, the nested markets approach takes an institutional view of the economy that understands transactions and economic exchanges as mediated by collectively negotiated disputes and consensus.

Our previous research on traditional markets in the Brazilian Northeast showed that trade practices and transactions are guided by bargaining as a social norm of economic action. This norm – a feature historically peculiar to the region related to its commercial tradition – operates as a tacit agreement between sellers and consumers who start their economic interactions by explicitly bargaining over foods offered. This possibility of negotiating and bargaining for prices ends up ascribing distinct patterns of governance to these markets, distinguishing them from others found in the same cities (Cassol 2018).

Finally, common pool resources can be related to the social networks approach. Insofar as these resources support processes of both product distinctiveness (culture) and establishment of social norms for economic interaction (institutions), they also provide for the development of interpersonal relations between the different actors that interact and exchange their products within food markets.

The Farmers Market of Passo Fundo, a medium-sized municipality located in the north of Rio Grande do Sul, Brazil, is an example, which we have discussed elsewhere (Cassol 2013; Schneider et al. 2016). This market, created by family farmers from that municipality, is today legitimized and reproduced due to the establishment of networks of interpersonal relations. These networks – based on direct contact between producers and consumers – strengthen inter-knowledge and friendship ties among the actors, ascribing quality and legitimacy to their products. Moreover, such interpersonal relationships act on the market strategies and the food prices, it being common to give discounts to known customers or to consumers who buy larger quantities, such as owners of groceries and minimarkets.

The nested markets perspective, therefore, is based on a heterodox reading of the markets, which aims to understand the various ways social actors across the world have organized themselves to build new spaces for food marketing and consumption. Asserting that these processes are neither linear nor standardized, this perspective innovates by analysing local agri-food markets in relation to global/conventional markets and revealing the social construction of markets through the analysis of governance patterns (standards and norms) and of the distinct features that reproduce them.

Final remarks

The purpose of this contribution was to connect the debates on sustainable agri-food markets with prominent approaches of the new economic sociology. It is worth highlighting some further considerations.

The first one refers to the need for rural studies to incorporate the analysis of the markets as such. As we have argued, most studies on agri-food markets have focused on their visible aspects, by analysing the exchanges and social interactions (networks) between producers and consumers that are established within these spaces. However, it is necessary to go further and take a step towards a "sociologization of food markets". This can be done by bring in the different sociological approaches to economics and the agri-food studies closer, as we have shown above. This convergence can help problematize how these spaces emerge and develop and, especially, investigate which actors and organizations control them and what forms of social differentiation contemporary (food) markets produce. This step forward will allow for advancing the analysis of the social commodification of agriculture.

The second consideration is related to the studies of economic sociology proper and the challenges posed to these approaches. As Wilkinson (2019) points out, the sociological studies of economic phenomena have met some significant problems. In particular, the analyses face difficulties in incorporating recent transformations in capitalist dynamics (and its markets), represented by the increasing digitalization and fragmentation of relations of labor and production. These transformations have impacted on both the forms of work and the use of money (financialization and marketization), concepts that are central to the new economic sociology and need to be better problematized (Wilkinson 2019). Thus, the rural studies – and even sociology – should strive to more and better theorize and analyse markets, as we argue here. This entails the need of new methodologies for analysing markets, such as the construction of typologies that differentiate how these spaces are built and given meaning in different regions. A first effort in this direction has been made by Schneider et al. (2016), who propose a typology of agri-food markets according to the type of marketing channel accessed by family farmers. This typology has been improved and has served as a starting point for the analysis of a set of different markets in the southern region of Brazil (Schneider et al. 2017).

The main point here is to recognize that markets, as social constructs, do not follow a general/universal pattern or model, as proclaimed by founding fathers of sociology (Marx 2017; Simmel 1972; Weber 1991). As they are social constructs, i.e., the outcomes of interactions, values, conventions, and norms shared by actors, the characteristics and governance patterns of markets vary according to the historical, cultural, political, and social contexts in which they emerge. This calls into question some assumptions and views that directly link markets to the capitalist system. In fact, in their sociological definitions, markets are beyond capitalism, they precede this system (Polanyi et al. 1957) and are often reproduced by means of non-capitalist values and practices (Mauss 1974; Bourdieu 2005).

Finally, a gap remains in the studies on agri-food markets regarding the development of indicators and variables for their analysis. As pointed out by Sonnino and Marsden (2006), studies on markets and agri-food systems still lack more robust and cohesive methodologies that could add to the several empirical analyses that have been conducted. Besides, the development of indicators to analyse markets might enhance references for better food policies by focusing both on sustainable practices of production and consumption. This may be useful to scale-up those practices and at the same time allow wider replication. Further, this could contribute to methodological issues around changes to contemporary markets and food systems. Again, this can be achieved by analysing agri-food systems making use of consolidated methodological approaches of economic sociology. Here is a research agenda for the future.

Questions for discussion

1. What types of markets can support social and sustainable agri-food practices?
2. How can different approaches of economic sociology contribute to understanding agri-food markets?
3. What are the ways farmers integrate into markets?

Note

1 Short food supply chains comprise a type of agri-food network that is widespread and extensively researched. These chains, fundamentally, demand the reduction of distances between producers and consumers and the reconnection between food and territory.

References

Allaire, G. The multidimensional definition of quality. In: Augustin-Jean, L., Ilbert, H. and Rivano, N. (Eds.) *Geographical Indications and International Agricultural Trade: the Challenge for Asia*, pp. 71–90. Basingstoke: Palgrave Macmillan, 2012.

Beckert, J. The social order of markets. *Theory and Society*, vol. 38, no. 3: 245–269, 2009.

Beckert, J. How do fields change? The interrelations of institutions, networks and cognition in the dynamics of markets. *Organization Studies*, vol. 31, no. 05: 605–627, 2010.

Beckert, J. Imagined futures: fictional expectations in the economy. *Theory and Society*, vol. 42: 219–240, 2013.

Beletti, M. and Mancini, L. The case of solidarity purchasing groups in the marche region, Italy. *Rivista Di Economia Agraria*, Anno vol. 70, no. 2: 185–207, 2015.

Bérard, L. and Marchenay, P. *From Localized Products to Geographical Indications: awareness and Action* Ressources des terroirs – Cultures, usages, sociétés. Bourg-en-Bresse: UMR Eco-Anthropologie et Ethnobiologie Centre national de la recherche scientifique Alimentec, 2008.

Blay-Palmer, A., Santini, G., Dubbeling, M., Renting, H., Taguchi, M. and Giordano, T. Validating the city region food system approach: enacting inclusive, transformational city region food system. *Sustainability*, vol. 10, no. 1680: 1–23, 2018.

Block, F. Relational work in market economies: an introduction. *Politics and Society*, 40(2), 135–144, 2012.

Boltanski, L. and Thevenot, L. *De La Justification*, Paris: Gallimard, 1991.

Born, B. and Purcell, M. Avoiding the local trap: scale and food systems in planning research. *Journal of Planning Education and Research*, vol. 26: 195–207, 2006.

Bourdieu, P. O campo econômico. *Política E Sociedade*, no. 6: abril de 2005.

Brunori, G. Local food and alternative food networks: a communication perspective. *Anthropology of Food*, vol. S2, 1–30: Mars 2007, From local food to localised food/De produits locaux a produits, 2007.

Brunori, G., Rossi, A. and Guidi, F. On the new social relations around and beyond food. analysing consumers' role and action in gruppi di acquisto solidale (Solidarity Purchasing Groups). *Sociologia Ruralis*, vol. 52, no. 1, 1–30. January 2012.

Burt, R. *Structural Holes: the Social Structure of Competition*. Cambridge: Harvard University Press, 1992.

Callon, M. (ed.) *The Laws of the Market*. Oxford: Blackwell Publishers, 1998.

Caron, P. *et al*. Food systems for sustainable development: proposals for a profound four-part transformation. *Agronomy for Sustainable Development*, 2018. doi: 10.1007/s13593-018-0519-1.

Cassol, A. Redes agroalimentares alternativas: mercados, interação social e a construção da confiança. Dissertation (Master in Sociology). Universidade Federal do Rio Grande do Sul. 2013.

Cassol, A. Instituições sociais e mercados alimentares tradicionais: barganha, preços, variedade, qualidade e consumo em feiras. Thesis (Doctorate in Sociology). Universidade Federal do Rio Grande do Sul, 2018.

Cruz, F. T. and Menasche, R. Tradition and diversity jeopardised by food safety regulations? The serrano cheese case, campos de cima da serra region, Brazil. *Food Policy*, vol. 45, 1–9, 2013.

DiMaggio, P., Powell, W. I., DiMaggio, P. and Powell, W. (Eds) *The New Institutionalism in Organizational Analysis*. 1–38. Chicago: University of Chicago Press, 1991.

DiMaggio, P. and Powell, W.I. The iron cage revisited: institutional isomorphism and collective rationality in organizational fields. *American Sociological Review*, vol. 48, 147–160, 1983.

Dobbin, F. Introduction: the sociology of the economy. In: Dobbin, F. (Ed.) *The Sociology of the Economy*, pp. 1–25. New York: Russell Sage Foundation, 2004.

Feenestra, G. W. Local food systems and sustainable communities. *American Journal of Alternative Agricultlura*, vol. 12: 28–36, 1997.

Fligstein, N. *The Architecture of Markets: an Economic Sociology of Twenty-First-Century Capitalist Societies*. Princeton: Princeton University Press, 2001.

Fonte, M. Knowledge, food and place. A way of producing, a way of knowing. *Sociologia Ruralis*, vol. 48, no. 3, 200–222, July 2008.

Fonte, M. Food relocalisation and knowledge: dynamics for sustainability in rural areas. In : Fonte, M. and Papadopoulos, A. G. (Eds.) *Naming Food after Places: food Relocalisation and Knowledge Dynamics in Rural Development*, pp. 1–35. Farnham: Ashgate, 2010.

Fourcade, M. Theories of markets and theories of society. *American Behavioral Scientist*, vol. 50: 1015–1034, 2007.

Gazzola, M. and Schneider, S. (Orgs). Cadeias curtas e redes agroalimentares alternativas: negócios e mercados da agricultura familiar. Porto Alegre, Ed. UFRGS, 2017.

Getz, A. Urban foodsheds. *Permac. Activist*, vol. 24: 26–27, 1991.

Goodman, D. Rethinking food production-consumption: integrative perspectives. *Sociologia Ruralis*, vol. 42, no. 4: 271–277, October 2002.

Goodman, D., Dupuis, E. and Goodman, M. *Alternative Food Networks*. London and New York: Routlege, 2012.

Goodman, M. The ethics of sustainable consumption governance: exploring the cultural economies of 'alternative' retailing. Environment, Politics and Development Working Paper Series. Department of Geography, King's College London, 2009.

Granovetter, M. The strength of weak ties. *American Journal of Sociology*, vol. 78, no. 6: 1360–1380, 1973.

Granovetter, M. Economic action and social structure: the problem of embeddedness. *American Journal of Sociology*, vol. 91, no. 3: 481–510, 1985.

Granovetter, M. The impact of social structures on economic outcomes. *Journal of Economic Perspectives*, vol. 19, no. 1: 33–50, 2005.

Guthman, J. *Agrarian Dreams: the Paradox of Organic Farming in California*. Berkeley, CA, USA,: Univ. of California Press, 2014.

Hebink, P., Ploeg, J. D. and Schneider, S. (Ed.) *Rural Development and the Construction of New Markets*. Haia: Routledge, 2015.

Hodgson, G. What are institutions?. *Journal of Economics Issues*, vol. XL, no. 1: 1–25, 2006.

Horlings, L. and Marsden, T. Exploring the "new rural paradigm" in Europe: eco-economic strategies as a counterforce to the global competitiveness agenda. *European Urban and Regional Studies*, vol. 21, 4–19, 2014.

Jennings, S., Cottee, J., Curtis, T. and Miller, S. *Food in an Urbanized World: the Role of City Region Food Systems in Resilience and Sustainable Development*. London: The International Sustainability Unit, The Prince of Wales Charitable Foundation, 2015.

Karpik, L. *L'économie Des Singularités*. Paris: Editions Gallimard, 2007.

Kremer, P. and Schreuder, Y. The feasibility of regional food systems in metropolitan areas: an investigation of Philadelphia's foodshed. *Journal of Agriculture, Food Systems and Community Development*, vol. 2: 171–191, 2012.

Krippner, G. The elusive market: embeddedness and the paradigm of economic sociology. *Theory and Society*, vol. 30: 775–810, 2001.

Lamine, C., Renting, H., Rossi, A., Wiskerke, J. S. C. and Brunori, G. Agri-Food systems and territorial development: innovations: new dynamics and changing governance mechanisms. In: Darnhofer, I. (Ed.) *Farming Systems Research into the 21st Century*, pp. 229–256. Dordrecht, The Netherlands: The New Dynamic. Springer, 2012.

Lang, T. and Heasman, M. *Food Wars: the Global Battle for Mouths, Minds and Markets*. London: Earthscan, 2009.

Marques, F. C., Conterato, M. A. and Schneider, S. *Construção De Mercados E Agricultura Familiar – desafios Para O Desenvolvimento Rural*. Porto Alegre: Ed. UFRGS, 2016.

Marsden, T., Banks, J. E. and Renting, H. Understanding alternative food networks: exploring the role of short food supply chains in rural development. *Environment and Planning A*, vol. 35: 393–411, 2003.

Marsden, T. and Renting, H. Uma réplica ao artigo: "Compreendendo as redes alimentares alternativas: o papel de cadeias curtas de abastecimento de alimentos no desenvolvimento rural". In: Gazzola, M. and Schneider, S. (Orgs) *Cadeias Curtas E Redes Agroalimentares Alternativas: negócios E Mercados Da Agricultura Familiar*, pp. 53–58, Porto Alegre: Ed. UFRGS. 2017.

Marsden, T. K. et al. Food supply chain approaches: exploring their role in rural development. *Sociologia Ruralis*, vol. 40: 424–438, 2000.

Marx, K. *O Capital: crítica Da Economia Política*, 2nd ed . São Paulo: Boitempo, 2017.

Mauss, M. Ensaio sobre a dádiva: forma e razão da troca nas sociedades arcaicas. In: Sociologia e Antropologia. São Paulo: EDUSP, 1974, V. 2, pp. 49–209.

Maye, D. and Kirwan, J. Alternative food networks. *Sociology of Agriculture and Food*, vol. 20: 383–389, 2010.

Mendras, H. *Sociedades Camponesas*. Rio de Janeiro: Zahar, 1978.

Milone, P. and Ventura, F. The visible hand in building new markets for rural economies. In: Hebink, P., Ploeg, J. D. and Schneider, S. (Eds.) *Rural Development and the Construction of New Markets*, Haia: Routledge. 2015. Chapter 3.

Muchnik, J., Biénabe, E. and Cerdan, C. Food identity/food quality: insights from the "coalho" cheese in the Northeast of Brazil. *Anthropology of Food*, vol. 4, 2005, 1–15.

Murdoch, J., Marsden, T. and Banks, J. Quality, nature, and embeddedness: some theoretical considerations in the context of the Food Sector. *Economic Geography*, vol. 76, no. 2: 107–125, 2000.

Nee, V. The new institutionalism in economics and sociology. In: Smelser, N. and Swedburg, R. (Eds.) *The Handbook of Economic Sociology*, 2nd ed., pp. 49–74, New York: Russell Sage Foundation, 2005.

Niederle, P. and Junior, V. *As Novas Ordens Alimentares*. Porto Alegre: Editora da UFRGS, 2018.

Oostindie, H. *et al*. The central role of nested markets in rural development in Europe. *Rivista Di Economia Agraria*, Firenze, vol. 65, no. 2, 2010, 191–224.

Ostrôm, E. *Governing the Commons: the Evolution of Institutions for Collective Action*. 280. Cambridge: Cambridge University Press, 1999. c1990.

Ostrôm, E.Beyond markets and states: polycentric governance of complex economic systems. *American Economic Review*, vol. 100: 1–33, 2010.

Ploeg, J. D. El proceso de trabajo agrícola y la mercantilización. In: Guzman, E. S. (Ed.) *Ecologia, Campesinato Y Historia*. España: Las ediciones de la Piqueta, 1992, 153–196.

Ploeg, J.D. *Camponeses E Impérios Alimentares: lutas Por Autonomia E Sustentabilidade Na Era Da Globalização*. Porto Alegre: Ed. UFRGS, 2008.

Ploeg, J.D.Newly emerging, nested markets: a theoretical introduction. In: Hebink, P., Ploeg, J. D. and Schneider, S. (Eds.) *Rural Development and the Construction of New Markets*, pp. 16–40. Haia: Routledge, 2014.

Ploeg, J.D. Mercados aninhados recém criados: uma introdução teórica. In: Marques, F. C., Conterato, M. A. and Schneider, S. *Construção De Mercados E Agricultura Familiar – desafios Para O Desenvolvimento Rural*, pp. 21–52. Porto Alegre: Ed. UFRGS, 2016.

Polanyi, K. *A Grande Transformação: as Origens De Nossa Época*. Rio de Janeiro: Campus, 1980.

Polanyi, K., Arensberg, C. and Pearson, H. *Trade and Market in the Early Empires*. Glencoe, IL: Free Press and Falcon's Wing Press, 1957.

Polman, N. *et al.* Nested markets with common pool resources in multifunctional agriculture. *Rivista Di Economia Agraria*, Firenze, vol. 65, no. 2, 2010, 295–318.

Pratt, J. Food values: the local and the authentic. *Critique of Anthropology*, vol. 27, no. 3, 2007, 285–300.

Raud, C. A construção social do mercado em Durkheim e Weber: análise do papel das instituições na sociologia econômica clássica. *Revista Brasileira De Ciências Sociais*, vol. 20, no. 57, fevereiro 2005, 127–142.

Schneider, S. et al. *A Dinâmica Dos Mercados Agroalimentares No Rio Grande Do Sul: mapeamento E Análise Socioeconômica*. Fundação de Amparo a Pesquisa do Estado do Rio Grande do Sul, projeto de pesquisa em andamento, 2017.

Schneider, S., Salvate, N. and Cassol, A. Nested markets, food networks, and new pathways for rural development in Brazil. *Agriculture*, vol. 6, no. 4: 1–19, nov 2016. doi: 10.3390/agriculture6040061.

Scott, J. and Carrington, P. *The Handbook of Social Network Analysis*. London: SAGE Publications, 2011.

Shanin, T. *Defining Peasants: Essays Concerning Rural Societies: Expolary Economies and Learning from Them*. Oxford; Cambridge, MA: Blackwell Publishing, 1990.

Shanin, T. The nature and logic of the peasant economy 1: a generalization. *Journal of Peasant Studies*, vol. 1, no. 1: 63–80, 1973.

Simmel, G. *Sociologia: estudios Sobre Las Formas De Socialización*. Madrid: Alianza, 1972.

Smelser, N. and Swedber, R. (Ed.) *The Handbook of Economic Sociology*. Princeton, New Jersey: Princeton University Press, 2005.

Sonnino, R. Embeddedness in action: saffron and the making of the local in southern Tuscany. *Agriculture and Human Values*, vol. 24: 61–74, 2007.

Sonnino, R. and Marsden, T. Beyond the divide: rethinking relations between alternative and conventional food networks in Europe. *Journal of Economic Geography*, vol. 6, 2006. 181–189.

Sonnino, R. and Marsden, T. Além da linha divisória: repensando relações entre redes alimentares alternativas e convencionais na Europa. In: Gazzola, M and Schneider, S. (eds). *Cadeias curtas e redes agroalimentares alternativas: negócios e mercados da agricultura familiar*. Porto Alegre, Ed. UFRGS, 2017.

Steiner, P. *A Sociologia Econômica*. São Paulo: Atlas, 2006.

Uzzi, B. Social structure and competition in interfirm networks: the paradox of embeddedness. *Administrative Science Quarterly*, vol. 42: 35–67, 1997.

Weber, M. *Economia E Sociedade: fundamentos Da Sociologia Compreensiva*. Brasília: Ed. da Unb, 1991.

Weber, M. *Historia Económica General*. 330 p. México: Fondo de Cultura Económica, 1997.

Whatmore, S. and Clark, N. Good food: ethical consumption and global change. In: Clark, N., Massey, D. and Sarre, P. (Eds.) *A World in the Making*, pp. 363–412. Milton Keynes, Bucks: The Open University, 2006.

White, H. Where do markets come from?. *American Journal of Sociology*, vol. 87, no. 3: 517–547, 1981.

Wilkinson, J. A new paradigm for economic analysis?. *Economy and Society*, vol. 26: 305–339, 1997.

Wilkinson, J. An Overview of German New Economic Sociology and the Contribution of the Max Planck Institute for the Studies of Societies. MPIfG Discussion Paper 19/3, Max Planck Institute for the Study of Societies, Cologne February 2019.

Zaneti, T. B. and Schneider, S. Ingredientes singulares à la carte: implicações do uso de produtos diferenciados na gastronomia contemporânea. *Anthropology of Food*, vol. 1: 1–20, 2016.

Zelizer, V. Human values and the market: the case of life insurance and death in 19th century America. *American Journal of Sociology*, vol. 84: 591–610, 1979.

Zelizer, V. The social meaning of money: "Special Monies". *American Journal of Sociology*, vol. 95, no. 2: 342–377, Sep., 1989.

Zelizer, V. *La Negociación De La Intimidad*. Buenos Aires: Fondo de Cultura Económica, 2009.

14

THE SYMBIOTIC FOOD SYSTEM

Marc Wegerif

Introduction

The word symbiosis originates form the Greek word *sumbiosis*, meaning companionship, which is drawn from the words *sun-*, together, and *bios*, life. It describes the way in which two or more organisms live together in relations that are usually of some mutual benefit, not necessarily equal and certainly involving contestation, but not predatory purely destructive relations between the actors.

The symbiotic food system is one organized around how people live their lives and without direct corporate, state, or development organization interventions. As with the peasant economy, the actors involved organize their economic activities to meet the needs of family reproduction, rather than being motivated primarily by an intention to increase returns on capital. It involves multitudes of small-scale actors who simultaneously maintain their autonomy and work together by drawing on existing practices, common cultural repertoires and personal relationships. At the heart of this working is the management of the tension between the individual striving to look after themselves and working in solidarity for the mutual benefit of the others involved.

This concept fills a gap in the debates on food systems that have tended to focus on the globally dominant corporate food system, on the one hand, or purposively created often local alternative food networks on the other. The symbiotic food system is neither purposively created, nor corporate. Importantly this food system, or elements of it, exists in many countries, plays a key role in the supply of food for many people, and provides an important market for many food producers.

This chapter will illustrate the concept by describing the symbiotic food system that feeds the majority of the 5 million residents of the coastal city of Dar es Salaam, in the East African country of Tanzania, located on the Indian Ocean between Mozambique and Kenya. Lessons from this example will be used to identify ways we can enhance the regenerative practices and opportunities that are intrinsic to such food systems.

Feeding Dar es Salaam

Mchapakazi is working with a hoe preparing one of his fields for planting just outside the village of Zombo, some 350 km inland from Dar es Salaam. As Fanana and I walk up he stops work and leans on his hoe with an easy smile. He is enthusiastic about his farming, it is a religious holiday and the temporary workers he hires are not in the field today, but Mchapakazi is. He gets two harvests a year and, next to the piece of land that he is working on, there are tall maize plants, a healthy green and the cobs of corn almost ready for picking. Mchapakazi shows us where he has planted different varieties of maize, marked with seed bags, to compare how each one grows. As well as buying improved seeds, he does his own seed selection for replanting the following year.

Fanana is also a farmer growing maize, sesame, and beans on four acres of land, two that he owns and two that he rents from another land-holder in the village. The two farmers are friends, a few evenings ago I had been with them and four others at a bar in the village. Their children, like almost all children in the village, go to the same school. They share information on farming and markets for their products. On many afternoons Fanana sits in the shade of a tree near the main road in the village playing cards and chatting with fellow village residents, most of them farmers. On some evenings he goes with his family to a nearby friend's house to watch television. That friend, as well as farming, is a butcher. The butcher buys cattle from farmers and pastoralists in the area, then slaughters and sells the meat locally. Fanana is one of his customers, buying meat from his friend to eat at home and sometimes his children also grill and sell meat near the bar in the evening.

Fanana and Mchapakazi use the maize they grow for home consumption and keep aside seeds for replanting, sometimes sharing or swapping seeds with other farmers. Maize that is left is sold to traders that take the maize to Dar es Salaam. In 2014 Fanana sold 25 sacks (just over 3 tons) of maize to these traders and Mchapakazi sold a similar quantity. When it makes sense, such as with the sesame harvest in 2014, they collaborate with other farmers to jointly hire a truck to take their produce to Dar es Salaam and sell it themselves. But the maize is almost always sold to traders who work with local *dalalis* (agents), many of whom are farmers themselves and from the same area. The *dalalis* collect the maize from various farmers until there is enough to meet the order from the trader. The trader then hires a truck to transport the maize either to a regional market where they sell to traders from Dar es Salaam, or straight to Dar es Salaam where, with the help of another *dalali*, they sell to *sembe* (maize meal) traders.

Mchapakazi and Fanana are typical of farmers from the 6 million farming households in Tanzania that each farm on an average of 1.3 hectares (3.2 acres) of land. Like other farmers they first learnt farming working in the fields of their parents and other relatives or friends and they produce food and other products to meet their own and their families' needs for food and an income.

I have started with the description of these farmers, in part because they grow maize that feeds Dar es Salaam and because these vignettes begin to reveal the way production and distribution of food is organized. One can see how food production is intertwined with the social relations and this occurs from farmers through to processors, retailers, and the urban eaters.

There are thousands of *sembe* traders in Dar es Salaam, each has their own brand printed on the sacks they use. They arrange the milling and packaging and then the sale and distribution of the *sembe* to wholesalers and to retail shops. One of the larger of these *sembe* brands is Chapa Asili (Brand nature/natural) with a mill located in Manzese, which is one of the maize trading and milling centers. Unlike most *sembe* traders, Chapa Asili have their own mill and a 3-ton truck. The company is owned and run by a husband and wife team and they employ 11 staff. They started in 2000 and Mosiya, the husband and joint owner, says they do not want to grow the business anymore, this size works for them. Most of the brands, like Enjo and Mama Bibi who I spent time with, do not own a mill, but rather pay for the use of a mill that serves a number of *sembe* traders. They also don't own any form of transport, instead they hire trucks to distribute their *sembe*. As well as selling *sembe*, all the millers dry and sell the *pumba* (bran) left from the milling process. This is a key ingredient in chicken and other animal foods sold mostly to urban and peri-urban farmers.

Chapa Asili have a high enough turnover to buy the 30 tons of maize needed to fill the largest, and most cost effective per ton, trucks bringing maize to Dar es Salaam. Enjo and Mama Bibi cannot afford to fill a truck alone, so they share truckloads of maize along with other *sembe* traders and through that collaboration pay the same transport price per ton as Chapa Asili. These are all family businesses and, just like the maize farmers, they all take home and eat some of the *sembe* they produce.

Chapa Asili buys maize from three suppliers that source it in the central regions of the country (Zombo village mentioned above falls into that area). Mosiya says there is good quality maize in the central regions; "the environment there is good for growing, they don't use chemicals" he explains. One of these suppliers is Maureen who is based in Dar es Salaam, but travels by bus and stays in local guest houses when she spends weeks at a time at markets in inland growing regions, such as the one at Kibaigwa in the Dodoma Region. I found her there spending her days sitting on a bench in the shade of a tree with other maize traders. These traders pass the time with gossip, jokes, and also discussing challenges in the industry and sharing information, such as on where there are good harvests or shortages of supply this year. Maureen buys from the farmers and local traders who deliver to the market until she has enough to fill an order. Sometimes, if she has a big order, the other traders she sits with and often has lunch with will help her by supplying the rest of the maize she needs. At other times she assists them in a similar way. It is also common for Maureen and the other traders to share transport by combining their loads to fill a truck. Maureen works together with her sister who stays in Dar es Salaam and is able to follow up with clients while Maureen is away. Maureen also has an assistant in Kibaigwa who helps find and negotiate for maize they need. This assistant intends to become a maize trader himself and is saving a little money while learning the trade from Maureen.

Martha and Mary Wholesaler (M&M) in Kinondoni, Dar es Salaam, is one of the buyers of Chapa Asili *sembe*. Mosiya says M&M are good customers and they pay on time. The shop is named after the daughters of the husband and wife couple who own and run it. Mama Martha is always sitting at the long counter that runs across the front of the shop. She and her husband started out with a small local *duka* (shop) and then expanded into wholesaling in 1999. They built up the business slowly, without loans, by saving and reinvesting in stock and have been in their current building since 2005. They never advertise and believe customers hear about them by word of mouth. Mama Martha knows Mosiya well and they have been buying from him for a long time, "customers like their *sembe*" she says.

Some eaters buy sacks of maize directly from the mills and wholesale shops, but *sembe* is primarily sold by local *dukas* that can be found within a few minutes' walk of most people's homes across the city. The *dukas* sell maize by weight, any weight the customer wants, measured from 50 kg sacks. The *dukas* are owner operated and most of the shop assistants who are employed are planning to start their own *dukas* in the future. They use their time as shop assistants to learn and save money. The *duka* owners know this and, in exchange for years of loyal and honest service, many help their assistants get started on their own. As well as selling maize and other food and household goods, these *dukas* create a public space where people have the opportunity to meet. It was around the *duka* in my street that I met my neighbors and heard the local news. The *duka* owners and their shopkeepers know everyone in the area, they provide credit to regular customers (as long as it gets repaid), and assist with things like keeping spare keys to your house.

The ordering of production and distribution of the main foods produced and eaten in Tanzania all follow similar modes and types of relations to those found in the maize-based examples shared above. Of course, there are differences due the nature of different crops and their processing. Rice, for example, is husked near the growing areas, unlike maize that is milled in the city. A key reason being that rice travels and lasts well husked, whereas *sembe* is much more vulnerable to damage than whole maize kernels. Also, rice husking produces very little bran, but lots of less useful chaff that is an environmental problem in densely populated areas and does not have a use in animal food, as the maize bran does. Despite these differences, we see the same role of traders and local *dalalis* in buying rice from farmers, the vast majority of whom operate at a small scale on only a few hectares of land. There is the same sharing of milling/husking machines by many traders. The same sharing of information and collaborating to share transport among the traders. And rice, while sold in markets more frequently than maize, is also sold at all the *dukas* in the city.

The very different kind of crop of green vegetables is also grown by small-scale farmers and trucked into Dar es Salaam from hundreds of kilometers away, as well as being grown in urban and peri-urban plots. The producers eat the vegetables they grow at home and share with neighbors when they have a surplus. They sell directly from their fields and trade through wholesale and then retail people's markets (also known as wet markets), or from small roadside fruit and vegetable stalls, known as *genge*. Fresh vegetables are also sold door to door by people on foot or on bicycles.

The people's markets accommodate many individual traders who run their enterprises side by side and also cooperate with activities such as sharing transport to go to wholesale markets, looking after each other's stalls, helping in child care, and contributing to costs of important social functions like weddings and funerals. Traders in people's markets, just like small-scale farmers, are colleagues as well as competitors, often living in the same communities under similar conditions. Their practices at home extend to the marketplace and vice versa; the spheres of reproduction and production overlapping. People's markets are also lively public spaces where people meet, eat, and have the opportunity to share and discuss with others. In fact, the social relations that customers have with the traders seems to be a greater determinant of who they buy from than factors like price, especially given that traders of particular products tend to all sell at the same price. The crop production and the final retail outlets differ, but the type of relations involved are similar to those found in maize and rice production and distribution.

The Tanzanian produced foods, such as maize, rice, potatoes, vegetables, etc. are consistently sold more cheaply at the people's markets and *dukas* than in the supermarkets, perhaps contributing to three international supermarket groups closing their operations in Tanzania since 2014. The markets and especially the *dukas* are not only cheaper, but more accessible due to being located close to where people live, having long opening hours and the flexibility to sell in whatever quantity is wanted at the time. A study of egg supplies in Dar es Salaam found them considerably cheaper in *dukas* than supermarkets and the egg suppliers to supermarkets got a similar price, but had to cover their own transport and supply on credit, compared to receiving cash at the farm/garden gate when selling to bicycle based traders that distribute to the *dukas* (Wegerif 2014). A study comparing raw milk supply through the symbiotic food system and a successful value chain project, supported by a responsible investment company, showed that the raw milk supply gave better prices to the dairy farmers (minimum of 58.7% higher) and better prices to the milk drinker (minimum of 16.6% lower) than the value chain initiative (Wegerif and Martucci 2019).

This economic competitiveness, in addition to social and environmental benefits, can be explained by the symbiotic food system having no or very low management overheads; surpluses being used in reproduction or reinvested into the enterprises without a cut going to shareholder or outside investors; family and apprentice workers keeping labor costs down; maximum utilization of equipment like mills and trucks through them serving many enterprises; and little or no spending on advertising as word of mouth and social networks secure customers.

Explaining this food system

The symbiotic food system includes and overlaps with forms of territorial markets that are advocated for by the Civil Society Mechanism of the World Committee on Food Security (CSM 2016) and have gained recognition over the last few years in policy positions, such as the New Urban Agenda (UN General Assembly 2017). These are markets serving the majority of small-scale farmers and operating within particular geographic areas; local, national, or regional. Territorial markets are also recognized as markets that cross the lines between what is referred to as formal and informal (CSM 2016). What the concept of the symbiotic food system brings to discussions on territorial markets is a further exposition and analysis of the mode of ordering and the nature of the social and economic relations involved in these particular food systems and the markets that are part of them.

The functioning of the symbiotic food system illustrates the social embeddedness of economic relations and also shows elements that can be found in peasant economic practices and common pool resource management as elaborated below.

The food-related economic transactions and production processes in the symbiotic food system take place within the framework of established social relations and norms, including of reciprocal giving and mutually beneficial collaborations (Granovetter 1992). The actors involved are not, however, simply automatons operating either within socially prescribed and immutable roles described by Granovetter (1985) as "over-socialized," nor as automatons responding purely to market forces in order to maximize utility, that Granovetter (1985) describes as "atomized, *under*socialized." The social and market structures that are part of the symbiotic food system create a framework within which actors have some room to maneuver and that they also engage with and reshape through their everyday practices, transactions, and social relations that take place within specific and changing contexts. These relations are not due to any intrinsic characteristics of those involved, rather they exist under particular circumstances and in a system where the tensions between self and mutual interest are finely managed. Those who step outside the limits of these relations are penalized, such as through ostracization that excludes them from the benefit of collaboration that they depend on. Even what appears to be charitable giving often has benefits, such as improved reputation and strengthened social networks (Mauss 1990).

Chayanov (1986) showed how the peasant economy works and has different motive forces than the capitalist economy. He argued, amongst other things, that it is driven by the interest of meeting the needs of reproduction of peasant families. It grows and produces not primarily in order to increase returns on capital (not that the farmer, certainly in Tanzania, is averse to making some money) as much as to feed and clothe growing families. This is reflected in most actors having little interest in growing their enterprises beyond that needed to meet family needs, which in turn leaves them willing to assist others in starting their own operations in the same sector. Another key element of the peasant economy is the effort of the actors involved to create circuits of production and distribution that give them greater autonomy from the corporate capitalist economic circuits (Van der Ploeg 2008; Van der Ploeg et al. 2012). These important characteristics can be found in the farmers in Tanzania and also in the many other enterprises that make up the food system these farmers are part of. This is not surprising in the Tanzanian context given that, in addition to working closely with farmers, many of those involved in the supply of food to Dar es Salaam, including urban retailers, have been or still are farming and at a minimum remain linked to rural farming families.

Research on common pool resource management has shown how people can work together to share and preserve limited resources with polycentric rather than hierarchical organization (Ostrom 2010). The mode of ordering in the symbiotic food system has similarities with the common pool resource management that people like Elinor Ostrom have focused on (Ostrom 1990), but differs in that it involves few formal agreements or management arrangements; there is rarely anything in writing. Collaborations emerge from practice more than as a consciously decided strategy and are often fluid and shifting. Transactions are agreed verbally and payments settled in cash, with witnesses rather than written contracts as the confirmation. This works under particular circumstances based on established norms and values among people working from common cultural repertoires. These are not fixed, but being constantly formed, taught to people entering into the food system, and reinforced in practice.

Essential to the symbiotic nature of the relationships is interdependence between the actors. This requires that they have some choice (i.e. that there is competition) not only about price and product, but also the social benefits. If there is only one supplier for a particular product, the interdependence is threatened as that supplier may feel little need to reciprocate in dealings with others who have no choice but to buy from him. On the other hand, if one actor has so much capital they can buy their way out of needing to collaborate with others that can also threaten interdependence; they can walk away from others and ostracization as a sanction, should they violate norms, will not affect them.

The particular circumstances in Tanzania that have created an enabling environment for this food system to emerge include the limited access to capital that has made collaboration essential for many traders. Historical constraints on foreign investments and on accumulation by local elites limited the extent of vertical integration and domination by a few players leaving opportunities, with low barriers to entry, for multitudes of small-scale actors, of fairly equitable status, to get involved in the food system (Wegerif 2018). Protection for agriculture in Tanzania, through import duties and other limitations on the importation of agricultural products, has also been important. While Tanzania has particular conditions, food systems similar to this play a significant role in other countries. For example, a recent study of the urban food systems in three countries – Kenya, Zambia, and Zimbabwe – found that, despite the presence of supermarkets, "the main and most frequent sources of food remained markets and traders (mostly informal) within their immediate neighbourhoods" (Battersby and Watson 2018, 5).

To summarise, the core elements of the symbiotic food system are that: 1) it is socially embedded in relations rooted in how people live together and their common cultural repertoires, including internal and social norms, but is also constantly being renegotiated in the actual relations between actors who work and trade together; 2) there is a high level of interdependence and reciprocity, although not always direct reciprocity, among people of relatively equitable social and economic relations with enterprises of a similar scale; 3) the primary driver of progress is people acting to meet their needs, rather than capital mobilized for higher returns, and growth happens through replication rather than scaling up; and 4) at the heart of the system is people finding ways to manage, with sanctions where needed, the tension between the striving for autonomy and social solidarity. This is all enabled by particular conditions, which can be made more or less enabling by, for example, particular policies, technology, and infrastructure. The next section will explore the regenerative elements of the symbiotic food system and how these can be enhanced and built on.

Enhancing the regenerative

Sustaining what we have now is important, but not enough. Many people in a city like Dar es Salaam need better food, greater security, and improved living conditions. Many farmers in Tanzania are already struggling to grow crops in soils that are depleted of nutrients and having to cope with the unpredictability of climate change driven weather patterns that make it hard for them to know when to plant and if what they plant will produce a harvest. Regenerative food systems are not about recreating the past, although there are many existing and past practices that can be learnt from and built on. They are food systems which take us into an improved future because they have built in processes of renewal and enrichment of the social, economic and ecological foundations they depend on.

The symbiotic food system already has strong sustainability characteristics and some regenerative practices with further potential to enhance these. I am going to focus here on a few of the strengths and opportunities for improved regenerative practices. In going into these I will be outlining a vision for a more regenerative food system and how we can move towards it.

End waste, build enriching cycles of reuse

We need a food system that eliminates waste through reducing the waste generated and reusing what waste there is for regenerative purposes. First, food waste is limited in the symbiotic food system through the incorporation of food recovery and redistribution in the everyday practices of the actors involved, rather than any external intervention. The lack of separation between the realms of reproduction and production means that often the food produced or traded for business is the same as that eaten and shared at home. The vegetable seller takes some home for lunch and dinner. The street food vendor eats and feeds her children with the food she cooks to sell and if she has enough she also shares with neighbors, or at least their children. Such sharing occurs within social networks and strengthens and enriches those networks. The practice of trading (or growing) what one eats, and eating what one trades, involves maximizing the reuse of resources and expands the level of autonomy from capitalist circuits of production and extraction of wealth.

The presence of food production – including horticulture, livestock keeping, and food processing – in and around the city creates opportunities for mutually enriching circuits for the reuse of food waste. Maize bran left after milling is locally used in animal feed. Blood collected in abattoirs is dried and becomes a source of protein in animal feed. Animal manure is sold or given away to be used to enrich soils in urban agriculture. Left-over food goes to chickens or other livestock. All these practices, that many people take for granted, can be both preserved and enhanced with awareness raising about their value and sharing of best practices.

One area for improvement is the handling of bulk waste, such as that generated at people's markets and largely made up of vegetable and fruit off-cuts. The municipalities collect this, but have not yet, despite some efforts and large potential, been successful in arranging the conversion into compost or other uses.

Most local foods are distributed in sacks or crates and then sold loose (unpackaged) in any quantity the buyer wants. For example, eggs are distributed in and sold from 30-egg cardboard trays that are reused many times (Wegerif 2014). The eater buys whatever quantity they want, counted from the tray that normally sits on the counter of the *duka*. Maize, rice, and cooking oil are measured out and sold in the quantities the eater wants. This approach reduces food waste at home and almost eliminates packaging, except that currently in Tanzania there is widespread use of plastic bags that many *duka* owners will give to their customers. There are people who have created an enterprise buying used sacks and buckets from the *dukas* and selling them in rural areas where they are used again to pack maize and other products. The already limited use of packaging can be improved on with intervention to stop the use of plastic bags and with encouragement of the existing practices with no single use packaging.

Enhanced agroecology for rejuvenated soils and farmer livelihoods

The primary production of food that feeds Dar es Salaam and indeed Tanzania, is by small-scale farmers already using at least low external input farming practices and default agroecological approaches; default because these build on historic farming practices and are shaped by a lack of capital for inputs, more than being a conscious commitment to agroecology. The opportunity for improvement is that such farmers find it easier to convert to fully agroecological approaches, because they are open to experimentation and not heavily locked into models dependent on high levels of external inputs (Altieri 2002). Further, many farmers and others in the food system are already concerned about soil degradation and the impacts of the long-term use of chemicals on food and soil quality. This is an opportunity to encourage the utilization of the best of current and growing knowledge of effective agroecological practices that can enrich, rather than deplete soils, reduce the contribution of agriculture to climate change, and leave farmers better able to survive the increasingly extreme weather conditions that are being brought by climate changes (Rosset et al. 2011).

Mdee et al. (2018) show, based on research into agroecological farming in Tanzania, how it is very possible to build on farmers' existing practices and networks for the successful adoption of improved agroecological practices. The main input is information and sharing between farmers and there is now evidence that farmers and soils have benefitted from this. The Cuban experience shows that this can work at a national level especially if linked to movement building and utilizing farmer to farmer extension (Rosset et al. 2011). It was also found in Cuba that the small-scale peasant farmers, similar to the majority in Tanzania, were the quickest to take up the improved agroecological practices.

Enhanced food

The symbiotic food system works well to make food accessible, especially to those in poverty, and resists the increasing distribution and consumption of highly processed foods that are causing so many health problems today. This can be enhanced with the expansion of more food enriching agroecological production practices, as mentioned above, and through appropriate food fortification and supportive food safety regulation. Initiatives, such as that by SANKU in Tanzania, after some time in development, now appear to be working and showing potential to reach significant numbers of people with a technology that importantly fits with the typical hammer mills, used by the thousands of *sembe* traders in Dar es Salaam (Mildon et al. 2015: see also http://projecthealthychildren.com/small-scale-fortification/).

Concerns about food safety are often raised in relation to what many call "informal" food production and marketing. There is room for improved regulation of food safety in Tanzania, provided it works to enhance and not undermine the practices of the majority of food producers and traders. This requires greater efforts to understand how people already manage food-borne risks and a differentiation between hazards in food and actual risk to people, that are often mitigated by people's practices. Based on 25 case studies from different parts of Africa, Roesel and Grace (2015, xv) found that in fact "food sold by the formal sector often has no better compliance with food standards than food sold in the informal sector."

Vibrant urban communities

A vibrant and safe city requires a careful mix of private and public spaces that protect autonomy and create ample opportunities for social interaction across class and cultural divides. Nodes in the food system perform an important function in this regard; the *dukas* in particular, along with the vegetable sellers and street food traders, are essential in creating good city streets, as described by Jane Jacobs in her classic work *The death and life of great American cities*. She explains how "[a] good city street neighbourhood achieves a marvel of balance between its people's determination to have essential privacy and their simultaneous wishes for differing degrees of contact, enjoyment or help from the people around" (Jacobs 1961, 59). At the *duka* you can meet people without having to invite them into your house. There is a sense of security that enables young children to play in the street and, even after dark, walk to the *duka* by themselves; the *duka* owner knows them and the house they come from. The *duka* and other food traders provide the "eyes upon the street" that Jacobs shows are so important; "eyes belonging to those we might call the natural proprietors of the street" (Jacobs 1961, 35).

The people's markets are also very important public spaces for social interaction, with the practice of people walking to these markets further enriching the interaction between people within neighborhoods. Keeping these within walking distance anchors communities and has positive environmental benefits. The space for the *dukas* and the markets needs to be preserved, and where missing created, to ensure *dukas* are in all streets and all people are within walking distance of markets. Infrastructure can be improved to make these existing spaces more people friendly, such as with improved roofing at markets, lighting, and sanitation.

Meaningful economic opportunities for people

The food system is a crucial part of any economy; in a country like Tanzania around 80% of the population derive their livelihoods from agriculture and food-related activities. The food system cannot provide incomes for all people, but it can and needs to make a significant contribution. Producing and distributing food in ways that reduce the number of income-generating opportunities will be counter-productive as it will leave more people unable to acquire the food they need, even if more food is grown. What is needed is wide access to meaningful economic activities, including to ownership and control of enterprises that operate at a human scale.

Economists, such as John Mellor (1999), have shown how growth in small-scale farm production and incomes is one of the best contributors to reducing poverty when compared to growth in other sectors and growth in larger scale farming (Mellor and Malik 2017). One of the main reasons for this is that small-scale farmers spend more locally than larger farmers and therefore increasing small-scale farmer incomes stimulates more local economic activity in the non-farm rural sector. This was most evident in my research when visiting the bustling small towns growing up around regional markets, like Kibaigwa in Dodoma region with its large grain market and in Ubaruku District in the Mbeya region due to the rice production and trade in that area. With farmers, traders, and transporters coming into such areas, a range of secondary services like agricultural supply shops, guest houses, bars, and restaurants emerge. One can see and feel the multiplier effects into the local non-farm economy that Mellor identifies with economic data.

The tax revenue from food trading is also an essential income for local and district governments in these rural areas. This continues in the urban centers where the multitudes of small-scale actors in the food system spread the economic opportunities and create vibrant market areas and keep business, which means "eyes" and social spaces, in the streets. These economic opportunities are more than just jobs, they are ownership opportunities. These are enterprises run by people who play a meaningful and responsible role in society and grow their autonomy and identity as they make their own decisions. The farmer decides when and what to plant. The *duka* owner decides what to buy and what mark-up to make, who to give credit to and who is not credit worthy. The maize trader makes decisions on quality, on price, and on which part of the country to go looking for more maize if there is a drought where they normally buy.

The wide spread of economic and ownership opportunities is achieved in the symbiotic food system by replication of enterprises, apprenticeship arrangements that bring people into a sector, and low capital barriers to entry. The valuing of the social interactions as much as the maximizing of profit keep enterprises at a human scale. Such practices need to be understood and promoted. Governments and development agents need to move away from the focus on scaling up and injecting capital to grow particular enterprises. Such approaches inevitably lead to a concentration of power in fewer hands. Increasing labour productivity can improve profits for a few, but means less opportunities for others. We need to value and respect a person not for how big their farm or company is, but for how many others they have helped to start their own farm or business.

Vision

Perhaps the most important benefit of identifying and documenting examples of the symbiotic food system in places like Dar es Salaam is that it can show us what is possible. It regenerates our imagination by showing us that there are other ways to organize food production and distribution. There are other ways to feed our large cities without the corporate dominated agro-industrial system that is driving increasing alienation, inequality, and environmental destruction. The symbiotic food system I have presented here is not perfect, but it exists and shows in practice a vision of how people can organize more regenerative food and agricultural systems that work for them.

Debates that arise

Growth or not

Some of what I see as working for the symbiotic food system, such as limiting capital inputs and not striving to maximize profits, flies in the face of much growth orientated economic development logic. Counter arguments for a future beyond growth are now gaining momentum (Fioramonti 2017: see also https://degrowth.org/2018/09/06/post-growth-open-letter/). The use of gross domestic product as a measure of progress is even more strongly criticized as arbitrary and irrelevant to real people's lives (Jerven 2011). I am not opposed to economic growth per se, especially in less developed countries like Tanzania, but strongly believe it is a mistake to prioritize economic growth as the main aim and measure of progress. Based on what I see in the practices of people supplying food to the residents of Dar es Salaam, I am arguing for a bottom up process, where people use collaboration as much as competition to build their knowledge and enterprises step by step through sharing, saving, and incremental improvements.

Agroecology also involves a process of gradual improvements, sometimes even initial losses in productivity, in order to get long-term and sustainable improvements in quality and quantity. Such processes involve putting aside aspirations for fast growth and instead require the valuing of social and community lives, seeds, and soils, and our contribution to these. This implies the need for a change in the vision of success that is promoted and the type of business management and entrepreneurship training that is provided. The small-scale owner and family operated enterprises that make up the symbiotic food system create decent livelihoods for many people, but create no rent seeking opportunities for large investors and the policy makers and politicians who serve them, which I believe is one of the main reasons they are often ignored.

Value chains

Value chain interventions have become ubiquitous in the development sector and seem to be part of almost all government and non-government development interventions in the food and agricultural sector. This is highly problematic, first because the logic of the value chain approach has been to link producers to "formal" and global markets (Gereffi et al. 2001). This overlooks the territorial markets that serve more eaters and farmers (CSM 2016) and risks tying small-scale producers into highly unequal relations with powerful corporate actors who they don't understand, but who are setting the terms of trade. Secondly, there is often a focus on removing what are referred to as "middle-men" and reducing transaction costs, which in reality means taking away income-earning opportunities from women and men traders who are part of the relationship-building glue holding the food system together. It will also tend, by removing actors in the interest of a narrow concept of economic efficiency, to reduce the positive multiplier effects into the non-farm rural economy that were explained above. Thirdly, there are few quality impact assessments showing the assumed development benefits of value chain interventions (Humphrey and Navas-Alemán 2010), while the studies that exist show that the poorest farmers are not reached as the farmers involved are ones with more assets and education (Seville et al. 2011). And fourth, the value chain analysis looks narrowly at the economic dimensions of transactions, thus missing and in doing so undervaluing the social and environmental benefits (or costs) and not situating the food system within its particular social context that it depends and impacts on.

Land grabs and farmer commercialization

The last ten years have seen an increasing drive to own or control large tracts of land for the expansion of corporate agriculture, normally capital intensive and high input mono-culture production, as well as for extractive industry purposes, such as mining. The majority of the resulting land deals have been in Africa and are a threat to local communities, small-scale farmers, and existing symbiotic food systems (Anseeuw et al. 2012). Increasingly small-scale farmers are under threat not just from land acquisitions, but from out-grower schemes that create dependency on seeds, other inputs, and markets controlled by corporations. Some interventions in the name of development cooperation are closely linked to the marketing of inputs and promote the "dominant frameworks of global agribusiness and capital accumulation" (Amanor and Chichava 2016). With this trend we see a move to private sector provision of agricultural extensions services that are only provided if linked to the promotion of agricultural methods that require particular products. It is essential, therefore, that the land rights of small-scale farmers are protected and state agricultural extension, not beholden to any corporate interests, is improved and focused on sustainable agroecological practices.

A strong or laissez-faire state?

While I celebrate the ability of many actors to start and run enterprises and believe that they should be given the space to do so, this should not be confused with a laissez-faire approach to government. The state has a very important role in regulating the economy and the food sector in particular, in order to create an enabling environment for the emergence and thriving of symbiotic food systems. What the state should not do is make direct interventions to create enterprises or promote particular forms of organization, even if cooperative. Such interventions tend to be misguided and undermine rather than enable people's own initiatives.

The state is needed in town planning and setting local by-laws to ensure the physical and regulatory space for food trading. State interventions, such as research and extension services, are needed to facilitate the identification and sharing of appropriate technology and the best agroecological practices between farmers. The state is also needed in the provision of education and health services and provision of social safety nets for the most impoverished and vulnerable groups. However well the food system runs it cannot provide for all needs. There is interesting further work to be done on how to combine a strong state with the creation of space for people's own initiatives. What is clear is that state policies and interventions should be designed with an in-depth understanding of how people organize within the food system and with the aim of enhancing not hampering that. Achieving this is not so easy, however, among other challenges the typical stakeholder and consultation processes, even when they do happen, miss the majority of people involved in symbiotic food systems as they are generally not organized into representative structures. At the same time many who are invited into these spaces, such as traditional farmers' associations, have been funded and influenced by corporate agribusiness, with leadership who have bought into the modernization paradigms that promise riches, at least for those at the top.

Alternative and short food networks

Many proponents of "alternative food networks" tend to focus on niche and local solutions, such as "short food supply chains" (cf. Renting et al. 2003), thus falling into what some have referred to as the "local trap" (Born and Purcell 2006). This risks overlooking food systems, such as those found in Tanzania, that are an important source of income for farmers in the hinterland and involve moving foods, especially the staple grains, over long distances yet are not corporate (Wegerif and Wiskerke 2017). As Forster and Escudero (2014) have argued, in order to feed our cities we need to have a dialogue that is not polarized between the ideologies of local and global.

The other focus, even when looking at more spatially dispersed "alternative food networks," has been to look at initiatives that have been purposively constructed, such as nested markets (Hebinck et al. 2015). These can hold interesting lessons and show what is possible, but they can also remain niche markets that have little to do with meeting the food needs of the majority of people. More attention needs to be given to looking at food systems, like the symbiotic one described in this chapter, that are organized by and feeding the majority of people, especially those in poverty.

Actions towards the more regenerative

The following are some suggested areas for action that can build on and enhance the regenerative potential of symbiotic food systems.

We need to refine and promote a clear vision for how the growing and urbanizing world population can be fed without the corporate and agro-industrial food system. This vision needs to value and through that reinforce, for those involved and for policy makers, the regenerative practices people are already engaged in. This requires further ethnographic research into how people in food systems in different parts of the world create their economic lives and respond to and reshape the systemic and external pressures and opportunities they are faced with (Hart 2015; Long 2001).

Programs are needed to identify and facilitate the sharing with and between farmers of the best of agroecological practices (Rosset et al. 2011) and these need to be organized to build on the existing, although not formalized, sharing that farmers do. Throughout the food system the creation of greater ecological awareness, building on actors existing concerns, will encourage the valuing of agroecological farming and other regenerative practices and products.

Town planning and regulations need to protect and create spaces for people's markets, *dukas*, urban agriculture, and the transport used to link these. Ensuring all people live within walking distance of markets reduces the environmental and other negative impacts of motorized transport and enriches community as walking to the market and shops creates more opportunity for people to interact. Likewise, improving space and provisions for bicycles increases the range for this form of zero emission transport that also facilitates more direct person to person interaction, compared to motorized transport.

Technology of an appropriate scale for the small enterprises in the symbiotic food system plays an important role in production, handling, and processing of food. The hammer mills, power tillers, and rice husking and sorting machines, most imported from China and India, are finding their way across Tanzania. There are processes, like milk-pasteurizing, where small-scale options are not yet being used, but could enhance the value of the widespread small-scale dairy herds. The promotion of such technology is an important area for intervention.

It is essential to protect the food and agricultural sector from the vagaries of international markets. Farmers need certainty for the long-term planning and commitments they have to make. This is not about protecting unproductive farmers, it is about stopping arbitrary factors such as exchange rate fluctuations destroying an industry that plays such an important role in society. It is also to avoid the race to the bottom that can result if farmers are forced to compete against producers in other countries who benefit from subsidies or from the extreme exploitation of labor and the environment.

If there is no strong voice for symbiotic food systems, they will likely continue to be neglected or undermined. Allies and new modes of mobilization are needed to increase the influence of actors in symbiotic food systems. Movements of the actors involved that cut across old divides from farmers to urban retailers could have potential given their common interests. New alliances can be explored between those in symbiotic food systems and those organizing for options like alternative food networks and the solidarity economy.

These are just a few ideas to start with. We need to continue to seek and build on the factors that enable the symbiotic relations and enriching food systems that serve the majority of people.

Discussion questions

1. What are the key factors that enable this food system to function?
2. What potential does this food system have to be regenerative of both ecology and society?
3. What elements of a symbiotic food system have you seen functioning beyond the examples this chapter shares?
4. Could such a food system sustainably meet the food needs of people in your country and why or why not?
5. If you were designing policies and program to improve food systems, what would you do to enhance and not undermine symbiotic food systems?

Further reading

CSM. (2016) *Connecting smallholders to markets: an analytical guide.* Rome: Civil Society Mechanism, World Committee on Food Security.

Jacobs J. (1961) *The death and life of great American cities*, New York: Vintage.

Van der Ploeg JD. (2008) *The new peasantries: struggles for autonomy and sustainability in an era of empire and globalization.* London: Earthscan.

Wegerif MCA and Martucci R. (2019) Milk and the city: raw milk challenging the value claims of value chains. *Agroecology and Sustainable Food Systems* 43: 1077–1105.

Wegerif MC and Wiskerke JS. (2017) Exploring the staple foodscape of Dar es Salaam. *Sustainability* 9: 1081.

References

Altieri MA. (2002) Agroecology: the science of natural resource management for poor farmers in marginal environments. *Agriculture, Ecosystems and Environment* 93: 1–24.

Amanor KS and Chichava S. (2016) South–south cooperation, agribusiness, and African agricultural development: Brazil and China in Ghana and Mozambique. *World Development* 81: 13–23.

Anseeuw W, Wily LA, Cotula L, et al. (2012) *Land rights and the rush for land: findings from the global commercial pressures on land research project*, Rome: ILC.

Battersby J and Watson V. (2018) *Urban food systems governance and poverty in African cities*, London: Routledge.

Born B and Purcell M. (2006) Avoiding the local trap: scale and food systems in planning research. *Journal of Planning Education and Research* 26: 195–2007.

Chayanov AV. (1986) *AV Chayanov on the theory of peasant economy*, Manchester: Manchester University Press.

CSM. (2016) *Connecting smallholders to markets: an analytical guide.* Rome: Civil Society Mechanism, World Committee on Food Security.

Fioramonti L. (2017) *Wellbeing economy: success in a world without growth.* Basingstoke: Macmillan.

Forster T and Escudero AG. (2014) *City regions as landscapes for people, food and nature*, Washington, DC: EcoAgriculture Partners, on behalf of the Landscapes for People, Food and Nature Initiative.

Gereffi G, Humphrey J and Kaplinsky R. (2001) Introduction: globalisation, value chains and development. *IDS Bulletin* 32: 1–8.

Granovetter M. (1985) Economic action and social structure: the problem of embeddedness. *American Journal of Sociology* 91: 481–510.

Granovetter M. (1992) Economic action and social structure: the problem of embeddedness (ch.2). In: Granovetter M and Swedberg R (eds) *The sociology of economic life.* Boulder, CO: Westview Press, 53–81.

Hart K. (2015) Human economy: the revolutionary struggle for happiness. In: Hart K (ed) *Economy for and against democracy.* New York and Oxford: Berghahn Books, 201–220.

Hebinck P, Schneider S and van der Ploeg JD. (2015) The construction of new, nested markets and the role of rural development policies: some introductory notes. In: Hebinck P, van der Ploeg JD and Schneider S (eds) *Rural development and the construction of new markets.* London and New York: Routledge, 1–15.

Humphrey J and Navas-Alemán L. (2010) *Value chains, donor interventions and poverty reduction: A review of donor practice*, IDS Research Reports, Brighton: Institute of Development Studies, 1–106.

Jacobs J. (1961) *The death and life of great American cities.* New York: Vintage.

Jerven M. (2011) The quest for the African dummy: explaining African post-colonial economic performance revisited. *Journal of International Development* 23: 288–307.

Long N. (2001) *Development sociology: actor perspectives.* London: Routledge.

Mauss M. (1990) *The gift.* London and New York: Routledge.

Mdee A, Wostry A, Coulson A, et al. (2018) A pathway to inclusive sustainable intensification in agriculture? Assessing evidence on the application of agroecology in Tanzania. In: *Agroecology and Sustainable Food Systems* 43(2): 1–27.

Mellor JW. (1999) Pro-poor growth: the relation between growth in agriculture and poverty reduction. Working Paper prepared for USAID/G/EGAD.

Mellor JW and Malik SJ. (2017) The impact of growth in small commercial farm productivity on rural poverty reduction. *World Development* 91: 1–10.

Mildon A, Klaas N, O'Leary M, et al. (2015) Can fortification be implemented in rural African communities where micronutrient deficiencies are greatest? Lessons from projects in Malawi, Tanzania, and Senegal. *Food and Nutrition Bulletin* 36: 3–13.

Ostrom E. (1990) *Governing the commons: the evolution of institutions for collective action.* New York: Cambridge University Press.

Ostrom E. (2010) Beyond markets and states: polycentric governance of complex economic systems. *American Economic Review* 100: 408–444.

Renting H, Marsden TK and Banks J. (2003) Understanding alternative food networks: exploring the role of short food supply chains in rural development. *Environment and Planning A* 35: 393–411.

Roesel K and Grace D. (2015) *Food safety and informal markets: animal products in sub-Saharan Africa.* Abingdon, Oxon: Routledge.

Rosset PM, Machín Sosa B, Roque Jaime AM, et al. (2011) The Campesino-to-Campesino agroecology movement of ANAP in Cuba: social process methodology in the construction of sustainable peasant agriculture and food sovereignty. *Journal of Peasant Studies* 38: 161–191.

Seville D, Buxton A and Vorley B. (2011) Under what conditions are value chains effective tools for pro-poor development. Accessed [21 August 2019]. Available from http://pubs.iied.org/16029IIED.html.

UN General Assembly. (2017) *New urban agenda: resolution adopted by the general assembly on 23 December 2016.* New York: United Nations.

Van der Ploeg JD. (2008) *The new peasantries: struggles for autonomy and sustainability in an era of empire and globalization.* London: Earthscan.

Van der Ploeg JD, Jingzhong Y and Schneider S. (2012) Rural development through the construction of new, nested, markets: comparative perspectives from China, Brazil and the European Union. *Journal of Peasant Studies* 39: 133–173.

Wegerif MCA. (2014) Exploring sustainable urban food provisioning: the case of eggs in Dar es Salaam. *Sustainability* 6: 3747–3779.

Wegerif MCA. (2018) An ethnographic exploration of food and the city. *Anthropology Today* 34: 16–19.

Wegerif MCA and Martucci R. (2019) Milk and the city: raw milk challenging the value claims of value chains. *Agroecology and Sustainable Food Systems* 43(10): 1077–1105.

Wegerif MC and Wiskerke JS. (2017) Exploring the staple foodscape of Dar es Salaam. *Sustainability* 9: 1081.

15

FOOD SHARING

Anna Davies

Introduction

Food sharing has been practiced by humans for millennia. Extensive research by evolutionary biologists and anthropologists has identified the manifold ways in which the collective and collaborative acquisition, preparation, and distribution of food have been used to ensure sustenance and structure relations within and between social groups historically (Kaplan and Gurven 2005; Jones 2007). As the unsustainability of our global food system has become incontrovertibly demonstrated, a resurgent interest in the practices of food sharing and its impacts has emerged. This interest moves beyond the studies of past and small-scale societies that have dominated attention to food sharing to date and focuses on contemporary food sharing which is increasingly mediated by digital information and communication technologies (ICT) and which takes place in multiple arenas, including cities (Davies 2019a). While international analyses of the goals of such ICT-mediated food sharing indicates that it is the intention of many initiatives to support the development of a sustainable, regenerative food system, the precise impacts of sharing are still to be evidenced empirically (Davies et al. 2018). As a result this chapter reflects on the practice and regenerative potential of contemporary food sharing, with a specific focus on those practices which are taking place beyond family and friendship networks and which are utilizing ICT to support their activities.

Before exploring the practices of food sharing, it is important to first consider the evolution of scholarly attention to it, delineating the foundational theories of food sharing that have been established. This is followed by the presentation of a working definition for examining contemporary food sharing and the contestations that remain in this definitional space. A typology of food sharing is then presented as a means to exemplify the diverse economies of food sharing that are admitted by the working definition. The main body of the chapter dissects illustrative examples of food sharing initiatives. It explores where the goals, practices, and impacts of these initiatives intersect with key characteristics of a regenerative food system that emphasizes closing loops to support human and environmental health, ensuring the protection of food cultures and sovereignty, and supporting a movement towards enhanced food democracy. The concluding section of this chapter adopts a reflective stance, identifying the main ways that food sharing might become classified as a regenerative practice and the steps needed to justify that classification.

Evolution of food sharing

While other species also share food, the complexity of food sharing amongst humans is unparalleled. Scholars widely agree that food sharing has been an important means not only to secure sustenance, but also to cement social relations, build resilience into communities, and allow for role specialization within society (Jaeggi and Gurven 2013). Within-family transfers of food shaped the division of labour and care, particularly with respect to age and gender, in ways which are still visible in many contemporary societies. However, food sharing that extends beyond nuclear familial groupings has also been identified, particularly amongst societies which are small-scale, hunter-gatherer, or forager-horticulturalist in character. In part this beyond-family food sharing emerged for pragmatic reasons because of the difficulties in preserving any surplus food. However, the bulk of societies studied for their beyond-family food sharing also had particular social structures which did not demand the same sorts of reciprocity or property ownership systems that predominate in contemporary western democracies (Kaplan and Gurven 2005). This has led to a suite of theories seeking to explain why sharing emerged in this way. As shown on Table 15.1, some theories highlight the toleration of begging and food theft within groups when food is abundant and the donation of food initially to close relatives in times of scarcity as exemplars of how food sharing is used to foster group resilience. Other theories emphasize the reciprocal dimensions and cooperative demands of sharing, arguing that people learnt to share as a result of numerous push and pull factors (Jones 2007). For example, sharing can be a pre-emptive response to avoid punitive treatment from others in the group or as a means to improve status within hierarchical social settings. However, much of the research on which sharing theories are based has been conducted within small-scale societies, particularly with hunter gatherers or groups that combine foraging with simple forms of horticulture. The justification for this focus is pragmatic, foraging societies often share food between families on a daily basis, providing a rich source of data on sharing practices. It is also driven by the disciplinary interests of evolution scholars, for while foraging as a primary means of food provisioning is increasingly rare and far removed from many contemporary experiences, the majority of human history is dominated by such food provisioning systems, with agriculture emerging only in the last 10,000 years. These reflective studies are certainly important for providing insights into the evolutionary dimensions of food sharing, most particularly with respect to the ways in which sharing performs highly socialized forms of interaction, but it is not clear what relevance they hold also for contemporary food sharing practices.

Extending the work of behavioral ecologists, psychologists and anthropologists have also sought to explain how sharing systems persist or transform over time as norms around sharing are negotiated. Here studies of transitional moments dominate, for example when foraging systems intersect with systems of settled agriculture and waged labour activities (Kaplan et al. 2012). In this context, geographical and cultural diversity are seen as key to the evolution of sharing systems as sharers seek to elevate gains from cooperation and minimise risks from free riding through sharing practices. This is important because such research begins to flesh out the dimensions of complex socio-political and economic phenomena also found in contemporary food sharing, identifying the range of different objectives that sharing fulfills for diverse actors and recognizing a dialectical relationship between individuals and structures in how sharing is performed. Despite this, food sharing

Table 15.1 Theories of food sharing

Theory	Characteristics	Key drivers
Reciprocal altruism	Food is given at one point in time in exchange for food at some later time.	Hunter gatherers focus on large, high-quality, nutrient-dense food which is difficult to acquire, leading to high variance in success When successful, more food is secured than can be consumed by hunters themselves, leading to waste Absence of safe storage for food
Co-operative acquisition and by-product mutualism	Individuals work together as a team to secure high value or hard-to-acquire foods, such as wild game.	Hard-to-acquire food often requires coordinated efforts of a number of individuals While an individual might be seen as the owner of acquired food if they found or killed the food source, sharing with those who participated in the hunt can be a means of rewarding cooperation and ensuring it is forthcoming in future hunts Trade-based reciprocal altruism where labour is rewarded with food Group production provides participants with higher per capita returns than gained as individuals
Tolerated theft and scrounging	Food is obtained by individuals through demands made to the generosity of those who acquire and control it (or by stealth).	Unequal access to food within groups leads to differential marginal value of additional food A hungry individual will be more cunning (or demanding) in order to obtain food An individual who has access to food and is not hungry is more likely to relinquish some of it It has been suggested that the sex-bias of hunting roles add additional weight to why food theft or scrounging might be tolerated May include elements of showing off from the food donor
Costly signalling	Food is shared as a means to demonstrate attractive character-istics in order to secure a partner, mate, or ally	Hard to obtain food is secured to demonstrate certain skills or characteristics Food shared may be ultimately sub-optimal from a calorific perspective Need to secure strong allies within a group Need to find a mate
Nepotism based on kin selection **Trait group selection**	Food is shared with kin Food sharing is done for the benefit of the group	Natural selection leads to sharing with those who have similar genetic material While food sharing may have costs to food donors, the benefits of their actions may lead to overall group benefits compared to groups without donors.

Source: Adapted from: Gurven, 2004

studies are still primarily focused on small-scale and isolated communities functioning on the edge or outside global trade systems, leaving much of the contemporary landscape of food sharing unexamined.

Placing food sharing as a practice in contemporary settings is fraught with complexity, not least because there is no agreed definition and therefore a lack of clarity about what types of activities, exchanges, and transactions count as legitimate acts of food sharing. With respect to sharing practices beyond food, it is the cultural specificity and evolutionary dynamism of sharing that is most clearly articulated (Belk 2010), with scholars also documenting a decline in sharing of many kinds as trends towards mass consumerism, privatization, and greater disposable income emerged across the globe in the 20th century (Gabriel 2013). The arrival of digital mobile platforms in the 21st century, however, brought a new wealth of possibilities to connect with others in unprecedented ways, sparking calls for more nuanced attention to contemporary sharing and leading to the emergence of a new term 'the sharing economy' (Botsman and Rogers 2010). While sharing is a social practice, the sharing economy has emerged as a term to describe a particular economic system in which assets or services are shared (for free or for a fee), typically by means of the internet. Despite the resurgence of attention to sharing generally, there are still definitional uncertainties about what exactly counts as food sharing.

Defining contemporary food sharing

While there is no agreed definition of food sharing in English the verb *to share* dates from the late 16th century. Sharing is defined by the *Oxford English Dictionary* (2019) as having a portion of something with others or giving a portion to someone, and is illustrated with food-based examples, such as 'he shared the pie with her' and 'they shared out the peanuts'. Beyond this, sharing is also defined as using, occupying, or enjoying something jointly with others, possessing a view or quality in common with others, or telling someone about something. To reflect the evolution of language and changing technologies of communication, the *Oxford English Dictionary* also includes the process of posting or reposting something on social media, a website, or application as a form of sharing. Building on this foundational reading, a working definition of food sharing can be outlined as follows:

> Having a portion of food with others or giving a portion of food to others; using, occupying or enjoying food (and food growing, cooking and eating spaces) jointly with others; possessing an interest in food in common with others or telling some-one about food, which includes knowledge and skills about food growing, cook-ing, eating and food redistribution.

Under this definition, the term food sharing can be used to refer to the joint or alternating use of a material or informational resource. This includes sharing food itself, in all its forms from seeds to products, but also sharing knowledge about food which might relate to growing, cooking, and storage practices and the sharing of spaces for growing and cooking together and food-related tools and utensils. It can refer to acts of dividing, distribution, and communication. The definition is loose in that it does not specify the mode or form that sharing should take. This has led to considerable contestation around whether sharing is an appropriate term to describe contemporary activities, particularly those which are for-profit enterprises which utilize highly sophisticated ICT to mediate their activities and which are typically collated under the term sharing economy. For example, advocates of the sharing economy, such as Botsman and Rogers (2010), have characterized sharing as a particularly beneficial way to make use of idling assets from cars to homes. For them sharing is primarily an efficiency mechanism which results in reduced waste and economic savings or income depending on the mode of sharing adopted. The social dimensions to sharing, so key to the theories outlined in Table 15.1, are largely absent from these readings of the sharing economy aside from general statements about how connecting people through exchanges (transactional or otherwise) helps to build community cohesion through interaction. Others argue for a more constrained definition of sharing which emphasizes the sociocultural dimensions and excludes the commercial transactions of large-scale sharing platforms or apps (Belk 2014). Much of this critical work brings a normative dimension to bear on sharing, imbuing it with notions of appropriate social interaction, collaboration, and generosity. In these narrower readings of sharing there are frequently assumptions made that it is pro-social and caring, but sharing in practice does not operate in a vacuum and it is infused with politics and uneven power relations. Essentially, whatever definition is adopted, sharing is performed according to a set of rules, tools, skills, and understandings that can change over time, across space, and depending on who is involved. Given this complexity it is useful to illustrate the diversity of what is shared, how it is shared, and the organizational forms that food sharing is taking, even if this can only ever provide a snapshot of dynamic food sharing practices.

Food sharing practices

The broad definition of food sharing set out in the previous section is useful in that it allows consideration of a diverse range of practices; termed diverse food sharing economies in homage to the rich body of literature emerging in relation to diverse food economies (Dixon 2011), but with an added focus on the role of socio-technologies, particularly ICT in shaping the ways sharing occurs (Davies et al. 2017a). Attention to ICT mediation is important for exploring contemporary sharing practices as it offers a technical fix to many challenges that typically constrain food sharing, such as the temporal limits of redistributing perishable goods and the spatial challenges of connecting people who are not necessarily co-located. Beyond the well-established benefits of being able to disseminate informational resources instantaneously and internationally, ICT can also be used to facilitate two-way connections, such as enabling donors and recipients to quickly match food offerings with needs.

Table 15.2 captures different aspects to food sharing, distinguishing between what is shared and how it is shared. The nature of what is being shared is carved into three core categories which comprise the bulk of food sharing initiatives identified through empirical research and which have distinct qualities (Davies, 2019). The food stuff category incorporates food in its many forms, from seeds and plants to highly processed food products, as well as tools and utensils which are used to grow, prepare, or redistribute food. Despite its diversity, what is shared under this category typically expresses a very material quality and is often a rival good, in that if someone is consuming or using it then it is not available to others. The food spaces category includes the physical sites where food sharing occurs, from land which is used to grow food together to the kitchens where collective cooking and eating take place. This category is restricted to place-bound and spatially delimited sites for sharing. The skills category captures the exchange of more intangible qualities; the skills, knowledge, and information related to food matters, from locating wild crops to setting up a surplus food redistribution network. What are shared in this category

Table 15.2 Food sharing typology

Mode of sharing What is shared	Collecting	Gifting	Bartering	Selling Not-for-profit	Selling For-profit
Food stuff *Including: seeds, plants, animals, unprocessed and processed food-stuff, utensils, food waste, compost*	Sharing food that has been foraged or gleaned, e.g. 510 fruits, USA	Providing food for free e.g. Food-Cloud, Ireland and UK	Swapping food and food devices, e.g. Adelaide Hills Produce Swap, Australia	Providing affordable food on a not-for-profit basis e.g. 4th Street Food Co-op, USA	Selling home cooked food that generates income beyond the costs of production e.g. Homemade, Australia
Food spaces *Including: sites for shared grow-ing, preparation, and eating spaces as well as phys-ical redistribution hubs*	Unofficial (guer-rilla) gardening of public open spaces e.g. Ele-phant and Castle roundabout, London, UK	Providing spaces for growing for free e.g. The Monroe Sharing Gar-dens, USA	Providing spaces where bartering can take place e.g. Community Shop, London	Providing spaces for people to grow food on a not-for-profit basis e.g. Mil-waukee Urban Gardens, USA	Providing spaces for supper clubs e.g. The Under-ground Supper Club, Ireland
Food skills *Including: shar-ing knowledge and experiences in relation to food growing, eating, redistribution, or disposal*	Sharing informa-tion about places where gleaning or foraging can occur e.g. Fallen Fruit, Los Angeles, USA	Providing skills around growing for free e.g. 3,000 acres, Australia	Providing opportunities to exchange information about food swapping e.g. Grow stuff, Australia	Providing work-shops around nutrition or growing, e.g. Hunger moun-tain co-op, Montpellier, USA	Providing opportunities for travellers to experience home cooked meals with locals, e.g. Viz Eat, Global

Source: Adapted from Davies et al. 2017a

are typically non-rival goods, such that sharing them with one person does not preclude sharing the same qualities with others.

Table 15.2 also provides exemplar initiatives to illustrate the sharing of stuff, spaces and skills in relation to four main modes of food sharing:

- **Collecting**: which refers to activities such as foraging, gleaning and skip surfing or dumpster diving, where edible food is collected from waste bins;
- **Gifting**: that includes bestowing something voluntarily and without compensation;
- **Bartering**: which involves the exchange of goods or services for other goods or ser-vices without using money; and
- **Monetary exchange**: where goods and services are exchanged for monetary payment, either for-profit or not-for-profit.

How initiatives choose to organize their activities is another important consideration as institutional arrangements can limit activities in particular ways. For example, charitable organizations are restricted from campaigning politically in many jurisdictions and this can sometimes affect capacities of initiatives to fully meet their stated goals to reorient the food system. In other cases, initiatives choose to have two different wings to their work, one may be for-profit, generating income to support other activities which may not be sustainable otherwise. Certainly, there are many ways to share, just as there are many motivations for, and outcomes from, doing so.

Food sharing in practice

Despite their innovation, the wealth of food sharing initiatives has historically been hard to identify due to their hyper-localized spheres of engagement and dependence (Cox 1998) and their small scale (Davies 2012). However, efforts are being made to map these initiatives internationally, thus creating greater visibility for their activities for those who already share, potential sharers and those charged with regulating sharing (Davies et al. 2017a). What this research reveals is that there is no single archetypal food sharing initiative as, despite the liberating capacities of ICT to overcome previous spatio-temporal constraints, the context in which food sharing initiatives emerge remains crucial to their practices. With this caveat in mind the following sub-sections focus on illustrative cases of food sharing with initiatives that explicitly seek sustainability from their actions in relation to growing, cooking, and eating and surplus food redistribution.

Collective growing

3,000 Acres is a network in Melbourne, Australia that shares land, knowledge, and skills through gifting. They provide a service which they describe on their website as making it 'easier for more people to grow more food in more places' (3,000 Acres website, 2019). Established in 2014, and drawing inspiration from a similar initiative 596 Acres based in New York, 3,000 Acres have been working to break down the barriers to urban food growing by influencing the public and private sector to rethink vacant land use as underutilized spaces for food growing, and by empowering community groups with the knowledge and skills they need to make it happen. Their overarching goal is to normalize collective food growing as a mainstream feature of healthy urban landscapes. This is driven not only by a desire to increase the incidence and volume of food grown by people together in urban areas, but also to reduce stress and increase feelings of calm which gardening has been shown to generate (Mitchell and Popham 2008; South et al. 2018). Importantly, the positive health effects of collective urban gardening are also equigenic, meaning that people who start out with worse health conditions experience greater levels of improvement when spending time in such spaces. Allied to the mental health benefits are the physical impacts of gardening as a low impact exercise that supports joint mobility and general fitness levels for people of all abilities. Beyond this, community gardens are flagged as important sites of nature-based productivity, not just of food but also for enhanced urban biodiversity and other ecosystem services (Clarke and Darrel 2015).

In collaboration with town planners, lawyers, residential developers, and web-developers, 3,000 Acres sought to identify and unlock pockets of vacant land to enable people to grow more food for themselves. Referring to the typology of food sharing developed earlier, they share the skills and knowledge (both online and face-to-face) needed to support collective growing activities. ICT for 3,000 Acres provides an effective and efficient means to collate, store, and communicate information about collective gardening activities. The website provides an open portal to explore (for those with access to the internet) information about how to identify a site for a community garden, how to organize with others to create a vision for a community garden, and sustain that garden financially and safely. The website also provides a means to connect and engage potential volunteers or donors to the initiative.

Through their experience of facilitating urban food gardens in Melbourne, 3,000 Acres identified a need to quantify the benefits of urban agriculture to deepen our understanding of urban agriculture's contribution to the environment and communities, to identify key areas for improvement and help to communicate the need for urban agriculture. They are developing a metric for measuring the health and social benefits of community gardens and are working with local authorities to encourage gardeners to measure their benefits through a citizen science initiative called 'backyard and all' which includes measuring kits with scales, recording sheets, and prizes. They are also supporting Melbournians to use an online toolkit developed by New York gardeners and sponsored by the New York City Community Garden Coalition in 2009. This forms part of the Farming Concrete project which seeks to measure how much food is grown in community gardens and urban farms. Between 2009 and 2012, Farming Concrete provided approximately 200 free scales, record keeping materials, training, and customized reports to New York City gardeners, who recorded harvests through their online platform. Farming Concrete's 2012 Harvest Report revealed the yield of more than 195 crop varieties from the data of 106 gardeners across the city. As seen with 3,000 Acres, Farming Concrete has used ICT to expand its territorial reach to engage urban food growers internationally developing a translocal ecosystem of food sharing (Edwards and Davies 2018). Farming Concrete contains 20 different methods for measuring, tracking, and analyzing the impacts of community gardens. These range from systems for weighing the pounds of vegetables harvested on a farm in a season to monitoring the number of times a visitor is made to feel happier as a result of walking through the garden gate.

Cooking and eating together

Eating alone has been demonstrated to have long-term negative health implications (Dunbar 2017), with loneliness identified as a key predictor of physical and mental health problems (Holt-Lunstad and Layton 2010). As a result, activities that foster interactions between people are increasingly valued for the social nourishment they can provide. Shared cooking and eating initiatives, as with the collective growing initiatives described above, provide opportunities for diverse interactions, from fleeting moments of encounter chopping vegetables alongside others, to deeper connections involving the sharing of intimate thoughts and feelings over regular meals eaten together.

In many cases, food sharing initiatives which focus on creating opportunities for people to cook and eat together are specifically focused on the social needs which predominate in the context in which they are located. In London, for example, Be Enriched run regular collective cooking and eating events in a number of locations to meet their goals of reducing inequalities, building community cohesion, and developing life skills amongst community members. Food is the centre of these events, but their overarching goal is broader, and listed on their website as 'enriching local life through connecting people through community activities and cultivating respect over a bite' (Be Enriched website, 2019). Meals are provided for free to anyone who attends and surplus food is used where possible to reduce food waste. In addition to providing sustenance at the dining events, Be Enriched also offers skill share events to encourage participants to make their own healthy, low cost food at home. While reporting on their sustainability impacts is currently limited, Be Enriched is helping to co-create an online tool to identify their sustainability worth in ways which are feasible, meaningful, and appropriate (MacKenzie and Davies 2019). However, there are particular challenges with pinning down the social sustainability impacts of food sharing where the affects and effects can be experienced differently amongst participants, can be fleeting, and hard to capture quantitatively. While cooking and eating together per se does not necessarily guarantee social sustainability or health benefits (Schor et al. 2016), researchers have demonstrated its potential to reduce social barriers relating to race, gender, and socioeconomic backgrounds, creating greater community cohesion as a result (Julier 2013).

Initiatives such as Open Table in Melbourne, Australia, also use ICT to provide open access and online information about community meals that take place in neighbourhoods across the city, but with a specific goal of destigmatizing the consumption of surplus food. Initiated in 2013 by a group of graduate students interested in sustainability who were inspired by a food sharing project in Sweden, Open Table began with a six-week pilot program in one location. By 2017 they were hosting seven community feasts every month using food collected from food rescue initiatives, such as Secondbite, as well as with food donations from local businesses (Edwards and Davies 2018).The monthly feasts focus on creating convivial moments for participants with a key focus on reducing social isolation, rather than providing alternative infrastructures of food security for vulnerable populations.

The goal of destigmatizing the consumption of surplus food is also the goal of O Allos Anthropos (translated as, the other human) which is based in Athens, Greece. Adopting an informal organizational structure, O Allos Anthropos shares prepared meals in shared kitchens using surplus food they collect or receive as food donations. They frame their endeavor as a society kitchen and the activities undertaken as acts of solidarity and consciousness raising. Similar goals are also visible in the multifunctional food sharing initiative the Skip Garden and Kitchen in London. The Skip Garden and Kitchen is the homebase of Global Generation, an educational charity established in 2004 which works to create healthy, integrated, and environmentally responsible communities. Fruits and vegetables are grown in mobile containers alongside a café which serves produce from the garden alongside nutritious seasonal food. In addition, the initiative provides work experience and employability programs to young people with special needs and refugees. Across their activities themes of ecology, education, and enterprise dominate, reflecting their core value articulated as 'I, we and the planet' and their mission to create the conditions for change (Davies 2019). In terms of evidencing progress towards their goals, the Skip Garden and Kitchen currently report on outcomes, such as numbers of people who have achieved certificates for completion of training programs or the number of opportunities provided to local children to come together around food.

In Berlin, Über Den Tellerrand is a social enterprise which shares food, kitchen spaces, knowledge, and meals. Its stated goal is to encourage face-to-face encounters between the local community and refugees in order to provide opportunities for people to learn from each other and discover diverse cultures, breaking down barriers and enhancing possibilities for understanding and harmony. However, standard sustainability assessment tools rarely provide indicators that might identify, capture, and monitor qualities of tolerance, inclusivity, and connectedness in communities. Instead, Über Den Tellerrand provide testimonials from participants in their annual reports which are then posted on their website and which highlight where activities helped generate responses which align with their stated goals. As with the other initiatives mentioned in this section, they predominantly use ICT as a means to organize and present information about food sharing alongside disseminating information about their activities, and recruiting new food sharers by illustrating and mapping their activities and opportunities to engage. The online component has become an essential feature of these initiatives in terms of their recruitment and dissemination activities, although it is the face-to-face elements which remain core to their goals and purpose. In other collective eating initiatives, particularly the for-profit initiatives such as VizEat and Eatwith, which offer collective eating experiences for travellers and economic opportunities for homecooks, it is sophisticated ICT, particularly interactive digital platforms, that are at the very core of connecting those who wish to come together over food.

Redistribution

The redistribution of surplus food is an area which has seen a dramatic increase in activities as the scale of global food loss and waste has become clear and it is the sector of food sharing that has adopted the most complex forms of ICT to mediate activities. This is unsurprising given the delimited time window in which food is simultaneously both surplus and edible. The connective capacity of digital platforms and apps provides the possibility of rapidly identifying and matching those with excess food to those in need of access. It can also provide a manageable mechanism for recording details of the transfer of surplus food from donor to recipient, providing digital traces that meet food safety requirements of identifying the origins and destinations of food for human consumption. Redistribution activities are, however, diverse and include the gleaning operations of Espigoladors in Barcelona, the community fridges of foodsharing.de in Germany, the mobile Food Justice Truck in Melbourne, and the fixed footprint of the Community Shop in London.

Ripe Near Me was established in Adelaide, Australia by co-founders who noticed the glut of seasonal fruits from public fruit trees in their city was not being consumed. Their goals are manifold, from encouraging food growing in urban areas, reducing food waste, and improving people's health and quality of life to encouraging more sustainable living and even microenterprises around growing food. More than simply seeing food as fuel, they see food as the catalyst 'to make the world a better place'. Utilizing the interactive capacity of open access online mapping, Ripe Near Me has expanded from one site in Adelaide and now has posts across Australasia, Europe, and North America with some urban harvests noted as far afield as Hawaii and Harare in Zimbabwe. Ripe Near Me facilitates harvesting of food on public lands (where this is permitted) alongside peer-to-peer harvesting where gardeners with crops to spare can offer their surplus for free or for a fee. There is no interpersonal intermediation offered by Ripe Near Me to facilitate donor–recipient relationships that other redistributive food sharing initiatives offer. It is very much an experiment with the generative capabilities of the technical mapping and exchange tool. As a result there is no publicly reported analysis of the impacts created.

Falling Fruit was established in Dublin in 2015 as an offshoot from a freecycling initiative We Share, which is a gift economy community group that uses a website to share skills, knowledge, stuff, and time, in a money-free environment. Rather than facilitating individual or peer-to-peer exchanges that emerge from the activities of Ripe Near Me, Falling Fruit focuses on redistributing surplus fruit and vegetables to charities and other social causes. They use a website to document their activities and to call out to growers with gluts of seasonal fruit and vegetables to donate and volunteers who have the capacity to transport the surplus food to those in need. To distribute their surplus effectively they liaise with other redistribution initiatives which have greater logistical infrastructures, such as FoodCloud. In contrast to the broader societal goals of Ripe Near Me, however, Falling

Fruit is very much focused on preventing food waste. With the aim of attaining zero waste, Falling Fruit ensures that food is eaten, stored, preserved, pressed, or fed to animals.

FoodCloud, which works with Falling Fruit, is a social enterprise from Ireland set up in 2012 to redistribute surplus food which is now operational nationwide in both the UK and Ireland. They have gained a public profile as being tech-innovators, winning accolades for their application of ICT for social good through their mediated digital platform which links donors of surplus food to recipients. It is this technical capacity and the buy-in of a major multinational retailer which has enabled the initiative to scale dramatically to reach more than 9,000 community groups. However, while FoodCloud would not be able to work at this scale without its use of ICT, it is the management of interpersonal relations between donors and recipients that is done by staff which sustains the system of surplus food redistribution. Their vision is a world where no good food goes to waste and their mission is to use food as a tool to empower people, bring communities together, and create a more sustainable food system. FoodCloud exists first and foremost to reduce the environmental impact of waste in the food supply chain. In the short term it concentrates on redirecting food from landfill towards people who are in need of food, but long-term they hope that the data they collect and pass on to retailers will be used to streamline acquisition systems to reduce the amount of surplus generated. While they are not in a position to require multinational companies to reduce their food waste in the light of their data, they are actively participating in policy shaping as members of a food loss and waste platform coordinated by the European Union to inform decisions on food waste policy.

As with other food sharing initiatives, FoodCloud tend to use simple output measures to demonstrate the impact of their activities. For example, they focus on numbers of groups engaged (indicating the scale and reach of their activities) and the weight of surplus food diverted from landfill. In 2019, their website reported that they helped 9,100 groups, saving 22,000 tonnes of food. Using simple conversion formulae they indicate that this provides 50 million meals, 72,727 tonnes of carbon savings, and €68.1 million in food budget savings to community groups. Although internal surveys of community partners are conducted annually, the difference these meals make to those who consume them is not currently reported externally.

Overall, it is clear that many food sharing initiatives, from collective growing activities to surplus food redistribution groups, articulate goals which indicate their desire to work within planetary boundaries, closing gaps within food systems which create food loss and waste to create more closed loop food systems that are frequently articulated as being the core of sustainable and regenerative food systems. However, while the goals are admirable, progress towards those goals tends to be only lightly monitored and reported. The final section of this chapter reflects on why this is the case.

Is food sharing sustainable and regenerative?

As Janelle Orsi and Emily Doskow surmise in their book *The Sharing Solution* (2009), sharing is seen as offering a means to save money, simplify your life, and build community. More than this, it is also seen as a way to live more sustainably and intimately with the environment, other species, and humanity. Here intimacy is seen as an important element of being human; allowing for essential relationships to be constructed. However, establishing the impacts that food sharing has on social, economic, and environmental sustainability is a challenge for a number of reasons, and not least because there is a lack of baseline data available. Incomplete, onerous, or contentious systems of measurement and reporting also play an important prohibitive role for food sharing initiatives.

Where data are collected by food sharing initiatives they are rarely shared openly and even when they are, as illustrated in the previous section, the data used tend to focus on outputs rather than outcomes or impacts. There have also been concerns raised that sharing may not always generate positive benefits. The bulk of these concerns about a shadowy side to sharing have been articulated in sectors other than food, with a focus on the precarity of income that sharers may be able to derive from sharing transactions and the negative knock-on effects on housing prices and availability through online accommodation sharing sites (Davies et al. 2017b). The monopolistic tendencies of venture-capital funded sharing economy platforms, and the exploitation of gray areas within regulation and taxation are also being raised as important issues for the future governance of sharing, raising questions about the extent to which these activities are contributing sufficiently to the maintenance of broader public goods. Social concerns have also been flagged, with the inclusivity of sharing practices questioned (Fitzmaurice and Schor 2018). Certainly, it is the case that sharing is replete with rules, even if these are often internally generated rather than externally driven. Nonetheless, in the food sharing sector specifically, major lines of tension between sharing initiatives and regulators revolve around health and hygiene, food safety and risk (Morrow, 2019).

Establishing sustainability impacts from food sharing can draw on a burgeoning suite of sustainability assessment frameworks designed specifically for food systems. However, these tools often fail to capture all the impacts from sharing and as such they provide only a limited picture of the impacts created. Instead, inspiration for the assessment of sharing's contribution to sustainability will need to look more broadly, to social, health, and education assessment tools and to toolkits designed to be appropriate to the types of initiatives that dominate (at least numerically) food sharing landscapes; grassroots, community driven, not for profit initiatives (MacKenzie and Davies 2019). Whatever systems are developed there needs to be a careful and reflective approach adopted, as measurement does not occur in a power vacuum. Impact reporting is, like sharing, itself a particular type of social practice whose performance is affected by the combination of rules, tools, skills, and understandings employed. Sustainability assessment tools for sharing will ultimately influence and define the very thing they are purporting to measure.

Food sharing initiatives do not, per se, provide a silver bullet in terms of developing a more sustainable and regenerative global food system, they are too diverse in constitution and dynamic in nature to make such a generic statement. Food sharing initiatives operate with, alongside, underneath, and beyond the dominant global commercial food system, in different ways depending on their goals and the context in which they are operating. As a result, the question should not be whether food sharing is sustainable, but rather how can we best capture and interrogate the impacts of food sharing to reveal any sustainability benefits and design a food system which supports those benefits. This means not only attending to how sharing meets the goals of regenerative food systems in relation to closed loop energy and nutrient systems for environmental sustainability, but also how they reconnect people to themselves, to others, and to the planet.

Discussion questions

- Should food sharing initiatives be governed by policy any differently from commercial food enterprises?
- Why is demonstrating the social impacts of food sharing so challenging?

- To what extent is the use of ICT by contemporary food sharing initiatives transformative?
- How have the goals of food sharing changed over time?
- Are existing theories of food sharing established for small-scale, hunter-gatherer communities still relevant for contemporary food sharing?

Acknowledgements

This chapter draws on empirical research conducted by a team of researchers as part of the ERC-funded SHARECITY project, Grant Agreement: 646883. Thanks are given to the funders, food sharing initiatives and researchers involved.

Further reading

Davies, A. R. (2019) *Urban Food Sharing*. Bristol: Policy Press.
Jones, M. (2007) *Feast: Why Humans Share Food*. New York: Oxford University Press.
Julier, A. (2013) *Eating Together: Food, Friendship and Inequality*. Urbana, IL: University of Illinois Press.
McLaren, D. and Agyeman, J. (2015) *Sharing Cities: A Cast for Truly Smart and Sustainable Cities*. Cambridge, MA: MIT Press.

References

Belk, R. (2010) 'Sharing', *Journal of Consumer Research*, 36(5): 715–734.
Belk, R. (2014) 'You are what you can access: Sharing and collaborative consumption online', *Journal of Business Research*, 67(8): 1595–1600.
Botsman, R. and Rogers, R. (2010) *What's Mine Is Yours*. New York: Harper Collins.
Cox, K. (1998) 'Spaces of dependence, spaces of engagement and the politics of scale, or: Looking for local politics', *Political Geography*, 17 (1): 1–23.
Clarke, L. and Darrel, J. (2015) 'Biodiversity and direct ecosystem service regulation in the community gardens of Los Angeles, CA', *Landscape Ecology*, 30(4): 637–653.
Davies, A. R. (2012) *Enterprising Communities: Grassroots Sustainability Innovations*. Bingley: Emerald Press.
Davies, A. R. (2019a) *Urban Food Sharing*. Bristol: Policy Press.
Davies, A. R. (2019b) 'Redistributing surplus food: Interrogating the collision of waste and justice', in N. Cook and D. Butz (eds) *Mobilities, Mobility Justice and Social Justice*. London: Routledge, pp. 250–262.
Davies, A. R., Edwards, F., Marovelli, B., Morrow, O., Rut, M. and Weymes, M. (2017a) 'Making visible: Interrogating the performance of food sharing across 100 urban areas', *Geoforum*, 86: 136–149.
Davies, A. R., Donald, B., Gray, M. and Knox-Hayes, J. (2017b). 'Sharing economies: Moving beyond binaries in a digital age', *Cambridge Journal of Regions, Economy and Society*, 10(2): 209–230.
Davies, A. R., Weymes, M. and MacKenzie, S. (2018) 'Communicating goals and impacts of urban food sharing', *Urban Agriculture Magazine*, 34: 38–40.
Davies, A. R., Cretella, A. and Franck, V. (2019) 'Regulating urban food sharing: Policy, practice and food democracy goals', *Politics and Governance*, 7(3): 8–20.
Dixon, J. (2011) 'Diverse food economies, multivariant capitalism, and the community dynamic shaping contemporary food systems', *Community Development Journal*, 46(1): 20–35.
Dunbar, R. I. M. (2017) 'Breaking bread: The functions of social eating', *Adaptive Human Behavior and Physiology*, 3: 198. doi:10.1007/s40750-017-0061-4.
Edwards, F. and Davies, A. R. (2018) 'Connective consumptions: Mapping Melbourne's food sharing ecosystem', *Urban Policy and Research*, 36(4): 476–495.
Fitzmaurice, C. and Schor, J. (2018) 'Homemade matters: Logics of opposition in a failed food swap', *Social Problems*, spx046 doi:10.1093/socpro/spx046
Gabriel, R. (2013) *Why I Buy: Self, Taste and Consumer Society in America*. Bristol: Intellect.
Gurven, M. (2004) 'To give and to give not: The behavioral ecology of human food transfers', *Behavioural and Brain Sciences*, 27(4): 543–559.

Holt-Lunstad, J. and Layton, J. B. (2010) 'Social relationships and mortality risk: A meta-analytic review', *PLoS Medicine*, 7(7) www.plosmedicine.org/article/info%3Adoi%2F10.1371%2Fjournal.pmed.1000316

Jaeggi, A. and Gurven, M. (2013) 'Natural cooperators: Food sharing in humans and other primates', *Evolutionary Anthropology*, 22: 186–195.

Jones, M. (2007) *Feast: Why Humans Share Food*. New York: Oxford University Press.

Julier, A. (2013) *Eating Together: Food, Friendship and Inequality*. Urbana, IL: University of Illinois Press.

Kaplan, H. and Gurven, M. (2005) 'The natural history of human food sharing and cooperation: A review and a new multi-individual approach to the negotiation of norms', in H. Gintis, S. Bowles, R. Boyd and E. Fehr (eds) *Moral Sentiments and Material Interests: The Foundations of Cooperation in Economic Life*. Cambridge, MA: MIT Press, pp. 75–113.

Kaplan, H., Schniter, E., Smith, V. and Wilson, B. (2012) 'Risk and the evolution of human exchange', *Proceedings Biological Science*, 279(1740): 2930–2935.

MacKenzie, S. and Davies, A. R. (2019) 'SHARE IT: Co-designing a sustainability assessment framework for urban food sharing initiatives', *Environmental Impact Assessment Review*, 79: 106300.

Mitchell, R. and Popham, F. (2008) 'Effect of exposure to natural environment on health inequalities: An observational population study', *The Lancet*, 372(9650): 1655–1660.

Morrow, O. (2019) 'Sharing food and risk in Berlin's urban food commons', *Geoforum*, 99: 202–212.

Orsi, J. and Doskow, E. (2009) *The Sharing Solution*. Berkeley: Nolo Press.

Schor, J. B., Fitzmaurice, C., Carfagna, L. B. and Attwood-Charles, W. (2016). Paradoxes of openness and distinction in the sharing economy, *Poetics*, 54: 66–81.

South, E. C., Hohl, B. C., Kondo, M. C., MacDonald, J. M. and Branas, C. C. (2018) 'Effect of greening vacant land on mental health: A citywide randomized controlled trial', *JAMA Network Open*, 1: 1–14.

Weymes, M. and Davies, A. R. (2019) '[Re]valuing surplus: Transitions, technologies and tensions in redistributing prepared food in San Francisco', *Geoforum*, 99: 160–169.

16

FINANCING FOOD SYSTEM REGENERATION?

The potential of social finance in the agrifood sector

Phoebe Stephens and Jennifer Clapp

Introduction

The regenerative capacity of food systems is profoundly shaped by the financial systems that serve them. Food and financial systems have been intimately entwined for centuries, although food studies scholars have only recently directed their full attention to this linkage. The concurrent 2008 food and financial crises prompted a closer look at the linkages between the sectors, as financial investors sought to profit from speculation in agricultural commodities, farmland, and agrifood equities investments (e.g. Fairbairn 2014; Ghosh 2010; Ouma 2016). These studies have focused on the extent to which the agrifood system has become 'financialized', with financial actors, institutions, and priorities becoming dominant in ways that reshape food systems (e.g. Clapp and Isakson 2018).

This work exploring the linkages between food and financial systems has prompted growing concern in both scholarly and policy communities about the ways in which financial investment in the sector is associated with problematic outcomes, including food price volatility, weakened land rights, and corporate concentration. Such outcomes on the ground suggest that the growing role of finance can diminish the resilience of food systems and their overall capacity for regeneration. Growing awareness of the potential for negative outcomes has prompted initiatives for more 'responsible' financial investment in the agrifood sector through initiatives such as voluntary codes of conduct and investor guidelines. These efforts have, on the whole, focused on a 'do no harm' approach to sustainability that is still rooted in profit maximization within the industrial food system.

Theorists and practitioners of social finance question whether negative outcomes are an inevitable result of financial investment in the food system. These scholars explore whether finance can be redeployed for more positive societal outcomes. Social finance seeks to invest for social and environmental return, rather than purely for financial gain. Though social finance has received far less attention in the academic literature on financialization in the agrifood system, there is value in bringing the two concepts together when examining this sector. Whereas most of the scholarship on financialization in the food system describes the ways in which finance interacts with various activities along the food chain, social finance offers potential solutions to the harmful effects of mainstream investment patterns and supports initiatives that reside outside of the mainstream industrial food system.

This chapter explores the theme of social finance and how, in the context of financialization in the agrifood sector, social finance could potentially support more regenerative food systems. We argue that regenerative food systems are those which are firmly rooted in local initiatives that explicitly seek to improve the capacity of food systems to provide positive environmental and social benefits that enable the sector not only to be more 'sustainable' (i.e. to enable the system to continue into the future without causing undue harm), but also to improve its capacity to regenerate ecosystems and social dynamics of food systems in ways that see continual positive improvement.

The chapter unfolds as follows. First, we provide a brief overview of the literature on the impact of financialization in the agrifood sector and the rise of 'responsible' investment in the sector. Second, we outline the ways in which social finance seeks to build not only more sustainable food systems, but specifically seeks to foster improvements that bolster the regenerative capacity of food systems by promoting initiatives outside of the mainstream industrial food system. Third, we present the case of FarmWorks Investment Co-op, based in the Canadian province of Nova Scotia, as a case study of the regenerative capacity of social finance for food systems. Fourth, we discuss the kinds of policy changes required for social finance to become a more dominant mode of financial support for the agrifood sector. Finally, we conclude with some reflections regarding potential contradictions and prospects for more regenerative types of agrifood finance.

Current patterns of agrifood financial investment fall short

Financial markets have been deeply enmeshed in the agrifood system for hundreds of years. The relationship is two-way. Financial markets have long provided much needed capital for farmers as well as for firms that operate along agrifood supply chains to enable their economic viability. Agrifood commodities, firms, and farmland have also served as lucrative investment opportunities for financial investors seeking a decent rate of return on their capital. While the relationship between food and finance has the potential to be mutually beneficial, it has also been fraught throughout history. Farmers have long expressed skepticism about the role of financial speculators who invested in agricultural commodities, for example, viewing them as forces that drive volatility in commodity prices (Martin and Clapp 2015).

Concern about the impact of commodity speculation on food prices became prominent during the 2008 food crisis. As the crisis unfolded, many analysts pointed to increased investment in financial derivatives such as commodity futures contracts as well as in new types of complex investment vehicles such as commodity index funds. The availability of these new investment products after the early 2000s fuelled investor interest in the sector, which coincided with sharp increases in food prices by 2008, prompting a number of analysts to conclude that speculative investment was a factor in the food price spikes (De Schutter 2010; Ghosh 2010; IATP 2008). The 2008 food crisis also increased awareness of the extent to which financial actors are also implicated in the global land rush, as pension funds and other institutional investors sought to increase their exposure to farmland through new complex financial instruments such as land investment funds (Fairbairn 2014). What set this new investment apart from previous historical episodes of speculation is that large-scale institutional investors have come to dominate these markets. In other words, pension funds, hedge funds, university endowments, and asset management companies have become large investors in the sector (Clapp 2019).

The growing interest by financial investors who were relatively new to the agrifood sector via new types of investment vehicles has been characterized by some analysts as 'financialization' of the food system. Financialization refers to an increased role for financial actors, motives, and institutions in determining and shaping activities in the broader economy (Epstein 2005; Krippner 2011; van der Zwan 2014). Financialization has taken three distinct forms as it has taken hold in the food system: it has transformed a range of activities across the agrifood sector into an arena for financial accumulation by investors; it has encouraged a prioritization of shareholder value within agrifood firms; and it has facilitated the permeation of financial activities and values into everyday food and agricultural provisioning (Clapp and Isakson 2018). This process of financialization within the sector has been associated with a range of effects, including the loss of land rights for many agricultural producers in some of the world's poorest countries; higher and more volatile food prices; corporate concentration; inequitable distribution of income among owners and workers in the sector; and a loss of autonomy for workers, farmers, and consumers (for an overview, see Clapp and Isakson 2018).

As awareness of the potential negative impacts of financialization in the food system has grown, so too have calls for more responsible financial investment in the sector (Hallam 2011; Clapp 2017). Such initiatives have sought to ensure that investors do not exacerbate potentially negative impacts, such as rising food prices, land grabbing, and environmental degradation. Calls for responsible investment have had some appeal in the agricultural sector, because many of the institutional investors that have a stake in the sector, such as pension funds, have long-term outlooks and passive investment strategies. Responsible investment approaches in farmland, for example, could help to ensure the long-term viability of those investments by ensuring that they are socially and ecologically sustainable, an important consideration given the illiquid nature of land as an asset (Scott 2013). In this sense, making 'responsible' investments is in the long-term interest of investors, while also reducing the potential for harm (Carroll and Shabana 2010).

Several prominent responsible agricultural investment initiatives emerged over the 2009–14 period. These include the Principles for Responsible Agricultural Investment (PRAI), led by Japan along with the World Bank, FAO, and UNCTAD, launched in 2010. The PRAI advance seven key principles to guide agricultural investments: (1) recognize and respect existing rights to both land and natural resources; (2) strengthen food security; (3) require transparency and good governance when acquiring land; (4) ensure consultation with and participation of those affected by the investment; (5) ensure economic viability; (6) promote positive social impacts; and (7) support environmental sustainability. The PRAI targets all types of agricultural investment, including investment from both public and private investors (FAO et al. 2010).

The Voluntary Guidelines on the Responsible Governance of Tenure of Land, Fisheries and Forests in the Context of National Food Security were launched in 2012 (FAO 2012; see also Seufert 2013). The Voluntary Guidelines (VGGT) were meant to guide investment in land, fisheries, and forests, with a view to protecting land and resource tenure rights, especially customary land rights for indigenous peoples and smallholders, and to safeguard the environment. The VGGT are relevant to financial investment in that they call on governments to protect tenure rights and request that all involved parties, including private financial investors, be respectful of those rights (FAO 2012). Coordinated by the FAO and overseen by the Committee on World Food Security (CFS), the VGGT were developed through a process largely viewed to be broadly inclusive and consultative (McKeon 2013). As such, the VGGT are widely seen as holding more legitimacy than the PRAI (Margulis and Porter 2013).

The CFS launched further discussions in 2012 with a view to developing yet another set of responsible agricultural investment guidelines that included land, but also encompassed other agricultural investment (Stephens 2013, 190). Adopted by the CFS in 2014, the Principles for Responsible Investment in Agriculture and Food Systems (PRIAFS, also referred to as the CFS-RAI) (FAO 2014), underline the role of small farmers as agricultural investors alongside corporate and financial investors. The CFS-RAI contain explicit language about the need to hold investors to account for any negative impacts of their investments (FAO 2014).

Other responsible investment initiatives have also emerged on the voluntary responsible investment landscape. These include the G8 New Alliance for Food Security and Nutrition's Analytical Framework for Responsible Land-Based Agricultural Investments; the UN Principles for Responsible Investment's (PRI) Principles for Responsible Investment in Farmland; the UN Land Policy Initiative's Guiding Principles on Large Scale Land Based Investments in Africa; the Global Compact's Food and Agriculture Business Principles; the OECD-FAO's Guidance for Responsible Agricultural Supply Chains; as well as numerous standards stylized for investment in specific commodities, including for soy, sugar, cotton, biofuels, etc. (GRAIN 2012; OECD and FAO 2016; World Bank et al. 2017).

These various responsible investment initiatives in the agrifood sector reflect a widespread interest to ensure that investment into the sector is socially and environmentally sustainable. But at the same time, these initiatives, based on the voluntary efforts of institutional investors to seek out responsible investments from the current products available through mainstream investment channels, have at best supported a 'do no harm' type approach, which maintains a strong motive to maximize financial returns while avoiding negative outcomes. In practice, these initiatives are inherently weak even at avoiding negative outcomes. The responsible investment initiatives in the agrifood sector have tended to be broad in scope and vague with respect to requirements, making it easy to claim adherence without changing much by way of practice. The PRAI, for example, is only one page long, and while the FAO's Voluntary Guidelines and the RAI-CFS are much more detailed and specific, all three operate only as guidance frameworks and do not have signatories, making it difficult to ascertain how many investors actually abide by them (Clapp 2017). The number of voluntary initiatives in the agricultural investment space has also multiplied rapidly, leading to confusion as they cover overlapping themes. For the casual observer, the differences between the PRAI, the Voluntary Guidelines, the CFS-RAI, and the Farmland Principles are not easily discernible (Margulis and Porter 2013).

The weaknesses of these responsible investment efforts have led some analysts to promote alternative financing initiatives, such as social finance, for the agrifood sector. Rather than banking on a sufficient number of institutional investors acting more responsibly in their global investment activities, these alternative initiatives seek to ground investment in sustainability by appealing to investors to fund specific sustainable agricultural initiatives at the local level.

Social finance

Social finance is an alternative way of conceptualizing finance that gained momentum after the 2008 financial crisis. It not only presents tools to align finance with social and environmental goals, but it also advances a progressive ethos about the way money is used (Nicholls 2010). Moving beyond responsible investing, it intentionally and proactively targets businesses that will provide measurable benefits to society rather than merely avoiding the worst offenders. It does so in a variety of ways including redrawing investment parameters and measuring investments according to social and environmental indicators.

Social finance is a growing field of research and practice aimed at supporting the success and spread of social innovations (Geobey et al. 2012, 151). Social innovation can be understood as: 'a complex process of introducing new products, processes or programs that profoundly change the basic routines, resource and authority flows, or beliefs of the social system in which the innovation occurs. Such successful social innovations have durability and broad impact' (Moore et al. 2012, 120). Such efforts go beyond the 'do no harm' approach, and as such have more potential to promote regenerative food systems.

By definition, 'regenerative' implies a more transformative process than 'sustainable.' Certainly, maintaining desirable characteristics over a period of time, or being sustainable, is necessary for the functioning of our food systems. But it does not adequately describe the changes that need to occur within agrifood systems to revitalize local economies, enhance biodiversity and soil quality, adapt to climate change, and improve the health of communities. Regenerative food systems, however, are about enhancing the vitality of natural and social resource bases over time (Dahlberg 1993). These systems emphasize local expressions, seeing niche activity as containing 'the adaptive possibilities that could offer stability to higher, more abstract levels of a system and resilience to the system as a whole' (DeLind 2011, 274). There is significant overlap between principles of local food and those of regenerative food systems. In both cases, supporting food systems that are contextually aware, collaborative, and self-reliant is deemed critically important.

There is no shortage of innovative, local alternatives to the industrial food system. And, as consumer interest in supporting a better food system grows, more and more novel approaches are arising. However, these promising initiatives frequently remain in the ideation or pilot stages because they lack resources to grow and sustain themselves. This is largely because mainstream economic structures present numerous barriers and disincentives for investing in these socially beneficial projects (Moore et al. 2012, 116). Market-based approaches to regenerate food systems unfortunately tend to 'employ narrow economic or production and productivity criteria to measure their "success"' (Dahlberg 1993, 80). Such hurdles are increasingly recognized by governments around the world, which have responded in recent years by developing social finance strategies to stimulate social innovation. For instance governments in Europe, Australia, the UK, and Canada are implementing social finance policies to cultivate an institutional environment that will allow communities to prosper from these much needed innovations.

The Government of Canada defines social finance as 'an approach to mobilizing private capital that delivers a social dividend and an economic return to achieve social and environmental goals' (Government of Canada 2015). Social finance looks to course correct existing resource flows to vitalize financially marginalized areas for individual and collective benefit. It involves a number of tools and approaches including community investment, ethical banking, alternative currencies, microfinance, social impact bonds, venture philanthropy, and impact investing (Rizzi et al. 2018, 805).

Investors may be drawn to social finance as a way of diversifying their portfolios and mitigating risk, but also because their investments hold promise for sparking 'a radical systems change' (Geobey 2014, 17). Indeed, the spectrum of what constitutes social finance and what motivates social financiers is mystifyingly broad. In an effort to bring some coherence to this emerging field, Nicholls (2010) put forward a three-part typology of social investment. Descriptions of the three types of social finance investments are provided in Table 16.1. Social finance can be applied to a variety of sectors and has featured prominently in supporting clean energy and poverty alleviation initiatives. It involves a range of actors from foundations to private investors, pension funds, individual community members, and governments. Similar to the well-established notion of strong versus weak sustainability (Neumayer 2013), there can be weaker social finance and stronger social finance.

Means-ends driven investments are primarily built on the desire to maximize financial return to investors, though social and environmental considerations still factor into the decision-making. Socially responsible investing falls under this category. We are sceptical about the degree to which means-ends driven social finance can effect profound change and thus ascribe them a weak social finance status. Funds that abide by this rationale often invest in large multinational firms that, granted, report on sustainability targets, but are ultimately vested in the growth of the industrial food system. For example, Closed-Loop is a social impact investment fund focused on improving recycling rates in the United States. The $100 million fund enjoys investment from some of the world's largest food and beverage multinationals including PepsiCo, Unilever, Walmart, Coca-Cola, and most recently, Nestlé Waters (Nestlé 2017). While improving recycling rates is a laudable goal, addressing the root causes that produce abundant plastic waste is not a focus of this fund nor of its investors. Sustainability in the food system, as considered by means-ends driven social financiers, aligns closely with proponents of the industrial model of sustainability. That is, food productivity must be increased to feed growing populations, farms must become more efficient at using natural resources, and the adoption of high-tech solutions is key to achieving these outcomes.

Values-driven social investments are significantly smaller in scale and tend to reflect a grounded approach to investment that helps to seed more transformational change. So far, this appears to be the strongest type of social finance. The Slow Money movement in the United States is an example of values-driven social finance that is focused on building regenerative food systems. The movement was started in 2008 by Woody Tasch, a socially conscious investor who believes that supporting local, regenerative food systems is one of the most powerful ways to address the social and ecological crises of our time (Scheer and Moss n.d.). Now a registered non-profit, Slow Money supports the formation of self-organizing local groups who determine the best ways to support their food systems (Slow Money Institute 2010).

Slow Money investors often describe themselves as nurture capitalists: 'fiduciaries that are working to balance financial returns with patient strategies for promoting carrying capacity, sense of place, and soil fertility' (Slow Money 2014). The vast majority of the 27 local groups loan money to food enterprises along the food value chain at low or no interest rates in an effort to regenerate local food systems. Since 2010, Slow Money chapters have invested US$66 million in almost 700 food enterprises across the United States and, to a more limited extent, in Canada (Slow Money Institute 2010). According to Tasch, one of the principal measures of success for the movement will be 'the extent to which we have

Table 16.1 Means-ends driven, systematic, and values driven social investment

1. *Means-Ends Driven Social Investment*	2. *Systematic Social Investment*	3. *Values-Driven Social Investment*
Focuses on maximizing returns to the owner of capital. This type of social investment consists of three categories of capital allocation: clean energy investments; socially responsible investment vehicles offered by mainstream fund managers; and venture philanthropy.	Reflects systemic investor rationality in owners of capital. This type of fund typically aims at balancing means-ends and values-driven rationality by seeking returns that benefit both the investor and the investee/beneficiary. This type includes: impact investments (typically in firms that offer high returns from operations in deprived areas or developing country settings); social enterprise investment; and government investment in social innovation.	Reflects a values-driven investor rationality. This rationality typically prioritizes the investee/beneficiary in terms of returns and often focuses on social and environmental impact and social change. This type consists of: mainstream philanthropy; community, mutual, and co-operative investment plus foundation Mission Related Investment; and social change investment.

Source: Reproduced from Nicholls 2010

catalysed substantial new capital flows to enterprises that create economic opportunity while respecting, protecting, and promoting the fertility of the soil' (Tasch 2008, 7). Values-driven social finance initiatives show the most promise for nurturing food systems towards regeneration. The challenge with the approach is its small scale.

Systematic social investment represents a mid-way point between means-ends and values-driven social finance. Some impact investing funds that target the food system fall within this category. While these funds are still motivated by a financial return, they work with investors with long-term visions and enough capital to weather short-term fluctuations. These funds invest with a goal of changing the food system and do so by establishing an impact framework through which to assess their activities. For instance, an evergreen impact investing fund in the Netherlands that is focused on food system change only invests in companies that benefit soil fertility, consumer health, and enhance fairness in the value chain. There are challenges with this approach, however, such as determining how to precisely measure the desired impacts. As well, these funds must still satisfy investors in order to continue to operate and are thus required to generate an attractive rate of return. Because financial incentives support dominant social structures, this type of fund– which seeks a competitive level of return – can only challenge the dominant structures to a limited extent. These funds attempt to excel within today's economic system while supporting a broader diversity of food enterprises.

Social finance in the food system: the case of FarmWorks Investment Co-operative

The primary Slow Money chapter in Canada, FarmWorks Investment Co-operative, provides valuable insights for the ways in which social finance is applied in practice to build regenerative food systems. In 2011, community members in the Canadian province of Nova Scotia recognized the opportunity of social finance to increase the region's local food supply and set up FarmWorks Investment Co-operative (FarmWorks n.d.a). FarmWorks is considered a social finance initiative because it mobilizes capital to achieve societal benefit alongside financial return. It best fits the description of a values-driven social investment because it relies almost exclusively on relationship lending and prioritizes social and environmental impact above profit.

FarmWorks operates as part of Nova Scotia's landmark Community Economic Development Investment Fund Program (CEDIF). The program came about because the majority of Nova Scotians' investment dollars were being funnelled to large economic centers in Canada instead of supporting the region (FarmWorks, 2019). CEDIF was set up in 1998 to recapture some of this investment – less than 2% of which was staying in the province, to build a more vibrant and resilient local economy (Farmworks.ca, n.d.b).. CEDIFs allow individuals to pool capital and invest in for-profit businesses in their communities. Investors receive a 35% tax credit as an incentive to participate in the program. If they choose to hold their investments in the CEDIF longer than five years, they are eligible for an additional 20% tax credit, and after ten years another 10% tax credit (Nova Scotia Department of Finance and Treasury Board 2018, p. 7). The maximum amount that any one individual can invest in a CEDIF is C$50,000. In the last five years, other Canadian provinces have started to set up their own version of the CEDIF model in an effort to revitalize local economies, particularly in rural areas.

The CEDIF model gained traction not only because Nova Scotians' investment dollars were leaving the province, but also because of a dramatic hollowing out of rural communities. The population of roughly one million inhabitants has been stagnant while youth out-migration is on the rise (The Canadian CED Network n.d.). This trend has exacerbated the issue of succession; there are fewer and fewer young people to take over family-run businesses. These unfortunate trends are at once fueling and being driven by the precarious economic situation. Farm populations in Nova Scotia have plunged from 58,000 to only 8,000, mirroring the declining number of farms from 12,518 to 3,905 over the last 50 years (Local Prosperity 2015). Understandably, employment in the local food sector is suffering, with a 20% decline from 2005 to 2012 (Local Prosperity 2015).

Currently, FarmWorks is the only CEDIF that invests along the food value chain. FarmWorks sees a unique role for local food in boosting the vibrancy and resilience of Nova Scotia's economy, particularly in rural areas. The organization believes that food production has a significant multiplier effect on local economies. In other words, 'a dollar spent on the local food system tends to circulate within the local economy many times over' (Stephens et al. 2019). FarmWorks believes that by prioritizing the local food economy, Nova Scotians will benefit as a whole. It argues that 'strategies that increase the availability of Nova-Scotian grown food will help improve the local economy' (FarmWorks 2017). These strategies demand financial investment, however. Gaining access to financing is often cited as a barrier for the start-up and expansion phases for small food enterprises. FarmWorks aims to fill a financing gap in order to support the region's local food economy, a key aspect of regenerative food systems, through the lens of values-driven social finance.

FarmWorks allows members to purchase common shares for a fixed period of five years in a diversified portfolio of businesses. As a CEDIF, those shares are eligible for a 35% Nova Scotia non-refundable Equity Tax Credit. These investments 'provide loans to farms, food processors, and value-added food · producers, helping to increase the viability and sustainability of agriculture and the security of a healthy food supply' (Farmworks.ca, n.d.b). As of June 15, 2018, FarmWorks had invested 2.8 million CAD in 89 companies across the province (Stephens et al. 2019). Kennedy et al. (2017) estimate that because of the multiplier effect of the local food sector, FarmWorks could generate between C$11.2 and C$20.8 million for Nova Scotia's economy. FarmWorks' clients see great value in the co-op's loans – attributing 70% of jobs generated to them. As FarmWorks' clients grow, they overwhelmingly tend to source from other local businesses, helping to develop a more resilient local economy (Kennedy et al. 2017). Social finance applied in this context goes beyond narrowly supporting sustainable production practices by strengthening the social and economic vitality of communities in Nova Scotia.

FarmWorks prioritizes 'relationship lending' and 'meaningful financial returns' (FarmWorks n.d.). Its lending criteria are less stringent than those of traditional financial institutions, enabling small enterprises that have non-traditional business models, such as those which take environmental and social sustainability into account along with economic profit, to access financing. FarmWorks members regularly make in-person visits to their clients to learn about how their businesses are doing. If they are struggling, FarmWorks offers mentorship for how to improve outcomes and connects the business owners to others in the community who may help support their success. Here again, the organization's approach demonstrates a commitment to regeneration as they go beyond merely monitoring sustainability outcomes towards building and strengthening of social capital. FarmWorks applies the principles of patient capital, meaning that its clients are not subjected to the pressures of 'growth at all costs,' allowing them to engage in practices that align with regenerative rather than industrial food systems, with their relentless focus on productivism and efficiency. As a social finance organization, FarmWorks seeks to create systemic change by intentionally channelling capital towards projects that will produce social and environmental as well as economic returns. In targeting the local food system, FarmWorks demonstrates the ways in which finance can be mobilized to regenerate both natural and social elements of the food system.

Making social finance a viable force

While the case of FarmWorks – and that of Slow Money more broadly – are inspiring, the amount they invest in building regenerative food system pales in comparison to financial investment in the industrial food system. According to some estimates, for example, the agricultural investments of pension funds alone was over US$ 300 billion in 2012 (Buxton et al. 2012, 2). Although agricultural investments, especially commodity futures, have seen some drop in investment in recent years due to depressed commodity prices, investments have shifted into private and listed equities in agrifood companies (Valoral Advisors 2015; Clapp 2019). By contrast, social impact investments remain tiny in terms of their size. This section explores what policies will encourage the growth of social finance to become a viable force in the food sector.

The case of FarmWorks demonstrates the need for government participation in creating incentives for investing in sustainable food systems. FarmWorks staff are adamant that the tax incentives available to investors through the CEDIF program substantially contribute to investor interest in the fund. The CEDIF model has been adopted in varying formats across several Canadian provinces. However, Canada's most populous province, Ontario, does not have anything comparable to the CEDIF program. For regions like Ontario that lack this type of government programming, investing in regenerative food systems is largely inaccessible to the average individual. It is clear that government has an important role to play in facilitating investments in sustainable food systems, and programs like CEDIF can help communities develop solutions well suited to their specific contexts.

More broadly, government funding is considered necessary for establishing a robust social finance market to foster social innovation. Raworth (2017) notes that state leadership is critical for catalyzing investments that will bring about the social and ecological changes required to comfortably live within planetary boundaries. In her view, 'the state, not the market, turns out to have been the innovating, risk-taking partner, not "crowding out" but "dynamising in" private enterprise' (Raworth 2017, 73). Indeed, government funding is often seen as a way of reducing risk for private investors or to seed a fund that could then attract funding from other organizations. This is why states often offer tax breaks and other incentives as a strategy for attracting investment to key sectors that it views as vital for its development and competitiveness. Such an approach with social impact investing '"signals" confidence in social finance to other investors' (Eggleton et al. 2018, 8).

Mazzucato (2015) argues that society tends to overlook the importance of government funding in spurring innovation and advances several key arguments that could improve outcomes of government investment. First, she argues that government is well-placed to make riskier investments in novel fields, playing the role of investor first and building an ecosystem of entrepreneurliasm that is necessary to address the complex challenges of the 21st century. For instance, the United States government generously funded the early days of the internet, which ultimately supported an explosion of technological innovation. Similarly, government funding in renewables helped to develop the industry, attract private investment, and bring down costs of these cleaner technologies. We have yet to see significant government investment in the food system to help shift the market towards a regenerative model, but experience in other sectors suggests that this is a pivotal step.

Second, the terms upon which governments invest in innovation also need to be revised, according to Mazzucato. Traditionally, governments have done a poor job at recouping their investments while private companies that benefit from initial public investments reap spectacular profits. Since citizens are backing these investments in social innovation, it stands that they should also experience rewards when they prove to be successful (Mazzucato 2011).

Governments are beginning to reconsider their role in innovation, and are starting to leverage social finance as a tactic for generating desirable social and environmental outcomes. In 2013, the G8 launched the Social Impact Investment Taskforce with a mandate of 'catalysing a global market in impact investment' (Social Investment Taskforce 2014). Since then, a number of national governments have established funds to support social innovation. In late 2018, the Canadian federal government announced the establishment of a C$755 million fund for social finance (MaRS 2018) that could, among other outcomes, motivate social investors to 'finance Indigenous social entrepreneurs to address challenges like food insecurity and clean energy generation' (McConnell Foundation 2018).

Conclusion

Governments are evidently embracing social finance as a tool for innovation, which can be interpreted as a positive development. However, it bears mentioning the risks and contradictions associated with this approach. Fetherston explains the rise in popularity of social finance in recent years: 'For governments continuing to feel the fiscal pinch of the global financial crisis, it offers a new source of revenue without an unpopular increase in taxation' (Fetherston 2014, 29). The rise of social finance in a context of tight budgets has led some scholars to question whether it represents a retraction of state responsibilities such as the provisioning of social services. If social finance investments replace public investments, then it may serve to further consolidate power in the hands of a few (wealthy investors). This unfortunate turn could present a host of implications such as limiting the social and environmental issues that are deemed 'worthy' of investment. The risks presented by social finance are well summed up by Rosenman (2017, 8),

> at stake is the question of whether social finance truly uses profits to engender a more holistic range of social values – as argued by the movement's proponents – or whether it allows financial logics to further dominate already-neoliberalizing models of social services provision and poverty regulation.

In this light, a glaring contradiction of social finance becomes clear: social finance paradoxically seeks to fix the negative impacts of financialization by extending finance's reach into previously untouched realms – thereby further spreading financialization, albeit in a mutated form.

Recognizing these risks and contradictions, we see social finance as playing a useful but limited role in shifting food systems towards greater regeneration. Weak social finance initiatives are likely to further entrench the existing neoliberal economic order, and potentially further financialize aspects of social life and environmental phenomena. However, strong social finance initiatives that are rooted in local communities, with the primary intention of regenerating systems may prove to be useful tools in addressing some of the world's most complex challenges including the food system. In either case, however, social finance operates in the existing neoliberal order and therefore engages in incremental rather than transformative change. To date, the application of social finance for regenerative food systems is under-researched and there are ample opportunities for exploring when and how it can be employed as a helpful intermediary towards greater transformation.

Discussion questions

1. To what degree can and should financial actors be made accountable for the social and environmental impacts of their investments?
2. Does social finance have transformative potential or is it unlikely to contribute to systemic change?
3. What role, if any, should the government play in supporting social finance initiatives?

Further reading

Clapp, J. and Isakson, R. S. (2018). *Speculative Harvests: Financialization, Food and Agriculture*. Halifax: Fernwood Press.

Holt-Gimenez, E. (2017). *A Foodie's Guide to Capitalism: Understanding the Political Economy of What We Eat*. New York: Monthly Review Press.

Rosenman, E. (2017). The Geographies of Social Finance: Poverty Regulation through the 'Invisible Heart' of Markets. *Progress in Human Geography*, Published online.

Stephens, P., Knezevic, I. and Best, L. (2019). Community Financing for Sustainable Food Systems: The Case of FarmWorks Investment Co-operative. *Journal of Canadian Food Studies* 6(3), 60–87.

Tasch, W. (2008). *Inquiries into the Nature of Slow Money*. White River Junction, VT: Chelsea Green Publishing.

References

Buxton, A., Campanale, M. and Cotula, L. (2012). *Farms and Funds: Investment Funds in the Global Land Rush*. IIED Briefing, January. London: IIED. Retrieved from pubs.iied.org/pdfs/17121IIED.pdf

Carroll, A. B. and Shabana, K. M. (2010). The Business Case for Corporate Social Responsibility: A Review of Concepts, Research and Practice. *International Journal of Management Reviews, 12*(1), 85–105.

Clapp, J. (2019). The Rise of Financial Investment and Common Ownership in Global Agrifood Firms. *Review of International Political Economy 26*(4), 604–29.

Clapp, J. (2017). Responsibility to the Rescue? Governing Private Financial Investment in Global Agriculture. *Agriculture and Human Values, 34*(1), 223–235.

Clapp, J. and Isakson, S. R. (2018). *Speculative Harvests: Financialization, Food and Agriculture*. Halifax: Fernwood Press.

Dahlberg, K. A. (1993). Regenerative Food Systems: Broadening the Scope and Agenda of Sustainability. In: P. Allen (Ed.), *Food for the Future*. New York: Wiley, pp. 75–102.

DeLind, L. B. (2011). Are Local Food and the Local Food Movement Taking Us Where We Want to Go? *Agriculture and Human Values, 28*(2), 273–383.

De Schutter, O. (2010). Food Commodities Speculation and Food Price Crises. UN Special Rapporteur on the Right to Food Briefing Note 02, September Retrieved from. www2.ohchr.org/english/issues/food/docs/briefing_note_02_september_2010_en.pdf

Eggleton, A., Petitclerc, C. and Seidman, J. (2018). *The Federal Role in a Social Finance Fund*. Ottawa, Senate Canada. Retrieved from https://sencanada.ca/content/sen/committee/421/SOCI/reports/SocialFinance_24thReport_FINAL_WEB_e.pdf

Epstein, G. (2005). Introduction: Financialization and the World Economy. In: G. A. Epstein (Ed.), *Financialization and the World Economy*. Cheltenham: Edward Elgar, pp. 3–16.

Fairbairn, M. (2014). 'Like Gold with Yield': Evolving Intersections between Farmland and Finance. *The Journal of Peasant Studies, 41*(5), 777–795.

FAO, IFAD, UNCTAD Secretariat, and World Bank Group. (2010). Principles for Responsible Agricultural Investment that Respects Rights, Livelihoods and Resources: Synoptic Version. Retrieved from www.fao.org/fileadmin/templates/est/INTERNATIONAL-TRADE/FDIs/RAI_Principles_Synoptic.pdf

Food and Agriculture Organization of the United Nations (FAO). (2012). *Voluntary Guidelines on the Responsible Governance of Tenure of Land, Fisheries and Forests in the Context of National Food Security*. Rome: Food and Agriculture Organization of the United Nations.

Food and Agriculture Organization of the United Nations (FAO). (2014). *Principles for Responsible Investment in Agriculture and Food Systems*. Adopted by the Committ-ee on World Food Security. Retrieved from www.fao.org/3/a-au866e.pdf

FarmWorks. (n.d.a). Home. Retrieved from http://farmworks.ca/home

FarmWorks (n.d.b) About. Retrieved from https://farmworks.ca/about/

FarmWorks. (2017). Business Plan, Board Manual Articles. Retrieved from http://farmworks.ca/about/business-plan/

FarmWorks. (2019). Investing in Nova Scotian Food. Retrieved from https://farmworks.ca/wp-content/uploads/2019/02/FarmWorks-2019-January-Eighth-Offer-web.pdf

Fetherston, J. (2014). Social Finance: Sorting Hope from Hype. *Kennedy School Review*. Retrieved from http://ksr.hkspublications.org/2014/08/09/social-finance-sorting-hope-from-hype/

Geobey, S. (2014). *Measurement, Decision-Making and the Pursuit of Social Innovation in Canadian Social Finance*. (Unpublished master's thesis) Waterloo, Ontario: University of Waterloo.

Geobey, S., Westley, F. R. and Weber, O. (2012). Enabling Social Innovation Through Developmental Social Finance. *Journal of Social Entrepreneurship, 3*(2), 151–165.

Ghosh, J. (2010). The Unnatural Coupling: Food and Global Finance. *Journal of Agrarian Change, 10*(1), 72–86.

Government of Canada. (2015). Social Finance. Retrieved from www.canada.ca/en/employment-social-development/programs/social-finance.html

GRAIN. (2012). Responsible Farmland Investing? Current Efforts to Regulate Land Grabs Will Make Things Worse. *Against the grain*, 22 August. Retrived from www.grain.org/article/entries/4564-responsible-farmland-investingcurrent-efforts-to-regulate-land-grabs-will-make-things-worse.

Hallam, D. (2011). International Investment in Developing Country Agriculture—Issues and Challenges. *Food Security*, *3*(1), 91–98.

Institute for Agriculture and Trade Policy (IATP). (2008). *Commodities Market Speculation: The Risk to Food Security and Agriculture*. Minneapolis, MN: ITAP. Retrieved from iatp.org/files/451_2_104414.pdf

Kennedy, C., Best, L., and Borgstrom, G. (2017). *The FarmWorks CEDIF: An Economic Overview Assessment*. BC Rural Centre.

Krippner, G. (2011). *Capitalizing on Crisis: The Political Origins of the Rise of Finance*. Cambridge: Harvard University Press.

Local Prosperity. (2015). Investing in Sustainable Food for Nova Scotians: FarmWorks. Retrieved from www.localprosperity.ca/wp-content/uploads/2015/04/Linda-FarmWorks-Local-Prosperity-2015.pdf

Margulis, M. E. and Porter, T. (2013). Governing the Global Land Grab: Multipolarity, Ideas, and Complexity in Transnational Governance. *Globalizations*, *10*(1), 65–86.

MaRS. (2018). MaRS Celebrates Federal Leadership with New $800M+ Commitment to Impact Investing. Press Release; 21 November. Retrieved from www.marsdd.com/media-centre/mars-celebrates-federal-leadership-with-new-800m-commitment-to-impact-investing/

Martin, S. J. and Clapp, J. (2015). Finance for Agriculture or Agriculture for Finance? *Journal of Agrarian Change*, *15*(4), 549–559.

Mazzucato, M. (2011). *The Entrepreneurial State*. London: Demos.

Mazzucato, M. (2015). The Innovative State: Governments Should Make Markets, Not Just Fix Them. *Foreign Affairs*, *94*(1), 61–68.

McConnell Foundation. (2018). Civil Society Leaders Applaud Government Commitment to Establish Social Finance Fund. Press Release, 22 November. Retrieved from www.newswire.ca/news-releases/civil-society-leaders-applaud-government-commitment-to-establish-social-finance-fund-701093632.html

McKeon, N. (2013). 'One Does Not Sell the Land upon Which the People Walk': Land Grabbing, Transnational Rural Social Movements, and Global Governance. *Globalizations*, *10*(1), 105–122.

Moore, M.-L., Westley, F. R. and Nicholls, A. (2012). The Social Finance and Social Innoation Nexus. *Journal of Social Entrepreneurship*, *3*(2), 115–127.

Nestlé. (2017). Nestlé Waters North America Announces $6 Million Investment in Closed Loop Fund. Press Release, 22 May. Retrieved from www.nestleusa.com/media/pressreleases/nestle-waters-north-america-closed-loop-fund-investment.

Neumayer, E. (2013). *Weak versus Strong Sustainability: Exploring the Limits of Two Opposing Paradigms* (4th ed.). Cheltenham: Edward Elgar Publishing.

Nicholls, A. (2010). The Institutionalization of Social Investment: The Interplay of Investment Logics and Investor Rationalities. *Journal of Social Entrepreneurship*, *1*(1), 70–100.

Organisation for Economic Co-operation and Development OECD and FAO. (2016). *OECD-FAOGuidance for Responsible Agricultural Supply Chains*. Paris: OECD. Retrieved from mneguidelines.oecd.org/OECD-FAO-Guidance.pdf

Nova Scotia Department of Finance and Treasury Board. (2018). Nova Scotia Equity Tax Credit Guidelines: Community Economic Development Investment Fund. Retrieved from https://novascotia.ca/finance/docs/ETC_Guidelines_-_CEDIFs_2018-04.pdf. Accessed on March 16, 2020.

Ouma, S. (2016). From Financialization to Operations of Capital: Historicizing and Disentangling the Finance–Farmland-Nexus. *Geoforum*, *72*, 82–93.

Raworth, K. (2017). *Doughnut Economics: Seven Ways to Think like a 21st-Century Economist*. London: Cornerstone.

Rizzi, F., Pellegrini, C. and Battaglia, M. (2018). The Structuring of Social Finance: Emerging Approaches for Supporting Environmentally and Socially Impactful Projects. *Journal of Cleaner Production*, *170*, 805–817.

Rosenman, E. (2017). The Geographies of Social Finance: Poverty Regulation through the 'Invisible Heart' of Markets. *Progress in Human Geography*, Published online.

Scheer, R. and Moss, D. (n.d.). What Is "Slow Money"? *Scientific American*. Retrived from www.scientificamerican.com/article/slow-money-small-local-food-enterprises/

Scott, M. (2013, January 22). Long-Term Investors Take an Interest in Farmland. *Financial Times*.

Seufert, P. (2013). The FAO Voluntary Guidelines on the Responsible Governance of Tenure ofLand, Fisheries and Forests. *Globalizations 10*(1), 181–186.

Slow Money (2014). State of the Sector Report: Investing in Small Food Enterprises. *Slow Money*. Retrieved from https://ek4t.com/wp-content/uploads/2014/11/Slow-Money-State-of-the-Sector-Report.pdf

Slow Money Institute. (2010). About Us. Retrieved from https://slowmoney.org/about

Social Investment Taskforce. (2014). Impact Investment: The Invisible Heart of Markets. Retrieved from www.ebanimpact.org/wp-content/uploads/2015/06/Report-of-the-SOCIAL-IMPACT-INVESTMENT-TASKFORCE-G8.pdf

Stephens, P. (2013). The Principles of Responsible Agricultural Investment. *Globalizations 10*(1), 187–192.

Stephens, P., Knezevic, I. and Best, L. (2019). Community Financing for Sustainable Food Systems: The Case of FarmWorks Investment Co-operative. *Canadian Journal of Food Studies, 6*(3), 60–87.

Tasch, W. (2008). *Inquiries into the Nature of Slow Money*. Vermont: Chelsea Green Publishing.

The Canadian CED Network. (n.d.). The FarmWorks CEDIF: An Economic Overview and Assessment. Retrieved from https://ccednet-rcdec.ca/en/toolbox/farmworks-cedif-economic-overview-assessment

Valoral Advisors. (2015). Institutional Investors Meet Farmers. *2015 Global Food and Agriculture Investment Outlook*. Issue 5, January. Retrieved from http://farmcompany.dk/wp-content/uploads/2016/09/2015-Global-Food-Agriculture-Investment-Outlook.pdf

van der Zwan, N. (2014). Making Sense of Financialization. *Socio-Economic Review, 12*(1), 99–129.

World Bank, UNCTAD, and Government of Japan. (2017). *The Impact of Larger-scale Agricultural Investments on Local Communities*. Agriculture Global Practice Discussion Paper 12. Retrieved from https://unctad.org/en/PublicationsLibrary/wb_unctad_2017_en.pdf

17

CITIZEN ENTREPRENEURSHIP

The making, and remaking, of local food entrepreneurs

Michael Carolan

Introduction

A major aim of this chapter is to think about regenerative food systems through the concept of "entrepreneurship" and draw from a mix of approaches from economic sociology and geography. The overarching research question animating this research was, how do locally-facing business owner-operators understand their roles as entrepreneurs, particularly in relation to their respective communities, and why do they hold the beliefs that they do? I intentionally avoided looking to test hypotheses. Rather, a grounded theory approach was employed, which I explain later when describing methods. I mention the approach here to prepare the reader for the manuscript's overall format, which is intentionally unconventional. The chapter's organization is more iterative, reflecting the reality that I did not enter into the field with a clear hypothesis and thus without a clear understanding of "the" relevant literature.

The field of socio-economic scholarship, dating at least as far back as Weber (2013) has sought to understand the constitutive elements of markets. One notable development occurred with the revival and refinement of Polanyi's (1957) argument that market exchange is embedded in social structures, an important corrective to the under-socialized *homo economicus* and the over-socialized *homo sociologicus* (e.g., Block 1990; Granovetter 1985; Hinrichs 2000). Economic sociology and geography have experienced a more recent growth in a field inspired by actor network theory and assemblage thinking (e.g., Callon and Muniesa 2005; MacKenzie and Millo 2003). What I appreciate about this approach is that it reminds us that social structures are not the only phenomena that play a role in sustaining and making market exchanges; a realization that ought to extend to how we think about sustaining and making of entrepreneurs.

The approach used in this chapter takes analytic inspiration from both of these literatures – social embeddedness and assemblage thinking. Together they prove good to think with, producing empirical insights that inform the chapter's discussion and conclusion about how policy and practices could be enacted to encourage the affording of *citizen entrepreneurs*.

The data animating this argument come from a longitudinal study of food entrepreneurs throughout the US state of Colorado, including farmers, ranchers, processors, venders, chefs, food bank administrators, and retailers. The meaning of "entrepreneur" will be explored below. I am therefore reluctant to give a standard/fixed definition of the concept. That said, I admit to having needed some understanding of the term when building the sample that drove and guided the selection of participants in the study. I was intentionally open with how the concept was originally operationalized, hoping the flexibility would yield unforeseen empirical fruit. The methods section describes some of the elements I was looking for when seeking out respondents.

The chapter proceeds as follows. The next section moves right into a discussion of methods – again, as the argument builds out of the data I need to engage immediately with the chapter's empirics. The remainder of the chapter unpacks how our understanding of entrepreneurship cannot be divorced from these agents' networks and practices and what this means for community development practitioners, activists, and policy makers.

Methods

This chapter is based on a multiyear research project that included food entrepreneurs throughout Colorado. Those interviewed either sold direct to consumers and/or they were linked up with local value chains. This chapter focuses only on entrepreneurs who had been in business less than five years at the point when first enrolled into the research project.

The sample consists of 49 respondents. Those interviewed were purposefully selected using theoretical and snowball sampling techniques. Theoretical sampling is central to grounded theorizing, as the sampling process is itself directed towards the generation and development of conceptual theory (Glaser and Strauss 1967). Following this practice, a sample is considered sufficiently robust when no new emergent themes appear and relationships are understood; what is known as theoretical saturation. The snowball sampling technique made it easy to extend the sample until saturation was achieved.

Table 17.1 describes the entrepreneurial mix of the sample. Farmers and ranchers described as a "vender" were also engaged in selling direct-to-consumers. Thus, the table should be read to indicate that, of the 14 in this category, four also sold directly to consumers. I am aware of the differences in risk profiles between farm-based businesses and off-farm food businesses, particularly in terms of the weather/climate uncertainties encountered by the former group. Most of those interviewed, however, had greenhouse operations – one even raised the majority of their produce with greenhouse and hydroponic technologies. So while I recognize that risk profiles, generally speaking, vary greatly between farm and off-farm businesses, I am not convinced that those difference were great enough in this study to justifying unpacking these categories further.

To understand the "processor" category requires an understanding of the state's Colorado Cottage Food Act. Similar to other states, this law allows very small-scale operations to produce things like cookies, spices, and dehydrated produce out of their homes for direct-to-consumer sales within the state without licensing or inspection. The Act applies only to "non-potentially hazardous" foods, which typically means items that do not require refrigeration. It also has a cap of $5,000 in net sales annually per product. The six venders of the processor category sold food in accordance with the Act. Non-vender processors owned a business where they cooked/baked/canned/etc. foods that they then sold to stores

Table 17.1 Sample demographics

Entrepreneurial type	
Farmer and/or rancher: 14 (14)	
Vender: 4 (5)	
Processor: 12 (8)	
Vender: 6 (4)	
Restaurateur: 9 (3)	
Chef: 4 (1)	
Retailer: 5 (5)	
Non-profit organizer: 5 (5)	
For-profit organizer: 4 (2)	
For-profit/Non-profit	
For-profit: 39 (28)	
Non-profit: 10 (9)	
Gender Breakdown[*]	
Female: 22 (20)	
Male: 27 (17)	
Ethnicity Breakdown[*]	
White: 36 (27)	
Black/African American: 6 (4)	
Hispanic/Latino: 5 (5)	
Asian American: 2 (1)	

t^1 n=49 (t^2 n=37)
* Self-identified

and/or restaurants. "Restaurateur" were owners of a restaurant, four of whom were also the establishment's chef. "Retailer" owned a store – grocery store, specialty shop, etc.

"Non-profit organizer" refers to anyone who helped non-profits get off the ground and/or who oversaw their operations (included in this category was one restaurateur, not counted earlier, who owned and operated a non-profit restaurant). Non-profit entrepreneurs were included in this research for two reasons: (1) I knew from past research (e.g., Carolan 2018b) that those in this category often thought of themselves as entrepreneurs, which led me to believe that interesting insights could be gleaned from this group if included; (2) I knew from past research that many non-profit entrepreneurs grapple with issues of resource (i.e., financial capital) scarcity, just as for-profit entrepreneurs do, and wanted to interrogate their struggle to make money. Lastly "for-profit organizer" is a catchall term for for-profit entrepreneurs interviewed who did not fit into the previously listed categories. An example of someone who fell into this category was someone who developed a business around a web-based culinary incubation platform (to provide any more detail would expose the entrepreneur to identification).

The following offers additional details about respondents' business structure, in terms of the "length" of their value chains and the nature (e.g., local facing) of their commitments. It is offered to provide readers with a better idea of how inclusion in the sample was determined. Among for-profit entrepreneur respondents: *farmer and/or rancher* – those interviewed generated at least 75 percent of their revenue by selling to markets within Colorado; *processor* – more than 90 percent of their inputs (a statement of value not volume) came from within the state and more than 90 percent of their products were sold within the state; *restaurateur* – at least half (a statement of value not volume) of their food was procured from within the state; *retailer* – independently-owned and a commitment (as stated in their mission) to local and/or Colorado procurement and community wellbeing. Among non-profit entrepreneur respondents: their classification as "local facing" hinged on servicing only Colorado communities and expressing a broader commitment (as stated in their mission or website) to connecting up with and supporting local food value chains.

Initial interviews occurred between 2013 and 2014. They were face to face, lasting on average 90 minutes. In addition to following a semi-structured, open-ended questionnaire, individuals were asked to verbally respond to a brief survey instrument, which I describe later while detailing longitudinal findings. Three years then transpired, after which time respondents were contacted and asked for a second interview. Only the data of those who were still in business are discussed in this chapter.

Semi-structured interviews started with basic stage setting questions – e.g., "Tell me about your business". Eventually, discussion moved to questions about the entrepreneur's goals and beliefs around business strategy, which included having them identify perceived strengths, weaknesses, threats, and opportunities that mediate the enterprise's success (the concept of "success" was also interrogated). If the interview had not already gone in this direction, I then asked respondents to talk about their financing story. The latter half of the interview consisted of a lengthy discussion about interactions with the community and how their business contributes to community "wealth", broadly conceived.

The second interview process looked much like the first. All respondents still in business after three years agreed to be re-interviewed. The principle aim of the second interview was to discern changes in attitudes, practices, networks, challenges, etc. The sample demographics of those participating in follow-up interviews are signified in Table 17.1 by the numbers in parentheses.

All interviews were conducted by me and were recorded, transcribed, and coded. Qualitative data analysis protocols were similar at both times. Two individuals and myself, trained in qualitative methods, independently coded the same two randomly selected interviews using NVivo software and any inconsistencies in coding were reviewed until consensus was reached. I coded all remaining interviews, using those initial codes as a guide.

Findings: profit, autonomy, and fluidity

This section is organized by subsection according to the following emergent themes: *profit*, where I explore how respondents grasped the concept and why; *autonomy*, where I detail how some respondents expressed autonomy-as-individualism while others located autonomy in commitments to interdependence and collaboration; and *fluidity*, which draws principally on the longitudinal aspects of the data, describing how even within the same individual the idea of *entrepreneurship*, as an identity and state of being, was unstable.

Profit: what is enough?

Credit and capital were frequently mentioned among respondents when asked to identify barriers to business success. This aligns with others' findings (e.g., Hamilton 2002; Cetorelli and Strahan 2006) and economic realities for small businesses post-Great Recession (Corner and Meyer 2013). An especially interesting element of these conversations came when strategies were discussed for overcoming those barriers, and how these enrollments with human (e.g., venture capitalists) and nonhuman (e.g., interest rates) elements shaped the type of entrepreneur they would be.

Those without adequate capital and lacking access to prime rate credit talked about pursuing, in the words of one respondent, "credit with less than ideal interest rates – stupid high rates, actually" (Lois, Processor). A number of respondents admitted to using, at some point in their business' life, credit cards to finance their operations. Four admitted to having a credit card balances in excess of $10,000, which they explained are accumulating interest at rates between 15 and 25 percent.

Lois, quoted earlier, owned a company that specialized in salsa and pizza sauce, which she sold to area restaurants and to a few specialty food stores. Beyond a "small" initial investment from a sister, used to help upgrade her kitchen space to make it compliant with regulatory requirements, Lois funded the operation entirely herself. "Some months the revenue is there; in other months, not so much", she told me. She has two credit cards, both with interest rates at around 20 percent, which she uses to cover shortfalls in revenue. In her words, "I prefer getting paid at the point of transaction; who wouldn't. ... Some of my customers are small businesses themselves, who are occasionally strapped for cash. ... I rely on my Visa to cover bills when I'm waiting for payment." Later, Lois admitted to using her credit cards to finance capital improvements, like the time she needed to get one of her commercial-grade refrigerators fixed – a $1,500 expense on a 20 percent interest bearing loan.

For empirical contrast, allow me to introduce Kirk. Kirk owned and operated a company that made gluten-free baked products, a venture that started in his mother's kitchen. Two years prior to being interviewed, Kirk was approached by venture capitalists. They wanted to invest in his business, which Kirk described as being at that time "a side gig". The investment allowed Kirk to expand operations significantly. It also came with tradeoffs.

Kirk and Lois, like numerous other respondents, could not disentangle how they thought and felt about profit from these associations with lenders, interest rates, and venture capitalists. Kirk explained how these connections "directly impact my profit-mindedness as an entrepreneur". At numerous points in the interview, he explicitly mentioned wanting to grow a business that was "more interested in reinvesting in community than in maximizing profitability." As evidence of this, he looked into investing in various programs associated with the Affordance Care Act (ACA), also known as Obamacare, like wellness programs and the Small Business Health Options Program (SHOP) – the latter is for small businesses (one to fifty full-time equivalent employees) that want to provide health and dental coverage to their employees. "When my investors caught wind [of these possible business expenses] they quickly put the kibosh to it," Kirk explained, adding, "They wanted to see a return [on their investment], so I'm forced, by association, to operate by that mindset too."

Lois made a similar observation, explaining how she would like to pay her employees more and donate a greater share of food to area non-profits. She even contemplated selling her food on a sliding scale, "for those", in her words, "less fortunate in the community". What keep her from doing this are, in significant part at least, those aforementioned credit card payments. In her words,

> I have to be incredibly mindful of my button line. If I don't make enough money, those credit card debts will only grow and my dream [her business] will go up in smoke. ... From the outside it might look like I'm some greedy capitalist, when in fact my actions and mindset are an extension of the credit card companies and the fact that banks won't lend me money.

Comments like this dovetail with the chapter's earlier-defined framework by bringing to the analytic surface examples of how the dog-eat-dog ideology attributed to the neoliberal entrepreneur is not necessarily a product of some inescapable logic that weighs on subjects equally but rather is an effect of diverse assemblages – Federal Reserve policies that make small business credit harder to come by, venture capitalists, monthly credit card bills, etc.

For contrast, while continuing to build the argument, I want to now introduce Michele. Michele owned and operated a small business that made specialty pasta. It was through her that I learned about merchant cash advances – also known as "fast cash". The process works something like the following. A loan is made to a business owner, taken out as an advance on future sales. The lender then makes automatic deductions from daily credit or debit card sales or by regularly deducting money from the business' bank account. The loan also comes with a hefty interest rate.

In Michele's case, she was given an advance of roughly $20,000 to help her make it through what she described as "a perfect storm" – an unexpected equipment breakdown coupled with some late payments from clients. To get the loan she was assessed close to $1,000 in processing fees. The lender then deducted a little more than $400 a day from her business' sales for 70 days. With fees, Faye paid back slightly less than $30,000, on a loan for $20,000 that lasted a little over two months. That is an effective interest rate in the *triple* digits.

A few months later, the brother of a customer who frequented her establishment approached her. Expressing an interest in investing, they eventually agreed on a partnership that made her business far less economically precarious. At the same time, Michele learned about a kitchen-sharing platform that gave food entrepreneurs access to affordable idle kitchen space. Being able to rent space by the hour, versus being locked into an "expensive commercial kitchen lease for equipment that was only used a few hours a week", saved Michele, in her words, "headache and money".

Both of these events greatly reduced the pressure she was under to be, in her words, a "jerk". As she explained,

> It was like having a weight lifted off my shoulders. I got into business to do something productive, for my community – to make a difference; not so I could be your stereotypical money hungry jerk. … If you create conditions for small businesses to prosper, they can turn a profit and stay in business and still serve *social* missions, maybe even make those community-building ends their priority.

Evidence suggests that Michele was able to pivot to serving more pro-social ends since having that "weight lifted" off her shoulders. Shortly after these events, her two employees "almost immediately" were given a "sizable raise" and she was able to create a price differentiation structure, allowing her to sell to some businesses at a reduced price – she mentioned two social enterprises in particular. As she told me, "I'm just looking to pay my bills and have a little left over for myself, which is so much easier to do now [that the aforementioned weight had been lifted]".

Autonomy: individualism vs. interdependence

A considerable body of agrifood scholarship documents tensions in how autonomy is understood, particularly among farmer groups (Coolsaet 2016; Carolan 2018a). The concept is important as it offers an analytic entry point into the holder's deeper assumptions about what it means to be a farmer, or, in this case, an entrepreneur. For example, among those holding individualistic views of autonomy, to be autonomous assumes a go-it-alone mindset. From this standpoint, neighbors and colleagues are natural competitors, those from whom independence must be sought as opposed to viewing them as potential collaborators.

As Dodd and Anderson (2007) argue, entrepreneurship is often understood, in the academy and beyond, as an individualistic practice, a position that reflects what they call the "individualized entrepreneur ideology" (p. 352). It is therefore understandable why social scientists are often critical of the concept, given this assumption that it is purely an expression of an individualist ontology – autonomy-as-individualism. Yet a central argument in economic sociology and geography literature, especially that inspired by the likes of Callon (e.g., 2016), is that *homo economicus* is neither pre-given nor natural. Rather, "it" – the fully autonomous, independent subject – is *made*.

Arthur manages farms located in urban and peri-urban settings. These organizations are non-profits. The produce and fruit raised in these spaces go to food banks and area restaurants. During his interview, Arthur lamented the few available subsidies and grants for enterprises like those he oversees. "If there would be more [money]," he explained, "they'd give us slack to innovate and outreach". When asked to say more about this, he confessed that "demand outstrips supply [for grants and subsidies], so I'm busting my butt writing grants for money I probably won't get." Adding, "If there were more money to go around, I might be able spend some time thinking about expanding the enterprise and engaging with the community, activities I can't afford at the moment."

In light of these comments, perhaps the commercial/non-commercial – or more specifically, for-profit/non-profit – dichotomy discussed so much in certain critical social scientific circles is a red herring. After all, Arthur, who oversaw non-profit enterprises, mentioned some of the same pressures you would expect a for-profit entrepreneur to confront – scrambling for money in a resource constrained environment, no time for community engagement, etc. The lack of available resources for non-profits has been repeatedly cited as a reason for why the scaling of local food production and consumption is often partially dependent on commercial practices (Bloom and Hinrichs 2011; Mount 2012). This scarcity, even for some non-profits, appears to be partially responsible for also instilling entrepreneurship subjectivities that "can't afford" to engage fully with the community. As in the previous subsection on profit, the degree to which one's entrepreneurial subjectivity was inward or outward looking proved partially an artifact of their (human/non-human) network. Those interviewed did not entirely choose to have an individual or collective outlook, but neither were those outlooks imposed upon them by some hegemonic structure from which there was no escape.

Building on this point, interesting parallels emerged between this research and arguments located in the feminist entrepreneurship scholarship literature (e.g., Dean and Ford 2017). The hegemonic masculinity classically associated with "successful" entrepreneurship – i.e., rationality, competition, profit maximizing (Nelson and Winter 1974) – is exclusionary toward women (Fielden and Hunt 2011) and other forms of masculinities, especially non-white, non-heteronormative masculinities (Ahl and Marlow 2012). As Dean and Ford (2017, 191) argue, "the diversity and subjectivity of the entrepreneurial leadership experience has, therefore, been obscured in so much of the writing on the entrepreneur".

This discussion is given added significance when looking at changes from t^1 to t^2 in terms of business persistence. Among female entrepreneurs interviewed at the beginning of the research, 91 percent (20 out of 22) remained in business when interviewed the second time, compared to a 63 percent (17 out of 27) persistence rate among male respondents.

This was not an artifact of significantly more men being located in, say, the "restaurateur" category, which had a t[1] gender breakdown of four females and five males. Sixty percent of restaurants do not make it to their one-year anniversary; 80 percent close before the five-year mark (Feloni 2014). This is a curious finding as it goes against much of the literature where masculine forms of entrepreneurship are valorized (Mirchandani 1999), assumingly because they are associated positively with "success", like business persistence.

Like the males interviewed, all female respondents expressed a desire to be innovative, creative, and forward looking. Not all of the women, however, immediately saw themselves as entrepreneurs (see also Dean and Ford 2017). This stands in striking contrast to male respondents, who all viewed themselves as entrepreneurs. Betty responded in the following ambivalent and somewhat confused way when asked if she would call herself an entrepreneur: "I'd like to think so but I doubt others would think so. I guess I would. Maybe. Maybe not."

When asked to explain why she felt this way, she made reference to "being passionate about innovating, but not always in ways that improve my business' bottom-line". An example of this innovation, which was based on creating collaborations versus being about beating out her competition, was a peer-to-peer lending platform that she was hoping to build that involved fellow business owners and members of the community. As Betty put it, when describing this platform:

> I think we forget the synergies that collaboration brings, like peer-to-peer learning. I've learned so much from other business owners – collaborations that have been mutually beneficial. Business doesn't have to be zero sum.

The fact that so many more female respondents hesitated when asked if they saw themselves as entrepreneurs suggests that their understanding of what it means to be one looks different compared to more conventional definitions. And this understanding brings with it different business strategies and practices, as evidenced by Betty's remark about how "we forget the synergies that collaboration brings, like peer-to-peer learning" – autonomy *through* interdependence. Perhaps these alternative strategies served the respondents holding them well, maybe better than the strategies wrapped up in more conventionally motivated (individualistic, profit maximization driven, etc.) entrepreneurs? Ultimately, that is a question for future research.[2]

How and *why*, then, did some respondents come to hold views of entrepreneurship that stand opposed to those where competition, rationality, and *homo economicus* are privileged? My encounter with Marcy is especially illustrative for purposes of answering this question.

Marcy owned and operated a small farm-to-table café. It was also, in her words, "bakery to table", as the bread she used came from a baker a few blocks away. At one point in our interview, when talking about financials, which included her revealing how she afforded the initial investment – the café was in a beautifully renovated century-old bank – she confessed, "I'd like to be able to tell you that I'm just a good person, but I got a lot of help". Later she added, "my business had been a team effort from the start and I'm working to keep that [collaborative] ball rolling." She admitted to receiving a "sizable inheritance" that allowed her to buy the building outright. This in turn gave her "the freedom to not have to think about my business' bottom line" – she operates by the business model where people pay what they can.

It was an important confession, as it reminds us to avoid uncritically demonizing (or, conversely, celebrating) entrepreneurs for what they individually do, such as whether they work to build collaborative relationships with other businesses and community members. As

Marcy reminded me, what you do as an entrepreneur, and whether you do it as an individual or as a member of a larger team, often has little to do with whether you are, in Marcy's words, "a good person" or not.

Fluidity: becoming entrepreneur

There is recognition among some scholars of entrepreneurship's heterogeneity (see e.g., Hmieleski and Ensley 2007; Dean and Ford 2017). Yet the issue of entrepreneurial identity fluidity remains largely unexplored. In fact, the literature continues to overwhelmingly view this group's identity as fixed.

The longitudinal data make it clear respondents' views about what it meant to be an entrepreneur changed from t^1 to t^2. Table 17.2 details some of this change, describing the results of the aforementioned brief survey that respondents were asked to verbally respond to at

Table 17.2 Survey results

	For-profit		Non-profit	
	Time 1, n=39	*Time 2, n=28*	*Time 1, n=10*	*Time 2, n=9*
Profit level sought				
Maximum	19 (49) / *12	**7 (25)**	NA	**NA**
Enough to get by	18 (46) / *15	**19 (68)**	NA	**NA**
Breakeven	2 (5) / *1	**2 (7)**	NA	**NA**
Importance of competitiveness for success ("How important is beating out other competitors?")				
1) Most important	15 (38) / *7	**7 (25)**	0 (0) / *0	**0 (0)**
2)	10 (27) / *7	**8 (29)**	1 (10) / *1	**0 (0)**
3) Moderately important	12 (31) / *12	**10 (36)**	1 (10) / *1	**1 (11)**
4)	2 (5) / *2	**2 (7)**	3 (30) / *2	**2 (22)**
5) Not important	0 (0) / *0	**1 (4)**	5 (50) / *5	**6 (67)**
Importance of collaboration for success ("How important is collaborating with similar businesses?")				
1) Most important	0 (0) / *0	**0 (0)**	8 (80) / *7	**8 (89)**
2)	4 (10) / *4	**8 (28)**	1 (10) / *1	**1 (11)**
3) Moderately important	20 (51) / *19	**19 (68)**	1 (10) / *1	**0 (0)**
4)	5 (13) / *2	**1 (4)**	0 (0) / *0	**0 (0)**
5) Not important	10 (26) / *3	**0 (0)**	0 (0) / *0	**0 (0)**
Interest in scaling up (i.e., national markets)				
1) Very interested	1 (3) / *0	**1 (4)**	NA	**NA**
2)	0 (0) / *0	**1 (4)**	NA	**NA**
3) Ambivalent	2 (5) / *2	**0 (0)**	NA	**NA**
4)	0 (0) / *0	**0 (0)**	NA	**NA**
5) No interest	36 (92) / *26	**26 (93)**	NA	**NA**
Rank reasons for being in business: n (%) ranked as most important				
Make a lot of money	17 (44) / *10	**5 (18)**	0 (0) / *0	**0 (0)**
Build vibrant community	12 (31) / *12	**11 (39)**	8 (80) / *8	**8 (89)**
Social justice	1 (3) / *1	**4 (14)**	2 (20) / *1	**1 (11)**
Environmental stewardship	7 (18) / *4	**6 (21)**	0 (0) / *0	**0 (0)**
Other	2 (5) / *1	**2 (7)**	0 (0) / *0	**0 (0)**

t^1 and t^2: n (%)

* Signifies location in the table of those at t^1 who remained in sample at t^2 (n = 28 / n = 9).

both times.[4] The sample in the table is broken up by "for-profit" and "non-profit" to create a more actuate – e.g., "apples to apples" – comparison between business types. The table also identifies numbers in t^t of the interviewees (n = 28/9) who were still in business at t^2.

While 49 percent of for-profit entrepreneurs surveyed reported wanting to "maximize" profit when first interviewed, 61 percent also reported that collaboration was at least a "moderately important" ingredient and 66 percent cited reasons other than to "make a lot of money" when listing their top reason for being in business. The qualitative data suggest that, echoing points already made, this "need" for profit maximization was an expression shaped significantly by network effects – e.g., high interest rates, high financial barriers to entry (e.g., leasing expressive commercial kitchen space), a lack of grants and subsidies. This apparent contradiction, between valuing both profit maximization and collaboration, could be expressed this way: many *needed* to make a significant return to stay in business even though they *wanted* to collaborate with others.[3]

The "need" to maximize profits decreased considerably by t^2, from 49 to 25 percent. Relatedly, "make a lot of money" dropped as the top reason for being in business – from 44 to 18 percent – while "build vibrant community", "social justice", and "environmental stewardship" saw increases in reporting in t^2. Part of this change can be explained in the fact that, by the second interview, those interviewed oversaw businesses that had been open for at least three years, which would suggest that they were more financially stable than when first interviewed (and a review of their financial situation – debt, revenue, etc. – backed this assertion up). Many thus talked about how, in the words of Jackie (Restaurateur), "the financial pressures aren't as great as they once were". This stability allowed them to deemphasize the bottom line (profit/revenue) and turn their attention outward, toward others and the community.

These attitudinal changes cannot be explained entirely by resource availability/stability, however. The *experience* of owning a locally-facing business seems to have played a role in making respondents less instrumental, individualistic, and inward-focused. By the second interview, respondents on the whole were expressing sentiments more in line with an entrepreneurship that was community centered, pro-social, and outward-focused. Representative quotes from respondents reflecting on their own change in attitudes from t^1 to t^2 include the following:

> If it wasn't crystal [clear] starting out, it is now. This isn't just a business within a community. ... As a member of this community, I've gotten to know its challenges and feel a responsibility to help overcome them. ... The people I employ, the taxes I pay, the food I donate to [the local school], these aren't some numbers on my QuickBooks [accounting] software. We're talking about people and places that know, that in some cases I've known since the day I was born.
>
> *(Alfred, Retailer)*

> I used to have a more Darwinian view of business, you know, survival of the fittest. [Chuckling] Naïve perhaps, but I learned; came to appreciate the business benefits of working together, with other businesses, with community leaders – everyone.
>
> *(Bill, For-profit organizer)*

Entrepreneurism was also reported as not closing off alternative avenues for political action among participants. This speaks to a major concern among many critical scholars, about how business-based responses to societal ills and community wellbeing engender a type of crowding out effect, where marketization leads to the belief among actors that markets offer *the only* avenue for social change (e.g., Szasz 2007). Rather, entrepreneurialism appears to have the potential to produce just the opposite effect, *broadening* views of what it meant to be a political subject and active (perhaps even an activist – Carolan 2017) citizen. To quote Nora (Farmer),

> I started this [business] with high-minded ideals, wanting to change the world and all that, by giving people a choice that doesn't involve Walmart. … It didn't take long to realize that you can only change the food system so much through markets. … There are some longstanding entrenched interests shaping markets. To change *that* you've got to think outside the business as usual box.

Shortly thereafter she talked about creating what she called "market hybrids". In her case that involved using her business to facilitate *non-market* collective organizing, like when she used her buildings to hold community meetings or as evidenced by her leveraging market-based relationships with customers (social and political capital) to lobby for change (e.g., emailing them to elicit support for social causes, providing discounts to those who attend charity music events on her property).

Before concluding this section, I want to make a few additional observations about the data in Table 17.2. Note the high failure rate among businesses between t^1 and t^2 who were owned by individuals seeking "maximum" profits – a 63 percent persistence rate compared to a rate of 88 percent among those seeking "enough to get by". Conversely, those expressing strongly pro-collaborative sentiments at t^1 seemed to perform better (as a function of remaining in business three years later) than those who did not. One hundred percent of those saying collaboration was very important (between "most" and "moderately" important) at t^1 remained in business at t^2, while 95 percent saying collaboration was "moderately" important at t^1 remained in business three years later, and only 30 percent remained in business at t^2 who initially said collaboration was "not important".

In the next section, I explore further what some of these trends and data points night mean.

Discussion and conclusion

In conventional terms, entrepreneurship boils down to the ability to exploit market opportunities (Shane and Venkataraman 2000). The goal of entrepreneurs, in this vision, is to generate maximum individual- and firm-level economic returns (Lepak et al. 2007). The extent to which society benefits from these activities is determined by the positive externalities therein produced – innovations, economic spillover/trickledown, etc. Phenomena like societal wellbeing, equity, and public health are never the principal motivators driving commercial entrepreneurship, which is why they can be negatively impacted by overly individualistic expressions of the identity (Harris et al. 2009; Mars and Schau 2017).

Because of the study's inclusion of only those involved in local and regional supply chains, it is worth asking if my sample is representative of entrepreneurs as a whole. My guess is that it is not. Future research could investigate the extent to which those involved in locally-facing enterprises enter into businesses for reasons and aims different from those entering into more conventional, nationally/globally facing supply chains. There are also metro/non-metro elements that ought to be investigated in the future – e.g., are entrepreneurs of businesses of short supply chains that traverse rural and urban environments different from those embedded entirely in metropolitan value chains (see e.g., Mars and Schau 2017)?

Part of the reason to expand the sample in the future is because this would allow us to better discern whether there is anything about locally-facing business practices *in themselves* that engender pro-social tendencies. This would help us better explain why the majority of respondents reported even stronger collaborative sentiments at t^2 than when first interviewed. Between the findings above and those detailed in Carolan (2017), which recorded attitudinal and behavioral changes among *consumers* of locally-facing alternative food platforms, there is considerable evidence supporting the thesis that there is indeed something about locally-facing business practices that elicit pro-social tendencies. But, again, more research is needed to tease out causal factors and impacts.

Levkoe (2011) identifies three elements necessary for a "transformative food politics": the transition to collective subjectivities, a whole system approach, and a politics of reflexive localism (avoiding the so-called local trap: Born and Purcell 2006). The entrepreneurship engendered by the practices and networks within which many of the respondents were embedded appears to align in various ways with all three of these elements. While the formation of collective/collaborative subjectivities was most clearly highlighted, respondents on the whole resisted seeing problems narrowly, as evidenced by their desire to change communities and not just "make a lot of money". In addition, the entrepreneurship expressed and practiced appeared to be grounded in a type of reflexive localism – e.g., recognizing that local ownership without collaboration and connectedness will not produce just, healthy, and resilient communities.

We know that a business' age shapes how entrepreneurs spread risk over time (Xiao et al. 2001), which is why I limited my sample to owner-operators of newer businesses, to approximate a better apple-to-apple comparison. As noted earlier, as businesses age and become well-capitalized and financially secure their owners and managers can afford to be less risk averse and focus on things that might cut into their bottom line, like paying their workers a liveable wage, exploring benefit (health care, retirement, etc.) options for employees, and making charitable donations. However, the data suggest that something more is happening to the entrepreneurs than simply this. First, as noted in the prior section, and in Table 17.2, those wanting "maximum" profit at t^1 had a lower business persistence rate than those who said they wanted to make "enough to get by". Conversely, those expressing strong pro collaboration sentiments performed better (as a function of being in business three years later) than those not expressing those sentiments. There appears to be something about the entrepreneurs – in terms of their embeddedness and assemblages – that helps to explain their pro-social sentiments, beyond just being well-capitalized and financially secure. Second, those sentiments became more pro-social between t^1 to t^2. And while financial security is unquestionably part of the explanation behind this, considerable evidence was provided suggesting that there are additional elements behind this shift in respondents' attitudes.

Before concluding, allow me to mention a few practical suggestions that could be gleaned from this research. Government officials can learn from these findings, noting especially that the value of local, and locally-facing in particular, business should not be reduced to bottom-line financials. Economic and business leaders and politicians speak a lot about tradeoffs. We need to expand that discussion to include having an honest conversation about what it means to populate businesses with entrepreneurs who seek to maximize profits (due in part to things like lending policies, interest rates, non scale neutral regulations, etc.), particularly in light of the pro-social tradeoffs that those sentiments and actions come at the expense of. This is *not* a critique of profits; any business, including non-profit businesses, needs to make money. The problem is that we cannot have an honest conversation about those tradeoffs because we have not done a very good job measuring and recording the non-market elements (e.g., social, political, cultural, and human capitals) that might be negatively impacted by aggressive profit maximizing practices. Such research could also better inform conversations around the tradeoffs between locally-facing and nationally/globally-facing businesses. Relatedly, when governments and practitioners provide entrepreneurship workshops, short courses, and online programs, they should think critically about the type of entrepreneurs – and by extension business structures (i.e., locally- vs. nationally/globally-facing) – they are hoping to afford through these events. These are all conversations that need to be had as policies and activities are pursued under the banner of rural wealth creation (Pender et al. 2014).

Related to what is mentioned in the prior paragraph, this research also emphasizes the "costs" to communities that arise from environments that are non-conducive to small businesses – e.g., high interest rates, a lack of grants and subsidies, non scale neutral regulations, lack of affordable land/commercial kitchen space/etc. These barriers come with the risk of making entrepreneurs who have little choice but to reject opportunities to work collaboratively and who are therefore making management decisions that are not always in the community's best interests. The last thing we ought to want is to create an environment where entrepreneurs feel like they have no option but to, as Michele put it, act like a "money hungry jerk". And while it is true that entrepreneurs might age out of that outlook as their business matures, that is far – *far* – from a guarantee.

Building on this point, the chapter sheds a spotlight on the subject of financing and lending. Loans by community banks in the US peaked in 2008, dropping drastically every year thereafter until 2011 (Corner and Meyer 2013). Since the Great Recession, traditional credit has dried up for small businesses. To quote a US Federal Reserve System research officer discussing the subject, "It's a totally different ballgame today, especially if you're looking for small-business financing. Most lenders, post-2008, are no longer community focused but are now Fed focused" (quoted in Carolan 2018b, 136–7). The *Fed focused* reference speaks to regulators' requirement, post-Recession, for banks to hold more capital against business loans than consumer loans, which has driven up the costs of small-business lending. The above data confirm this view, showing that resource and credit scarcity is driving small business owners into lending arrangements (e.g., "fast cash", credit cards) that are directly linked to non pro-social entrepreneurial attributes.

In sum, we need to continue to understand the values and identities of farm and food business owners and how they connect up with community goals, commitments to inclusivity, and economic realities (e.g., regulatory and lender regimes). And then, work to engender better alignment across all those spheres.

Discussion questions

1. How is entrepreneurship gendered?
2. How can we engender markets that lead to more pro-social encounters and communities?
3. How does lending contribute to socially negative (and positive) behavior among businesses?

Notes

1 The two "other" responses came from ranchers, who answered "lifestyle" – the rancher/farmer way of life was their top reason for being in business.
2 Some men also expressed these collaborative leanings. Yet, again, not one male questioned their standing as entrepreneurs.
3 Respondents regularly conflated "profits" with "revenue", recognizing that, technically speaking, profits are revenues minus expenses. It was actually therefore *revenue* maximization that many respondents were expressing a need for in order to remain in business.
4 The complete questions recorded in the table are the following.

- In general, what level of profit do you hope to achieve through your business: maximum; enough to get by; enough to breakeven?
- In general, what level of importance do you place on competitiveness for business success? In other words, how important is beating out other competitors: 1 (most important ingredient) to 5 (not important)?
- In general, what level of importance do you place on collaboration for business success? In other words, how important is working with and learning from similar businesses: 1 (most important ingredient) to 5 (not important)?
- What is your interest in scaling up your operation to someday tap into national markets: 1 (very interested) to 5 (no interest)?
- Rank the reasons for being in business, from 1 to 5 in order of their importance: make a lot of money; build vibrant community; social justice; environmental stewardship; other. (Note: the number reported in the table reflects the reason ranked as most important.)

Further reading

Carolan, M. 2019. Capitalizing on financing ecologies: The world making properties of peer-to-peer lending through everyday entrepreneurship. *Geoforum* 102: 17–26.
Clark, J., and M. Record 2017b. Local capitalism and civic engagement: The potential of locally facing firms. *Public Administration Review* 77(6): 875–887.
Mars, M., and H. Schau 2017. What is local food entrepreneurship? Variations in the commercially and socially oriented features of entrepreneurship in the Southeastern Arizona local food system. *Rural Sociology*. DOI: 10.1111/ruso.12197

References

Ahl, H., and S. Marlow 2012. Exploring the dynamics of gender, feminism and entrepreneurship: Advancing debate to escape a dead end? *Organization* 19(5): 543–562.
Austin, J., H. Stevenson, and J. Wei-Skillern 2006. Social and commercial entrepreneurship: Same, different, or both? *Entrepreneurship Theory and Practice* 30(1): 1–22.
Block, F. 1990. *Postindustrial Possibilities: A Critique of Economic Discourse.* Berkeley, CA: University of California Press.
Bloom, J.D. and C.C. Hinrichs 2011. Moving local food through conventional food system infrastructure: Value chain framework comparisons and insights. *Renewable Agriculture and Food Systems* 26(1): 13–23.
Born, B., and M. Purcell 2006. Avoiding the local trap scale and food systems in planning research. *Journal of Planning Education and Research* 26(2): 195–207.
Callon, M. 2016. Revisiting marketization: From interface-markets to market agencements. *Consumption Markets and Culture* 19(1): 17–37.
Callon, M. and F. Muniesa 2005. Peripheral vision: Economic markets as calculative collective devices. *Organization Studies* 26(8): 1229–1250.
Carolan, M. 2017. More-than-active food citizens: A longitudinal and comparative study of alternative and conventional eaters. *Rural Sociology* 82(2): 197–225.

Carolan, M. 2018a. Justice across real and imagined food worlds: Rural corn growers, urban agriculture activists, and the political ontologies they live by. *Rural Sociology* 83(4): 823–856.

Carolan, M. 2018b. *The Food Sharing Revolution: How Start-ups, Pop-ups, and Co-ops are Changing the Way We Eat*, Washington, DC: Island Press.

Cetorelli, N., and P. Strahan 2006. Finance as a barrier to entry: Bank competition and industry structure in local US markets. *Journal of Finance* 61(1): 437–461.

Clark, J., and M. Record 2017a. Local capitalism and civic engagement: The potential of locally facing firms. *Public Administration Review* 77(6): 875–887.

Connelly, S., S. Markey, and M. Roseland 2011. Bridging sustainability and the social economy: Achieving community transformation through local food initiatives. *Critical Social Policy* 31(2): 308–324.

Coolsaet, B. 2016. Towards an agroecology of knowledges: Recognition, cognitive justice and farmers' autonomy in France. *Journal of Rural Studies* 47: 165–171.

Corner, G., and A. Meyer 2013. Community bank lending during the financial crisis, Federal Reserve, St. Louis. www.stlouisfed.org/Publications/Central-Banker/Spring- 2013/Community-Bank-Lending-during-the-Financial-Crisis, last accessed December 20, 2017.

Dean, H., and J. Ford 2017. Discourses of entrepreneurial leadership: Exposing myths and exploring new approaches. *International Small Business Journal* 35(2): 178–196.

Dodd, S., and A. Anderson 2007. Mumpsimus and the mything of the individualistic entrepreneur. *International Small Business Journal* 25(4): 341–360.

Feloni, R. 2014. Food network chef Robert Irvine shares the top 5 reasons restaurants fail. *Business Insider.* February 25, www.businessinsider.com/why-restaurants-fail-so-often-2014-2, last accessed December 25, 2017.

Fielden, S., and C. Hunt 2011. Online coaching: An alternative source of social support for female entrepreneurs during venture creation. *International Small Business Journal* 29(4): 345–359.

Glaser, B., and A. Strauss 1967. *The Discovery of Grounded Theory: Strategies for Qualitative Research.* New York: Aldine.

Granovetter, M. 1985. Economic action and social structure: The problem of embeddedness. *American Journal of Sociology* 91(3): 481–510.

Hamilton, N. 2002. Putting a face on our food: How state and local food policies can promote the new agriculture. *Drake Journal of Agriculture and Law* 7: 407–442.

Harris, J., H. Sapienza, and N. Bowie 2009. Ethics and entrepreneurship. *Journal of Business Venturing* 24 (5): 407–418.

Hinrichs, C.C. 2000. Embeddedness and local food systems: Notes on two types of direct agricultural market. *Journal of Rural Studies* 16(3): 295–303.

Hmieleski, K., and M. Ensley 2007. A contextual examination of new venture performance: Entrepreneur leadership behavior, top management team heterogeneity, and environmental dynamism. *Journal of Organizational Behavior* 28(7): 865–889.

King, R., and R. Levine 1993. Finance, entrepreneurship and growth. *Journal of Monetary Economics* 32 (3): 513–542.

Lepak, D., K. Smith, and M. Taylor 2007. Value creation and value capture: A multilevel perspective. *Academy of Management Review* 32(1): 180–194.

Levkoe, C.Z. 2011. Towards a transformative food politics. *Local Environment: The International Journal of Justice and Sustainability* 16(7): 687–705.

MacKenzie, D. and Y. Millo 2003. Constructing a market, performing theory: The historical sociology of a financial derivatives exchange. *American Journal of Sociology* 109(1): 107–145.

Mars, M., and H. Schau 2017. What is local food entrepreneurship? Variations in the commercially and socially oriented features of entrepreneurship in the Southeastern Arizona local food system. *Rural Sociology* DOI: 10.1111/ruso.12197

Mirchandani, K. 1999. Feminist insight on gendered work: New directions in research on women and entrepreneurship. *Gender, Work and Organization* 6(4): 224–235.

Mount, P. 2012. Growing local food: Scale and local food systems governance. *Agriculture and Human Values* 29(1): 107–121.

Nelson, R., and S. Winter 1974. Neoclassical vs. evolutionary theories of economic growth: Critique and prospectus. *The Economic Journal* 84: 886–905.

Pender, J.L., B.A. Weber, T.G. Johnson, and J.M. Fannin eds. 2014. *Rural Wealth Creation.* New York: Routledge.

Roelvink, G. 2010. Collective action and the politics of affect. *Emotion, Space and Society*, 3(2): 111–118.

Shane, S., and S. Venkataraman 2000. The promise of entrepreneurship as a field of research. *Academy of Management Review* 25(1): 217–226.

Szasz, A. 2007. *Shopping Our Way to Safety: How We Changed from Protecting the Environment to Protecting Ourselves*. Minneapolis, MN: University of Minnesota Press.

Tolbert, C., T. Lyson, and M. Irwin 1998. Local capitalism, civic engagement, and socioeconomic well-being. *Social Forces* 77(2): 401–427.

Tolbert, C., T. Lyson, M. Irwin, and A. Nucci 2002. Civic community in small-town America: How civic welfare is influenced by local capitalism and civic engagement. *Rural Sociology* 67(1): 90–113.

Weber, M. 2013 (1903) *The Protestant Ethic and the Spirit of Capitalism*. New York: Merchant Books.

Xiao, J.J., M.J. Alhabeeb, G.S. Hong, and G.W. Haynes 2001. Attitude toward risk and risk- taking behavior of business-owning families. *Journal of Consumer Affairs*, 35(2): 307–325.

18

COFFEE MICRO-MILLS IN COSTA RICA

A non-cooperative path to regenerative agriculture?

Maria del Milagro Nuñez-Solis, Christopher Rosin, and Nazmun Ratna

Introduction

In this chapter, we examine coffee production in Costa Rica as an insightful case study of regenerative agriculture. While the challenges of a volatile global market and an intensively managed ecosystem to sustainable coffee production are well documented, the emergence of certification schemes promoting greater social (e.g. Fair-Trade) and/or environmental (e.g. Bird-Friendly, Carbon Zero) benefits drew our collective attention as having the potential to improve the sustainability, if not the regenerative nature, of coffee production in Costa Rica. As is often the case, however, reality had already outpaced our interests. Milagro's discovery during fieldwork in the Tarrazu region that household investment in coffee micro-mills was increasingly taking the lead in alternative production chains forced us to reassess our beliefs and understandings regarding the composition of regenerative agriculture. The fact that these same households were operating outside cooperative marketing structures and abandoning their pursuit of certification directly challenged our embracing of such mechanisms as important factors in the development of regenerative agriculture. Instead, we were obliged to re-examine the potential for individualized, market-based strategies to contribute to the pursuit of regenerative agricultural as a food utopia (Stock et al. 2015)

To assess the role of micro-mills as agents of regenerative agriculture, we must first elaborate our measuring stick. Ultimately, a regenerative agriculture must offer the potential for producers to realize a viable livelihood. Our perspective on livelihoods is influenced by our engagement with the sustainable livelihoods literature – and in particular its recent developments in the context of capability approach pioneered by Sen (1999), and the work by Gibson-Graham (2006b) on the community economies that underlie collective wellbeing. A viable livelihood extends beyond material needs, to include the empowerment of individuals so that they are free to make choices they value the most and can realize a positive contribution to the collective by doing so. It also comprises a reciprocal engagement with the non-human environment that acknowledges the benefits of enhanced (and not just sustained) function and capacity of the socio-ecological community. As noted above, our definition of regenerative agriculture is unquestionably utopian – we do not expect to see it achieved. We do, however, present it as an ideal against which we can assess the achievements of a particular agri-food system.

Our challenge in the remainder of the chapter is to make a convincing argument that the experimentation associated with the innovation of the micro-mill among coffee households in Costa Rica is demonstrably aligned with the ideal of a regenerative agriculture. The evidence to support our argument is drawn from a series of qualitative interviews with members (both male and female) of coffee producing households completed between February and May 2018. In these interviews, the participants described their experimentation as thriving as a result of the new commercial relationships with specialty coffee roasters from East Asia, Europe, and the United States of America (US). Through the direct connection to roasters, coffee households have learned to manage their plantations to utilize quality differentiations recognized by buyers, to coordinate activities within households, and to share knowledge with the community. Despite the reduced importance of certification schemes in these direct relations, we also have found evidence of continued attention to the environmental impacts of coffee production extending to interests in invigorating biodiversity in plantations and across the landscape. However, before investigating the emergent empowerment of coffee households and the women of these households, we first review the context of coffee production in Costa Rica. This review demonstrates both the contribution of the coffee cooperatives to regenerative agriculture as well as its shortcomings that eventually led to the experimentation with micro-mills. We conclude the chapter with a discussion of the potential of micro-mills to realign coffee production in Costa Rica along a trajectory toward regenerative agriculture.

Coffee and the promise of development

Coffee and coffee farming have long been central to Costa Rican pursuits of a more regenerative agriculture. The national identity was founded in the image of a rural middle class of family farmers dependent on coffee coupled with a homogeneous and egalitarian society inherited from colonial times. A notable outlier in a Central American region with a long history of inequality, war, and poverty, the societal conditions in Costa Rica allowed the coffee "peasantry of the nineteenth and early twentieth centuries to transform itself into employer, self-sufficient householder, and employee classes" (Gudmundson 2014).

By the second half of the twentieth century, however, the coffee processing mills and export channels were in the hands of a powerful national oligarchy. In response, a Coffee Defense Movement of small and medium-sized farmers was born (Acuña 1987). One of their first achievements was a 1933 law that provided for annually fixed coffee prices that varied according to quality and regional designation. By the late 1950s, members of the defense movement had become the founders of cooperatives. The creation of farmer cooperatives occurred at a similar time as most of Costa Rica's social-democratic and progressive reforms.

Within this context of progressive social reforms, coffee organizations initiated a development strategy incorporating their vision of a regenerative path for coffee production. At the international level, Costa Rica contributed to the formation of the International Coffee Agreement (ICA). The ICA operated as a quota system for producing and consuming countries imposing some level of price stability in the volatile coffee commodity market. On the national stage, small-scale coffee producers negotiated fairer market conditions with the government, resulting in the foundation of coffee cooperatives. Likewise, the national banking system instituted programs for farmers to access credit through cooperatives. At the same time, large investments were made in extension and research projects, specifically funded by USAID as part of their policies to expand the green revolution in Latin America.

In Costa Rica, the green revolution promised to enhance community wellbeing by "modernizing" practices and improving the competitive advantage in coffee production. The main changes involved the introduction of dwarf varieties such as *caturra* and *catuai*, replacing high-quality and low-production varieties with average cup-quality and high-yield ones and facilitating increased density of plantations from 1100 to 4500 bushes per *manzana*.[1] The new management practices also included an associated agrichemical package of herbicides, pesticides, and inorganic fertilizers. As a result, harvest volumes doubled and the country achieved world record yields (Gudmundson 2014). The 1970s and 1980s thus became known as a golden age for Costa Rica's coffee producers. These technological innovations combined with State social welfare programs helped Costa Rica to consolidate the position of family-owned farms in contrast to the rest of Latin America (Babin 2012).

The limits of the regenerative

The golden age of coffee production in Costa Rica was short-lived, having depended on economic measures and environmental practices that were not viable in the long term. In 1989, international political economic pressures contributed to the dissolution of the ICA, corresponding with a shifting interest of consuming countries in promoting free trade. As a result, producing countries lost control over coffee prices and farmers became subject to the New York Stock Exchange's Coffee price (C-price), which is characterized by high volatility. During the past 30 years, this situation has had a strong impact on the Los Santos region where Tarrazu coffee is produced. Los Santos farmers receive a price premium of approximately US\$20 above the C-price due to their high-quality beans.[2] This is not, however, sufficient to provide a viable livelihood for households.[3] In fact, it confirms Daviron and Ponte's (2005) assessment that coffee, as a global commodity, is a paradox in which farmers scarcely derive a livelihood from the commodity that provides retailers and roasters ample profits.

The scope of regenerative coffee extends beyond commodity prices, however, to include the fuller complexities of the agri-food system. In pursuing more viable coffee production, Costa Rica must also address unsustainability of farming practices inspired by the green revolution. Environmental consequences, especially related to biodiversity, became apparent as the coffee landscape changed from a traditional forest-like to an unshaded plantation (Perfecto and Vandermeer 2015). *El cerco*, the traditional plantation with shared space for fruit trees, *musas*, subsistence horticulture, and forest, disappeared with the adoption of dwarf varieties, putting household food security at risk. Deforestation, while increasing the planting area, constricted migratory bird habitation, exacerbated soil erosion and pests (such as leaf rust), and reduced the diversity of coffee varieties.

The highly prescribed management of the intensive plantations and the inability to engage directly in the coffee market both constrain farmers' agency. Danilo, a micro-mill owner, commented that "Costa Rica's coffee production lives under two realities: you produce volume; or you look for your own management techniques and concentrate on producing quality". Coffee farmers are forced into such stark options as cooperatives and commercial mills have adopted the "volume coffee system" in which the farmers' role is reduced to cultivating, picking, and delivering the coffee berry. The resulting system in which value chain stages related to milling techniques and buyer contracts are the responsibility of the cooperatives or mills is roundly criticized by Tarrazu's farmers.

Cooperatives and certifications

Los Santos has a strong history of choosing cooperatives as the main modality of enterprise, with electricity, financial services, and agricultural production operating under this framework. In the case of coffee, Lucas mentioned, "Cooperatives are the ones that act as a regulator for transnational coffee buyers here, so they don't come and do whatever they want". What happens, however, when such social enterprises grow in capital and membership and are still linked to a commodity market that generates little value for producers? New Institutional Economics identifies the problem within traditional cooperatives that have poorly defined voting rights over capital and the allocation of benefits to members, leading to free-riding, control, and influence problems (Chaddad and Cook 2004). This situation is exacerbated in a country where clientelism is common in its institutional system (Sobrado and Rojas 2006). For farmers, it is expressed as a lack of fairness and a dogmatic adherence to the cooperative as an institution. In Evelio's words:

> People have grown accustomed to not seeing the reality. … The word "coopera-tive" gets polarized when we have an enterprise valued in the millions of dollars in capital and assets. … So, [it seems] we have a capitalist enterprise instead of a cooperative. A cooperative is founded for the development of both parties; but it is inconceivable that one of the parties grows in a disproportionate manner and the other descends into an immoral inequality. … There is no way that the person that is giving the principal resource [coffee] is going through the situations we are right now and [we] farmers are quiet on our farm bearing with it.

Coffee farmers' reasons for leaving the cooperatives and establishing a micro-enterprise were many. For Tano, it was an issue of pursuing new opportunities:

> When I began to produce organic, I went to talk to the director to see if they were going to receive my coffee. I told him, "I want to promote organic coffee and I already passed the 5 years of transition". His answer was, "no we can't. It's too complicated".

It is also apparent that coffee certifications – largely associated with the cooperatives or commercial mills – have not contributed to regenerative coffee production. Whereas development agencies and some academics saw certifications as a pathway to regenerative practices, empirical research has shown mixed results (Lyon 2009; Jaffee 2014). Certifications for coffee are largely initiated in the Global North to set traceability standards and assure consumers of minimum standards of quality, respect for basic human rights, and environmental outcomes. They were expected to foster an "alternative market" with stable and higher prices and enhanced wellbeing for coffee communities (David et al. 2016). By the 2000s, all cooperatives and commercial mills in Los Santos were engaged with mainstream certifications such as Rain Forest, Café Practices, and Fair-Trade. However, farmers are critical of how price premiums have been allocated, subject to the structural limitations of cooperatives. Ronny's experience is an important example:

10 years ago the director of the cooperative brought the idea of differentiated coffees. It was called "sustainable coffees". Seventeen coffee producers began with the
project. We were engaged; but it resulted in a very unpleasant experience. Our
production levels dropped from 350 fanegas to 82; our finances felt apart. ... The
worst of all was that the promised price premium never came. We changed to
a new program, Starbucks' Café Practices, the same discourse that we were going
to receive a differentiated price, and again the premium price never came.
I remember Starbucks people here doing research and us investing in all the things
the certification required. ... My farm became like a forest, with very low productivity and none of a premium price that could compensate. ... I was disappointed;
but the good thing we achieved was to put into our heads the idea of being environmentally conscious when working our land.

The current state of the coffee agri-food system in Costa Rica appears far from the idealized
engine of an empowered, rural middle class envisioned in the 1950s, with neither the
formation of cooperatives nor the introduction of green revolution technologies ensuring its
economic or ecological viability. These challenges are, however, also engendering a new
form of experimentation among coffee producing households.

Micro-mill households: more-than-active food producers?

Micro-mill households are family-owned enterprises, with farms ranging from 3 to 20
hectares. They have invested in basic equipment to crush, dry, and package coffee berries.
The objective is to sell micro-lots directly to the specialty coffee market overseas. Buyers
pay according to their own assessment of the coffee quality, delinking earnings from the
C-price. Many of the micro-mill households interviewed have dropped out of cooperatives
and conventional "volume coffee" production. Their actions anticipated the rejection of the
inherited unsustainable coffee production practices, while also experimenting with different
ways to challenge the *status quo*.

Carolan (2017a, 2017b) has used the concept of "more-than-active food citizens" to
distinguish people who, rather than limiting themselves to being food consumers, undertake
actions towards the improvement of their foodscapes. Similarly, we picture micro-mill
households as "more-than-active food producers" in contraposition to farmers whose actions
are limited to the current coffee system: holding a cooperative membership, being satisfied
with discussions in the annual assemblies, and accepting the faith dictated by the
cooperatives in respect to their coffee livelihoods. Micro-mill households, by comparison,
are actively experimenting in the pursuit of fairer market relations. They seek to discover
the workings of the world of coffee beyond the gates of a *recividor*[4] and the means to realize
the environmental advantages of producing quality rather than volume.

Likewise, micro-mills have become a coffee enterprise that expands the diversity of
economic opportunities in Los Santos. Gibson-Graham (2006b) distinguishes sites of
economic difference in communities where the economy is not pre-configured by specific
types of enterprises, forms of payments, or transactions. Instead, non-market and non-
financial social relations coexist with market-led initiatives, opening opportunities for co-
experimentation, new economic identities, and networks. Micro-mill households are linked
to specialty coffee roasters, a movement known as the "Third Wave"[5] of coffee. Their aim
is to set just and sustainable relations with coffee producers and communities through
empathetic relations focused on quality and direct trade (Gyllensten, 2017). Third Wave

roasters buy high-quality micro-lots of coffee from specific farms using direct contact with suppliers to ensure traceability. Such contact also acts as a mechanism for sharing knowledge and working hand-to-hand with the household to promote desirable artisanal processes. Josue describes these buyers as:

> People that are just like us or even smaller [a micro-enterprise]. They are people that just began with a roaster, even paying for rent and all the services. People think that, because they are from Japan or the United States, they have a lot of money; but most of our buyers are small roasters that have 2 or 3 cafes.

These global buyer–farmer relations show that empathetic markets are not limited to initiatives such as consuming local. Carolan (2017b) argues that, beyond concentrating on the "local distance" of food, we should reflect on its "social distance". The objective is to create foodscapes where social wellbeing and empathy are the drivers of relations. Buyers and micro-mill households achieve such relations with buyers traveling to the origin, establishing long-term relations with family-based enterprises, and negotiating prices that recognize the qualities of coffee. Furthermore, some volunteer on the coffee farms contributing to coffee picking, helping in the milling processes, and doing communal work (e.g., planting parks, painting churches) to learn more about coffee livelihoods and sustainable farm practices. Ronny captured the impact of these relations, stating "Our effort. That is what the buyer values. Our effort". Such producer–buyer relations differ from "cold market relations". Ramiro acknowledges the buyer's act of "sending us coffee packages so we can see how our coffee is being sold. To me that's like a trophy, the result of our efforts are in those bags". Luis considers it a learning opportunity, "This year a Korean came with a coffee processing idea and we ended up doing his experiment. Then a Japanese buyer came and gave us new ideas. So we learned from them."

Micro-mills households' self-awareness and women empowerment

An essential element of micro-mill households' activities as more-than-active food producers is the emergent process of experimentation. In part, they are motivated by low coffee prices. "We couldn't continue giving our coffee to a transnational. We needed to look for an alternative. ... I always tell people that, if we had continued producing conventional coffee, we would already be bankrupt" summarized Monica's justifications. Micro-mills, therefore, offer a mechanism for the economic empowerment of coffee-producing households in Los Santos.

The pioneers of experimentation with micro-mills were La Candelilla Estate (owned by eight families) and Cafesito (an individual), both of which were established in 2000.[6] La Candelilla had the financial resources to gain the legal permits for industrial mills. After earning Starbucks' highest category for quality coffee from a mill, a Black Apron, the families invested the associated reward in technological innovation, becoming the first coffee enterprise to process high-quality micro-lots of coffee and reduce processing wastage. As Danilo remarked, "if people were to take their coffee to be prepared at a conventional mill, they were risking the loss of at least 4 quintals of green coffee, because it gets stuck in different parts of such big machineries".

By contrast, Cafesito's experimentation process was rooted in a commitment to produce organic coffee. In the owner's words:

Learning was the greatest difficulty. I used to ask people at the traditional mills about the processes, and their reality was very different. The way to learn was here, hands on; and another difficulty was that I needed to have a low profile because there was a big cooperative just by my side that wouldn't like it.

Critics such as Fisher (2017) and Daviron and Ponte (2005) consider efforts to de-commoditize coffee through the intervention of specialty coffee buyers to be illusive given the failure to address the paradox of the coffee commodity chain. This argument holds that, despite higher prices, retailers and roasters continue to claim most of the benefit from the symbolic values while producers realize only a small premium on the material value of coffee. The micro-mill households refer, however, to the value of their experiences within the specialty coffee world, rather than decrying the unfairness of global economic forces. In particular, they embrace the potential to set a price floor for their coffee (as opposed to depending on the C-price and a negotiated premium subject to the cupping score). Maritza sees it as a form of motivation:

We think the love we put into our farm and the coffee processing is acknowledged by the client. We try to do things better every year. … When they come here, they recognize that by feeling the soil, watching the trees. It's like they're falling in love.

The extent to which buyers claim the symbolic value from producers is subject to debate. From the producers' comments, realizing symbolic value is not so elusive in the Los Santos case. Manuel's experience shows a different understanding:

I never realized the things that were coming. I got into this; but other things came that made it more interesting. That is why I feel passionate about it: I like to welcome people, be a good host, drink a good coffee, talk about coffee, have a nice dinner and create an experience out of all this.

Likewise, Ana speaks for many micro-mill households when noting that participating in the cooperative system had constrained agency and knowledge:

We did not know the treasure we had in our farms. … We never had the opportunity to meet the buyers while in the cooperative; [and] since we left the cooperative, we know what happens to our coffee after we deliver it. We know which coffee goes to which buyer. … With the cooperative, there was no coffee differentiation. We did not have exotic varieties or add any value to it.

More significantly, women[7] have assumed a more empowered role within the micro-mill households. Conventional coffee households in Costa Rica follow the traditional role of a male as the head of household in charge of all farming activities, household income and expenditure, and land-use. This is true even in cases where the land is an asset inherited by a woman. Women would perform the household chores, family care, and any work related to the coffee activity – especially during harvesting time – would be considered unpaid help.

By comparison, micro-mill households have become a space where women are finding opportunities for greater participation. They demonstrate agency in the management and use of their income as well as in decision-making within the family enterprise, and in processing and management tasks. They showed more participation in coffee sector activities and off-farm entrepreneurial initiatives (e.g., tourism and local marketing of roasted coffee). For Lina and Rita, two sisters in charge of all micro-mill activities, the major opposition they faced came from their community:

> a buyer wouldn't say, "we are not going to buy your coffee because you are women." That does not happen. … It's more related to the culture of this town, saying that we couldn't do it because we are women; but, to some extent, I have seen that it has turned into admiration. [People saying,] "That man's daughters were able to do it. We should do it too".

Women are using a specific initiative to participate in coffee training activities. Damaris' experience is representative of that of other women in this context:

> When we began, I took one training on coffee ovens. … There were no other women when I began. Men would be murmuring because I was there; but, since I like to talk, they got used to me. Now you can see a lot more women at coffee events: wives, daughters; but, when I began, it was me and 30 other men.

Maritza has engaged more in a conscious process of fighting Los Santos' "machista" culture. She states that, as an outsider from San Jose, she had to find different strategies for acceptance within her husband's family. It was necessary to show people she knows about coffee. She refers to her experience saying,

> Yes, I have broken the "machismo" barrier; but even though I'm like that [an empowered women], my husband has known how to manage the situation and even taken advantage of it. I feel he has been one of the few that has given me my place. If he wouldn't give me the opportunity or define roles, that would have meant fighting against him too.

Nonetheless, "machismo" and gender roles persist in Costa Rican coffee activities, meaning that the participation of women in Los Santos coffee production requires structural changes. That said, drawing inspiration from *second wave feminist movement* thinking, Gibson-Graham (2006a) argues that "where there is an empowered woman, a small revolution is happening". Thus, the emergent gender relations in micro-mill households represent an important example of women's fight for more significant influence and position in the coffee commodity chain. There remain, however, many challenges as Tania explains:

> I have two disadvantages: I'm a woman and I'm young. At the beginning, people would not take me seriously. In the first place, it is very hard to learn how to manage a small enterprise and I have to assume the extra challenge of people taking me seriously just because I'm a young woman. That means more work. I feel society is changing, [but] not as fast as I would like it to.

Community

Most micro-mill households are fourth generation coffee producers, with acute awareness of the efforts of their grandparents and parents to create better market conditions within the cooperative movement. When asked how they collaborate with their communities, their answers focused on aspects such as employment, better salaries during harvest, revitalization of the economy, improved international coffee image, or promotion of local tourism. Throughout the conversations, participants reflected on caring, sharing, and solidarity among coffee farmers. Evelio and Rosa shared some of the experiences they have had:

> We consider the motivation we give to other families – to believe this can be done – is an act that benefits others. We have had the good fortune to meet many people that, in hard moments, remind us that it can be done, to keep on going … After we took this step, many people have asked us to show how they should begin. It's not one or two; it has been like six new micro-mills.

One of the biggest struggles involves efforts to build an association. The first attempt began in 2013, but lasted for only three years. It included more than 40 local micro-mill households who wanted to build a shared packing facility for green coffee and to host an annual coffee fair where people around the country could learn about the different coffees from the region. Gustavo suggested their main weakness was that "the association exclusively focused on organizing the fair" and, as Tano mentioned, "after each of the three fairs, there were financial losses". Despite this failure, a common topic in the interviews and a product of our focus group was the importance of uniting to directly ship their coffee and, thereby, limit the power of local and international traders. As Nelson argued:

> There is still a long way we need to go. We need to find the way for our kids to also become entrepreneurs, to finish a university career and be the ones going abroad to sell the coffee. If only one family tries to do this, it is going to be really hard. We need to unite. We used to have that association and we left it aside.

The micro-mill households are clear that the only way to achieve certain goals and solutions is through collaboration, which includes cooperatives as well. Although one cooperative suspended micro-mill owners and accused micro-mills of disloyalty, the households are optimistic that they can work together. Ramiro explained the current relations by saying, "I do not get why cooperatives, with the logistics they have, with all their infrastructure, why they don't sell all the coffee produced by micro-mills. They have everything, but instead they war with us."

Farming and environment practices

To this point, our analysis has addressed the potential contribution of micro-mill experimentation to regenerative social dynamics at the household, community, and international scales. It would be remiss, however, not to reflect on the extent to which such experimentation involves environmental outcomes associated with the emergence of a more regenerative coffee foodscape. While our research did not involve ecological analysis, an established literature points to the crucial role of coffee management practices in the provision of ecosystem services[8] and the establishment of biodiversity refuges (Perfecto and Vandermeer 2015). In order to account for the environmental implications of micro-mill experimentation, we examine how micro-mill households express their environmental subjectivities.

Agrawal (2005) proposes the concept of environmentalities to account for the subject positions created in response to the governance of environmental resources. Assessing a case of community forestry in India, he determined that people assumed more environmentally aware exploitation of forest resources when decentralized governance attributed greater agency to the community. By comparison, micro-mill households in Los Santos have assumed new environmentalities in response to their emergent roles and associated possibilities within the coffee commodity chain. The basic knowledge of how to manage farms in a sustainable manner came from their early engagement with coffee certifications, as Manuel recalls, "climate change was something I always have cared about. When I was part of the cooperative I always tried to be part of Café Practices and Rainforest certifications." However, their interest in these practices was discouraged by the lack of compensation for their investment in the form of better prices or recognized quality standards. Furthermore, their efforts were not respected by the cooperatives who mixed certified coffee with undesignated product of lower quality. The situation was exacerbated by the arrival of leaf rust disease in 2011, which affected more than 68% of Costa Rican coffee plantations and reduced yields by 38% (Banch 2013).

The influence of market certification schemes was reinforced by more recent State intervention that recognizes the importance of coffee in "payment for ecosystem services" (PES) programs. The implementation of PES has directed actions towards greenhouse gas mitigation and agro-ecological practices for coffee. Nonetheless, micro-mill households credit their closer engagement within the specialty coffee market as the primary motivation behind farming practices that contribute towards a more regenerative agriculture. The emergent market relations are a platform for recognizing their sustainable practices and provide sufficient profit to facilitate reinvestment in the plantation. According to Ronny:

> We began to prepare for climate change 20 years ago and now it is a strength of our farm. … One thing the coffee buyer likes is the way we treat our plants and properties. We have a protected [forest] area, we protect the water, we work with microorganisms and we have a lot of fauna. So they like that.

Motivations for using sustainable environmental practices vary among micro-mill households. For Lucas, sustainable practice is an issue of common sense:

> We care for the environment. Because of climate change we are losing nature, and what are we going to leave for the next generations? It's an issue of being responsible. … I need to protect the animals and the birds because they are part of the diversity that Earth needs for surviving.

Focusing on quality rather than volume has an important role in reducing agrichemical inputs. In this context, practices have emerged to exploit sustainable and organic techniques in order to achieve better cupping scores. Lina summarizes the changes through her observations that, "The coffee plant seems a lot healthier; but this is because of the type of care we give to them. Yields are lower with these techniques, but they realize better quality and that is what we care about." Similarly, Maritza and Nelson commented, "You will see coffee farms with a very good yield, but it is unshaded coffee. We know those plants will weaken very quickly. Our plants might not give excessive yields, but they are healthier." A study of the trade-offs between increased productivity, sustainability, and high-quality flavour profiles in Tarrazu (Castro-Tanzi et al. 2012) supports the practices of micro-mill households. Farmers with high yield systems had poorer soils because of plant nutrient extraction and farmers compensated with inorganic fertilizers, resulting in soil acidification that affected production and quality.

Environmental techniques used by micro-mill households include organic soil fertilizers and compost produced with the dry coffee pulp. Foliar fertilizers are also made using microorganisms collected from leaf litter and N, CaO, Mg salts. They encourage each other to replace herbicides with manual weed control. In addition, they conduct soil analyses every two years, build terraces to reduce soil erosion, plant live fences and trees for semi-shaded and shaded coffee, use agro-ecological pest controls, and reuse water for milling activities. Their explanation of these changing practices indicated a belief that their plantations were regenerative. For example, Santiago commented, "Yes, when you use shade and use the machete to cut bad weeds, it looks better. You can see more organic material. As a whole the farm benefits.. Josue notes regenerative results of using compost: "Yes, the soil regenerates if you have enough compost. Your soils do regenerate." Likewise, many of them express a sense of pride in not using herbicides. According to Rodrigo,

> I always use our neighbour as an example. He does everything that doesn't need to be done: there the soil is like moss because of the herbicides, the rivers do not have even one tree, just a string of water passes through the rocks. On our farm, we have two springs and they are protected by forest. All the organic material that goes to the coffee comes from the pigs, the hens and the brush.

Their decision-making with regard to farming practices is an expression of their agency within an agri-food system dominated by agrichemicals and high-intensity practices. Luis described the value of their local knowledge compared to that of a commercial agronomist:

> There is no better agricultural consultant [ingeniero] than us. Only we know the coffee plots we have, what is going wrong and what needs to be done. We can ask a consultant, but we take what we consider to be good and use it. We are the ones that have learned those things.

Rodrigo offers examples of such decisions:

> I see people every year using insecticides to "cure" the soil, but I never have done it. It smells horrible, like that thing called *Conter.*[9] We have not even tried to use it, because the little animals and birds eat it and they die.

Of equal relevance is Danilo's perception of the coffee farm as the basis for food security, "To me a coffee farm is a 'cerco' like my grandparents used to call it. It had bananas, casava, arracache, sweet potatoes."

The extent to which agro-ecological based agriculture is accepted best practice in the Costa Rican coffee sector is another challenge. Micro-mill households remain committed to them due, in part, to the stable income they receive within the specialty coffee market. All of the farming techniques associated with agro-ecological practice require more labour and dedication to the farm, demands that many coffee farmers cannot meet because of off-farm employment required to compensate for coffee low prices.

Conclusion

Through our investigation of the Los Santos foodscape and the Costa Rican coffee system, we understand regenerative agriculture as a trajectory towards a food utopia. For both the country and the coffee farmers, regenerative strategies have evolved in response to historical circumstances. What once appeared as a pathway to a desired outcome (i.e., green revolution technologies and international coffee agreements), was later challenged by unforeseen consequences (environmental degradation and fraught global trade relations). In an effort to realign coffee production along the utopian trajectory, coffee producers and cooperatives are experimenting with innovations that attribute new qualities to their product. Our analysis also illustrates that pathways for regenerative agriculture can be initiated by the State or private actors and networks. The experimentation of the micro-mill households is a prime example of the latter in which individual action has enabled the empowerment of farmers and household members along a new trajectory towards a more regenerative coffee system. As stated in the introduction, our criteria for regenerative agriculture include enhancement of democratic food production, community and household wellbeing, caring for the non-human including ecological regeneration and market relations where surplus is humanized. The market-led experimentation with micro-mills has enabled collaborative market relations, increased participation of women, facilitated interest in sustainable environmental practices, enhanced self-awareness, and invigorated market agency.

While direct economic and non-economic benefits accrue to the households, experimentation with micro-mills involves hard work, compromise among family members and even financial sacrifice. In recounting the benefits of specialty coffees, participants focused on the agency they have acquired. Adding value to their coffee has allowed them to access better prices; but they also value their new knowledge of coffee processing practices. Likewise, the reduced migration rates among young family members as the processing activities of coffee become more attractive is identified as an improvement in family wellbeing. Not least important has been the empowerment of female household members within a culture that considers women incapable of managing coffee related activities.

The environmental and community benefits are not as tangible based on the research conducted. There is clear evidence that the economy of empathy created through specialty coffee markets provides strong incentives to adopt agro-ecological practice, although the outcomes have not been measured. This enterprise model also creates empathetic relations within the participants' wider community, although at this stage of experimentation, evidence of an emergent shared economy or community-being-in-common (Gibson-Graham 2006b) is relatively weak. The interviews did not identify an explicit mechanism of collaboration among buyers, traders, and micro-mill households with a direct impact on the local community. That said, a strong undercurrent of community responsibility and a desire to share successful knowledge and practice flows through the discourse of the micro-mill households, suggesting that their experimentation is aligned with a food utopia that comprises a comprehensive form of regenerative agriculture.

Discussion questions

1. How can researchers account for social dimensions of regenerative agriculture and what theoretical approaches can be used to investigate agricultural realities and case studies?
2. What mechanisms are available to coffee producing communities in their interactions with buyers that would empower the creation of more cohesive and equitable community market relations associated with the specialty coffee system?

3. What insights does the experience of the Costa Rican coffee households provide for analyses of regenerative agriculture that acknowledge the potential for producers to realize wellbeing benefits irrespective of the form of market relations (i.e., capitalist, cooperative, etc.)?

Notes

1 One manzana equals to 7500m^2.
2 Tarrazu's coffee is known as Strictly Hard Coffee (SHC) Arabica, which indicates that (while green) it will not lose its flavours in storage.
3 In 2018, cooperatives paid US $160 per fanega (46kg of green coffee beans). Production costs for that fanega total $115 in inputs, labour, and taxes.
4 This is the name of the place where they deliver the coffee berries.
5 Fisher (2017) identifies three waves of coffee, including: First Wave marked by buyer demands for quality and unadulterated product beginning in 1950s, followed by increasing price competition among retailers in the 1960s; Second Wave, in the 1970s, with the emergence of Starbucks and the "latte revolution" and consumer demand for variety in origin, roast and preparation. The Second Wave also involved increased attention to social conditions through Fair-Trade certification and "sustainable coffees" and emergence of "specialty coffee".
6 The first micro-mill to ever exist in Central America was in Tarrazu and went bankrupt in 1998 due to management problems.
7 Women's empowerment from an economic perspective refers to the capacity of women to exercise agency or control over their life in terms of decision-making, income and its investment, time use, access to means of production and political participation (Pepper 2016–17; Meemken and Qaim 2018).
8 "Shade trees perform important ecological functions in the agroecosystem, such as providing organic matter and in the case of nitrogen-fixing trees, increasing the amount of nitrogen in the soil. They are also involve with microclimate regulation, wind protection, weed suppression, refuge for natural enemies and many other ecological function and ecosystem services" (Perfecto and Vandermeer 2015, 27).
9 Refers to the insecticide *Counter FC 15% G.*

Further reading

Carolan, M. (2017). More-than-active food citizens: A longitudinal and comparative study of alternative and conventional eaters. *Rural Sociology*, 82(2), 197–225. doi:10.1111/ruso.12120
Gibson-Graham, J. K., J. Cameron, and S. Healy (2013). *Take Back the Economy* (Vol. 1). Minneapolis, MN: University of Minnesota.
O'Hara, C., and F. Clement (2018). Power as agency: A critical reflection on the measurement of women's empowerment in the development sector. *World Development*, 106, 111–123. doi:10.1016/j.worlddev.2018.02.002
Stock, P., M. Carolan, and C. Rosin (2015). *Food Utopias. Reimagining Citizenship, Ethics and Community.* New York: Routledge.

References

Acuña, V.-H. (1987). La ideología de los pequeños y medianos productores cafetaleros costarricenses (1900–1961). *Revista de Historia*, 1987(1), 137–159.
Agrawal, A. (2005). *Environmentality. Technologies of Government and the Making of Subjects.* London: Duke University Press.
Babin, N. (2012). *Agrarian Change, Agroecological Transformation and the Coffee Crisis in Costa Rica.* Doctor of Philosophy in Environmental Studies, University of California, Santa Cruz. Retrieved from https://escholarship.org/uc/item/29h9p44k
Banch, O. (2013). *XX Informe Estado de la Nacion en Desarrollo Humano Sostenible. Agricultura y sostenibilidad.* San Jose, Costa Rica: Estado de la Nacion.

Carolan, M. (2017a). More-than-active food citizens: A longitudinal and comparative study of alternative and conventional eaters. *Rural Sociology*, 82(2), 197–225. doi:10.1111/ruso.12120

Carolan, M. (2017b). *No One Eats Alone: Food as a Social Enterprise*. Washington, DC: Island Press.

Castro-Tanzi, S., T. Dietsch, N. Urena, L. Vindas, and M. Chandler (2012). Analysis of management and site factors to improve the sustainability of smallholder coffee production in Tarrazú, Costa Rica. *Agriculture, Ecosystems and Environment*, 155, 172–181. doi:https://doi.org/10.1016/j.agee.2012.04.013

Chaddad, F. R., and M. L. Cook (2004). Understanding new cooperative models: An ownership control right typology. *Review of Agricultural Economics*, 26(3), 348–360.

David, L., R. Juliane, and M. Stephan (2016). The political dynamics of sustainable coffee: Contested value regimes and the transformation of sustainability. *Journal of Management Studies*, 53(3), 364–401. doi:10.1111/joms.12144

Daviron, B., and S. Ponte (2005). *The Coffee Paradox. Global Market, Commodity Trade and the Elusive Promise of Development*. London: Zed Books.

Fisher, E. (2017). *Quality and Inequality: Taste, Value, and Power in the Third Wave Coffee Market* (Vol. 17/4). Cologne: Max-Planck Institute for the Study of Societies.

Gibson-Graham, J. K. (2006a). *End of Capitalism (As We Knew It): A Feminist Critique of Political Economy*. Minneapolis, MN: University of Minnesota Press.

Gibson-Graham, J. K. (2006b). *Postcapitalist Politics*. Minneapolis, MN: University of Minnesota Press.

Gibson-Graham, J. K., J. Cameron, and S. Healy (2013). *Take Back the Economy* (Vol. 1). Minneapolis, MN: University of Minnesota Press.

Gudmundson, L. (2014). On green revolutions and golden beans: Memories and metaphors of Costa Rican Coffee Co-op Founders. *Agricultural History Society*, 88(4), 538–565. doi:10.3098/ah.2014.088.4.538

Gyllensten, B. (2017). *Micro Mills, Specialty Coffee and Relationships. Following the Supply Chain from Costa Rica to Norway*.

Jaffee, D. (2014). *Brewing Justice. Fair Trade Coffee, Sustainability, and Survival*. Berkeley, CA: University of California Press.

Lyon, S. (2009). "'What good will two more trees do?" The political economy of sustainable coffee certification, local livelihoods and identities. *Landscape Research*, 34(2), 223–240. doi:10.1080/01426390802390673

Meemken, E.-M., and M. Qaim (2018). Can private food standards promote gender equality in the small farm sector? *Journal of Rural Studies*, 58, 39–51. doi:10.1016/j.jrurstud.2017.12.030

Pepper, A. (2016–2017). *Value Chain Development, Gender and Women's Empowerment in Ghana*. Ndiaye, W. (Ed.). Dakar, Senegal: World Food Program. Retrieved from https://docs.wfp.org/api/documents/WFP-0000022433/download/

Perfecto, I., and J. Vandermeer (2015). *Coffee Agroecology. A New Approach to Understanding Agricultural Biodiversity, Ecosystem Services and Sustainable Development* (Vol. 1). New York: Routledge, Taylor & Francis group.

Sen, A. (1999). *Development as Freedom*. New York: Oxford University Press.

Sobrado, M., and J. Rojas (2006). *America Latina: Crisis del Estado clientelista y la construccion de republicas ciudadanad*. Heredia, Costa Rica: EUNA.

Specialty Coffee Association, S. (2017). Protocols and best practices. Retrieved from https://sca.coffee/research/protocols-best-practices/

Stock, P., M. Carolan, and C. Rosin (2015). *Food Utopias. Reimagining Citizenship, Ethics and Community*. New York: Routledge.

19

COMMONS AND COMMONING TO BUILD ECOLOGICALLY REPARATORY FOOD SYSTEMS

Tomaso Ferrando

Enough of 'more of the same but with a nicer face'

Despite the lack of a single definition of sustainability, the idea that 'a sustainable future is possible' increasingly shapes the political, practical, and intellectual imaginary of public and private actors across the transnational food system. However, since the 2030 Agenda for Sustainable Development and the 17 Sustainable Development Goals (SDGs) were officially embraced in 2015 by all the Member States of the United Nations, transnational corporations, and multiple civil society organizations, the number of people suffering from hunger has constantly increased, returning to levels of a decade ago (WHO 2018a). Similarly, the production of negative externalities by the global agri-food system (in the form of greenhouse gases, depletion of soil and other resources, loss of biodiversity, etc.) appear unstoppable.

From farm to fork, the food system is failing to achieve the social and environmental goals enshrined in the sustainable paradigm. It may sound as a failure, but not for everyone: large companies are consolidating upstream and downstream the phase of agricultural production; shareholders are rewarded with the distribution of increasing profits; financial investors are enlarging their wealth by betting on commodity markets, future production, and the necessity of land. In this context of tensions and incoherence, sustainability as an attempt to do things better seems incapable of challenging the reproduction of patterns of accumulation and inequality. On the contrary, it seems to be compatible with them.

Take the example of coffee, which is known to be one of the most traded 'food commodities' in the world: international traders and roasters understood, probably earlier than policy makers and academics, that climate change and the uncontrolled exploitation of soil and water may compromise future production. In one word, they realized that short-term and unconstrained market-based approaches to coffee production exclusively dictated by the desire to increase production, expand markets, and generate more profit could produce a future with no more farmers (because of the Green Revolution-like effect of dependency on inputs, the increased cost of production, and the intensification of global competition) or no more coffee (because of the exhaustion of nature). The solution? Implementing 'environmentally and socially 'sustainable' practices' that guarantee the reproduction of coffee berries on trees and the permanence of farmers on their land. Sold as a win-win-win solution (for industry, planet, and small-scale producers), this approach may guarantee the survival of people and the planet but it is not addressing the underlying and historical inequalities that characterize a very concentrated food chain where farmers are completely dependent on buyers. Moreover, it ignores the intersectionality of gender, race, and class More importantly, sustainable practices that guarantee production, export and wages do not depart from the idea that food is anything more than a commodity to be sold and bought rather than an essential component of human lives and the outcome of a complex ecological system (Vivero Pol et al. 2018). Even worse, the search for a quick fix rather than the promotion of systemic transformations legitimizes the extraction and accumulation of value by a few actors who trade, roast, and retail coffee beans produced all over the world.

In this context, I interpreted the editors' invitation to think about the shift away from sustainability into regenerative food systems as the recognition of the insufficiency of the current ideological framework and the desire to go beyond the 'more of the same but with a better face' approach to people and planet. If sustainable practices are simply conceived as the need to identify the point of maximum exploitation of soil and people without compromising their reproduction, there can be no regeneration because there is no emancipation from the ideas and practices that subordinate nature to people and create hierarchies between groups of people. A sustainable food system constructed around greener and fairer practices would simply postpone planetary extinction or the rebellion against the actors responsible for it. Thus, the change must be deeper than a mere comparative aspiration to something better than we have: we need to think of a just, fair, and ecological food system based on radical new premises.

To imagine a regenerative food system, we must be ambitious and challenge notions that are often taken for granted and normalized. In particular, we should: a) abandon the dualistic idea of nature and society as separate and adopt a vision of the relationship between nature and society based on the idea of an interconnected ecology; b) move away from the obsession with progress and growth and conceive a food system that is capable of achieving future inter-generational justice while being rooted in the redressal of historical injustices; c) question the commodity-based understanding of food and realize that ecological and reparatory justice cannot be achieved in a context where food, an essential element of life and a gift of nature, is treated as nothing more than a 'thing'. The notions of commons and commoning that are introduced in this chapter provide a static and dynamic opportunity to move away from sustainability and think about socio-environmental regeneration as based on different premises for different future horizons.

Because a radical shift requires a strong awareness of the present and a powerful imagination, this chapter begins with a brief account of the non-regenerative nature of the dominant food regime based on expanding corporate control and the priority of financial investors and financial motives over the needs of people and planet (Raworth 2017). In this context, the next section presents sustainability discourses as an opportunity not to address the historical and structural problems but to reproduce the current patterns of extraction, subordination, and accumulation. Then, the chapter looks backward to suggest that no regenerative future can be constructed without taking seriously the colonial origins of global food and the multiple commodifications (of nature, labour, gender, food, etc.) that underpin the capitalist food system. The final section offers a vision of a regenerative future based on the two pillars of multiple food systems as a commons (as a web of interconnected human and non-human actors) and commoning (as the process of interacting with each other, nurturing nature, and – more importantly – moving towards socio and environmental justice). In this vision, food is a non-commodity at the center of an ecological organization structured around the principles of anti-colonialism, anti-patriarchy, equality, social justice, and the recognition of the inherent co-construction of nature and society as intrinsically connected.

Embracing sustainability, but for whom?

In September 2015, 193 heads of state adopted the 2030 Agenda for Sustainable Development and the 17 Sustainable Development Goals. A quick research for the words 'sustainable food' on Web of Science shows a constant (SDGs) increase from the 992 academic articles published in 2015 containing them to 1,111 in 2016 and 1,625 in 2018 (Web of Science 2019). At the same time, big food companies are #EmbracingSustainability (Coca-Cola 2019) and promoting projects aimed at integrating socio-environmental elements in their business structures. For example, companies representing almost 30% of the US food and beverage market (including Unilever, Campbell Soup, Smithfield Farmers, Walmart, and Kellogg's) have pledged their commitment to the SUSTAIN toolbox, a series of "technologies and practices, data, and advisory information on sustainable field nutrient management and efficiency, water management and soil health" (Grady 2016). Others have been focusing on water risks (Ceres 2018), waste, gender, hunger, and any of the other SDGs, that are often, picked and prioritized according to the company's profile and image. The underpinning narrative, clearly visible on Cola-Cola's sustainability page, is that 'Profitability is important, but not at any cost. People matter. Our planet matters. We do business the right way by following our values and working toward solutions that benefit us all' (Coca-Cola 2019).

However, in the three years since the SDGs were officially embraced by states, corporations, and civil society organizations, the number of people suffering from hunger has constantly increased, returning to levels of a decade ago (WHO 2018a). Of these, the majority is represented by small-scale farmers and urban dwellers who have lost access to the means of production. Hunger is not the only expression of a global food system incompatible with the long-term survival of people and planet. In 2016, the percentage of adults aged 18 years and over who were overweight reached the historic level of 39%, with 13% obese people (WHO 2018b). In Mexico, where in 1980 7% of the citizens were obese, the figure reached the staggering height of 20.3% in 2016, an increase that has been explained by the liberalization of the food market and the arrival of hyper-processed corporate food and beverages (including that same Coca-Cola that is embracing sustainability as a core tenet of its business practices). On the production side, the same farmers and ranchers in the USA who are asked by large-scale corporations to adopt sustainable practices saw a 45% drop in net farm income between 2013 and 2016 and, after a small increase in 2017, a new decline of almost 15% in 2018 (USDA 2018). In the Global South, the very low price for some food 'commodities' like coffee is leaving farmers with no alternatives to selling under-cost or taking the streets to openly manifest their disappointment (Efe-epa 2018).

From farm to fork (or, better, to landfill), the whole global food system seems to be suffering: with some significant exceptions. Anheuser-Busch (AB InBev), a beverage multinational, produced about 612.57 million hectoliters of beer (Statista 2019) in a world where one out of nine people lack access to safe water (WHO and UNICEF 2017), generated $56 billion in revenues and $7.9 billion in record profits, with a significant increase in sales in Sub-Saharan Africa, Latin American, and Asia. In the same year, Nestle, the second largest food and beverage company in the world, produced revenues of $91 billion, with profits of $7.3 billion (lower than the $8.6 billion recorded in 2017), and in May 2018 concluded a $7.2 billion alliance with Starbucks coffee to accelerate the grow and global reach of the brand. And while Coca-Cola was embracing sustainability, it also reached the seventh place in the food and drink sector for 2017, with profits of $1.4 billion. In 2018 alone, the beverages company announced of the purchase of Costa Coffee for $5.1 billion realized with the support of Rothschild & Co., Goldman Sachs, Morgan Stanley and Deutsche Bank, large-scale financial investors and banks which acted as advisers or joint sponsors and got a slice of the pie (Business Insider 2018).

Overall, the diffusion of the SDGs narrative and the emphasis of sustainable food chains has been combined with a significant surge in corporate profits, a spike in mergers and consolidation across sectors and levels of the food network (Food Engineering 2018; iPES-Food 2017), an increase in the amount of value captured by supermarkets and international retailers (Willoughby and Gore 2017) and a stronger participation of financial investors and speculators (Chadwick 2019; Clapp and Isakson 2018; Ferrando 2018). Straight-jacketed by the assumptions of economic growth and the normalization of capitalist modes of organizing society and nature, the shift towards sustainability seems incapable (or disinterested) in challenging the patterns of accumulation that are the material expression of a vision based on the enclosure of nature, the alienation of workers' labour, and the translation of the world into monetary terms. Any attempt to move beyond the limits of the mainstream conception and implementation of sustainability in the food system needs, therefore, to unveil its links with the Cartesian understanding of nature as separate from society that was functional to the subordination of nature and the consolidation of the capitalist food regime. A critical look at the genealogy of the contemporary food systems is thus needed to identify continuities and gaps: more importantly, it helps us identify the structural aspect of the current food system that must be changed if the aim is to build a future that not only helps nature and people to survive but that is truly regenerative.

A monopsony built on colonialism and multiple commodifications

Food, planet, and humanity are inherently interconnected. Their relationship has been changing through the centuries, along with it the way in which food and nature have been perceived, defined and dealt with. The history of the food regime and the regime-based approach to food give visibility to a long trajectory, almost 600 years, characterized by struggles, tensions, and interactions among peoples, laws, power, violence and nature Friedman and McMichael 1989; Friedman 1993, 2015, 2016; McMichael 2009, 2013). It starts with the colonial project, the Caravels and the scramble for the 'New World', it passes through the industrial revolution, the mechanization of agriculture, and the need to feed the growing urban labour force, and then reaches the contemporary world of the World Trade Organization, cheap transportation, and hyper-financialized extraction of rent from the food chain (Patel and Moore 2018). Rather than being static, the contemporary food regime is the expression of everything that took place before. To understand the present and transform it, we thus need to realize the importance of the past and the institutions that have brought us here (Fakhri 2014).

Today's international food system is deeply rooted in the colonial project and its ideological and material consequences (Patel and Moore 2018). Trade and investment patterns reproduce the global division of labour and capital that has been constructed through centuries of uneven development, discrimination, racism, and patriarchy. In particular, the current distribution of agricultural land and the development of the productivist agricultural system can be traced back to the time of colonies and the militarization of the Cold War era. For example, Feronia Inc, an agribusiness company operating in the Democratic Republic of Congo since 2009 is justifying its right to operate more than 30,000 hectares of land on the basis of the 1911 concession that the Lever Brothers (later Unilever) obtained from the Belgian State (Feronia 2019). Similarly, the Badische Anilin- und Soda-Fabrik (BASF) company that was central to the generation of ammonia and its commercialization at the beginning of 1913, was originally involved in the provision of supplies for agricultural purposes and then in the realization of the gunpowder that sustained the fighting in World War I (Melillo 2012). Similarly, from 1965 to 1969, the Monsanto Company was one of the nine wartime US government contractors manufacturing the Agent Orange that was used by the US military as a defoliant in the Vietnam War (Monsanto 2017).

The link between the past and the future of the food system is even clearer if we think about the invisible and intangible, i.e. the intellectual and ideological premises that characterize the different regimes described by Friedmann and McMichael (1989). The colonial food system, the state-led agricultural 'green revolutions', the corporate food chains, and the financialized world of nowadays would have not been the same without a shared conception that (some) people and the surrounding world are 'things' up for grab. The legal construction and enforcement of slavery, the enclosure of land in Europe, the economic coercion of factory and farm workers all over the food chain, the artificial creation of *terra nullius* in the 'New World', the subordination of women and the obliteration of reproductive labour that is essential to the survival of the human species (Federici 2018), the use of chemical fertilizers and pesticides and several other processes that characterized the last 600 years of food regimes share ideologies and practices that see nature and people (especially women and non-white) as appropriable and translatable in monetized commodities (Capra and Mattei 2015). Once they are commodified, these 'things' are 'disengaged from their makers and at the mercy of market transactions. Things are exchanged for money so that the people and the activities behind them can be forgotten; the commodity is available for use or further transactions' (Tsing 2015a: 22). In the food system, the multiple commodifications of 'things' that make food possible (land, water, soil, productive and reproductive labour, etc.) determined the transformation of food into a commodity and the normalization of the idea that the food system in a mere matter of inputs and outputs disentangled from its ecology and interconnected web of relationships Patel and Moore 2018; (Maughan and Ferrando 2018).

The continuum of these historical and ideological frameworks represents, I believe, the background of today's corporate claims for a sustainable global food system and, to a larger degree, of the promotion of public-private partnership as the pathway towards the Sustainable Development Goals and of the optimism behind the possibility of a coexistence between different understandings of food and agriculture. In the private accounts of sustainability, silence is cast on the unequal distribution of values and resources, the reproduction of historical injustices, the genealogy of accumulation of wealth and opportunities. Wilful ignorance is exercised to turn a blind eye on the anti-emancipatory nature of a world where people and nature are defined through their exchange value. For sure, SDG 10 fixes as an objective the reduction of income inequality, but a focus on people's income overlooks the role that wealth inequality and centuries of uneven development have in allocating opportunities and defining socio-economic hierarchies (Smith 1984). Thus, if the aim is to reduce the productive gap without addressing structural concerns, citizens and the planet can be brought to a level of sufficiency (enough to eat, enough biodiversity, enough growth, formal equality, etc.) without being brought to a level of justice and equality (Moyn, 2018), Social and envrionmental conditions are brought to a level of sufficiency, but the overall food system continues operating within the existing paradigmatic framework and historical (mis)distribution. By avoiding questions such as 'Who got what, and who should pay for that?' (Patel and Moore 2018), we do not engage with the systemic and structural issues behind the failures of the current food system and we do not create the space for transgressive responses.

Let's take as an example the Round Table on Sustainable Palm Oil (RSPO). In the last ten years, the palm industry has come under serious criticism both for the environmental consequences of logging, for the social consequences of transforming food-producing areas into monoculture, and for the grabbing of communities' land (Paiement 2017). The 2008 RSPO Principles and Criteria for Sustainable Palm Oil Production,[1] the RSPO Certification System, the auditing system, and the creation of a supply chain approach to the issue represented the sector's response. Today, the scheme has been subscribed to by banks and investors, consumer goods manufacturers, environmental and conservation NGOs, oil palm growers, palm oil processors and traders, retailers, social and development NGOs, and supply chain group managers. The eight principles are clear and easy to understand: 1) commitment to transparency; 2) compliance with applicable laws and regulations; 3) long-term economic and financial viability; 4) use of appropriate best practices by growers and millers; 5) environmental responsibility and conversation of natural resources and biodiversity; 6) responsible consideration of employees, and of individual and communities affected by growers and mills; 7) responsible development of new planting; 8) commitment to continuous improvement in key areas of activity (RSPO 2013).

However, what does it mean in practice? Feronia Inc. is a RSPO member since December 2017. In its 2019 public commitment toward RSPO, the company stresses the role that RSPO will play in consolidating the sustainability of the plantation and improving its interactions with stakeholders and the whole chain. Most of sustainability critiques have focused on whether Feronia Inc. is complying with its commitment, i.e. implemented a productive process in its 30,000 hectares of plantations that respects the workers, uses the best practices available, and refrains from logging more trees (Feronia 2019). In this context, the company feels confident and comfortable adopting a narrative that stresses the role that it had in saving the Unilever oil palm plantations from 'extinction' and making sure that once productive land that was going to be lost to nature is now efficiently and sustainable cultivated (Feronia 2019). From the regenerative perspective that I adopt in this chapter, something is clearly missing from the picture. First, we are told that the end of palm oil monoculture in the middle of the RDC tropical forest would have equaled the catastrophic impact of an asteroid: an extinction would have affected the large-scale plantation and nature's idleness and unproductive dynamics would have taken over. Secondly, the focus on sustainable conservation of monoculture omits a bigger piece of the puzzle it dismisses the original subtraction of land from local communities and the original transformation of biodiverse forest into a repetitive series of identical trees. It ignores the impact that existing monoculture has on the surrounding forest and the food system, including on the food security of workers who have now little time to provide for themselves and their family. It normalizes the transformation of nature and people into sources of monetary value for someone else.

In the absence of diverse and imaginative thinking (Shiva 1993), the notion of sustainability constructed by the RSPO and implemented by Feronia is functional to the reproduction of the mainstream vision of the future as defined by the current constraints, and therefore neither reparatory nor emancipatory. The focus is on how to make future better than the present, and not on the reasons behind the diffusion of the oil palm at the time of colonialism and the industrial revolution, let alone its ecological and redistributive implications. What about the practices and non-commodified connections with the nature that were destroyed and replaced to make space for the plantation? Why should local communities choose between working for a salary or migrating, rather than being given the opportunity to define their own present and future? Can we praise companies and narratives that look forward without questioning the standpoint of who is speaking and the ecological implications of their vision?

A similar consideration can be proposed with regard to the SDGs and their transformative/emancipatory potential of the global food system. Of the 17 priorities and 169 targets, several are connected with food and could potentially be leveraged to foster a transition towards a regenerative food system. However, two points must be noticed: the goals as the agreement between states are inevitably operating within the totalizing and neo-colonial framework of Eurocentrism, sovereign imperialism, and international law (Anghie 2007). From a food system perspective, the creation of the 'third world' (later 'developing') obliterated the existence of colonial and historical responsibilities (Escobar 2007). Similarly, the paradigm of the free market as a cornucopia for people and the embracement of international trade for food security hides the underlying inequality in the distribution of value and power across the food regimes and enforces the idea of food as a global marketable commodity (Fakhri 2014). At the same time, diversity and uniqueness were integrated and adapted to the needs of long-distance trade and consumerism rather than given legal and political spaces where the multiplicity of embedded and situated food knowledges could be autonomously expressed (Haraway 1988; Mies and Shiva 2014). To say that world hunger will be halved by 2050 is a commendable purpose and should be fully embraced: yet, it seems rather optimistic to expect the dominant approach to sustainability as a capitalist feature to do more than feeding and providing sufficiency. Let's not expect a historically redistributive approach that pushes for land redistributions, reparation for colonial and climate responsibilities, the recognition and enforcement of food sovereignty as superior to the goals and mechanisms of world trade, nor for the adoption of different visions of food based on its multiple meanings and its socio-ecological component (Vivero-Pol 2017). If the problem lies with the paradigmatic premises of the global food system as a non-ecological place for commodities exchange, it is from there that we have to start.

Commons and commoning for regenerative food systems

There is little doubt that capitalism as a socio-economic system is failing people and the planet (Moore 2015). Planetary boundaries and social foundations of a flourishing society are disregarded and continuously violated (Raworth 2017). The global food system, structured around corporations and financial capital, is not an exception: it is environmentally and socially broken. It is treating nature as an object and people like productive figures, or malleable consumers at the best. More importantly, it thrives out of the commodification of food and the food system and uses its rhetoric and images to make invisible the ecological complexity behind every bite we take. When food is a thing rather than the visible part of a web of life (Capra 1997), when history does not matter and when the present is defined according to its monetary value, different premises and different assumptions are needed. First of all, we need to abandon the vision of the top-down global food system and engage with the construction of bottom-up food systems with unique features and their own dynamics. Secondly, we need to make the effort of replacing the existing conceptions of food and the food system with the idea of the food system as a commons and the act of commoning the food systems as a continuous interaction between nature and society based on the premises of reparative ecology (Patel and Moore 2018). In a nutshell, we need to undo the Copernican revolution and the idea of a center around which everything rotates (knowledge, ideals, paradigms, food, value, money, etc.).

To understand the transformative potential of commons and commoning, it is important to differentiate among the multiple theories of commons that have been proposed in the last decade. This leads to the realization that that they are not all the same and that radical and systemic change can only come with the adoption of the most political declination of the terms. Since Elinor Ostrom's work in the 1990s (Ostrom 1990), the idea of the commons has been deployed as a catch-all concept (Perilleux and Nyssens 2016), often infusing the term with an aura of social progressiveness and virtues of horizontal and fair governance (Verhagen 2015). The acritical diffusion of the term risks making it an empty slogan. As Rodotá already warned in 2013, if 'everything is a commons, nothing is a commons' (Rodotá 2013, 8).

If we are imagining a food system that is not only environmentally sustainable but also capable of supporting ecological and regenerative processes and achieving historical and future justice, we must thus be careful with accepting economic conceptions of the term like the one proposed by Ostrom (1990). They only superficially engage with the redistributive, historical, and justice potential of the notion. Constructed around the axes of excludability and rivalry, the economic understanding of the commons that has become particularly popular is often used to define a large set of human and natural systems that are 'sufficiently large that it is difficult, but not impossible, to define recognized users and exclude other users altogether' (Ostrom 2009). These common-pool resources, such as fisheries, forests, lakes, and oceans, are seen in terms of their management and resilience to the major ecological challenges.

Surely, the proof that resources can be managed collectively and not be irreparably deployed challenges the dominant vision of the commons as a *terra nullius* with no rules beyond selfishness and competition among users whose greed inevitably exhaust the opportunities for future generations (Hardin 1968). Despite this intellectual achievement, the proof that land, fisheries, forests, and other 'natural resources' can be successfully managed by communities and the conclusion that Hardin was wrong when he proposed the idea of the *Tragedy of the Commons* still say very little about social justice, distribution of resources, equality of opportunity. In particular, it does not challenge how that specific allocation of resources was obtained nor questions the long-term social resilience of the new system that has been put in place. What if the herders in Hardin's example were contract farmers who can only access a tiny percentage of the market-value generated by the sale of the wool? What if their right to food was severely affected by the decision to use the common land to raise livestock rather than to achieve food sovereignty? What if the land had originally been grabbed from a native community and allocated to settlers? These concerns disappear behind the environmentally sustainable governance of a common pool resource.

To think about contemporary examples, there is no 'commons' or 'commoning' when a fridge is left in the middle of the street so that anonymous citizens moved by charitable feelings can leave any sort of food – including that purchased at a low cost in large-scale discounts – to other anonymous citizens. Similarly, we should not talk about commons or commoning when a food bank uses mislabeled products of a large cereal multinational company (probably obtained at very low cost from large monoculture and containing excessive amounts of sugar) to feed children in breakfast clubs. For sure, these practices have been allowing several families to survive and improve their immediate conditions. However, the diffusion of these practices does not challenge the underlying reasons behind the unequal distribution of food and financial resources nor the lack of a welfare state that protects, respects, and fulfills the essential right to food and nutrition. More importantly, corporate charity and bottom-up emergency aid dependent on the mainstream food system do not challenge the idea that food is a final object of consumption rather than a political act. The covid-19 food collapse proved that hunger lurks behind the corner of millions of people in the world. In the short-term, it must be addressed by any means. However, long-term solution must be radical, transformative, ecological, and fully democratic: ecologically regenerative food systems cannot be based on the acceptance of the existing limits and the reproduction of the same forms of dependencies and marginalization.

To apply a regenerative idea of commons and commoning to the food systems means, in my opinion, to imagine that all material components (seeds, land, soil, water, labor, food, etc) and non-material goods (culture, knowledge, personal relationships, biodiversity, etc.) that build a food system shall be jointly developed and maintained by a community, shared according to democratically defined rules that are redistributive and historically reparatory, and based on the recognition of the constant interaction and interdependence between nature and society as co-constructed (Moore 2015). For this reason, it is necessary to think about the commons not as a static item, a well-defined space or a 'thing', but rather the product of the practice of 'commoning'. Commons and commoning are, according to the more political vision of the commons, two indissoluble components of a radical transformation of the present: the commons do not exist in isolation but are the process of commoning that creates them (Dardot and Laval 2014). It is 'commoning' that confers on a material, or non-material, common resource its commons consideration and its emancipatory character (Dardot and Laval 2014). Commoning is about human/nature continuous inter-relationships (Bollier and Helfrich 2015) and, therefore, the human-made consideration of what a commons is can only be embedded in the diversity and partiality of people, places, and times (Friedmann 2015). Commoning the food system is the action of cultivating, processing, exchanging, selling, cooking, and eating together. Commoning is about asking who produces what, what are the values that the food system is satisfying, who has what, who has responsibility, and what institutions (legal, political, cultural, etc.) are needed to respect the planetary boundaries and *at the same time* strengthen the social foundations of society.

The dynamic thinking behind commoning has the imaginative power to create new/old traditions, review laws, and establish a different legal and political institutional framework (Charbonnier and Festa 2016; Dardot and Laval 2014; Mattei and Capra 2015; Ruivenkamp and Hilton 2017). Not surprisingly, the consolidated duopoly of the industrial food system (the state and the food market) feels threatened. Expansion, capital remuneration, and extraction of private value from the food system are incompatible with self-organized communities and social food movements based on non-commodified paradigms that challenge the globalized free market of food and the idea itself that food and the food system can be appropriated, controlled, monopolized, and profited from.

Commoning the food systems means recognizing that it is not inevitable that land is privately owned, financially invested, or considered as something else from its soil and ecology. It means challenging the enclosure of seeds, biodiversity, labour, and value, the increase in inequality, and the schizophrenia of the food system that are consequence of a specific vision of time, people, animals and planet. There are alternatives to the fact that agricultural choices are made on the basis of who can pay more (ethanol producers, cattle farmers, or human beings), that food is seen as any other tradable good and that agricultural policies are constructed without considering the fact that agriculture is intrinsically connected with food and – therefore – with health, rights, education, environment, and several other aspects of life that transcend production. A regenerative transition is thus more about re-commoning the food systems rather than starting from scratch. Re-commoning the food system challenges the multiple privatization of the commons that characterized the recent history of food and aims to the establishment of regenerative, anti-colonial, and de-commodified forms of food production (agro-ecology), along with their systems of governance (food democracies and food ecologies) and the underlying political horizons (food justice and food sovereignty).

In the complexity of the contemporary food regime, it is not possible to point to one leverage point or one-size-fits-all solutions. It would be presumptuous and disrespectful of the diversity that the commons and commoning want to foster and support. However, the transition must be pushed from below as much as it concerns a redefinition of macro-structures. Change is represented by territorial experiences like Mondeggi Bene Comune, where abandoned public land was occupied, a cooperative established, agro-ecology introduced, the space open to the community, and the harvest was exchanged with workers and sold in 'informal' street markets at accessible prices (Maughan and Ferrando 2018). But change must also take place at the macro level, challenging and subverting the premises of the world food market, a transnational space made of layers of law and regulations that is pretentiously considered to be flat and even and where the exchange of fetishized commodities has no past and no future. Equally, the flows of international investments in the food sector must be re-commoned and re-thought: is it enough to adopt the best conventional agricultural practices and to pay workers the legal minimum if thousand hectares of land are privatized, fenced, transformed into monoculture,e and the regenerative capacity of the soil transformed into millions of dollars that increase the bank accounts of corporations and the global rentier elite? These are just few of the multiple directions that we will explore if we reimagine and re-common the food systems, both in our daily lives as food actors and at the level of international laws and organizations. Commons and commoning are about thinking ecologically at the interconnection between food, people, and planet, acting with awareness of the past and aiming at present and future socio-environmental justice through historical reparation and long-term imagination. Given its potential for conviviality and its deep roots in the reproductive power of nature, food is a perfect agent of change (McMichael 2009): we need to act now, or it will be too late.

Conclusions

There is no clear remedy to the inequality and imbalances that characterize the global food system and that threaten the survival of people and planet while enriching the coffers of a few individuals and corporations. For sure, it is important to resist the trap of the 'one-size fits all solution' and to reject the idea that it is enough to think about food differently. This chapter has suggested that two of the systemic causes behind the social and environmental costs of the global food system are the unquestioned acceptance of food as a commodity and the adoption of a forward-looking attitude to transformation that dismisses the importance of the past. It is essential to take Patel and Moore's invitation to imagine and implement food systems that are ecologically reparatory (2018) seriously, i.e. thinking collectively at forms of combining people and planet around food production and consumption that are based on the recognition of the historical origins of the existing inequalities and on the inevitable and inherent connection between nature and society as co-constructed and co-dependent.

If the goal is to imagine and construct food systems (and economies) that are reparatory and regenerative, there is little doubt that the ideas and practices of sustainability embraced by large corporate actors, crystallized in the Sustainable Development Goals and progressively implemented in national and international law have failed. Instead of addressing the systemic causes of social and environmental struggles, the narratives of future improvements have narrowed our imagination and legitimized the idea that no radical transformation is needed. After the covid-19 food collapse, we can no longer believe that the social and environmental foundations of the capitalist food system are solid. In the context of corporate sustainable food, it is enough to improve the existing system from within, despite the centuries of exploitation, inequality, and appropriation that underpin the current distribution of labour, wealth, power, and opportunities. For sustainability as sufficiency, we should be satisfied with creating a food system that does not starve people and does not destroy the planet instead of pursuing the horizon of equality and ecology beyond the existing constraints (Moyn 2018). When we accept sustainability as sufficiency we refuse to look outside of the fishbowl of accumulation, growth, historical inequality, and subordination of nature in which we are swimming (Kapur 2018).

We need to tip the fishbowl. Some help may come from imagining, practicing, and engaging with food and the food system as both a commons (in the political sense of an ecological organization based on principles of justice, equality, redistribution, anti-colonialism, de-commodification, and anti-patriarchy) and organizing in the continuous process of commoning (in the sense of a non-static interaction between people and planet based on historical reparation, the respect of socio-environmental limits, mutual respect and the construction and reproduction of food systems and food practices that are ecologically regenerative). Commons and commoning are visions, practices, and aspiration based on a de-commodified, anti-enclosure, and historically rich understanding of the food system. Yet, they are not clear solutions or pre-existing institutions that can be imitated or transplanted around the world. When thinking about commons, commoning and reparatory ecology, we must have three things in mind.

First, the adoption of a commons-paradigm and the desire to talk about generative and regenerative dynamics should not give the impression that the capitalist food system is extraneous to generative and reproductive practices or exclusively based on the exploitation and irreversible consumption of nature and society. On the contrary, feminist approaches to capitalism have clearly showed its dependency on the appropriation of natural processes, the so-called 'raw materials' (let's think of plants' ability to grow and produce fruits) and reproductive practices (both of animals and human beings) (Haraway 2008; Mies and Shiva 2014; Tsing 2015a). As a matter of fact, 'Capitalists are unable to *make* most of their resources', but 'make use of animal digestion and plant photosynthesis without having any clue how to shape these processes, despite the sophisticated engineering of plants and animals' (Tsing 2015b). Similarly, the industrial revolution, colonialism, and the construction of the colonial trade of food and slaves were built upon the enclosure of land and nature all over the world (from the English commons to the so called 'New World'), the appropriation of soil and nutrients, and the subordination of human beings and both their productive and reproductive labour. Recognizing the role that generative processes play in the replication of capitalism as an expansionary and resilient form of organization of society and nature creates the possibility of thinking of regenerative practices as something that breaks with the subordination of nature and society. This is why commons as a static concept must be enriched with commoning as a dynamic, ecological, historically aware and redistributive interaction between people and the planet.

Secondly, a vision of the future food system cannot be disentangled from its past and present: in order to build a food system on the paradigm of the commons and commoning it is essential to realize the present legacy of historical creation and distributions of value, power and resources. Commons and commoning can help imagining a food system that responds to the needs of 'reparation ecology' (Patel and Moore 2018), i.e. the recognition of historical and current exploitations of people and nature and the need to redress them through a redefinition of socio-environmental relationships rather than by mere monetary compensation. A regenerative food system cannot be rooted in its colonial and oppressive past. Trade patterns, financial flows, and food practices that depend on a hundred years of uneven development (Smith 1984) cannot be swept under the carpet (Davis 2002; De Waal 2018). Mainstream visions of sustainability accept that we have to aim towards the Pareto optimal in the context of the current distribution of resources and power: what matters is not the initial distribution of value, power, and resources between bargaining parties, but the achievement of the best solution for both of them. If you have been deprived of your land and obtain a job in the company that is now operating it, lucky you! Commons and commoning challenge this assumption and a regenerative vision of the food system should do the same.

Finally, when we embrace the subversive and transformative paradigms of commons and commoning as opposed to the sufficiency of sustainability , attention must be paid to the multiple ways in which food systems are inter-connected with gender, race, energy, nature, equality, justice, etc. The relevance and distributive impacts of the intersectionality behind the food system cannot be fully understood from above and only by looking at food. Rather, it requires the recognition and support of grass-roots organizations and their struggles aagainst the multiple yokes of patriarchy, capitalism, and colonialism, within and without the food system. For example, there is a lot to learn from the indigenous peoples reclaiming food as a political action of self-determination, socio-economic development, and reconstruction of subordinated identities (Natifs 2018). Commons and commoning cannot, by themselves, build ecologically reparatory food systems: yet, their disruptive and subversive potential can provide the political glue and the imaginative horizon to challenge and change premises, assumptions, and discourses that are too often perceived as inevitable and undisputable.

Discussion questions

1. Can food systems be regenerative without redressing the historical violence, multiple injustices (race, class, gender, etc.) and dispossessions that underpin it?
2. Why do we consider food, the essence of life and a gift of nature, a commodity?

3. Shall we praise corporate pledges towards environmental sustainability in the context of increasing socio-economic inequality and food injustices?
4. Are we ready to take the role of capitalism seriously when thinking about regenerative food systems?

Note

1 RSPO Principles and Criteria are developed and revised every five years. The latest version of the RSPO Principles was released in 2013.

Further reading

Capra, F. 1997, *The Web of Life* (Toronto: Anchor Books).
Grady, B. 2016, From Kellogg's to Unilever, A Quiet Revolution in Sustainable, Farming. https://www.greenbiz.com/article/kelloggs-unilever-quiet-revolution-sustainable-farming
Holt-Giménez, E. 2017, *A Foodie's Guide to Capitalism* (New York: Monthly Review Press).
Patel, R. and Moore, J.W. 2017, *The History of the World in Seven Cheap Things* (New York: Verso).
Raworth, K., 2018, *The Doughnut Economics* (London: Random House Business Books).
Vivero Pol, J.L., Ferrando, T., De Schutter, O. and Mattei, U. 2018, *The Routledge Handbook of Food as a Commons* (London: Routledge).

References

Anghie, T., 2007, *Imperialism, Sovereignty and the Making of International Law* (Cambridge: Cambridge University Press).
Bernstein, H., 2015, Food regimes and food regime analysis: A selective survey, BICAS Working Paper.
Bollier, D., and Helfrich, S., 2015, Overture, in Bollier D. and S. Helfrich (eds.), *Patterns of Commoning* (Amherst, MA: Commons Strategy Group and Off the Common Press).
Business Insider, 2018, http://uk.businessinsider.com/coca-cola-costa-coffee-deal-banks-advising-2018-8
Capra, F., 1997, *The Web of Life* (Toronto: Anchor Books).
Capra, F. and U. Mattei, 2015, *The Ecology of Law: Toward a Legal System in Tune with Nature and Community* (Oakland, CA: Berrett-Koehler Publishers).
Ceres, 2018, Feeding Ourselves Thirsty, https://feedingourselvesthirsty.ceres.org/
Chadwick, A., 2019, *Law and the Political Economy of Hunger* (Oxford: Oxford University Press).
Charbonnier, P. and D. Festa, 2016, Introduction. Biens communs, beni comuni, in Charbonnier P. et al. (eds.), *Traduire et introduire*, (Paris: Tracés, hors-série).
Clapp, J. and R. Isakson, 2018, *Speculative Harvests* (Halifax: Fernwood Publishing).
Coca-Cola, 2019, How Coca-Cola is #EmbracingSustainability, www.coca-colacompany.com/stories/how-coca-cola-is-embracingsustainability
Dardot, P. and C. Laval, 2014, *Commun, essai sur la révolution au XXIe siècle* (Paris: Le Découverte).
Davis, M., 2002, *Late Victorian Holocaust* (London: Verso Books).
De Waal, A., 2018, *Mass Starvation: The History and Future of Famine* (Cambridge: Polity Press).
Efe-epa, 2018, Colombian coffee growers protest falling prices, www.latinxtoday.com/309_english-news/5663730_colombian-coffee-growers-protest-falling-prices.html
Escobar, A., 2007, Worlds and knowledges otherwise, *Cultural Studies*, 21(2), 179–210.
Fakhri, M., 2014, *Sugar and the Making of International Trade Law* (Cambridge: Cambridge University Press).
Feronia, 2019, Land policy, www.feronia.com/sustainability-policies/view/land-policy
Ferrando, T., 2018, The financialization of the transnational food chain: From threat to leverage point? *Transnational Legal Theory*, 9(3–4), 316–342.
Ferrando, T. and J.L. Vivero-Pol, 2017, Commons and 'commoning': A 'new' old narrative to enrich the food sovereignty and right to food claims. *Right to Food and Nutrition Watch*, 2017, 50–56. www.righttofoodandnutrition.org/files/02.rtfanw-2017_eng_17_12_article-5_web_rz.pdf

Food Engineering, 2018, Food and beverage mergers and acquisitions trends, www.foodengineeringmag.com/articles/97299-food-and-beverage-mergers-and-acquisitions-trends

Friedmann, H., 1993, International political economy of food: A global crisis, *New Left Review*, 197, Jan./Feb., 29–57.

Friedmann, H., 2015, Governing land and landscapes: Political ecology of enclosures and commons, *Canadian Food Studies*, 2(2), 23–31.

Friedmann, H., 2016, Commentary: Food regime analysis and agrarian questions: Widening the conversation, *Journal of Peasant Studies*, 43(3), 671–692.

Friedmann, H. and P. McMichael, 1989, Agriculture and the state system: The rise and decline of national agriculture, *Sociologia Ruralis*, 19(2), 93–117.

Hardin, G., 1968, The tragedy of the commons, *Science*, 162(3859), 1243–1248.

Haraway, D., 2008, *When Species Meet* (Minneapolis: University of Minnesota Press).

Haraway, D., 1988, Situated knowledges: The science question in feminism and the privilege of partial perspective, *Feminist Studies*, 14(3), 575–599.

iPES-Food, 2017, *Too Big to Feed: Exploring the Impacts of Mega-Mergers, Concentration, Concentration of Power in the Agri-Food Sector* (International Panel of Experts on Sustainable Food Systems).

Kapur, R., 2018, *Gender, Alterity and Human Rights Freedom in a Fishbowl* (London: Edward Elgar).

Maughan, C. and T. Ferrando, 2018, Land as a commons: Examples from the UK and Italy, in Vivero-Pol J.L., T. Ferrando, O. De Schutter and U. Mattei (eds.), *The Routledge Handbook of Food as a Commons* (London: Routledge), 329–341.

McMichael, P., 2009, A food regime genealogy, *Journal of Peasant Studies*, 36(1), 139–169.

McMichael, P., 2013, *Food Regimes and the Agrarian Question* (Halifax: Fernview).

McMichael, P., 2016, Commentary: Food regime for thought, *Journal of Peasant Studies*, 43(3), 648–670.

Melillo, E., 2012, The first green revolution: Debt peonage and the making of the nitrogen fertilizer trade, 1840–1930, *American Historical Review*, 117(4), 1028–1060.

Mies, M. and V. Shiva, 2014, *Ecofeminism* (2nd edition, London: Zed Books; 1st edition, 1993).

Monsanto, 2017, Statements: Agent Orange: Background on Monsanto's involvement. Harroway, April 7, https://monsanto.com/company/media/statements/agent-orange-background/

Moore, J.M., 2015, *Capitalism in the Web of Life* (Verso, London).

Moyn, S., 2018, *Not Enough: Human Rights in an Unequal World* (Cambridge: Harvard University Press).

Natifs, 2018, North American traditional indigenous food systems, www.natifs.org/indigenous-food-lab

Ostrom, E., 1990, *Governing the Commons: The Evolution of Institutions for Collective Action* (New York: Cambridge University Press).

Ostrom, E., 2009, *A Polycentric Approach to Climate Change*, Policy Research Working Paper WPS 5095. (Washington, DC: World Bank).

Paiement, P., 2017, *Transnational Sustainability Laws* (Cambridge: Cambridge University Press).

Patel, R. and J.W. Moore, 2018, *A History of the World in Seven Cheap Things: A Guide to Capitalism, Nature, and the Future of the Planet* (Berkeley, CA: University of California Press).

Perilleux, A. and M. Nyssens, 2016, Understanding cooperative finance as a new common, Discussion Paper 2, IRES.

Raworth, K., 2017, *Doughnut Economics* (London: Penguin Books).

Rodotá, S., 2013, Constituting the commons in the context of state, law and politics, ECC Report, http://boellblog.org/wp-content/uploads/2013/10/ECC-Rodota-keynote.pdf.

RSPO, 2013, Principles and criteria for the production of sustainable palm oil 2013 (RSPO).

RSPO, 2019a, Members: Feronia, www.rspo.org/members/5284/Feronia-Inc.

RSPO, 2019b, How RSPO certification works, https://rspo.org.

Ruivenkamp, G. and A. Hilton, 2017, *Prospectives on Commoning* (Chicago, IL: Zed Books).

Shiva, V., 1993, *Monoculture of the Mind* (London and New York: Zed Books).

Smith, N. 1984, *Uneven Development: Nature, Capital and the Production of Space* (Athens: University of Georgia Press).

Statista, 2019, Production volume of Anheuseer-Buch InBEV, www.statista.com/statistics/269114/production-volume-of-anheuser-busch-inbev-by-region/

Tsing, A., 2015a, *The Mushroom at the End of the World* (Princeton, NJ: Princeton University Press).

Tsing, A., 2015b, Salvage accumulation, or the structural effects of capitalist generativity, Society for Cultural Anthropology, https://culanth.org/fieldsights/salvage-accumulation-or-the-structural-effects-of-capitalist-generativity

USDA, 2018, U.S. net farm income forecast to decline in 2018, www.ers.usda.gov/data-products/chart-gallery/gallery/chart-detail/?chartId=76952

Verhagen, E., 2015, La forge conceptuelle. Le 'commun' comme réinterprétation de la propriété, *Recherches Sociologiques et Anthropologiques*, 46(2), 111–131.

Vivero-Pol, J.L., 2017, The idea of food as commons or commodity in academia: A systematic review of English scholarly text, *Journal of Rural Studies*, 53, 182–201.

Vivero-Pol, J.L., T. Ferrando, O. De Schutter and U. Mattei, 2018, *The Routledge Handbook of Food as a Commons* (London: Routledge).

Web of Science, 2019, Basic research from all databases 1900–2019: Sustainability, http://apps.webof knowledge.com/Search.do?product=UA&SID=F1iVvRu2xBMn2h5ZAl2&search_mode=General Search&prID=57b81416-66db-4d0d-8380-d768b642177b>

WHO, 2018a, Global Hunger continues to rise, new UN report says, www.who.int/news-room/detail/ 11-09-2018-global-hunger-continues-to-rise-new-un-report-says

WHO, 2018b, Obesity and overweight, www.who.int/news-room/fact-sheets/detail/obesity-and-overweight

WHO and UNICEF, 2017, *Joint Monitoring Programme: Progress on Drinking Water and Sanitation, Update and MDG Assessment* (Geneva: WHO).

Willoughby, R. and T. Gore, 2017, *Ripe for Change: Ending Human Suffering in Supermarket Supply Chains* (London: Oxfam).

20

FORGING BY FORAGING

The role of wild products in shaping new relations with nature

Mikelis Grivins

Introduction

Wild product foraging – the gathering of edible products that are not cultivated – remains a remarkably poorly understood mode of people's engagement with nature. However, almost everywhere there are still groups of people engaging in wild product picking. Furthermore, recently there have been several indications that these products have acquired new popularity – either as part of foodie culture, newly discovered traditional/cultural roots, search for healthier diets, etc. (Reyes-Garcia et al. 2015; Stryamets et al. 2015; Wirsum 2017; Wirsum et al. 2018). The complex set of reasons fuelling the revival of foraging illustrates the diverse meanings and roles wild products can hold. Thus, the interpretations associated with wild products are not intrinsic properties of these products but rather a construct created within a particular social context. However, while the role of the product can shift, in broad terms, the practice of wild product picking remains the same everywhere. Thus, while meanings can change, the foundation upon which these meanings are built is stable. The chapter illustrates how the practice of wild product foraging strengthens the nature connectedness of people and how nature connectedness introduces new altruistic reasons for individuals to engage with nature responsibly. Thus, if considered from the perspective of individual motivations, foraging can generate support for as well as be a part of regenerative food systems.

This chapter focuses on the linking properties wild product picking can possess: the ability of wild products to bridge and heal connections that are needed to restructure consumption patterns; to reintroduce meaningfulness in food supply; to facilitate a better understanding of nature; and to reinstate nature as a significant aspect of the perception of contemporary social reality and self (to raise nature connectedness). The chapter pursues two goals. First, it aims to illustrate how wild product picking bridges the gaps and connects categories that are often seen as contradictory (such as traditional and modern, the local and the global, the environment and people, and the past and the present). Second, the chapter strives to analyse those properties of wild products that have allowed them to become an element connecting these ideas. Finally, this chapter discusses how such linkages can help to move closer to regenerative food systems.

In this chapter only edible flora and related products are considered. The concept of wild products as it is operationalized here is not necessarily an outcome of the wilderness. Often these products grow in otherwise systematically constructed environments, and a wild product is just one way that nature manifests itself in a particular environment. Wild products are not the opposite of cultivated products either. For instance, apple picking may occur in abandoned orchards or other previously cultivated territories that are largely abandoned now. Some other territories may still be cultivated, yet with a purpose different from generating pickable flora. Foraging in parks is an example of this practice. Thus, stretching the interpretation of what wild is, this chapter addresses products that are not systematically cultivated for large-scale harvesting. This definition simultaneously stresses two things: the way and the purpose of growing these products as well as the collecting practices related to these products. The definition thus distances the chapter from most of the literature that sees wild products as part of new forest management models, discussing the historical significance of picking, or associating wild products with conservationism. The chapter addresses one aspect of the social role of foraging. Foraging, picking, and gathering are used as synonyms here.

The chapter is based on 35 interviews with wild product pickers in Latvia (Male [M] = 4; Female [F] = 17), Estonia (M = 2; F = 1), the UK (M = 2; F = 3), and the Netherlands (M = 5; F = 1). The interviews were conducted in 2018 and represent various groups of foragers, focusing on various plants (berries, mushrooms, and teas) and different engagement levels (in terms of regularity, engagement with commercial foraging). From the respondents interviewed, 9 were younger than 30, 15 were in the age group between 30 and 50, and 11 were older than 50. No respondents younger than 18 were interviewed. Outside Latvia, foragers were found via recommendations. In Latvia, respondents were found via social media and recommendations, or addressed while foraging. The interviews have been recorded, transcribed, and coded.

This chapter consciously provides a very Western perspective on wild products. There is an ongoing heated debate on the role of wild products in the context of the Global South. However, addressing this conversation would mean introducing conflicts and issues that, unfortunately, would be too lengthy for this chapter (see, for example, Pullanikkatil and Shackleton 2019; Shackleton et al. 2011). In this chapter I acknowledge that the conflicts present in communities exposed to high pressure to commercialize wild products generate processes and notions that reverse the positive impacts this chapter associates with wild products. The chapter focuses on the micro level – discussing individual experiences.

Environmental connections

The literature discussing wild products has had a very narrow perspective in terms of how wild products should be interpreted. Much of the literature focuses on historical (Kalle and Sõukand 2012; Kujawska et al. 2015; Svanberg 2012) and traditional (Bardone and Pungas-Kohv 2015; Łuczaj et al. 2013a) wild product related practices and knowledge; analyzes the potential these products have as part of ecosystem services (Schulp et al. 2014; Wirsum 2017) or of new forest management practices (Hubert et al. 2017; Miina et al. 2010; Turtiainen et al. 2011); inspects the role these products have in ensuring livelihoods for local communities (Grivins and Tisenkopfs 2018; Turtiainen and Nuutinen 2012) and emerging lifestyles. Furthermore, with some exceptions (see Ludvig et al. 2018; Schulp et al. 2014; Wirsum 2017), research has addressed the role wild products have at the local level. These perspectives have generated an oversimplified picture that links wild products mainly with the environment, past, localness, and traditions, avoiding any functional role these products may have in the contemporary world. Because of the oversimplification, wild products have seemed to be of secondary importance.

This stance is in stark contrast to arguments proposed by authors who theorize relations between humans and nature. A somewhat controversial biophilia hypothesis suggests that humans have an imminent inner pull towards nature (Beery and Wolf-Watz 2014; Schultz 2001). This approach allows thecontroversial claim that foraging is just a manifestation of this pull. The less provocative nature connectedness approach suggests that meaningful encounters humans have with biophysical surroundings cause a change in their attitude toward practices creating environmental concerns (Beery and Wolf-Watz 2014; Nisbet and Zelenski 2011). The connectedness is related to the level of exposure to nature, which then manifests itself through how integrated one feels with nature, how much one cares, and how much one is ready to commit to nature. The recognition that nature fulfills a role in improving a person's wellbeing will strengthen the connectedness (Davis et al. 2009). Environmental concerns facilitate an adaptation of nature as an interconnected part of the self (Schultz 2001), resulting in "nature identity" – a nature related aspect of self-perception which co-exists and shapes other identities a person has. As Schultz (2002) puts it, one does not need to feel included by nature in order to engage with pro-environmental activities. However, without the connection, the individual engaging in these activities will want to see personal benefits emerging from the practice. Thus, connectedness with nature introduces altruism as an argument. The interlinkages between nature identity and other aspects of a person's life eventually transform into new forms of how everyday life is lived.

Foraging, as a practice linking a person with the surrounding environment, causes the emergence of an environmental identity. Consequently, the foraging practice – as a link connecting a person with nature – is heavily influenced by and shapes the person's other

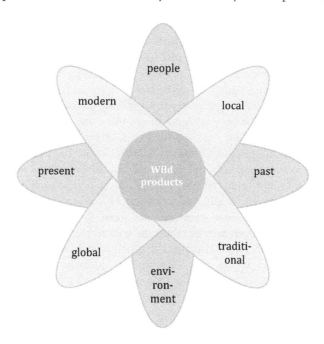

Figure 20.1 The binaries linked by wild products.

experiences. The interviews discussed in this chapter reveal how the categories named earlier – the environment, localness, traditionality, and past – intertwine with those representing a person's everyday life – people, global, modern, contemporary. These different categories mix, creating entirely new ways for engagement, bridging connections, and creating new ways for nature to manifest in the contemporary world.

The following sections provide an analysis of the connections, presenting them as pairs of ideas coexisting in foraging: the environment and people, the local and the global, the past and the present, traditional and modern (Figure 20.1).

Environment and people

> Of course, it is expensive to pick. Just to get to our spot – it takes fuel, it takes time. And sometimes all you find is just a small basket of mushrooms. However, you also get joy from being in the forest, moving away from the beaten path, and from encountering butterflies. It is an aesthetic pleasure. This cannot be measured.
>
> *(Woman in Latvia, 55)*

While there are at least some data on the effects foraging has on the environment, there is little information on how it affects people. In his famous work *The Omnivore's Dilemma*, Pollan (2006) takes time to illustrate how he struggled to find chanterelles, the mushroom that is very distinctive and, arguably, easy to recognize. In all four countries, mushroom pickers interviewed in the course of this study reported that the ability to spot wild mushrooms comes with practice. One has to have a trained eye to notice that in the moss, among colourful wild plants and old dry leaves, there are mushroom heads. This requires training and repetition. One has to know what one is looking for, and accompanying signs may help with spotting the particular product. The stories pickers told during interviews revealed how they had started to learn natural signs indicating the proximity of the wanted plant. Some guidance is usually inherited from the older generation, while some finding skills are acquired through practice – from trial and error.

Foragers tend to be conservative when it comes to choosing a place to pick wild goods. Returning to the same place again and again, pickers learn to recognize possible hazards, and they learn not to be afraid of them. If they continue to come back to the same wild area year after year, they learn the geography of the place, they learn how not to get lost, they start noticing where various wild animals live, and pay attention to other particular aspects of the chosen wilderness spot. People picking herbal tea plants report that they slowly learn to recognize supporting plants, spatial and environmental nuances indicating that what they search for is near. Finally, some of the respondents report that they have learned to distinguish particular smells, thus unlocking new senses to interact with the wild. Certain aromas might seem obvious when one talks about, for example, flowers. However, respondents claim that they have unlocked the same skills to recognize and find mushrooms. Thus, the engagement with nature transforms the forager and creates new, more personal connections to nature that are based on new knowledge, new skills, and new ways to interact.

The local and the global

Most of the foraged products never travel far. They end up being consumed somewhere close to the place where they were picked. There is, of course, evidence of some truly global enterprises trading wild goods and truly global wild products, such as wild harvested cork (Pettenella et al. 2016); wild bilberry (Grivins et al. 2016); and various mushrooms. The globalization of wild products can have all sorts of adverse effects on foragers' communities and on the habitats where these products grow (see Laird et al. 2010). However, the existence of a couple of products that have been captured by global industries does not necessarily illustrate the potential of wild products to connect the local and the global. The relationship between foraging and migration does it much better.

In-depth interviews and academic literature suggest (see Ceuterick et al. 2007, 2011) that engagement with foraging and reliance on wild products tend to transcend geographical boundaries. Both short- and long-term migrants, if they have had foraging experience, often continue to collect wild products after arriving in the destination country. Some might suggest that this is due to the economic vulnerability of migrants: foraging allows them to overcome financial hardship. However, there are also other reasons for the practice to travel along with people. In interviews conducted both in the Netherlands and the UK, foraging migrant communities constitute a reoccurring theme. Some respondents admired the traditional knowledge migrants have. However, more often people discussed the ownership of and the rights of migrant communities to engage with wild products.

At the same time, respondents with migration experience had a completely different take on the issue. One story illustrating an experience of a Russian migrant family captures the overall sentiment reoccurring in similar stories. After moving from a forested region in Russia to the seashore in the UK, the whole family started to collect sea plants. Even when the relatives preserving the original foraging knowledge passed away, the family continued to forage. For them, foraging was a way to maintain a memory of who they were. In every other aspect of life, they followed the traditions of the local communities, yet they chose to preserve this link to wilderness as part of their identity. This link to the past is the reason for why some of the migrating groups decided to continue to forage. Wilderness and links to wilderness constitute for them a way to maintain a sense of connectedness in an otherwise rapidly changing context. Thus, for these people, wild products bridge the gap between what they know and the challenges of their new environment. Therefore, once established, these linkages to wilderness prevail as a flag post in an otherwise rapidly changing world. The same is most likely true for the people who continue to forage in the same spot year after year – while the world changes, the practice remains as it was.

The past and the present

In most cases, the plants respondents pick, they have learned from the elders of the family in their childhood. It is the same with foraging spots. If not abruptly broken, relations with the environment move at a much slower pace than most other experiences of modern life. This allows for an extensive collection of memories to accumulate around foraging practices and the spot where one forages. For example, during interviews people tended to recall foraging trips they had made with their grandparents. Many of the interviewees who had grown up in the Republics that used to be occupied by the Soviet Union talked about officially organized foraging trips. Wild products can connect generations and experiences of one's own life. As one interviewee explained:

> I have been interested in my grandma's herbal tea picking knowledge since my childhood. She used to read to me her notes on what each herb is for. I also saw

how she gathers plants for herbal teas. Nobody else in my family was doing it. Now she is old and she cannot walk the distances that she used to walk and now I am the one gathering teas.

(Female from Latvia, 25)

The role of cross-generational knowledge exchange cannot be stressed enough. The knowledge can be about edible products, the ways of preparing these products, or the best spots to collect them. As one respondent, a woman in her twenties from Latvia, states: "My dad knows all the best mushroom spots. If I want to go mushroom picking – I ask him to take me." On the other hand, as illustrated by the quote above, some products are typically collected by just one person for the whole family. In this case, the older generation not only serve as the preservers of plant-related knowledge but are also the suppliers of these products. The process of passing knowledge related to these products is much more intimate; it is not just the knowledge that is passed on, but also a responsibility, the wellbeing of relatives.

Finally, it is worth noting that for many of the interviewed people picking and wild product-related knowledge emerge as a symbol of particular ethnic belonging and specific traditional knowledge. In Latvia and Estonia particularly, respondents often substantiated their willingness to pick wild products by saying something along the lines of "all Estonians do that," "it is the Latvian in me," "he's a Russian, and he knows these particular recipes," etc. The knowledge needs foraging presupposes link the practice to well-established categories of social relations and self-identification and belonging. This increases the value of the practice and creates additional reasons for a person to feel connected to nature.

Traditional and modern

A modern sceptic would say that the moon phases are nonsense. But it is not so. The moon phases have a massive effect on how mushrooms grow. It is a fact. If it is a crescent moon, then mushrooms will be full of worms, and it is not worth it to go in the forest.

(Woman from Latvia, 43)

A long line of studies generated by European ethnobotanists illustrates that foraging is seen as a very traditional activity. The general idea behind this assumption is that the historical exposure to nature has produced a knowledge that does not have an equivalent today. This, of course, at least to some extent, is true. The comparative studies assessing current and historical knowledge of wild products serve as clear evidence for this claim (Kalle and Sõukand 2012; Łuczaj et al. 2013b). However, modernity and technological advances have introduced new dimensions to how people interact with nature. The knowledge does not need to be encapsulated in a couple of wise persons. Digital technologies ensure that it is available when needed.

I told her that I don't have a cloudberry spot. She mentioned that her mom had a cloudberry spot in Krievu bog near Smiltene, but she could not tell me the exact location because it's the place where her uncle forages now. Yet, I had enough information – I went home and started to study maps and information online. The area she named was huge – but, of course, we found the spot.

(Woman from Latvia, 55)

Maps, information on soil structure, GPS, etc. can be used to fill the gaps in traditional knowledge. Meanwhile, books, guided educational picking tours, mobile apps, and mutual support groups on social media aiming to help with identifying a particular plant are all there to assist the contemporary forager. These are the instruments usually named as responsible for reviving foraging among foodies and other local groups. Some respondents suggested that availability of the new support instruments offered a sense of safety, which allowed them to focus more on nature.

However, most clearly the presence of modern means can perhaps be witnessed in how pickers interact with the picked products. Wild products have become an inspiration to improvise. Availability of new kitchen equipment, creative cooking as a means of self-expression, and wider availability of information create a context where known recipes are challenged and changed. One respondent recalled the difficulties she went through while trying to learn to deep-freeze mushrooms. She finally had to learn to dehydrate the mushrooms to avoid mushrooms turning into mush after defrosting. Some foragers talk about pulverized mushrooms, fermented herbal teas and teas turned into oil, formic acid mixed with birch sap syrup, etc. These people push the boundaries of how wild products can be used just because they can.

Consequently, foraging and wild products penetrate various fields of modern life. On the one hand, this has allowed nature to remain a recognizable part of the lived reality, where otherwise it may have ended up pushed into the background. On the other hand, this underlines the benefits that can be associated with nature.

Unique properties of wild products

Nature connectedness allows foragers to embed the foraging practice in contemporary reality, thus allowing nature to manifest itself through various aspects of a person's life. Being part of a person's life, nature also ensures that it is something to care about. Through these characteristics, foraging might become a strong element of regenerative food systems. However, while the chapter has shown the social processes that allow this to happen, so far it has had very little to say regarding what wild product properties are crucial in forging these connections. The interview data allows identification of four aspects characterising the wild that may shed light on how wild products create the link – the rootedness, unpredictability, commonness, and permanence of wild products.

Rootedness

Part of the uniqueness of wild products is the ties these products have to a particular environment. These products are a manifestation of the nature of a place, scenery, and time. Even managed, heavily modified spaces and locations used for other specific purposes are not entirely lost to vigilant foragers. As one respondent stated, "it is no secret … you can always find raspberry shrubs under power lines." Or, "to my surprise, I found ceps in my yard, right under our oak tree." Nature, in this regard, is unpredictable. One can easily imagine finding the best mushroom spot in the middle of the forest. However, strawberries, raspberries, or any other edible plants may start growing in an urban parking lot, park, next to train lines, or in other heavily modified landscapes. In several interviews respondents claim that they have found booty right in the city where they least expected it. Wild products can be found wherever nature manages to manifest itself.

People may try to do their best to replicate the environment where their favourite products grow. However, more often than not, they fail to cultivate the conditions wild products need. And even when they succeed, they get a completely different plant – one that requires an entirely different interaction. It is quite ironic that the find after the search is among the most significant rewards for a mushroom picker, yet most of these pickers also try to come up with a way to control where the desired mushrooms would grow. Wild products are embedded in a wild environment. Therefore, even the most sincere attempts to collect these products will require significant engagement with nature.

Unpredictability

Wild products are characterized by a high level of unpredictability. On the macro level, there have been attempts to introduce models explaining the prevalence of one or another wild product in a particular year or area (see Bonet et al. 2014; Kilpelainen et al. 2016; Turtiainen et al. 2013). However, this knowledge becomes obsolete when regarded at the level of an individual picker. One can know the best berry spots, yet, most likely, one will struggle to predict which places will be best and how much product there will be each year.

The shifting nature of spots where the wild products can be found was a reoccurring theme in the interviews with pickers. Some perennial plants (like wild chestnuts and apples) will be fixed to one place. However, for products such as raspberries changes are much more pronounced: it is a cycle where these berries grow for a while in a glade and then disappear to reappear again in other glades. For some others, it is a slow movement across space. Meanwhile, for other products, it is the constant unpredictability that presupposes constant search. Thus, yet again wild products emerge in this description as an unknown or at least as an element that is hard to predict. Pickers cannot change this, and thus the search for wild products requires conscious engagement that, in turn, causes connectedness.

Commonness

There are tensions between forest owners, foragers, and groups promoting the preservation of wildlife (see Górriz-Mifsud et al. 2015; Górriz-Mifsuda et al. 2017), and the running discussion on how to regulate access to wild products may end in an introduction of a fee for foraging at least in some EU countries. However, wild products are currently freely accessible in most places in Europe. Apart from macro factors shaping accessibility to wild products, there are also micro aspects influencing the accessibility. These micro aspects take the shape of beliefs, tacit rules associated with a particular area, or individual agreements. For example, some foragers collect booty only on the land where they know the owner. In another interview, a respondent explained that, in his private forest, there is a field of wild strawberries that all other foragers leave untouched because it is the favorite spot of the forest owner himself. However, there are practically no preconditions for pickers to engage with wild products.

The commonness translates into a deep engagement: every place where there is something to collect invites the forager to interact. The forager can engage with nature everywhere. One respondent explained how she always brings some pine cones, pretty branches, or maybe some flowers back home. These practices, of course, can be discussed in the context of their effect on nature. However, the bonding potential the constant interaction with nature has should be considered as well. Every place that invites the forager to pick also serves as a reminder of the links one has to nature.

Permanence

Despite the dramatic biodiversity loss the world is witnessing, there is a permanence in the presence of wild products. For cultivated products, market processes, regulations, crop sequence, etc. will affect farmers' choices. However, for wild products, the products growing are always there without the need for human support. The same can be said about the engagement with wild products – picking practices have existed long before the current foragers discovered the joy of foraging. The fact that most of them refer to their older relatives as mentors introducing them to foraging attests to this. Several respondents have described foraging as slow time, as a form of meditation, a time for themselves. There is a permanence to wild products that is independent and does not need humans. Although this thought may seem too philosophical to be considered seriously, the interviewed respondents stated that they talk to nature, forests, plants, and trees. The themes and issues raised by these conversations seem to repeat from one interview to the next: greeting the natural (forest, meadow, bog), asking for permission to take what nature has to offer, saying thanks for what it has given to the picker. The relations each forager has with nature are very personal.

Conclusions

Domestication and cultivation can be considered a project of control of the otherwise unpredictable surroundings. The wild and engagements with the wild are the opposite of this process: the wild repels control. The wild in its nature is the uncontrolled and unpredictable part of our reality. Because of this, practices engaging wilderness have unique characteristics. Thus, in many ways, foraging offers an experience that is qualitatively different from the general direction the modern reality is taking us. Any serious attempt to restructure the contemporary food system so that it would regenerate the broken ecosystems should take into consideration the factor of control. Foraging as a practice allowing engagement with the uncontrolled part of our reality exposes one to the wilderness, teaches the forager to interact with an uncontrollable part of reality and, by doing so, forges a much more meaningful relationship with food.

Foraging increases environmental connectedness and strengthens the environmental identity. This happens due to the unstructured nature of the wilderness. The chapter illustrates how connectedness and the environmental identity penetrate spheres of modern reality, thus facilitating broader implications: engagement with wild products ensures that the environment becomes more sensible and present; knowledge observed locally can globalize, broadening the scope of the engagement with nature; stronger connections linking experiences are established; and, finally, foraging allows well-known practices to be linked with new ways of doing things.

This chapter has addressed only the cases where people forage to gather foodstuffs. For the most part, foraging is just another channel to access food and diversify the contemporary food system. What this chapter illustrates is the layers of meaning foraging brings into the food supply process and the connectedness to nature this process encourages. Because the experiences have broader implications for the way reality is perceived, it is possible to suggest that the beliefs and ideas these practices cause to emerge will rub on to other fields of the food system.

Thus, a critical engagement with wild products can help us to move closer to regenerative food systems. First of all, engagement can be reintroduced back into food systems – by ensuring that what is consumed is perceived as being a part of nature and complex systems rather than just a product. Second, regenerative food systems can be approximated by facilitating care for the natural. And, finally, food systems can be diversified with local, place-sensitive practices.

Discussion questions

1. Can concepts like "environmental connectedness" be helpful to discuss the changes in attitudes dominating in the ever more urbanizing world?
2. What relations there are between socio-economic context, ideological development trajectories, culture, and environmental connectedness?
3. Should we look at foraging as a practice that can provide significant social, economic, and environmental benefits in Western countries or should it be approached only as a viable option for the indigenous communities living close to nature?
4. Can environmental identity emerge in contexts that otherwise are supportive towards exploitative use of natural resources?

Acknowledgments

This paper has financially benefitted from the ERAF Post-doctoral Research Support Program project Nr. 1.1.1.2/16/I/001 research application Nr. 1.1.1.2./VIAA/1/16/155.

Further reading

Laird, S.A., McLain, R.J., Wynberg, R.P. (2010). *Wild Product Governance: Finding Policies that Work for Non-Timber Forest Products.*, London: Earthscan.
Shackleton, S., Shackleton, C., Shanley, P. (eds.). (2011). *Tropical Forestry Non-Timber Forest Products in the Global Context*. Berlin, Heidelberg: Springer-Verlag.

References

Bardone, E., Pungas-Kohv, P. (2015). Changing values of wild berries in Estonian households: Recollections from an ethnographic archive. *Journal of Baltic Studies*, 46(3): 319–336. https://doi.org/10.1080/01629778.2015.1073916
Beery, T.H., Wolf-Watz, D. (2014). Nature to place: Rethinking the environmental connectedness perspective. *Journal of Environmental Psychology*, 40: 198–205.
Bonet, J.A., Gonzalez-Olabarria, J.R., De Aragon, J.M. (2014). Mushroom production as an alternative for rural development in a forested mountainous areas. *Journal of Mountain Science*, 11(2): 535–543.
Ceuterick, M., Vandebroek, I., Pieroni, A. (2011). Resilience of Andean urban ethnobotanies: A comparison of medicinal plant use among Bolivian and Peruvian migrants in the United Kingdom and in their countries of origin. *Journal of Ethnopharmacol*, 136(1): 27–54. 10.1016/j.jep.2011.03.038
Ceuterick, M., Vandebroek, I., Torry, B., Pieroni, A. (2007). The use of home remedies for health care and well-being by Spanish-Speaking Latino immigrants in London: A reflection on acculturation. In: Pieroni, A., Vandebroek, I. (eds.). *Traveling Cultures and Plants. The Ethnobiology and Ethnopharmacy of Migrations*. Berghahn, Oxford, pp. 145–165.
Davis, J.L., Green, J.D., Reed, A. (2009). Interdependence with the environment: Commitment, interconnectedness, and environmental behavior. *Journal of Environmental Psychology*, 29(2): 173–180.
Górriz-Mifsud, E., Domínguez-Torres, G., Prokofieva, I. (2015). Understanding foresttowners' preferences for policy interventions addressing mushroom picking in Catalonia (North-East Spain). *European Journal of Forest Research*, 134(4): 585–598.

Górriz-Mifsuda, E., Goviglib, V.M., Boneta, J.A. (2017). What to do with mushroom pickers in my forest? Policy tools from the landowners' perspective. *Land Use Policy*, 63. https://doi.org/10.1016/j.landusepol.2017.02.003

Grivins, M., Tisenkopfs, T. (2018). Benefitting from the global, protecting the local: The nested markets of wild product trade. *Journal of Rural Studies*, 61: 335–342. https://doi.org/10.1016/j.jrurstud.2018.01.005

Grivins, M., Tisenkopfs, T., Stojanovic, Z., Ristic, B. (2016). A comparative analysis of the social performance of global and local berry supply chains. *Sustainability*, www.mdpi.com/2071-1050/8/6/532

Hubert, P., Hujala, T., Kurttila, M., Wolfslehner, B., Vacik, H. (2017). Application of multi criteria analysis methods for a participatory assessment of non-wood forest products in two European case studies. *Forest Policy and Economics*. https://doi.org/10.1016/j.forpol.2017.07.003

Kalle, R., Sõukand, R. (2012). Historical ethnobotanical review of wild edible plants of Estonia (1770s–1960s). *Acta Societatis Botanicorum Poloniae*, 81(4). https://doi.org/10.5586/asbp.2012.033

Kilpelainen, H., Miina, J., Store, R., Salo, K., Kurttila, M. (2016). Evaluation of bilberry and cowberry yield models by comparing model predictions with field measurements from North Karelia, Finland. *Forest Ecology and Management*, 363: 120–129. https://doi.org/10.1016/j.foreco.2015.12.034

Kujawska, M., Luczaj, L., Typek, J. (2015). Fischer's Lexicon of Slavic beliefs and customs: A previously unknown contribution to the ethnobotany of Ukraine and Poland. *Journal of Ethnobiology and Ethnomedicine*, 11: 85. 10.1186/s13002-015-0073-8

Laird, S.A., McLain, R.J., Wynberg, R.P. (2010). *Wild Product Governance: Finding Policies that Work for Non-Timber Forest Products*. London: Earthscan.

Ludvig, A., Weiss, G., Sarkki, S., Nijnik, M., Živojinovič, I. (2018). Mapping European and forest related policies supporting social innovation for rural settings. *Forest Policy and Economics*, 97: 146–152. https://doi.org/10.1016/j.forpol.2018.09.015

Łuczaj, Ł., Kohler, P., Piroznikow, E., Graniszewska, M., Pieroni, A., Gervasi, T. (2013b). Wild edible plants of Belarus: From Rostafiski's questionnaire of 1883 to the present. *Journal of Ethnobiology and Ethnomedicine*, 9(21). https://doi.org/10.1186/1746-4269-9-21

Łuczaj, Ł., Zovko Končić, M., Miličević, T., Dolina, K., Pandža, M. (2013a). Wild vegetable mixes sold in the markets of Dalmatia (Southern Croatia). *Journal of Ethnobiology Ethnomediciene*, 9: 2. https://doi.org/10.1186/1746-4269-9-2

Miina, J., Pukkala, T., Hotanen, J.-P., Salo, K. (2010). Optimizing the joint production of timber and bilberries. *Forest Ecology Management*, 259(10): 2065–2071. https://doi.org/10.1016/j.foreco.2010.02.017

Nisbet, E.K., Zelenski, J.M. (2011). Underestimating nearby nature: Affective forecasting errors obscure the happy path to sustainability. *Psychological Science*, 22(9): 1101–1106.

Pettenella, D., Vidale, E., Da Re, R., Baskent, E.Z., Bouriaud, L., Corradini, G., Gorriz, E., Japelj, A., et al. (2016). D3.3. Trends, rural impacts and future developments of regional WFP market. Deliverable of StarTree project. Available in (29.10.2018): www.star-tree.eu/images/deliverables/WP3/D%203.3.pdf

Pollan, M. (2006). *The Omnivore's Dilemma. A Natural History of Four Meals*. London: Penguin Press, Bloomsbury.

Pullanikkatil, D., Shackleton, C.M. (eds.). (2019). *Poverty Reduction through Non-Timber Forest Products*, Sustainable Development Goals Series. Berlin: Springer Nature.

Reyes-Garcia, V., Menendez-Baceta, G., Aceituno-Mata, L., Acosta-Naranjo, R., Calvet-Mir, L., Domínguez, P., Garnatje, T., Gómez- Baggethun, E., et al. (2015). From famine foods to delicatessen: Interpreting trends in the use of wild edible plants through cultural ecosystem services. *Ecological Economics*, 10.1016/j.ecolecon.2015.11.003

Schulp, C.J.E., Thuiller, W., Verburg, P.H. (2014). Wild food in Europe: A synthesis of knowledge and data of terrestrial wild food as an ecosystem service. *Ecological Economics*, 105: 292–305. https://doi.org/10.1016/j.ecolecon.2014.06.018

Schultz, P.W. (2001). The structure of environmental concern: Concern for self, other people, and the biosphere. *Journal of Environmental Psychology*, 21: 1–13.

Schultz, P.W. (2002). Inclusion with nature: The psychology of human–nature relations. In: Schmuck, P., Schultz, W.P. (eds.). *Psychology of Sustainable Development*. Kluwer Academic, Boston, MA, pp. 61–78.

Shackleton, S., Shackleton, C., Shanley, P. (eds.). (2011). *Tropical Forestry Non-Timber Forest Products in the Global Context*. Berlin, Heidelberg: Springer-Verlag.

Stryamets, N., Elbakidze, M., Ceuterick, M., Angelstam, P., Axelsson, R. (2015). From economic survival to recreation: Contemporary uses of wild food and medicine in rural Sweden, Ukraine and NW Russia. *Journal of Ethnobotany and Ethnomedicine*, 11(53). https://doi.org/10.1186/s13002-015-0036-0

Svanberg, I. (2012). The use of wild plants as food in pre-industrial Sweden. *Acta Societatis Botanicorum Poloniae*, 81(4). https://doi.org/10.5586/asbp.2012.039

Turtiainen, M., Miina, J., Salo, K., Hotanen, J.P. (2013). Empirical prediction models for the coverage and yields of cowberry in Finland. *Silva Fennica*, 47(3): 10.14214/sf.1005

Turtiainen, M., Nuutinen, T. (2012). Evaluation of information on wild berry and mushroom markets in European Countries. *Small-Scale Forestry*, 11(1): 131–145.

Turtiainen, M., Salo, K., Saastamoinen, O. (2011). Variations of yield and utilisation of bilberries (Vaccinium myrtillus L.) and cowberries (V. Vitis-idaea L.) in Finland. *Silva Fenica*, 45(2): 237–251. http://dx.doi.org/10.14214/sf.115

Wirsum, K.F. (2017). New interest in wild forest products in Europe as an expression of biocultural dynamics. *Human Ecology*, 45(6): 787–794.

Wirsum, K.F., Wong, J.L.G., Vacik, H. (2018). Perspectives on non-wood forest product development in Europe. *International Forestry Review*, 20(2): 250–262. https://doi.org/10.1505/146554818823767546

21

SOCIAL PROCESSES OF SHARING AND COLLECTING SEEDS AS REGENERATIVE AGRICULTURAL PRACTICES

Archana Patnaik and Joost Jongerden

Introduction

The Green Revolution fostered crop productivity through the use of high yielding varieties (HYVs) in combination with agro-chemicals (Bazuin et al. 2011; Power 2010; Thrupp 2000; Tilman et al. 2001; Rundgren and Parrott 2006). One of the environmental consequences of this production strategy was genetic erosion (Shiva 1991, 2016; Singh 2000; Thrupp 2000), since the high yielding varieties with a narrow genetic basis replaced a diversity of varieties used and saved by farmers (Peres 2016). In this chapter, we discuss this genetic erosion as part of a metabolic rift, and, reflecting on seed sharing practices of farmers in India, we discuss possibilities to move beyond this metabolic rift and build regenerative agricultural practices.

The interaction between nature and the human production process where growth and reproduction are possible without hampering the life systems is characterised as metabolic. According to Vandana Shiva (1991: 244), a metabolic rift occurs in the 'shift from ecological processes of reproduction to technological processes of production'. In the technological transformation in seed-production, in particular hybridization, seeds lose their reproductive and thus regenerative capacity. Other scholars have argued that an 'essential form of resistance, and one antidote to the problems of the Green Revolution, is to reclaim the means of production' (Jacques and Jacques 2012: 2986). Reclaiming seed is one of the ways to reclaim production and, as we will argue, addresses the problem of the rift.

In debates on reclaiming seeds, the possibility of sharing seeds is given a high priority (Kloppenburg 2014). Scholars like Sthapit (2013) and Kloppenburg (2014) have claimed that seed sharing is fundamental to the development of seed sovereignty. Wittman et al. (2010: 11) emphasized the importance of having access to and control over seeds 'as essential building block of food sovereignty'. It is against these backgrounds that this chapter discusses the centrality of seeds and sharing for addressing the metabolic rift and developing regenerative agricultural practices.

In this chapter, we first examine the idea of metabolic rift and metabolic fit, and then we reflect on the Indian scenario considering seeds. We go on to examine how different scholars have analyzed the conservation of seeds as commons and the implications of this for metabolic rift and describe the methodology employed for the analysis. Next, we reflect on cases of restoration practices and, based on the cases, we consider whether and the extent to which the local and regional production practices restore, rebuild, and regenerate the production process, thus mending the rift. Finally, we conclude the analysis with a consideration of what is required to make agricultural practices regenerative.

Metabolic rift, metabolic fit, and seeds

Environmental degradation caused by conventional agriculture has been conceptualized in terms of metabolic rift (Foster 1999; Wittman 2009). Deriving from Marx, Foster (1999) argued that the exchange between the production system and nature under modern capitalism has been increasingly harmful for nature, disrupting its ability to recover and reproduce. An additional factor leading to the metabolic rift according to Wittman (2009: 808) was the delocalization of agriculture, which 'entailed a thoroughgoing rupture with old ecological relations of production'. Thus, not only the changes in the production system through use of chemical fertilizers and pesticides have created (and continually recreate) the rift but also the breakdown in the local food system due to demands created by the globalized food production and distribution system. Local and regional production processes, especially small-scale agriculture, are based on the principle of maintaining the socio-ecological metabolism, in which nutrients derived from the soil during agricultural production are later replenished (Wittman 2009). This has been disrupted through the introduction of conventional agricultural practices. Considering production processes in the agricultural sector, therefore, choices where metabolic relations between nature and production systems are approached in terms of local and regional production processes imply possibilities for metabolic fit.

According to McMichael (2006, 408), peasant movements 'are the most direct expression of the crisis created by dispossession and ecological commodification, especially insofar as these movements manifest themselves in a diversity of responses to 're-spatialise' the social and economic relations in the corporate food regime'. For his part, Kloppenburg (2014) emphasizes that any form of resistance to the corporate control of food production has to take into consideration farmers' sovereignty over seeds that form the core of agricultural production. Wittman et al. (2010: 11) voice the same opinion, asserting that '[a]ccess to and control over seeds is an essential building block of food sovereignty'.

Thus, in order to mend the rift created and constituted by the conventional farming practice of Green Revolution (HYV) agro-industrial mono-cropping aimed solely at maximizing production, it is essential to consider the sovereignty of farmers in respect of seeds. Since peasant movements are considered as a site of resistance to conventional agriculture, we will reflect on the act of resistance wherein farmers have come together with non-governmental organizations (NGOs) to mend the rift in the agricultural production processes. Importance here will be given to rebuilding approaches to agro-ecological systems, reflecting on the local and regional production processes in India where a fit between nature and production system is aimed at through sustainable agricultural practices.

Seeds, resistance, and the Indian context

In India, the practice of conserving traditional varieties and using them for cultivation is not something that appeared with the debates about metabolic rift and need for sustainable farming practices. On the contrary, conserving seeds for sharing and planting in the following season is a much used practice of doing agriculture in India. According to Sthapit (2013, 18), the informal seed systems that operate between farmers are 'considered good traditional practices for seed security and therefore, ensuring food sovereignty'. Other scholars have emphasized how seeds become regenerative resources when managed as commons under the control of farmers (Shiva 1991). Thus, creating informal seed exchange networks not only addresses the agro-ecological problem but also creates conditions for mending the rift.

The metabolic rift in respect of seeds in India came about through the introduction of HYVs in the mid-1960s, which increased the dependence on external agencies for seeds (Shiva 2016). In addition to this, as Shiva (1991, 244) points out, seeds tend to lose their regenerative capacity when there is a 'shift from ecological processes of reproduction to technological processes of production', e.g. hybridization. Thus, the changed role of seeds from being treated as commons (Patnaik et al. 2017) shared with fellow farmers through informal seed networks to being regarded as commodities for buying and selling on the market led to a deepening of the rift. 'Farmers only can save two kinds of seed; composite/ HYVs or local varieties', stated Ghose (2005, 7), where HYVs are 'purchased regularly, anywhere from every two to three years, while the latter can be saved indefinitely'.

Essentially, one might say, the use of HYVs creates an opportunity to increase crop production but also dependence, while their non-uptake or discontinuation represents a form of resistance to the logic of the market. As elsewhere, HYVs and the associated practices leading to metabolic rift were widely employed among the farmers in India during the period of the Green Revolution. However, they were also resisted in India, and the new ways of doing agriculture were also referred to as a means for the corporate world to exert control over agriculture. This corporate control of seeds was challenged by several movements in India, such as the Beej Bachao Andolan (Save the Seeds Movement) in 1982, which brought people in Garhwal, Uttarakhand, together to revive the use of traditional or landrace seed varieties. Several NGOs – like Navadanya, the Deccan Development Society, the Genetic Resource Energy Ecology Nutrition (GREEN) Foundation, and Sahaja Samrudha, to name a few – also continued to resist the corporate control of seeds and encouraged farmers to save and cultivate the traditional varieties.

In the following sections, we discuss three cases from India where farmers along with NGOs have developed an informal arrangement to save and conserve seeds. These NGOs aim to diminish the dependence of farmers on external agencies for seeds, and their activities to achieve this can be mapped as reviving, restabilizing, and rebuilding to promote sustainable production practices. Rebuilding approaches to agro-ecological systems are further understood here following Reed's (2007) idea of whole systems and living systems. This is a holistic approach, one that gives importance to understanding the system in its entirety while recognizing the interconnectedness of its different parts in their complex interrelationships. We look at the interconnectedness of various aspects of the agricultural production process here, focusing on the techniques of conservation, sharing, and cultivation of seeds. Seeds are at the heart of the agricultural production process. Thus, we will be taking seeds as a lens to reflect on the local and regional production processes in India in the context of metabolic rift and (re)fit.

Community conservation of seeds, its social implications, and metabolic fit

In situ conservation of plant genetic resources (seeds) through community-based efforts has been analysed by various scholars in terms of practices that help to conserve agrobiodiversity (Shrestha et al. 2005, 2006, 2013; Thrupp 2000; Vernooy et al. 2015a). Through the conservation of different landrace varieties, these practices mend the rift of genetic erosion created by the monocropping approach implied by the cultivation of HYVs. Conserving seeds through *in situ* practices create the conditions for metabolic exchange between nature and the production system.

For example, access to seeds creates possibilities for their sharing and thence multifarious recombinations of their genetic materials. This recombination of genetic materials is a historical practice of cultivation that produces agronomic resilient varieties over time in form of landrace varieties or farmer-developed crop varieties (Kloppenburg 2008, 2010). Thus, seeds conserved by communities also act as sources for the development of resilient varieties contributing to the gene pool and thence addressing the rift created by the intensification of agricultural production through monocropping.

Scholars also argue that the community conservation of seeds contributes much more than just the maintenance of agrobiodiversity and metabolic fit. Seed conservation practices determine various kind of relations through seed networks creating related forms of agricultural socialities – and in the context of agro-industrial socialities, these are different, alternative, oppositional, if not exactly new. As Aistara (2011) notes, seed networks among Costa Rican farmers involve humans and non-humans creating a space for resistance to corporate monopoly. Da Via (2012, 230) explains how seed networks are created through informal exchanges in Europe as 'a concrete expression of the practice and politics of re-peasantization'. And Patnaik et al. (2017) have established how the management and conservation of seeds in community seed banks by a marginalized community in India has created a space of commons. Thus, seed conservation and sharing through seed networks not only facilitates the development of metabolic relations between nature and production processes but also creates spaces through which different forms of agricultural socialities become possible.

These social implications are essential when we analyse seed conservation and sharing in communities through seed networks following Reed's (2007) whole systems and living systems categories. Essentially, these analyse sustainability in the design and development field in terms of a move towards restoration, reconciliation, and regeneration, which can play an important role in agricultural production processes. For example, this approach emphasizes the *place* where stakeholders create a whole system of mutually beneficial and thus regenerative relationships. Introduced by Robert Rodale, a leading proponent of organic farming, the idea of regenerative agriculture takes a living systems approach to agriculture as a complex whole with its different parts and their relationships. For Rodale (1984, 294), a regenerative 'farm must be able to produce with few off-farm fertility inputs', meaning that, among other things, '[c]apture of nitrogen from the air and use of minerals from the soil are essential'.

While this systems thinking stresses the importance of the conservation of different units as a whole, Reed's (2007) notion of whole systems and living systems 'recognizes that the entirety is interconnected, and moves us beyond mechanics into a world activated by complex interrelationships – natural systems, human social systems, and the conscious forces behind their actions' (Reed 2007, 675). It is in order to understand agricultural production process in this whole system and living systems thinking that we will reflect on community practices in which restoration processes are effected through seed conservation and management practices that employ seed banks, focusing on the relationship between humans and nature to describe the reconciliation process and reflecting on the metabolic value thus created.

Methodology

For this study, we analyze regional food production systems where seeds are conserved by the communities. Three cases of seed conservation and sharing through communities of farmers with the help of NGOs are considered. These are mostly informal arrangements that save and conserve seeds collectively. One case of community seed banks (CSBs) will be analysed, organized by the Deccan Development Society (DDS), an NGO in Zaheerabad Mandal, which is a sub-district of Medak in the southern state of Telangana. The DDS CSBs are managed by women from a marginalized community of the Dalit caste (the lowest in the caste hierarchy). Farmers associated with DDS are mostly small-scale farmers (with less than a hectare of land) promoting millet cultivation and through that food sovereignty.

Key informants (associated with DDS for ten to fifteen years) were interviewed in September 2013 for information on the management and functioning of the CSBs. Each DDS community seed bank is managed by a women's group known as *sangham* (voluntary group), with one woman appointed as its head. To gain in-depth information, five focus group discussions (FGDs) were conducted with *sangham* heads covering 33 different villages. Further, unstructured interviews were conducted with ten *sangham* members from different villages, and the first author also visited the homes of three women in one village (Pastapur, where the DDS project office is located). In addition, a semi-structured interview of over an hour was held with one of the founding members of the DDS in order to gain information on the historical context of the CSBs. Secondary sources, such as government reports, DDS reports, articles and websites featuring DDS and the CSBs, were analysed to expand the primary sources and establish the context in which the struggle to food sovereignty was initiated.

In addition to the DDS CSBs, we look at the activities of two other NGOs, which run organizational seed banks (OSBs) in Odisha, India. The OSBs were created as a result of local farmers' resistance to the mode of production inherent in conventional agricultural practices and rejection of their external dependence on markets, institutes, and external agencies for seeds. The first of these NGOs that we discuss is Loka Samabaya Pratisthan in Khurda, and the second is Sambhav in Nayagarh district. Registered under the Society Act of India (1860), these NGOs practice organic farming. The farmers associated with these NGOs are based in an interior part of the country and mostly small-scale farmers.

The first NGO, Loka Samabaya Pratisthan, was visited during April 2013 and the second, Sambhav, during March 2013. During these visits, NGO founders and farmers associated with them were interviewed. Fifteen farmers linked to each NGO were interviewed using a semi-structured interview method to gain a holistic perspective of what metabolic rift and the repossession of seeds meant to them. Participant observation was carried out while attending various workshops on the conservation of agrobiodiversity through seeds at which both the NGOs were represented. These workshops provided spaces where farmers, scientists, and NGO activists from all over India came together and shared their views on saving seeds for biodiversity conservation. The various participant NGOs and farmers had similar objectives and backgrounds as those of the two NGOs studied here.

These workshops were further used to conduct unstructured interviews with an additional ten farmers from different NGOs attending the workshop to showcase their conserved varieties, which enriched the study perspective and helped in understanding the meaning of seed conservation and repossession to grassroots NGOs in India. In addition to this, the founders of both the NGOs were interviewed for additional information for over an hour. Thus, information from over 40 interviews in total is employed here.

CSBs and restoration practices of the DDS

CSBs are 'locally governed and managed, mostly informal, institutions whose core function is to maintain seeds for local use' (Vernooy et al. 2015b, 2). The DDS CSBs were established with the aim of conserving, maintaining, and reviving the traditional varieties of millet. First, the women's *sanghams* (voluntary groups) were formed and designated the task of collecting and then conserving seeds. Women from the *sanghams* divided the tasks among themselves and started procuring traditional millet seeds to build their resource base. The source for this was their social capital, their networks of community, and inter-community relationships. Procuring seeds from social networks like this is a long-standing, informal practice used by communities across the world (see Almekinders et al. 1994; Chambers and Brush 2010; Coomes 2010; Pautasso et al. 2013).

In order to build the resource base, *sangham* members started collecting seeds from their mothers, relatives, friends, and neighbours. These social networks were then expanded by creating new networks with others, such as friends' friends, distant relatives, seed savers, and farmers from other villages. This practice of collecting seeds, not only brought different people across different places into social relations based upon the collection and sharing of resources, but also helped in expanding and building the existing networks as a resource base. At the material level, these informal, seed-collection social networks created a pool of millet seed types, which became the foundation of the DDS CSBs. Through these efforts, the DDS has retrieved over 80 landraces over the years.[1]

Once storage was completed, *sangham* members started sharing the conserved seeds with other farmers. They did this based on the principle of double-the-return, in which farmers pledge to return twice the amount of seeds they borrow, thus increasing stock levels. Thus, community efforts at DDS were able to rebuild, maintain, and extend the resource base through seed-sharing and conservation, contributing thereby to agrobiodiversity. Seed conservation through CSBs revives and regenerates the traditional seed system but also broadens it for future ecological systems and cycles. For example, *sangham* members use sustainable practices to keep and cultivate the seeds stored in their CSBs. Employing their traditional, indigenous knowledge, the women use bamboo baskets covered with mud and cow dung paste to store the seed, which they also mix with neem leaves to protect against pests. These traditional remedies of pest protection during seed conservation are eco-friendly and economic (Mehta et al. 2012). So, the seed conservation practices of the DSS members create in the network of CSBs a system that reintegrates features of the traditional agricultural knowledge system, reinstating efficient, eco-friendly mechanisms for agricultural production.

Sangham members described the use of vermicompost for their fields, which they believe helps in restoring soil quality or health. Through this application, earthworms are used to convert organic waste into nutrient rich vermicast (Jansirani et al. 2012). Vermicompost is a 'nutrient-rich, microbiologically-active organic amendment that results from the interactions between earthworms and microorganisms during the breakdown of organic matter' (Lazcano and Domínguez 2011, 2–3). Thus, the DDS CSB members employ agricultural production processes that rebuild the existing soil structure and ecological systems, restoring the soil for cultivation. They also use cow dung and neem cakes as fertilizers and cow urine as a pesticide, thereby avoiding synthetic products.

If we analyse these choices made to increase soil health (thence its fertility, or productivity), we find them to be complementary to nature, creating a metabolic relation between nature and the agricultural production system. The farming practices employed by these women in their cultivation of millets comprise a blend of traditional, indigenous and of modern sustainable farming practices. So, by building the resource base, rebuilding it, and extending it, the DDS CSB system maintains the metabolic relation between nature and the production system, fitting the latter to the former. Further, using methods that regenerate soil, agriculture, and the environment using indigenous knowledge operates as an alternative to the conventional farming practices.

OSBs and restoration practices

The NGOs Loka Samabaya Pratisthan and Sambhav both use an informal social network to procure seeds for conservation and sharing through their OSBs. The Loka Samabaya Pratisthan founder explained that initially he had started looking for seed varieties himself and later appointed people to collect varieties using their informal networks of farmers and NGOs (first from different villages and then from different states). Similarly, members of Sambhav collected seeds from all over India using their informal social networks. Seed fairs in nearby villages or districts, farmers, individuals, and organizations visiting Sambhav all served as sources of seed collection. Apart from the social networks of farmers associated with these NGOs, their founders also collected seeds from seed fairs and used their own social networks for enrichment of the seed collection at their seed banks. So, like DDS, both Loka Samabaya Pratisthan and Sambhav used their social capital to build the resource base.

The resource base created at Loka Samabaya Pratisthan caters to the need for seeds of hundreds of farmers across India, whom the founder also trains in organic farming techniques.[2] The founder has collected over 350 varieties of rice since the inception of Loka Samabaya Pratisthan. It was found during the interview with him that the organization has partnered with Living Farms, another NGO working in the backward districts of Odisha to distribute seeds among farmers interested in cultivating the traditional varieties. Thus, we find that the resource base of Loka Samabaya Pratisthan is also expanded through informal social networks.

Sambhav has also been able to conserve many varieties of rice – nearly 500, according to Khetarpal (2018). In 2017, one of the founders of Sambhav, Ms. Sabarmatee, received the *Nari Shakti Puraskar,* India's highest civilian honour for women, for her contribution to women's empowerment, by training farmers in organic techniques. Ms. Sabarmatee highlighted the use of informal networks of seed sharing and the goal of encouraging farmers to 'adopt a seed'. Through this 'adoption', farmers would treat seeds as their children and become responsible for the sustenance and ultimately the maintenance of seed (so species) diversity.

The informal social networks of seed collection and sharing thus established further helped the NGOs in creating a pool of landrace seed varieties – rice in the case of Loka Samabaya Pratisthan; rice, vegetables, and fruits in the case of Sambhav. Both the NGOs shared the conserved varieties with other farmers based on the principle of double-the-return, exchange, or barter. The hundreds of varieties now being stored at these OSBs is the result of a continuous procurement and conservation. Further, having a pool of resource helped the NGOs to start practicing agriculture using sustainable agricultural practices. Once the means of production or reproduction (the landrace seeds) was at the OSBs, farmers associated with the NGOs also started cultivating and producing these varieties (so more seeds).

As in the DDS case, in both these NGOs farming practices were used that regenerate soil and agriculture. For example, both the NGOs used natural inputs, like neem cakes and cow dung. Such practices are attuned with maintaining the metabolic relationship between nature and the production system. Further, seed conservation by the two NGOs revived the traditional seed system and seed sharing. Seeds in these cases were shared within their social networks and across different villages, thus building and rebuilding the social networks through the OSBs and sustaining the related ecological systems and cycles.

Local and regional practices as restoring, rebuilding, and regenerating approaches

Summarizing the efforts of the three NGOs, we find social processes of seed sharing and collecting that help the farmers utilize sustainable farming for cultivation, ultimately restoring, rebuilding, and regenerating agricultural practices, especially for the small-scale farmers. In each of the three cases investigated, first, the landrace varieties were restored using social networks and social relations of farmers and associated members of the NGOs, and then, efforts were geared towards rebuilding the metabolic relations between nature and agriculture. In order to achieve a regenerative function, the following three steps were followed:

i) Build a resource base of landrace seeds in form of CSBs or OSBs;
ii) Extend the resource base through social networks of seed sharing and conservation;
iii) Practice sustainable farming, maintaining the metabolic relation between nature and the production process.

Almekinders et al. (1994), Chambers and Brush (2010), Coomes (2010), and Pautasso et al. (2013) have all described the practices of seed sharing through informal social ties as a long-standing practice. The three cases discussed here offer examples of new developments of this, of how the organization of social processes of seed collecting and sharing led to regenerative practices of (re)production. Again, it is to be noted that the landrace varieties can be saved indefinitely, reflecting the regenerative nature of these seeds, which can further be cultivated using non-synthetic fertilizers and pesticides leading to regenerative agricultural production systems. With the regenerative resources (landrace seeds) come rebuilding practices of cultivation employing sustainable farming techniques and indigenous knowledge. The combination of all these factors together created sustainable agricultural practices among the seed saving and sharing communities discussed.

The need for open spaces and regenerative approaches

The local and regional production practices cited in the above cases are able to restore, rebuild, and regenerate agricultural systems because of the informal arrangements through which they conserve and share the means of (re)production, the seeds. Community seed saving and sharing practices as reflected in these cases operate as arrangements in which seeds are treated as commons. This treatment of resources as commons created conditions for the exchange and sharing of the resources through informal seed networks. Informal exchange and sharing forms the basis for sustaining local and regional production systems. This stands in sharp contrast to the orientation of capital(ism) in which property claims are made to the genetic information contained in and defining the new varieties developed in laboratories by corporations, implying the ownership of seed (to be exploited for maximal financial gain).

As scholars like Aoki and Luvai (2007), Kloppenburg (2010, 2014), and Ramanna and Smale (2004) have pointed out, intellectual property rights (IPRs) create barriers in the sustainable use of plant genetic resources (PGRs). Further, as Roa-Rodríguez and van Dooren (2008, 181) have discussed, the changed usage of PGRs moves them from a

> space in which these resources were, by and large, open to all and could not be enclosed by any individual, towards a space in which resources are readily available for appropriation for commercial interests in a way that limits and sometimes prohibits the rights of other users.

In the three cases discussed here, landrace varieties were conserved and shared outside the purview of IPR, as a result of which conservation and sharing became easy. But this does not hold for other varieties, like breeders' varieties and genetically modified varieties, which are protected under the legal regime of IPRs. In our three cases, it was precisely the treatment of the landrace varieties as a common resource available in relatively open spaces that made the resources regenerative and created possibilities for regenerative practices. From the three Indian cases, it is evident that, in order to have sustainable agricultural production systems, it is essential to collect, save, and share seeds freely, without legal restriction.

Apart from being shared and conserved as a common resource, the seeds in these case studies brought farmers from different places together into a social process of sharing and collecting seeds. This process extended farmers' existing social networks, creating a space of commons. Beyond the idea of seeds as physical or information resources to which there is a common access – and more in the sense of the employment of these, among others, in social relationships (i.e. of commoning) – the idea of a space of commons here refers to a 'socio-economic or more broadly cultural space in which the marginalized but empowered community encounters and negotiates a common lived experience' (Patnaik et al. 2017: 178). In the examples from India, the CSBs and OSBs bring together and develop small-scale farming communities with the common goals of cultivating millet and other landrace varieties using sustainable farming practices. In all the three cases, the farmers who participate in seed sharing and conserving activities share a common lived experience with other farmers. The farmers have in common not just the goal of conserving varieties but also of negotiating their subjectivities with others outside this space. They develop an autonomy in relation to them.

Basically, these farmers challenge and diminish the monopoly over resources by conserving and then using seeds for agricultural production themselves. They denounce individuals, communities, and organizations, public and private, that practice conventional agriculture, do not support this agricultural production system, and do not encourage the bottom-up small-scale-oriented, community-based, self-directed sharing and conservation of seeds and all that this entails. Further, seed sharing among farmers from different communities broadens the space of commons as farmers become related to each other through what Aistara (2011, 494) calls a 'new culture of relatedness'. The network of seed sharing scales up to bring farmers from all over India into relationship 'through the common management of other biological species – the plants and their seeds' (Aistara 2011, 494). Thus, in these cases, apart from reviving the traditional varieties, farmers aim at developing a future-oriented understanding of the production system where resources are shared and brought together into the space of commons.

Apart from the three cases reflected in this chapter, we can observe instances in India where attempts are being made to formalize a certain space of commons. For example, the Millet Network of India (MINI) and the Organic Farming Association of India (OFAI) can be seen as formal representations of the space of commons. MINI is a network of communities and organizations from all over India that produce millets, and OFAI is a nationwide organization of organic farmers. Farmers associated with MINI and OFAI are brought into social relationship through defending their common goal of sustainable agriculture. Thus, farmers associated with these networks have shared aims and negotiate their subjectivities with others placed outside this space. For example, MINI and OFAI lobby government agencies for the rights of the farmers associated with them and in that defend the common goal of promoting sustainable agricultural practices. Here, farmers and communities across India linked to MINI and OFAI are related through a common lived (politico-socioeconomic) experience and thence growing a new culture of relatedness, and they gain an opportunity through this space to translate their struggle and resistance at a national level. Thus, the activities of conserving landrace varieties and sharing them with other farmers suggest scaling-up possibilities for local commons through the wider space of commons.

Conclusions: moving a step ahead – the regenerative agricultural system

The pathway of the 'Green Revolution' that seeks to foster crop productivity and increase food production has created a metabolic rift. This has resulted in an appeal for sustainable and regenerative production processes. As Dahlberg (1991, 337) stated, '[t]he concepts termed agroecology, permaculture, and regenerative agriculture emerged in the environmental and the post-oil-embargo era, drawing heavily on ecological and systems theories'. Further, scholars like Rodale (1984), Northbourne (1940), and Scofield (1986) have given importance to systems thinking in order to make agriculture regenerative where the conservation of different units is considered as a whole and valued. In the cases of regenerative seeds (landrace varieties) discussed in this chapter, however, we see that in order for systems to be regenerative, we need to consider the means by which they are sustained. Arrangements through which basic resources, such as seeds, are managed, conserved, and utilized in the (re)production system are important for the development of a metabolic fit between nature and agriculture, leading to further, sustainable farming practices. Thus, seeds managed as commons and cultivated using sustainable methods can be considered regenerative.

Further, we find that in order to address the metabolic rift in the agricultural production processes, a whole system and living systems thinking is important. In all the three cases, we found that the agricultural production process was thought of as whole, with seeds forming the entry point to the system. Through the usage of regenerative resources (landrace varieties) and sustainable cultivation practices, communities in all the three cases integrated themselves into the system, creating different interrelationships. In addition, it was found that the farmers in these cases practicing sustainable farming through seed sharing and exchange expanded their social networks and thus built and rebuilt the social networks, creating a space of commons and further maintaining agrobiodiversity. The seed conservation practices in the CSBs and OSBs reintegrated traditional agricultural knowledge. Thus, a whole system and living systems thinking is reflected in the production practices of all the three cases, and this thinking promotes the metabolic fit of regenerative (re)production systems.

In fact, a clear, sequential pattern emerged in all the three cases through which the sustainable agricultural production system became regenerative. First, efforts were geared towards building a resource base to be used for production; then, attempts were made to extend the resource base through social networks of seed sharing and conserving; finally, through the sustainable farming practices, the metabolic relation between nature and agriculture was regenerated. Regeneration was possible because these steps helped in rebuilding the metabolic relationship negatively impacted by the conventional agricultural practices.

In addition to this, we found that the conservation and sharing of landrace varieties and use of sustainable farming methods helped communities to interact and rebuild their farms as coherent units. In such an understanding, the interactions between nature and agricultural production form a whole system and living systems perspective that becomes a central concern. The evidence of this chapter suggests that seeds, their reproduction, and sharing practices are important constituents in these interactions, and therefore in the regeneration of agricultural systems. Seed sharing and collection through the space of commons can lead to the restoration, rebuilding, and regeneration of agricultural practices informed by traditional, indigenous knowledge in ways that are beneficial for small-scale farmers. Scholars should investigate further the practices and methods that redesign the relationship between nature and production systems, and by doing so address the rift for a better understanding of regenerative agricultural practices.

Discussion questions

1. How are arrangements through which basic resources, such as seeds, are managed, conserved, and utilized in the (re)production system important for bringing in metabolic fit between nature and agriculture creating sustainable farming practices?
2. What are the social implications of seed conservation and sharing for communities involved in the activity through informal seed networks?
3. Can the local and regional agricultural production practices restore, rebuild, and regenerate the production processes mending the metabolic rift?
4. How do seeds managed as commons and cultivated using sustainable methods promote regenerative agricultural systems?

Acknowledgements

The first author would like to thank the Deccan Development Society, Loka Samabaya Pratisthan, Sambhav and all its members especially Mr. P.V. Satheesh, Mr. Suresh, Mrs. Jayasri Cherukuri, Mr. Natabar Sarangi and Ms. Sabarmatee for their willingness to accommodate the needs of the research. A special thanks to all the farmers who devoted their valuable time providing insights into different areas of the research and who 'contribute to' and 'help in' maintaining the commons. The fieldwork and research was conducted as part of The Netherlands Organisation for Scientific Research (NWO) WOTRO funded project.

Notes

1 See DDS official website for details www.ddsindia.com/www/default.asp accessed 22 April 2019. Also, see Almekinders et al. (1994), who have also looked at how seed exchanges and sharing among farmers obtain new and lost varieties.
2 See the official website of the Global Green Grants Fund for details: www.greengrants.org/2011/11/02/a-retired-teacher-seeds-organic-farming-in-india/[Accessed 30 June 2015].

Further reading

Aistara, G. A. (2011). Seeds of kin, kin of seeds: The commodification of organic seeds and social relations in Costa Rica and Latvia. *Ethnography*, 12(4): 490–517.

Da Via, E. (2012). Seed diversity, farmers' rights, and the politics of repeasantization. *International Journal of Sociology of Agriculture and Food*, 19(2): 229–242.

Kloppenburg, J. (2014) Re-purposing the master's tools: The open source seed initiative and the struggle for seed sovereignty. *Journal of Peasant Studies*, 41(6): 1225–1246.

Patnaik, A., Ruivenkamp, G. T. P., and Jongerden, J. P. (2017). Marginalized community, space of commons and autonomy. *Journal of Rural Studies*, 53: 173–181.

Reed, B. (2007). Shifting from 'sustainability' to regeneration. *Building Research and Information*, 35(6): 674–680.

Works cited

Aistara, G. A. (2011). Seeds of kin, kin of seeds: The commodification of organic seeds and social relations in Costa Rica and Latvia. *Ethnography*, 12(4): 490–517.

Almekinders, C., Louwaar, N. and De Bruijn, G. (1994). Local seed systems and their importance for an improved seed supply in developing countries. *Euphytica*, 78(3): 207–216.

Altieri, M. A. (2009). Agroecology, small farms, and food sovereignty. *Monthly Review*, 61(3): 102–113.

Aoki, K. and Luvai, K. (2007). Reclaiming common heritage treatment in the international plant genetic resources regime complex. *Michigan State Law Review*, 35(1): 35–70.

Badgley, C., Moghtader, J., Quintero, E., Zakem, E., Chappell, M. J., Aviles-Vazquez, K. … Perfecto, I. (2007). Organic agriculture and the global food supply. *Renewable Agriculture and Food Systems*, 22(2): 86–108.

Bazuin, S., Azadi, H. and Witlox, F. (2011). Application of GM crops in sub-Saharan Africa: Lessons learned from green revolution. *Biotechnology Advances*, 29(6): 908–912.

Bezabih, M. (2008). Agrobiodiversity conservation under an imperfect seed system: The role of community seed banking schemes. *Agricultural Economics*, 38(1): 77–87.

Bezner Kerr, R. (2013). Seed struggles and food sovereignty in northern Malawi. *Journal of Peasant Studies*, 40(5): 867–897.

Bourdieu, P. (1985). The social space and the genesis of groups. *Theory and Society*, 14(6): 723–744.

Bourdieu, P. (1989). Social space and symbolic power. *Sociological Theory*, 7(1): 14–25.

Brundtland, G. (1987). Our common future: Report of the 1987 World Commission on Environment and Development. *United Nations, Oslo*, 1: 59.

Chambers, K. J. and Brush, S. B. (2010). Geographic influences on maize seed exchange in the Bajío, Mexico. *The Professional Geographer*, 62(3): 305–322.

Chiverton, P. A. and Sotherton, N. W. (1991). The effects on beneficial arthropods of exclusion of herbicides from cereal crop edges. *Journal of Applied Ecology*, 28: 1027–1039.

Coomes, O. T. (2010). Of stakes, stems, and cuttings: The importance of local seed systems in traditional Amazonian societies. *The Professional Geographer*, 62(3): 323–334.

Da Via, E. (2012). Seed diversity, farmers' rights, and the politics of repeasantization. *International Journal of Sociology of Agriculture and Food*, 19(2): 229–242.

Dahlberg, K. A. (1991). Sustainable agriculture: Fad or harbinger? *BioScience*, 41(5): 337–340.

Delêtre, M., McKey, D. B. and Hodkinson, T. R. (2011). Marriage exchanges, seed exchanges, and the dynamics of manioc diversity. *Proceedings of the National Academy of Sciences*, 108(45): 18249–18254.

Demissie, A. and Tanto, T. (2000). Dynamic participatory approach to the use of plant genetic resources. *Progress Report ETH/93/GEF31*. Institute of Biodiversity Conservation and Research, Ethiopia, Addis Ababa.

Foster, J. B. (1999). Marx's theory of metabolic rift: Classical foundations for environmental sociology. *American Journal of Sociology*, 105(2): 366–405.

Ghose, J. R. (2005). The right to save seed. Working Paper 13, *Rural Poverty and the Environment Working Paper Series*. Ottawa: International Development Research Centre.

Godfray, H. C. J., Beddington, J. R., Crute, I. R., Haddad, L., Lawrence, D., Muir, J. F., ... Toulmin, C. (2010). Food security: The challenge of feeding 9 billion people. *Science*, 327: 812–818.

Jackson, L., van Noordwijk, M., Bengtsson, J., Foster, W., Lipper, L., Pulleman, M. ... Vodouhe, R. (2010). Biodiversity and agricultural sustainability: From assessment to adaptive management. *Current Opinion in Environmental Sustainability*, 2(1–2): 80–87.

Jacques, P. and Jacques, J. (2012). Monocropping cultures into ruin: The loss of food varieties and cultural diversity. *Sustainability*, 4(11): 2970–2997.

Jansirani, D., Nivethitha, S. and Singh, M. V. P. (2012). Production and utilization of vermicast using organic wastes and its impact on Trigonella foenum and Phaseolus aureus. *International Journal of Research in Biological Sciences*, 2(4): 187–189.

Jarvis, D. I., Hodgkin, T., Sthapit, B. R., et al. (2011). An heuristic framework for identifying multiple ways of supporting the conservation and use of traditional crop varieties within the agricultural production system. *Critical Reviews in Plant Sciences*, 30(1–2): 125–176.

Khetarpal, S. (2018). Diversfied farming. *Business Today*, 23September. businesstoday.in (Accessed 7 May, 2019).

Kloppenburg, J. (2008). Seeds, sovereignty, and the Vía Campesina: Plants, property, and the promise of open source biology. Paper prepared for the Workshop on Food Sovereignty: Theory, Praxis and Power. November 17–18, 2008.

Kloppenburg, J. (2010). Impeding dispossession, enabling repossession: Biological open source and the recovery of seed sovereignty. *Journal of Agrarian Change*, 10(3): 367–388.

Kloppenburg, J. (2014). Re-purposing the master's tools: The open source seed initiative and the struggle for seed sovereignty. *Journal of Peasant Studies*, 41(6): 1225–1246.

Kumbamu, A. (2009). Subaltern strategies and autonomous community building: A critical analysis of the network organization of sustainable agriculture initiatives in Andhra Pradesh. *Community Development Journal*, 44: 336–350.

Lazcano, C. and Domínguez, J. (2011). The use of vermicompost in sustainable agriculture: Impact on plant growth and soil fertility. *Soil Nutrients*, 10(1–23): 187.

Lewis, V. and Mulvany, P. (1997). *A Typology of Community Seed Banks*. Chatham: Natural Resource Institute, Project A 595: 47.

Mäder, P., Fliessbach, A., Dubois, D., Gunst, L., Fried, P. and Niggli, U. (2002). Soil fertility and biodiversity in organic farming. *Science*, 296(5573): 1694–1697.

Marsden, T., Murdoch, J. and Morgan, K. (1999). Sustainable agriculture, food supply chains and regional development: Editorial introduction. *International Planning Studies*, 4(3): 295–301.

Matson, P. A., Parton, W. J., Power, A. G. and Swift, M. J. (1997). Agricultural intensification and ecosystem properties. *Science*, 277(5325): 504–509.

McMichael, P. (2006). Peasant prospects in the neoliberal age. *New Political Economy*, 11(3): 407–418.

Mehta, P. S., Negi, K. S., Rathi, R. S. and Ojha, S. N. (2012). Indigenous methods of seed conservation and protection in Uttarakhand Himalaya. *Indian Journal of Traditional Knowledge*, 1(2): 279–282.

Northbourne, L. (1940). *Look to the Land*. London: J. M. Dent.

Patnaik, A., Ruivenkamp, G. T. P. and Jongerden, J. P. (2017). Marginalized community, space of commons and autonomy. *Journal of Rural Studies*, 53: 173–181.

Pautasso, M., Aistara, G., Barnaud, A., et al. (2013). Seed exchange networks for agrobiodiversity conservation. A review. *Agronomy for Sustainable Development*, 33(1): 151–175.

Peres, S. (2016). Saving the gene pool for the future: Seed banks as archives. *Studies in History and Philosophy of Science Part C: Studies in History and Philosophy of Biological and Biomedical Sciences*, 55: 96–104.

Power, A. G. (2010). Ecosystem services and agriculture: Tradeoffs and synergies. *Philosophical Transactions of the Royal Society of London B: Biological Sciences*, 365(1554): 2959–2971.

Pretty, J. (2008). Agricultural sustainability: Concepts, principles and evidence. *Philosophical Transactions of the Royal Society of London B: Biological Sciences*, 363(1491): 447–465.

Ramanna, A. and Smale, M. (2004). Rights and access to plant genetic resources under India's New Law. *Development Policy Review*, 22(4): 423–442.

Reed, B. (2007). Shifting from 'sustainability' to regeneration. *Building Research and Information*, 35(6): 674–680.

Reganold, J. P., Papendick, R. I. and Parr, J. F. (1990). Sustainable agriculture. *Scientific American*, 262(6): 112–121.

Roa-Rodríguez, C. and van Dooren, T. (2008). Shifting common spaces of plant genetic resources in the international regulation of property. *Journal of World Intellectual Property*, 11(3): 176–202.

Rodale, R. (1984). Alternative agriculture. *Journal of Soil and Water Conservation*, 39(5): 294–296.

Rundgren, G. and Parrott, N. (2006). *Organic Agriculture and Food Security*. Bonn: IFOAM.

Sandhu, H. S., Wratten, S. D. and Cullen, R. (2010). Organic agriculture and ecosystem services. *Environmental Science and Policy*, 13(1): 1–7.

Schneider, M. and McMichael, P. (2010). Deepening, and repairing, the metabolic rift. *The Journal of Peasant Studies*, 37(3): 461–484.

Schoonbeek, S., Azadi, H., Mahmoudi, H., Derudder, B., De Maeyer, P. and Witlox, F. (2013). Organic agriculture and undernourishment in developing countries: Main potentials and challenges. *Critical Reviews in Food Science and Nutrition*, 53(9): 917–928.

Scofield, A. M. (1986). Organic farming – The origin of the name. *Biological Agriculture and Horticulture*, 4: 1–5.

Shiva, V. (1991). *The Violence of the Green Revolution: Third World Agriculture, Ecology and Politics*. Pengany, Malaysia: The Third World Network.

Shiva, V. (2016). *The Violence of the Green Revolution: Third World Agriculture, Ecology and Politics*. Lexington, KY: University Press of Kentucky.

Shrestha, P., Gezu, G., Swain, S., Lassaigne, B., Subedi, A. and de Boef, W. S. (2013). The community seed bank: A common driver for community biodiversity management. In de Boef, W. S., Subedi, A., Peroni, N., Thijssen, M. and O'Keeffe, E. (eds.) *Community Biodiversity Management: Promoting Resilience and the Conservation of Plant Genetic Resources*. London and Sterling: Earthscan, 109–117.

Shrestha, P., Subedi, A., Rijal, D., et al. (2005) Enhancing local seed security and on-farm conservation through community seed bank in Bara district of Nepal. In: Sthapit, B. R., Upadhyay, M. P., Shrestha, P. K. and Jarvis, D. I. (eds.) *On-Farm Conservation of Agricultural Biodiversity in Nepal, Vol. 2 Managing Diversity and Promoting Its Benefits*, Proceedings of the Second National Workshop, Nagarkot, Kathmandu, 25–27 August 2004, IPGRI, 70–76.

Shrestha, P., Subedi, A., Sthapit, S., Rijal, D., et al. (2006). Community seed bank: Reliable and effective option for agricultural biodiversity conservation. In Sthapit, B. R., Shrestha, P. K. and Upadhyay, M. P. (eds.) *Good Practices: On-Farm Management of Agricultural Biodiversity in Nepal*. Kathmandu: NARC, LI-BIRD, IPGRI, and IDRC, 41–44.

Singh, R. B. (2000). Environmental consequences of agricultural development: A case study from the green revolution state of Haryana, India. *Agriculture, Ecosystems and Environment*, 82(1): 97–103.

Spiertz, J. H. J. and Ewert, F. (2009). Crop production and resource use to meet the growing demand for food, feed and fuel: Opportunities and constraints. *NJAS-Wageningen Journal of Life Sciences*, 56(4): 281–300.

Srivastava, P., Singh, R., Tripathi, S. and Raghubansh, A. S. (2016). An urgent need for sustainable thinking in agriculture – An Indian scenario. *Ecological Indicators*, 67: 611–622.

Sthapit, B. (2013). Emerging theory and practice: Community seed banks, seed system resilience and food security. In Shrestha, P., Vernooy, R. and Chaudhary, P. (eds.) *Proceedings of a National Workshop Community Seed Banks in Nepal, Past, Present, Future*. Pokhara, Nepal: The Development Fund/ IFAD/BioversityInternational, Canada, Asia, Oxfam, 16–40.

Tansley, A. G. (1935). The use and abuse of vegetational concepts and terms. *Ecology*, 16(3): 284–307.

Thrupp, L. A. (2000). Linking agricultural biodiversity and food security: The valuable role of agrobiodiversity for sustainable agriculture. *International Affairs*, 76(2): 283–297.

Tilman, D., Fargione, J., Wolff, B., D'Antonio, C., Dobson, A., Howarth, R., … Swackhamer, D. (2001). Forecasting agriculturally driven global environmental change. *Science*, 292: 281–284.

UNCTAD. 2006. *Trade and Environment Review*. New York: UN. www.unctad.org/en/docs/ditcte d200512_en.pdf

Van der Ploeg, J. D. (2008). *The New Peasantries: Struggles for Autonomy and Sustainability in an Era of Empire and Globalization*. London, Sterling: Earthscan.

Vernooy, R., Shrestha, P. and Sthapit, B. (2015a). Origins and evolution. In Vernooy, R., Shrestha, P., and Sthapit, B. (eds.) *Community Seed Banks: Origins, Evolution and Prospects*. Abingdon, Oxon: Routledge, 11–19.

Vernooy, R., Shrestha, P. and Sthapit, B. (2015b). The rich but little known chronicles of community seed banks. In Vernooy, R., Shrestha, P., and Sthapit, B. (eds.) *Community Seed Banks: Origins, Evolution and Prospects*. Abingdon, Oxon: Routledge, 1–8.

Wittman, H. (2009). Reworking the metabolic rift: La Vía Campesina, agrarian citizenship, and food sovereignty. *Journal of Peasant Studies*, 36(4): 805–826.

Wittman, H., Desmarais, A. and Wiebe, N. (2010). The origins and potential of food sovereignty. In Wittman, H., Desmarais, A. and Wiebe, N. (eds.) *Food Sovereignty: Reconnecting Food, Nature and Community*, Halifax, NS: Fernwood, 1–14.

22

ENABLING MORE REGENERATIVE AGRICULTURE, FOOD, AND NUTRITION IN THE ANDES

The relational *bio-power* of "seeds"

Patricia Natividad, María Cristina Omonte Ferrufino, María Mayer de Scurrah, and Stephen Sherwood

Introduction

Rural development initiatives do not just seek *sustainable* solutions (i.e., results that continue or prolong over a period of time in relatively static or linear form), but also more *regenerative* ones (outcomes that renew and revitalize productive processes in ways that grow, expand, and diversify), ultimately contributing to the enhancement of people's material needs, but also their self-esteem and a sense of ownership, autonomy, and creativity – what we understand as the subjectivities of catalytic, lasting social change and development. In agronomy and health, one approach that is commonly called for in the literature is agro-biological and nutritional "diversification" – of the processes involved in on-farm production, consumption, circulation, and exchange for multiple purposes of health, wealth, and environment as well as the social.

In this age of broad-scale socio-biological decline in regions such as the highland Andes, as per Carolan (2011), we propose a look at agrobiodiversity and nutrition as an embodied form of inter-dependence and co-existence in and through food. Inherent in this *relational* perspective is a criticism over the common depiction of agrobiodiversity in the modernist literature as well as in public policy as an inanimate object and commodity, thereby creating the abstraction that agriculture, food, and nutrition are the product of a series of highly instrumental, independent, and linear chain-like linkages composed of discrete value. Instead, here we understand the "seed" as an embodiment of human-nonhuman *biopower* of genetic resources found in plants, animals, and microbes. In considering agrobiodiversity as part of an emergent, aesthetic order (rather than a natural one), the state of agriculture and health at any given moment is understood as the outcome of a value achieving process based on unfolding human-nonhuman legacies that are laden with potential – for harvesting sunlight and the provision of fiber, food, and energy as well as the generation of social worth and economy.

In this chapter, we employ a relational perspective to shed fresh light on three strategic interventions in food diversification as a means of helping rural people in the remote Andes to address their health concerns: 1) the multiple-purpose re-introduction of high-protein legumes to address nutritional deficiencies in vulnerable infants and mothers as well as soil fertility in Potosí, Bolivia, 2) the promotion of native potato landraces with high iron, zinc, and vitamin C in Huancavelica, Perú, and 3) the introduction of a vegetable food-basket or *canasta* as a means of creating demand and culture for nutrient-rich vegetables during the first "1,000 days of life" in Imbabura, Ecuador. In reflecting on these experiences, we ask, how is agrobiodiversity part of life regenerating forces of process and the emergence of more regenerative food and nutrition?

Malnutrition and the life-structuring potential of seeds

According to the Pan American Health Organization (PAHO), many women in poor regions of the highland Andes begin pregnancy in a condition of poor nutrition, which translates into a delay in intrauterine growth of the fetus. As a consequence, infants and young children in rural areas commonly start life with stunting and an increased susceptibility to disease, which can require special care and draw on the precious time and resources of families as well as public services. This situation is commonly attributed to the limited access of families to an adequate quantity and quality of food, to inadequate conditions of potable water and hygiene, and health care.

Being the only complete food during the first six months of the child's life, breast milk provides high-quality nutrients that can be absorbed easily, while protecting a child from infections and disease (León-Cava et al. 2002; UNICEF 2005). As a result, the World Health Organization recommends exclusive breastfeeding for at least the first six months of a child's life, and ideally for two years, and supplementing with a diet of nutritious foods.[1] Well-nourished children tend to be healthier, more productive, and more capable at learning; while malnourished children tend to have less capacity to learn and to be productive, which in turn, can contribute to a pernicious cycle of poverty in families and in the community.

As per the work of Reyes-García and Benyei (2019) that identifies multiple pathways of linking agrobiodiversity and maternal health and breastfeeding, here we utilize the seed as a metaphor that encapsulates an interactive, largely plant-based means of socio-biological and socio-material potential, in this case for enabling rural families to address concerns over malnutrition of highly vulnerable mothers, infants, and children. As Aistara (2019) explains, the social research on agriculture and food has largely overlooked a relational perspective when seeking to understand agrobiodiversity, leading to at least two consequences. First, when considering the social value and "life" of seeds, the identity and qualities of the seed taken on specific significance to the user and can provide an important basis for shaping her or his identity and sense of being. Secondly, with the perception of genetic resources as centers around which social networks emerge, seeds enter the realm of ownership, power, inclusion, and exclusion.

Moreover, agrobiodiversity is not a stable phenomenon. Rather, agrobiodiversity is the result of endlessly evolving interactions between people and their associations, whether in processes of production, consumption, circulation, health, sustainability, or equity (as well as their antipodes). When extracted from its social or environmental situation, for example, when leaving a field or plate and entering a laboratory or gene bank, only a limited number of the multifaceted and highly nuanced socio-biological and material qualities of agrobiodiversity survives. As a result, here we understand agrobiodiversity, as embodied in a seed, as a promising form of relational *biopower* that is both life-conserving and life-structuring.

Enabling more regenerative nutrition in the Andes: three projects

Yanapai: improving nutrition through potato biofortification

The Chopcca people live in highland communities that are situated between 3,400 and 4,500 meters above sea level, including 13 populated centers of Huancavelica, Peru. The population of the region is about 10,500 people, of which the vast majority are native Quechua speakers. During the period of civil unrest in 1980–1992, the Chopcca refused to allow either the Shining Path revolutionaries or the government's military into its communities. As explained in Roel-Mendizabel and Martinez-Vivanco (2013), today, the tenacious Chopcca spirit of resistance is captured by its people's unusual commitment to wearing traditional dress.

In large part tied to the extreme environment and living conditions of the highlands, Huancavelica has the highest rate of chronic malnutrition in Peru at 54.6% (INEI 2012). Height to age data taken for children under 3 years of age indicates chronic malnutrition among children at 44.2%. Agrarian reform arrived in Chopcca communities in the early 1970s, and presently, the distribution of land is based on a mixture of family-owned and collective property. The highland climate is marked by a dry season from June to August, with morning temperatures commonly below 0°C, and a wet season from September to May. The chief economic activity is small-scale family farming, based mainly on the cultivation of potato and barley as well as a suite of complementary crops, such as field bean, pea, oca, olluco, mashua, and tarwi or lupine bean. In addition, families commonly rear limited livestock, including sheep, cattle, and pigs as well as smaller animals in and around their homes, such as guinea pigs and chickens.

During the rainy season the Chopcca collect sundry leafy herbs, such as yuyo (*Brasica campestris*), olluco leaf, potato leaf and some families grow wild, *sacha* cabbage. Some vegetables such as onions, carrots, celery, squash are obtained either through barter or currency exchange at a weekly farmers' fair in the district capital, Paucará. The largest populated center of the Chopcca community, Ccasapata, organizes a weekly fair, where people can find vegetables, fruits, llama fat and viscera, and dried, salted fish as well as haberdashery and clothing.

Between 2011 and 2015, Grupo Yanapai, in collaboration with the National Institute of Nutritional Research, implemented the project, "Agrobiodiversity and Nutrition for Food Security in Chopcca Communities, Huancavelica". In 2010, about 42% of children under 5 years of age in the project area experienced malnutrition. The objective of this action-research intervention was to address food insecurity, in particular of vulnerable girls and women through enhanced functional diversity of its staple food source: potato. Strategies to improve agrobiodiversity included the introduction of potato cultivars with high iron and zinc content and new cultivars of traditional Andean roots and tubers, the promotion of mixed varieties with diverse disease tolerance (a traditional practice), tarwi, field beans, barley, and cultivated pastures (ryegrass with red clover) for feeding guinea pigs and chickens. In addition, Yanapai provided specialized, on-hand training for women and mothers in child nutrition, largely based on improved traditional recipes for meeting the nutritional requirements of infants between 6–36 months of age.

Yanapai's ex-post evaluations found that the lasting result of this approach was a marginal increase in the adoption of new potato, oca, mashua, and tarwi varieties, a tendency to raise a greater number of chickens for egg production, more precise information among women in the use, and revaluation of alternative food sources found in their farming, useful for improving the nutrition of their children and family. Nevertheless, measurable results in dietary changes were limited, although the sample showed a general decrease in malnutrition. The project identified significant changes that were not necessarily attributable to its activity, including a decrease in the number of farms under cultivation as well as an increase in the emigration of men and young families and other confounding factors. For example, soups, a traditional source of complementary feeding, actually were discouraged by certain nutritionists, who explained, "They [soups] are filled with liquid", arguing that the broth needed to be made more substantial with vegetables, carbohydrates, and meat. Participants explained that animals were considered a money-saving device for emergencies, so sacrificing them for child nutrition was deemed risky.

The process of introducing potatoes with high nutritional content was slow due to the need of lengthy field trials of three or more years in time. As a result, the new materials only arrived at the end of this assessment, and hence, their potential nutritional benefit for children and mothers was yet to be determined.

Despite favorable results in increased agrobiodiversity and knowledge tied to the training activities, the situation of children who failed to meet minimal nutritional requirements did not substantially change over the three years of the project. In part, this was attributed to the substantial contextual challenges of achieving healthy family nutrition in Huancavelica, in particular as a result of the harsh environmental conditions of the dry, barren highlands, limited access to potable water, and dietary preferences towards high carbohydrate foods as well as the limited timeframe of the project. One confounding factor was the fact that the most nutritious food products, such as tarwi, barley, potatoes, poultry, and eggs, commonly held the highest value in the market. Yanapai found that increased income from the sale of high value farm products as well as the generation of off-farm income, including temporary migration and direct payments from social programs, often did not have a measurable effect on improving maternal or child nutrition.

As published in Arce et al. (2016), Yanapai ultimately found that under the uniquely harsh conditions of rural Huancavelica, Chopcca farming was only partially capable of providing sufficient production for meeting the household-level energy, iron, and zinc nutritional demands (Figure 22.1). Of the tested interventions (increasing potato yield, introduction of biofortified potato, and the promotion of guinea pigs), the study identified that a mixed strategy held the greatest promise for reducing nutrition gaps. The research concluded that production potential of high-altitude Andean agriculture based on low-fertile land and essentially no irrigation was inherently low. As a result, household food security depended on not just effective agronomic interventions, but also the strategic mobilization of off-farm income opportunities and associated food procurement.

World neighbors: legumes for soil fertility and nutrition

Located in the isolated, precipitous, and semi-arid, highland mountains of Bolivia, the department of Potosí contains the highest indicators of rural poverty and food insecurity in the Americas. According to government statistics, over 96% of families do not meet their basic food needs, and child malnutrition ranges from 40 to 60%. Depending on elevation, typical crop rotations in the area include potato or maize as the first crop after fallow, followed by fava

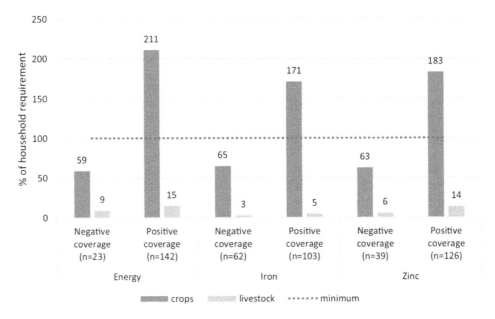

Figure 22.1 Contribution of crop and livestock production to the energy, iron, and zinc balance for households with a positive and negative coverage for each nutritional parameter. Dotted line (y=100%) represents basal household-level demand for full coverage.

Source: Arce et al. 2016

beans, small grains (wheat, barley, and forage oats), quinoa, and tarwi, followed by two to six years of soil "resting" or recovery. Sheep, cows, and llamas are important as economic assets, sources of meat and draft power as well as for their manure for agriculture. Overgrazing and the shortening of fallow periods of fragile hillside soils, however, commonly contributes to land degradation and decreasing crop yields. In addition, seasonal labor migration, mostly of men to nearby Argentina and Brazil, has created an acute labor shortage in rural villages.

The activity reported here took place in three major phases unrolled between 2005 and 2013. Working with Cornell University and local farmer experimenters, World Neighbors initiated action-research on agrobiodiversity as a means of strengthening the relationships between food security, soil health, and legume-based food and forage crops. Collaborating agencies included Bolivia's Forage Research Center (CIF), the Pairumani Center for Ecological Plant Genetic Research (CIPF), and a government-supported Hillside Agriculture Project (PROLADE) as well as the administrative and logistical support of state-based municipalities (*alcaldías*) and indigenous-based sub-municipalities (*sub-alcaldías*).

The first phase (2005–9) of the program emphasized the introduction of legumes in order to improve not only family diet, but also soil fertility. The most promising studied dual-use species were: broad bean (*Vicia faba*), pea (*Pisum sativum*), bean (Phaseolus vulgaris), tarwi (*Lupinus mutabilis*), and peanut (*Arachis hypogaea*). In addition, the project conducted trials on the following green manures solely for soil fertility improvement: arquilla (a wild legume, *Parocela pacense*), hairy vetch (*Vicia dasycarpa*), and forage oats (*Avena sativa*). The assumption was that the introduction of legumes would result in higher crop yields as a result of increased nitrogen fixation in soils as well as greater nutrition as a result of increased consumption of legumes in the family diet.

Between 2005 and 2008, 394 farmer-led variety trials were carried out, with the participants from each altitudinal zone involved in the selection of materials with the highest yield, the best adaptability, and culinary acceptance as well as N-fixation and biomass production (for example, see Figure 22.2). Similarly, 40 on-farm trials were established with vetch, tarwi, beans, and peas to improve soil fertility through biomass production. The project provided improved seeds, chemical inputs, tools, and fences for the plots as well as notebooks for farmers to record the performance of trials. The technical team carried out the follow-up and advice to the farmers, who were in charge of crop management. In all, World Neighbors held 470 field visits, 267 community workshops with men and women, and 16 cross-visits and learning tours. Meanwhile, the team of nutritionists and nurses trained women in legume-based cooking and nutrition, and they helped to form 12 mothers' clubs.

A second phase (2009–2010) focused on the barriers that mothers faced to improve the feeding practices of infants and young children, involving 195 households from the 13 communities involved in the initial phase. Between June 2009 and January 2010, a Nutrition PhD student from Cornell University led workshops based on the modified version of the Improved Practice Essays (EPM) based on Dickin et al. (1997). The action-learning agenda focused on nutrition education, with emphasis on how to improve the dietary practices of children under 2 years of age by means of available foods, breastfeeding,

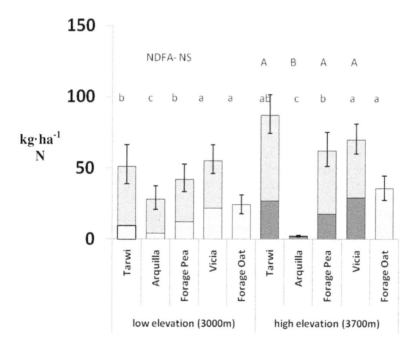

Figure 22.2 N soil stock (bottom light section of bar) plus fixed atmospheric N (top darker section of bar) of four species at two highland altitudes at sites in Northern Potosi. Capital letters denote statistically equal means for Nitrogen derived from N$_2$ fixation (Ndfa). Lower case letters denote statistically similar means for Ndfs. NS signifies No Significant Differences.

Source: Vanek 2011

and complementary feeding. The intervention methodology incorporated innovative visual tools, including child drawings and videos. In 2010, the team took part in a critical self-assessment of its work, leading to the launch of a third phase.

From 2010-13, the project reduced the intervention communities to five, with activities focusing on strengthening the earlier work in breastfeeding, complementary feeding, and dietary diversity. An additional issue, family support, was added as a new priority based on the results and reflections of the previous phases. Nutrition education workshops continued, with the difference that in this phase they were more dynamic, interactive, and organized around the employment of visual tools, including Participatory Video, Visualization of Processes and Participatory Programs (VIPP), and Participatory Action Research (IAP), recognized for promoting a democratic, horizontal, and creative participation of all participants. In addition, these activities involved the entire family: women, men, and children. Three workshops were held for each theme. The first workshop documented local knowledge; the second introduced scientific knowledge (comparing it with local knowledge and generating a dialogue about both), and the third involved a consultation with participants on changes that were necessary for improving infant and family feeding. In addition, the project added two new strategies: 1) "family accompaniment", which consisted of home stays of highly vulnerable families, during which project staff accompanied a family in its daily chores, with the objective of documenting, observing, and reinforcing key messages; 2) "native food day", which involved the preparation of traditionally nutritious foods and discussions of the importance of food in local culture.

With regard to the utilization of agrobiodiversity, and in particular legume-based green manures for soil fertility improvement, subsequent research concluded that soil management in rural Northern Potosi was oriented towards food production on a yearly timescale, whereas soil erosion and rangeland degradation accrued over decades (Vanek and Drinkwater 2013). Animal manure applications, and to a lesser extent the use of legume-based green manures, were sufficient to mitigate erosion impacts on crop yields, at least at present. As a result, soil degradation was not as swiftly apparent and could not be factored into short-term decision-making. Researchers found that management nested within environmental constraints, such as soil erosion and fertility loss, drove soil nutrient sustainability. They determined that the time-lag between management and long-term degradation was a principal sustainability challenge for farming in severe Andean highland conditions.

World Neighbors' ex-post evaluation corroborated the complexity of improving child nutrition in rural villages, where heavy workloads for mothers limited ability to prepare nutritious foods or to have the rest and time required for breastfeeding. Meanwhile, parents had come to believe that modern, processed foods were healthier and more prestigious. This reflection on the three phases led to three major insights. First, increases in food production did not necessarily translate into household-level improvements in nutrition. Second, the approach of working with mothers to improve nutrition was not enough to enable substantial change in health practices. Each family member influenced the possibility of health and disease. Although the mother commonly was primarily responsible for the care of children during the first years of life, the child's diet and nutrition depended on negotiations among adult members of the household, in particular the husband and mother-in-law. As a result, intra-family relationships merited special attention. Finally, the emphasis on improving mothers' cognitive knowledge in nutrition was deemed helpful, but insufficient in isolation of the contextual barriers in family and the community.

World Food Program: "the first 1,000 days of life"

In Ecuador, 23.9% of children under 5 suffer from chronic malnutrition. In rural highlands, these figures climb to over 50% of all children (Freire et al. 2014). A quarter of children are deficient in micronutrients, such as iron, zinc, or vitamin A, which can lead to chronic anemia. One-third of children between 5 and 11 years of age and more than 60% of the adult population between 19 and 59 are overweight or obese. Today, the double-burden of malnutrition – simultaneous under- and over-nutrition – is well established in both urban and rural Ecuador.

Operating from within the framework of the United Nations' Sustainable Development Goals and the "Zero Hunger Challenge" initiative, the World Food Program (WFP), in collaboration with Ecuador's Coordinating Ministry for Social Development (currently the Secretariat for Whole Life Planning), the Ministry of Economic and Social Inclusion, the Ministry of Public Health, the Ministry of Agriculture, and the Provincial Government of Imbabura, implemented the "Food and Nutritional Security" project in five parishes of Ibarra and Cotacachi. This project strategically targeted the "First 1,000 Days of Life", an effort to address the food and health monitoring needs during a woman's pregnancy as well as during the first year of a newborn child. This was addressed through regular medical check-ups, the provision of a diverse family diet by means of a regular food basket or *canasta*, and frequent capacity-building activities.

In order to diversify diets, the project sought the co-responsibility of beneficiary families in the constitution and delivery of a monthly fresh food basket per family, valued at $40 per month over a period of 15 months. The products offered in the basket were selected based on identified nutrient gaps of vulnerable people in the area and locally available foods, including both traditional Andean crops and European vegetables. As a result of concern over rising rates of overweight/obesity, the project also sought to decrease the consumption of carbohydrates.

Ex-post evaluation surveys identified an increase in the variety of fresh food in the diet of participating families, including fruits, vegetables, legumes, and animal-based proteins found in poultry, eggs, and meat and dairy products. As presented in Figure 22.3, this led to positive tendencies in anthropometric measurements of infants and children. The curves represents the weight for standard age made by the World Health Organization and the data of the beneficiary population surveyed by the Minimum Acceptable Diet. Children initially identified in a state of severe malnutrition were lifted to a moderate level of malnutrition. The evaluation found that trends in consumption were related to direct participation in the nutrition project, with an overall decrease in the consumption of fats and sugars that was significant. The project observed a reduction in the consumption of cereals, with a concomitant increase in the consumption of legumes as a source of energy and protein.

Subsequent critical review found that the delivery of monthly food baskets linked with nutrition-sensitive capacity-building and household visits led to an increase in the number of medical controls and a diversification in the family diet in ways that could improve the health of pregnant or lactating women with children under 2 years of age. When consulted about the reasons for success, project beneficiaries emphasized the importance of close collaboration with people working at the different ministries and institutions in the area. These agencies contributed logistical competence and organization stability as well as complementary financial resources to support nutrition activities, while allowing community leaders to establish needed relationships for other community concerns, such as improving roadways and schools. Nevertheless, the onerous logistical demands of a fresh food basket

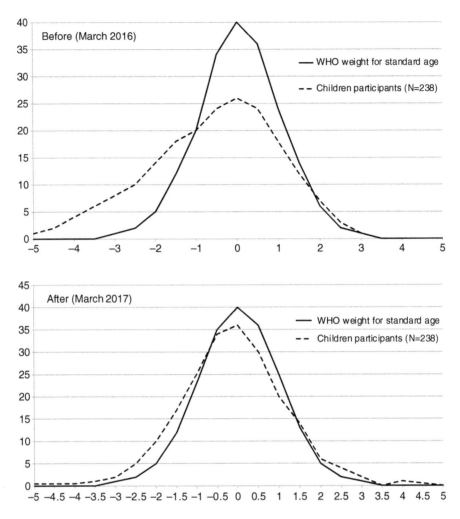

Figure 22.3 Changes in anthropometric measurements of children between the ages of 6–24 months of age involved in the 1,000 Days Project.

Source: WFP project survey

scheme raised concerns over dependence on externally based project support, placing into question the long-term viability of the work.

In response, the WFP found the up-front investment of financial and political resources necessary to "prime the pump" of demand for diverse, fresh foods in the project area. At the time of this research, it was experimenting with mechanisms to avoid or overcome dependence. For example, WFP increased the involvement of leaders and their organizations in the implementation of the food basket distribution system. The project strategically involved farmers and community health promoters in its training activities and monitoring and evaluation system as well as the design and implementation of subsequent corrective measures. Future priorities included the need to identify novel ways of strengthening producer-consumer ties, for example in administrative and financial management of the basket scheme, the creation of joint consumer-producer organizations, and special attention to new commercial opportunities.

Discussion

Investment in process

Each project sought to creatively utilize agrobiodiversity to address food security concerns, be it through strategy of biofortification in a long-standing staple crop (potato) as a means of addressing priority deficiencies (in particular, iron and zinc), the strengthening of legumes in production systems for dual purposes of improving soil fertility and nutrition (proteins and fats as well as feeding animals for meat), and diversifying diet by means of the regular production and distribution of diverse, fresh-food baskets (the *canastas*). The outcomes of this activity, however, were not always predictable or straightforward.

In the case of Northern Potosi, sometimes there was a conflict between the competing objectives of improving soil fertility and meeting immediate family nutrition needs, for example, when wanting to turn in cover crops at maximum nitrogen contribution of 80% flowering. Additionally, some of the most promising legumes, such as the green manure hairy vetch, were exotic and difficult to independently reproduce. Yanapai was successful in identifying biofortified materials, but the most nutritious potato was not always the most productive, tasty, or commercially attractive. In the case of WFP, the *canasta* system generated heavy logistical demands and products were not readily available from local producers, causing the project to purchase products from outside the area.

Faced with challenges in the form of acceptance, relevance, participation, and impact, each project introduced a number of processed-based innovations as a means of "narrowing distance" between the experience, needs, interests, and motivations of its project beneficiaries as well as the project staff itself. With the help of a PhD student, World Neighbors introduced Participatory Video, Visualization of Processes and Participatory Programs (VIPP), and Participatory Action Research (IAP). The WFP prioritized beneficiary monitoring of its training activities, and the direct involvement of beneficiaries in subsequent innovations. Meanwhile, Yanapai found the need to renew and strengthen community leadership and organization.

Despite the "high cost" of participatory development, for World Neighbors and WFP, attention to the quality of process was a necessary means of enabling innovation through "creating trust", "building confidence", and "enhancing local ownership" of learning-action processes. According to the World Neighbors' project coordinator, "We sought to organize our work around the rhythms of the community." In all cases, over time the demands of beneficiaries led to major changes in project priorities, designs, and the investment of resources. Through such means, distances – temporal, geographic, social, and otherwise – between project and intended beneficiaries were narrowed. Rather than seeds being used as an end, they became a means. Rather than pushing or imposing an externally defined agenda, the priority became bringing forth and co-generating a desired future – one that was healthier, more sustainable, more socially equitable and just. Over time, each of the three projects worked in its own way with the life force in agrobiodiversity to strengthen certain strategic relations – with soil, human body, neighbors, and difficult-to-reach institutions, thereby enabling previously neglected or unavailable potentials for transformation.

Hidden associations

Each of the projects erected its own conceptual borders dividing insides from outsides, families by household, youth from adults, mothers from fathers, indigenous first nations from moderns, traditional foods from modern food, soils from plants, varieties from other types of potato, health from disease. The Euclidean model of explanation continually assumes that threats (and solutions) come from the outside, rather than thinking of the present actuality as simply part of the state of things. A territory continually undergoes change wrought by mutable organisms and other agencies, transforming material states, social norms, and organization. The three cases presented here show that agrobiodiversity and food can be fundamental elements of this endless forging of the present.

In categorization of life, for example in creating closures around organisms and in creating limits of good and bad practice, farmers, development practitioners, researchers, agency officials, and others became involved in biopolitics. This happened in favor of certain worldviews and interests, including economics, for example, when determining a household or neighborhood healthy or sick, indigenous, naming a variety Andean, high in iron or zinc, or labeling a process productive or participatory. While there were degrees of truth in such determinations, as per the findings of past scientific activity and the rigors of good application of scientific method, such categorization was inherently partial and temporary. According to traditional Andean cosmovision, a potato, not unlike other organic forms, inevitably is in a continual state of (de)composition. What today constitutes the form of a potato, tomorrow may become part of an entirely new form: a soup, a petri dish auger, or a starch. Shining a light on a certain moment of that dynamic effectively hides others.

Hinchliffe et al. (2013) find that such geometrical mapping is selective, exclusive, and political. In the case of agrobiodiversity, it is strategically biopolitical. The resulting typology brings forth a certain world, with all of its contours of color, flavor, and taste, for example, at the cost of other possibilities. The introduction of modern agriculture and food in the 20th century is how Andean cosmology historically became unsettled and displaced by modernity. More recently, social activists have organized in alternative food networks as a form of sub-political counter-movement. Each project experienced confounding dynamics of each – pre-planned and emergent, modern and traditional, lay and scientific – at work in its activity.

The practice of agriculture, food, and health, not unlike other moments in reality, is fundamentally holomorphic and infinitely differentiable. As such, its characterization is inevitably partial and temporary. Nevertheless, bodies of science in agriculture and health have radically and strategically sought to reduce agriculture, food, and health (as well as other forms of life) to constituent elements, such as the farm, the producer, and consumer, a series of nutrients, fats, and amino acids as well as certain commodity forms, weights, flavors, and tastes.

Borders dividing realities are not just lines of difference, but also sites of encounter and contact, in particular among living organisms. Even though the potato may be self-pollinating, varieties compete in other ways – for example, with insects, weeds, and pathogens in the field as well as with micro-organisms in the soil, moisture, and nutrients. Similar to climate, market forces, the movement of genes, discourses, and narratives, the present is the product of the intensity of associations between and among organisms, for example, food and the body, pathogen and the host, a plant and the soil. Through workshops, field trials, cross-visits, and other encounters, the projects played with borderlines to expose participants to previously unseen or neglected phenomena, thereby unleashing the potential of fresh experience and creativity on the present.

Human-nonhuman subjectivity

Present-day strategies of addressing the extreme poverty and marginalization of the people in remote areas of the highland Andes commonly have proven ineffective and inadequate. This situation demands new ways of thinking, organizing, and doing. In order to "step outside the box" of present-day agriculture and food, we argue for an exploration of the human-nonhuman relational interactions, transactions, and transformations at the edges of development. As demonstrated in each of the projects, a population of individuals living and acting in a family and community does not become underfed and sick alone. In Northern Potosi, for example, disease and hunger is the product of centuries of socio-biological and material interactions to the point where poverty and premature death are not an isolated event, but rather an all-too-common reproduction, if unwanted, in households across the landscape.

From the work reported here, nutrition and health cannot simply be achieved by walling in nutrients or walling off an external world of pathogens and other invaders. Instead, health must be attained in and through daily living and being. As such, (ill-)health is understood as fundamentally relational – i.e., an entangled interplay among environments, pathogens, and hosts (including humans). Returning to the work of Hinchliffe et al. (2013) on the biopolitics of "infected life", the task of development for regenerative food involves less the establishment of walls or borderlines between malnourishment and nourishment and the control of infectious disease and more the enabling of socio-biological and material territories that favor health and wellbeing.

Each case presented here found untapped energy in agrobiodiversity for shaking up the present, but this potential did not rest merely in classical class-based categorizations of people's experience, as commonly depicted in the development literature. Rather, the possibility of change rested at the dynamic territorial edges of living and being in the household, on the pathways of the village, and in the hillsides. Through human-nonhuman encounters of knowledge, affect, and skill in food and agriculture, the projects diversely assembled relational biopower found in and among plants, humans, microbiology, and the landscape, thereby generating new subjective entanglements and associations.

Conclusions: the relational bio-power of seeds

According to the work presented here, progress towards more regenerative agriculture and food is not necessarily achieved through the *extensification* of experience (i.e., an outward growth or scaling in number, area, or size), but rather through the *intensification* (i.e., a "deepening" or diversification of experience) of the entities of which they are presently a part – the genetics of existing, yet largely underutilized potato varieties, the strategic use of legumes for both harvesting atmospheric nitrogen for soil fertility improvement and the consumption of fats and proteins, and novel utilizations of the surrounding institutions and social relationships in a watershed. In so doing, participants came to disrupt the notion that marginalization and poverty were, as commonly argued in the development literature and politics, the inevitable product of genetics, race, the "the capitalist system", or simply bad luck.

Each initiative pursued a unique pathway to utilizing agrobiodiversity as a high potential, self-replicating force for development. For example, in seeking to mobilize the nutritional heterogeneity inherent in native potato varieties, Yanapai localized source of effective biofortification and addressing iron and zinc deficiencies. World Neighbors fostered the utilization of legumes to address protein and fat deficiencies while seeking to address concerns over soil fertility and degradation, and the WFP enabled conditions for the installation of a community food basket as a social innovation for "priming the pump" of direct purchasing.

For the World Neighbors' project in Northern Potosi, improving process involved the introduction of new interactive methodologies that sought to strengthen the ties and associations between the project and local practice and social dynamics. Similarly, for Yanapai in Huancavelica and WFP in Imbabura, this involved the ability to set aside technical priorities and to create or improve fit between the project and participating communities in ways that enhanced local leadership over the governance of food.

Depictions of agrobiodiversity in the scientific and development literature are inevitably partial. Experiences with project beneficiaries and the critical reflection presented here lead us to raise questions over spatial segregation between people and their agrobiodiversity, for example with regard to nutrition and the body, the body and its food, food and its genetics, soil and agriculture. For more regenerative food and agriculture, interventions must fully embrace the depth and breadth of human-nonhuman potentialities enabled (and disabled) through people's inevitable living and being in and through seeds and agrobiodiversity.

The present state of biodiversity in agriculture, food, and nutrition is not the product of local or global phenomena, but rather simultaneously each: a highly situated, though infinitely contextualized, organic encapsulation of a particular moment in life – a singularity. As a biological form, the seed is not composed of a part or whole, but rather it is composed of overlapping and penetrable entities capable of continual reproduction. In this sense, we find that seeds are fundamentally regenerative. Owning infinitely diffuse boundaries, agrobiodiversity is a potentially powerful point of entry to both understanding socio-material and biological development as it is for engaging and intervening in it. Add water, and a seed takes on a life of its own!

Discussion questions

1. How are genetic resources (i.e., seeds) part of the (re)generating forces of life?
2. How is human-seed subjectivity involved in constituting an unsustainable present, in terms of growing ill-health, social inequality, and environmental decline?
3. How do people strategically enable, through agrobiodiversity or seeds, essential relationships of health and sustainability, both within families, neighborhoods, and social networks as well as between people and their natural environments?

Note

1 For example, see: www.unicef.org/spanish/nutrition/index_24824.html.

Acknowldgements

The McKnight Foundation's Collaborative Crop Research Program financed the three projects presented here. The authors would like to thank the respective teams at Yanapai, World Neighbors and World Food Programme for their contributions as well as the insightful commentary of Claire Nicklin and Steven Vanek on an initial draft. Any lingering mistakes belong to the authors.

Further reading

Sherwood, S., A. Arce and M. Paredes (eds). 2017. *Food, Agriculture and Social Change: The Everyday Vitality of Latin America*. London: Earthscan/Routledge. A summary is available at: www.ileia.org/2017/04/18/vitality-everyday-food/

Willett, W., J. Rockström, B. Loken, M. Springmann, T. Lang, S. Vermeulen, et al. 2019. Food in the anthropocene: The EAT–*Lancet* Commission on healthy diets from sustainable food systems, 393(10170): 447–492. A summary is available at: https://eatforum.org/eat-lancet-commission/eat-lancet-commission-summary-report/

Zimmerer, K.S. and S. de Haan (eds). 2019. *Agrobiodiversity: Integrating Knowledge for a Sustainable Future*. Cambridge, MA: Massachusetts Institute of Technology and Frankfurt Institute for Advanced Studies. Chapters are available at: https://esforum.de/publications/sfr24/Agrobiodiversity.html

References

Aistara, G.A. 2019. Seed relations: Placemaking through ecological, social and political networks as a basis for agrobiodiversity governance. in Zimmerer, K.S., and S. de Haan (eds). *Agrobiodiversity: Integrating Knowledge for a Sustainable Future*. Cambridge, MA: Massachusetts Institute of Technology and Frankfurt Institute for Advanced Studies, pp. 283–306.

Arce, A., H. Creed-Kanashiro, M. Scurrah, R. Ccanto, E. Olivera, D. Burra, and S. De Haan. 2016. The challenge of achieving basal energy, iron and zinc provision for home consumption through family farming in the Andes: A comparison of coverage through contemporary production systems and selected agricultural interventions. *Agriculture and Food Security*, 5(23): 1–19. doi: 10.1186/s40066-016-0071-7.

Carolan, M. 2011. *Embodied Food Politics*. Surrey, England and Burlington, USA: Ashgate.

Dickin, K., M. Griffiths, and E. Piwoz 1997. *Designing by Dialogue: A Program Planners' Guide to Consultative Research for Improving Young Child Feeding*. Washington, DC: Health and Human Resources Analysis Project.

Freire, W., et al. 2014. The double burden of undernutrition and excess body weight in Ecuador. *American Journal of Clinical Nutrition*, 100(6): 1636–143S.

Hinchliffe, S., J. Allen, S. Lavau, N. Bingham, and S. Carter. 2013. Biosecurity and the topologies of infected life: From borderlines to borderlands. *Transactions of the Institute of British Geographers*, 38: 531–543.

INEI (Instituto Nacional de Estadística e Informática). 2012. *Encuesta Demográfica Y De Salud Familiar-ENDES 2011*. Lima, Perú: Instituto Nacional de Estadística e Informática.

León-Cava, N., C. Lutter, J. Ross, L. Martin. 2002. *Cuantificación de los Beneficios de la Lactancia Materna: Reseña de la Evidencia*. Washington, DC: Organización Panamericana de la Salud (OPS). 188 pp.

Reyes-García, V., and P. Benyei. 2019. Exploring pathways to link agrobiodiversity and human health. in Zimmerer, K.S., and S. de Haan (eds). *Agrobiodiversity: Integrating Knowledge for a Sustainable Future*. Cambridge, MA: Massachusetts Institute of Technologyand Frankfurt Institute for Advanced Studies, pp. 225–240.

Roel-Mendizabel, P., and M. Martinez-Vivanco. 2013. *Los chopcca de Huancavelica Etnicidad y cultura en el perú contemporáneo*. Lima, Peru: Ministeria de Cultura, p. 310.

UNICEF, 2005. *Hacia la promoción y el rescate de la lactancia materna*. Caracas, Venezuela: UNICEF.

Vanek, 2011. Legume-phosphorus synergies in mountain agroecosystem: Field nutrient balances, soil fertility gradients, and effects on legume attributes and nutrient cycles in the Bolivian Andes. PhD Dissertation, Ithaca, NY: Cornell University, p. 171.

Vanek, S. J. and Drinkwater, L.E., 2013. Environmental, social, and management drivers of soil nutrient mass balances in an extensive Andean cropping system. *Ecosystems*, 16: 1517–1535. 10.1007/s10021-013-9699-3.

Vanek, S. J., A.D. Jones, and L.E. Drinkwater. 2016. Coupling of soil regeneration, food security, and nutrition outcomes in Andean subsistence agroecosystems, *Food Security: the Science, Sociology and Economics of Food Production and Access to Food, Springer; The International Society for Plant Pathology*, 8 (4): 727–742, August.

23

CIRCULAR FOOD ECONOMIES

Stefano Pascucci

Introduction

In this chapter, I discuss the emerging concept of 'circular economy' within the wider debate on 're-thinking food systems'. With this purpose in mind, I have adopted a 'food system design' perspective, highlighting how this debate is becoming progressively more polarized and ambiguous, creating de facto two narratives, each leading to the identification of very different *food futures*. In order to introduce the two narratives and to disentangle their key elements, I will make use of few key (design) questions and namely: (i) What has circular economy to do with re-thinking food systems? (ii) For whom are we (re-)designing food systems? What are our design intentions? And finally (iii) at what scale will the 're-designed' system operate?

In tackling these questions I will make use of various examples of 'circular practices' as they are emerging and unfolding in the empirical contexts in which the circular food economy narratives are taking shape. In so doing I will identify pathways for re-designing food systems, giving us the opportunity to discuss the reflexive and transformational ambitions (and potentials) of these narratives, the (im)possibilities of their reconciling, and to question how to define food futures in more general terms. In short, I will talk about circular food economies as a *plural*, *multiple*, *diverse* phenomenon and concept.

The point of departure in the intellectual journey I am presenting in this chapter is to make sense of these two different circular food economy narratives. What are they? And why should we care? In the next section I will describe the narratives in further detail. But to start, we can think about the first narrative as the set of policies, research agendas, and corporate strategies revolving around the capacity of circular economy to 're-design' so-called linear food systems, defined as the current large-scale and highly industrialized systems of food production, distribution, and consumption (Pascucci and Duncan 2017). In this narrative a circular food economy is a system that relies on practices such as: (i) closing loops of key nutrients, like water, nitrogen, or phosphorus, (ii) cascading materials, like recycling fibers for several purposes and usages before their disposal or incineration, (iii) applying bio-based technologies and recovering energy from biological materials, for example through anaerobic digestion or composting (Stahel 2016; Ellen McArthur Foundation 2019). In this narrative circular is defined as 'opposed' to linear, to emphasize the importance of eliminating and designing out the concept of waste. In this narrative 'circular' addresses the problem of resource extraction and exploitation. In this narrative a circular food economy is a food provisioning system designed around the *principles and practices of an industrial ecology*.

The second narrative, instead, takes into account agricultural and communitarian practices aiming at enhancing soil health, biodiversity, and large nutrient bio-cycles as key planetary boundaries (Pascucci and Duncan 2017). It considers these practices connected and embedded in wider social practices, in fact combining an ecological worldview with a social justice perspective to define 'regenerative food systems'. In this narrative, regenerative is part of various and diverse food cultures, which inform what people do, their practices in fact. The dominant perspective is around the idea of fostering food systems based on regenerative agriculture, understood both as a 'political movement' and as a set of social practices, while circular economy is not yet fully defined or understood. Sometimes it is even contested or neglected. In this narrative a circular food economy is a food provisioning system designed around the *principles and practices of an agro-ecology*.

At the origin of the debate: the principles of circular economy

Circular economy has emerged as an approach that celebrates *regenerative and restorative* design, and is based on the principles that resources need to circulate in closed loops; that renewable energy should be used where possible; and that diversity should be celebrated. In other words a circular system draws on, and fits within, local natural systems (Webster 2013; Ellen McArthur Foundation 2013; Ghisellini et al. 2016). In contrast to a 'linear approach' to designing an industrial system, circular economy proposes to identify and operate in cyclical metabolisms (Ellen MacArthur Foundation 2013). From this perspective and since its origin, circular economy has been framed as a vision to re-design industrial systems around a set of principles and practices such as (i) *closing loops* of nutrients and creating rich feedback flows of materials and information, and fostering *regenerative* approaches; (ii) *sharing* and *optimizing* use of resources; (iii) *innovating* by *dematerializing* and exploring the potentials of *new technology*, for example to transport materials and design products (Webster 2013; Ellen MacArthur Foundation 2015; Stahel 2016; Pascucci and Duncan 2017).

Closing loops and using regenerative approaches is maybe the most prominent principle of circular economy design. Closing loops and regenerating deal with *design flows of healthy nutrients* (Webster 2013). They point to the need to design production, distribution, and consumption processes using renewable energy and materials, taking into account the properties of eco-systems, thus managing to return biological nutrients safely back into nature and its cycles, enhancing the quality of water, air, and soil (Braungart and McDonough 2002; Webster 2013). A regenerative circular system is able to produce and distribute products avoiding the use of fossil fuels, while maximizing the use of healthy materials, enhancing eco-system services from production to consumption (Ellen MacArthur Foundation 2013). In this way, circular economy aims to inspire transition towards a post-carbon/post-fossil-fuelled society, and it demands a re-think of the way we associate energy production and consumption with industrial systems (Webster 2013).

Sharing and optimizing relate to the idea of streamlining and seeking efficiency, and collaborating, networking, and sharing key resources (Ellen MacArthur Foundation and McKinsey Center for Business and Environment 2015). A system based on sharing resources aims at reconciling efficiency and resilience through adaptive optimization processes that require a *system thinking approach* and flexibility in terms of technology, practices, and capabilities used (Webster 2013). Sharing and optimizing along the supply chain also deal with prolonging the life-span of key materials, for example, reusing and up-cycling packaging (Ellen MacArthur Foundation and McKinsey Center for Business and Environment 2015).

Dematerialize and use new technology look at circular economy as an enhancer of innovative possibilities (Ellen MacArthur Foundation and McKinsey Center for Business and Environment 2015). For example, packaging represents a resource-intense component of current industrial systems. Reducing the use of materials and energy for packaging products is a strategy to dematerialize. Use of alternative systems to deliver products to consumers as inputs along the supply chains, for example via a more intense use of virtual and ICT-based platforms, can be seen as a way of combining dematerializing and use of new technologies. Virtual value chains and online shopping are currently the practices leading towards the combination of new technologies and dematerialized delivery systems (Ellen MacArthur Foundation and McKinsey Center for Business and Environment 2015).

A circular food economy as an industrial ecology

The first narrative of a circular food economy designed as an industrial ecology is emerging from the implementation of the above mentioned principles into practices to re-think conventional food systems, also defined as 'linear' or 'extractive' (Ellen MacArthur Foundation 2019). The starting point of this narrative is the identification of the challenges faced by 'linear food systems' as 'socio-technical problems' that have reached a critical stage due to the scale of operation of these systems. From this perspective, circularity offers the opportunity to identify 'technological fixes at system level' rather than 'at product or company level'. In other words, it offers the opportunity to tackle the current global socio-ecological crisis related to our food systems by looking at shifting the scale of solutions. It is about matching problems and potential solutions at a global, complex, and systemic scale.

The assumption in this narrative is that part of the challenges faced by current food systems is due to the fact that they have been designed in a 'linear way' (Ellen MacArthur Foundation 2019). This means that in a 'linear food system' natural resources are extracted, made into products (food, feed, or fiber), consumed, and disposed of, generating waste, detrimental emissions, and pollution (Jurgilevich et al. 2016; Ellen MacArthur Foundation 2019). While these systems can be highly resource efficient and productive in the short and medium run, the drive to specialize and increase the scale of operation, thus to standardize and streamline processes, often leads to over-reliance on a few productive varieties and an over-dependency on external inputs, including biological materials, technologies, and infrastructures (Webster 2013). A linearly designed food system, like any other industrial system or economy, has embedded the tensions inherently present in 'linear approaches', namely, being 'extractive by design'. On one hand, in an 'extractive' economy there are unprecedented growth and provisioning of gains, for example in terms of agricultural productivity. On the other hand, an 'extractive' economy eventually faces the reduction of (biological and cultural) diversity, an increase in the intensification of resource exploitation (Marsden and Farioli 2015), and the challenge of increased resource scarcity (Webster 2013; Stahel 2016). In the extractive design there is no guarantee that the short-term gains, although very large and consistent, are equally shared and accessed by everyone. Such an extractive design usually 'regenerates' itself by shifting the focus to the type of resources to be extracted and exploited. This identifies a pattern in which periods of short-term abundancy are followed by periods of progressive scarcity, and then by the research and identification of new resources to extract and exploit (Gunderson and Holling 2001). The question is to understand how a circular economy approach is going to break this 'vicious' cycle typical of a linear and extractive economy. More specifically, how can a circular economy approach to design food systems become different from an extractive and linear one, and how can this approach eventually offer systemic solutions to our 21st-century food crises?

The answers to these questions lie in the idea of transforming a linear and extractive food economy, based on large-scale exploitation of fossil resources, labor, energy, soil health, and ecosystem services, into a new circular food economy that works like an innovative, dynamic, adaptive, technology-driven, and intensely connected industrial ecology (Stahel 2016; Ellen MacArthur Foundation 2019). In this economy food producers, distributors, and consumers develop (economic) relations that ensure that key natural resources are used and safely returned into the biosphere, generating (new or improved) ecosystem services, protecting (and possibly enhancing) biodiversity, perhaps guided by the principles of sustainable intensification (Tittonell 2014; Oliver et al. 2015). A circular food economy that works like an industrial ecology might be able to tackle one of the main challenges of a linear food economy, that is the use of key elements, such as phosphorus, nitrogen, and water, as non-renewable resources (Jurgilevich et al. 2016). In fact, while in principle these resources are all renewable, the rate and scale at which we use them in industrialized and large-scale agricultural and food production systems is such that they need to be extracted or mined from the earth in their fossil form (Pascucci and Duncan 2017). In a circular food economy, instead, nutrients are recovered after feed or food consumption, for example by extracting phosphorus, nitrogen, and water from food waste, urine, and manure, for example through bio-based technology, bio-composting, or anaerobic digestion (Blades et al. 2017; Chojnacka 2017). Material reutilization supports the development of a bio-based economy, in which technical nutrients, like plastics, can be substituted by bio-based products. Moreover, this economy is designed to use renewable energy, from farming to food consumption. Therefore, it inspires us to re-think the type of energy used in the food production and distribution processes, since current industrialized agriculture and food systems are energy-intensive (Ellen MacArthur Foundation 2019).

If we think about how this narrative foresees the 'transition' from an extractive to a circular food economy, we can frame it as a sort of new, extended, and up-scaled 'green revolution'[1] in which a set of bio-based technological practices, and related social and institutional infrastructures, are designed to increase 'productivity and resource use efficiency' of food provisioning systems (Marsden 2013; Marsden and Farioli 2015). At the same time, in this transition to a bio-based and technology-driven food economy, the corporate space, e.g. large agribusiness conglomerates and multinationals, remains dominant in regulating the (economic) relations between food production, distribution, and consumption. Also while food provisioning is coupled with renewed capacity of the system to (re)generate (rather than exploit) ecosystem services, thus designing an economy aligned with ecological values, food products remain inherently commodities whose values are prevailingly defined by markets and trading relations.

Therefore, the question remains on how to reconcile a corporate dominated and still commodified (bio-based) food economy with the intension to align this economy with regenerative principles and practices. Would not a circular food economy based on new principles and practices also need new actors to be more effective? How can a 'new green revolution' tackle the socio-ecological crisis that the 'old green revolution' did not fix?

A circular food economy as an agro-ecology

The answers to these questions are at the heart of the second narrative around circular food economy. This narrative is based on the perspective of taking into account *soil health, biodiversity, ecosystem services,* and *celebrate diversity* as the key pillars to designing any food economy. In this narrative circularity connects to the intention to design food systems aligned with the large cycles of nutrients while keeping use of natural resources in food provisioning systems within planetary boundaries. It also identifies agricultural and food-related practices as inherently embedded in and connected with social practices (Pascucci and Duncan 2017). They are in fact part of agrarian and food cultures, and embedded in specific socio-ecological contexts. They are 'place-based' and 'community-oriented' (Marsden 2013). In this narrative, the regenerative capacity of an ecosystem is a key aspect in designing food systems coupled with agricultural practices that consider maintaining and restoring cycles of key nutrients. This is ensured by using as low as possible external inputs, maximizing diversity within the systems, adopting synergic and mutualistic relations rather than forcing the system to be maintained at an 'imposed simplified order' against the natural tendency toward entropy, diversity, and stability (Altieri et al. 1983). There is a dominant biomimetic and ecological worldview in this approach, complemented with a social justice perspective (Rhodes 2012). Increasing productivity is not subordinate to achieving a just, fair, and safe access to food to everyone. Often these practices imply that farming and food provisioning are part of a wider network of social and political relations between food producers and consumers. A circular food economy in this narrative works like an agro-ecology.

Moreover, in this narrative, circularity also connects with the principle of celebrating diversity instead of specializing, selecting, and standardizing. Celebrating diversity promotes a rethinking of the way we approach food in a more general and broader sense. In an agro-ecological approach food systems are designed as a rich and diverse socio-ecological web, and not just to deal with reduction of (food) waste and to maximize resource use and recovery, nor as just a new way of tackling corporate social responsibility (Pascucci and Duncan 2017). Instead, an agro-ecological approach to a circular food economy is about inviting actors involved in the food system to think about local communities, justice, and power unbalances, as well as collaboratively designing rules and decision-making mechanisms to govern the food system. To a certain extent, the call to celebrate diversity means to encourage actors participating in in the food economy to think about how to foster collaborative and place-based interactions, and to democratize food systems (Marsden 2013; Pascucci and Duncan 2017). As such, a circular food economy is concerned with the maintenance of a balanced relation between the biophysical, technological, and socio-economic components of the economy (Marsden and Farioli 2015). For example, productivity is seen as the capacity of an agricultural system to sustain yields and optimize the use of local resources while minimizing any negative environmental and socio-economic impacts of agricultural practices.[2] In fact, this narrative is centred on the concept of *regenerative agriculture* as 'an approach to food and farming systems that regenerates topsoil and increases biodiversity now and long into the future'.[3] Regenerative practices carefully manage cycles of nutrients and enhance their availability and quality, enhance ecosystem services, increase resilience to climate fluctuation, and strengthen the health and vitality of farming communities (Sherwood and Uphoff 2000; Rhodes 2012). A circular food economy of this type is based on communities rather than corporations and market-based (economic) relations. It relies on small-scale processes and adaptation to local conditions instead of designing large-scale and 'easy to standardize' processes. In fact, a key design principle in this narrative is restoring and regenerating 'ecological health' of food systems in order to contribute to realizing a safe, just, resilient, and sustainable food economy (Rhodes 2012).

Exemplary cases of circular food economies

In this section, I have selected exemplary cases from the two narratives in order to carve out their similarities and differences. In general terms in both narratives actors operating in circular food economies seem to focus on practices that help them to manage key cycles of nutrients/materials in order to maintain food provisioning within planetary boundaries. However, as already indicated in the previous sections, the two narratives involve different actors. Mostly large agribusiness companies and multinationals have contributed to the first narrative. These actors have framed their practices more explicitly as circular, identifying what they do as contributing to transition into 'a circular economy' and connected to closing loops of resources (Webster 2013). Instead the second narrative has been supported prevailing by regenerative agriculture pioneers, agro-ecology practitioners, and activists, and includes a variety of small-scale projects operating in both urban and rural contexts. These actors have not always identified themselves, and what they do, with circularity or circular economy. In my view it is important to note that, despite these differences, both narratives have used some of the 'circular economy' principles, and framing, as a way to 'provoke change' and to re-think, re-design, and re-organize current food systems, at farm, supply chain, or regional level (Pascucci and Duncan 2017). In other words, principles of circularity have been used as means to an end in order to re-imagine and re-configure food provisioning: for example, to gain competitive advantages by innovating products, processes, and business models, as in the case of agribusinesses and food companies, or to introduce social innovations, as in the case of the regenerative agriculture and agro-ecology initiatives (Pascucci and Duncan 2017).

Despite the political use of terminology, here what matters is what 'actors operating in the system do'. By looking at their practices, in fact, we can create the conceptual and ontological basis to understand both the industrial ecology and agro-ecology narratives as the context in which plural, multiple, and diverse circular food economies take place. In the former, the terms 'circular' and 'circularity' are used more explicitly, generating consensus among practitioners, while in the latter these terms are and will probably remain somehow contested and contentious. Despite these differences, in both narratives it is possible to identify *three typologies of practices* used in relation to the intention to create a 'circular food economy'. These practices can be related to (i) *closing loops of nutrients,* (ii) *enhancing resource recovery through designing novel food products and processes,* and (iii) *fostering regenerative agriculture and soil health.* The first typology identifies the tendency to engage with circular economy in a sort of reactive fashion, for example, to tackle problems generated by 'linear systems', to remediate, mitigate, and cope with an existing 'dysfunctional reality' through re-engineering processes related to use of materials and nutrients. The other two typologies, instead, identify the tendency to engage with circular economy in a rather proactive fashion, using creativity, reflexivity, and innovativeness in order to embed 'circular thinking' in the design intentions. In the next sections, I will present some exemplary cases that illustrate these typologies in both narratives.

Closing loops of nutrients

Practices around closing loops of nutrients are arguably the most diffuse, diverse, and relevant in both narratives on circular food economies. Some of these practices relate to recycling and reuse of food packaging. Other practices connect to food waste management and valorization of biological waste streams, particularly through bio-based technologies, bio-composting, bio-energy production. A third set of practices take place in relation to closing loops of key nutrients at the agricultural stage of the food provisioning, and therefore they deal particularly with farming practices. Re-thinking strategy around food packaging, as well as recycling and reusing materials related to food production, distribution, and consumption have been introduced and supported mainly by large agribusiness corporations. Often this has happened in collaboration with small and medium food companies and supply chain partners, including retailers. These practices have the strategic intent to develop new business models along different stages of the food supply chain and they are sometimes described through the perspective of circular business models (Short et al. 2014; Borrello et al. 2016). For example Danone has launched three large-scale projects on managing plastics cycles (in collaboration with Veolia), water, and milk use related to key products (McKinsey 2016). Another dairy giant like Arla Foods has instead identified in the 'Zero Waste' vision its way to support a transition into a circular food economy. This vision revolves around the idea of introducing recyclable packaging, reducing food waste, and valorizing waste from production through bio-based processes[4] (see Box 23.1 below). Recently Coca Cola has launched a similar program to increase their capacity to reuse plastics, and to implement a circular economy agenda throughout its supply chain.[5] In the South-West of England, a recently founded research project has tested various strategies to manage close loops of nutrients in small and medium food enterprises operating in the dairy and bakery sector.[6]

Box 23.1   Closing loops to manage waste – Arla Foods: Zero Waste Program

Case description:

Arla Foods has introduced the Zero Waste Program as part of their commitment to work responsibly throughout the supply chain with their Environmental Strategy 2020, which includes a zero waste vision. The vision is to tackle waste along the supply chain and when needed to treat it as a resource to be reused or recycled.

Key circular practices:

– Recyclable packaging to achieve 100 percent recyclable packaging by 2020 by focusing on cooperation with suppliers, researchers and partnerships with key customers, and by evaluating and selecting the right packaging in relation to design and materials. Arla is engaged in development projects for facilitating recycling with the City of Copenhagen to recycle milk cartons and plastics.

– Reduce food waste to help consumers bring down their food waste by 50 percent by easier ahead planning in food purchases and through guides on making full use of products, e.g. online tips and tricks for using leftovers, weekly dinner schedules, and climate friendly recipes. Another method is optimal packaging in terms of portion size and ability

---

to be completely emptied by consumers. Arla participates in EU's FUSIONS project to reduce food waste through social innovation.

- Waste from production,aims to eliminate waste to landfill from production by using waste products for animal feed or biogas production, cooperating with waste management vendors or suppliers to recycle or reuse solid waste. An example is a new developed technology from Arla's Food Ingredients to use leftover acid whey from yoghurt as ingredients for regular food rather than dumping into land farming or feedstock, thereby fine-tuning the value chain and product life cycle.

Source: European Territorial Futures, http://ec.europa.eu/environment/circular-economy/index_en.htm

A number of projects have developed strategies to close loops of nutrients in relation to food waste, particularly in urban contexts or related to urban farming. Many of these projects have been supported by the European Union policy agenda to define strategies to tackle food waste through circular economy.[7] In the 'Cities and Circular Economy for Food' report the Ellen MacArthur Foundation has indicated improving the capacity of cities to manage food waste as one of the priorities in the circular economy agenda worldwide.[8] Several practices linking closing loops of nutrients with valorization of food waste are presented in the report, showing how this issue has become central in the circular agenda of several cities and regional authorities (Ellen MacArthur Foundation 2019). Using closing loops strategies to design out food waste is not confined to corporate social responsibility agendas supported by large food companies but has also been practiced by several NGOs, social enterprises, charities, and public-private partnerships. For example, Zero Waste Europe is a large network organization that connects and supports a vibrant network of 29 national and local NGOs promoting the so-called 'Zero Waste' strategy as a way to make Europe more sustainable. Local groups are responsible for promoting the strategy, managing and monitoring the network of Zero Waste municipalities, and engaging with companies and decision-makers.[9] The Waste and Resources Action Program (WRAP) in the UK provides another example of how circular economy has been directly applied to find solutions to food waste issues in urban contexts[10, 11](see Box 23.2).

Box 23.2   Closing loops with social innovation: Waste and Resources Action Program (WRAP)

Case description:

WRAP works with governments, businesses, and communities to deliver practical solutions to improve resource efficiency. Their mission is to accelerate the move to a sustainable, resource-efficient economy by (i) re-inventing how we design, produce, and sell products; (ii) re-thinking how we use and consume products, and (iii) re-defining what is possible through re-use and recycling.

Key circular practices:

WRAP is a catalyst for positive economic and environmental action. They work uniquely, and by design, in the space between governments, businesses, communities, thinkers, and individuals – forging powerful partnerships and delivering ground-breaking initiatives to support more sustainable economies and society. WRAP is working with organizations in the food and drink industry to create economic and environmental value from reducing food waste and tackling issues around water scarcity across the supply chain. WRAP supports three key sets of practices:

– Citizen Food Waste Prevention: projects enabling citizens to change their behavior, and take real action to reduce household food waste through (local-based) campaigns.
– Business Food Waste Prevention: this is an action focused on providing practical tools for producers, manufacturers, and retailers to find economic and environmental value through cutting their food waste, water usage, and carbon footprint.
– International Food and Drink: this action is supporting international projects aimed at cutting food waste across the globe. WRAP uses its expertise and evidence to create shared vision and tailored, targeted programs that help deliver sustainability goals.

Source: WRAP, http://www.wrap.org.uk/

Valorization of biological waste streams is the key strategy for the development of various agro-parks. Inspired by industrial symbiosis principles they focus on closing material loops, and to produce bio-based materials (e.g. bio-plastics) and energy (Nuhoff-Isakhanyan et al. 2017). These parks are set up and managed in order to create an integrated system in which ties between companies are created on the basis of shared materials (i.e. waste industrial streams) and energy (Zwier et al. 2015). Several examples of agro-parks have been developed in Europe in both urban and rural contexts. Progressively, these agro-industrial clusters are emerging all over the world, particularly in emerging economies such as China, Brazil, and India, and more recently in Africa. They are often designed as industrial clusters operating as an industrial symbiosis such that one waste stream from a company can be used as key resource input for another company. Recently this approach is finding novel applications, for example by varying the scale of the 'metabolism' and by allowing the actors operating in the symbiosis to be located in different regions. An interesting approach in this sense is offered by a public-private partnership project called AgroCycle. This is a Horizon 2020 research and innovation project addressing the recycling and valorisation of waste from the agri-food sector.[12] The project takes a holistic approach to understanding and addressing how to make best use of the full range of waste streams associated with the agri-food industry, including: bio-fuels, high value-added biopolymers, energy, and microbial fuel cells (Figure 23.1).

Recently a large dairy company, Friesland Campina, in partnership with the social enterprise Circle Economy, has tested a similar approach. In a pilot project they developed different pathways to transition into circular dairy farming systems[13]. In this project alternative technologies and agricultural practices have been investigated to close loops of nutrients. One of the pathways has been associated with practices of 'optimized grazing', in which land productivity is increased through combining biological and technological approaches. An alternative pathway has been associated with practices of 'extensive grazing', which instead relies on biological processes and organic farming methods to close the soil-plant-animal-nutrient cycle locally.

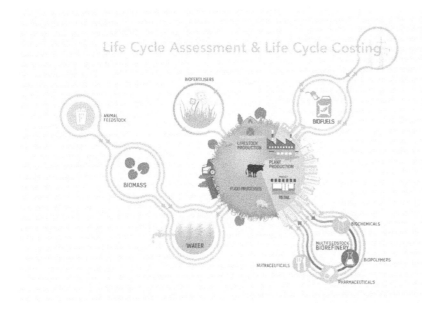

Figure 23.1 AgroCycle: creating new metabolisms of nutrients through closing loops.
Source: www.agrocycle.eu/

Enhancing resource recovery through designing novel food products and processes

This second set of practices also focuses on tackling the problem of food waste and resource recovery but through a design perspective. These practices look into technology and innovation to identify a different approach to use and reuse of materials and energy associated to food production and distribution. They are concerned to the achievement of social and environmental goals through the introduction of new (circular) business models and they stimulate creativity and new form of engagement between and among actors of the food system, for example through the creation of innovation eco-systems (Pascucci and Duncan 2017). A countless number of small and medium food enterprises, micro-enterprises, and start-ups have been experimenting around using alternative sources of nutrients or by investing in bio-based technologies to enable more efficient energy-recovery from biological waste streams. For example, during the last decade a network of new food companies was born around the idea of using food waste as feed for insects that eventually are used to produce feed for animals and proteins. The International Platform of Insects for Food and Feed (IPIFF) is an EU non-profit organization that represents the interests of the insect production sector towards EU policy makers, European stakeholders, and citizens.[14]

Originally created in 2012, the association is today composed of 50 members. Most IPIFF members are European small and medium size enterprises who produce insects for the European market.[15] The association also welcomes insect-producing companies located outside Europe, research institutes, and other actors along the food supply-chain. Other examples in this sector include Agriprotein,[16] Ynsect,[17] and Protix BV.[18] The use of insects potentially impacts not only the way food waste is managed and recycled, but effectively offers a way to upcycle it by creating large-scale proteins production. Although the introduction of proteins from insects in western diets has proven problematic (de-Magistris, Pascucci, and Mitsopoulos, 2015), its application to feedstock and particularly to aquaculture and poultry seems instead quite successful and potentially disruptive for these sectors.

Another area of very intense experimentation is the one around novel food ingredients based on re-engineering, reuse, and upcycling of biological waste streams. Planetarians, for instance, is using defatted seeds and solid food waste streams to produce high-protein and fiber ingredients.[19] At the same time, companies are testing technologies to turn waste streams for large-scale agricultural production into new fibers and biomaterials. Pinetex is a successful example of upcycling waste streams from pineapple production (www.ananas-anam.com/). Ricehouse operates in the segment of rice production waste streams and designs and engineers novel bio-materials for the construction sector.[20] In general both the textile and building industries are becoming areas in which businesses are developing novel approaches to upcycle waste streams from agricultural production or food waste. This experimentation is not confined to the corporate world and has more to it than just technological applications. The UK-based GrowUP start-up,[21] for example, combines principles of closing loops with community engagement in order to foster social innovation, particularly when it comes to food and water waste, access to nutritious food products, and application of technology solutions to food production in urban contexts. Imperfect is a US-based start-up that collects fruit and vegetables from farmers when they are non-selected by buyers due their appearance and cosmetics.[22] This produce is delivered to customers through a veggie-box scheme, instead of ending up in a landfill. But similar projects can be found in several cities and have assumed various forms, from projects run by food banks to campaigns against food waste. EndFoodWaste.org is the website of a social movement that was born around the Ugly Fruit and Veg campaign.[23]

Initiatives revolving around the concept of vertical farming are another example of projects oriented to design new food systems by using innovation and technological development to create closed loops of materials and energy. A well-known example of this type of approach is offered by the Philips – City farming solutions project.[24] The Association for Vertical Farming (AVF) openly endorses circular economy and closed loop thinking as a key strategy to develop the sector in the future.[25] AeroFarms has been indicated as one of the most disruptive business models in food production and fully scaled up vertical farming, claiming to be inspired by circularity and closed loop thinking (Box 23.3).[26]

Box 23.3 Designing circular vertical farming systems – AeroFarms

Case description:

AeroFarms is focused to transform agriculture by building and operating environmentally responsible farms throughout the world to enable local production at scale and nourish our communities with safe, nutritious, and delicious food. AeroFarms recently began growing at the world's largest indoor vertical farm and new global headquarters in Newark, NJ. AeroFarms is rapidly scaling up due to the tremendous demand for locally grown, delicious, produce. They are currently developing farms in multiple US states and on four continents.

Key circular practices:

AeroFarms has been working to set up a new standard for totally-controlled agriculture since 2004. It operates in a way to disrupt traditional supply chains by building farms on major distribution routes and near population centres.

- Use of disruptive technology based on growing vegetables without sun or soil in a fully-controlled indoor environment. AeroFarms optimised a patented aeroponic growing system for faster harvest cycles, predictable results, increased food safety and less environmental impact. In this way the company is able to defy traditional growing seasons by enabling local farming at commercial scale all-year round.
- Definition and use of a new standard for traceability by managing produce from seed to package.
- Design of resource-efficient systems based on optimized closed-loops of nutrients that are able to use 95% less water than field farmed-food and with yields 390 times higher per square foot annually.

Source: Aerofarms.com

The number of innovative projects claiming to use principles of circularity to design novel food products and processes is indeed growing and leading towards technology-based and social innovations.

Fostering regenerative agriculture and soil health

Regenerative agriculture and regenerative farming practices have recently become a central part of the debate on circularity and food systems (Ellen MacArthur Foundation 2019). Regenerative agriculture is a system of farming principles and practices that increases biodiversity, enriches soils, improves watersheds, and enhances ecosystem services (www. regenfarm.com). Several initiatives on regenerative agriculture are rapidly emerging at the interface of the agribusiness corporate domain and social enterprises and grassroots movements. For example, Danone has recently launched a large-scale campaign to support regenerative agriculture with the aim to improve soil health practices in its 140,000+ network of farmers.[27] The campaign has already resulted in the development of the Soil Health Initiative, a collaborative research project based in the US.[28] General Mills is also following the trend of 'incorporating' regenerative agriculture practices in large agribusiness operations and sustainability strategies, with a target of dedicating one million acres to regenerative agriculture by 2030.[29] The Balbo Group, one of the largest organic producers of sugarcane and a prominent agribusiness conglomerate in the Latin-American landscape, has recently embraced a full-scale approach based on regenerative principles in light with a transition into a circular food economy.[30]

The Regenerative Organic Alliance is another example of this type of large-scale initiative based on regenerative agriculture. It promotes the participation of farmers and food producers in a global movement in which soil health, animal welfare, and social fairness are the key guiding principles to be used to design food systems.[31] The Alliance is also promoting a certification program coupled with a learning platform to facilitate the transition into regenerative practices. 'FoodTank' is a non-profit organization which actively connects projects and initiatives around regenerative agriculture and sustainable food production systems, promoting actions to reduce food waste and recovery materials along the food supply chain.[32] A similar approach is adopted by learning platforms like RegenFARM (see Box 23.4). The list of small-scale and community-oriented initiatives based on regenerative agriculture and agro-ecology framed as circular projects is indeed growing and almost impossible to fully map out at this stage.

Box 23.4 Enhancing soil health with smart and regenerative agriculture – Regenfarm

Case description:

RegenFARM enables farmers and farmland investors to determine the most productive and profitable way to use their natural capital assets anywhere in the world, making them resilient to the impacts of climate change, and a participant in the developing circular economy.

Key circular practices:

RegenFARM is an Internet of Things (IoT) Platform farm design tool-based on proven regenerative agriculture methods using:

- Big data from agritech, industry and other sources.
- Algorithms integrating and analysing data designing 'key-line' farms.
- High performance computing to simulate digital twin farm design in real-time.
- IoT platform hosting the design tool and accelerating scope and scale.

Source: Regenfarm.com

Food futures: transition pathways to circular food economies

In this concluding section I will try to explain how the emergence of diverse circular food economies and the related exemplary cases are part of a wider debate on the 'future of food'. To define these food futures though, I need to use the above-mentioned narratives, cases, and practices and position them against some 'utopian considerations'. In so doing I will try to reconnect the debate on circular economies with the emerging literature on food futures and utopias (Stock et al. 2016). This debate also entails different worldviews and visions on how to tackle societal challenges related to food security, climate change, and planetary boundaries. This debate is related to the way we conceptualize and apply changes and innovation in designing global food provisioning systems. I have indicated two narratives shaping the debate on circular food economies and an economy of food that works like an industrial symbiosis as opposed to an economy of food that works like an agro-ecology. Although we have seen that regenerative principles are commonly used in both narratives, as well as social and technological innovation, in my view three concepts make these narratives distinct and potentially lead to alternative food futures.

The first concept refers to the role of *commodification* in the design approach. When we are designing products, processes, and systems in which food is a commodity then the approach to circularity is also dominated by it. In my view this is the distinct logic used in what I have defined as the narrative of a circular food economy as an industrial ecology. The inclusion of regenerative agricultural practices in large-scale agribusiness operation is part of a 'strategy of change' in which the idea that food will end being traded as a global commodity has not been challenged. In the so-called second narrative, instead, the interest for circularity aligns with the 'critique' of the intensive process of commodification of food. In this narrative, closing loops of nutrients, designing new products, and applying regenerative principles is part of a political and social agenda aiming at profoundly transforming food systems by de-commodifying food.

The second concepts refers to the *scale* at which our design thinking is applied. In the first narrative there is an urgency to move into systemic solutions to tackle global challenges. Large-scale operations and scaling up potentials are key issues considered in all the innovations triggered by circular economy in that space. When experimenting around new packaging solutions large agribusinesses, food processors, and retailing companies, but also cities and public authorities, are all interested in solutions that can be scaled-up easily and rapidly. When thinking of using insects to feed livestock, companies like AgriProtein or Ynesct are testing business models to engage with global partners and markets. In the second narrative, instead, the scale is subordinated to the scope. Instead of systemic solutions, practices of circularity are seeking holistic approaches. Often the scope includes adding multiple functions to economic and social activities revolving around food provisioning. In this narrative small group and community is the scale at which the design thinking takes place.

The third concept refers to the *nature of innovation* and *change* that the design thinking ought to trigger. In the first narrative, innovation, change, new business models, and practices relate to circularity predominantly framed and understood as technologically driven. An industrial ecology works like a large and coordinated industrial symbiosis of 'engineered relationships'. It is not just the heavy application of technologies to agricultural or food processing practices that makes this approach technologically driven, but the essence of how social and economic relationships are subordinate to functional relations. This approach makes this narrative also aligned with the wider narrative on so-called *sustainable intensification* of agriculture and food provisioning (Tittonell 2014) and the debate of food place-making and the difference between bio-based and eco economy (Marsden 2013). In this narrative, in fact, resource efficiency is the key objective to achieve higher productivity and the application of technologies and support systems to food provisioning is the way to realize that. In the second narrative, innovation and change align with social and political processes. In fact they are part of grassroots principles, embedded in eco-cultures or alternative cultures, which openly challenge the status quo of current food provisioning systems (Böhm et al. 2014). This second approach makes this narrative also aligned with the wider narrative of so-called *ecological intensification* in which resource effectiveness is the key objective to achieve high productivity (Tittonell 2014). Therefore, if we look at these key conceptual dimensions we can identify two potential pathways towards food futures, and how circular food economies may contribute to them. In Table 23.1, I have summarized the key identified differences of the two pathways and how they are conducive to different food futures.

The first pathway indicates a potential transition towards a circular food economy that works like a *globalized industrial ecology*. In this 'food future' circular bio-based food systems

Table 23.1 Pathways to transition in circular food economies and their contribution to food futures

Characterisation	Pathway 1: Towards a circular food economy that works like a globalized industrial ecology	Pathway 2: towards a circular food economy that works like a networked agro-ecology
Current circular economy paradigm	Circular bio-based food systems	Regenerative food systems
Dominant worldview	Cradle-to-cradle/industrial ecology	Biomimicry/agro-ecology
Dominant circular approach	Closing loops/planetary boundaries	Soil health/socio-ecological diversity
Dominant logic	Productivity	Resilience
Strategic approach	Economy of scale	Economy of scope
Type of resource use	Resource efficiency	Resource effectiveness
Dominant actors	Corporates	Communities
Type of innovation	Technology-driven	Social innovation
Design thinking	Systemic	Holistic
Wider narrative	Sustainable intensification	Ecological intensification

Source: The author

are designed through the principles of industrial ecology and aim at closing loops of key nutrients and working within the boundaries of the planet. This is a food future in which food systems are increasing productivity through economies of scale, enhanced resource recovery, and efficiency. In this scenario corporates become even more the dominant actor in the operating systems, and commodification of food is therefore the dominant logic in the system. In this scenario innovation is mostly technology-driven while system changes are pursued to achieve systemic solutions to global challenges. This food future is aligned with several scenarios identified by the sustainable intensification debate and a transition into a bio-based economy (Marsden 2013).

The second pathway indicates a potential transition towards a circular food economy that works like a *networked agro-ecology*. It is dominated by small-scale communities interested in developing biomimetic and regenerative practices to foster a holistic approach to agricultural production and distribution. In this scenario resilience is the dominant logic and economy of scope and resource effectiveness the way to achieve it. The type of change follows social innovation patterns. This food future is aligned with several scenarios identified by the ecological intensification debate and what has been identified as a transition into an eco-economy (Marsden 2013).

It is hard to predict, at this stage of the debate, which of the narratives, and food futures, will become more prominent and dominant, whether the narratives will converge into a 'unified' narrative, and whether new narratives will emerge. Empirical evidence from the cases seems to indicate that if a transition to a circular food economy is to shape the future of food, then it will be more likely led by large agribusinesses and corporate actors, rather than a network of small-scale and community-based initiatives. It is therefore more likely that the first type of narrative will influence a transition from a linear to a circular food economy in the years to come. This is probably due to the fact that in this transition pathway the circular design principles and practices do not challenge the core principles and practices of the current linear food economy. In fact, in this type of transition food commodification, large-scale operations, and technology-driven innovation will still be the dominant logics of the food economy. Evidence also indicates that some of the principles and practices characterizing the second narrative will be likely included and absorbed in the first one. For example, it is particularly interesting to observe how quickly the principle and practices related to regenerative agriculture have been embedded in large-scale operations led by corporate actors. While regenerative was a term confined in alternative and grassroots communities only few years ago, it is now extensively used in the framing of bio-based industrial ecology projects. In fact, it is used to identify circular economy and circularity in more general terms (Webster 2013; Ellen MacArthur Foundation and McKinsey Center for Business and Environment 2015; Stahel 2016). Still it is debatable whether any circular food economy scenario will emerge at all. So far, circular economy inspired initiatives, in both narratives and examined empirical contexts, still represent a 'niche' and a relatively negligible share of how we produce, distribute, and consume food worldwide. Food provisioning systems are still predominantly wasteful, energy- and resource-intensive, and lack a fair and just access to food for everyone.

Discussion questions

1. What are the key principles and practices of a circular food system?
2. What has circular economy to do with re-thinking food systems?
3. Whom for are we re-thinking food systems? What are our design intentions?
4. How is the future of food looking like in a circular food economy?
5. Will we be able to observe plural, multiple, diverse circular food economies in the future?

Notes

1 The term 'green revolution' is used in literature to define a set of research and technology transfer initiatives, occurring between 1950 and the late 1960s, that increased agricultural production worldwide, particularly in the developing world, beginning most markedly in the late 1960s (Hazell 2009). The so-called 'green revolution' resulted in the adoption of new technologies, including high-yielding varieties (HYVs) of cereals, especially dwarf wheats and rice, in association with chemical fertilizers and agro-chemicals, and with controlled water-supply (usually involving irrigation) and new methods of cultivation, including mechanization (Farmer 1986).
2 http://agroeco.org/
3 www.regenerativeagriculturefoundation.org
4 https://www.arla.com/company/responsibility/environmental-strategy/zero-waste/
5 https://www.ellenmacarthurfoundation.org/case-studies/increasing-post-consumer-plastic-content-in-packaging
6 https://www.circularfood.net/
7 http://ec.europa.eu/environment/circular-economy/index_en.htm
8 https://www.ellenmacarthurfoundation.org/assets/downloads/Cities-and-Circular-Economy-for-Food_280119.pdf
9 https://zerowasteeurope.eu/
10 https://www.wrap.org.uk/
11 https://www.wrap.org.uk/content/wraps-vision-uk-circular-economy-2020
12 http://www.agrocycle.eu/#project
13 http://www.circle-economy.com/case/the-circular-dairy-economy/

14 https://ipiff.org/wp-content/uploads/2020/02/18-02-2020-IPIFF-Position-Paper-on-the-F2F.pdf
15 http://ipiff.org/about-ipiff/
16 https://agriprotein.com/
17 http://www.ynsect.com/en/
18 https://protix.eu/
19 https://www.planetarians.com/
20 https://www.ricehouse.it/eng-home
21 http://growup.org.uk; https://www.imperfectproduce.com/
22 https://www.imperfectproduce.com/
23 http://www.endfoodwaste.org/ugly-fruit—veg.html
24 http://www.lighting.philips.com/main/products/horticulture/press-releases/Philips-commercializ
     ing-city-farming-solutions-based-on-LED-light-recipes.html
25 https://vertical-farming.net/
26 https://aerofarms.com
27 https://www.danone.com/impact/planet/regenerative-agriculture.html
28 http://www.danonenorthamerica.com/news/regenerative-agriculture/
29 https://www.generalmills.com/en/News/NewsReleases/Library/2019/March/Regen-Ag
30 https://www.ellenmacarthurfoundation.org/case-studies/regenerative-agriculture-at-scale
31 https://regenorganic.org/
32 https://foodtank.com/

Further readings

Benyus, J. M. (1997). *Biomimicry: Innovation Inspired by Nature*. New York: HarperCollins Publishers Inc.
McDonough, W., and Braungart, M. (2010). *Cradle to Cradle: Remaking the Way We Make Things*. New York: North Point Press.
Schlosser, E. (2012). *Fast Food Nation: The Dark Side of the All-American Meal*. Boston, MA: Houghton Mifflin Harcourt.
Webster, K. (2017). *The Circular Economy: A Wealth of Flows*. Cowes, Isle of Wight, UK: Ellen MacArthur Foundation Publishing.

References

Altieri, M. A., Letourneau, D. K., and Davis, J. R. (1983). Developing sustainable agroecosystems. *BioScience*, 33 (1), 45–49.
Blades, L., Morgan, K., Douglas, R., Glover, S., De Rosa, M., Cromie, T., and Smyth, B. (2017). Circular biogas-based economy in a rural agricultural setting. *Energy Procedia*, 123, 89–96.
Böhm, S., Bharucha, Z. P., and Pretty, J. (Eds.). (2014). *Ecocultures: Blueprints for Sustainable Communities*. Abingdon, Oxon: Routledge.
Borrello, M., Lombardi, A., Pascucci, S., and Cembalo, L. (2016). The seven challenges for transitioning into a bio-based circular economy in the agri-food sector. Recent patents on food. *Nutrition and Agriculture*, 8 (1), 39–47.
Braungart, M., and McDonough, W. (2002) *Cradle to Cradle; Remaking the Way I Make Things*. New York: North Point Press.
Chojnacka, K. (2017). Bio-based fertilizers: A practical approach towards circular economy. *Energy Procedia*, 12389–12396.
de-Magistris, T., Pascucci, S., and Mitsopoulos, D. (2015). Paying to see a bug on my food: How regulations and information can hamper radical innovations in the European Union. *British Food Journal*, 117 (6), 1777–1792.
Ellen MacArthur Foundation. (2013). Towards the circular economy: An economic and business rationale for an accelerated transition. Available at: www.ellenmacarthurfoundation.org/assets/down loads/publications/Ellen-MacArthur-Foundation-Towards-the-Circular-Economy-vol.1.pdf (last access 24/ 08/2019).
Ellen MacArthur Foundation. (2019). Cities and circular economy for food. Available at: www.ellenma carthurfoundation.org/assets/downloads/Cities-and-Circular-Economy-for-Food_280119.pdf (last access 29/ 08/2019).

Ellen MacArthur Foundation and McKinsey Center for Business and Environment. (2015). Growth within: A circular economy vision for a competitive Europe. SUN in collaboration with the Ellen MacArthur Foundation and McKinsey Center for Business and Environment. Available online at: www.ellenmacarthurfoundation.org/assets/downloads/publications/EllenMacArthurFoundation_Growth-Within_July15.pdf (last access 24 August 2019).

Farmer, B. H. (1986). Perspectives on the 'green revolution' in South Asia. *Modern Asian Studies*, 20 (1), 175–199.

Ghisellini, P., Cialani, C., and Ulgiati, S. (2016). A review on circular economy: The expected transition to a balanced interplay of environmental and economic systems. *Journal of Cleaner Production*, 114, 11–32.

Gunderson, L., and Holling, C.S. (2001). *Panarchy: Understanding Transformations in Human and Natural Systems*. New York: Island Press.

Hazell, P. B. (2009). *The Asian Green Revolution*. IFPRI discussion paper, 911, 35, 3–9, available at: https://www.researchgate.net/publication/239807423_The_Asian_Green_Revolution (last access: 12 June 2019).

Jurgilevich, A., Birge, T., Kentala-Lehtonen, J., Korhonen-Kurki, K., Pietikäinen, J., Saikku, L., and Schösler, H. (2016). Transition towards circular economy in the food system. *Sustainability*, 8 (1), 69.

Marsden, T. (2013). Sustainable place-making for sustainability science: The contested case of agri-food and urban–rural relations. *Sustainability Science*, 8 (2), 213–226.

Marsden, T., and Farioli, F. (2015). Natural powers: From the bio-economy to the eco-economy and sustainable place-making. *Sustainability Science*, 10 (2), 331–344.

McKinsey. (2016). Toward a circular economy in food. *McKinsey Quarterly*, February. Report available at: www.mckinsey.com/~/media/McKinsey/Business%20Functions/Sustainability/Our%20Insights/Toward%20a%20circular%20economy%20in%20food/Toward%20a%20circular%20economy%20in%20food.ashx (last access 04/04/2019).

Nuhoff-Isakhanyan, G., Wubben, E. F., Omta, O. S., and Pascucci, S. (2017). Network structure in sustainable agro-industrial parks. *Journal of Cleaner Production*, 141, 1209–1220.

Oliver, T. H., Heard, M. S., Isaac, N. J., Roy, D. B., Procter, D., Eigenbrod, F., Freckleton, R., Hector, A., Orme, C. D. L., Petchey, O. L., and Proença, V. (2015). Biodiversity and resilience of ecosystem functions. *Trends in Ecology and Evolution*, 30 (11), 673–684.

Pascucci, S., and Duncan, J. (2017). From pirate islands to communities of hope. In *Sustainable Food Futures: Multidisciplinary Solutions*, Duncan, J. and M. Bailey (eds.), New York: Routledge, pp. 186–200.

Rhodes, C. J. (2012). Feeding and healing the world: Through regenerative agriculture and permaculture. *Science Progress*, 95 (4), 345–446.

Sherwood, S., and Uphoff, N. (2000). Soil health: Research, practice and policy for a more regenerative agriculture. *Applied Soil Ecology*, 15 (1), 85–97.

Short, S. W., Bocken, N. M., Barlow, C. Y., and Chertow, M. R. (2014). From refining sugar to growing tomatoes: Industrial ecology and business model evolution. *Journal of Industrial Ecology*, 18 (5), 603–618.

Stahel, W. R. (2016). The circular economy. *Nature News*, 531 (7595), 435.

Stock, P. V., Rosin, C., and Carolan, M. (2016). Food utopias: Performing emergent scholarship and agri-food futures. In *Biological Economies: Experimentation and the Politics of Agri-food Frontiers*. Abingdon, Oxon, and New York (US): Routledge, pp. 212–224.

Tittonell, P. (2014). Ecological intensification of agriculture – Sustainable by nature. *Current Opinion in Environmental Sustainability*, 8, 53–61.

Webster, K. (2013). What might I say about a circular economy? Some temptations to avoid if possible. *World Futures*, 69 (7–8), 542–554.

Zwier, J., Blok, V., Lemmens, P., and Geerts, R. J. (2015). The ideal of a zero-waste humanity: Philosophical reflections on the demand for a bio-based economy. *Journal of Agricultural and Environmental Ethics*, 28(2), 353–374.

24

A DIGITAL "REVOLUTION" IN AGRICULTURE?

Critically viewing digital innovations through a regenerative food systems lens

Kelly Bronson

Introduction

This chapter invites readers to think carefully about what might stay the same under the so-called digital "revolution" in agriculture and is driven by the premise that "regenerative" food systems are ones which fundamentally break from the *status quo* and thus "remediate the economic, social and environmental damage from the existing, dominant food system" (Blay-Palmer and Koc 2010, 223; Dahlberg 1993, 1994). The dominant discourse suggests that digital tools for collecting big data and analyzing them can drive a sustainability revolution in food production (and practices along the entire food chain). Mike Stern, President and Chief Operations Officer for The Climate Corporation, claims that we are on the cusp of a third revolution in agriculture where "digital agriculture, driven by the application of data science to new and ever-evolving data sets, will transform the future of farming in more profound ways than hybrid corn and biotechnology changed farming in the 20th century" (Stern 2019). Drawing on qualitative interviews and digital ethnography, this chapter details how the current trajectory for digital agriculture is one which supports the continuation of large-scale, low-value crop farming amended for more judicious use of chemicals and water. Therefore, digital agricultural tools are not regenerative but rather, at least in their current economic and legal infrastructures, are reproducing a number of social and cultural food system challenges.

Background: precision agriculture and sustainability

There is widespread hope that the collection of agricultural data will bring sustainability to food production practices, especially as these data get aggregated into big datasets. At present, big agricultural data are being collected via remote and near sensing technologies which are currently in use across North American, European, Australian, and Chinese farms (and indeed across the food system or supply chain) (Faulkner and Cebul 2014; Li et al. 2014; Sundmaeker et al. 2016). There is by now a well-developed space-based infrastructure for environmental surveillance where public and private satellites collect data relevant to agriculture. Yet many agricultural data are being collected on operating farms by "precision" machinery equipped with built-in sensors (see Schimmelpfennig 2015).[1] Environmental data being collected by precision equipment reflects one of the key features of big data: the collection of data by unconventional sources (boyd and Crawford 2012). Instead of a farmer testing soil moisture by hand and logging soil data in a spreadsheet, for example, precision tractors fitted with sensors can automatically measure various aspects of soil quality. After sensors embedded on farm equipment (or in some cases on drones) collect the on-farm data, then GPS tracking of field positions allows for the generation of maps displaying spatial variability of the features under consideration (Scholten et al. 2013). Precision agriculture (PA) can be thought of beyond just the material artifact used to collect the data but rather as "an approach" to agricultural decisions – one that uses monitoring and measurement of farm-level environmental data (including data on production practices) in order enable more precise agricultural decision-making (McBratney et al. 2005).

Proponents of this precision approach believe it will help farmers address the environmental impact of farming and meet environmental challenges such as global climate change. Weersink and colleagues write,

> Agriculture stands on the cusp of a digital revolution, and the same technologies that created the Internet and are transforming medicine are now being applied in our farms and on our fields. … The promise of these technologies is more food, produced on less land, with fewer inputs and a smaller environmental footprint.
>
> *(2018, 19)*

Big data can be analyzed by computer algorithms that glean information enabling more precise decisions, which is thought to lead to sustainability gains by a reduction of scarce (e.g. water) or harmful (e.g. chemicals) agricultural inputs. An early – 2004 – literature review of academic work on PA

> confirm[ed] the intuitive idea that PA should reduce environmental loading by applying fertilizers and pesticides only where they are needed, and when they are needed. Precision agriculture benefits to the environment come from more targeted use of inputs that reduce losses from excess applications and from reduction of losses due to nutrient imbalances, weed escapes, insect damage, etc.
>
> *(Bongiovanni and Lowenberg-Deboer 2004)*

As indicated by the word *should* here, most studies of PA evaluating environmental impact continue to do so only indirectly, by assuming a reduction in chemical use under PA equates with overall environmental gain (see Gebbers and Adamchuk 2010; cf. Akhtman et al. 2017). Some studies point to broader sustainability gains from PA, such as more ethical human and non-human animal relations on dairy farms (e.g. Scholten et al. 2013). Nonetheless, the link between precise information gleaned from big data and sustainability dominates the literature on PA and is thought to be so profound that it represents a "paradigm shift" from production-based agricultural goals to sustainability (Rossel and Bouma 2016, 71):

> Last century, during the "Green Revolution," the use of synthetic fertilizers contributed to increased agricultural production. However, their use did not reflect local soil and water conditions because recommendations were developed for larger

agro-ecological zones. They only focused on increased productivity, neglecting any adverse environmental consequences. ... Using soil sensors in agriculture can fundamentally change this approach by allowing innovative "bottom-up" approaches that characterize local soil and environmental conditions in space and time, improving the efficiency of production to maximize farm incomes and minimize environmental side effects.

Similarly, industry actors have declared PA an altogether different way of doing business: the goal of maximizing profit via the sale of chemical and seed inputs is said to be replaced by the goal of selling positive social and environmental outcomes via the sale of big-data-generated information. Tobias Menne, head of Bayer's Digital Farming, put it this way in a blog post for World Food Day in 2018:

> Before, selling more products meant more business for a company like Bayer; whereas in future, the fewer products we sell the better, because we're selling outcome-based services. With sensor devices, we can learn a lot more about what is and is not helping crops and livestock and create a better way of doing things.

Enthusiasm for precision agriculture's sustainability potential is not only shared among many academic scientists and industry but also among development agencies such as the World Bank (see Kim 2015) and governments who are funding large-scale big data projects. For instance, the European Commission has made broad commitments to digital innovations for the collection of farm-level data across member countries. The Internet of Food and Farm 2020 project (IoF2020) explores the potential of IoT-technologies for European farming with the goal to build a lasting innovation ecosystem that fosters the uptake of precision agriculture as one "vital step towards a more sustainable food value chain. With the help of IoT technologies higher yields and better quality produce are within reach. Pesticide and fertilizer use will drop and overall efficiency is optimized" (n.p./online). One example of a project furthered under this EC funding is RHEA, which is developing ground and aerial robots equipped with sensors for collecting data on chemical use; the goal is to reduce harmful agricultural inputs by 75 percent (see Vieri et al. 2013). In Australia, the Commonwealth Scientific and Industrial Research Organization (CSIRO) is developing a digital platform for aggregating and mining data from PA equipment. The project is called *Digiscape* and it aims to "solve multiple knowledge shortfalls in the land sector simultaneously ... by building a common big data infrastructure that will support next generation decision making and transform agricultural industries and environmental action" (n.p./online). Neither the United States or Canada has anything as comprehensive as IoF2020 or *Digiscape* although the National Institute of Food and Agriculture has tracked the adoption of PA since the late 1990s and the US Department of Agriculture continues to invest in a variety of extension as well as industry-public research and development activities related to PA. In Canada, a much-celebrated recent Canadian federal budget flagged agriculture as an area ripe for investment in digital innovation and the potential development of a common analytics platform (Barton/Advisory Council on Economic Growth/GOC, 10).

Theoretical perspective and method

Amidst these declarations that a digital "revolution" in food production is leading to environmental and economic sustainability, this chapter takes up the broad research question: *What is indeed sustained – as in, what remains intact – under current innovation-led agricultural shifts?*

Asking this question is motivated by a theoretical and indeed normative commitment to a regenerative food systems approach which aims to "remake both natural and social systems over time" (Dahlberg 1994, 175). As Kenneth Dahlberg puts it, regenerative is not sustainable, and indeed the rubric offers advantages over that of sustainability in part because it "calls for the inclusion of issues of social justice, intergenerational equity and inter-species balance" (1994, 175). Regenerative is a rubric for thinking beyond what was and what is to radical imaginings which can transform food systems into community-based food webs that are equitable, just, resilient, inclusive, and regenerative (Blay-Palmer and Koc 2010, 224). In line with this literature on regenerative food systems, I interrogate the regenerative potential of digital agriculture vis-à-vis power and equity. Viewing food system health beyond a narrow focus on environment and economy, I look into the ways by which current innovation-led shifts in food production may be reproducing and stabilizing historically inequitable social relations within the food system – specifically distributions of power and authority which have historically disadvantaged small-scale and diversified production. A number of high-level and empirically grounded reports have demonstrated that food, and wider socio-ecological systems, are threatened by the hegemony of large-scale, low-value commodity production and a lack of cultural and bio-diversity (see IPES 2016). A regenerative framework is meant to formalize "a systems approach" which envisions "the full dimensions of diversity" (Dahlberg 1994, 175).

I used two methods to interrogate the regenerative potential of digital agriculture between May 2017 and April 2018. First, I conducted 40 unstructured qualitative interviews with funders, designers, and users (farmers) of digital agricultural technologies in North America. I asked interviewees open-ended questions about their practice, motivations, and goals in relation to digital agriculture. The funders and designers are scientists and engineers (computer scientists, computational biologists, statisticians, geo-position specialists, agricultural engineers); corporate spokespeople; activists. The farmers are from across North America and were all recruited via a call for users of "digital agricultural technologies" that was sent across email list-serves of a range of farm and food networks. The farmers who responded were predominantly based in the Mid-West (6), with some representation from Ontario, Canada (3), and one farmer from Quebec. Interviews were conducted by phone between January 2016 and June 2018 and recorded. The interviews were then transcribed and coded inductively, the key themes organized using the software program NVivo Pro 11. All interviewees were rendered anonymous in the chapter unless they asked not to be. Second, I used digital ethnographies – or several months spent with a variety of digital agricultural tools (hardware like sensors, digital platforms, online maps) as well as their privacy and access agreements. In these engagements I asked questions about how these tools, in their material forms and modalities, may be disrupting or reproducing current food system relations.

Results

My research findings suggest that the majority of digital innovations applied to food production are currently designed and governed in ways which foster hegemonic food system characteristics and relations.

Corporate power and concentration

Commercial tools for collecting, managing, and "mining" agricultural data are currently structured such that data and its systems are centralized and tightly controlled within corporations; this could allow for the unfair advantage of corporate over other food system actors (e.g. producers). For example, the Canadian agribusiness, Farmers Edge, is described by its founder and CEO, Wade Barnes, as a "leader in *independent* data management" (YouTube, Farmers Edge Our Story, emphasis mine) because the company has invested in a private network of sensors extending across over 4,000 farms in North America, Australia, and Brazil as well as a private constellation of satellites (via a partnership with Planet Labs). Corporate data scientists explained to me in interviews their need for "predictable" access to up-to-date data and also a pursuit of accuracy. To maximize accuracy, starting in 2012, Farmers Edge (formerly dominated by agronomists) partnered with hardware manufacturers and data and computer scientists to develop company-controlled, proprietary data collection devices ("plug-in" sensors for farm machinery) and corporate protected algorithms for mining datasets also controlled by the corporation and usable by in-house experts. "We are in the business," Barnes says, "of decision ag … right now in precision agriculture there are lots of people collecting data but fewer people using good that data to make smart decisions on the farm."

This technical configuration – tight corporate control over farm-level data and a hierarchizing of knowledge (in-house experts for hire by farmers) – is mirrored in other corporate technologies I studied. Commercially collected agricultural data (and its infrastructures) are predominantly housed "in" the cloud, on servers owned or controlled by input or machinery companies. We know that these farm-level data are used to "teach" predictive algorithms but the full extent of their use is obfuscated from farmers and the general public as it is currently governed by the corporation's own privacy and access agreements, which promise to manage privacy breaches by allowing only aggregated data to be used by undisclosed third parties. As with so much personal data, those privacy and access agreements I read do not specify the particular uses of agricultural data (O'Neill 2016). We do know that until very recently Monsanto was a recipient of data which are passively collected from every new John Deere tractor – called "precision" tractors – and we can infer they are used for corporate gain such as profile development for targeted marketing. Isabelle Carbonell suggests that such data uses, structured by legal arrangements between John Deere and seed/chemical companies (there have been 13), "give Monsanto a privileged position with unique insights into what farmers are doing around the clock, on a field-by-field, crop-by-crop basis into what is currently a third or more of the US farmland" (Carbonell 2016, 2; ETC Group 2016). Data scientists working for agribusinesses explained to me in interviews how restricted data use answers to technical problems of potentially unreliable and inaccurate data, yet many also admitted that such restriction reduces the end user's range of options by preventing easy access to data.

Not only are the corporate uses of big agricultural data obfuscated by privacy and access agreements but so is the means by which advice is generated for the farmer. Bayer/Monsanto's FieldScripts platform, for example, is delivered to farms exclusively through a corporate-certified seed dealer network. Farmers who are interested in using this technology until recently were required to "buy in" with data: a minimum of three years of raw corn/soybean yield data. Licensing this platform allows farmers to meet with their nearest seed dealer and enter their farm-level data into a FieldScripts database. The database makes use of a proprietary, field-tested algorithm that purportedly identifies which seeds are the "best match" for a field's conditions and then creates a variable rate seeding "prescription." The "prescription," administered by the seed dealer, consists of recommendations that purportedly match the conditions of a farmer's field to one of Bayer/Monsanto's hybrid seeds and proprietary chemicals –

products bought as part and parcel of this "prescription," also through the seed dealer. That the means by which the "data-driven" "prescription" is achieved are invisible to the farmer raises ethical questions when the recommendation necessarily tethers farmers to Bayer/Monsanto (only their products are recommended).

Interviews with farmers who are using the corporate data systems indicated to me that they share in the technical ethos of data scientists working in commercial contexts – one which sees farmers as businesspeople eager to cut down on the presentational overhead and presumed cognitive work (not to mention the digital skillset) required to engage with data directly. A small handful of these farmers expressed a concern over corporate or government ("big brother") access to intimate details of the farm (via big data), saying

> if all of these advisors have all of this information collected, and they share it amongst themselves, they'll have much more information than the farmers have and it could greatly influence marketing and just how farmers are sold on various inputs, you know?

At the same time, this farmer was uninterested in having access to or engaging with unprocessed data or even peeking behind the corporate protected algorithms used to generate advice. One Canadian data scientist put it this way:

> Farmers don't give a crap about our operational monitoring here. They want their auto steers to work, they want the GPS systems to work, they want the services that maybe they subscribe to to give them the best advice and information on "hey it's shaping up to be a real dry summer, how should I deal with this?"

Regardless of whether users perceive that they get something valuable from the commercial configurations for agricultural data, they give unequal benefit to agribusinesses, which have operated as privileged food system actors with a variety of social and environmental consequences (see Lang and Heasman 2004). As ETC Group's Neth Daño puts it, "They all [seeds/chemicals, machinery, plant genomics companies] meet in the Cloud, ... It's all about who can profit most from the control of data."

Productivism

Commercially developed data and their systems are helping those farmers working within a "productivist" strategy – maximizing commodity export crop output (Buttel 2003; Kneen 1995, 69) – amend their practices for the more judicious use of chemicals and water. One farmer using a commercial platform called Climate Fieldview put it this way:

> I could just go out there and slap it [herbicide] on and be happy with it but I wanted to do the best job I could and not waste a bunch of spray. Now, when you waste spray you overlap and whatnot, it's also potentially a pollution, so you know you don't want to do that ... Just enough to do the job in the right place. That's what this tool helps me do.

Beyond large-scale commodity farmers like this one, the major commercial tools are not useful. For one, just as with genetically engineered seed systems, corporate digital agricultural tools focus on a selection of major agronomic commodity crops versus horticultural crops such as vegetables and fruits (Welsch and Glenna 2006). Because of their relative value, agronomic crops such as corn, canola, or soy are typically planted on extremely large acreages and for a host of reasons (land cost, environmental variation) there is an east–west split fragmenting land size across North America and subsequently the market for agricultural machinery. In mid-western Canada and the US there is, typically, emphasis on commodity cropping, with whole regions now dominated by wheat, corn, or canola. Given the low returns on commodity crops, there is a related tendency toward industrialism – to manage the farm like a business – and toward large farms. An average farm in Saskatchewan, Canada, is 1,700 acres whereas in Ontario, Canada, it is 750 acres.

Agribusinesses investing in digital agriculture are currently making little attempt to overcome these historic patterns of variation in land size and strategy, which subsequently map onto different technological needs for farm machinery. Expensive pieces of equipment such as the newest tractors and combines best suit large holdings of over 1,000 acres where turnaround at the edges of fields is easier, where there is a lack of variation and topography and where there is more capital available for investment in equipment than with smaller farms. The data which are used to build the digital maps within the Farm Command platform come from plug-in sensors that work on machinery only used by industrial farms. And in order to make good on the advice generated from Farm Command, one also needs machinery allowing for "variable rate" application of inputs like chemical pesticides (otherwise knowing that a particular area of one's farm needs a particular application load would be of little use). One western Canadian grain farmer describes the cost barrier to this use of on-farm environmental data:

> Auto-steering for seeding using GPS is a no-brainer. ... As soon as we could have something steer parallel straight lines up and down a field ... um, you know there was no overlap, so you're running a 55' drill in parallel patterns in a field ... so minor variation meant loss and so there were savings when you're not overlapping and over-seeding. ... The larger you are, if you're hand-steering and you're overlapping by two feet every time, it doesn't take very long before you start to add up quite a bit of uh overlap.
>
> But the thing about field-mapping is, well it requires some very expensive technology to do a variable fertilizer application. Data helps you determine which areas of the field are the least productive. And then as you go through your soil testing you can soil test those quadrants and then you can see if they require different applications of fertilizer. But in order to do that you have to have application equipment which is quite expensive, which is variable rate technology.

Like many agricultural technologies – from Jethro Tull's seed drill to GMOs – Farm Command data infrastructures actually feed into the bifurcation of foodways (Tanahill 1973). Standardizing the environment by turning to mono-cropping was historically necessary for large agricultural machinery and was as much a precondition as a product of industrial farming. Similarly, the maps created within the Farm Command platform are made meaningful only if one adheres to a rigid conventional farming strategy of seeding in neat rows separated by areas of soil "cleaned" of weeds. The "crop health maps" generated via Farmers Edge private satellites display "variability" in growth measured as a general impression of plant density. Said differently, the maps use colour to give the farmer a gestalt view of their yield where colour indicates areas that might require attention (increased fertilizer, for example) in order to increase the density of growth. Such environmental mapping will fail to advise an organic farmer, for instance, whose seedlings may be surrounded by plastic or mulch weed cover.

There is a built-in disincentive for for-profit scientists to explore the kinds of problems and farm strategies which occupy unconventional farms (e.g. organic). As one agronomic economist interviewed for this study put it: "Of course industry is interested [to design technologies for] large farmers, they are the ones with money to pay." Another representative for a very large agri-business put it this way:

> There's not that much regard for smaller family farms … it's not that [big businesses] don't care, it's that they don't know they should care. Smaller farmers aren't as profitable … I think we're currently targeting farmers who spend countless hours in a cab and not with their families.

A shift to data-driven farming, therefore, would currently demand a high level of social innovation among corporations and/or among farmers who do not use large, expensive machinery, who do not seed in neat rows, and who do not grow commodity crops. Moreover, this realization of digital farming assumes farmers do not enjoy being in the field, and thus does not account for those choosing farming as a lifestyle.

Regenerative technological and agricultural systems

While the commercial realization of digital agriculture supports a more sustainable productivist food system, there is another model for its realization. There are activist groups of farmers and data and other scientists working on technologies that they feel will help regenerate agricultural, technological, and wider social systems. Exemplary here is the "farm management" platform called Farm OS, which is open source and supported by a loosely organized and transient group self-describing as "non-hierarchical."[2] Farm OS is being developed for those farmers working outside of the dominant productivist strategy – "alternative" or "unconventional" producers such as agro-ecological growers or market gardeners. One developer working on Farm OS talked in detail about the "blind-spots" of public and private sector scientific efforts that current focus on the collection of farm-level environmental data on corn and soy, saying, "It's pretty insane the lack of data and understanding." Michael Stenta, a sort of leader in this community, says that he hopes to represent all of the detail on unconventional farms:

> On these farms there is a lot of things going on – it's often more complex than on larger farms. … As I was harvesting and working on these farms I was thinking about how to track what was happening. And I got hooked on this problem: how to represent enough aspects of farming in a generalized way and how to include information from cheap sensors and public data?
>
> *(YouTube video)*

Farm OS is also explicitly meant to regenerate food, technological, and wider social systems through what interviewees called its "development methodology": all of the code is visible and freely available, anyone can install the platform or host the system, and also anyone can contribute by writing code and developing novel features. One computer scientist currently working on Farm OS describes how regeneration is a guiding motivation behind this decentralization of data and expertise:

I'm sure it's been very obvious so far but I do believe that key piece of creating brand new systems that are resilient is part of having systems that are decentralized. They are interconnected. My hope is that we can both have our tools and our communities reflecting each other.

Michael Stenta put it this way in interview: "Along with the software, we are also trying to build a *community* around the software" (emphasis mine):

> The goal is to create a diverse knowledge base that individuals can build upon. The reason its open source is so we can build a global community around it. To serve as a platform for farmers but also researchers and service providers. Data and knowledge ownership is also an important piece of this ... a lot of the commercial software systems don't give access or control over farm-level environmental data. You sign that away.

Dorn Cox, who also assumes a leadership role with Farm OS, puts it this way:

> Oh, uh, well ... I ... think it's all about essentially agriculture as a shared human endeavor and public participation in science and um, and production through environmental improvement, so that's sort of the one thing and that there's expressions of that through open source, open science hardware and software systems ... and then farming itself.

Thus far, under this development methodology, a variety of contributors have shaped the Farm OS platform with interesting distinctions from the commercially developed tools. Data are collected for field mapping and other purposes using open satellite data and other publicly available data, such as US Department of Agriculture soil data. However, Farm OS allows for the collection of any type of farm data by any means. For instance, farmers can log their "assets" and it is up to them to decide what constitutes an asset. Of those farmers using Farm OS, assets appear to be animals, plantings (crops), equipment, labourers, compost piles, mushroom or soil substrate, maple stands or groves within a farm field, among others. Farm OS is being developed in close connection with the farmers using it, not just because some (though not many) of those farmers are also writing code but because the data scientists explicitly call on user feedback. One computer scientist working on the platform put it this way:

> What we care about is this idea of shared common, whether it's things like shared information, shared resources or community building. There is a sense of collective action. There is a sense of responsibility, not just to yourself but the environment that you're working in and tools that we build are responsive to needs. ... I hear farmers talk about ... or like in my grad work I did a lot of qualitative research trying to learn from farmers what that goal is, what they care about, what they're interested in doing in sustainable agriculture. I would hear their stories and learn more about their practice.

Farm OS has an analog in Farm Hack: a loosely tied network of do-it-yourself technology builders and self-described hackers motivated to make tools for small-scale and unconventional agriculture for whom "good farm equipment is often too expensive" (from

NOFRA conference presentation and GODAN video). One prominent hack which potentially unites Farm OS and Farm Hack is the DIY soil sensor. Dorn Cox is leading a comprehensive implementation at Wolf's Neck Farm of DIY soil sensors for measuring a host of variables, some similar to those measured by the commercial sensors. Michael Stenta describes this initiative as a "big collaborative effort indicative of open and collaborative science … we have folks from USDA, EPA and commercial farming and software and hardware developers." While many of the variables currently under consideration by this group (e.g. pH and moisture) are similar to those variables for which commercial sensors grab data, Cox describes how his team desires to move beyond the "extractive" scientific approach of agri-businesses (he mentions Monsanto) towards a "systems" and "regenerative" perspective on environmental data, including data on soil systems:

> So, we have millions of years of genetic material that's adapted to create life on Earth pretty much everywhere (*laughs*). There's something that grows everywhere, so there's value in that … but where that intersects with the current digital world is that we can now exchange knowledge of complexity and how all those genetic materials express themselves … And that's bacterial as well as plants and animals, too. I mean, we're really looking at that whole range – bacterial/fungal relationship. The whole fungal world is still blowing my mind (*laughs*) how important it is!

Cox put it succinctly later in the interview: "Agriculture isn't rocket science, it's actually far more complex."

Discussion: how to enable regenerative agricultural transitions

The vision of regenerating food, technological, and wider social systems via big data is currently marginalized and this reveals how emergent agricultural innovations intervene in long-standing food political struggles. Food studies scholarship has pointed to the environmental and social consequences of historic asymmetry in the competition between productivist versus alternative "food regimes" and the technologies supporting these (DeSchutter 2015; Friedmann 2009; Friedmann and McMichael 1987; Lang and Heasman 2004). Just as with previous technologies like genetically modified seed systems, digital agriculture's designers and scientists working in the private sector are better organized, better funded, and more influential with government agencies than those working outside of industry. Because government and industry have historically devoted more money to the development of technologies which are meant to solve productivist agricultural problems, like boosting yield, there is momentum behind this model for the realization of digital agriculture. There is a significant promotion engine (PR, advertising, an academic journal *Precision Agriculture*) bolstering the funding and adoption of digital tools for large-scale commodity producers.

Still, the future of digital agriculture is not yet solidified into a concrete socio-technical system and there is time to carefully shape digital innovations and their infrastructures for a diversity of food system actors; it has become clear that fostering diversity of farm strategies and sizes, among other kinds of diversity, is key to meeting food system and environmental crises (see IPES 2016). Here are three suggestions: One, the centralization of data collection and management enlists digital agricultural tools as "vehicles of corporate supremacy" (McMichael 2009, 140) and bold governance decisions need to be taken toward regulating the usages of personal (in this case farm-level) data in the interests of the many instead of the few. A model for such bold governance could be the General Data Protection Regulation, in effect since May 25 2018 in the European Union, which is an attempt to set stringent rules around the corporate uses of personal data with an eye toward forcing large technology firms to make more visible the ways they share data with other firms (see https://eugdpr.org). Two, tight corporate control over agricultural data is as much a manifestation of historic patterns of consolidation among agribusinesses as it feeds into these patterns of corporate power and corporatization of the food system. Legal measures need to be taken to seek redress for pre-existing patterns of consolidation among agribusinesses (notably, John Deere and Monsanto/Climate Corporation/Bayer), which enable a level of interoperability that appears to call inexorably for streamlined and standardized data systems and tight data control. Three, those environmental and food activists which mobilized around genetically engineered seed systems would do well to participate more actively in discussions around how dominant digital agricultural technologies and their infrastructures might further food system inequities. Critical public discourse could push funders and designers, among others, to reflect on the normative aspects and *purposes* of innovation. Why fund or design this tool and not this other? Who exactly stands to benefit from this specific R&D direction?

Discussion questions

1. How does the author define "sustainable" for the purpose of this chapter? Was this definition surprising to you?
2. What are the sustainability benefits of digital innovations, according to proponents?
3. What are some of the negative socio-environmental consequences of digital innovations as they currently are being applied to food production?

Notes

1 Comprehensive adoption studies have yet to be completed in many countries besides the US. The Ministry of Agriculture and Agri-food in Canada contracted a survey on adoption in 2015 completed by an agricultural engineer Dan Steele which showed less adoption relative to the US.
2 The group includes data and computer scientists volunteering in their off hours, researchers from government (US Department of Agriculture, Extension and Conservation) and academia (e.g. Tufts), a variety of farmers most of whom are unconventional (market gardeners, no-till planters).

Further reading

Akhtman, Y., E. Golubeva, O. Tutubalina, and M. Zimin 2017. "Application of Hyperspectral Images and Ground Data for Precision Farming," *Geography, Environment, Sustainability* 10: 117–128. 10.24057 /2071-9388-2017-10-4-117-128.

boyd, D. and K. Crawford. 2012. "Critical Questions for Big Data: Provocations for a Cultural, Technological, and Scholarly Phenomenon," *Information, Communication and Society* 15: 662–679.

Bronson, K. and I. Knezevic 2016. "Big Data in Food and Agriculture," *Big Data and Society* 3: 1–5.

Carbonell, I. 2016. "The Ethics of Big Data in Big Agriculture," *Internet Policy Review* 5.

Carolan, M. 2017. "Publicising Food: Big Data, Precision Agriculture, and Co-experimental Techniques of Addition," *Sociologia Ruralis* 57: 135–154.

DeSchutter, O. 2015. "Starving for Answers: Why Hunger and Thirst Don't Have to Doom the World," *Financial Post*. http://fp-reg.onecount.net/onecount/redirects/index.php?action=gettokens&js=1&sid=&return=https%3A%2F%2Fforeignpolicy.com%2F2015%2F07%2F20%2Fstarving-for-answers-food-water-united-nations%2F&sid=ujbgnkdjdpooc3p94c974car35 (Accessed 3 October 2019).

References

Adamchuk, S., I. Viacheslav and R. Gebbers 2010. "Precision Agriculture and Food Security," *Science* 327, no. 5976: 828–831.

Albritton, Robert. 2009. *Let Them Eat Junk: How Capitalism Creates Hunger and Obesity*. Winnipeg, MB: Arbeiter Ring.

Bijker, W., T. Hughes and T. Pinch. 2012. *The Social Construction of Technological Systems, Anniversary Edition*. Cambridge, MA: MIT Press.

Bishop, K. and A. Phillips 1993. "Seven Steps to Market: The Development of the Market-Led Approach to Countryside Conservation and Recreation," *Journal of Rural Studies* 9, no. 4: 315–338.

Blay-Palmer, A. and M. Koc 2010. "Imagining Sustainable Food Systems: The Path to Regenerative Food Systems," in *Imagining Sustainable Food Systems: Theory and Practice*, edited by Blay-Palmer, A., 223–246. Burlington, VT: Ashgate.

Bongiovanni, R. and J. Lowenberg-Deboer 2004. "Precision Agriculture and Sustainability," *Journal of Precision Agriculture* 5, no. 4: 359–387.

Bowker, G. 2005. *Memory Practices in the Sciences*. Cambridge, MA: MIT Press.

Buttel, F. 2003. "Environmental Sociology and the Explanation of the Environmental Reform," *Acoustics, Speech, and the Signal Processing Newsletter, IEEE* 16, no. 3: 306–344.

Cloke, P. and M. Goodwin. 1992. "Conceptualising Countryside Change: From Post-Fordism to Rural Structured Coherence," *Transactions of the Institute of British Geographers* 19, no. NS17: 321–336.

Cox, S. 2002. "Information Technology: The Global Key to Precision Agriculture and Sustainability," *Computers and Electronics in Agriculture* 36, no. 2: 93–111.

Dahlberg, K. 1993. "Regenerative Food Systems: Broadening the Scope and Agenda of Sustainability," in *Food for the Future: Conditions and Contradictions of Sustainability*, edited by Allen, P., 75–102. New York: John Wiley & Sons.

Dahlberg, K. 1994. "A Transition from Agriculture to Regenerative Food Systems," *Futures* 26, no. 2: 170–179.

Davis, G. 2007. "History of the NOAA Satellite Program," *Journal of Applied Remote Sensing* 1, no. 1: 012504.

DeSchutter, O. 2015. "Don't Let Food Be the Problem: Producing Too Much Food Is What Starves the Planet," *Financial Post* (July/August). http://foreignpolicy.com/2015/07/20/starving-for-answers-food-water-united-nations/ (Accessed August 2018).

Edwards, P. 2010. *A Vast Machine*. Cambridge, MA: MIT Press.

ETC Group. 2016. "Year End Status of the Agribusiness Mega-Mergers, Software v. Hardware, Deere and Co. Is Becoming Monsanto in a Box," Annual report, December. www.etcgroup.org/content/deere-co-becoming-monsanto-box (Accessed September 2018).

Faulkner, A. and K. Cebul. 2014. "Agriculture Gets Smart: The Rise of Data and Robotics," *Cleantech Agriculture Report, Cleantech Group*. May 2014. www.cleantech.com/wp-content/uploads/2014/07/Agriculture-Gets-Smart-Report.pdf (Accessed August 2018).

Friedmann, H. 2009. "Feeding the Empire: The Pathologies of Globalized Agriculture," *Socialist Register* 41: 124–143.

Friedmann, H. and P. McMichael. 1987. "Agriculture and the State System: The Rise and Fall of National Agricultures, 1870 to the Present," *Sociologia Ruralis* 29, no. 2: 93–117.

Gebbers, R. and V. Adamchuk. (2010). "Precision Agriculture and Food Security," *Science* 327, no. 5967: 828–831.

Gilpin, L. 2015. "How Big Data Is Going to Help Feed Nine Billion People by 2050," *Tech Republic*. www.techrepublic.com/article/how-big-data-is-going-to-help-feed-9-billion-people-by-2050/ (Accessed August 2018).

GODAN: Global Open Data for Agriculture and Nutrition. n.d. www.godan.info (Accessed August 2018).

Government of Canada. 2017. "Budget in Brief: Skills and Innovation," Last modified March 22, 2017. www.budget.gc.ca/2017/docs/bb/brief-bref-en.html#section1 (Accessed August 2018).

Gustafson, S. 2016. "The Digital Revolution in Agriculture: Progress and Constraints," *International food policy research institute*, January 27, 2016. www.ifpri.org/blog/digital-revolution-agriculture-progress-and-constraints (Accessed August 2018).

Halfacree, K. 1999. "A New Space or Spatial Effacement? Alternative Futures for the Post-Productivist Countryside," in *Reshaping the Countryside: Perceptions and Processes of Rural Change*, edited by N. Walford, J. Everitt and N. Derril, 67–76. New York: CABI Publishing.

Heaton, T. and D. Brown 1982. "Farm Structure and Energy Intensity: Another Look," *Rural Sociology* 47, no. 1: 17–31.

IPES, International Panel of Experts on Sustainable Food Systems. Report to the United Nations, June 2016. www.ipes-food.org/images/Reports/UniformityToDiversity_FullReport.pdf

Kim, Jim Yong. 2015. "Future of Food: Shaping a Climate Smart Global Food System," http://documents.worldbank.org/curated/en/645981468189237140/pdf/100046-WP-PUBLIC-dislcose-7am-10-8-15-Box393216B.pdf

Kneen, B. 1995. *From Land to Mouth, Understanding the Food System*, 2nd Edition. Toronto, ON: NC Press.

Lang, T. and M. Heasman. 2004. *Food Wars, the Global Battle for Mouths, Minds and Markets*. London: Routledge.

Lesser, A. 2014. "Big Data and Big Agriculture," *Gigaom Research*. https://gigaom.com/report/big-data-and-big-agriculture/ (Accessed September 2018).

Levidow, L. and S. Carr. 2007. "GM Crops on Trial: Technological Development as Real-World Experiment," *Futures* 39, no. 4: 408–431.

Li, X., S. Chen and L. Guo. 2014. "Technological Innovation of Agricultural Information Service in the Age of Big Data," *Journal of Agricultural Science and Technology* 6, no. 4: 10–15.

Lowe, P., J. Murdoch, T. Marsden, R. Munton and A.z Flynn. 1993. "Regulating the New Rural Spaces: The Uneven Development of Land," *Journal of Rural Studies* 9, no. 3: 205–222.

Marsden, T., R. Munton, S. Whatmore and J. Little. 1986. "Towards a Political Economy of Capitalist Agriculture: A British Perspective," *International Journal of Urban and Regional Research* 10, no. 4: 489–521.

Marx, L. and M. Roe-Smith. 1994. *Does Technology Drive History? The Dilemma of Technological Determinism*. Cambridge, MA: MIT Press.

McBratney, A., B. Whelan, T. Ancev and J. Bouma 2005. "Future Directions of Precision Agriculture," *Precision Agriculture* 6: 7–23. 10.1007/s1111 9-005-0681-8.

McMichael, P. 2009. "A Food Regime Genealogy," *Journal of Peasant Studies* 36, no. 1: 139–169.

Menne, T. 2018. "Smart and Sustainable: Digitalisation Helps Farmers to Grow More with Less," *Media Planet*. www.globalcause.co.uk/world-food-day/smart-and-sustainable-digitalisation-helps-farmers-to-grow-more-with-less (Accessed August 2018).

Mirowski, P. 2011. *Science Mart: Privatizing American Science*. Cambridge, MA: Harvard University Press.

Mooney, P. 1998. *My Own Boss? Class, Rationality and the Family Farm*. New York, NY: Routledge Press.

Moore Lappe, F. 1971. *Diet for a Small Planet*. New York: Ballantine Books.

Muller, B. 2008. "Still Feeding the World? The Political Ecology of Canadian Prairie Farmers," *Anthropologica* 50, no. 2: 389–407.

Poppe, K, S. Wolfert, C.N. Verdouw and A. Renwick 2015. "A European Perspective on the Economics of Big Data," *Farm Policy Journal* 12, no. 1: 11–19.

Reif, L. 1987. "Farm Structure, Industry Structure, and Socioeconomic Conditions in the United States," *Rural Sociology* 52, no. 4: 462–482.

Rossel, V. and J. Bouma. 2016. "Soil Sensing: A New Paradigm for Agriculture," *Journal of Agricultural Systems* 148: 71–74.

Schimmelpfennig, D. 2016. "Farm Profits and Adoption of Precision Agriculture," ERR217, US Department of Agriculture, Economic Research Service, October 2016. www.ers.usda.gov/web docs/publications/80326/err-217.pdf?v=42661 (Accessed August 2018).

Scholten, M.C., I.J.M. de Boer, B. Gremmen and C. Lokhorst. 2013. "Livestock Farming with Care: Towards Sustainable Production of Animal-source Food," *Wageningen Journal of Life Sciences* 66: 3–5.

Sonka, S. 2015. "Big Data: From Hype to Agricultural Tool," *Farm Policy Journal* 12, no. 1: 1–9.

Stern, M. 2019. "The (Re)Evolution is Real: Digital Tools Will Transform Farming," www.precisionag.com/digital-farming/the-reevolution-is-real-digital-tools-will-transform-farming/

Sugimoto, C., H. Ekbia, and M. Mattioli. 2016. *Big Data Is Not a Monolith*. Cambridge, MA: MIT Press.

Sundmaeker, H., C. Verdouw, S. Wolfert and L. Perez 2016. "Internet of Food and Farm 2020," in *Digitising the Industry: Internet of Things Connecting Physical, Digital and Virtual Worlds*, edited by Friess, Vermesan O., 129–151. Gistrup, Denmark, and Delft, the Netherlands: River Publishers.

Tanahill, R. 1973. *Food in History*. New York: Three Rivers Press.

Vieri, M. L., M. R. Riccardo, and D. Sarri. 2013. "The RHEA Project Robot for Tree Crops Pesticide Application," *Journal of Agricultural Engineering* 44(s1): 359–362.

Welsch, R. and L. Glenna 2006. "Considering the Role of the University in Conducting Research on Agri-Biotechnologies," *Social Studies of Science* 36(6): 929–942.

Weersink, A., E. Fraser, D. Pannell, E. Duncan and S. Rotz. 2018. "Opportunities and Challenges for Big Data in Agricultural and Environmental Analysis," *Annual Review of Resource Economics* 10: 19–37.

Wilson, G. 2001. "From Productivism to Post-Productivism and Back Again? Exploring the (Un) changed Natural and Mental Landscapes of European Agriculture," *Transactions of the Institute of British Geographers* 26, no. 1: 77–102.

Winner, L. 1986. "Do Artifacts Have Politics?" *Daedalus* 109, no. 1: 121–136.

World Economic Forum. 2018. Open forum ASEAN, Ha Noi, September. www.weforum.org/events/world-economic-forum-on-asean (Accessed August 2018).

25

FROM WEEKEND FARMING TO TELEPHONE FARMING

Digital food pathways in Africa

Joseph Macharia

Introduction

This chapter explores the relationship between digital technologies, emerging medium-scale farmers, and the phenomenon of telephone farming in the contemporary context of agricultural regeneration across Africa. Increasingly, digitization is impacting upon work and life in a range of ways, yet the influence of digitization within farming processes remains underexamined. This chapter aims to start filling this gap by looking at the practices of Kenyan farmers who use digital technologies to manage their farm from a distance, a practice termed "telephone farming". Telephone farming involves using digital artifacts such as mobile phones to manage and coordinate farming processes from a distance and as such migrating some of the traditional physical activities of farming to virtual environments, which is described as process virtualization (Overby 2008). Drawing from an affordances perspective (Majchrzak and Markus 2013) this chapter examines how an emerging category of "telephone farmers" uses digital technologies such mobile phones to virtualize key farming processes. The use of digital artifacts and the technology affordances it generates along spatial constraints, contextual, and social dimensions are also investigated. Preliminary findings from interviews with 25 Kenyan telephone farmers suggest that material features of mobile phones offer three technology affordances related to spatiality, relationality, and contextuality, which enables telephone farmers to virtualize some farming processes along the value chain. These findings from work in progress suggest that a new pathway of farming is emerging in Kenya, which involves the use of mobile phones to carry out farming as an enterprise remotely. Understanding the context behind these trends and the challenges being faced by African farmers embracing agro-food technologies sheds light on the factors that will contribute to sustainable regenerative food system of Africa in the future.

Background

In order for the case study drawn upon in this chapter to be meaningfully understood, it is necessary to understand a number of factors changing the practice of agriculture within Africa.

First, we need to look at the implications of digital technologies for farming in Africa and differentiate the needs and uses of digital technologies within the agricultural sector in a developing country context. Second, this chapter briefly examines the current debate in the literature on the emerging trend of medium-scale farming across Africa (Anseeuw et al. 2016; Jayne et al. 2016; Jayne et al. 2015a; Scoones et al. 2018; Sitko and Jayne 2014). The so-called "missing middle" farmer is an important factor to understand when looking at farming beyond the subsistence level, as this group of farmers is injecting new energy into food production networks across Africa. Finally, the phenomenon of "telephone farming" within Kenya is briefly explained, linking the discussion of digital technologies in the agriculture sector and the medium-scale farmer trends, by providing a concrete example of medium-scale farmers using mobile phones to carry out farming as a business from a distance.

Digital technology and agriculture

Various scholars recognize the potential of digital technologies in enabling agricultural productivity, resilience, sustainability, and management (Aker et al. 2016; Cox 2002; Deichmann et al. 2016; Oliver et al. 2010). A sustainable regenerative food system of the future will involve a range of agro-food-based technologies and, as Carolan has emphasized, understanding these technologies requires looking beyond the technology itself and focusing on the socio-technical implications of these technologies on people and the agricultural sector (Carolan 2017). In the developed countries context, the agro-food-based technologies in the design and testing phase include: the use of robots/machines in precision agriculture, exploring the role of big data in agriculture (soil, climate, weather, market, and insurance data), and internet-based platforms used by food activists which seek to promote more local, sustainable, and equitable food systems.

In the developing countries context, most of the existing literature mainly looks at the role of digital technologies from the perspective of the small-scale farmer and looks at the use of these farmers in using mobile phone and internet in connecting to commercial markets, accessing agricultural extension support (Aker 2011; Donner and Escobari 2010; Jensen 2007). For instance, a study carried out with Kerala fishermen in India found that the use of mobile phones has positive outcomes on the earnings of fishermen by reducing price volatility and waste (Jensen 2007). Similarly, Aker (2011) who studied African small-scale farmers found that farmers experienced cost and time benefits by using digital technologies to access extension services. In addition to marketing, Deichmann et al. (2016) notes digital artifacts such as mobile phones provide access to online agricultural extension services, which has potential to raise on-farm productivity by providing knowledge about new tools, methods, or seeds. The contribution of information communication technologies (ICT) to socioeconomic development remains debatable (Donner and Escobari 2010; Etzo and Collender 2010), but their use is now ubiquitous within society and so they will play a role in future food systems. Existing literature thus suggests that digitization in agriculture in the developing country context is largely connected with processes occurring via a mobile phone such as gaining market access or market understanding, accessing extension services virtually and connecting with other farmers through the use of ICTs.

Farm size and cost influence the type of digital technology adopted. Large-scale farms, which are more predominant in the developed country context are more likely to be able to afford more costly digital technologies such as robots and access to software packages using artificial intelligence based on data harvesting to inform farm practices. Smaller farms, such as those predominantly found in developing countries, are using online platforms and mobile phone applications and affordances to enhance their farm practices with the rise of the digital revolution in agriculture.

Emerging medium-scale farming

Across the African agriculture landscape, a new type of farmer is emerging. This farmer is not a subsistence small-scale farmer nor a large-scale multinational company. The term "missing middle" (Leenstra 2014) "emergent investor farmer" (Jayne et al. 2015a) refers to the emergence of a new type of farmer who is farming a medium size of land as a business enterprise mostly from a distance. While small-scale farmers tend to farm for subsistence purposes, medium-scale farmers are farming to make profit and as such their investments, both in terms of input and labour, are generally higher than small-scale farmers. Jayne et al. (2016) define medium-scale farmers as farmers holding between 5 and 100 hectares (ha) while (Anseeuw et al. 2016) defines medium-scale landholders/farmers as farmers with a total landholding of between 5 and 50 ha. In the African context, different governments have different interpretations of medium-scale farms and tend to recognize the smaller end of medium-scale farms as those encompassing land sized between 5 and 20 ha (Makumire et al. 2013). Scholarly literature on medium-scale farmers remains limited, due to the previous focus of agricultural scholarship and governmental policy within Africa on the impacts of small-scale or large-scale farming on rural economies (Collier 2008).

Medium-scale farmers have emerged organically as opposed to being encouraged by international or national government policies. While medium-scale farming has always existed on some level across Africa, current interest in such ventures is being driven by the rapid expansion of "investor farmers" documented since 2000 (Jayne et al. 2016). In this context, investor farmers are the local professionals who invest in farming as a business. Existing literature broadly associates the rapid emergence of medium-scale farmers in Africa with several developments such as global food crisis, improved market access, mechanization, and multiparty democracy that gives more voice to farmers and national land reforms programs in some countries (Anseeuw et al. 2012; Jayne et al. 2016; Leenstra 2014; Sitko and Chamberlin 2015; Sitko and Jayne 2014).

According to Jayne et al (2016), there are two pathways into medium-scale farming. The first pathway involves expansion by small-scale farmers who successfully graduate to medium-scale farming through expansion of their farming size and operations (Anseeuw et al. 2016; Jayne et al. 2014; Muyanga and Jayne 2014). The second pathway involves investor farmers, which Sitko and Jayne (2014) describe as "lateral entry" into agriculture, implying that they entered farming without any prior experience. These farmers use non-farm capital earned mainly from full-time employment or other business in urban areas and invest in farm enterprises in the rural areas. According to Jayne et al. (2016), 60% of farmers from this second pathway are urban-based, while 35% are rural-based elites (whose parents tend to be affluent). The emergence of medium-scale farmers across Africa is changing the African food system. It is changing the crops grown (crops for market as opposed to consumption), the sophistication of farming being practiced driven by investment into farming innovations and technologies, and it is expected to bring change at the rural economy level.

Telephone farming

The final piece of the puzzle to understand in the African agriculture sector is the proliferation and use of mobile phones for a wide range of purposes including agriculture purposes. The term "telephone farming" has been used in East Africa to describe farming that primarily is controlled through mobile phone from a distance (Fleming et al. 2016). This farming is characterized by farmers who are not physically present in the farm to perform and monitor daily activities required to run a farm, as they often live and have salaried work in urban areas. They engage in farming as a strategy of livelihood diversification in order to meet increased living costs associated with educating children, supporting dependent relatives, and retirement investment preparation (Leenstra 2014).

Historically, the term "telephone farmers" was associated with the African elite farmers who benefitted from transfer of farms from the colonial white farmers after decolonization in early 1960s. Despite lack of smart phones then, this term was used to associate absent elite farmers with their farms. They were also referred to as "brief case farmers", "suitcase farmers", "weekend farmers" (Foeken and Owuor 2008). Such transfers were influenced by African political elites interested in gaining access to farm land as a productive resource and the government interest in shaping the economic structure to ensure a smooth transformation of colonial Kenya to independence (Leo 1984). Within Kenya, under the guidance of the World Bank and the British government, the government handed over productive farmland previously held by white settlers to local people, with the aim of avoiding disruption to economic performance. This led to transfer of large farms, benefitting the well-educated high-ranking civil servants, politicians, and business people living in the urban areas. These farmers were criticized for benefitting from government support without actually improving farming productivity since they were not fully engaged in farming like other small-scale farmers. Leo (1984, 193) described this group of farmers as follows:

> They – and many others like them elsewhere in Kenya – became what some administrative officials referred to as telephone farmers, people who concentrate on more lucrative activities while farming over the weekend and by telephone. Unproductive telephone farmers while failing to increase the commercial opportunities and infrastructure in rural areas that would be beneficial for the more productive small-scale farmers.

This critique is based on the belief that small-scale farmers would be better managers of land as their livelihoods are tied to the land. This rationale has, however, not played out in practice, with the majority of the world's poor living in agricultural communities (80% of the extreme poor and 75% of the moderate poor). This chapter argues that the agriculture sector, just like any other successful sector, needs the people engaged within it to hold relevant education or business experience, access to capital to invest in farming ventures, and a passion for farming and the land in order for the sector to regenerate.

More recently, the term telephone farmers has been used to describe medium-scale farmers in full-time employment or with alternative income from non-farm activities, who live and work in urban areas, and simultaneously engage in rural farming as an enterprise (Fleming et al. 2016; Leenstra 2014; Majchrzak and Markus 2013). In telephone farming, the farmers are not present in the farm to perform and monitor daily activities. A study by Fleming et al. (2016) compared education, farm size, age, monthly income, and crop production characteristics of small-scale and telephone farmers and found that the median age of a telephone farmer was 34 years, compared to 60 years of small-scale farmers in Kenya. The study found similarities among education levels (high school completion at a minimum) but differences among the risk-taking behaviors between the two groups, with telephone farmers more willing to take additional investment risks to improve farm productivity.

According to Leenstra (2014) and Makumire et al. (2013), there are several challenges facing telephone farming in Kenya. The first challenge is the balancing of the full-time job with farming enterprise. In telephone farming, there is lack of time to dedicate to the enterprise due to challenges in balancing the management of the farm along with salaried work and family and personal commitments. The second challenge is the use of poorly skilled and thus poorly paid employees to run the farm. Farm employees often have no technical agriculture or business training and often lack the skills and motivation to run the farm in an entrepreneurial manner. The third challenge is lack of trust between the farm workers and the telephone farmer, which was a strong theme in the results of this study. Telephone farmers face all such challenges due to the spatial constraints in the farm locations. However, Williams et al. (2011) argue that digital technologies such as mobile phones can support to overcome such spatial constraints.

Traditionally, farming is geographically bound in that the farmer and the farm are inexorably linked and the farm and farmer usually co-located. However, in telephone farming, the farmer is absent or away from the farm and thus coordination and supervision of the farm process is mediated by technology. This chapter demonstrates that the use of digital technologies such as mobile phones can enable farmers to overcome spatial-related constraints in farming enterprises. Digital artifacts such as smartphones are viewed as enablers in overcoming spatial constraints in farming. This study attempts to understand how digital technologies and people interrelate. By doing so, it problematizes the sociotechnical context of telephone farming and the specific needs of telephone farming.

Theoretical background

This chapter draws upon the technology affordances perspective (Majchrzak and Markus 2013; Strong et al. 2014) to help examine the use of mobile phones in enabling process virtualization in farming. A technology affordances perspective is suited to examining the present study since it allows the researcher to sketch the precise nature of a technology (Majchrzak and Markus 2013) and it is appropriate for researchers interested in unrecognized roles of emerging technology (Majchrzak and Markus 2013). This allows the researcher to go beyond the technology functionalities to theorize digitally enabled actions and their outcomes (Majchrzak and Markus 2013; Strong et al. 2014) such as in telephone farming.

Technology affordance is an opportunity for action (Hutchby 2001) "an individual or organization with a particular purpose can do with a technology" (Majchrzak and Markus 2013, 1) which offers an explanation of a technological artifact's use and the related consequences for individuals' behavior (Majchrzak and Markus 2013). There is a distinction between technology affordances and technology features. Technology features are the designated functionalities inbuilt into the technology and the technology affordances lens identifies the symbiotic relationships between human action and technological capabilities (Majchrzak and Markus 2013; Zammuto et al. 2007). Debate still exists on whether the affordances are embedded on the technology artifact or they emerge in the interaction between the user and the artifact (Fayard and Weeks 2014; Zheng and Yu 2016). Existing information system (IS) literature has two perspectives on understanding technology affordances.

The first perspective views affordances as action potential intended and embedded in technology artifacts by the designer (Majchrzak and Markus 2013; Markus and Silver 2008). Existing studies on this perspective focus on identifying functional affordances in a specific technological artifact (Majchrzak and Markus 2013). In the same vein, Strong et al. (2014) extended the focus on this perspective into understanding of how such affordances are actualized by users. The second perspective views affordances as "emergent from sociomaterial practices that involve technology" (Zheng and Yu 2016) – that is, affordances do not exist in technology, but as emergent phenomena. This is a recent perspective of affordances in the sociomateriality research (Bygstad et al. 2016) and theorizes affordances for practice (Fayard and Weeks 2014) that are "contingent upon the purpose of human agency as well as historical and socio-institutional settings" (Zheng and Yu 2016, 292). This study continues this focus on affordances. Thus this chapter seeks to reshape the debate on the regenerative food-based technologies, from what technology a farmer looks at to what socio-technical forms technology engenders. In other words "affordances are not just something that can be designed for and be intended but are emerging through use and actions" (Thapa and Sein 2018, 798). The studies argue that affordances emerge through use and actions.

According to Orlikowski and Scott (2008), the affordances of technology are shaped by social practices, in particular those social practice(s) it enables. Sociomaterial practices are considered spaces within which people engage with the materiality of technological artifacts to produce various outcomes (Orlikowski and Scott 2008). Affordances are therefore not exclusive properties of either the actor or a given technology but a constituent of the relationship between people and the material artifacts with which they come in contact through a set of social practices (Hutchby 2001). To capture the affordances of different technologies, it is important to focus on the social practices they enable. The features of technologies are "materialized" only if their use by telephone farmers is consequential in how these farmers carry out management practices of their farms from a distance. Affordances are derived from capabilities.

Methodology

The sample consisted of 25 telephone farmers from Nairobi, Kenya. Data were collected through 25 in-depth, semi-structured interviews with all the informants. Informants were selected on the basis of fulfilling the following criteria: employed or with a main income from non-farm activities while simultaneously engaged in farming as enterprise, engaged in farming but not residing on-farm for its day-to-day running and supervision, and utilizing digital technologies in the farm either as a system of the farm or farm management through smart farming. Participants were identified through purposive sampling, with possible contact established through social media platforms. The interview focused on the uses of digital technologies in managing a farm from a distance. The questions were based on the affordances theoretical framework, while allowing space for other themes and issues to emerge. The interviews continued until no new ideas were suggested by the interviewees and the emerging themes were fully explored, i.e. there was a saturation in the responses from the interviewees. For the analysis the emerging themes and key ideas of each interview were distilled according to the three foci of the interview and the related theoretical framework. The patterns and key differences that emerged are described in the results section. All the interviews were audio recorded with the consent of the participants, and the recordings transcribed. Thematic analysis of data was followed, with familiarization with data, generation of initial codes, then searching and reviewing themes, naming themes, and then building constructs.

Findings

Data analysis gives rise to three virtualizing practices that enable telephone farmers to carry out farming from a distance. These practices provide understanding relative to farming outside the traditional farming arrangements where the farmer is based in the farm as a full-time activity. All of these virtualizing practices are intertwined with diverse use of digital technologies. The next section describes the enabling roles played by these digital technologies.

Reducing spatial constraints

Traditionally, farming has been seen as the main source of a farmer's income and the farm location as the main location of work (Vik and McElwee 2011). Telephone farming changes this paradigm by having an urban professional using capital earned from non-farm sources to invest in farming activities from a distance. In order for such practices to take place, spatial constraints must be overcome so they can farm from a distance. Travelling from the city to the farm every day is not possible as telephone farmers have full-time work and family commitments in urban areas, preventing them visiting the farm on a very frequent basis. Participants recognized that mobile phones played a role in overcoming spatial constraints. One informant explicitly recognized that "new technology where we have phones … you can coordinate everything over the phone other than being in there present" (TF07).

Mobile phones enabled farming by a distance as they reduced the number of physical visits to the farm. One respondent (TF06) explained that previously they "would have probably travelled maybe twice a month to go and check how the crops are doing how the animals are"; however they now are able to coordinate all of these activities from their office in the city. Telephone farming thus decouples the spatial and temporal conditions from one another. One can engage in farming without investing time to travel to the farm.

Participants also used technology to monitor farm activities. Cameras and sensors enabled telephone farmers to see farm processes in real time. One participant explained that they used their phone to check in on farm activities and that the

> advantage of ICT on the farm in terms of monitoring, surveillance on the farm, such that instead of being told that the animals are being milked when I am in the city almost 200 km away, with the touch of a button I can monitor on the cameras what is happening.
>
> *(TF04)*

Technology has thus made temporal boundaries fluid and also plays a role in enhancing monitoring ability of farming enterprises.

Enhancing trustworthiness

One significant challenge for telephone farmers is a lack of trust between telephone farmers and farm managers, and the difficulty in locating and keeping trustworthy and skilled farm employees. Trust is an important issue in telephone farming. Despite digital technology enabling communication and interactions in telephone farming, the telephone farmers interviewed indicated lack of trust within their virtual team network. 'Being a telephone farmer the greatest challenge is having employees that you can trust. If we are able to get the right type of combinations of employees who can do work with integrity, telephone farming will thrive" (TF21).

Many of the informants used a network approach to increase their trust in farm operations. The informants identified a range of people whom they interacted with in order to receive and verify farm information (Figure 25.1). All informants had a farm manager who acted as their central point of contact. In addition, informants identified

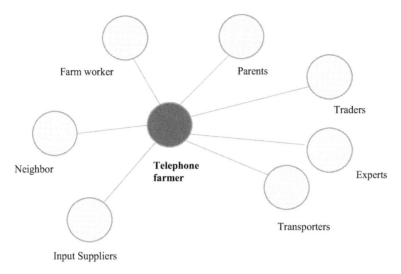

Figure 25.1 Network of telephone farmer.

a range of other actors whom they contacted regarding farm operations, including: parents, friends, neighbors, farm workers, experts, farm input suppliers. "You realise the phone is very important because I talk to my farm workers. I have two workers. I talk to them every day and also my parents are in close proximity to be able to see what is happening." (TF04).

Some of the participants use parents as a "third eye" aimed at confirming the truth as communicated by others.

> I trust that my parents won't swindle me. Even when I am in Nairobi and they are there supervising, I am sure the work will be done. they will ensure the labourers do exactly as advised, so, it is an enterprise of trust. (TF11)

Other participants utilize the good relationships they have with their neighbours by engaging them to provide information about the farm enterprise.

> I engage my neighbours on security of course. They tell me what's going on. If someone comes to the farm and picks some produce, one or two of my neighbours will call and ask if I have authorized it. You cannot trust anyone 100%. (TF01)

Within this network, the telephone farmer communicates with the players at varying frequencies depending on the roles and the relations they have. Interactions take place via telephone calls, video calls, SMS, and photo SMS. Mobile phones thus enabled verbal and visual messages to be conveyed, with the visual messages being used to confirm verbal updates.

Enacting farming-personal-work balance

Telephone farmers face two challenges in achieving work-life balance: first, they struggle to balance farm management with other full-time working commitments and secondly they struggle to balance double work commitments with personal and family commitments. In terms of balancing full-time work and telephone farming, one participant remarked:

> This is challenge but I feel like my employer is getting a raw deal. Because once in a while I have to use the office Wi-Fi for my personal farming business, I have to get out of the office to engage with my local vet. So, it is stealing half of work.
>
> *(TF10)*

As technology develops and allows work to be carried out at all times from all locations, previous time-bounded hours of work disappear. While this brings benefits in terms of flexibility and arguably efficiently, it also brings challenges in managing work-life balance. As telephone farmers carry their mobile phones with them at all times, they are on call 24 hours a day. Telephone farmers thus never really switch off from work. This trend is experienced beyond the telephone farming context and applies to anyone who checks work emails on their personal phone. Telephone farmers recognized that their farming activities crept into personal time and acknowledged the tensions this caused with family members. "My wife hates my farm worker because we are always on the phone when I enter the car. I will call him when I'm home he will call me when I'm at work" (TF16).

Telephone farmers did however identify some solutions for achieving better balance by setting boundaries to keep telephone farming separate from other commitments. Some of the participants utilize their "down time" to carry out farming activities: "when I'm waiting to go for a meeting or where I'm in a meeting and it hasn't started. I basically use phone to get more information about agriculture" (TF04).

Discussion

This chapter has sought to understand how digital technologies are changing farming practices in Kenya. The preliminary results provide evidence of the practice of telephone farming in Kenya. Telephone farming is dependent upon mobile phones and the different affordances that they offer such as: communication, access to digital platforms for marketing or networking purposes, and applications for monitoring farm activities. The development of digital infrastructure has laid the foundations for telephone farming and is acting as an external enabler of entrepreneurship in African farming (Friederici and Graham 2018). Affordances of various digital technologies for telephone farming can be understood for how their use enables virtualization of farming processes. By enabling different migration of farming processes from physical to virtual environments, the usage of digital technologies generates affordances for virtualizing farming process.

Telephone farmers do however face a range of barriers when farming remotely, including time pressure and trust issues related to finding reliable farm employees whom they can rely upon to manage farm operations in their absence. Digital technologies alone do not enable process virtualization in farming enterprises. Instead, telephone farmers implemented various combinations of face-to-face, trust-based relationships and a unique local knowledge, combined with mobile phone affordances such as picture messages and cameras, to overcome various constraints on engaging in farming from a distance.

While digital technologies are enabling telephone farmers, not all individuals working in the city are engaged in farming from a distance. The majority of those engaging in telephone farming seem to have some cultural embeddedness to farming and are still attached or connected to the rural areas, which generally arises from growing up in rural farming communities. Those who are not motivated by a passion for farming or with no rural connection (i.e. most family members have migrated to urban areas) may find it difficult to practice telephone farming as they will have difficulty establishing trust without family, friend, or professional networks in rural areas.

Existing literature notes that the increasing presence of medium-scale farmers has largely been ignored by government and international organizations (Anseeuw et al. 2016; Jayne et al. 2016; Jayne et al. 2015b). Existing literature also shows that Africa's labour force is diversifying away from subsistence farming (Yeboah and Jayne, 2018) and new private actors such as telephone farmers are investing heavily in areas of agricultural commercialization (Sitko and Jayne 2014). This implies that telephone farming is contributing to the transformation of African agriculture.

These preliminary results have policy implications:

–   Agriculture policy within Kenya needs to recognize a shift within agriculture which is seeing farming from a distance (telephone farming) and farming being carried out as a business enterprise (medium-scale farming).
–   Government data collection should be modified to take account of these emerging practices and should collect data regarding farm size, crop, and market destination.
–   The international community, both donor agriculture agencies and trade bodies, need to support medium-scale and telephone farming initiatives and increase data collection on these emerging agricultural practices.
–   Literature tends to conclude that medium-scale farmers provide benefits to rural and national economies (Jayne et al. 2016). As such, consideration needs to be given to how to support telephone farmers. This study did not identify any barriers imposed by government which prevent telephone farming, however consideration should be given to developing or supporting initiatives which aim to improve market access and provide digital extension services, noting that government may not be the best providers of these services, with many existing successful online agricultural platforms in existence run by private practitioners.
–   Telephone farming has the potential to increase competition for rural land. There is a need to ensure that land for telephone farming is acquired fairly, with consent of landowners and appropriate compensation paid.
–   There is a need to strike a balance between overregulation of telephone farming and no regulation of telephone farming. It is likely that telephone farmers are not currently paying full tax on farming enterprises, which may be one factor driving entrepreneurship in the sector. Care should be taken in introducing any reforms regarding tax, as onerous tax obligations may stifle and or destroy the sector.
–   Farm labourers working on farms managed by telephone farmers should be earning the established minimum wage, which in 2018 is around $132 USD per month.

Conclusion

This chapter explored how telephone farmers are using digital technologies such mobile phones to virtualize key farming processes. All participants shared the experience of enacting process virtualization in farming, drawing from digital technologies such as mobile phones. Digital technologies have noticeable roles here, based on subjective ease of use. It's important to note that the use of digital technologies has changed when, where, and how farming is carried out. The affordances lens provides a base for capturing the roles played by digital technologies in facilitating process virtualization in telephone farming. This chapter identifies telephone farming as one of the emerging alternative foodscapes being shaped by technology. Digitalization can change business processes or models that result from use of a digital technology (Nambisan et al. 2017). Digital technologies are promoting agricultural transformations, thus reshaping the debate on how we think and talk about agro-food-based technologies.

While these findings are specific to the Kenyan context, it is suggested that the influence of digital technologies on migration of farming processes to a virtual environment is of general relevance when seeking to understand of the effects of digital technologies on the increasing practice of medium-scale farming in developing countries. As discussed above, technology used in agriculture tends to divide along developed and developing country lines and findings from this study will be more transferable to countries with emerging medium-scale farm activities, who are likely to fall in the developing country grouping. However, like any other qualitative research, this study suffers from limitations. The insights into telephone farming raise questions of generalizability on whether the findings can apply to other communities and countries. While the phenomenon of telephone farming has been reported in other African countries, it is hard to exclude the possibilities of other factors in our research settings that might have influenced the evolution of the observed processes. The ultimate goal was to extend the affordance theory in the context of digital agriculture. Thus more research is needed in order to confirm whether these ideas hold when subjected to quantitative inquiry in other jurisdictions. As studies on medium-scale farmers come largely from Africa, further studies from Asia, the Pacific, South, and Central America on medium-scale farmers would help provide some insight into emerging global trends in agricultural transformation.

Discussion questions

1. Could digital technologies be an enabling mechanism of regenerative food systems in Africa?
2. Who is a telephone farmer?
3. How should agricultural and development policy support the emergence of telephone or medium-scale farmers?

Further reading

Jayne, T., Chamberlin, J., Traub, L., Sitko, N., Muyanga, M., Yeboah, F. K., … Nkonde, C. (2016). Africa's changing farm size distribution patterns: The rise of medium-scale farms. *Agricultural Economics*, *47*(S1), 197–214.

Aker, J. C. (2011). Dial "A" for agriculture: A review of information and communication technologies for agricultural extension in developing countries. *Agricultural Economics*, *42*(6), 631–647.

Leenstra, M. (2014). From suitcase farmers to telephone farmers. In: *Digging deeper: Inside Africa's agricultural, food and nutrition dynamics* (pp. 217–231). Leiden: Koninklijke Brill NV.

Majchrzak, A., & Markus, M. L. (2013). *Methods for policy research: Taking socially responsible action* (Vol. 3). Newbury Park: SAGE publications.

Carolan, M. (2017). Publicising food: Big data, precision agriculture, and co-experimental techniques of addition. *Sociologia Ruralis*, *57*(2), 135–154.

References

Aker, J. C. (2011). Dial "A" for agriculture: A review of information and communication technologies for agricultural extension in developing countries. *Agricultural Economics, 42*(6), 631–647.

Aker, J. C., Ghosh, I., and Burrell, J. (2016). The promise (and pitfalls) of ICT for agriculture initiatives. *Agricultural Economics, 47*(S1), 35–48.

Anseeuw, W., et al. (2012). *Transnational land deals for agriculture in the global South.* Analytical Report Based on the Land Matrix Database, (The Land Matrix Partnership 2012). (CDE/CIRAD/GIGA, Bern/Montpellier/Hamburg). Available at http://landportal.info. Accessed May, 2019.

Anseeuw, W., Jayne, T., Kachule, R., and Kotsopoulos, J. (2016). The quiet rise of medium-scale farms in Malawi. *Land, 5*(3), 19.

Bygstad, B., Munkvold, B. E., and Volkoff, O. (2016). Identifying generative mechanisms through affordances: A framework for critical realist data analysis. *Journal of Information Technology, 31*(1), 83–96.

Collier, P. (2008). *The bottom billion: Why the poorest countries are failing and what can be done about it.* New York: Oxford University Press.

Cox, S. (2002). Information technology: The global key to precision agriculture and sustainability. *Computers and Electronics in Agriculture, 36*(2), 93–111.

Deichmann, U., Goyal, A., and Mishra, D. (2016). Will digital technologies transform agriculture in developing countries? *Agricultural Economics, 47*(S1), 21–33.

Donner, J., and Escobari, M. X. (2010). A review of evidence on mobile use by micro and small enterprises in developing countries. *Journal of International Development, 22*(5), 641–658.

Etzo, S., and Collender, G. (2010). The mobile phone 'revolution' in Africa: Rhetoric or reality? *African Affairs, 109*(437), 659–668.

Fayard, A.-L., and Weeks, J. (2014). Affordances for practice. *Information and Organization, 24*(4), 236–249.

Fleming, K., Kouassi, A., Ondula, E., and Waweru, P. (2016). Toward farmer decision profiles to improve food security in Kenya. *IBM Journal of Research and Development, 60* (5/6), 6: 1–6: 10.

Foeken, D. W., and Owuor, S. O. (2008). Farming as a livelihood source for the urban poor of Nakuru, Kenya. *Geoforum, 39*(6), 1978–1990.

Friederici, N., and Graham, M. (2018). The bounded opportunities of digital enterprises in global economic Peripheries. Available at SSRN 3249499.

Hutchby, I. (2001). Technologies, texts and affordances. *Sociology, 35*(2), 441–456.

Jayne, T. S. et al. (2014). Is the scramble for land in Africa foreclosing a smallholder agricultural expansion strategy? *Journal of International Affairs, 67*(2), 35.

Jayne, T., et al. (2016). Africa's changing farm size distribution patterns: The rise of medium-scale farms. *Agricultural Economics, 47*(S1), 197–214.

Jayne, T. S. et al. (2015a). Africa's changing farmland ownership: The rise of the emergent investor farmer. In 2015 Conference, August 9–14, 2015, Milan, Italy: International Association of Agricultural Economists.

Jayne, T. S., et al. (2015b). *Africa's changing farmland ownership: Causes and consequences.* No. 1098-2016-88851. 2015.

Jensen, R. (2007). The digital provide: Information (technology), market performance, and welfare in the South Indian fisheries sector. *Quarterly Journal of Economics, 122*(3), 879–924.

Leenstra, M. (2014). From suitcase farmers to telephone farmers. In: *Digging deeper: Inside Africa's agricultural, food and nutrition dynamics* (pp. 217–231). Leiden: Koninklijke Brill NV.

Leo, C. (1984). *Land and class in Kenya.* Toronto: University of Toronto Press.

Majchrzak, A., and Markus, M. L. (2013). Technology affordances and constraints in Management Information Systems (MIS). In E. Kessler (Eds.), *Encyclopedia of Management Theory* (pp. 832–835). Los Angeles, CA: Sage Publications.

Makumire, T., Nijhoff, and de Vries, K. (2013). *Unlocking the potential of telephone farmers.* Wageningen: WUR/CDI.

Markus, M. L., and Silver, M. S. (2008). A foundation for the study of IT effects: A new look at DeSanctis and Poole's concepts of structural features and spirit. *Journal of the Association for Information Systems, 9*(10/11), 609.

Muyanga, M., and Jayne, T. (2014). Effects of rising rural population density on smallholder agriculture in Kenya. *Food Policy, 48*, 98–113.

Nambisan, S., Lyytinen, K., Majchrzak, A., and Song, M. (2017). Digital innovation management: Reinventing innovation management research in a digital world. *Mis Quarterly*, *41*(1).

Oliver, Y., Robertson, M., and Wong, M. (2010). Integrating farmer knowledge, precision agriculture tools, and crop simulation modelling to evaluate management options for poor-performing patches in cropping fields. *European Journal of Agronomy*, *32*(1), 40–50.

Orlikowski, W. J., and Scott, S. V. (Singer-songwriters). (2008). Sociomateriality: Challenging the separation of technology, work and organization. *The Academy of Management Annals*, *2* (1), 433–474 .

Overby, E. (2008). Process virtualization theory and the impact of information technology. *Organization Science*, *19*(2), 277–291.

Scoones, I., Mavedzenge, B., and Murimbarimba, F. (2018). Medium-scale commercial farms in Africa: The experience of the "native purchase areas" in Zimbabwe. *Africa*, *88*(3), 597–619.

Sitko, N., and Chamberlin, J. (2015). The Anatomy of medium-scale farm growth in Zambia: what are the implications for the future of smallholder agriculture? *Land*, *4*(3), 869–887.

Sitko, N. J., and Jayne, T. (2014). Structural transformation or elite land capture? The growth of "emergent" farmers in Zambia. *Food Policy*, *48*, 194–202.

Strong, D. M., Johnson, S. A., Tulu, B., Trudel, J., Volkoff, O., Pelletier, L. R., ... Garber, L. (2014). A theory of organization-EHR affordance actualization. *Journal of the Association for Information Systems*, *15*(2), 53.

Thapa, D., and Sein, M. K. (2018). Trajectory of Affordances: Insights from a case of telemedicine in Nepal. *Information Systems Journal*, *28*(5), 796–817.

Vik, J., & McElwee, G. (2011). Diversification and the entrepreneurial motivations of farmers in Norway★. *Journal of Small Business Management*, *49*(3), 390–410.

Williams, M. D., Mayer, R., and Minges, M. (2011). *Africa's ICT infrastructure: Building on the mobile revolution*. Washington, DC: World Bank.

Yeboah, F. K., and Jayne, T. (2018). Africa's evolving employment structure. *The Journal of Development Studies*, *54*(5), 803–832.

Zammuto, R. F., Griffith, T. L., Majchrzak, A., Dougherty, D. J., and Faraj, S. (2007). Information technology and the changing fabric of organization. *Organization Science*, *18*(5), 749–762.

Zheng, Y., and Yu, A. (2016). Affordances of social media in collective action: The case of free lunch for children in China. *Information Systems Journal*, *26*(3), 289–313.

26

RURAL–URBAN LINKAGES

Michael Woods

Introduction

The fifth floor of the Museum aan de Strom (MAS) in Antwerp teems with objects and artifacts, pictures, maps, and infographics that represent the city's relationship with food. There are examples of 16th-century kettles and 18th-century tableware, models of fishing boats, and paintings and photographs not only of market gardens outside the city's walls and haystacks in the Flemish countryside, but also of Canadian grain fields, African banana plantations, and a Brazilian sugar factory, drawing the connections between urban food consumption and rural food production. As the book accompanying the exhibition observes,

> Cities have been hungry for centuries. They are scattered throughout the world but are always dependent upon rural areas for survival and are shaped, far more than we think, by food – and not just in social and cultural terms, but also spatially, economically and politically. Like voracious 'monsters' they devour harvests from near and far, but are also places where, for centuries, crops and have been transformed into culinary specialties that acquire, in turn, added value … It is a universal aspect of urbanity that simultaneously makes every metropolis unique and different, for all cities have their own special connection with food.
>
> *(Beyers and van Damme 2016, 6)*

Food is at the core of the rural–urban relation. As agglomerations of population where land is a prized and contested asset, cities have a limited capacity to feed themselves and have always relied on the importation of food from rural areas that in turn have become characterized by agriculture. Historically, the food consumed by a city was provided predominantly by its immediate hinterland, and it is no coincidence that the world's first great urban civilizations developed in fertile farming regions. With the progression of time, however, food has been sourced over increasing distances and through ever more complex supply chains, as diets have diversified, trade expanded, technologies improved, and a global agrifood system established. These developments have not only changed how and what cities eat, but they also have stretched rural–urban interactions over longer distances, creating dependencies between non-adjacent localities. Thus, today, a global countryside feeds an increasingly urbanized global population.

Yet, the sustainability of the current global food system has been brought into question by the challenges of the climate crisis, concerns around environmental degradation and biodiversity loss, and growing public awareness about food quality, health effects, and ethics. Activist food movements have emerged advocating responses ranging from agroecology to veganism, and food sovereignty to organic farming; whilst the agro-industrial sector has continued to develop its own technological solutions to food security concerns, with advances in genetic engineering, precision farming techniques, and digital agriculture. Each of these pathways involves changes to how and where food is produced, as well as to what and where we eat, and thus impacts on the configuration of rural–urban relations.

This chapter considers the significance of rural–urban linkages in current and future food systems. It first briefly elaborates the historical evolution of food markets and supply chains, and the increasing complexity of the rural–urban relations with which they are associated, as well as the challenges to the contemporary global food system. The chapter then proceeds to outline four different scenarios for rural–urban interactions in sustainable food futures, highlighting intersections with wider social and economic processes. Finally, the chapter concludes by briefly reflecting on the potential and limitations of different approaches to reconfiguring rural–urban relations in more sustainable and regenerative food systems and questions that consequently need to be considered by social scientists engaging with these developments.

Rural–urban interactions and the globalization of food systems

Urban food systems have moved a long way from the idealized model of von Thünen's concentric ring model, with cities supplied by radiating circles successively providing horticulture and dairying; forestry for firewood and building materials; arable land for cereals; and livestock grazing. In practice, cities have always supplemented hinterland agriculture with food sourced from more distant regions, whether luxury commodities such as spices, or meat from livestock herded by drovers from peripheral regions to cities such as London for sale and slaughter. Technological developments in railways, shipping and refrigeration in the 19th century further extended the range of food provisioning, establishing connections between major cities and regions that came to specialize in the supply of milk, vegetables, or fruit to particular urban markets (Freidberg 2009). At the same time, public health concerns combined with competition for land in rapidly expanding industrial cities to squeeze out agriculture, creating a spatial division of labour between the countryside as the site of food production and the city as the locus of food consumption.

By the start of the 20th century, the networks supplying European and North American cities had become global in scope, involving nascent transnational agrifood corporations that pioneered vertical integration from the farm to the shop, and providing the markets and capital to sustain the expansion of large-scale commercial agriculture in Australia, New Zealand, and parts of North and South America and Africa. At first these elongated commodity chains were shaped by geopolitics, through colonial ties and preferential trade deals, such that it was still possible to identify stable relations between cities and specific producer regions. Later trade liberalization, however, together with the consolidation of global agrifood corporations with multinational operations, turned agricultural sectors into foot-loose industries, with production concentrated in sites determined by cost efficiencies rather than by environmental conditions or market adjacency.

The integration of the global food system has not only locked farmers into global commodity chains, but it has also changed the dynamics of food distribution and consumption within rural areas. Farmers that are producing under contract to a food producer, exporter, or retailer do not have produce to sell locally, and in many rural regions the infrastructure for localized supply chains has been compromised by the closure and consolidation of abattoirs, dairies, and markets. Supermarkets have inserted themselves into rural localities and become the major suppliers of food in these districts. Accordingly, the geographical logic of food supply networks has been to some extent reversed, with rural districts now dependent on urban areas for the supply of food routed through airports, ports, processing plants, and distribution depots commonly located on the edge of cities.

Although geographical provenance remains important to some aspects of the global food system, in most cases the transparency of rural–urban food relations has been substantially obscured by the proliferation of mass-produced processed food and the agglomeration of smaller national and local agrifood companies into transnational corporations – including transnational retailers such as Tesco and Walmart. It is therefore not surprising that studies indicate that many urban residents do not know where their food comes from, in either general or specific terms.

The globalized food system has in many respects been remarkably successful in enabling the world to adapt to the increasing urbanization of the population. It has delivered a largely stable supply of diverse, cheap food to urban residents who do not have the capacity to produce food themselves, and has contributed to decreasing global rates of hunger and malnutrition and increasing life expectancy. Yet, these undoubted benefits have incurred social and environmental costs, and critics have questioned the long-term viability of the system.

The pressure comes in part from the ongoing trend of urbanization. At around the same time as the world's population became majority urban for the first time in 2007 a combination of weather events, political unrest, and financial speculation contributed to a spike in global food prices, leading several significant wheat- and rice- producing countries to temporarily ban exports. The effects were particularly felt in highly urbanized countries in Asia and the Middle East with limited domestic agricultural industries. As a consequence, state agencies and large corporations in states such as Kuwait, Singapore, South Korea, and the United Arab Emirates increased investment in agricultural land in Africa, Australia, and parts of the former Soviet Union to secure reliable sources of food outside world market mechanisms, in a wave of so-called 'land-grabs'. In Africa in particular the investments were frequently controversial for the displacement of local farmers and the effective diversion of crops, land, and water resources from supplying local populations to provisioning distant cities.

The food 'crisis' of 2007 and subsequent land-grabs helped to highlight the question of global food security in public and political discourse, with the projected global population of 9 billion people in 2050 – including more than 6 billion living in cities (double the global urban population in 2005) – given prominence as an imperative for action (Tomlinson 2013). For the corporate agrifood sector the figure was deployed as justification for intensifying the current food system, with calls to increase global food production by 70–100 per cent, assisted by biotechnology such as genetic modification. Critics, however, argued that the current food system is part of the problem, producing inequalities that are fundamentally unstable and unsustainable. Groups such as La Via Campesina, representing peasant and smallholder farmers, instead developed the concept of food sovereignty, founded on principles of localism. In a potential paradox, food sovereignty asserts both the right to food of all people, and the right of producers to control the distribution of the food that they produce. These assertions imply that a greater proportion of food should be retained in producer regions – especially in the Global South – with a reduced supply to world markets, and hence to cities. By implication, therefore, food sovereignty necessarily requires the relocalization of food production in and around urban areas.

The tendency to relocalization is further supported by critiques of the environmental sustainability of the globalized food system in relation to the climate crisis. From one perspective, the flexibility inherent in a foot-loose model of agricultural production could provide resilience for global supply networks as changing climate conditions alter the geographical distribution of crop and livestock farming. Yet such a perspective ignores the displacement of claims on environmental resources such as water that are intrinsic to the global food system. Moreover, the globalized food system itself directly contributes to the climate crisis through carbon emissions from transport, agrochemical production, and intensive livestock farming. As countries move towards policies for carbon neutrality, the mass importation of food may need to be reconsidered and alternatives of more sustainable, low-carbon local production explored and supported.

After centuries in which the trajectory of food distribution has been to integrate both cities and rural producer regions into ever longer, more complex global networks, the challenge of developing more sustainable and regenerative food systems may necessitate a radical reversal, with significant implications for rural–urban linkages. The next section examines four scenarios for how such changes might unfold.

Towards sustainable food systems: four scenarios

Claire Lamine (2014) observed that questions of sustainable agriculture are commonly approached through one of two paradigms, either a sustainable development paradigm 'which focuses on the interaction between agriculture and the environment to the detriment of food issues' (p. 41), or a relocalization paradigm that 'claims closer links between agriculture and food, considering that these are also good for the environment' (pp. 41–2). Rationales for developing sustainable food systems are not necessarily concerned with issues of space and distance – they can focus on climate change, carbon reduction, soil or water conservation, pollution, biodiversity, animal welfare, food quality, or social justice in terms that are not spatialized – but objectives of sustainability are frequently elided with the relocalization of food systems. As Lamine notes, the 'prevailing argument is that a relocalisation of production and consumption is more sustainable in ecological, economic and social terms owing to shorter distances, fewer intermediaries, more direct links between producers and consumers, and less industrial processing' (p. 42).

With a majority urban world population, the logic of this argument points to a reconcentration of food production in the rural areas immediately surrounding cities, reversing the dynamic of the current global food system in which regions with most cost efficient production supply worldwide markets. Accordingly, a move towards more sustainable food systems is likely to involve a reworking of the geographies of food systems and of rural–urban relations within them. However, there multiple different ways in which this could be achieved, depending on interpretations of sustainability, the prioritization of different environmental outcomes, the types of agriculture adopted, and dynamics of consumer behavior and public policy. This section thus discusses four scenarios or pathways for sustainable agriculture in respect to rural–urban interactions: reconnecting the rural hinterland; the return of urban agriculture; peri-urban intensive farming; and reruralization. The first three emphasize different approaches to relocalizing food production close to cities and are not necessarily mutually exclusive; whilst the fourth scenario contests the assumption that food production needs to move closer to cities, and promotes a more radical reworking of rural–urban relations. Each of these scenarios builds on initiatives and trends that can already be observed, but each also faces challenges and limitations in becoming more widely adopted.

Scenario 1: reconnecting the rural hinterland

References to the relocalization of food are most commonly associated with reconnecting urban consumers with food produced in the rural hinterlands of their cities. As DuPuis and Goodman (2005) have noted, the concept of 'eating locally' has been popularized by food writers and activists since the 1990s and commodified in urban food culture through restaurants, specialist shops, and markets. As such, food localization is at least in part a consumer-led, market-based movement, but it can also be promoted through public policies, with a number of cities and regions across the world adopting local food plans or strategies, in many cases under the framework of the Milan Urban Food Pact that commits signatory cities to developing sustainable food systems. As well as supporting branding and marketing of local foods and the development of infrastructure to facilitate local food systems, public policy can also directly contribute to the shortening of supply chains through food procurement, notably for schools and hospitals (Izumi et al. 2010; Lever et al. 2019).

Whilst definitions of 'local' vary, in some cases defined by distance, in others referring to a state or region, a recurrent theme in food relocalization is the establishment of a direct connection between the farmer or food processor and the consumer, bypassing the anonymity of the global food system. Direct transactions may be made through on-farm sales (as well as on-farm restaurants, cafes, and food evenings), with customers frequently travelling out from towns and cities, as well as through farmers' markets that typically involve farmers and producers travelling to sell at markets in nearby towns and cities. With over 8,000 farmers' markets in the United States alone, and similar networks in many other countries from Brazil to Taiwan (as well as more traditional food markets that persist in many countries in the Global South and parts of Europe), farmers' markets can be found in many small and medium-sized towns but have also been established in larger cities. The long-standing Union Square Greenmarket in New York, for example, attracts up to 140 stallholders four times a week, including farmers from Long Island and the Hudson Valley. These may travel from 200 km or more outside the city, but nonetheless represent the agricultural hinterland of the metropolis. In other, less densely populated, cases, the maximum range of farmers eligible for a farmers' market may be more tightly defined.

Alongside farmers' markets and on-farm sales, connections have also been established between urban consumers and rural producers through the framework of Community Supported Agriculture (CSA), which arguably forms the closest and most permanent rural–urban relationships. Although CSA schemes vary in format and practice, the core principle is that members of the scheme pay a subscription to the farm at the start of a season. This provides the farm with working capital and a guaranteed income, and in return members receive a share of the farm's harvest, often through a 'box scheme' with regular deliveries of seasonal produce. In some cases, CSA members might themselves participate in work on farm, or contribute to farm governance and decision-making, and in such instances CSA arguably goes beyond reconnecting farmers and consumers to provide opportunities for urban consumers to sample or perform a farming lifestyle.

The CSA movement started with two farms in the United States in 1986 and had expanded in the USA to 6,200 farms by 2014 (Paul 2018). CSA schemes can be found in every state of the US, however there is a tendency for them to be located in more populous states and close to major cities – reflecting the requirement for a stable and sizeable local market. Although members of a CSA need not necessarily live locally to the farm, the practicalities of delivering produce shares and the ethos of most CSA projects means that they generally do. Hence, CSA tends to reproduce a rural–urban linkage between rural farmers and urban consumers. In recent decades, the CSA model has been exported from the United States to other urbanized countries, and not only in Europe. In China, for example, there are estimated to be over 500 CSA farms, commonly located on the edge of major cities such as Beijing, Chengdu, and Shanghai and responding to urban middle-class desires for locally-grown food and concerns over food safety (Ding et al. 2018; Krul and Ho 2017). The Little Donkey Farm on the western fringe of Beijing is widely recognized to have been the first CSA farm in China, established in 2008, and reflects the demands of its urban members with a hybrid model that combines a delivery box scheme with opportunities for members to cultivate their own plots of land.

A scenario projected forward from the present food relocalization movement might therefore anticipate future cities being fed by food grown within their region, or a radius of say 100 or 200 km, supplied through a mix of local shops, restaurants, farmers' markets, and – at the most participatory end of the scale – community supported agriculture schemes. Yet, studies suggest a number of challenges involved in upscaling current models of food relocalization to mainstream urban food supply. Farms engaged in local food systems are a minority in the agricultural sector. In 2015, for instance, there were just under 115,000 farms in the United States selling directly to consumers, which is around 5 per cent of all farms in the US, including 41,000 selling at farmers' markets and 7,400 involved in CSA schemes (USDA 2016).

Moreover, these farms are spatially and sectorally concentrated. Over half (53 per cent) of farms in the United States with direct sales are located in metropolitan counties, and two-thirds (67 per cent) of direct sales are from farms in metropolitan counties (USDA 2016). In contrast, farms in remoter rural areas without a large population center have less opportunity to develop direct sales because of the lack of local market. This includes farming regions that historically supplied particular cities with commodities such as wheat, meat, or milk, but which are excluded by the emphasis on distance in food relocalization. Similarly, farms engaged with the food relocalization movement tend to be focused on fruit and vegetable cultivation, poultry farming for eggs, or producing cheese or pies – foods that are practical for small-scale production and can be sold profitably in small amounts. Farms focused on larger-scale commodity production – of crops such as wheat, corn, and soy, or large-scale poultry, beef, pork, or dairy production – have less opportunity to sell into local markets, and continue to be predominantly contracted to large food processors and retailers. As such, despite the growth of food relocalization, many farms in the hinterlands of cities are not connected into local food systems.

The engagement of urban consumers is also uneven, with participants in CSA and customers at farmers' markets largely drawn from more affluent, middle-class residents. Locally-grown food is generally more expensive than mass produced food, and frequently requires more time and commitment from the consumer – whether in volunteering at a CSA farm, or planning meals around seasonal produce – and CSA schemes can experience attrition of membership (Galt et al. 2019). Moreover, sites for local food consumption within cities, including restaurants and farmers' markets, can be associated with gentrification, potentially contributing to the displacement and exclusion of less affluent communities (Carolan 2011; DuPuis and Goodman 2005). At the same time, although premium prices for locally-grown food have helped to raise incomes *from farming* for some farmers, several studies have indicated that farm households engaged in local food sales are less likely to adopt other diversification and pluriactivity strategies to supplement agricultural income such that the financial viability of the farm can continue to be precarious (Paul

2018). Thus, whilst the food relocalization movement has been important in demonstrating the demand and potential for reconnecting urban consumers with sustainable agriculture in city hinterlands, it would need to move beyond its current modes of delivery if it were to fully meet the requirements of urban food security.

Scenario 2: the return of urban agriculture

The second scenario shares many principles with the first, but has a different spatial dynamic, focusing not on connecting urban consumers and rural farmers but on reviving practices of food-growing in cities. As Neilson and Rickards (2017) observe, food production in urban spaces encompasses a wide range of models including 'rooftop gardens, guerrilla gardens, urban apiaries, city farms, allotments, micro-livestock keeping, community and institutional gardens' (p. 295), some of which have a continuous presence in cities as private domestic cultivation of fruit and vegetables for household use, others of which represent initiatives for larger-scale and more commercial production. It is the latter that might properly be described as urban agriculture and which mark a breach in the rural–urban spatial division of labour that was enforced in much of the Global North with the expansion of industrial cities, as detailed in the previous section. It is perhaps significant, therefore, that some of the most notable examples of urban agriculture are associated with deindustrializing cities such as Detroit and Oakland (McClintock 2014; Walker 2016).

In Detroit, for instance, around 1,500 community and school gardens and urban farms have been established on vacant plots, supported by local government policies extending back to the late 19th century but particularly promoted by the 'Farm-a-Lot' initiative adopted in 1981, which permitted residents to grow food on vacant lots, and the Detroit Urban Agriculture Ordinance in 2013, which formalized the land use categories of 'urban garden' and 'urban farm' and allowed small-scale producers to sell produce from stalls on their land. In addition to communal gardens and farms – many motivated by social justice, food poverty, and sustainability concerns – individual households have used the ordinance to acquire vacant plots and operate micro-farms. The urban farming tradition in Detroit has drawn on the agricultural knowledge of migrants from the rural south of the USA and most participants are from the city's majority black American population. As such, urban agriculture in Detroit has a very different socio-demographic profile to the rural American farming community. Indeed, whereas the food relocalization movement has been critiqued for its middle-class bias, in many cases city farms and community gardens are located in lower-income neighbourhoods and involve members of working-class and ethnic minority communities.

Yet, there are exceptions. Walker (2016) argues that Vancouver's promotion of urban farming on community gardens is part of an economic development and place-marketing strategy to brand the city as green and sustainable. High land values in Vancouver have made finding land for urban agriculture challenging and although tax incentives have encouraged vacant plots to be made available for food-growing, such spaces tend to be temporary. With key support for Vancouver's urban agriculture provided by middle-class 'foodies' interested in local, fresh, organic produce, Walker notes that 'the lifestyle element of this discourse tends to glass over the food insecurities faced by many in Vancouver' (2016, 171). Even in Detroit, there are concerns over the increasing involvement of white stakeholders and investors in urban agriculture, including the leasing of land by the city for larger commercial farms, with suggestions that the more formalized approach to urban agriculture embodied in the 2013 ordinance could act as a driver of gentrification and the displacement of black American communities (Paddeu 2017; Safransky 2014).

Outside the Global North, urban agriculture has a more continuous presence and can play an important role in food systems. In cities such as Ouagadougou in Burkina Faso and Tamale in Ghana, studied by Bellwood-Howard et al. (2018), urban agriculture encompasses both 'open field' farming – including previously rural farms subsumed by urban expansion – and backyard farming, growing crops including maize, okra, rice, lettuce, and other vegetables. In other contexts, urban agriculture includes backyard livestock rearing, notably of pigs, goats, and poultry. Households engage in urban food-growing in part for domestic consumption, with surpluses being sold through markets to generate additional income and contributing to urban food supply. In this way, urban agriculture may arguably be positioned as an expression of 'repeasantization', with individual households reconnected with food-growing in a distributed food production system, but in very different geographical settings to traditional peasant farming. Indeed, in many cities of the Global South, urban agriculture has expanded with the arrival of rural migrants – including peasant farmers displaced by land-grabbing and the consolidation of commercial agriculture in rural areas – who have transplanted their farming practice. Furthermore, urban settings can be attractive for small-scale farming because of access to urban infrastructure including electricity and water for irrigation (Bellwood-Howard et al. 2018).

The revival of urban agriculture in diverse cities around the world represents a more radical shift in the spatialization of farming than the food relocalization movement, involving a deconstruction of the discursive rural–urban divide and a 'ruralization' of urban land and food systems. With urban agriculture often practiced by lower-income residents, including recent rural migrants, it is arguably also more socially inclusive and thus more directly contributes to incorporating sustainable agriculture into urban food security and food sovereignty. Yet, with competition for land, space constraints, and regulation by urban by-laws and planning codes, urban farming is restricted in scope and potential. These limitations tend to reinforce the application of more sustainable farming practices in urban agriculture, but without economies of scale, and with production partly for domestic consumption, urban farming tends not to deliver sufficient returns to be a financially viable prospect in highly competitive urban land markets with high land values and rents. As such, extensive urban agriculture is only a realistic scenario in cities where there is an oversupply of land relative to demand for industry, services, or housing, such as Detroit.

Scenario 3: peri-urban intensive farming

The first two scenarios, around food relocalization and urban agriculture, were bottom-up movements informed by ideological stances of sustainability and social justice and incorporating ideas from agroecology, organic farming, permaculture, and similar models for sustainable agriculture. They demonstrate the potential for connecting urban consumers with sustainable agriculture but, as discussed above, they face limitations in their capacity to fully meet the demands of urban food systems. The third scenario, in contrast, reflects a top-down approach that starts from a different standpoint on sustainability, asking how a predominantly urban population can be fed in a future post-carbon society and adjusting agricultural systems to fit. This question leads to a model in which food production is concentrated in peri-urban areas, to minimize transport requirements, but involves far more intensive forms of agriculture than envisaged in either of the preceding scenarios. In order to achieve large-scale sustainable food production the model utilizes technologies such as precision farming and digital agriculture that are commonly eschewed in the more romanticized notions of farming valorized in the food relocalization movement.

A notable example of this approach can be found in the Zero Carbon Britain project, which presents a blueprint for how the United Kingdom could move to a carbon-neutral economy and society by 2030 (Kemp and Wexler 2010). In its chapter on land use and agriculture, Zero Carbon Britain proposes a radical reorganization of the food system, linked to shifts towards a more plant-based diet, with an 80 per cent reduction in sheep and dairy cattle numbers and a 90 per cent reduction in beef cattle. Rural land currently employed for livestock grazing would largely converted to 'decarbonisation' activities, including forestry (for carbon sequestration) and the cultivation of energy crops such as miscanthus and short-rotation coppice willow. Arable land farmed for animal feed would in turn be mostly repurposed for food crops, with nitrogen-fixing legumes planted as alternative feedstocks. Meanwhile, peri-urban areas and vacant urban land would be used for 'especially-intensive food production and semi-recreational or educational livestock' (Kemp and Wexler 2010, 212), including 'intensive livestock units' for pigs and poultry, and increased production of protected horticultural crops 'taking advantage of the decarbonized energy supply' (Kemp and Wexler 2010, 212).

Prototypes of the intensive agricultural units that would populate urban and peri-urban land in this scenario are already operating, such as Thanet Earth. Located in London's extended peri-urban zone in Kent, Thanet Earth is Britain's largest horticultural operation, with six large greenhouses producing salad vegetables year-round, including 12 per cent of the UK's tomato crop, on a 90 hectare site. The farm uses hydroponic technology to irrigate and cultivate crops, employs natural pest control to minimize chemical pesticide use, and obtains energy from a combined and heat and power plant that recycles waste heat and carbon dioxide. Another example is a floating dairy farm constructed in Rotterdam harbour in 2018, which houses 40 dairy cattle on a water-borne platform producing 800 litres of milk a day for the city. The cows are fed on food waste collected from the city and duckweed grown under the platform and milked by robotic milking machines, with power supplied in part through solar panels.

Proponents of such schemes contend that they are the future of agriculture with the potential to feed an expanded, urban-based population. Yet, the development of this scenario would need to overcome challenges including public skepticism towards 'industrial foods' and opposition to landscape impacts. Full implementation of the Zero Carbon Britain plan would dramatically change the appearance of the British countryside, disrupting the pastoral aesthetic of the rural idyll and eroding local rural cultures centred on livestock farming, and consequently would face fierce opposition from rural residents, farming lobbies, and countryside preservation campaigners. In peri-urban areas, the proliferation of intensive agricultural units is similarly likely to be contested. Thanet Earth has received complaints from local residents about light pollution and the visual impact of its greenhouses in the landscape; whilst the development of intensive livestock units has generated conflict in peri-urban areas on both aesthetic and animal welfare grounds (Butt and Taylor 2018).

Scenario 4: reruralization

The previous three scenarios all make the assumption that a future sustainable society will be primarily urban and that future sustainable food systems will therefore involve bringing agriculture closer to the city in some way. An alternative view, reflected in this fourth scenario, asserts the contrary belief that cities are not sustainable in a post-carbon society and that future populations will need to deurbanize and move closer to sites of food production for survival.

The association of rurality with self-sufficiency and sustainable lifestyles has been a key driver of the 'back-to-the-land' movement extending back to the 1960s, in which ex-city dwellers opted out of urban life and relocated to smallholdings often in more remote rural regions such as Vermont in the United States, west Wales in Britain, and south-west France (Halfacree 2006). The capacity to grow their own food using environmentally sensitive methods was a core attraction for back-to-the-landers, and many subsequently became pioneers of organic farming, agroecology, and other sustainable agriculture approaches, as well as active figures in the relocalization of food systems in their adopted regions. More recently, a trend has been observed in several countries of mostly young people leaving professional jobs in cities and seeking to enter farming, again commonly motivated by concerns around climate change and food quality. Unlike earlier back-to-the-landers, these 'new farmers' tend to be found in peri-urban areas, from where they can still access urban social networks and markets (and in some cases still live in cities), and where small plots of land can be accessed. In I-lan county, south-east of the Taiwanese capital city of Taipei, for example, a loose grouping of new farmers – many of them young women – work plots of land as small as 0.2 hectares that are often due to be developed as weekend homes for wealthy urbanites but which have been rented out during a statutory pre-construction rest period. The food they produce, predominantly rice, is mainly exchanged or sold through their social networks, thus contributing in only a very minor way to the urban food system, but fulfilling the participants' desires to know where their food came from and to be doing something practical for sustainability.[1]

In addition to individual counterurbanizers, reruralization also includes the formation of intentional communities in rural settings that are founded on principles of low environmental impact and self-sufficiency, in which sustainable agriculture plays a core role. For instance, Halfacree (2011) identifies among examples of alternative settlements in Wales the cases of Tir Penrhos Isaf in Gwynedd, operated as a permaculture holding, and Ty'r Eithin in Carmarthenshire, focused on biodynamic farming, as well as the better known Lammas project in Pembrokeshire that is engaged in constructing a new eco-village with nine smallholdings clustered around a community hub, village green, and millpond. The Lammas eco-village is operated on permaculture principles, with the smallholdings growing fruit and vegetables, raising livestock and keeping bees primarily to produce food for the community, with energy sourced from a combination of hydropower, solar power, wind turbines and biomass, and water from a private spring and rainwater harvesting. The project has an explicit educational objective as an exemplar for sustainable rural communities to be replicated elsewhere.

Back-to-the-landers, environmentally-conscious new farmers, and low-impact intentional communities are all engaged in forms of sustainable agriculture framed within a notion of expressly rural resilience. In part, the vision that they share is premised on the low-density population of rural areas, such that the model of sustainable living that is espoused is necessarily small scale. Accordingly there are limits to the extent to which it can be expanded and to the population that could be supported. Thus, whilst the trajectories of reruralization participants involve a rejection of urban living for themselves – and possibly skepticism about the sustainability and resilience of large cities – they do not offer a viable pathway for feeding the majority urban population. They might, however, indicate how sustainable rural communities could be maintained alongside a food system that refocuses mainstream food production closer to cities.

Conclusion

This chapter has explored how moves towards sustainable and regenerative agriculture intersect with the demands of a majority urban global population and the potential reconfigurations of rural–urban linkages in food systems that might result. The urbanization of the global population has been facilitated by an integrated and industrialized global food system that disconnects consumers from agriculture, but which is not environmentally sustainable. A transition to more sustainable forms of farming is likely to involve the relocation of food production back closer to urban markets, including the reinvigoration of urban and peri-urban agriculture. Indeed, the rural–urban fringe has emerged as a key locus for sustainable agriculture initiatives, not only because of the proximity to urban consumers, but also because of other structural conditions that create space for experiments with alternative food systems. Land protected for agricultural use by green-belt or farmland preservation schemes, for instance, may become available for small-scale alternative farming if it can neither be worked profitably for conventional agriculture nor sold for development. The precarities of alternative food networks, meanwhile, means that many participants are in effect part of the 'gig economy', constantly looking for 'gigs' through which to sell or promote produce and commonly also holding down other off-farm jobs, made easier by access to urban labour markets.

However, an over-emphasis on peri-urban areas can neglect questions about what happens to remoter rural regions, in which the population is too small to support sophisticated local food systems and where agriculture had been developed to supply distant urban markets. There is no necessary reason why such regions cannot still be linked into urban food networks based on sustainable agriculture. Lamine (2014) for example cites the Ecovida network in Brazil as evidence that 'reconnection beyond geographical distance' can also be achieved, with consumers 'in touch with distant farmers for products that cannot be produced in their region' and regional networks 'linked through delivery routes in order to offer more diversity in the product range' (p. 49). Such connections however require imaginative thinking beyond emphases on relocalization.

Indeed, each of the four scenarios discussed in this chapter for the reconfiguration of rural–urban relations around sustainable agriculture presents both opportunities and challenges. The food relocalization movement has reconnected urban consumers and rural producers, but exhibits spatial, sectoral, and consumer biases that limit its scope to displace mainstream food supply networks. Urban agriculture can be more socially inclusive, but is constrained by competition for land in cities. The development of intensive peri-urban farming as part of a carbon neutral agricultural system may have the capacity to feed mass urban populations more sustainably, but requires compromises on some aspects of sustainability as well as on landscape aesthetics. Rerualization, as practiced by back-to-the-land migrants, may offer a model of how sustainable agriculture might be organized in more remote rural areas, but is unlikely to offer an alternative to urban living for the majority of the population.

As such, a future sustainable food system is likely to involve a combination of these approaches. The most advanced regional food plans are already preparing for this prospect through an integrated perspective that goes beyond simply promoting local food. Lamine (2014, 54) again provides an example in the Biovallée project in the Drôme valley in France, which is 'focused not only on agriculture and agrifood chains, but much more generally on urban planning, transport [and] ecological building' around the concept of closing ecological cycles.

Food and rural researchers have an important part to play in helping to facilitate the development and implementation of such strategies, with a number of research questions that still need to be explored and addressed. In particular, there is a need for more holistic analysis of the urban food systems of specific cities, identifying where the food comes from, the interactions with transport, energy, and waste infrastructure, and the environmental costs. We need research to better understand the spatial and social dynamics of different forms of sustainable and regenerative agriculture, and how these place limitations on their development. We need to examine public attitudes towards land use and landscape changes, from urban farming to intensive protected agriculture to the reforestation of grazing land, and how support can be mobilized around options for sustainable food systems. Finally, we require large-scale quantitative analysis of the future food demands of the global urban population and the potential of elements of sustainable and regenerative agriculture to contribute towards these, mapping out figuratively and geographically a blueprint for sustainable food security.

Discussion questions

1. Will urban or rural areas offer the more sustainable lifestyles in a post-carbon future and what will this mean for the supply of food?
2. What are the principal incentives and obstacles for participation by farmers in local food networks?
3. How might increasing food production in cities and in peri-urban areas close to cities have impacts on both rural and urban environments?

Note

1 This example is taken from fieldwork conducted in Taiwan in January 2015 with Ho-Chia Chueh, National Taiwan University, and funded by the European Research Council and the Taiwan Ministry of Science and Education.

Further reading

DuPuis, M. and Goodman, D. (2005) Should we go 'home' to eat? Towards a reflexive politics in localism, *Journal of Rural Studies*, 21: 359–371.
Lamine, C. (2014) Sustainability and resilience in agrifood systems: reconnecting agriculture, food and the environment, *Sociologia Ruralis*, 55: 41–61.
Neilson, C. and Rickards, L. (2017) The relational character of urban agriculture: competing perspectives on land, food, people, agriculture and the city, *Geographical Journal*, 183: 295–306.
Paul, M. (2018) Community-supported agriculture in the United States: social, ecological, and economic benefits in farming, *Journal of Agrarian Change*, 19: 162–180.
Walker, S. (2016) Urban agriculture and the sustainability fix in Vancouver and Detroit, *Urban Geography*, 37: 163–182.

References

Bellwood-Howard, I., Shakya, M., Korbeogo, G. and Schlesinger, J. (2018) The role of backyard farms in two West African urban landscapes, *Landscape and Urban Planning*, 170: 34–47.
Beyers, L. and van Damme, I. (eds). (2016) *Antwerp à la Carte: On Cities and Food*. Antwerp: MAS.
Butt, A. and Taylor, E. (2018) Smells like politics: planning and the inconvenient politics of intensive peri-urban agriculture, *Geographical Research*, 56: 206–218.
Carolan, M. S. (2011) *Embodied Food Politics*. New York: Routledge.

Ding, D., Liu, P. and Ravenscroft, N. (2018) The new urban agricultural geography of Shanghai, *Geoforum*, 90: 74–83.

DuPuis, M. and Goodman, D. (2005) Should we go 'home' to eat? Towards a reflexive politics in localism, *Journal of Rural Studies*, 21: 359–371.

Freidberg, S. (2009) *Fresh: A Perishable History*. Cambridge, MA: Harvard University Press.

Galt, R. E., Bradley, K., Christensen, L. O. and Munden-Dixon, K. (2019) The (un)making of 'CSA people': member retention and the customization paradox in Community Supported Agriculture (CSA) in California, *Journal of Rural Studies*, 65: 172–185.

Halfacree, K. (2006) From dropping out to leading on? British counter-cultural back-to-the-land in a changing rurality, *Progress in Human Geography*, 30: 309–336.

Halfacree, K. (2011) 'Alternative' communities in rural Wales, in P. Milbourne (ed.) *Rural Wales in the Twenty-First Century*, Cardiff: University of Wales Press, pp. 65–88.

Izumi, B. T., Wynne Wright, D. and Hamm, M. W. (2010) Market diversification and social benefits: motivations of farmers participating in farm to school programs, *Journal of Rural Studies*, 26: 374–380.

Kemp, M. and Wexler, J. (eds). (2010) *Zero Carbon Britain, 2030: A New Energy Strategy*. Machynlleth: Centre for Alternative Technology.

Krul, K. and Ho, P. (2017) Alternative approaches to food: community supported agriculture in urban China, *Sustainability*, 9: 844.

Lamine, C. (2014) Sustainability and resilience in agrifood systems: reconnecting agriculture, food and the environment, *Sociologia Ruralis*, 55: 41–61.

Lever, J., Sonnino, R. and Cheetham, F. (2019) Reconfiguring local food governance in an age of austerity: towards a place-based approach? *Journal of Rural Studies*, 69: 97–105.

McClintock, N. (2014) Radical, reformist and garden-variety neoliberal: coming to terms with urban agriculture's contradictions, *Local Environment*, 19: 147–171.

Neilson, C. and Rickards, L. (2017) The relational character of urban agriculture: competing perspectives on land, food, people, agriculture and the city, *Geographical Journal*, 183: 295–306.

Paddeu, F. (2017) Demystifying urban agriculture in Detroit, *Metropolitics*, 14 December 2017, www.metropolitiques.eu/Demystifying-urban-agriculture-in-Detroit.html (accessed 1/8/19).

Paul, M. (2018) Community-supported agriculture in the United States: social, ecological, and economic benefits in farming, *Journal of Agrarian Change*, 19: 162–180.

Safransky, S. (2014) Greening the urban frontier: race, property and resettlement in Detroit, *Geoforum*, 56: 237–248.

Tomlinson, I. (2013) Doubling food production to feed the 9 billion: a critical perspective on a key discourse of food security in the UK, *Journal of Rural Studies*, 29: 81–90.

USDA. (2016) Direct farm sales of food, census of agriculture highlights, ACH12-35/December 2016, www.nass.usda.gov/Publications/Highlights/2016/LocalFoodsMarketingPractices_Highlights.pdf (accessed 1/8/19).

Walker, S. (2016) Urban agriculture and the sustainability fix in Vancouver and Detroit, *Urban Geography*, 37: 163–182.

27

PLANNING REGENERATIVE WORKING LANDSCAPES

Cheryl Morse, Caitlin Morgan, and Amy Trubek

Dynamic landscapes

Land is a commodity with assigned value which can be bought and sold. It is chunked into parcels which have owners and managers who make decisions about its uses. By contrast, landscapes stretch across property boundaries. They include multiple land covers, built environments, uses, and topographies. They connect rather than parse. Like water, pollutants, animals, seeds, and soils, people often move through landscapes with no regard for abstract boundary lines. Individuals experience landscapes through everyday embodied interactions and can develop strong emotional attachments to them (Wylie 2005; Carolan 2008; Morse et al. 2014). In this way, landscapes have public and community dimensions, even when all the land they encompass is privately owned. Landscapes, then, are a useful way to think through not only the agricultural and ecological aspects of food systems, but their affective, cultural, and social dimensions as well.

In recent years, scholars have theorized landscapes as dynamic sets of ongoing interactions amongst diverse actors, rather than as static pieces of ground on which humans inscribe meaning and conduct activities. Tim Ingold proposed the notion of "taskscapes," an idea which posits landscape as the outcome of multiple tasks which he defines as "any practical operation, carried out by a skilled agent in an environment, as part of his or her normal business of life" (2011, 195). Paul Cloke and Owain Jones (2001) applied the taskscape idea to an analysis of an apple orchard in southern England. Their account included the actions of humans but also the influences that ideas about country life, tools, machines, and other nonhumans had on the ongoing production of the orchard as a place. They concluded that "places are dynamic entities, coconstituted by human and nonhuman actants" (2001, 650). This approach allowed them to include the social, the market, the historical, and the ecological into a single narrative of place making. This kind of analysis also highlights the dynamic and performative aspects of landscape, made through activity (Wylie 2007; Morse et al. 2014; for an overview of the theories associated with this perspective, see Waterton 2013). We suggest that analyses of agricultural practices and food systems may benefit from a landscape perspective that acknowledges the ongoing material engagement of people and nonhumans as well as the spatial dimensions of place-making which spill over parcel boundaries. A landscape perspective helps us better assess not only how food landscapes are produced, but also how they may be promoted and revitalized.

The hidden landscape in regenerative agriculture literature

In his 2017 essay, "The imperative for regenerative agriculture," Christopher Rhodes recommends several farming practices including holistic management, permaculture, and keyline subsoiling. While each is tailored to a particular kind of farming, they all work to build soil, generate biodiversity, and increase ecosystems service provision such as water filtration and carbon fixation. In our view, they also take a landscape perspective, meaning that each practice relies on a range of diverse environmental actors. Each system attempts to draw on the contributions of natural processes. Therefore their scale of operations extends beyond a single monocropped field managed to reduce biodiversity, to a complex system that may include multiple land covers containing multiple land uses, microbes, animals, and companion plants and any number of interactions between each. Social relations and cultural factors are implicit yet foundational to a landscape perspective on regenerative agriculture, an observation noted by K. Dalhberg in 1993: "Regenerative approaches seek to understand how to reinstate and regenerate over the long term not only local cropping systems and farm families, but also rural communities, landscapes, and regions" (section 1.2). Dahlberg's definition of regenerative agriculture also drew attention to systems change over time, and the contextual dimensions of natural and cultural change, meaning that particular places may develop unique food systems. In the following section we review two areas of scholarship which similarly take multidimensional approaches to analyze landscapes, and which could help enrich systems thinking in regenerative agriculture.

Multifunctionality and ecosystems services approaches

A landscape perspective is present in two fields concerned with human–nature interactions, scholarly inquiries which have developed more or less independently in recent decades: multifunctionality and ecosystem services. Multifunctionality attempts to measure or in other ways account for the many outcomes of a particular landscape, beyond the commercial products it may produce (Parris 2004). Multifunctionality assessments include values, services, and outputs (Wilson 2010) and have been used to measure the functionality from the scale of an individual farm (Lovell et al. 2010) to an entire region (Palang et al. 2004). As the concept has matured, multifunctionality advocates have moved from listing a landscape's services to consideration of the interaction of processes, including interactivity, synergistic effects, and integrative systems (Selman 2009). In an essay on planning multifunctional landscapes, Paul Selman writes

> Much of the visual charm, social vibrancy, and environmental integrity of cultural landscapes derive from a mosaic of land uses that complement each other, generally as a result of fortunate accident. Emerging policy approaches often aim to recapture this kind of serendipitous, dynamic, and self-reinforcing interaction, promoting the reinforcement of "regenerative" landscapes and the rehabilitation of "degenerative" ones.
>
> *(2009, 47)*

However, the multifunctionality literature has yet to produce empirical studies that document the regenerative outcomes of agricultural and food activities at the landscape scale.

The multifunctionality approach has much in common with ecosystems services, which emerged from a recognition that traditional economic models did not account for the "goods" that natural systems produce, nor the harm caused by environmental degradation. The Millennium Ecosystem Assessment groups ecosystem services – understood as the benefits that humans derive from nature – into four main categories: provisioning (like food and water), regulating (like flood and disease controls), supporting (like nutrient cycling), and cultural (like recreation or spiritual connection) (Millennium Ecosystem Assessment n. d.). Because ecosystem services emerged largely from the fields of ecology and conservation, the focus is often on wild landscapes, although there is also extensive literature on agricultural services such as crop pollination (see, for example, Kremen et al. 2007; Ricketts et al. 2008; Potts et al. 2010; Garibaldi et al. 2013). There is debate within the field about the questions of monetary valuation (Luck et al. 2009); quantification in general (Boerema et al. 2016); and conservation for its own sake versus for humanity's (Mace 2014). Despite its attempt to understand and account for the ways in which humans benefit from landscapes, the literature still tends to parse different functions into discrete categories, and often relies on monetary valuation as a primary way to measure ecosystems' benefits. Some recent work has tried to reintegrate the landscape level into evaluation for better predictions on ecosystem service provisioning (Mitchell et al. 2015).

Our reading of the multifunctionality and ecosystems services literatures suggests that there is much to be gained by drawing them together in order to develop novel ways to track the economic, ecological, cultural, and spatial dimensions of agricultural systems in specific environments. Empirical analyses such as these, which acknowledge the spatial and social particularities of place, could then inform bottom-up food systems policy making. We suggest this as a practical approach to building public support for regenerative agriculture that must necessarily work across property boundaries. In the following section we describe a discourse which aims to incorporate diverse landscape values, activities, and outcomes into rural development planning, one that seems to have broad appeal.

Working landscapes

The terms "working forests," "working lands," and "working landscapes" have become increasingly popular amongst scholars, planners, and the public in the United States. Steven Wolf and Jeffrey Klein (2007) located the origin of the term in a controversy over the sale of a large tract of forest land along the northern border of New England and New York. Their research revealed that the ambiguity of the term "working forests" allowed for people with diverse views on appropriate uses of forests to come together to successfully produce policy. Stakeholders could variously define work as the work that forests perform, or the forest as a workplace for loggers and others. Perhaps because of its elasticity and its conjuring of traditional rural livelihoods, popular usage of "working" terms now describes a range of very different activities. Scholars use the term to explain initiatives amongst diverse interest groups to achieve land use agreements and policies in the Western United States (Charnley et al. 2014) and the kind of desirable landscapes that both newcomers and long-term residents of rural regions can agree upon (Abrams and Bliss 2013). Cannavo (2007) uses "working landscapes" in a planning context to imagine environments in which human activity can take place within ecological bounds. Taken together, existing definitions of "working landscapes" seem to aim for diverse human uses (multifunctionality) of landscapes alongside efforts to protect and enhance existing ecological functions (ecosystem services). The goals of working landscapes and efforts to promote them may potentially offer insight to the regenerative agriculture movement. In the case study that follows, we outline a working lands policy in the state of Vermont and describe one example of how it articulated with the growing artisan cider industry. We use the analysis to consider the possibilities and drawbacks of a landscape approach to food systems policy making and regenerative agriculture.

Vermont's food and forest landscapes

Vermont is a small state – in terms of both population and territory – located in the New England region of the northeastern United States. Although the majority of its land cover is mixed forests, Vermont is known for its agrarian landscape and artisan food products such as cheese, ice cream, maple syrup, and craft beer. Dairy farming dominated Vermont's agricultural economy for most of the 20th century, yet making a living in Vermont's cold climate and hilly terrain often meant that farmers also engaged in multiple productive activities such as making maple syrup, cutting firewood, and keeping an orchard for fresh fruit, vinegar, or cider. Forest-based production, therefore, was a component of the agricultural household economy. However, as some dairy farms grew larger, farmers narrowed their scope of operations to making milk. Similarly, apple orchards grew to serve wholesale markets, and maple sugar makers developed their operations into specialized year-round businesses with thousands of taps. By the end of the 20th century, dairy farming was still the largest sector of Vermont's agricultural production, but the overall food system had begun to diversify, with large increases in the percentages of organic dairy farms, organic vegetable operations, and very small farms of all kinds (United States Department of Agriculture 2017). These trends have continued into the early 21st century while conventional dairy farming has faced difficult conditions.

Tourism development activities in Vermont have always been linked to landscape change. Contemporary artisan food and beverage production, farm to plate programs, and agri-tourism activities have come to define the state, in keeping with Vermont's image as an agrarian place. This geographical imagination has been actively marketed since the late 19th century when state leaders turned to tourism as a strategy to counteract the economic and social impacts of out-migration (Brown 1995; Hinrichs 1996; Harrison 2006). Vermont's tourism industry grew out of agricultural and rural crisis, and purposefully drew on the bucolic view of compact villages, small farms, and meadows to attract visitors. The irony of the pastoral view was that it was the product of at least two stages of deforestation, and over the course of the 20th century, forests returned.

Understanding the close association of tourism, farming, and forest-based food and fuel production in Vermont is essential to our interpretation of a particular land use and economic development policy that recently emerged in the state, and to our broader point about the importance of taking a landscape approach to regenerative food systems.

Vermont's working lands policy

In 2012 Vermont's state legislature passed Act 142, the Working Lands Enterprise Initiative (WLEI). The program grants public funds to businesses and service providers to boost entrepreneurialism in the agricultural and forest-products sectors. Between the years 2013–17, the program distributed nearly $6 million amongst nearly 203 projects, a not insignificant amount for a state with a population of 625,000 residents. Funded initiatives range from an on-farm kitchen for kimchi production to an elderberry product feasibility study to a softwood pellet mill. The program estimates that, over the course of its existence, the WLEI's funded projects have generated $31 million in additional sales for the Vermont economy (Working Lands Enterprise Initiative 2019).

The WLEI is a remarkable achievement for several reasons. First, the Act and the advocacy that led up to its introduction was the result of efforts by a coalition of diverse stakeholders from the agricultural, forest industry, conservation, and community sectors (Vermont Council on Rural Development 2016) – groups that do not always easily collaborate. Second, the state legislature has funded the program each year since its establishment, years when the state budget has been under great strain. Clearly legislators feel this is a cause worthy of their support; working lands seems to capture strongly-held values. Third, the policy attempts to guide a particular kind of landscape vision through promotion rather than regulation. Vermont does not have state-level land use planning, other than a law which requires large-scale developments to undergo environmental review. Most planning is conducted at the municipal level, meaning Vermont's small towns and handful of small cities hold the authority to design their own town plans and determine their land use zoning. Some towns choose to do neither. Rather than attempting to increase land use diversity through regulating zoning or creating new forest and agriculture rules at the state level, the WLEI promotes diversification through direct funding of particular practices. This is a "carrot" instead of a "stick" approach. Lastly, the Act solidifies support for itself by making the case that Vermont's landscape is the result of its diverse land uses and that these activities shape the state's economy, cultural identity, and social life:

> Vermont's unique agricultural and forest assets – its working landscape – are crucial to the state's economy, communities, character, and culture. These assets provide jobs, food and fiber, energy, security, tourism and recreational opportunities, and a sense of well-being. They contribute to Vermont's reputation for quality, resilience, and self-reliance.
>
> *(Act 142 2012, 1)*

This language crafts a vision of Vermont's future by calling upon a diversified landscape of the past. It defines the activities that produce the Vermont landscape, yet these days the vast majority of Vermonters do not make their livings from farming or forest-based work. Those who do, like farmers, loggers, and craft beer makers, tend to be siloed, participating in only one kind of land-based work. Still, the landscape itself remains multifunctional, with diverse land use activities taking place in close spatial proximity to one another. One of the implicit assumptions of the WLEI is that proximal activities will become productive edges where synergies begin to take place, where traditional activities might return in new ways. For example, an organic vegetable farmer partners with a neighboring cheesemaker to feed food scraps and whey to pastured heritage pigs, closing a gap in nutrient cycling and developing a new artisan pork business enterprise. While WLEI does not explicitly mention regenerative agriculture as one of its aims, it places its faith in the belief that multifunctional outcomes emerge from diversified working landscapes, and that these will contribute to proper stewardship of the land in the future (Morse 2019). In the following section we focus on one sector – cider production – which is undergoing tremendous growth.

Old orchards and new ciders

The production of craft beverages, including beer, switchel, kombucha, spirits, wine, maple sap drinks, and cider, is booming in Vermont (Vermont Farm to Plate 2019). The Working Lands Initiative has contributed to this development; they have funded bottling machines, tools for making aging barrels, and research into apple market optimization for hard cider production. Here we focus on the changing roles of apple orchards in Vermont over time and show the ways in which small and commercial apple orchards persist in Vermont's landscape yet wax and wane in economic significance. In the following section we offer a case study of how a Working Lands Enterprise grant impacted one, and then two cider makers. We use this case study to point out how direct investment has the potential to generate knock-on effects and to suggest that greater attention to particular geographies could produce even greater value in regenerative food systems.

Apples are not native to the Americas. They were brought to the western hemisphere by English settlers. Apples, as food writer Rowan Jacobsen (2014) points out, have one of the largest genomes of any food plant. If you plant a seed, you create a new variety. In the vastness of the North American continent, literally thousands of varieties of apples emerged. By the 1700s, most New England homesteads had apple trees planted nearby, and this tradition remained for two hundred years. The fruit from these trees was for home use; there were often six to twelve varieties planted. Pressing fresh cider from cultivated and wild apples was important to the homesteading life of this period. Fermentation produced other important products such as hard cider, applejack, and cider vinegar. In much of the US, these homestead-based operations began to decline in the 19th century with the population shift from rural to urban areas.

Northern New England was also witness to such transformations over the course of the 19th century, but small-scale and subsistence agriculture persisted. By the late 19th century, there was a shift to growing apples commercially for both food and drink, providing apples and apple products to urban dwellers. By 1899, 55 million gallons of hard cider were sold in the US (Watson 1999, 31). With Prohibition and rural flight, production dropped to 13 million gallons only 20 years later (Watson 1999, 30). Those involved with cultivating apples began producing fresh eating apples (also known as hand fruit) like the newly discovered McIntosh. Apple trees remained part of the landscape, even as the botanical varieties and human purposes for the fruit changed.

In the early 20th-century Vermont, small homestead orchards continued to fulfill a variety of purposes for the household, but commercial orchards produced only eating apples, not fruit for beverages. By the mid-20th century, these commercial apple orchards came to be centered in Vermont's Addison County, which borders on Lake Champlain and has a relatively mild climate for the region. The largest commercial orchards were planted in the 1970s, in response to a growing urban demand for fresh fruits, and thus most of this newer wave of orchards produced the popular dessert apples of that time: Empires, MacIntosh, Red Delicious. Addison County's "one hundred acre" orchards shipped apples all over the United States and some also made fresh cider for local consumption. By the early 2000s, however, these large orchards were struggling, due to increased competition from the even larger orchards in Washington and Oregon, and the stronger presence of apple juice concentrate from China. Orchards remained a component of Vermont's 20th-century landscape but their purposes adapted to changing social and economic conditions.

The most recent changes to Vermont's apple orchards involve a fascinating 21st-century revival of hard cider, present in both the New England region and nationally. Hard cider effectively disappeared over the course of the 20th century, with less than 300,000 gallons (national total) commercially produced in 1990 (Watson 1999, 31). An uptake in interest in the 1990s became a full-blown trend in the early 21st century. In 2015, 55 million gallons of hard cider were produced nationally (Fabien-Ouellet and Conner 2018). Vermont has emerged as a leader in hard cider production and cider diversification. The state has the highest production of bottled hard cider, produced by cider makers working at multiple scales, from the independent orchard-based makers who purchase some or all of their apples, to the second-largest cider brand in the US (Fabien-Ouellet and Conner 2018). A variety of craft hard ciders are now available from makers located across the state: ginger and coriander, rose, berry-infused, aged in whiskey barrels, and a new dessert drink called "ice cider."

The apples necessary for this boom in production come from diverse orchards. Commercial orchards are responding to the demand for cider apples by transitioning away from sweet apples to varieties such as Northern Spy, Golden Russet, and Dabinett which are drier and have more tannins. Apples are imported from outside the state and even outside the country, from both large commercial operations and small traditional cider apple orchards. A third source of apples is the small homestead and abandoned orchards which contain some of the older varieties of trees that fell out of favor in the 20th century. The case study that follows begins in one such highly diverse yet small homestead orchard, and leads to the production of ice cider, with assistance from the Working Lands Enterprise Initiative.

Lost orchards, state funding, and cider networking: a case study

Amy Trubek (one of the authors of this chapter) and her partner, Brad Koehler, purchased their 19th-century farmstead in Addison County in 2002. Both are trained chefs and Trubek is a food anthropologist. One of the selling points of the home was its 3+ acre orchard, with hundreds of trees, including over 80 varieties of apples. The previous owner, a local doctor, had developed the orchard as much for variety as commercial viability, hence the tremendous variety of fruit. Koehler and Trubek realized the demand for Vermont-made artisan food and drink meant that there could be an opportunity to use their many apple varieties in a new way. In 2009, Koehler began making Windfall Orchards hard cider and ice cider, a drink that was developed in the Eastern Townships of Quebec several decades ago. It is made by freezing cider (outside in winter), then melting the cider, pouring off the water, and fermenting the resulting concentrate. This process produces a sweet, intensely flavored dessert wine with a high alcohol content. The production of Koehler's ice cider is place-based and particular, relying as it does on freezing winter conditions and a blend of several heirloom apple varieties. It is also a labor-intensive process. Windfall Orchards ice cider has always been made in collaboration with a business partner, another ice cider producer who encouraged Koehler to move beyond pressing fresh cider.

After pressing apples and bottling the ciders with equipment suitable for a small fresh cider operation but not as good for the larger volume needed for ice cider and hard cider, Koehler applied for one of the new Working Lands Enterprise Investment Grants in 2013. He was encouraged to do so by a farmer friend who was also a representative of the Vermont House, a member of the WLEI board, and his primary ice cider partner. He applied for new pressing equipment that would also him to conduct custom pressing for others. The grant application process required letters of support from others who might benefit directly or indirectly from the grant receipt. One of Koehler's letters came from another emerging cider operation in Addison County. Koehler was successful in his application, and the $9,500 grant allowed Windfall Orchard to become more efficient in their own production and to conduct custom pressing for its neighboring cider business. Over the following years the two companies shared cider making knowledge, equipment, and marketing opportunities. The neighboring company has expanded rapidly, and now sells its craft ciders across the country and employs a dozen people. This company, along with Koehler, have also actively promoted the revival of "lost apples," that is, locating old varieties in abandoned orchards and old homesteads and working with area commercial orchards to grow them again. Meanwhile, Windfall Orchards continues to produce hard cider, ice cider, and perry (an alcoholic drink made from pressed pears) at a scale that suits a small-scale operation.

The importance of people, place, and human–nature interactions in food landscapes

This case study of the impacts of a single small grant from WLEI illustrates several themes that are central to our perspective of the possibilities for regenerative working landscapes. The encouragement Koehler received to apply for the WLEI grant demonstrates the efficiency of a small agricultural innovation community, and how the close connections between politicians, program leaders, and farmers allowed for the development of momentum in new projects. A small injection of funding enabled not only the purchase of equipment, but for the knowledge exchange and development of expertise amongst cider makers, and contributed to the growth of a second company. Social relations are foundational to food-based entrepreneurship, and to building the new skills required for new food and forest-based livelihoods.

Culture, in particular the narrative of working landscapes, played a key role in the success of these cider ventures. The WLEI initiative justifies its existence on the basis of a history of small-scale agriculture and forest products production. Such diversified activity is not only central to Vermont's economy, they say, but is at the heart of the state's identity as a rural place. Just as agricultural promoters did at the end of the 19th century, today's state promoters draw on a bucolic identity to sell its food and forest products (Hinrichs 1996). With their labels featuring rustic images of trees and old-timey fonts, cider makers connect their new products to old landscapes. Both directly and indirectly through the WLEI grant programs, food and forest entrepreneurs draw on a particular cultural geographic imagination of the past to build contemporary livelihoods.

Place mattered in this story. Geographic proximity was essential to the equipment and knowledge sharing between the two cider makers. The place of Addison County held the new and old orchards which provided the fruit, but it also contained people with the cider-making know-how that could be developed. We can also consider in this case study the taskscape (Ingold 2011) of cider production and the diverse activities cider making gathers together: old and new orchard tending, bottling, marketing, communicating, and developing new products.

Cider production depends on the dynamic quality of human–environment interactions. Orchards, originally established by people, have persisted in Vermont for over 200 years, sometimes carefully pruned to produce the most abundant harvest, sometimes left to survive on their own in a forgotten field. Whatever their state, their physical presence has made possible commercial sales of dessert apples, and the crafting of high-end artisanal beverages. Each arrangement requires both humans and orchards to respond to the demands and conditions of the time. Such interaction shows a temporal dimension to food landscapes which is not present for annual crops. Trees take a long time to grow, but they tend to last a long time too and because of this, Vermont cider makers have been able to capitalize on bringing back old and developing new skills, products, and apple varieties.

Orchards blur the boundary between traditional categories of agriculture and forestry, between human tending and wild growth, and the temporal categories of past and present. Ours is not a story that starts with a grand idea of restoring and replenishing the soil but instead tells about the human side of regenerative systems: skill building, ingenuity, and adapting to new social and economic conditions. In this chapter we have intentionally focused on the social and development dimensions of regenerative agriculture, an area of research that we feel demands further exploration.

Planning regenerative working landscapes

Vermont's Working Lands policy offers some insight into progressive policy making for regenerative agriculture. This policy draws on a firmly established rural identity and "working landscapes" language that is flexible enough to include the livelihoods of diverse food and forest products producers. It aims to be inclusive. It seeks to encourage multiple land uses (multifunctionality) and both material (jobs and products) and non-material ecosystem services (bucolic views and heritage) by directly funding, rather than regulating land-based enterprises. The program's services grants (not discussed in detail here) fund programs that build skills, both traditional skills and those required to conduct new forms of agricultural and forest work. Vermont's program hopes to enhance infrastructural and social capacity. This kind of approach may be useful to other organizations which seek to build capacity into a geographic region without imposing rules. The important caution is that attention must paid to scale.

Each year the WLEI funds projects in nearly each of Vermont's fourteen counties, spreading the potential for capacity building across the entire state. This is important for political reasons. However, this approach may overlook the maximizing effects of funding projects in close proximity to one another. Perhaps the co-location of funded projects could produce additional knock-on effects. To achieve ecological and environmental synergies in a multifunctional landscape, activities must be in close proximity (Selman 2009). In the example of the artisan pork production mentioned earlier, the cheesemaker and vegetable farmer (both earlier recipients of WLEI grants which helped develop their original businesses) learned that they had to locate the grazing pigs a maximum distance of twelve miles from the cheesemaking facilities because the trucking fees to move whey further were too high. Closing a nutrient cycling gap and capitalizing on their existing resources was only feasible in close proximity. The story of the cider makers suggests that the equipment and information sharing that were essential to the companies' growth was similarly dependent on close proximity. We suggest that those seeking to operationalize the concepts of multifunctionality and ecosystems services keep in mind the importance of distance, time, and scale in developing cultural, social, and ecological relationships.

Food systems research and advocacy tend to be conducted within a single industry – vegetable farming, specialty crops, farmer's markets, citrus crops, cheese making. Moving from a food or product focus to a landscape perspective opens up the possibility for collaboration amongst diverse neighboring land-based activities. A landscape view can take into account the services and possibilities of cropland, wetlands, forests, orchards, and the built environment, and can potentially put them in dialogue with one another. Temporal dimensions may also be best accommodated with a landscape view; the regional harvest of annual, perennial, and biennial food crops should be timed alongside the harvests of timber, firewood, leaf litter, and even fresh and saltwater fish. Regenerative systems which seek to build soil, biodiversity, and healthy human and nonhuman ecosystems will rely on diverse elements such as these. They will also rely on careful planning which will require public support, place-based knowledge of farmers, ecologists, and foresters, and engaged political leaders. These are relationships best built at the community scale around a shared physical landscape, or place-based activism (Martin 2003).

Scholars can assist in promoting a landscape perspective in regenerative agriculture by conducting truly interdisciplinary research that draws together knowledge and methods from seemingly disparate fields. This is a difficult task. However, planning that results in diversified working landscapes requires ecological, environmental, geographic, social, cultural, and economic insights. The field needs case studies of regenerative efforts across property boundaries in order to pilot new theories and practices. We argue that the social and cultural dimensions of this kind of community and landscape planning are the least understood, and this could be an important starting point. Finally, it is essential that the multiple values and cultural traditions present within communities are deeply considered in such studies, not to reify some imagined past cohesive culture but to ensure that the diverse individuals who constitute "the public" feel a sense of attachment to the shared vision put forward in the planning effort.

Discussion questions

1. What could define the cultural, ecological, and economic dimensions of a regenerative food system in your region?
2. Under what conditions or in which locations are multiple uses of landscapes incompatible or impossible? In other words, must some ecosystem services exclude others?
3. Can successful landscape planning take place outside regulation? And if so, by whom and at what scale?
4. What social conditions and workplace skills are required to build emerging regenerative working landscapes?

Further reading

Lovell, S. T., S. DeSantis, C. A. Nathan, M. B. Olson, V. E. Mendez, H. C. Kominami, … W. B. Morris. 2010. Integrating agroecology and landscape multifunctionality in Vermont: An evolving framework to evaluate the design of agroecosystems. *Agricultural Systems* 103 (5):327–341. doi: 10.1016/j.agsy.2010.03.003.

Morse, C. E. 2019. Faith and doubt in an American working landscape: The importance of scale, work, and place in rural development planning. *Society & Natural Resources* 32 (2), 150–166. doi: 10.1080/08941920.2018.1511021.

Rhodes, C. J. 2017. The imperative for regenerative agriculture. *Science Progress* 100 (1):80–129.

Selman, P. 2009. Planning for landscape multifunctionality. *Sustainability: Science, Practice, and Policy* 5 (2):45–52.

Wolf, S. A. and J. A. Klein. 2007. Enter the working forest: Discourse analysis in the Northern Forest. *Geoforum* 38 (5):985–998. doi: 10.1016/j.geoforum.2007.03.009.

References

Abrams, J. and J. C. Bliss. 2013. Amenity landownership, land use change, and the re-creation of "working landscapes". *Society & Natural Resources* 26 (7):845–859. doi: 10.1080/08941920.2012.719587.

Act 142. 2012. An act relating to preserving Vermont's working landscape. State of Vermont Statutes. Title 6. H. 496, Section 1. Available at: www.leg.state.vt.us/docs/2012/Acts/ACT142.pdf.

Boerema, A., A. J. Rebelo, M. B. Bodi, K. J. Esler and P. Meire. 2016. Are ecosystem services adequately quantified? *Journal of Applied Ecology* 54 (2):358–370. doi: 10.1111/1365-2664.12696.

Brown, D. 1995. *Inventing New England: Regional Tourism in the Nineteenth Century*. Washington, DC, and London: Smithsonian Institution Press.

Cannavo, P. 2007. *The Working Landscape: Founding, Preservation, and the Politics of Place*. Cambridge, MA: MIT Press.

Carolan, M. S. 2008. More-than-representational knowledge/s of the countryside: How we think as bodies. *Sociologia Ruralis* 48 (4):408–422. doi: 10.1111/j.1467-9523.2008.00458.x.

Charnley, S., T. Sheriden and P. Nabhan. 2014. *Stitching the West Back Together: Conservation of Working Landscapes*. Chicago, IL, and London: University of Chicago Press.

Cloke, P. and O. Jones. 2001. Dwelling, place, and landscape: An orchard in Somerset. *Environment and Planning A* 33 (4):649–666.

Dahlberg, K. 1993. Regenerative food systems. In *Management of Agricultural, Forestry, and Fisheries Enterprises* (Vol. 2, pp. 175–189). Encyclopedia of Life Support Systems (EOLSS). Paris: UNESCO.

Fabien-Ouellet, N. and D. Conner. 2018. The identity crisis of hard cider. *Journal of Food Research* 7 (2):54–68.

Garibaldi, L. A., I. Steffan-Dewenter, R. Winfree, M. A. Aizen, R. Bommarco, S. A. Cunningham … A. M. Klein. 2013. Wild pollinators enhance fruit set of crops regardless of honey bee abundance. *Science* 339 (6127):1608–1611. doi: 10.1126/science.1230200.

Harrison, B. 2006. *The View from Vermont: Tourism and the Making of an American Rural Landscape*. Burlington, VT: University of Vermont Press.

Hinrichs, C. 1996. Consuming images: Making and marketing Vermont as distinctive rural place. In *Creating the Countryside*, edited by E. Melanie DuPuis and P. Vandergeest (pp. 259–278). Philadelphia, PA: Temple University Press.

Ingold, T. 2011. *The Perception of the Environment: Essays on Livelihood, Dwelling and Skill*. London: Routledge.

Jacobsen, R. 2014. *Apples of Uncommon Character*. New York: Bloomsbury.

Kremen, C., N. M. Williams, M. A. Aizen, B. Gemmill-Herren, G. LeBuhn, R. Minckley … T. H. Ricketts. 2007. Pollination and other ecosystem services produced by mobile organisms: A conceptual framework for the effects of land-use change. *Ecology Letters* 10 (4):299–314. doi: 10.1111/j.1461-0248.2007.01018.x.

Lovell, S. T., S. DeSantis, C. A. Nathan, M. B. Olson, V. E. Mendez, H. C. Kominami, … W. B. Morris. 2010. Integrating agroecology and landscape multifunctionality in Vermont: An evolving framework to evaluate the design of agroecosystems. *Agricultural Systems* 103 (5):327–341. doi: 10.1016/j.agsy.2010.03.003.

Luck, G. W., R. Harrington, P. A. Harrison, C. Kremen, P. M. Berry, R. Bugter … M. Zobel. 2009. Quantifying the contribution of organisms to the provision of ecosystem services. *BioScience* 59 (3):223–235. doi: 10.1525/bio.2009.59.3.7.

Mace, G. M. 2014. Whose conservation? *Science* 345 (6204):1558–1560. doi: 10.1126/science.1254704.

Martin, D. G. 2003. "Place-framing" as place-making: Constituting a neighborhood for organizing and activism. *Annals of the Association of American Geographers* 93 (3):730–750. doi: 10.1111/1467-8306.9303011.

Millennium Ecosystem Assessment. N.d. Ecosystems and their services. In *Ecosystem and Human Well-being: Synthesis*. Washington, DC: Island Press. Available at: www.millenniumassessment.org/documents/document.300.aspx.pdf

Mitchell, M. G. E., A. F. Suarez-Castro, M. Martinez-Harms, M. Maron, C. McAlpine, K. J. Gaston … J. R. Rhodes. 2015. Reframing landscape fragmentation's effects on ecosystem services. *Trends in Ecology and Evolution* 30 (4):190–198. doi: 10.1016/j.tree.2015.01.011.

Morse, C. E. 2019. Faith and doubt in an American working landscape: The importance of scale, work, and place in rural development planning. *Society and Natural Resources* 32 (2):150–166.

Morse, C. E., A. M. Strong, V. E. Mendez, S. T. Lovell, A. R. Troy and W. B. Morris. 2014. Performing a New England landscape: Viewing, engaging, and belonging. *Journal of Rural Studies* 36:226–236. doi: 10.1016/j.jrurstud.2014.09.002.

Palang, H., H. Alumae, A. Printsmann and K. Sepp. 2004. Landscape values and context in planning: An Estonian model. In *Multifunctional Landscapes*, Volume 1, *Theory, Values and History*, edited by J. Brandt and H. Vejre (pp. 218–233). Boston, MA: WIT Press.

Parris, K. 2004. Measuring changes in agricultural landscapes as a tool for policy makers. In *Multifunctional Landscapes*, Volume 1, *Theory, Values and History*, edited by J. Brandt and H. Vejre (pp. 193–218). Boston, MA: WIT Press.

Potts, S. G., J. C. Biesmeijer, C. Kremen, P. Neumann, O. Schweiger, and W. E. Kunin. 2010. Global pollinator declines: Trends, impacts and drivers. *Trends in Ecology and Evolution* 25 (6):345–353. doi: 10.1016/j.tree.2010.01.007.

Ricketts, T. H., J. Regetz, I. Steffan-Dewenter, S. A. Cunningham, C. Kremen, A. Bogdanski … B. F. Viana. 2008. Landscape effects on crop pollination services: Are there general patterns? *Ecology Letters* 11 (5):499–515. doi: 10.1111/j.1461-0248.2008.01157.x.

Selman, P. 2009. Planning for landscape multifunctionality. *Sustainability: Science, Practice, and Policy* 5 (2):45–52.

United States Department of Agriculture. 2012. *Census of Agriculture*, volume 1/chapter 1, State Level Data, Vermont. www.agcensus.usda.gov/Publications/2012/Full_Report/Volume_1,_Chapter_1_State_Level/Vermont/. Accessed September 29, 2018.

United States Department of Agriculture. *Census of Agriculture*. 2017 State and County Profiles – Vermont. Available at: https://www.nass.usda.gov/Publications/AgCensus/2017/Online_Resources/County_Profiles/Vermont/. Accesssed March 20, 2020.

Vermont Council on Rural Development. 2016. *Working Landscapes Partnership Council: 2011–2012*. Available at: www.vtrural.org/programs/policy-councils/workinglands

Vermont Farm to Plate. 2019. Available at: www.vtfarmtoplate.com/plan/chapter/hard-cider-spirits-and-wine. Accessed May 2.

Waterton, E. 2013. Landscape and non-representational theories. In *The Routledge Companion to Landscape Studies*, edited by P. Howard, I. Thompson and E. Waterton (pp. 66–75). London and New York: Routledge.

Watson, B. 1999. *Cider: Hard and Sweet*. Hanover, NH: Chelsea Green Press.

Wilson, G. A. 2010. Multifunctional "quality" and rural community resilience. *Transactions of the Institute of British Geographers* 35 (3):364–381. doi: 10.1111/j.1475-5661.2010.00391.x.

Wolf, S. A. and J. A. Klein. 2007. Enter the working forest: Discourse analysis in the Northern Forest. *Geoforum* 38 (5):985–998. doi: 10.1016/j.geoforum.2007.03.009.

Working Lands Enterprise Initiative. 2020. *History of the Initiative*. https://workinglands.vermont.gov/history-initiative. Accessed March 20, 2020.

Wylie, J. 2005. A single day's walking: Narrating self and landscape on the South West Coast Path. *Transactions of the Institute of British Geographers* 30 (2):234–247. doi: 10.1111/j.1475-5661.2005.00163.x.

Wylie, J. 2007. *Landscape*. London: Routledge.

28

URBAN FOOD PLANNING

A new frontier for city and regenerative food system builders

Rositsa T. Ilieva

Not having to plan for food in cities has, for more than a century, been celebrated as a sign of human progress and one of the key markers of modern urban life. And yet food systems and cities shape one another and, in doing so, manifest in space – the subject matter of urban planning. In fact, cities evolve hand in hand with their foodsheds and in this food-city coevolution it is hard to imagine a transition to regenerative agrifood systems without a transition to regenerative cities. This chapter further develops this argument by drawing on current literature and practices of *urban food planning* – the intentional practice of developing new, and amending existing, urban policies, plans, regulations, and physical spaces to achieve healthier, more environmentally sound, and equitable urban food environments. It offers ten reasons as to why planning for regenerative food systems is a vital new frontier in city (and agrifood system) planning, and points to how urban planners and other urban professionals can engage with food systems in their practice. The concluding part of the chapter calls attention to a few unsolved dilemmas in this emergent field and invites readers to reflect on some of the priority items on urban food planning's agenda for research and practice.

Introduction: urban food planning rising

Cities eat, a lot. Every year, between 4 and 6 million tons of food flow through the streets of global cities like New York (The City of New York 2013), London (City Limits n.d.), Beijing (Kennedy et al. 2015; University of Ontario n.d.), and Paris (Barles 2009). Food is constantly being trucked, distributed, consumed, disposed of, and even grown, on city streets and within neighborhoods. Food binds human and ecological communities together, creates a sense of place and belonging, keeps us healthy (or sick), and ultimately affects a city's wealth and ability to thrive. Yet, urban food systems have seldom been elevated to the status of a public infrastructure nor have they developed as a specialty in the urban planning profession.

Not having to plan for food in cities has, for more than a century, been celebrated as a sign of human progress and one of the key markers of modern urban life. As several observers have noted (Steel 2009), with the rise of new transportation technologies – railway in the 19th century and automobiles in the 20th century – local food systems were readily pushed away from urban and peri-urban communities and effectively excluded from Western city-building practices. Thus, the fact that food systems – functionally more vital to a city's existence than other systems that planners traditionally plan for – are not front and center in urban planning today is not surprising.

And yet food systems and cities shape one another and, in doing so, manifest in *space* – the subject matter of urban planning (Hall and Tewdwr-Jones 2011). From the micro-scale spaces food takes up in our bodies, refrigerators, working desks, or waste bins, to the meso-scale of food distribution infrastructures and related city traffic, competition for land, commercial corridors, and rising (or plummeting) property rents. Western city foodsheds are, furthermore, shaping urban communities at the macro scale as well. In fact, what modern urbanites devour, inevitably shapes the livelihoods, ecosystems, and even urban development patterns of communities around the globe – New York City's craze for avocados, for instance, is remaking rural towns in the Mexican "avocado belt" (Burnett 2016), whereas London's appetite for tomatoes (Ough 2017) is stretching the limits of the vast greenhouse fields in the Netherlands, Spain, and Morocco, some of which are, in turn, reinventing the tomato crop and the agrifood industry (Netherlands Foreign Investment Agency 2017) as a whole in order to stay competitive.

In this food-city coevolution it is hard to imagine a transition to regenerative agrifood systems without a transition to regenerative cities. And, by the same token, cities are unlikely to get closer to resilient and sustainable futures by staying predatory and oblivious to the geographies of the local and global food infrastructures that sustain them. On several occasions already, and commonly at the brink of environmental health crises, cities have momentarily awakened to the untapped potential of civic food landscapes to redesign the relationship between cities and agrifood systems to secure a healthier and more fulfilling urban experience. From their college textbooks urban planners and architects might recall notable exemplars of regenerative city models such as Benjamin Richardson's ideal city of health Hygeia (Richardson 1876), Ebenezer Howard's town-country magnet, Patrick Geddes's place-work-folk triad in the "natural region," or Frank Lloyd Wright's "Broadacre City" – all pointing to a "third" way to urban and human development.

Visionaries at the cusp of the first (manufacturing) and second (assembly-line) industrial revolutions dared to submit to their contemporaries that recuperating the urban, human scale of food systems is all but a sign of backwardness and, in fact, it is cities' best chance of securing long-term prosperity. Simply put, planning for regenerative cities goes hand in hand with planning for regenerative food systems.

As we are now traversing a third (digital) industrial revolution, and urban sprawl is unfolding at a planetary scale, cities are re-awakening to their dysfunctional metabolisms and, once again, entertaining the possibility of using food systems as a lever for a more harmonious human existence and spatial development. In the early 20th century, urban social reformists propelled the rise of *urban planning*; today, in the early 21st century, a global collective of community *food* advocates, environmental activists, policymakers, economists, sociologists, geographers, architects, urban planners, and other urban professionals, are effectively propelling a new niche and approach to the art of designing and caring for cities – *urban food planning* (Moragues-Faus and Morgan 2015).

But what is *urban food planning*? In a nutshell, urban food planning is the intentional practice of developing new, and amending existing, urban policies, plans, regulations, and physical spaces to achieve healthier, more environmentally sound, and equitable urban food environments. It is a new frontier in city (and agrifood system) planning and the focus of this chapter.

The rest of the chapter further develops this argument by drawing on current literature on the topic and urban food planning scholarship and experiences in Global North cities. The next section delves into the rationale for urban food planning and confronts the reader with ten basic reasons *why* walking the distance between regenerative food systems and urban planning is a fruitful pursuit and the empirical question of *how* urban planners and other urban professionals can engage with food systems in their practice. Lastly, the chapter synthesizes some of the still open questions and unsolved dilemmas and invites readers to reflect on some of the top priority items on urban food planning's agenda for research and practice.

Engaging with urban food planning: ten reasons why

The time is ripe for a shift from planning to sustain cities to planning for regenerative socio-ecological-technological systems that sustain human and other species' habitats in tandem (McPhearson et al. 2015). Urban food systems offer a unique entry point to achieve that, while addressing some of the profession's early omissions. In fact, a growing momentum of grassroot and institutional innovations, at the margins of planning systems around the world, point to at least *ten reasons why* 21st-century planners should engage with urban food systems planning in their work (Table 28.1).

The gist of public policy is to work for the common good and safeguard the public interest. A newly codified rule, or set of rules, often results from government stepping in to solve an issue that, if left unattended, will persist, or even exacerbate, over time and lead to irreversible damage to society. Except for food safety and waste disposal regulations, the urban food system is rarely depicted as in need of government intervention. Evidence of the dysfunctional and degenerative relationship between cities and agrifood systems, however, abounds. While the level of complexity, sophistication, and efficiency of modern food systems is astounding, if we just look close enough or stepped far back enough, it will become clear that the current food-city regime is everything but serving the public interest.

In fact, contemporary agrifood systems have evolved to maximize efficiency, standardization, scale, and profit and have thus allowed the feeding of an ever-increasing urban population. Yet the transition of large swaths of the system from the primary (agricultural) to the secondary

Table 28.1 Ten reasons for urban food planning

1. **Food systems are not serving the public interest**
2. **Cities' metabolism is wearing agrifood systems out**
3. **Food is a fundamental city infrastructure**
4. **Planners have been sitting on this idea for more than a century**
5. **Food systems can help planners plan**
6. **Planners can help food systems thrive**
7. **Public food systems are already being planned every day**
8. **Demand for urban food systems planning is on the rise**
9. **There is a growing community of food planning entrepreneurs**
10. **Political spaces for urban food systems planning are expanding**

(industrial) economic sector was accomplished at a "hidden" social and environmental cost which 21st-century cities are starting to reckon with. If in preindustrial times climate dictated the course of agriculture, today, the opposite is also true. Agricultural industries are responsible for one-third of the greenhouse gases emissions (GHGs) on the planet and are a chief contributor to climate change. While "food miles" and transportation are less consequential when compared to farming and production, in the US, food distribution and individual trips to grocery stores amount to about 20% of the overall GHGs of the sector, with the average food item traveling 1,500 miles from source to plate.

Longer supply chains, however, also mean more intermediaries, with consequences for both farmers and consumers who pay the cost at both ends of the chain. Over the past several decades, the rapid inflation of the "middle" of the food chain has more than halved the farmer's share of the food dollar from about from 41 cents in 1950 to just 17.4 cents in 2013 (Schnepf 2015). Stretching the journey from farm to plate has also created greater need for refrigeration, preservatives, and packaging. It is estimated that, between 1997 and 2002, as much as 80% of the increase in energy flows in the US were attributed to the food system, mostly due to increased production of processed goods (Canning et al. 2010). The annual rate of increased energy consumption in the food processing sector in the US has been about 8.3% and this trend is expected to remain steady in the next decade (Canning et al. 2010). Most of this energy is derived from nonrenewable sources and fossil fuels (Pfeiffer 2009).

Packaging, and packaging waste, are another consequence of our current, nonregenerative food systems. Every year, in New York City alone, nearly 100 pounds (or about 45 kg) of non-bottle rigid plastics are thrown away by every household and this increased by 10 pounds between 2005 and 2017 (DSNY, 2018). Much of the plastics production relies on the petrochemical industry and nonrenewable energy sources. What is more, globally, of the 8,300 metric tons of plastics produced since 1950, only 7% have been recycled as of 2015. Plastic waste has critical implications for public and environmental health and the safety and security of our food systems. For instance, plastic products may be mistakenly ingested by marine animals and livestock and jeopardize entire ecosystems. Toxic metal elements used to fortify plastic bags and make them more resistant can be freed up during the breakdown of the material and contaminate fish and other food later proposed for human consumption.

In fact, environmental and human health are interlocked in ways that are not always outright and easy to grasp. The regenerative function of our food supply has been impaired also through the proliferation of ready-made, low-cost, tasty products packed with sugar (or substitutes), sodium, or fat and offering a very low nutritional value. The allure and convenience of "empty-calorie" foods and beverages in the urban food system has led to an unprecedented rise in noncommunicable diet-related diseases (NCDs) like hypertension, diabetes, and obesity worldwide, but especially in developed and emerging economies cities. Globally, 87% of NCDs occur in high-income countries (Bloom et al. 2011) but a rapid transition to western diets in middle-income and emerging countries is contributing to an accelerated diffusion of NCDs in those regions as well. For instance, before 1980, less than 1% of China's youth population was affected by diabetes, 33 years later, a staggering 11.6% were affected by diabetes and 36% were exhibiting prediabetes conditions (Wang et al. 2017). These are higher than the US's rates – 9% and 26% respectively (CDC 2017).

The current food regime's influence on human health affects cities and nation' economies too. It is estimated that the economic impact of the top five NCDs could reach $47 trillion by 2030, translating to a 5% loss of the 2010 global GDP. For lower income communities – who are disproportionately targeted by cheap, unhealthy food and drinks options – the impacts of the disruption of the health and wealth cycle will be disproportionately higher.

Cities' metabolism is wearing agrifood systems out

By 2050, two-thirds of the world population will be calling cities their home. This means that we are about to see more of two interlocked transactions – trading food *for* shelter – through the conversion of prime agricultural land into urban development – and trading nature *for* food – through the conversion of wild habitats into farmland. Thus, while soil is a renewable resource, productive land is becoming increasingly scarce and land use contested (Kim et al. 2015; Lambin 2012). Because of shrinking farmland reserves and dwindling labor in the agricultural sector, to ensure their long-term food security, some countries – like China, Egypt, UAE, India, UK, and US – have started purchasing valuable farmland abroad – a practice often referred to as "land grabbing" (Rulli et al., 2013). In fact, research indicates that urbanization of arable lands in the US has decreased agricultural productivity by 1.6% or the equivalent of meeting the caloric needs of 16.5 million people (Imhoff et al. 2004). Recent studies have also been able to quantify the "urban pollution island effect" for urban regions by studying the specific chemicals associated with urbanization in an urban watershed (Sun et al. 2013).

What is more, contemporary urban development models are still lagging behind in closing the loop of resources (e.g., food, water, energy) utilized during the construction and throughout the lifecycle of a building or a neighborhood. The separation and recycling of organic waste can help regenerate soils in cities, reduce the use of chemical inputs and minerals runoff by introducing compost for landscaping and agriculture purposes, decrease methane emissions from the breakdown of organic waste in landfills, and reduce carbon dioxide emissions associated with the production of chemical fertilizers (Wood and Cowie 2004; Zhou et al. 2010). Further, on-site recycling of greywater and backwater is still the exception and prevents cities from conserving finite nutrients – like phosphorous – which our food chain depends on. Half of the world food supply would have not been possible without phosphorous. Alarmingly, scientists estimate that current phosphorous reserves will be exhausted within the next 80 years (Faradji and de Boer 2016). Lastly, the limited integration of on-site energy production within cities and the emphasis on large-scale solar and wind farms put energy and farming in competition and, in some instances, further jeopardize integrity of urban food systems.

The everyday practices with which urban residents engage – from food choices and shopping for groceries to cooking and disposing of food scraps and packaging – also contribute to some of the pernicious bonds between cities and food systems. Meat-centered diets, for instance, fuel greater water consumption, the accelerated encroachment of farming on natural habitats, and methane emissions from livestock operations.

Estimates show that methane gas – a greenhouse gas associated with bovine meat production – is 25 times more potent than carbon dioxide over a hundred-year period (IPCC 2007), and thus has a decisive role in determining the pace of global warming. Looking only at emissions, however, may not be as fruitful since researchers in the US caution that, even if all Americans went vegan, this would reduce the country's footprint only by 2.6% (White and Hall 2017). Yet, different diets also affect land consumption differently. If cities lessened their appetite for ruminant meat (from animals with a four-chambered stomach such as cattle), for instance, and replaced it with monogastric meat (from animals with a single-chambered stomach such as pigs and chickens) their land use would decrease, the smallest land use footprint being achieved through a vegan diet (Van Kernebeek et al. 2016). Moreover, on average, the production of one kilogram of bovine meat requires 15,415 liters of water whereas one kilogram of vegetables requires only 322 liters (Mekonnen and Hoekstra 2010). This is significant, considering that globally per capita meat consumption is on the rise, reaching

43 kg/person per year in 2014 – or more than double 1961 rates (Ritchie and Roser 2017). From this holistic viewpoint, researchers agree that, to feed a population likely to reach 10 billion people by 2050, a transition to a new dietary pattern, whereby consumption of red meat and sugar are half the current levels, is imperative (Willett et al. 2019).

Lastly, the convenient practice of using disposable plastic grocery shopping bags is also harming both human and environmental health, as well as cities' food systems and economies. Every year, about 91,000 tons of single-use shopping plastic and paper bags are thrown away in New York City alone. This costs the city $12.5 million to dispose of every year (Garcia 2014) and, as noted in the previous section, plastic bag waste has detrimental impacts on aquatic life and the integrity of the food chains and ecosystems on which cities' sustenance depends.

Food is a fundamental city infrastructure

Food is a fundamental city infrastructure which pervades, and shapes, all four key urban functions – dwelling, work, recreation, and transportation – codified by modern city planners during the first half of the 20th century (Gold 1998). Failing to recognize this makes planning for more sustainable cities, and for regenerative food systems, futile endeavors. Acknowledging that the food system has been absent from the planning profession simply because "too big to see" (Steel 2009) is a first step toward a more honest assessment of what should or shouldn't be in the remit of city governments and urban planners' responsibilities.

In fact, food-related *transportation*, including food waste collection, makes up an important share of city traffic and thus is consequential for urban transportation planning. Every day, hundreds of trucks and vans bring food to city supermarkets, restaurants, farmers markets, food pantries, and soup kitchens, as well as to large institutions like schools, colleges, hospitals, and correction facilities. Other vehicles are entering the city to deliver foods directly to large wholesale distribution centers and food hubs. Yet other fleets of vans and bicycles shuttle between restaurants and emergency food providers and homeless shelters, recovering donated uneaten or unsold food and redistributing it to those most in need.

An increasing share of internal city food trips is also associated with the rapid growth of e-commerce and demand for home deliveries of groceries and meals. In NYC, for instance, more than half of residents receive home deliveries of prepared food at least a few times a month and almost a third use online shopping for groceries, liquor, or household staples (NYC Department of Transportation 2018). This increases demand for distribution space for e-commerce as well as space for loading and unloading on the city's sidewalks which affects both automobile and pedestrian traffic (Port NYC and NYCEDC 2018). Lastly, urban traffic is also affected by food-waste related transportation – from curbside solid and organic food waste collection to haulers of used cooking oil from fast-food restaurants for the production of biodiesel fuel. Individual consumers trips to grocery stores, restaurants, and food banks also contribute to and shape pedestrian, transit, and automobile mobility and influence the planning of all other urban systems.

Likewise, food businesses are integral part of commercial and recreational city zones. In fact, global cities like New York, London, and Paris are home to tens of thousands of commercial food establishments – from grocery stores to cafes, restaurants, mobile food carts, and food trucks. Informal food vendors are part of a city's food scene as well and play an important role in shaping the public realm and the urban environment in spaces of central concern to urbanists and city planners. In fact, food jobs make up an important part of a city's economy. Considering food service, grocery, and wholesale businesses alone in New York City, these make nearly 10% of the overall employment of the city (New York State Department of Labor 2019).

Manufacturing districts across different city boroughs are home distribution centers for goods, including food, which then are moved through last-mile delivery networks. Today, some of those districts house both global and regional food distribution and processing hubs, helping smaller scale farmers aggregate their produce and reach high-volume demand from urban markets. Commercial kitchens and food business incubators are also frequent enterprises residing within city boundaries, part of the urban food system infrastructure and contributing to the local economy. More recently, with the decommissioning of former industrial districts and repurposing of some manufacturing buildings, rooftop and indoor urban farming operations are becoming integrated inside cities as well.

Lastly, food is also an integral infrastructure in residential urban zones. Cities like New York, Baltimore, Detroit, Portland, and Seattle in the US, Toronto and Vancouver in Canada, and London and Berlin in Europe have extensive networks of food-producing gardens which effectively serve and shape the built environment. New urban districts devoting nearly half of the available land to urban farming, public housing projects with rooftop greenhouses and farms, and school farms as educational and urban amenities are increasingly dotting the landscape of residential districts and interacting with energy, water, transportation, and waste management city systems and thus merit full recognition as an urban infrastructure.

Planners have been sitting on this idea for more than a century

Recalibrating the balance between built up and open space by weaving productive landscapes back into the urban fabric is an idea as old as modern city planning. Building healthier communities meant ensuring fresher air and more opportunities for outdoor activities and vegetable gardens, orchards, and street markets provided all of this in addition to sustenance and nutrition. Since the beginning of the 20th century, when town and country planning was still a social movement in the UK, urban theorists and innovators have entertained this idea and used it as a keystone for an entirely new way of city building. Ebenezer Howard's polycentric garden city regions with ample agricultural belts, the urban region with an agricultural heart envisioned by Dutch spatial planners, and every family's right to 1-acre farmland in Frank Lloyd Wright's Broadacre City, are all part of the legacy of bold planning ideas developed in the aftermath of the industrial revolution, the new possibilities offered by mass train and automobile transportation, and the unruly urbanization that followed both.

Over the past century, as the institutionalization of city and regional planning progressed and, and societies saw their distancing from food – agriculture, manufacturing, organic waste, and even cooking – as sign of progress and civilization, the urban food system's component of planning's bold ideas was dropped. And, while it is true that urban planners – through their decisions on housing, transportation, sanitation, and other urban systems – continued to shape the city-regional foodshed, the impetus for using local food infrastructures as a lever for more harmonious and healthier built environments withered. Today, at the turn of the 21st century, theorists of sustainable and resilient urban development call for a turn to "strong sustainability": a normative framework which demands both technological and social innovations and holistic rather than siloed problem-solving approaches. Food, unlike any other urban system, is suited to craft strategies for strong sustainability. It is time to take urban food planning out of hibernation.

Food systems can help planners plan

The first century of contemporary city and regional planning aided industrial cities to overcome the unhealthy and unsanitary conditions inherited from the industrial revolution, develop state-of-the-art underground infrastructures (water, gas, electricity), and, during the postwar periods, guide the reconstruction of entire districts and neighborhoods. Early contemporary urban planners developed theories and principles for the rational organization of human activities in space – to avoid nuisance and conflict between uses like residences and factories – but also meeting demand for housing, employment, public transportation, green spaces, and community services like schools, hospitals, churches, and community centers. While the goal was to provide a minimum standard of each of those services to all, not infrequently, implementation was skewed by the inequalities embedded in the larger political and socioeconomic context in each city.

Participatory and communicative planning theories in the second half of the past century sought to remedy those disparities, focusing on the social and political processes of decision-making but distanced planners from the physical environment – planners' distinct competency. It also raised doubts about the unique contribution of the profession and whether its independent status from other disciplines such as urban geography, urban sociology, transportation economy, engineering, or political science, among others, is justified. In fact, planners have since strived for "something more" (Davoudi and Pendlebury 2010) to distinguish themselves from other professions. More recently, with rising concerns about the environmental sustainability of ever-expanding urban regions and the imperative of resilient urban development, there has been a renewed interest in the spatial dimension of city planning. Community food systems offer a compelling space for planners to advance social, economic, and environmental goals while bringing about equitable and regenerative city infrastructures.

As other observers have argued, planning claims a holistic approach to the management and design of urban systems and the credibility of the profession relies on planners' abilities to bridge disciplines and cross institutional silos. It is an interdisciplinary field whose experts are versed in the interdependencies between multiple urban infrastructures – and the policies that regulate them – and anticipating potential unintended consequences of their decisions. The fact that food is an inherently ubiquitous urban infrastructure – accompanying and interacting with a myriad of other infrastructures and everyday social practices – makes it an excellent entry point to pursue planning's comprehensive task while enabling planners to further sharpen their cross-disciplinary skills.

Further, the acknowledgment of healthy, equitable urban food systems as "commons" (Vivero-Pol 2017) – or a public good on par with clean air and water – and the consequent mandate to take food environments into consideration while vetting land use planning decisions may provide further normative guidance and legitimacy to planning. Food-sensitive urban planning would also help amplify efforts to safeguard food security, disaster preparedness, and public and environmental health, while building a sense of place and belonging across diverse urban communities.

A stronger link between housing and community food systems would also be beneficial for economic planning. A recent study, focusing on inequitable food access in New York City, found that planning for new food retail development on the 50 city-owned properties where public housing is located would potentially result in between $6 and $9 million in additional annual revenue for the City (Husock 2016).

Planners can help food systems thrive

While planners have limited powers and depend upon multiple other policy and political decisions made by city, regional, and national government officials, a food-sensitive lens on urban development has the potential to trigger cascades of small-scale, positive, changes throughout the urban foodshed. In other words, planners can and do contribute to the creation of regenerative agrifood chains. For instance, city and regional planners can channel the progressive urbanization of open space and productive farmland resulting from population growth in emerging economies and from migration, including due to natural disasters and climate change, in a way that minimizes environmental impacts. Planners can also heighten attention to rules and practices that aid the preservation of prime agricultural land and urban watersheds. For instance, the localization of large new infrastructures like highways, airports, or freight terminals can be grounded in suitability analyses taking into account the ecological, cultural, and economic make up of existing urban and peri-urban food systems and farming operations.

Additionally, by partnering with academic institutions, government planning agencies, and climate resilience offices can research alternative models for urban development and test "third" ways to urbanize open spaces to meet need for housing and commercial activities. The development of new urban districts or the infill of existing urban areas can be guided to incorporate, rather than replace or ignore, community food systems and opportunities to strengthen them. Shielding open space from development within cities through the attentive analysis of ground-level activities and community needs and services is an important step toward the introduction of productive urban landscapes citywide. Building codes and zoning regulations controlling the use of ground-level and rooftop open spaces can be amended so that the design for productive land uses can be encouraged from the outset of any new urban transformation. Square feet and walking distance standards, that have been applied to planning for other urban amenities like parks and urban green space, can be extended to promote equitable access to healthy, affordable, culturally appropriate food options. As with the separation of harmful, industrial land uses to protect public health, zoning codes could be revised to halt or inhibit the saturation of lower-income, minority neighborhoods with unhealthy food marketing and high-calorie, low-nutrient fast foods.

Finally, while personal transportation is a minor contributor to GHGs in the food system the current shift to online grocery shopping – a multibillion-dollar industry projected to make up to 20% of total grocery shopping in the US by 2025 (Wakeland et al. 2012) – will have consequential ramifications for urban food systems, city traffic, and the allocation of land for warehouses and distribution centers in and around cities. Additionally, recent research reveals that 42% of people in the US eat to-go foods while in transit. What do these trends mean for the design of regenerative urban food systems and cities? With their interdisciplinary training, and involvement in decision-making and control across multiple urban systems, planners are uniquely positioned to tackle such inter-sectoral emerging challenges.

Public food systems are already being planned every day, anyway

Planners would be wise to engage with food systems also because public food systems are already being planned every day, anyway. Public food systems include all publicly-funded meals and related services and infrastructures which govern the food procurement of institutions like public schools, governmental agencies, senior centers, day care, prisons, and hospitals, among others. Scholars have often referred to the aggregate of these practices as the "public plate" and called attention to the roles that local governments already play in shaping the food system and its health and environmental outcomes.

The scale of publicly funded food supply puts public food systems at a distinct advantage when weighing the influence of different levers for systemic change at the local level. For instance, in New York City, every day, 1.1 million meals are being prepared, distributed, and eaten by students attending public schools. In fact, the decisions that go into each step are key entry points for the transition to regenerative food systems. The Urban School Food Alliance of which NYC is part – which currently serves 584 million meals per year worth $755 million – has recently been successful in concurrently shifting school food procurement in Dallas, Baltimore, Chicago, Orlando, Boston, Los Angeles, Ft. Lauderdale, Miami, and Philadelphia – to antibiotics-free poultry and introduced compostable trays in school cafeterias. The scale is such that an alliance between only a handful of those schools has made a dent in both the food production and food packaging industries.

Public food systems are also occurring in specific spaces and places whose accessibility, design, and physical characteristics affect the relationship between cities' youngest residents and infrastructures that nourish them. Research has demonstrated that the interior design – furniture, colors, and dining style – of the spaces where food is being served affects participation rates and determines the outcome of free and healthy food programs. Architects and designers can work with schools and other public institutions to ensure that publicly subsidized food systems serve those most in need and help eliminate stigma. Further, in some schools there is not enough room for everyone to have a meal at the same time, which leads to lunch being served closer to morning hours thus undermining the reach of the programs. This is a spatial and organizational problem. An assessment of the available spaces, inside and nearby public buildings, and investment in options that would allow equal access for all can be carried out by inter-departmental teams of which planners can and should be part of.

Lastly, local government officials, including urban planners, make myriads decisions about multiple urban systems – from public housing to public transit and green infrastructure – every day, which may well be food system planning practices "in disguise." The up-zoning of a neighborhood, for instance, may attract capital and economic activity but make the current food environment devoid of affordable food options for long-term residents. Some urban food planning scholars have developed in-depth case studies to examine this seldom discussed consequence of urban transformation and conceptualized it as an instance of "food gentrification" (Cohen 2016). Conversely, a new public transit route may positively reconfigure the geography of food access independently from the availability of fresh, affordable food options in close proximity. In fact, marketing research shows that, today, grocery shoppers in the US are more likely to seek for deals and make purchases at multiple locations.

Demand for urban food systems planning is on the rise

Twenty years ago, when planners and food system planning advocates Jerry Kaufman and Kami Pothukuchi (2000) sought to awake the planning community to the fact that food systems are integral to the profession's function, few practitioners sympathized with the idea. Main barriers included the lack of clear indications that the food system was in need of fixing, an institutional environment that signaled that food issues are a corporate or federal government matter, the belief that integrating food into urban planning made sense only in rural areas, and the concern that planners were not trained to interfere with the urban food system. A more recent survey, which scanned US planning agencies and departments in 2015 (Raja 2015), confirmed that a formal mandate for urban food systems planning was still the exception rather than the norm, but that the concept was less alien to planners compared to a couple of decades ago. This is not surprising given the upsurge in interest in city-level food system initiatives across multiple spheres of urban governance including academic research, public policy, private firms, and civil society.

Researchers' curiosity about the interface between food systems and urban geography and planning has notably increased over the past two decades, and so have planning journals editors' views of the topic. Since 1999 contributions in planning publications have gone from a handful per year to an average of more than 20 per year in the period 2008–2018 (Ilieva 2016). Special issues centered on food systems planning in journals like *International Planning Studies* (2009), *Built Environment* (2017), and *Landscape and Urban Planning* (2018) were released, testifying to the growing community of planners and geographers entering this domain of research. Additionally, in-depth explorations of the topic have started coming out of the sole domain of MS theses and PhD dissertations, as critical as these are, with the publication of a series of edited volumes and research monographs. Examples of this newer tier of academic contributions include *Sustainable Food Planning* (2012), *Urban Food Planning* (2016), *Sustainable Urban Agriculture and Food Planning* (2016), *Integrating Food into Urban Planning* (2018), and *Urban Food Systems Governance and Poverty in African Cities* (2018).

Further, demand for researchers and professionals versed in food systems planning is rising not merely inside academic institutions, but in government agencies and businesses as well. In fact, the proliferation of academic publications on the integration of food into planning was paralleled by similar growth in government-issued or commissioned reports, strategies, and plans for city and regional food systems. Over the past 20 years, more than 80 urban and regional food system strategies, stating specific goals and objectives local administrations should pursue, were released including by cities such as New York, Seattle, London, Toronto, Vancouver, and Amsterdam and regional planning authorities like the Delaware Valley Regional Planning Commission. Other local administrations, like Philadelphia, Chicago, and Baltimore have included food system priorities in their long-term comprehensive sustainability plans, while others still have commissioned resiliency assessments to gauge the city's food system ability to withstand extreme weather events and flooding. New York's *Five Borough Food Flow* study (New York City Mayor's Office of Recovery and Resiliency 2016), the *Baltimore Food System Advisory Report* (Biehl et al. 2017), and Boston's (ICIC 2015) and Toronto's (Zeuli et al. 2018) *Resilient Food Systems, Resilient Cities* assessments speak well to these emerging efforts.

There is a growing community of food planning entrepreneurs

The lack of an established community of practice, and fear of being in this "alone," used to commonly deter professionals from entering the field. Not anymore. Today, on both sides of the Atlantic, there are active food systems planning groups within established academic and professional planning associations – such as the American Planning Association (APA) and the Association of Collegiate Schools of Planning (ACSP) in the US and the Association of European Schools of Planning (AESOP) in Europe. All of which have annual meetings where graduate students and planning practitioners from the public and private sectors present their work in the different spheres of urban food systems planning. Additionally, within AESOP, there is a subgroup of doctoral students who organize parallel workshops and webinars at the Association's annual Sustainable Food Planning Conference and invite contributions from food planning scholars and practitioners from around the world.

The Food Systems Planning Interest Group (FIG) within APA has also actively worked to identify and showcase urban and regional food planning practice through their initiative "Faces of Food Systems Planning" (APA FIG n.d.) – featuring interviews with active food planning practitioners from across North America. To date, there is a catalog featuring nearly 30 food systems planners and their unique career pathways and accomplishments. Some of them were also recently recognized in the July 2017 issue of APA's magazine *Planning* as ambassadors of the new generation of "millennial planners" (Holeywell 2017) and the unique perspectives they are bringing to the discipline and practice of city and regional planning, such as urban food as an infrastructure and part of the commons.

The rising need for expertise in multiple facets of the urban food system – from growing to sourcing, distribution, and disposal – noted in the previous section has also driven an upsurge in private organizations, often serving as consultants to government agencies that still do not have sufficient capacity to extensively investigate and plan for city-regional food systems. Examples of these organizations, and places where the community of food planning practitioners now stretches to, include the Initiative for a Competitive Inner City (ICIC) (who authored the Boston and Toronto's resiliency studies noted above), Karen Karp & Partners in New York City (frequent sponsor of APA FIG's annual national meetings), and even global architecture and engineering firms like Arup and AECOM who have occasionally hired experts in food systems planning and sustainable agriculture to aid their master planning services.

Political spaces for urban food systems planning are expanding

Already, food systems planning pioneers have accomplished what, just 20 years ago, seemed out of reach. The 2015 Milan Urban Food Policy Pact – signed by more than 190 mayors from around the world – is a good example. When the APA and AESOP food planning workgroups were formed, the landscape of urban food planning was still largely made of isolated episodes of success and scattered innovations. Almost everyone thought that it would be a long time before more than a handful of cities, let alone a global network of mayors, got to include food system commitments in their local policies and plans. Yet, in a matter of only a few years, hundreds of individuals working at universities, local and global nongovernmental organizations, and government institutions mobilized to carve out new political spaces for food systems planning and make the improbable possible. Most recently, in December 2019 the APA's Food Systems Planning Interest Group (APA-FIG) announced that it is becoming an official APA division in 2020 (APA-FIG 2019).

In practice, successes like this stand on the shoulders of decades of community activism and the work of grassroots organizations such as the Community Food Security Coalition in North America (disbanded in 2012) which connected, and often gave the impetus for, city, county, and state food policy councils in the US and Canada. Today, at the Johns Hopkins University's Center for Livable Future, there is a monitoring unit which tracks the trajectory of these food governance innovations and provides them with capacity building and other services. From the yearly reports the Center publishes (Bassarab et al. 2019), it is evident that the number of these organizations, no matter how limited in their operations, has steadily risen from just a handful in the 1990s to more than 300 today. In the UK, the Sustainable Food Cities network brings together nearly 60 cities that have adopted or are working toward an urban food system strategy or plan, as well as a food metrics or indicator framework.

Some of them, such as the advisory food policy councils in Los Angeles and Chicago, have been able to effectively influence policymaking and include local food system policies into mainstream planning documents and food procurement regulations. Both the City of Los Angeles and the City of Chicago (and Cook County), for instance, adopted the Good Food Purchasing Policy (GFPP) – requiring them to adhere to higher economic, environmental, nutritional, labor, and animal welfare standards. And the 2040 metropolitan plan for Chicago included a separate section on local food, including targets on healthy food access. Importantly, the City of Baltimore, which was conferred the Milan Pact Award in 2016 for its many accomplishments in bringing a resilient food systems perspective into planning, not only has an extensive food policy initiative within the city's urban planning department, but also dedicated food access and food resiliency planners on staff.

Thinking deeper: tackling barriers and limitations

Although urban food planning scholarship and action are getting closer to mainstream every year, this emergent field is still a dynamic, and in many ways precarious, niche of innovation. Pioneer community and regional food system planners still encounter colleagues who oppose or, even worse, remain indifferent to the value of integrating healthy and regenerative food system goals into the profession's established tasks and competencies. But as history of science shows – early adopters would do well to not give in to destructive criticisms and peer pressure.

The longevity and credibility of this nascent field ultimately depend not so much on fencing off external criticisms but on the ability of its frontrunners, as well as newcomers, to inject a healthy dose of skeptical optimism into their work. So far, and rightly so, the overwhelming part of urban food planning research has focused on throwing light on the benefits of re-engaging with food environments in local policy and planning, and only seldom pointing to "traps" or slippery slopes of which planners need to be wary.

As food systems planning is coming of age and a campaign is underway to make it an official division of the American Planning Association, it is key to ponder on some of the barriers and limitations to its normalization. Listed below are a few seeds for thought that could be helpful in expanding this line of work within the field.

Semantic traps

No planner needs to be convinced that language and discourse are key to building trust in planning process and a precondition for effective deliberation. Yet the impact of different ways in which planners advocate for the need for regenerative, community food systems work in different locales is seldom discussed in food planning literature. Which terms in the food planning vocabulary are neutral across multiple constituencies and which provoke strong opposition or even rejection? Where it is better to talk about cleanliness and efficiency instead of sustainability and where of human health instead of ecosystems and climate resiliency? Going forward, food planners will benefit from documenting more intentionally these nuances and turning them from barriers into levers for change.

Two steps ahead

Steel (2009) argues that we have ignored food as an urban system because it is "too big to see." To make matters worse, the food system is also interlocked with all other basic urban systems from housing to transportation, parks, and sanitation. Many of the limitations of food systems planning stem from missing those links. For instance, developers and grocery store owners may be hesitant to work with governments, even if incentives are provided; or certain selection parameters, like square footage, may exclude some communities and put others at advantage, not always matching the highest need; additionally, private companies that oversee the management of some of properties may impose private policies that run against allowed land uses and incentives for gardening and food growing in those same areas; outdoor activities need indoor spaces as well, e.g., for supplies; new bus stops or routes may fail due to low ridership; and simply imposing a requirement for fresh food options for bodegas, say in the licensing process, may be bound to fail due to lack of storage, refrigeration, clientele interest, or inadequate supply chains.

There are reasons why things operate the way they do, which transcend the boundaries of the single garden, food store, or school cafeteria and the budgets and decisions made by their managers and staff. Learning from these experiences and training food system planners to think two steps ahead in problem-solving situations, especially complex in the food system, will go a long way in fortifying the profession's position. Put simply, asking more often "What can go wrong?" and crash-testing food planning ideas on a smaller scale would prevent pioneer food planning scholars and practitioners from erecting more barriers that we started with.

Food planning in disguise

Food planning leaders must broaden the scope of their analysis and have their eyes peeled for instances of food planning "in disguise." A simple way to get started is to take a look at the second-order hurdles that fledgling food system planning initiatives – from securing land tenure for a community garden to establishing a new shuttle service for grocery shopping or permitting a new farmers market downtown – have already stumbled upon. Those are often due to existing planning and other regulations that cities must abide by. Thus, the avenue to including equitable and regenerative food system principles in city building necessarily passes through "seeing" food in all policies. There has already been progress on this font, but we can do more and document the food-policy link and impacts across a wider range of food system planning spheres, from field to fork.

Giving time time

Most sociotechnical transitions take up to half a century to fully unfold and some health, environmental, and equity benefits of public policies take a decade or more to manifest and become measurable. Judging food planning initiatives' outcomes on their ability to deliver within a single mayoral cycle is thus counterproductive and bound to bring about shortsighted decisions and frustration. Additionally, the journey from issues to policies is commonly tortuous and, at times complicated by multiple legal battles, and so takes time itself. For food system planners this translates into the need to become versed in managing community and stakeholder expectations early on in the planning process. Failing to clearly communicate this may jeopardize the important work and overarching goal of codifying food equity goals into local laws and regulations.

Concluding remarks

In a way, urban food planning heralds the rise of a new cohort of "millennial" planners refusing to keep the old town–country, agri-food systems–city systems dichotomy intact and accept it as the state of affairs in the discipline. It is also a wakeup call about the twin, widely unquestioned, evils that come with high GDPs – cities and lifestyles that run on fast, unhealthy diets and pernicious environmental footprints. The last two decades of groundbreaking food planning scholarship have made it easier for planners to, once again, tweak the "town-country magnet," to use Ebenezer Howard's term. We better not let it slip through our fingers this time.

Discussion questions

1. What is not being measured is invisible to policymakers. How can food systems planners help make the role and importance of community food systems measurable? What tools and metrics would be most beneficial from farm to plate to compost bin? How can we capture and communicate the social and cultural benefits of community food systems which defy most metrics?
2. Who is in charge of urban food systems planning? Besides urban planners and allied professionals who else should be engaged in including goals of healthy, just, and sustainable food systems in all policies? What is the role of ordinary citizens? What does urban food democracy look like? Which cities are leaders in food democracy and what can we learn from them? What are some successful mechanisms for building capacity and nurturing citizen food systems planners alongside experts and professionals?
3. Almost 20 years have passed since the Pothukuchi and Kaufman's paper was published. What have we accomplished so far and what should be the goals for community and regional food systems planning for the next two decades?

Further reading

Cabannes, Y., and Marocchino, C. (eds). (2018). *Integrating Food into Urban Planning*. London: UCL Press; Rome, FAO.

Ilieva, R. T. (2016). *Urban Food Planning: Seeds of Transition in the Global North*. New York: Routledge.

Morgan, K. (2013). The rise of urban food planning. *International Planning Studies, 18*(1), 1–4.

Pothukuchi, K., and Kaufman, J. L. (2000). The food system: A stranger to the planning field. *Journal of the American Planning Association, 66*(2), 113–124.

Sonnino, R. (2009). Feeding the city: Towards a new research and planning agenda. *International Planning Studies, 14*(4), 425–435.

References

APA FIG. (n.d.). *Faces of Food Systems Planning*. Retrieved from https://apafig.wordpress.com/faces-of-food-systems-planning/

APA-FIG. (2019). APA-FIG is becoming an official APA division! December 17. Retrieved from https://us3.campaign-archive.com/?u=f68ca3048f5760c3ab2d691fb&id=840897beee

Barles, S. (2009). Urban metabolism of Paris and its region. *Journal of Industrial Ecology*. doi:10.1111/j.1530-9290.2009.00169.x.

Bassarab, K., Santo, T., and Palmer, A. (2019). *Food Policy Councils Report 2018*. Retrieved from https://assets.jhsph.edu/clf/mod_clfResource/doc/FPC%20Report%202018-FINAL-4-1-19.pdf.

Biehl, E., Buzogany, A., Huang, A., Chodur, G., and Neff, R. (2017). *Baltimore Food System Resilience Advisory Report*. Retrieved from www.jhsph.edu/research/centers-and-institutes/johns-hopkins-center-for-a-livable-future/_pdf/projects/resilience/Baltimore-Resilience-Report.pdf

Bloom, D. E., Cafiero, E. T., Jané-Llopis, E., Abrahams-Gessel, S., Bloom, L. R., Fathima, S., … Weinstein, C. (2011). *The Global Economic Burden of Noncommunicable Diseases*. Geneva: World Economic Forum.

Burnett, V. (2016, November 17). Avocados imperil monarch butterflies' winter home in Mexico. *The New York Times*. Retrieved from https://www.nytimes.com/2016/11/18/world/americas/ambition-of-avocado-imperils-monarch-butterflies-winter-home.html

Canning, P. et al. (2010). *Energy Use in the U.S. Food System*. Washington, DC: United States Department of Agriculture. Economic Research Service.

CDC. (2017). *New CDC Report: More than 100 Million Americans Have Diabetes or Prediabetes*. Washington, DC: CDC.

City Limits. (n.d.). *Resource Flow Analysis Results*. Retrieved from www.citylimitslondon.com/down loads/Results.pdf

Cohen, N. (2016). *Feeding or Starving Gentrification: The Role of Food Policy*. New York: CUNY Urban Food Policy Institute.

Davoudi, S., and Pendlebury, J. (2010). Centenary paper: The evolution of planning as an academic discipline. *Town Planning Review, 81*(6), 613–646. doi:10.3828/tpr.2010.24.

DSNY. (2018). *2017 Waste Characterization Study*. Retrieved from https://dsny.cityofnewyork.us/wp-content/uploads/2018/04/2017-Waste-Characterization-Study.pdf

Faradji, C., and de Boer, M. (2016, February 11). How the great phosphorus shortage could leave us all hungry. *The Conversation*. Retrieved from http://theconversation.com/how-the-great-phosphorus-shortage-could-leave-us-all-hungry-54432

Garcia, K. (2014). *Testimony of Kathryn Garcia*. Commissioner of the New York City Department of Sanitation, Before the New York City Council Committee on Sanitation and Solid Waste Management, Intro No. 209 – A Local Law to Amend the Administrative Code of the City.

Gold, J. R. (1998). Creating the Charter of Athens CI AM and the functional city, 1933–43. *Town Planning Review*. doi:10.3828/tpr.69.3.2357285302gl032l.

Hall, P., and Tewdwr-Jones, M. (2011). *Urban and Regional Planning* (Fifth). New York: Routledge.

Holeywell, R. (2017). A new course: Millennial planners – like their peers in other professions – are taking over the workforce. How do these young professionals value and approach their work? *Planning*, July, 12–21. Retrieved from: https://www.planning.org/planning/2017/jul/newcourse

Husock, H. (2016). *Turning Food Deserts into Oases: Why NY's Public Housing Should Encourage Commercial Development*. New York: Manhattan Institute.

ICIC. (2015). *Resilient Food Systems, Resilient Cities: Recommendations for the City of Boston*. Boston, MA: ICIC.

Ilieva, R. T. (2016). *Urban Food Planning: Seeds of Transition in the Global North*. New York: Routledge.

Imhoff, M. L., Bounoua, L., DeFries, R., Lawrence, W. T., Stutzer, D., Tucker, C. J., and Ricketts, T. (2004). The consequences of urban land transformation on net primary productivity in the United States. *Remote Sensing of Environment*. doi:10.1016/j.rse.2003.10.015.

IPCC. (2007). Table TS.2. Lifetimes, radiative efficiencies and direct (except for CH4) global warming potentials (GWP) relative to CO2. In *Climate Change 2007. The Physical Science Basis: Working Group I Contribution to the Fourth Assessment Report of the IPCC*, p. 33. Paris: IPCC. Retrieved from https://www.ipcc.ch/site/assets/uploads/2018/05/ar4_wg1_full_report-1.pdf.

Kennedy, C. A., Stewart, I., Facchini, A., Cersosimo, I., Mele, R., Chen, B., … Sahin, A. D. (2015). Energy and material flows of megacities. *Proceedings of the National Academy of Sciences of the United States of America*. doi:10.1073/pnas.1504315112.

Kim, D. H., Sexton, J. O., and Townshend, J. R. (2015). Accelerated deforestation in the humid tropics from the 1990s to the 2000s. *Geophysical Research Letters*. doi:10.1002/2014GL062777.

Lambin, E. F. (2012). Global land availability: Malthus versus Ricardo. *Global Food Security*. doi:10.1016/j.gfs.2012.11.002.

McPhearson, T., Andersson, E., Elmqvist, T., and Frantzeskaki, N. (2015). Resilience of and through urban ecosystem services. *Ecosystem Services*. doi:10.1016/j.ecoser.2014.07.012.

Mekonnen, M. M., and Hoekstra, A. Y. (2010). *The Green, Blue and Grey Water Footprint of Farm Animals and Animal Product*. Delft: UNESCO-IHE.

Moragues-Faus, A., and Morgan, K. (2015). Reframing the foodscape: The emergent world of urban food policy. *Environment and Planning A*. doi:10.1177/0308518X15595754.

Netherlands Foreign Investment Agency. (2017). The Netherlands has basically reinvented the tomato. Quartz, February 17. Retrieved from https://qz.com/907971/the-netherlands-basically-reinvented-the-tomato

New York City Mayor's Office of Recovery and Resiliency. (2016). *Five Borough Food Flow: 2016 New York City Food Distribution and Resiliency Study Results*. New York: City Mayor's Office.

New York State Department of Labor. (2019). *Labor Statistics for the New York City Region*. NYC Current Employment Statistics (CES) Latest Month. Retrieved from www.labor.ny.gov/stats/nyc/

NYC Department of Transportation. (2018). *Mobility Report, New York City*. Available: http://www.nyc.gov/html/dot/downloads/pdf/mobility-report-2018-print.pdf.

Ough, T. (2017). The UK's favourite vegetable? *Broccoli*. Retrieved from The Telegraph website: www.telegraph.co.uk/food-and-drink/news/uks-favourite-vegetable-broccoli/

Pfeiffer, D. (2009). *Eating Fossil Fuels: Oil, Food and the Coming Crisis in Agriculture*. Gabriola Island, BC: New Society Publishers.

Port NYC and NYCEDC. (2018). *Freight NYC: Goods for the Good of the City*. Retrieved from www.nycedc.com/sites/default/files/filemanager/Programs/FreightNYC_book__DIGITAL.pdf

Pothukuchi, K., and Kaufman, J. L. (2000). The food system: A stranger to the planning field. *Journal of the American Planning Association*, 66(2), 113–124.

Raja, S. (2015, April 3). Why all cities should have a Department of Food. Retrieved December 10, 2015, from The Conversation website: http://theconversation.com/why-all-cities-should-have-a-department-of-food-39462

Richardson, B. (1876). Modern sanitary science – A city of health. *Van Nostrand's Eclectic Engineering Magazine*, *14*, 31–42. Retrieved from http://urbanplanning.library.cornell.edu/DOCS/rich%27son.htm

Ritchie, H., and Roser, M. (2017). Meat and seafood production and consumption. doi:10.1088/1748-9326/aa6cd5.

Rulli, M. C., Saviori, A., and D'Odorico, P. (2013). Global land and water grabbing. *Proceedings of the National Academy of Sciences of the United States of America*. doi:10.1073/pnas.1213163110.

Schnepf, R. (2015). *CRS Report: Farm-to-food price dynamics*. Washington, DC: Congressional Research Service. Retrieved from https://fas.org/sgp/crs/misc/R40621.pdf

Steel, C. (2009). *Hungry City: How Food Shapes Our Lives*. London: Random House.

Sun, J. L., Chen, Z. X., Ni, H. G., and Zeng, H. (2013). PBDEs as indicator chemicals of urbanization along an urban/rural gradient in South China. *Chemosphere*. doi:10.1016/j.chemosphere.2013.01.036.

The City of New York. (2013). Other critical networks – food supply. In *A Stronger, More Resilient New York*, Chapter 13. New York: City of New York.

University of Ontario. (n.d.). *Energy and material flows of megacities*. Retrieved from https://sites.ontariotechu.ca/sustainabilitytoday/urban-and-energy-systems/Worlds-largest-cities/energy-and-material-flows-of-megacities/beijing.php

Van Kernebeek, H. R. J., Oosting, S. J., Van Ittersum, M. K., Bikker, P., and De Boer, I. J. M. (2016). Saving land to feed a growing population: consequences for consumption of crop and livestock products. *International Journal of Life Cycle Assessment*. doi:10.1007/s11367-015-0923-6.

Vivero-Pol, J. L. (2017). The idea of food as commons or commodity in academia. A systematic review of English scholarly texts. *Journal of Rural Studies*. doi:10.1016/j.jrurstud.2017.05.015.

Wakeland, W., Cholette, S., and Venkat, K. (2012). Food transportation issues and reducing carbon footprint. Food Engineering Series. doi:10.1007/978-1-4614-1587-9_9.

Wang, L., Gao, P., Zhang, M., Huang, Z., Zhang, D., Deng, Q., … Wang, L. (2017). Prevalence and ethnic pattern of diabetes and prediabetes in China in 2013. *JAMA – Journal of the American Medical Association*. doi:10.1001/jama.2017.7596.

White, R. R., and Hall, M. B. (2017). Nutritional and greenhouse gas impacts of removing animals from US agriculture. *Proceedings of the National Academy of Sciences of the United States of America*. doi:10.1073/pnas.1707322114.

Willett, W., Rockström, J., Loken, B., Springmann, M., Lang, T., Vermeulen, S., … Murray, C. J. L. (2019). Food in the anthropocene: The EAT–Lancet Commission on healthy diets from sustainable food systems. *The Lancet*. doi:10.1016/S0140-6736(18)31788-4.

Wood, S., and Cowie, A. (2004). A review of greenhouse gas emission factors for fertiliser production. *IEA Bioenergy Task*, *38*(June), 20. Retrieved from www.leaftc.co.uk/downloads/cc/GHG_Emission_

Fertilizer_Production_June2004.pdf%5Cnpapers2://publication/uuid/2BF3C5E9-C678-4A99-AA6A-5FCDE15367B7

Zeuli, K., Nijhuis, A., and Gerson-Nieder, Z. (2018). *Resilient Food Systems, Resilient Cities: A High-Level Vulnerability Assessment of Toronto's Food System*. Retrieved from www.toronto.ca/legdocs/mmis/2018/hl/bgrd/backgroundfile-118076.pdf

Zhou, W., Zhu, B., Li, Q., Ma, T., Hu, S., and Griffy-Brown, C. (2010). CO2 emissions and mitigation potential in China's ammonia industry. *Energy Policy*. doi:10.1016/j.enpol.2010.02.048.

29

CRADLE TO CRADLE

The role of food waste in a regenerative food system

Tammara Soma

Introduction

Concepts around conspicuous consumption (Trigg 2001), the throwaway society (Cooper 2005), and planned obsolescence (Bulow 1986) have in some cases been mobilized to reflect and explain the current state of our society. A society in which bodies of water around the world are contaminated with industrial waste (Davis 2012), where fish are filled with microplastic (Lusher et al. 2013), and specific to the chapter, a society in which approximately one-third of food produced for human consumption is wasted globally (FAO 2011). It has been argued that in answering these questions as it relates to the role of food, we may find answers to the broader questions. Namely as Mostafavi argues, "what kinds of foods are we consuming and in what manner?" and also "what are we doing to ourselves?" (2010, 36). The multi-faceted answers to Mostafavi's questions may be harrowing based on empirical data around diet-related health problems (Hawkes 2006), issues around junk food (Schlosser 2012), the growing trend towards convenience pre-packaged foods (Warde 1999), the growth of factory farms (Weis 2013), and labour exploitation in the field (Weiler et al. 2016), among others. Mostafavi also adds, that "if we don't see the garbage of our culture, both literally and metaphorically, then we are not confronting the reality of what that garbage actually says about us" (Mostafavi 2010, 36). This wastage of food includes collateral in the form of wasted resources, energy, water, labour, and loss of biodiversity (FAO 2014). According to the Food and Agriculture Organization, the amount of food that is currently wasted is equivalent to the greenhouse gas emissions of the third largest country in the world, behind the United States and China (FAO 2014). However, debates and questions around what is exactly meant by food and what is "waste" are complex: laced with nuances around culture, class, income, and the power behind the ability to categorize what is "food" and what is "waste" (Shilling 2013; Soma 2017a). The impact of food waste differs greatly between regions in the global South (Papargyropoulou et al. 2014; Soma 2017b) and the global North (Lazell 2016; Parizeau et al. 2015). In the global South, where landfills are often open dumpsites, methane generated from food waste has acted as a "ticking time bomb" in creating landfill fires and fatal landslides, the victims of which include children, many of whom live and work on landfill sites (Lavigne et al. 2014).

Dominant solutions to address the global food waste problem, especially as it relates to consumers, have primarily focused on the importance of creating more consumer awareness (WRAP 2014; van der Werf et al. 2018). Leading scholars in the field of food waste studies however caution (and in many cases rightly so) against the neoliberal tendency for policy recommendations to concentrate blame on the individual consumer (see Evans 2011) and instead explore the conduits of divestment (Gregson et al. 2007) and love/care relationships around the domestic food provisioning which in some cases lead to wasting (Watson and Meah 2012). The concept of the throwaway society has been highly contested in both waste and food waste literature (Gregson et al. 2007; O'Brien 2007; Evans 2014). O'Brien argues that the myth of a "throwaway culture" is premised on the idea that there is a "crisis" of waste and a failure of waste management policy (2007, 83). On the issue of questioning the existence of a waste crisis, I would depart from O'Brien and agree with Hawkins (2012), in the sense that I believe there is empirical evidence to demonstrate the existence of multiple waste crises, most of which falls on the shores, soil, water, and bodies of marginalized communities (Pastor et al. 2001; Clapp and Isakson 2018). However, beyond multiple waste crises, one may argue that there is also a food and agricultural crisis, which the notable Wendell Berry in his 1977 book *The Unsettling of America: Culture and Agriculture* identified as a crisis of culture – an industrial culture, which is based on exploitation (see Dahlberg 1993) and waste.

The concept of regenerative agriculture coined by Robert Rodale in 1983 encouraged approaches concerned with the long-term regeneration of crops, communities, landscapes, and regions, as well as the intersection between natural and social systems (Dahlberg 1993). Such a perspective based on long-term thinking is not alien to Indigenous ontologies, based on the seven generation principles (Clarkson et al. 1992). Beyond the specific context of agriculture, the concept of a regenerative food system refers to a system that is based on the principles of a closed loop food system, covering all processes including production, processing, distribution, consumption, and disposal (composting, etc.) and everything in between. A regenerative system is interested in connecting remaining nutrients from the by-products of consumption to regenerate food production (more specifically), and nourish the natural environment (animals, plants, biodiversity) more broadly. It can be argued therefore that the paradigm of "waste" is the antithesis of a regenerative and sustainable food system. Yet a waste regime is embedded in the industrial agriculture model and "is therefore definitive within the cultural logic of capitalist production," specifically in a capitalist food system based on accumulation (Giles 2015, 81).

The concept of waste as "resource" (Moore 2012) which in this chapter will be employed with caution, will also be used as a framework to explain key concepts relevant to the management of food waste such as recycling and reuse. I use the terms "cradle to cradle" and closed loop to define the principles of regenerative food system and to unpack the definition of "waste." In this chapter I will answer the following questions:

1) How can we redefine "waste" in the context of moving towards a regenerative food system?
2) How can waste be managed better in a regenerative food system?
3) What practices or technologies can help address the challenge of food waste?

By reframing the concept of waste and challenging the categorization of what is "food" and what is "waste," I hope to provide alternative platforms and explore alternative worldviews, systems, and methodologies that may reshape the ways in which we, as a society in the Anthropocene, view and value food.

(Re)defining food waste

Waste can be defined in varied ways (Moore 2012). Evans has posited that it is "a bit peculiar to suggest that waste matters, especially when it is generally understood as a void – the worthless, redundant, rejected and discarded afterwards of how we live our lives" (2011, 707). Yet waste does matter. As Gille (2012) noted, the economy is not simply a place where value begets value, it is also a space where value begets waste, waste begets value, and waste begets waste. In the process of understanding "value" and undertaking the task of re-defining waste, the task would not be complete without engaging the seminal work of Mary Douglas (2002). According to Douglas, dirt is defined as "matter out of place" and things are defined as "dirt" or "pollutants" not because they are unhealthy in-and-of-themselves, but because they transgress particular cultural categorizations. Reflection on waste can be compared to Douglas' reflection on dirt, which "involves reflection of order to disorder, being to non-being, form to formlessness, life to death" (2002, 7). In understanding these binaries, it clear that defining food waste is not a clear-cut process. In fact, categorizations and definitions around food waste is replete with contradictions. As the old adage goes, one person's waste is another person's treasure. According to Moore, "waste is best thought of as a parallax object" or an object that disturbs the smooth running of things (2012, 780). In her extensive review of the waste literature, Moore explores the ways that waste is conceptualized by various scholars (2012). This includes among others the concepts of waste as hazard, waste as resource, waste as (non-Marxian) commodity, waste as manageable object, waste as risk, waste as fetish, and many others. The concept of "waste as fetish" is especially relevant to this chapter. According to Moore, "to think of waste as fetish is to propose that wasted objects contain, and thus have the power to reveal, the uneven political and economic relations of capitalist production" (2012, 790). In this chapter, it is useful to familiarize oneself with the common definitions around food waste employed by leading international institutions and researchers.

In general, the term *food waste* is defined as waste occurring at the end of the food chain during the retail and consumer stage, while the term *food loss* refers to the decrease in edible food mass taking places at the production (farm), postharvest, and earlier processing stages in the food supply chain (Parfitt et al. 2010). In their definition that is informed by a political economy and human-oriented perspective, Alexander et al. (2013, 473) refer to food waste as a "failure to use potentially edible items to satisfy human hunger, as well as to the inefficient use of plants' energy content and nutrients for human purposes." There are of course other definitions of food waste, with O'Brien (2012, 196–7) declaring that food waste is simply "capitalist surplus" and an imaginary construct. One definition by Lee and Soma (2016, 248) considers food waste "to be any discarded organic material that was intended for consumption by humans, regardless of its ultimate fate" (for example: composting, anaerobic digestion). The authors argue that this definition emphasizes prevention and is based on an understanding that the original intention and purpose of the food was for human consumption, which should be distinguished from effort around diversion. In addition to food loss and food waste, there are also sub-categories within food waste, as noted in Table 29.1.

Questions of what is "potentially avoidable" and what is "unavoidable food waste" become complex when embedded within the context of culture. For example, corn smut is a plant disease caused by the fungus *ustilago maydis* which impacts corn by causing the corn to be filled with tumour-like blisters and a burned appearance. While corn infested with a visually unappealing fungus may be considered an unavoidable food waste in many countries, in Mexico, corn smut or *huitlacoche* is considered a delicacy. As such, in the

Table 29.1 Avoidable, potentially avoidable, and unavoidable food waste

CATEGORIES	DEFINITION
Avoidable Food Waste	Food and drink thrown away because it is no longer wanted or has been allowed to go past its best. The vast majority of avoidable food is composed of material that was, at some point prior to disposal, edible, even though a proportion is not edible at the time of disposal due to deterioration (e.g. gone mouldy). In contrast to "possibly avoidable" (see below), the category of "avoidable" includes foods or parts of food that are considered edible by the vast majority of people.
Potentially Avoidable Food Waste	Food and drink that some people eat and others do not (e.g. broccoli stalk), or that can be eaten when prepared in one way but not in another (e.g. orange rind). As with "avoidable" waste, "possibly avoidable" waste is composed of material that was, at some point prior to disposal, edible.
Unavoidable Food Waste	Waste arising from food and drink preparation that is not, and has not been, edible under normal circumstances. This includes pineapple skin, apple cores, meat bones, tea bags, and coffee grounds.

Source: adapted from WRAP 2009 *Household Food and Drink Waste in the UK.*

process of re-defining what is food and what is waste, it is important to include diverse cultural perspectives, or what I term as "cultural genius" to stretch the imagination and boundaries of what is possible when it come to the full utilization of food (leaf to root or nose to tail).

In defining what is food and what is waste, Evans highlights the complex intersection of everyday food practices in shaping food consumption and food wasting, in the following definition (2014, xv):

> the passage of "food" into "waste" occurs "as a more or less mundane" consequence of the ways in which practices of everyday and domestic life are currently carried out, and the various factors that shape the prevailing organization of food consumption.

While this definition does not specifically mention issues around equity, class, and privilege in the ability to consume and waste food, it poignantly identified food wasting as influenced by various factors that shape everyday life. (For a specific analysis around food wasting and issues of equity and class see Soma, 2017a.) In essence, by asking us to understand the factors that shape everyday practices, Evans is asking us to consider broader systemic and structural issues that mold the production, distribution, selling, consumption, and wasting of food. In this case, re-defining modern waste (as it relates specifically to food) requires a broader understanding and analysis of – to borrow the spiritual framework employed by Douglas (1966) – the "temple" of the modern industrial food system (Patel 2007). Namely, we need to consider how modern food provisioning infrastructures (food production, processing, retail) shape the rules and systems that define what is "food" and what is "waste." In the following section, I will focus primarily on how factors such as the long-distance global food supply chain supported by the "temple" of modern retail have reshaped our relationship to food and as such severed our ability to return nutrients to, nourish, and regenerate our food systems.

Food as vibrant matter: contradictions within a globalized commodity-based food system

In the book *Hungry City: How Food Shapes Our Lives*, Steel argues that waste is a matter of attitude, "it is in our nature only to value things we have to struggle for – what comes easily is easily tossed" (2008, 281). Her analysis is astute, especially in the general context of cheap and overabundant food supply in the global North. For example, (especially in the global North) we are spending less of our annual incomes on food than with any previous generation (Carolan 2011). The percentage of disposable income spent on food in the United States dropped to 9.8 percent in 2005 from 13.9 percent in 1970 (Carolan 2011). However, this cheap and abundant food system comes at a price. As Carolan (2011) noted, there are genuine environmental, economic, and social costs to the ways in which industrialized societies view, value, and toss food. In 2002, the Food and Agriculture Organization (FAO) calculated that we produce enough food for every person to consume 2,720 kilocalories (kcal) per day (2002, 9). Obviously, this caloric amount goes beyond the needs of an average individual. However, despite overproduction, as Giles (2015) noted, there is a persistent faith in the orthodoxy of increase, especially by major international institutions (see FAO, 2012). Scholars such as Godfray and Garnett (2014) and Beddington (2009) continue to repeat the mantra of increasing production under the term "sustainable intensification." The chorus of increasing production amidst increasing wastage is baffling, yet it fits within the pattern promoted by the industrialization of agriculture via the green revolution. A system of cheap commodified food is premised upon the economic bottom line without considering that dollar values are insufficient to reflect the loss of biodiversity and the intrinsic value of food, which in some cultures and spiritual practices is far from a commodity, but rather is a relation to be honoured with rules around mutual respect and responsibilities (Todd 2014).

In a system bent on standardization, mechanization, short-term efficiency, overproduction, and cheapness, food poses a host of problems due to its intrinsic nature. Both food and waste are dynamic categories that are socially constructed, are vibrant, are tied to moral and ethical questions, and are embedded in larger questions of social, economic, environmental, and political justice. It is both a living organism and can be categorized as an inelastic demand which poses problems in a capitalist-based consumption and production system. In the mainstream industrial western paradigm, food is framed as a passive commodity, the purpose of which is to be consumed or ingested. However, far from being passive, food has material agency. Bennett's (2009) work on "Edible Matter" is important in shifting the hierarchy of consumption – or what she termed "the conquest model of consumption" – towards the material agency of food and how it impacts us (Bennett 2009, 133). According to Bennett (2009), our thoughts on political agency have inadequately considered the material and political agency of food. She argues that there is material and agentic capacity in food, namely the vital power of nonhuman "actants" in the bodies of vegetables and minerals that is not restricted to the human actors (Bennett 2009, 133). Within the "body" of food (and as such I would similarly argue within the body of food waste) there exists a potentiality that includes "the negative power to resist or obstruct human projects" as well as "the active power to exert forces and create effects" (Bennett 2009, 133). An example of the ways in which the intrinsic, living, and vibrant matter of food resists or obstructs human projects of mechanization and standardization, is the fact that food – to our dismay – rots, wilts, and bruises. To the "dismay" of machines, foods are also diverse in shapes, colours, and tastes. As such, food makes the process of standardization and homogenization very challenging, which in turn leads to wasting (Gille 2012).

However, a new generation of food biotechnologists, researchers, and companies are putting their best efforts into changing this resistance and these so-called "limitations" by developing and marketing genetically modified foods that would defy natural processes. Such products include the Arctic® Apple, an apple developed by Okanagan Specialty Fruits® that is sometimes sold in pre-sliced convenience packs and will not brown. There is also a line of non-browning potatoes, pink lycopene infused pineapples, and more. Arctic® Apple has been heavily marketed as a food waste solution, arguing that the product is "slicing into food waste" by encouraging more children to eat more of their apple (in the pre-sliced non-browning form) and that it reduces overall food waste by preventing "that dreaded browning" as you bite into the apples (Brooks 2018). The company argues that apples going brown result in people binning a perfectly edible food. Interestingly, rather than interrogate and address the values and lack of competency that lead to the wasting of a perfectly edible apple, the solution from a technological angle is rather to focus on controlling natural processes. In the effort to control food, we should also consider that food has unpredictable agentic capacity. For example, there is unpredictable agentic capacity in the ability of "particular fats to act in different ways with different bodies and with different intensities, even within the same body at different times" (Bennett 2009, 137). This unpredictability shifts the power in how we recognize and value food's material vitality as well as agentic capacity to transform individuals and affect the environment. Recognizing this agency should lead us to a path of humility. Alas, embedded within the global industrialized food system is a *distancing* process (both spatially and mentally) that has allowed us to commodify and as such waste food. We should seriously ask whether the solution to food waste is for us to develop fruits, plants, and meat that never rot, brown, or wilt? Are we, as Douglas indicated, trying to impose "system on an inherently untidy experience?" (2002, 5).

Indeed, the harnessing and manipulating of natural systems has been the *modus operandi* of our increasingly distanced and globalized food supply chain. Consider that today, the average plate of food consumed in North America and Europe has travelled approximately 1,500 miles before it is consumed (Clapp 2012). When we pick a mango from the supermarket, rarely do we consider that embedded within that mango is the energy, water, resources, and inputs from another country. To transport and move food with all the water, energy, resources, and land embedded in the product, entails the development of massive and complex global logistical food supply chains that are increasingly tangled in a digital financialization model connected to global stock markets (Clapp and Isakson 2018) and international trade regulations via the World Trade Organization (WTO). WTO rules distorting prices have threatened rural livelihood by increasing food dumping in the global South (Ritchie et al. 2003). Not only does this practice drive farmers out of business, but it may also cause significant food loss at the farm level.

The role and concept of *distancing* is key to this chapter and to the valuation (both undervaluation and in some cases overvaluation) of food and waste. Distancing refers to the "separation of production and consumption decisions, both of which impede ecological and social feedbacks" (Princen 2002, 104) or the "separation between primary resource extraction decisions and ultimate consumptions decisions" (Princen 2002, 116). Specifically, the process of distancing contributes to the severing of nutrient feedback, pushes overconsumption, and shifts the nourishing and beneficial role of organic by-products (food scraps), at a smaller more manageable scale, into a toxic global burden. Distancing and the moral discourse around waste is connected to the field of ethical consumption and Marxist critique of capitalism. Marxist thoughts on the politics of consumption reframe commodity fetishism as a hypothesis about the deleterious effects of affluent consumers having no knowledge about the origins of the goods that they consume (Barnett et al. 2010). In this view, as outlined by Barnett et al. (2010), it is assumed/suggested that by reconnecting locations of production, networks of distribution, and acts of consumption, the alienating effects of modern capitalism can be exposed. Further, it is assumed that the key to motivating action lies in informing people so that they can recognize their entanglement in the complex networks of commodification and accumulation. The process of *distancing* perfectly frames this phenomenon whereby the contemporary political economy of food breaks the feedback loop and externalizes cost. Scale and space matter for the recycling of the nutrient and feedback loop. I will illustrate this with the case of a household food waste study in Indonesia. Through this case study, I will also outline and provide examples on how the field of food system planning (Pothukuchi and Kaufman 2000; Soma and Wakefield 2011) may help in re-framing the values around food and waste and the rebuilding of a regenerative food system based on a cradle to cradle/closed loop food system approach.

Scale: the role of food systems planning and words of caution on the "waste as a resource" paradigm

Rarely do we see policy and articles around the issue of food and waste focusing on degrowth, the need to sacrifice, or the need to practice constraint in consumption (for exceptions see Giles 2015; Kallis et al. 2012). This is due to the prevalence of the productionist paradigm or what Carolan identifies as the "ecological modernization theory" (2004). From the perspective of ecological modernization theory, there is no need to address, constrain, reduce, sacrifice consumption, namely because problems related to consumption can be solved through more efficient industrial and ecological production. With a focus on alternative/"green" production, examples of which include "sustainable intensification" (Godfray 2014), "climate smart agriculture" (World Bank 2017), donating corporate food waste and surplus to the poor (for a critique of this model see Fisher 2017), and investment in depackaging technologies (WRAP 2009), challenging the pattern and growth in consumption becomes irrelevant (Carolan 2004). As Gille argues, "solutions to the 'food waste problem' limited to technological innovation and a few sites or even countries will prove insufficient and will likely exacerbate existing inequalities" (2012 27).

In discussing potential solutions to food waste, a popular concept in waste management literature is the notion of recycling and reuse. The concept of waste as a resource (Moore 2012) is relevant to the processes around the reuse and recycling of food waste. According to Evans (2011), reuse is what happens once goods have gone through the first cycle of consumption, reached the point of disposal and entered another cycle rather than being sent to the landfill. An example of reuse is "secondhand consumption," which in the context of food can include the consuming of leftovers or the donation of leftover/surplus food, for example through food rescue (Giles 2015) in the form of community refrigerators, food banks, food sharing apps. The practice of dumpster diving or freeganism can also be considered as reuse (Barnard 2016). Recycling is a form of reuse that involves some form of material transformation between the first and second cycle uses of an object (Evans 2011). In the context of food waste, an example of recycling would be the transformation of food waste into compost that can be used as a fertilizer or soil conditioner (Hoornweg et al. 1999). These key concepts in waste scholarship and the idea of "waste as resource" might be useful when considering interventions to reduce food waste. However, I would like to throw a word of caution in the mobilization of the "waste as a resource" paradigm, namely because scale and space matter. Scale is what differentiates backyard composting (the use of a small bin in the backyard) from centralized composting (processing approximately >40,000 tons/year) where millions of dollars in upfront capital (Hoornweg et al. 1999) and fossil fuel are needed to move, manage, and process organic waste and where contamination to the feedstock becomes a massive problem (Refed n.d.). In focusing on converting food waste into valuable outputs, there is a danger when scale is not taken into account. Alexander et al. cautioned that "when food waste's disposal becomes productive (i.e., value creating), it demands that more food becomes wasted" (2013, 473).

The issue of scale is particularly important in the field of city and regional planning, especially in the process of developing a regenerative closed loop food system. As a food system planner (Soma and Wakefield 2011), I aim to integrate food system consideration in my academic and professional planning work. Food system planning is useful in the process of building a regenerative food system and in connecting/re-connecting the nutrient feedback loop. This is because food system planning is concerned with the "chain of activities connecting food production, processing, distribution, consumption, and waste management, as well as all of the associated regulatory institutions and activities" (Pothukuchi and Kaufman 2000, 113). Planners of the past, such as Ebenezer Howard, have integrated principles of food system planning, and the objectives of closed loop food systems in their planning documents. Noteworthy is the classic Garden City proposal developed in 1898 which integrated local food system considerations and natural metabolism in food production and the management of nutrients from food scraps into its plan. The Garden Cities plan is constrained in scale, namely that the population of each garden city should be capped ideally at 32,000 people and that it will be developed in clusters, to ensure self-sufficiency and proper nutrient recycling of waste. Once a cluster reaches the cap, another garden city would be developed. In the Garden City proposal, Howard from the very beginning planned for a circular food system whereby the flow of raw and cooked food from collective kitchens and dining halls was to be collected and recycled as fertilizer for farms (Pothukuchi and Kaufman 2000). As I mentioned, the issue of scale is critical in reconnecting the severed nutrient feedback loop from food waste. According to Raja et al. (2008), an ideal community food system:

> promotes the use of environmentally sustainable method for producing, processing and distributing food. By favouring local distribution networks over global, the consumption of fossil fuel is minimized. In a similar vein, minimal packaging of food and composting of food leftovers is encouraged to reduce the impact on land-fills ... a community food system facilitates residents' access to healthful, affordable, and culturally appropriate foods at all times.
>
> *(Raja et al. 2008, 4)*

Prior to 2007 (when the American Planning Association policy guide on community and regional food planning was published) planners were generally unaware that local land use planning decisions strongly affect people's ability to access food and their ability to manage food waste sustainably (e.g., residential developments on prime farmland, grocery stores only accessible for those with access to cars, food deserts, restrictions on urban agriculture, ban on community composting). The following case study in Indonesia will illustrate the severance of the nutrient feedback loop, and potential solutions from a food system planning perspective.

Case study Bogor: Indonesia

In this section, I will outline my case study in Bogor, Indonesia (a more detailed account of the study is published in the journal *Built Environment*, see Soma 2017b). This example will outline the points of contention, opportunities, and conflict, in viewing food waste as a resource, as well as identify the root problems that have made it more difficult to build a regenerative closed loop food system. To better understand how we can sustainably manage food waste and connect the feedback loop, it is important to understand the role of packaging and the transformation of food provisioning through a long-distance supply chain reflected in the supermarket model. The question of food packaging is first and foremost a game of "which came first: the chicken or the egg?" In this sense, we can ask "which came first, the birth of plastic packaging to support a long-distance food supply chain, or the long-distance food supply chain giving birth to a rise of plastic food packaging?" To answer the two final research questions: "How can waste be managed better in a regenerative food system?" and "What practices or technologies can help address the challenge of food waste?" I will elucidate several examples from the City of Bogor, Indonesia.

The City of Bogor, Indonesia, is a rapidly urbanizing city located 60 km south of Indonesia's capital Jakarta. I conducted my doctoral fieldwork in Bogor between May 2014 and October 2015 and conducted a mixed methods study. The first phase of the research included a qualitative study employing ethnographic tools with 21 households divided into n=7 upper income, n=7 middle income and n=7 lower-income households, as well as n=12 key informant interviews with supermarket managers, waste collector, city planners, mobile vegetable vendor, and more. The second phase of the study included household surveys of 323 households consisting of n=154 (low-income), n=107 (middle-income) and n=62 (upper-income households). In Indonesia, rapid urbanization has exacerbated the issue of land scarcity, with the paving over of prime agricultural farmland and urban development on spaces where low-income community members used to grow their food. There are also space restrictions due to land scarcity and sprawl, which makes it more difficult for households to manage their food waste sustainably. As Ayu (pseudonym), a low-income respondent, noted:

> Before I used to grow cassava, bananas, corn … now the land has been used to build those big houses … near my house there used to be trees, *rambutan* trees, banana trees, cassava, different types of trees, there were some folks who planted spinach, tomatoes and other vegetables. When we needed food, we just picked it. Now it's so difficult …

With the loss of local farmland, increasingly, Indonesians are becoming more dependent on modern supermarkets and hypermarkets. For example, by 2005, 30 percent of food purchased by Indonesians was purchased from modern supermarkets (Reardon and Hopkins 2006) and findings from my household survey in Bogor found that 93.5 percent of high-income and 70.1 percent of middle-income respondents respectively shop for their daily foods at modern supermarkets (Soma 2019). These modern food retail development in the form of big box stores are gobbling up more and more land, resulting in less spaces to grow food.

Concurrently, modern consumption has led to "modern" packaging, replacing traditional biodegradable packaging such as bamboo and banana leaf. Foods that were traditionally wrapped in banana or *pandan* leaf (*pandanus amaryllifolius*) are now packaged in Styrofoam, and a variety of plastics. Bogor residents also used to bring reusable bags to shop in the form of *bongsang*, a bag made of woven bamboo or cloth bags. With the rise of cheap plastic, it is becoming harder and harder to find anyone shopping with *bongsang* or a reusable bag in general.

My study found that 59.7 percent of upper-income, 43 percent of middle-income, and 26.6 percent of low-income respondents knew how to compost. However, 92.6 percent of respondents stated that they never compost their food waste (Soma 2019). This is no surprise considering the lack of space and complexity posed by multiple waste streams and packaging waste (all of which were once biodegradable as exemplified by the banana leaf). Sarah, a middle-income respondent, provided an insightful account of the historical transition from on-site regenerative practices of food waste management and the current difficulties around managing waste.

> Before, until the 1980s, you could pretty much dig and put the garbage in a hole … Yes, dig a hole and you put the waste in … but what becomes problematic now is the packaging. Before, there was only a small amount of plastic and tin can waste.

The type of food packaging promoted by the modern retail complex and global food supply chain is critical in further severing the nutrient feedback in Indonesia, and makes it more challenging to manage waste on site. The scale of the food packaging waste also pushes the waste management of food-related waste to the realm of municipal waste collection. Most problematic in the Indonesian case is the ways in which policy makers have attempted to push the burden of food packaging management on the poor. This is all done within the paradigm of "waste as a resource" and illustrates the problem of the ecological modernization/productionist paradigm mindset, as well as the issue of scale. As the head of Bogor's waste management stated:

> There is a law UU No 18, 2008 that packaging waste is the responsibility of the producer. It is part of extended producer responsibility to pick up the packaging waste or to provide incentives to whomever can manage that waste … in the city of Bogor, those packaging wastes are residue. It cannot be processed in our temporary dumpsite and communal 3R sites … So, we try to encourage those packaging waste to become arts and crafts. We introduce this to the public in our training programs. Because it's our job to educate, we inform the public that packaging waste if cut nicely can be arts and crafts that are saleable …

It is clear that, instead of addressing the structural causes of the waste crisis, which is rooted in the creation and growth of non-biodegradable packaging, Indonesian policy makers instead insist on framing packaging waste as a resource in the form of arts and crafts. While in small amounts it may be possible to reduce waste by recycling packaging waste into saleable arts and crafts, with the industrial scale at which food packaging is produced and wasted, the logistics of individual residents scavenging for plastic packaging waste to be made into purses, wallets, and other arts and crafts is simply improbable. In addition, arts and crafts waste-related training programs in Bogor are often tailored as economic opportunities for the urban poor. As such it is worth questioning whether those who are expected to manage the waste and provide solutions are those who are poor. Within the context of unequal and uneven waste collection (in Bogor, only 68 percent of waste is collected by the municipality) packaging waste pollutes farmland, destroy crops in times of flooding (BBSDLP Indonesian Ministry of Agriculture 2018), and clogs waterways. To reconnect the nutrient feedback loop, agricultural farmland must be protected from both urban development and the crisis of packaging waste. Urban lands should also be allocated to supplement the self-sufficiency and food security of residents and urban lands for food production should also integrate organic waste management in the form of composting (both windrow and vermicomposting). Additional food scraps (again, scale is key) can be fed to urban livestock including chicken, small-scale urban catfish aquaculture, and ducks. Most importantly, a revitalization of traditional biodegradable food packaging and the practice of bringing reusable bags for shopping would support in reducing wastage and promote a more regenerative food system.

Conclusions

In this chapter I have outlined how waste can be managed better in a regenerative food system. I have also unpacked the definition of food waste and the concept of "waste as a resource." While defining waste as a byproduct or a resource is useful at a particular scale (mostly small to medium scale), at a larger scale it simply encourages more wasting and worsens the problem by not addressing the structural causes due to overproduction and overconsumption. I have also outlined low-cost practices and provided examples from the global South that can help reconnect the severed nutrient feedback. As I noted in the case study, in countries with a lack of waste infrastructure, non-biodegradable food packaging can act as a barrier for more sustainable food waste management such as home-based, backyard, or neighbourhood-based composting. In essence, the existence of cheap and ubiquitous non-biodegradable packaging and land scarcity has resulted in the need for Indonesians (particularly) and the broader society (more generally) to move toward a more centralized, complex, and long-distance waste collection system that keeps waste "out of sight and out of mind" at least for a privileged few. Future research should explore the topic of modern food consumption and pay a particular attention to the role of food packaging in the food system. Concerns over the cost of managing food waste should also be coupled with consideration for the associated cost of municipal waste collection and the environmental impact caused by the generation of food packaging waste.

While the premise of disposable plastic food packaging is that it helps protect food from being wasted during travels from farm to distant tables, the more important premise is the idea that food should continue to be branded and shipped from distant places, which will further disconnect the food waste nutrient feedback loop and therefore create barriers in the development of a regenerative food system. In addition, the examples provided in this chapter also highlight the power relations that shape and influence the definition of waste. Further studies should explore the emerging rise of zero waste grocery store initiatives around the world and the ways in which these stores may facilitate a more localized, transparent, regenerative, and less wasteful food system. While these zero waste store initiatives are currently located in the global North, the reusable and zero waste model was commonplace in many traditional markets of the global South before the advent of cheap plastic packaging. As such, future research should also explore alternative solutions from diverse cultures and geographies in the global South.

Discussion questions

1. How can food waste contribute to regenerative agriculture, while recognizing the need to also prevent food waste? Consider the definitions of food waste outlined in this chapter.

2. What are factors that have caused distancing and made it more difficult to return organic nutrients back into the soil?
3. Are there similarities and learning lessons from the case of Indonesia outlined in this chapter for other countries?

Further reading

Evans, D. (2014). *Food Waste: Home Consumption, Material Culture and Everyday Life*. London: Bloomsbury Publishing.

Lee, K., and Soma, T. (2016). From "farm to table" to "farm to dump": Emerging research on household food waste in the global south. In Anderson, C., Brady, J., and Levkoe, C (eds.) *Conversation in Food Studies* (pp. 243–266). Winnipeg: University of Manitoba Press.

Parfitt, J., Barthel, M., and Macnaughton, S. (2010). Food waste within food supply chains: Quantification and potential for change to 2050. *Philosophical Transactions of the Royal Society B: Biological Sciences, 365*(1554), 3065–3081.

References

Alexander, C., Gregson, N., & Gille, Z. (2013). Food waste. In Murcott, A., Belasco, W., & Jackson, P. (eds). *The Handbook of Food Research*. London: Bloomsbury Publishing, pp. 471–483.

Barnard, A. V. (2016). *Freegans: Diving into the Wealth of Food Waste in America*. Minneapolis, MN: University of Minnesota Press.

Barnett, C., Cloke, P., Clarke, N., and Malpass, A. (2010). *Globalizing Responsibility: The Political Rationalities of Ethical Consumption*. London: John Wiley & Sons.

BBSDLP Indonesian Ministry of Agriculture. (2018). Selamatkan Pertanian Indonesia dari Sampah Plastik. Retrieved July 14th 2018 from: https://bbsdlp.litbang.pertanian.go.id/ind/index.php/laya nan-mainmenu-65/info-terkini/792-selamatkan-pertanian-indonesia

Beddington, J. (2009). *The Perfect Storm* (p. 1). Government Office for Science. Retrieved from: webarc hive. nationalarchives. gov. uk/20121212135622/www. bis. gov. uk/assets/goscience/docs/p/per fect-storm-paper. pdf. Slide show

Bennett, J. (2009). *Vibrant Matter: A Political Ecology of Things*. Durham, NC: Duke University Press.

Brooks, J. (2018). *Slicing into Food Waste with Arctic® Apple*. Retrieved March 20th 2020 from: https:// www.arcticapples.com/slicing-into-food-waste-with-arctic-apples/

Bulow, J. (1986). An economic theory of planned obsolescence. *Quarterly Journal of Economics, 101*(4), 729–749.

Carolan, M. S. (2004). Ecological modernization theory: What about consumption? *Society and Natural Resources, 17*(3), 247–260.

Carolan, M. (2011). *The Real Cost of Cheap Food*. London, UK: Earthscan Publications Ltd.

Clapp, J., and Isakson, S. R. (2018). *Speculative Harvest*. Halifax: Fernwood Publishing.

Clapp, J. 2012. *Food*. Cambridge: Polity Press.

Clarkson, L., Morrissette, V., and Regallet, G. (1992). *Our Responsibility to the Seventh Generation: Indigenous Peoples and Sustainable Development* (p. 63). Winnipeg: International Institute for Sustainable Development.

Cooper, T. (2005). Slower consumption reflections on product life spans and the "throwaway society". *Journal of Industrial Ecology, 9*(1–2), 51–67.

Dahlberg, K. A. (1993). Regenerative food systems: Broadening the scope and agenda of sustainability. In Allen, P. (ed.) *Food for the Future* (pp. 75–102). New York: John Wiley & Sons.

Davis, C. (2012). The politics of "fracking": Regulating natural gas drilling practices in Colorado and Texas. *Review of Policy Research, 29*(2), 177–191.

Douglas, M. (2002). *Purity and Danger: An Analysis of the Concept of Pollution and Taboo*. Abingdon, Oxon: Routledge (first publisghed 1966).

Evans, D. (2011). Blaming the consumer–once again: The social and material contexts of everyday food waste practices in some English households. *Critical Public Health, 21*(4), 429–440.

Evans, D. (2014). *Food Waste: Home Consumption, Material Culture and Everyday Life*. London: Bloomsbury Publishing.

FAO. (2002). *Reducing Poverty and Hunger: The Critical Role of Financing for Food, Agriculture and Rural Development*. Food and Agriculture Organization, Internaitional Fund for Agricultural Development, World Food Programme. Retrieved March 20th 2020 from: http://www.fao.org/3/Y6265e/y6265e00.htm

FAO. (2011). *Global Food Losses and Food Waste: Extent, Causes and Prevention*. Rome: FAO.

FAO. (2014). *Food Wastage Footprint Full Cost Accounting: Final Report*. Rome. Retrieved July 14th 2018 from: www.fao.org/3/a-i3991e.pdf

Fisher, A. (2017). *Big Hunger: The Unholy Alliance Between Corporate America and Anti-Hunger Groups*. Cambridge, MA: MIT Press.

Giles, D. B. (2015). The work of waste-making: Biopolitical labour and the myth of the global city. In Marshall, J. P., and Connor, L. H.(eds) *Environmental Change and the World's Futures* (pp. 95–109). Abingdon, Oxon: Routledge.

Gille, Z. (2012). From risk to waste: Global food waste regimes. *The Sociological Review*, *60*, 27–46.

Godfray, H. C. J., and Garnett, T. (2014). Food security and sustainable intensification. *Philosophical Transactions of the Royal Society B: Biological Sciences*, *369*(1639), 20120273.

Gregson, N., Metcalfe, A., and Crewe, L. (2007). Moving things along: The conduits and practices of divestment in consumption. *Transactions of the Institute of British Geographers*, *32*(2), 187–200.

Hawkes, C. (2006). Uneven dietary development: Linking the policies and processes of globalization with the nutrition transition, obesity and diet-related chronic diseases. *Globalization and Health*, *2*(1), 4.

Hawkins, G. (2012). The performativity of food packaging: Market devices, waste crisis and recycling. *The Sociological Review*, *60*(2_suppl), 66–83.

Hoornweg, D., Thomas, L., and Otten, L. (1999). Composting and its applicability in developing countries. *World Bank Working Paper Series*, *8*. Retrieved from: www.eolss.net/Sample-Chapters/C10/E5-15-07-05.pdf

Kallis, G., Kerschner, C., & Martinez-Alier, J. (2012). The economics of degrowth. *Ecological Economics*, *84*, 172–180.

Lavigne, F., Wassmer, P., Gomez, C., Davies, T. A., Hadmoko, D. S., Iskandarsyah, T. Y. W., … Pratomo, I. (2014). The 21 February 2005, catastrophic waste avalanche at Leuwigajah dumpsite, Bandung, Indonesia. *Geoenvironmental Disasters*, *1*(1), 10.

Lazell, J. (2016). Consumer food waste behaviour in universities: Sharing as a means of prevention. *Journal of Consumer Behaviour*, *15*(5), 430–439.

Lee, K., and Soma, T. (2016). From "farm to table" to "farm to dump": Emerging research on household food waste in the global south. In Anderson, C., Brady, J., and Levkoe, C. (eds.) *Conversation in Food Studies* (pp. 243–266). Winnipeg: University of Manitoba Press.

Lusher, A. L., McHugh, M., and Thompson, R. C. (2013). Occurrence of microplastics in the gastrointestinal tract of pelagic and demersal fish from the English Channel. *Marine Pollution Bulletin*, *67*(1–2), 94–99.

Moore, S. A. (2012). Garbage matters: Concepts in new geographies of waste. *Progress in Human Geography*, *36*(6), 780–799.

Mostafavi, M. (2010). Why ecological urbanism? Why now?. In *Ecological Urbanism* (pp. 12–53). Zurich: Lars Müller Publisher.

O'Brien, M. (2007) *A Crisis of Waste? Understanding the Rubbish Society*. London: Routledge.

Okanagan Specialty Fruits. (2018). Slicing into food waste with Arctic® Apples. Retrieved July 14th 2018 from: www.arcticapples.com/slicing-into-food-waste-with-arctic-apples/

Patel, R. (2007). *Stuffed & Starved: The Hidden Battle for the World Food System*. Brooklyn, NY: Melville House Publishing.

Papargyropoulou, E., Padfield, R., Rupani, P. F., and Zakaria, Z. (2014). Towards sustainable resource and waste management in developing countries: The role of commercial and food waste in Malaysia. *International Journal of Waste Resources*, *4*(3), 2–7.

Parfitt, J., Barthel, M., and Macnaughton, S. (2010). Food waste within food supply chains: Quantification and potential for change to 2050. *Philosophical Transactions of the Royal Society B: Biological Sciences*, *365*(1554), 3065–3081.

Parizeau, K., von Massow, M., and Martin, R. (2015). Household-level dynamics of food waste production and related beliefs, attitudes, and behaviours in Guelph, Ontario. *Waste Management*, *35*, 207–217.

Pastor, M., Sadd, J., and Hipp, J. (2001). Which came first? Toxic facilities, minority move-in, and environmental justice. *Journal of Urban Affairs*, *23*(1), 1–21.

Pothukuchi, K., and Kaufman, J. L. (2000). The food system: A stranger to the planning field. *Journal of the American Planning Association, 66*(2), 113–124.

Princen, T. (2002). Distancing: Consumption and the severing of feedback. In Princen, T., Maniates, M., and Conca, K. (eds) *Confronting consumption.* Cambridge, MA: MIT press, pp. 103–131.

Raja, S., Born, B. M., and Russell, J. K. (2008). *Planners Guide to Community and Regional Food Planning.* Chicago, IL: American Planning Association.

Reardon, T., and Hopkins, R. (2006). The supermarket revolution in developing countries: Policies to address emerging tensions among supermarkets, suppliers and traditional retailers. *The European Journal of Development Research, 18*(4), 522–545.

ReFed. (n.d.). *Centralized Composting.* Retrieved July 14th 2018 from: www.refed.com/solutions/central ized-composting

Ritchie, M., Murphy, S., and Lake, A. B. (2003). *US Dumping on World Agricultural Markets: Can Trade Rules Help Farmers?* WTO Watch Trade Observatory, IATP. Retrieved July 14th 2018 from: www. eldis.org/document/A12039

Schlosser, E. (2012). *Fast Food Nation: The Dark Side of the All-American Meal.* Boston, MA: Houghton Mifflin Harcourt.

Shilling, C. (2013). Series editor's introduction. In Evans, D., Campbell, H., and Murcott, A. (eds.) *Waste Matters: New Perspectives on Food and Society* (pp. 1–4). London: John Wiley & Sons.

Soma, T. (2017a). Gifting, ridding and the "everyday mundane": The role of class and privilege in food waste generation in Indonesia. *Local Environment, 22*(12), 1444–1460.

Soma, T. (2017b). Wasted infrastructures: Urbanization, distancing and food waste in Bogor, Indonesia. *Built Environment, 43*(3), 431–446.

Soma, T., & Wakefield, S. (2011). The emerging role of a food system planner: Integrating food considerations into planning. *Journal of Agriculture, Food Systems, and Community Development, 2*(1), 53–64.

Steel, C. (2008). *Hungry City: How Food Shapes Our Lives.* London, UK: Chatto & Windus.

Todd, Z. (2014). Fish pluralities: Human-animal relations and sites of engagement in Paulatuuq, Arctic Canada. *Etudes/Inuit/Studies, 38*(1–2), 217–238.

Trigg, A. B. (2001). Veblen, Bourdieu, and conspicuous consumption. *Journal of Economic Issues, 35*(1), 99–115. doi:10.1080/00213624.2001.11506342.

van der Werf, P., Seabrook, J. A., and Gilliland, J. A. (2018). Food for naught: Using the theory of planned behaviour to better understand household food wasting behaviour. *The Canadian Geographer/ Le Géographe Canadien. 63*(3), 478–493.

Warde, A. (1999). Convenience food: Space and timing. *British Food Journal, 101*(7), 518–527.

Watson, M., and Meah, A. (2012). Food, waste and safety: Negotiating conflicting social anxieties into the practices of domestic provisioning. *The Sociological Review, 60*(2_suppl), 102–120.

Weiler, A. M., Otero, G., and Wittman, H. (2016). Rock stars and bad apples: Moral economies of alternative food networks and precarious farm work regimes. *Antipode, 48*(4), 1140–1162.

Weis, T. (2013). *The Ecological Hoofprint: The Global Burden of Industrial Livestock.* London: Zed Books.

World Bank. (2017). *Climate Smart Agriculture.* Retrieved July 14th 2018 from: www.worldbank.org/en/ topic/climate-smart-agriculture

WRAP. (2009). *Household Food and Drink Waste in the U.K. Final Report.* Retrieved July 14th 2018 from: www.wrap.org.uk/sites/files/wrap/Household_food_and_drink_waste_in_the_UK_-_report.pdf

WRAP. (2014). *Strategies to Achieve Economic and Environmental Gains by Reducing Food Waste.* Retrieved April 29th 2019 from: www.wrap.org.uk/sites/files/wrap/WRAP-NCE_Economic-environmental-gains-food-waste.pdf

30

CONTROVERSIES AROUND FOOD SECURITY

Something difficult to swallow

Antonio A. R. Ioris

Problematizing the problem

Much has been said, and there is more to be added, about food and agriculture. Food now is big business and the business of food is constantly changing. People in urban areas, but also quite a few in the countryside, increasingly rely on supply chains dominated by large supermarkets that trade food and goods coming from all over the planet. That means a significant distance between producers and consumers, making seasons and local traditions irrelevant, homogenizing tastes, and including many new players who were not involved before (e.g. freight ship companies, logistics personnel, lorry drivers, international lawyers and bankers, among others). The socioecological impacts of intensive, high yield commercial food production – what in Brazil and Latin America is simply described as 'agribusiness' (Ioris 2016) – are therefore borne thousands of kilometers away from the spots where food is consumed. In addition, despite systematic campaigns for healthier eating and active lifestyles, a significant proportion of the global society now ingests something that vaguely resembles, but is not really food as our ancestors knew it. More people regularly eat, both at home and in fast-food restaurants, heavily processed food of questionable nutritional value and harmful ingredients. What is on offer on most market shelves is industrialized organic matter that results from the combination of raw material and numerous chemical substances, which looks like food, has images of food on the package, but is essentially different. Michael Pollan addresses this unsettling conundrum and suggests a basic criterion to 'locate' food: 'don't eat anything your great grandmother wouldn't recognize as food' (Pollan 2008: 148). This provocative, half-joke remark illustrates how 'food' has transmuted and is now associated with things that have only a tenuous similarity with what was eaten by countless previous generations.

In a context where food, as experienced before, is increasingly disfigured and metamorphosed into something else, the question of food security goes beyond issues of access, affordability, and self-sufficiency. The semiotics and the social construction of relations around food suggest that the agenda of food security needs to incorporate and react to many layers of complexity. The problem of food has been somehow dislocated from crop fields and national markets and, consequently, food insecurity has a much wider range of causes and repercussions. This debate is certainly not trivial. There are regular, almost daily new stories about food, hunger, trade, safety, and so on somewhere in the planet, that seem to annul our ability to think critically and react to mounting demands and distortions. We feel overwhelmed and impotent, particularly because the growing acceptance of American-style (junk) food is fuelled by investments in marketing, including dishonest advertisements aired during young children's programs (Rahill et al. 2019; Truman and Elliott 2019; Velazquez et al. 2019). The problem is that, like other major contemporary challenges, food insecurity is growing in scale and complexity, but it is hard to make sense of. The common human reaction is to acknowledge the magnitude and urgency of the problem, but carry on regardless.

It is necessary to situate the controversy in its right time and spatial setting. Food scarcity and hunger have always been major human problems, serving to justify wars and grassroots rebellions. However, it was really in the second half of the 20th century – the so-called Age of Development, since Truman's Four Point Speech of 1949 – that food insecurity became a matter of global concern. The Food and Agriculture Organization (FAO) of the United Nations was established just before the end of the Second World War (in 1943 at Hot Springs, Virginia) and many conferences have been held over the last decades – especially the 1948 meeting when the Havana Charter was signed, the 1974 World Food Conference, the 1960–94 GATT trade negotiations, and the 1996 World Food Summit. Food security is now an integral component of diplomatic activity and international development strategies. The most recognized international publication on food and nutrition, *The State of Food Insecurity and Nutrition in the World* (SOFI) by FAO, IFAD, UNICEF, WFP, and WHO (2017: ii), reported that:

> In 2016 the number of chronically undernourished people in the world is estimated to have increased to 815 million, up from 777 million in 2015 although still down from about 900 million in 2000. After a prolonged decline, this recent increase could signal a reversal of trends. The food security situation has worsened in particular in parts of sub-Saharan Africa, South-Eastern Asia and Western Asia, and deteriorations have been observed most notably in situations of conflict and conflict combined with droughts or floods.

And about the related issue of obesity and malnutrition:

> Multiple forms of malnutrition coexist, with countries experiencing simultaneously high rates of child undernutrition, anaemia among women, and adult obesity. Rising rates of overweight and obesity add to these concerns.[1] Childhood overweight and obesity are increasing in most regions, and in all regions for adults. In 2016, 41 million children under five years of age were overweight. The number of conflicts is also on the rise. Exacerbated by climate-related shocks, conflicts seriously affect food security and are a cause of much of the recent increase in food insecurity.[2]

Interestingly, this specific document offers a comprehensive assessment of the global and regional situation, but is very brief on causes, responsibilities, and political disputes (this is obviously the style of the consensus-seeking United Nations initiatives). A critical part of the puzzle, hidden behind statistics and assessments, is how food security is conceptualized and acted upon. It is true that the concept has evolved significantly in recent decades, since the World Food Conference (1974) defined food security as the 'availability at all times of adequate world food supplies of basic foodstuffs to sustain a steady expansion of food consumption and to offset fluctuations in production and prices'. That was extended in a report of the FAO director general of 1983: 'ensuring that all people at all times have both physical and economic access to the basic food that they need'. Those notions were later revised and included the household scale in the 1986 World Bank Report on Poverty and Hunger. The 1996 World Food Summit reaffirmed the multidimensional basis of food security and called for policies more focused on the promotion and recovery of livelihood options. More recently, the Committee on World Food Security (CFS) claimed that

> [f]ood security exists when all people, at all times, have physical, social and eco-nomic access to sufficient, safe and nutritious food to meet their dietary needs and food preferences for an active and healthy life. The four pillars of food security are availability, access, utilization and stability. The nutritional dimension is integral to the concept of food security.
>
> *(FAO 2009)*

Yet, the majority of definitions of security adopted around the world focus on issues restricted to notions of availability, adequate diet, and stable supply, typically betraying a technocratic, narrow perspective, and evading the crucial political basis of food insecurity. For instance, Naylor (2014, 375) defines food insecurity as 'a situation that exists when people lack secure access to sufficient amounts of safe and nutritious food for normal growth and development and an active and healthy life … It may be chronic, seasonal or transitory'. Much more needs to be said on this, although first it is necessary to revisit the prevailing lines of reasoning before we expand the discussion and open up the conversation.

Prevailing approaches to food security

Instead of an exegesis of individual concepts, our goal in this section is to address the shortcomings of the main lines of argument and identity key gaps in those constructions. The aim is to consider the discursive processes by which food security ideas are constructed, which also both reflect disputes between different social groups and inform the formulation of policies and responses to the phenomenon of food insecurity. It is not our intention either to entail an epistemological or philosophical battle around the definition of food security, but it is important to observe that what is missing in most definitions is the connection, across scale, of food with daily life and global politico-economic and ideological systems. Food security is a global question with regional (such as the European level), local, and personal ramifications. In schematic terms, there are three main positionalities from which the debate takes place at different, interconnected scales.

Market-based productivism

The most common reaction to the pressures of food security is the productivist paradigm (De Schutter 2014; see also Lang and Heasman 2015). Basically, the argument goes, if there is a lack of food, the answer is to produce more and make food more easily available in time and space (while issues of distribution and socio-spatial inequalities are much less important). Productivism betrays a strong influence of Western positivism and its search for the universal, superior 'truth' to be brought to the rest of humankind. The narrative is that, because of steady population growth and less significant productivity gains, there is a growing threat to the ability of entire countries and regions to feed themselves, but with rising prices of basic food commodities the response was to produce more. This is evidently the principal rationality adopted by diplomacy, national governments, and the corporate business sector. It directly transforms food insecurity – without asking questions about past legacies, injustices, and responsibilities – into a source of political gain (in the form of promises made by politicians), the legitimization of government strategies (as response to social demands), and profits (as investments and production platforms will need to be funded and goods sold in the market). An important facet of the productivist response to food insecurity is the claim that the attention should be focused on technology, machinery, more land to be cultivated, and more inputs to be transformed into higher outputs (especially in terms of caloric output). In that way, agriculture's cultural and ecological dimensions are disregarded. Agriculture is, in practice, equated to biochemistry, engineering, and business administration, as much as food is reduced to a long table of nutrients rather than an important element of family and community relations. Those excuses pave the way to technological fixes that, in the end, represent a form of Malthusianism by the backdoor. Carolan (2013, 2) rightly interprets that food security 'has been hijacked by a vocal and powerful minority' who translate it into narrow, productivist policies.

The focus on unrestrained incorporation of new areas and intensification of technology is driven also by economic thinking about agricultural modernization, a model that was introduced at the end of the 19th century in the Western countries and has been expanding to the most remote parts of the world since the launch of the Green Revolution (Patel 2013). During most of the 20th century, agricultural development, justified by the need to curtail food insecurity, relied on direct support by the state, an approach that showed signs of exhaustion during the so-called financial crisis of the state in the 1980s. The alleged excesses and insufficiencies of the classical productivist model of economic growth in the post-war decades led to the return of neoliberal strategies designed already in the 1930s. The apparatus of the state remained firmly in control of policies and supporting schemes, but the rhetoric shifted to a hybrid platform of 'agroneoliberalism' based on the supposed advantages of increased market space (Ioris 2018). Evidently, the state never left the scene and exerts full control over food production policies (in the wealthy western world various forms of subsidy and monetary incentives continued more or less unabated). The developmentalist mentality continues intact, but now in the form of 'market productivism' that combines a neoliberalizing ideology with sustained state support (Potter and Tilzey 2007). Multilateral agencies, such as the FAO, WTO, and the World Bank, redirected their modus operandi and required that borrowing of funds for agricultural development must be now accompanied by liberalizing policies, including trade deregulation and structural adjustment programs.

It should be noted that productivism remains hegemonic and underpins most agriculture activity around the world, but clearly failed to resolve the problem of food insecurity. On the contrary, it has resulted in increasingly levels of farmer indebtedness, market risks, and financial speculation, demonstrated by the power of transnational corporations and the grabbing of land resourced by foreign investors (Clapp 2019; Haller 2019; McMichael 2015). Due to horizontal and vertical restructuring tendencies that produce ever-bigger corporations in charge of seed, agri-chemicals, fertilizers, agricultural data, animal genetics, and farm machinery industries, power imbalances have become more acute, and there are higher levels of social and environmental unsustainability (IPES 2017). The influence of huge oligopolistic food producers and mega distributors has often been facilitated by the intervention of neoliberalized governments under the ideology of market-based efficiencies (Otero et al. 2018). The growing power of agri-food corporations evidently aggravates farm dependency and class polarization, such as the exploitation of labor and migrants (Wolf and Bonanno 2014). At the same time, the contradictions and manifest failures of the productivist agenda (both in its developmentalist and neoliberal tendencies) has led to reactions and the search for alternatives, as in the case of the sustainability, post-productivist paradigm.

The sustainability/post-productivist paradigm

With the declining economic role of agricultures in so-called post-industrial countries, a new argument began to emerge and scholars started to argue that agriculture was embarking on a post-productivist or multifuncionality phase, as much as the environmental question had reached an ecological modernization stage and the economy a service-based status (Evans et al. 2002; Michel-Villarreal et al. 2019; Omoto and Scott 2016; Robinson 2018). According to this (mainly British) literature, while productivist agriculture is intensive, expansionist, and industrial driven, constantly trying to boost production of a single crop using a large area, dependent on state support and aiming to reach national self-sufficiency, a post-productivist model (triggered by regulatory reforms, such as the adjustments of the CAP-related policies) is focused on diversification, pluriactivity, quality instead of quantity, and an environmentally friendly agriculture. It also includes an encouragement of activities that 'consume' the countryside, such as recreation, tourism, and the conservation of cultural and natural heritages (Ilbery 1998). The contention in favour of a post-productivist, multifunctional agriculture has parallels with the search for more sustainable farming. Instead of the highly impacting productivist approach, post-productivism has been described as the pursuit of sustainable farming systems (Wilson and Burton 2015). The solution to ensure food security should then observe sustainability concerns and be more people-centred, avoiding the degradation of systems and their ability to provide human needs in the long term (McDonald 2010). Sustainability authors denounce the real costs of 'cheap food' as the super-exploitation of workers and the environmental passivity produced by mainstream agriculture but not incorporated in the selling price. The sustainability of agriculture is related to the capacity of an agroecosystem to maintain production through time, that is, remain stable under a given set of economic and environmental circumstances (Arulbalachandran et al. 2013).

There is growing realization that the most of the commercial agri-food systems developed over the past half-century have proved to be clearly unsustainable, resistant to reform, and fraught with problems, such as their failure to reduce rural poverty and address power imbalances in food chains (De Schutter 2017). At face value, it seems that the shortcomings of input-intense agriculture are self-evident (at least to a large proportion of those questioning its long-term prospects) and sustainability could be achieved with a more diversified type of agriculture that delivers high-quality goods and services with lower use of chemical inputs. In practice, however, calls for sustainability are often undermined by the multiple continuities between 'conventional' and 'alternative' production systems, which lead to an uncertain transition from one model to the other (Walford 2003). As happened in many other areas of social activity, there was some intellectual space for self-criticism, but inevitably the same dualist and utilitarian biases that informed the productivist mindset were replicated. Basically, the sustainable food paradigm entails a more efficient use of resources and the mitigation of negative impacts on natural and human capital. It is about striking the balance between the production of goods and services and the rate of natural resources consumption, but it is much less obvious how that might be achieved, which means a depoliticization of the debate (Redclift 1997). It is often associated with organic markets, where local farmers can meet the customers on regular basis. Calls for food and agriculture sustainability, just like post-productivism, are fraught with contradictions and shortcomings. For instance, the second Sustainable Development Goal aims to reach zero hunger (SDG2 = 'End hunger, achieve food security and improved nutrition and promote sustainable agriculture'), but different donors and international development agencies have adopted conflicting strategies and all claim to be contributing towards the same goal, often ignoring the concrete geographical context and the deep causes of food insecurity, including the perverse legacies of the productivist paradigm (Blesh et al. 2019; Jones et al. 2019).

Unanswered questions therefore persist about the definition of minimum thresholds of an agriculture production system considered sustainable. Likewise, if sustainability involves maintaining some features and accepting the exchange of others for some economic gain, who decides what can be affected and what is non-substitutable? Another serious trouble is the tendency to occupy the margins of the agricultural system and the emphasis on local, secondary markets, instead of offering an alternative that challenges hegemonic agribusiness and is at the same time able to replace current supply chains. In terms of food security, supposedly sustainable or organic food systems could represent a significant improvement because of the use of traditional farming inputs, the repudiation of agrochemicals and industrialized fertilizer, reduced packaging, etc., but the focus is on local, small-scale production, normally (but not necessarily) associated with higher costs and less convenience (more time to prepare). More importantly, if sustainability is reduced to low-impact production and 'organic' farming techniques, it is easy for conventional distribution chains and large supermarkets to incorporate it as a form of niche-market food. Supermarkets have combined the selling of standard goods (considered cheaper) with some shelf space for luxurious goods (often imported from 'exotic' parts of the world) and for organic, more sustainable food. Sustainability is reduced to a personal choice about where and how to consume, which may have some impact on production patterns, but certainly fails to provoke any significant change in agriculture that leads to higher food security and benefit wider society.

Food justice, food rights, and community-based responses

A third main discursive response to the problems of insecurity is focused on the ethical and human rights dimension of food security. This epitomized by calls for food justice, which entail more than mere distributive action, but also require the recognition of the political voice and the representation of all people in decision-making and public policies on production, consumption, and distribution of food, as well as the normative connections between food-related practices and collective self-determination (Scoville 2015). It is not difficult to perceive the cross-references between food justice and environmental justice, which both demand a fair treatment of all people, regardless of race, colour, national origin, or income, with respect to the development, implementation, and enforcement of regulatory frameworks. The departure point of this third perspective is the abundant evidence around the world of the connections between poverty, social inequalities, and food insecurity. Food insecurity is thus interpreted as a socio-political problem in particular historical and geographical contexts, which cannot be resolved with better productivity and market globalization. Because of the accumulation of state and market failures, hunger and malnutrition are not distributed randomly, but concentrated in certain areas and among certain groups. For instance, UNICEF (2017) estimate that nearly half of all deaths in children under 5 are attributable to undernutrition, translating into the loss of about 3 million young lives a year (associated with the increased frequency and severity of infectious diseases); despite important gains in recent decades, high levels of mortality continue to be found especially in South Asia (48 per 1,000 live births) and Sub-Saharan Africa (78, with a peak of 95 in West and Central Africa).

The Right to Food is not a new concept, and was first recognized in the UN Declaration of Human Rights in 1948. In 1996, the formal adoption of the Right to Adequate Food marked a milestone achievement by World Food Summit delegates. It pointed the way towards the possibility of a rights-based approach to food security. Currently over 40 countries have the right to food enshrined in their constitution and FAO estimates that the right to food could be judicial in some 54 countries (McClain-Nhlapo 2004). According to Knuth and Vidar (2011), at least 56 national constitutions already protect the right to food in some form or another, which means a protection of the right to food as a justiciable right or in the form of a directive principle of state. In 2004, a set of voluntary guidelines supporting the progressive realization of the right to adequate food in the context of national food security were elaborated by an Intergovernmental Working Group under the auspices of the FAO Council. In parallel, an emerging and very influential concept is food sovereignty, coined by members of the international peasant movement La Vía Campesina in 1996, which challenges the role of markets and corporations and reaffirms the basic rights of those who produce, distribute, and consume food to formulate policies and be meaningfully involved in decision-making. In 2007, the Forum for Food Sovereignty (with representatives from small and peasant farmers, artisans, indigenous peoples, landless peoples, rural workers, pastoralists, forest communities, among other groups) which took place in Mali approved a declaration stating that 'food sovereignty is the right of peoples to healthy and culturally appropriate food produced through ecologically sound and sustainable methods, and their right to define their own food and agriculture systems' (Declaration of Nyéléni, available at: https://nyeleni.org/IMG/pdf/DeclNyeleni-en.pdf).

The agenda of food justice has paved the way for the organization of farmers' markets, as well as agroecologically managed farms, community-supported agriculture initiatives, fair trade and organic food suppliers, etc. which are all attempts to connect producers and consumers and cherish the importance of place-based agri-food chains. However, there is a common risk of local farmers' markets becoming restricted to better informed, high-income shoppers in search of better quality food, but oblivious to wider food insecurity trends and the nutritional challenges of the majority of the population. The romanticism of localized food chains leads to serious biases and represents a form of elitism by the backdoor behind the good intentions on the part of farmers, facilitators, and consumers. A similar distortion, that also tempers the impact of food justice agenda, was the appropriation of the food sovereignty by the International Assessment of Agricultural Science and Technology for Development, an intergovernmental panel under the sponsorship of the United Nations and initiated by the World Bank in 2002. Its synthesis report describes food sovereignty as 'the right of peoples and sovereign states to democratically determine their own agricultural and food policies' (IAASTD 2009), which is a rather technocratic definition empty of the political content that characterizes the activity of La Vía Campesina and other critical grassroots movements. The confusion and limitations of these approaches will be examined in the following section.

Why is food security so elusive?

The three main paradigms about agri-food systems, briefly mentioned above, have filled a lively debate about agriculture production and (qualitative and quantitative) food security, in academic, policy-making, and private sector domains. Food is a constant topic in contemporary public debates and food security, even in affluent western countries, remains a major source of concern for governments, farmers, and consumers. The prominence of food insecurity can be demonstrated, for example, by the simultaneous manifestation of both hunger and obesity derived from the same agri-food system. However, despite the relevance of the debate, the most common outcome is a sort of unspoken impasse: the food problem is acknowledged, remains high on the agenda, but it is hard to see where effective solutions and meaningful changes would come from. Effective solutions seem blocked by the fact that there are companies and groups making huge sums of money from the dominant food production and distribution model (Ioris 2015). It means that food insecurity, as much as other socio-economic distortions, results from deliberate decisions and investments in technology and production chains, and not from their absence. There is food insecurity around the planet, from megalopolises in the Global North to the remotest corners of the Global South, because food has been appropriated, resignified, and transformed into a quick-profit strategy, controlled by the application of Western science and technology (transforming food into commodity-food), that serves a universe of alienated and disconnected eaters (who themselves are treated just as consumers).

The consequence is a (sometimes noisy) discomfort among the better off about what they are eating and sheer hunger and malnutrition among half of global population. The maelstrom with the apparent elusiveness of food security is aggravated by the constant bombardment of information about nutrition-related diseases (including cancer, diabetes, and heart problems), environmental impacts caused by intense agriculture, and the failure of official responses. Food insecurity has important similarities with the confusing rhetoric about other mega-questions in the world, such as climate change, racism, migration, and terrorism. The persistent gap between political and economic strategies and the frustration of civil society with the lack of tangible answers is one of the most direct challenges to representative democracy and public policy-making today. It is therefore important to explore the root causes of the global food crisis and understand grassroots responses, which could open up entirely different opportunities and lead to comprehensive solutions to the problem of hunger, health, and the environment (Holt-Giménez 2010).

First of all, most of the discussion has been reduced to questions of production, distribution, access, or affordability, neglecting that food security constitutes a field of disputes and source of dissension. The meaning of food security has mutated over the last half-century, mirroring the evolving views on development theory and practice, but many still think in terms of productivist goals and fail to agree that food problems are essentially political issues of first magnitude (Shaw 2007). A range of interests and hidden agendas exists behind the benign calls for food security. While around 820 million people continue to suffer from hunger and another good share of the global population struggle with obesity-related health issues, many continue to profit from the widespread condition of food insecurity (FAO 2019). The concept of food security has often been manipulated and used to boost the stronger interests of corporations, banks, large-scale landowners, and allied politicians, as during the 'golden age' of developmentalism during the post-World War II decades when international development became a global project. This spurious gain is accrued either directly (from the manipulation of assistance programs) or indirectly (from the maintenance of the current agri-food model).

Since the time of Kennedy's Alliance for Progress, food aid has been used to tackle hunger in emergency situations and achieve food security. However, 'food aid', as well as the increasing rhetoric of 'food assistance', are donor-driven strategies that first of all promote domestic and geopolitical interests of donor countries. It helps to maintain the price of agricultural commodities and remove surplus production from the market at the expense of subsidies paid by taxpayers (Brett 2010). Food aid may lead to some short-term alleviation, but also disrupts production systems and local markets in the receiving countries, while increasing their dependence on further donations (Nagoda 2017). Indirectly, food aid or food assistance, as urgent initiatives in the pursuit of food security, can even reinforce a productivist excuse for the mobilization of more land, chemical inputs, and GMOs, which (as mentioned above) are ultimately production factors increasingly controlled by transnational corporations and powerful landowners.

A very influential line of reasoning, particularly among the UN agencies, is Amartya Sen's theorization of entitlements and of command over food, which seems to present a way forward but in effect falls short of dealing with the deep institutional and political sources of food insecurity (Sen 1991). This defence of food security is constructed in the abstract and decontextualized, absent from concrete political economic and sociocultural contexts. Likewise, given the hegemonic nature of global agribusiness, powerful actors often invoke the rhetoric of entitlements in order to maintain privileges and state concessions. Like in the case of the sustainability argument (discussed above), food security from the perspective of entitlements is inadvertently rendered into an apolitical matter, minimizing both the structural causes and the lived experience of hunger, as well as the related problems of overconsumption and wastage of food.

Conceptualizations such as these tend to neglect that the long-lasting problems of food, which have pervaded the history of all human societies since before the ancient civilizations, mutated into a problem of 'insecurity' only in the course of the capitalist modernization of the world. The advance of capitalism entailed an ontological shift from (old) starvation to (modern and persistent) food insecurity. It is because of the intrinsic features of capitalism that food scarcity (as much as poverty and human degradation) remains firmly entrenched amid abundant stocks of food, sophisticated technologies, and global wealth. Food has become a mere element of economic systems and food policy just a topic for top-down economic policies. People who need to eat reduced to mere consumer, food to nutrient, agriculture to agribusiness, meal to organic matter. The insecurity of food supply is not an isolated phenomenon, but it is an element of a wider multiplicity of scarcities that characterize market globalization; in that sense, the naturalization of food deficits in the official policy-making discourse (away from political, economic, and ideological causes) overlooks interconnected mechanisms of political differentiation and socioeconomic exploitation that influence the production and allocation of food.[3]

That indicates the role of a non-essentialist interpretation of multiple scarcities and the need to address the totality of the experience of scarcity (Ioris 2012). Food insecurity is, basically, the result of the concurrence of two main driving-forces unleashed by the growing commodification of everything: first, the reduction of agriculture to agribusiness and, second, the disconnection of people from the sources, the provision, and the content of their food. In relation to the first main driver of food insecurity, for many thousands of years agriculture was not merely a human process employed to produce food and raw material, but the expression of particular culture, the manifestation of accumulated knowledge and the basis of social relations taking place in specific socioecological settings. With the advance of capitalist relations of production, profound changes took place, initially in the countryside of Western European countries and then most of the world was inserted into the sphere of influence of modern capitalist agriculture. Even areas in the Global South with the predominance of family farming, and suffering from the consequences of land displacement, soil degradation, and various other environmental injustices, are indirectly affected by pro-agribusiness policies (as in the case of the Common Agricultural Policy that combines subsidies and support programs for agriculture operated by the European Union).

The containment of agriculture within the narrow boundaries of agribusiness has involved, in general terms, the appropriation and privatization of land and other commons, the expulsion of large contingents of the population to work in urban areas, and the specialization of production according to the demands of industries and cities. In the history of capitalism, agriculture and farmers have always taken a twofold subordinate position, combining the subordination (exploitation) of labour to capital and the countryside to the city. This phenomenon can be described as

> a movement from food-as-nutrition and agriculture-as-social-integration to a situation in which agri-food operations are carried out primarily to circulate and accumulate capital. The ideological and practical reduction of food to the realm of commodities, exploitation and profit also represents a decisive barrier to the reso-lution of nutritional and environmental problems. In synthetic terms, this is a gradual shift, which began at the end of 19th century, from *agriculture-cum-food* to *agriculture-cum-agribusiness*.
>
> *(Ioris 2017, 21)*

Due to scientific developments, in the last few decades new agricultural techniques have exponentially accelerated the erosion of social relations and food as life enrichment in favour of agriculture as business and profit. Such exogenous technologies were, in the spirit of the Green Revolution, meant to transform the ecological conditions of the soil and dramatically alter the genetic makeup of organisms, instead of focusing on the much more sustainable adaptation of plants and animals to their ecosystems. It is a very disconcerting that what is normally described as modern and superior agriculture is in effect a narrow and impoverished form of agriculture, determined by market rules and political bargains that, in the end, cause and perpetuate food insecurity. As demonstrated by Clapp and Fuchs (2009), the food systems around the world are increasingly affected by the corporate-dominated global systems and corporations are involved at all stages along the production chain, compromising small farmer livelihoods, environmental quality, food security, and consumer sovereignty. The result is that *agriculture-cum-agribusiness* is fundamentally anti-food, anti-people, and anti-future, as it is inescapably led by the logic of the circulation of capital and short-term profits. Food insecurity derives here from the mistaken delegation of something so basic and precious as food to the exclusive realm of money-making. One madness of the world today, among many others, it to transfer the control and the choices of what we eat or ingest in our bodies to nameless players with explicit but selfish agendas: plantation farmers, supermarket managers, scientists, bureaucrats, unelected regulators, among others.

Food insecurity, as dealt with by most of the global community today, is a clear sign of the highly risky and limited perspectives of the increasingly capitalization of agriculture; in simple terms, the more agribusiness, the higher the risks of food insecurity. Instead of the managerial focus on access and availability of food that underpin the aforementioned definitions, the decisive sources of food insecurity are really located in the capitalist relations of production and reproduction based on the perpetuation of symbolic and material forms of political control, which serve to maintain the primacy of exchange-value over other values and to justify exploitation as the basis of profit-making. In other words, food insecurity as such is something that can be found in a world shaped by capitalist logic of production and exchange (different than the also tragic situations of food scarcity and food-related conflicts in pre-capitalist societies). Just as liberal capitalism has increasingly undermined liberal democracy (because of the internal contradictions of capitalism, the drive for expropriation, exploitation, commodification, and accumulation), an agri-food system dominated by financialization trends doesn't allow for genuine prospects of fair food security.

That is even more noticeable in the early 21st century when liberal democracy, as adopted in western countries and replicated around the world, shows signs of electoral fatigue and indifference, eroding representative institutions, disruptive lobbying, manipulation of parliamentarian procedures, sidelining minorities through political correctness, among other problems (Tam 2018). The relation between people and elected politicians is worryingly determined by the influence, the values, and the language of large business and transnational banks and corporations (the British case is emblematic, due to the enormous share of the banking sector in the national and, particularly, London-based economy). For instance, in 2016 the USA electoral process produced one of the most troubling aberrations with the election of a controversial billionaire for president (himself a famous consumer of fast-food who has been involved in sex scandals and suspicious businesses), representing the direct and unqualified takeover of democracy by large business. A subset of that trend is the reduction of agriculture to agribusiness, food to processed, commodified food, eaters to supermarket consumers. Following this logic, it is not surprising that the hegemonic thinking about food security is pervaded by quick-fix solutions that cancel the possibility of rupture and, ultimately, perpetuate the causes of insecurity.

The second main driver of food insecurity is a direct extension of the anterior: food has become something abstract, taken for granted, and disconnected (disembedded) from basic cultural and socioecological concerns, given that the problem is basically reduced to production and purchase operations mediated by the market. As long as people have money, they assume that some sort of food will be available for buying. This simplistic, mono-dimensional thinking about food expands not only in urban areas, but also affects farmers and rural dwellers who also increasingly rely on local vendors (supplied by corporate-controlled supply chains). The aberrant consequence is that the question of food is largely equated to the holding of money and economic power, provided that even when people (farmers in Western countries included) cultivate what their families eat they are likely to be food insecure. The majority doesn't have the knowledge and have minimal opportunity to cultivate something for their own kitchens. Contemporary society is to a greater extent separated and unaware of the origin, substance, and practices behind what they eat. Their experience, in most cases, goes as far as supermarket shelves, local markets, or fast-food restaurants. This condition obviously leaves low-income people very vulnerable to the vagaries of the market, as in the case of the food crisis the followed the crash of global markets in 2008 when food prices doubled or tripled, and eventually reduced again to the pre-crisis level of 2006 (Magdoff and Tokar 2010). In sociological terms, this problem is directly related to both the concentration of power in the hands of corporations and supermarkets, and also the centuries-long process of peasant displacement and land commodification.

The disconnection between people and their food is, effectively, a process of alienation caused by social stratification and similar to the alienation between the worker and the product of their work described by Marx (1976). The alienation of people from their own labor is a distortion that happens in the concrete historical context of capitalism, which is a crucial pillar of an economy that creates and concentrates wealth by force at the expense of the majority. The workers (the non-capitalist sectors of society) are manipulated and involved in a process of exploitation and control, although they retain the superior social and ethical ground. Marx is evidently talking about the wider process of the advance of capitalism and industry, but it is also directly relevant for agricultural capitalization. The process is fraught with injustices and perversities in which

> the worker stands on a higher plane than the capitalist from the outset, since the latter has his roots in the process of alienation and finds absolute satisfaction in it whereas right from the start the worker is a victim who confronts it as a rebel and experiences it as a process of enslavement.
>
> *(Marx 1976, 990)*

Marx was concerned with agency and alienation at the personal, micro-scale level when he described the capitalism himself/herself involved and constrained by the same process. Interestingly, the same process of alienation involves and undermines the worker and also the capitalist. In his words,

> the self-valorization of capital – the creation of surplus-value – is therefore the determining, dominating and overriding purpose of the capitalist; it is the absolute motive and content of his activity. And in fact it is no more than the rationalized motive and aim of the hoarder – a highly impoverished and abstract content which makes it plain that the capitalist is just as enslaved by the relationship of capitalism as is his opposite pole, the worker, albeit in a quite different manner.

Having considered some of the fundamental elements of the food security controversy – especially the narrowness of agriculture as mere agribusiness and the ubiquitous alienation of people from food and food sources – in the final section below we will briefly explore what alternative, just food systems could look like.

The way forward: a full plate of food

From the above, it can be concluded that food insecurity is a complex, politically sensitive problem that continues to inflict much suffering and to undermine claims of democracy and justice. If there is a major food crisis today, it has been constantly manipulated and presented as a non-political crisis that is supposedly overcome through the incorporation of more production areas and more input-intense technologies. In any case, as pointed out by Harvey (2014), crises don't make change, but they require reaction and fight. Food security is part of the pursuit of wider human security, which necessarily includes a different, more inclusive and egalitarian, basis of economic production, property relations, interaction between humans and non-humans, democratic management of collective assets and issues, and so forth. The risky condition of present-day agri-food systems is certainly a serious question, but it is not an isolated or exclusive problem. On the contrary, 'the food issue must, then, be situated historically with respect to particular phases of capital accumulation in the world economy and its uneven impact upon peripheral economies' (Watts 2013, 5). For instance, the emphasis of national policies on cash crops for export exacerbates socio-economic tensions, disturbs land tenure relations, and aggravates food insecurity. Likewise, it is necessary to connect pressures such as population changes and growing social inequalities, changing food diets and consumption patterns, price oscillation (as in the first decade of the 21st century), technological packages (biotechnology and digital techniques), and environmental degradation (climate change and soil erosion). The response to those challenges requires a proper understanding of the totality of politico-economic relationships and of the internal dialectics between the multiple, multi-scale components of a profoundly unequal and unsustainable socio-economic condition. There are crucial synergies, for example, between hunger and poverty, which create true 'spaces of vulnerability' determined by particular political, economic, and institutional factors (Watts and Bohle 1993). The construction of higher levels of food security depends on a twofold agenda: reclaiming agriculture from agribusiness and reinstating the centrality of good, locally produced food in daily life.

Therefore, food security depends, first of all, on the ability of peasant family farmers (the real producers of food, cf. Shiva 2016) to maintain their activity in the long term, which is related to problems such as land access, fair market transactions, just payment of rural laborers, the removal of control over food by supermarkets and transnational corporations, the enhancement of peasant associations, etc. The reaffirmation of agriculture as primarily the source of food, and not profit, is evidently a major and difficult political question. In addition, food security depends on the offer of a 'full plate', not only in terms of quantity, but quality (in terms of nutrition, safety, freshness, and according to local culture and the autonomous wishes of producers and consumers). Full plate is in fact a perfect metaphor of the totality of relations underpinning food security. Good food is 'just food', instead of the products manipulated and commercialized by corporations. Food security requires rethinking food, revisiting agriculture, which ultimately requires rethinking the world. Those two mega-agendas will have to incorporate cultural, economic, agrarian, and technological differences, but in general terms the task is similar in countries of both the Global North and the Global South. However, the non-Western parts of the world seem to have much more to offer and a lot to teach. This is perhaps the moment to return to common sense and appreciate food as food. As demonstrated by Descola (1996, 74), 'in common with all societies not governed by market prices, the Achuar [a group of indigenous peoples in the Amazon] rule out lucrative transactions where food is concerned'.

Discussion questions

1. What are the connections between food security, environmental justice, and meaningful social inclusion?
2. Why has the neoliberalization of agribusiness aggravated food insecurity and worsened socioecological degradation?
3. Is it possible to expect higher levels of food security without significantly reducing corporate influence on democracy?

Notes

1 The report elsewhere adds (p. 19): 'The global prevalence of obesity more than doubled between 1980 and 2014. In 2014, more than 600 million adults were obese, equal to about 13 percent of the world's adult population. The prevalence is higher on average among women (15 percent) than men (11 percent).'
2 The relation between climate-related crises and food insecurity goes much beyond irregular rainfall and exceptional temperature. In effect, those climatic adversities have been historically maximized by the impacts of colonization and the priorities of international market transactions (Davis 2002).
3 In the UK and USA, food banks have become a temporary and controversial safety net to the most vulnerable social groups, such as unemployed and homeless people.

Further reading

Carolan, M. 2013. *Reclaiming Food Security*. Routledge: London and New York.
Magdoff, F. and Tokar, B. (eds). 2010. *Agriculture and Food in Crisis: Conflict, Resistance, and Renewal*. Monthly Review Press: New York.
Schanbacher, W.D. 2019. *Food as a Human Right: Combatting Global Hunger and Forging a Path to Food Sovereignty*. Praeger: Santa Barbara, CA.
Shiva, V. 2016. *Who Really Feeds the World? The Failures of Agribusiness and the Promise of Agroecology*. North Atlantic Books: Berkeley, CA.
Watts, M.J. 2013. *Silent Violence: Food, Famine, and Peasantry in Northern Nigeria*. University of Georgia Press: Athens, GA, and London.

References

Arulbalachandran, D., Mullainathan, L. and Latha, S. 2013. Food Security and Sustainable Agriculture. In: *Sustainable Agriculture Towards Food Security*, Arulbalachandran, D. (ed). Springer: Singapore. pp. 3–13.
Blesh, J., Hoey, L., Jones, A.D., Friedmann, H. and Perfecto, I. 2019. Development Pathways toward 'Zero Hunger'. *World Development*, 118, 1–14.
Brett, J.A. 2010. The Political-Economics of Developing Markets versus Satisfying Food Needs. *Food and Foodways*, 18(1–2), 28–42.
Carolan, M. 2013. *Reclaiming Food Security*. Routledge: London and New York.
Clapp, J. 2019. The Rise of Financial Investment and Common Ownership in Global Agrifood Firms. *Review of International Political Economy*, 26(4), 604–629.
Clapp, J. and Fuchs, D. (eds). 2009. *Corporate Power in Global Agrifood Governance*. MIT Press: Cambridge, MA, and London.
Davis, M. 2002. *Late Victorian Holocausts: El Niño Famines and the Making of the Third World*. Verso: London and New York.
De Schutter, O. 2014. The Specter of Productivism and Food Democracy. *Wisconsin Law Review*, 2014 (2), 199–233.
De Schutter, O. 2017. The Political Economy of Food Systems Reform. *European Review of Agricultural Economics*, 44(4), 705–731.
Descola, P. 1996. *The Spears of Twilight*. Trans. J. Lloyd. Flamingo: London.
Evans, N., Morris, C. and Winter, M. 2002. Conceptualizing Agriculture: A Critique of Post-Productivism as the New Orthodoxy. *Progress in Human Geography*, 26(3), 313–332.
FAO. 2009. *Reform of the Committee on World Food Security: Final Version*. Document CFS:2009/2 Rev.2. FAO: Rome.
FAO. 2019. *The State of Food Security and Nutrition in the World 2019*. FAO: Rome.
FAO, IFAD, UNICEF, WFP and WHO. 2017. *The State of Food Security and Nutrition in the World 2017: Building Resilience for Peace and Food Security*. FAO: Rome.
Haller, T. 2019. The Different Meanings of Land in the Age of Neoliberalism: Theoretical Reflections on Commons and Resilience Grabbing from a Social Anthropological Perspective. *Land*, 8(7), 104.
Harvey, D. 2014. *Seventeen Contradictions and the End of Capitalism*. Profile Books: London.

Holt-Giménez, E. 2010. Foreword. In: *Food Security, Nutrition and Sustainability*, Lawrence, G., Lyons, K. and Wallington, T. (eds). Earthscan: London and Sterling, VA. pp. xxiii–xxiv.

IAASTD. 2009. *Agriculture at a Crossroads: A Synthesis of the Global and Sub-Global IAASTD Reports*. International Assessment of Agricultural Knowledge, Science and Technology for Development: Washington, DC.

Ilbery, B. (ed.). 1998. *The Geography of Rural Change*. Pearson/Prentice Hall: Harlow.

Ioris, A.A.R. 2012. The Geography of Multiple Scarcities. *Geoforum*, 43(3), 612–622.

Ioris, A.A.R. 2015. Cracking the Nut of Agribusiness and Global Food Insecurity: In Search of a Critical Agenda of Research. *Geoforum*, 63, 1–4.

Ioris, A.A.R. 2016. Rent of Agribusiness in the Amazon: A Case Study from Mato Grosso. *Land Use Policy*, 59, 456–466.

Ioris, A.A.R. 2017. *Agribusiness and the Neoliberal Food System in Brazil: Frontiers and Fissures of Agro-neoliberalism*. Routledge: London.

Ioris, A.A.R. 2018. The Politics of Agribusiness and the Business of Sustainability. *Sustainability*, 10(5), 1648.

IPES. 2017. *Too Big to Feed: Exploring the Impacts of Mega-Mergers, Consolidation and Concentration of Power in the Agri-Food Sector*. IPES-Food: Brussels.

Jones, R., Wham, C. and Burlingame, B. 2019. New Zealand's Food System Is Unsustainable: A Survey of the Divergent Attitudes of Agriculture, Environment, and Health Sector Professionals towards Eating Guidelines. *Frontiers in Nutrition*, 6, 99.

Knuth, L. and Vidar, M. 2011. *Constitutional and Legal Protection of the Right to Food around the World*. Right to Food Studies. FAO: Rome.

Lang, T. and Heasman, M. 2015. *Food Wars: The Global Battle for Mouths, Minds and Markets*. 2nd edition. Routledge: London and New York.

Magdoff, F. and Tokar, B. (eds). 2010. *Agriculture and Food in Crisis: Conflict, Resistance, and Renewal*. Monthly Review Press: New York.

Marx, K. 1976 [1867]. *Capital*. Vol. 1. Trans. B. Fowkes. Penguin: London.

McDonald, B.L. 2010. *Food Security*. Polity: Cambridge.

McClain-Nhlapo, C. 2004. *Implementing a Human Rights Approach to Food Security*. 2020 Africa Conference Brief. Policy Brief 13, IFPRI: Washington, DC.

McMichael, P. 2015. The Land Question in the Food Sovereignty Project. *Globalizations*, 12(4), 434–451.

McMurtry, J. 1999. *The Cancer Stage of Capitalism*. Polity: London.

Mendras, H. 1984. *Le Fin des Paysans*. Actes Sud: Paris.

Michel-Villarreal, R., Hingley, M., Canavari, M. and Bregoli, I. 2019. Sustainability in Alternative Food Networks: A Systematic Literature Review. *Sustainability*, 11(3), 859.

Nagoda, S. 2017. Rethinking Food Aid in a Chronically Food-insecure Region: Effects of Food Aid on Local Power Relations and Vulnerability Patterns in Northwestern Nepal. *IDS Bulletin*, 48(4), 111–124.

Naylor, R.L. (ed). 2014. *The Evolving Sphere of Food Security*. Oxford University Press: Oxford.

Omoto, R. and Scott, S. 2016. Multifunctionality and Agrarian Transition in Alternative Agro-Food Production in the Global South: The Case of Organic Shrimp Certification in the Mekong Delta, Vietnam. *Asia Pacific Viewpoint*, 57(1), 121–137.

Otero, G., Gürcan, E.C., Pechlaner, G. and Liberman, G. 2018. Food Security, Obesity, and Inequality: Measuring the Risk of Exposure to the Neoliberal Diet. *Journal of Agrarian Change*, 18, 536–554.

Patel, R. 2013. The Long Green Revolution. *The Journal of Peasant Studies*, 40(1), 1–63.

Pollan, M. 2008. *In Defence of Food: The Myth of Nutrition and the Pleasures of Eating*. Penguin: London.

Potter, C. and Tilzey, M. 2007. Agricultural Multifunctionality, Environmental Sustainability and the WTO: Resistance or Accommodation to the Neoliberal Project for Agriculture? *Geoforum*, 38, 1290–1303.

Rahill, S., Kennedy, A., Walton, J., McNulty, B.A. and Kearney, J. 2019. The Factors Associated with Food Fussiness in Irish School-aged Children. *Public Health Nutrition*, 22(1), 164–174.

Redclift, M. 1997. Sustainability and Theory: An Agenda for Action. In: *Globalising Food*, Goodman, D. and Watts, M.J. (eds). Routledge: Abingdon. pp. 333–343.

Robinson, G.M. 2018. New Frontiers in Agricultural Geography: Transformations, Food Security, Land Grabs and Climate Change. *Boletín de la Asociación de Geógrafos Españoles*, 78, 1–48.

Scoville, J.M. 2015. Framing Food Justice. In: *Just Food: Philosophy, Justice and Food*, Dieterle, J.M. (ed.). Rowman & Littlefield: London and New York. pp. 3–20.

Sen, A. 1991. Public Action to Remedy Hunger. *Interdisciplinary Science Reviews*, 16(4), 324–336.

Shaw, D.J. 2007. *World Food Security: A History since 1945*. Palgrave Macmillan: Basingstoke.

Shiva, V. 2016. *Who Really Feeds the World? The Failures of Agribusiness and the Promise of Agroecology.* North Atlantic Books: Berkeley, CA.

Tam, H. 2018. *Time to Save Democracy: How to Govern Ourselves in the Age of Anti-Politics.* University of Chicago Press: Chicago, IL.

Truman, E. and Elliott, C. 2019. Identifying Food Marketing to Teenagers: A Scoping Review. *International Journal of Behavioral Nutrition and Physical Activity*, 16(1), 67.

UNICEF. 2017. *The State of the World's Children 2017: Children in a Digital World*. UNICEF: New York.

Velazquez, C.E., Daepp, M.I.G. and Black, J.L. 2019. Assessing Exposure to Food and Beverage Advertisements Surrounding Schools in Vancouver, BC. *Health and Place*, 58, 102066.

Walford, N. 2003. Productivism Is Allegedly Dead, Long Live Productivism: Evidence of Continued Productivist Attitudes and Decision Making in South-East England. *Journal of Rural Studies*, 19, 491–502.

Watts, M.J. 2013 [1983]. *Silent Violence: Food, Famine, and Peasantry in Northern Nigeria.* University of Georgia Press: Athens, GA, and London.

Watts, M.J. and Bohle, H.G. 1993. The Space of Vulnerability: The Causal Structure of Hunger and Famine. *Progress in Human Geography*, 17(1), 43–67.

Wilson, G.A. and Burton, R.J.F. 2015. 'Neo-Productivist' Agriculture: Spatio-Temporal versus Structuralist Perspectives. *Journal of Rural Studies*, 38, 52–64.

Wolf, S.A. and Bonanno, A. (eds). 2014. *The Neoliberal Regime in the Agri-Food Sector: Crisis, Resilience, and Restructuring.* Earthscan: London and New York.

INDEX

Page numbers in *italic* refer to figures. Page numbers in **bold** refer to tables. Page number followed by 'n' refer to notes.